When should I travel to get the best airfare?
Where do I go for answers to my travel questions?
What's the best and easiest way to plan and book my trip?

frommers.travelocity.com

Frommer's, the travel guide leader, has teamed up with **Travelocity.com**, the leader in online travel, to bring you an in-depth, easy-to-use resource designed to help you plan and book your trip online.

At **frommers.travelocity.com**, you'll find free online updates about your destination from the experts at Frommer's plus the outstanding travel planning and purchasing features of Travelocity.com. Travelocity.com provides reservations capabilities for 95 percent of all airline seats sold, more than 47,000 hotels, and over 50 car rental companies. In addition, Travelocity.com offers more than 2,000 exciting vacation and cruise packages. Travelocity.com puts you in complete control of your travel planning with these and other great features:

Expert travel guidance from Frommer's - over 150 writers reporting from around the world!

Best Fare Finder - an interactive calendar tells you when to travel to get the best airfare

Fare Watcher - we'll track airfare changes to your favorite destinations

Dream Maps - a mapping feature that suggests travel opportunities based on your budget

Shop Safe Guarantee - 24 hours a day / 7 days a week live customer service, and more!

Whether traveling on a tight budget, looking for a quick weekend getaway, or planning the trip of a lifetime, Frommer's guides and Travelocity.com will make your travel dreams a reality. You've bought the book, now book the trip!

Frommer's

Great Outdoor Guide to Arizona & New Mexico
1st Edition

Also Available:

Frommer's Great Outdoor Guide to Northern California
Frommer's Great Outdoor Guide to Southern New England
Frommer's Great Outdoor Guide to Vermont & New Hampshire
Frommer's Great Outdoor Guide to Washington & Oregon

Great Outdoor Guide to Arizona & New Mexico
1st Edition

by Lesley S. King

Hungry Minds, Inc.
An International Data Group Company
New York, NY · Cleveland, OH · Indianapolis, IN

About the Author

Lesley S. King grew up on a ranch in northern New Mexico, where she still returns on weekends to help work cattle. A freelance writer and photographer, she's a contributor to *New Mexico Magazine* and an avid kayaker and skier. She has written about food and restaurants for *The New York Times*, the Anasazi culture for United Airlines' *Hemispheres* magazine, ranches for *American Cowboy*, and birds for *Audubon*. She is writer and host of *Written on the Wind*, a television documentary series. She is also the author of *Frommer's Santa Fe, Taos & Albuquerque* and *Frommer's New Mexico*.

Hungry Minds, Inc.
909 Third Ave.
New York, NY 10022
www.frommers.com

Copyright © 2001 Hungry Minds, Inc. All rights reserved. No part of this book may be reproduced or transmitted in any form or by any means, electronic or mechanical, including photocopying, recording, or by any information storage and retrieval system, without permission in writing from the Publisher.

FROMMER'S is a registered trademark of Arthur Frommer. Used under license.

ISBN 0-02-863591-4
ISSN 1531-7609

Editor: Myka Carroll
Production Editor: Donna Wright
Photo Editor: Richard Fox
Design by Madhouse Studios
Cartographer: John Decamillis
Production by Hungry Minds Indianapolis Production Services

Special Sales
For general information on Hungry Minds' products and services please contact our Consumer Care department: within the U.S. at 800-762-2974, outside the U.S. at 317-572-3993 or fax 317-572-4002. For sales inquiries and reseller information, including discounts, bulk sales, customized editions, and premium sales, please contact our Customer Care department at 800-434-3422.

Manufactured in the United States of America.

5 4 3 2 1

Contents

List of Maps xiii

Map Legend xiv

Introduction xvii

1 The Basics 1
   Before You Go 4
   Getting Underway 7
   Ballooning 7, Bird Watching 8, Boardsailing & Sailing 8, Caving 9, Climbing 10, Cross-Country Skiing 11, Downhill Skiing & Snowboarding 11, Fishing 12, Hikes & Backpack Trips 13, Horseback Riding 14, Mountain Biking 18, Road Biking 20, Scuba Diving 20, Sea Kayaking 20, Snowshoeing 21, Swimming & Tubing 21, Walks & Rambles 21, White-Water Kayaking & Rafting 22, Wildlife Viewing 23

   Where to Stay 23
   Leave No Trace: A Final Note About Preservation 24

FEATURES
Hantavirus Pulmonary Syndrome 5
Canyoneering Basics 14
Choosing an Outfitter 16

2 Arizona Grand Canyon Country 25
   The Lay of the Land 26
   Orientation 28
   Parks & Other Hot Spots 29
   Grand Canyon National Park 30
   What to Do & Where to Do It 33
   Bird Watching 33, Caving 35, Climbing 35, Cross-Country Skiing & Snowshoeing 36, Downhill Skiing 37, Fishing 38, Hikes & Backpack Trips 38, Horseback Riding 49, Mountain Biking 50, Road Biking 53, Swimming 54, Walks & Rambles 54, White-Water Kayaking & Rafting 55, Wildlife Viewing 57

Campgrounds & Other Accommodations   57

FEATURES

On the Horizon: New Ways to Enjoy the Grand Canyon   31
California Condor   34

3 Arizona Indian Country 62

The Lay of the Land   64

Orientation   66

Parks & Other Hot Spots   66

What to Do & Where to Do It   72

Bird Watching 72, Climbing 72, Fishing 73, Hikes & Backpack Trips 73, Horseback Riding 77, Mountain Biking 78, Road Biking 79, Scuba Diving 80, Sea Kayaking 81, Walks & Rambles 81, White-Water Rafting 84, Wildlife Viewing 84

Campgrounds & Other Accommodations   84

FEATURES

Draining Lake Powell?   68
Ancient Anasazi   77

4 Arizona's West Coast 88

The Lay of the Land   91

Orientation   91

Parks & Other Hot Spots   92

Organ Pipe Cactus National Monument   94

What to Do & Where to Do It   96

Bird Watching 96, Boardsailing & Sailing 98, Fishing 98, Hikes & Backpack Trips 99, Horseback Riding 101, Mountain Biking 102, Road Biking 103, Sea Kayaking 103, Swimming 104, Walks & Rambles 104, Wildlife Viewing 105

Campgrounds & Other Accommodations   107

FEATURES

The London Bridge   90
El Camino del Diablo   106

5 Arizona Red Rock Country 109

The Lay of the Land   110

Orientation   112

Parks & Other Hot Spots   113

What to Do & Where to Do It   114
Ballooning 114, Bird Watching 115, Climbing 116, Fishing 116, Hikes & Backpack Trips 118, Horseback Riding 125, Mountain Biking 126, Road Biking 131, Swimming & Tubing 132, Walks & Rambles 132, Wildlife Viewing 135

Campgrounds & Other Accommodations   136

FEATURE

The Arizona Trail   123

6 Arizona's White Mountains 139

The Lay of the Land   140

Orientation   141

Parks & Other Hot Spots   142

What to Do & Where to Do It   143
Bird Watching 143, Boardsailing & Sailing 143, Cross-Country Skiing & Snowshoeing 144, Downhill Skiing 145, Fishing 145, Hikes & Backpack Trips 148, Horseback Riding 152, Mountain Biking 153, Road Biking 157, Swimming 158, Walks & Rambles 158, White-Water Kayaking & Rafting 160, Wildlife Viewing 161

Campgrounds & Other Accommodations   162

FEATURE

The Return of the Wolf   161

7 Arizona's Sky Islands 165

The Lay of the Land   166

Orientation   167

Parks & Other Hot Spots   168

Saguaro National Park   171

Chiricahua National Monument   172

What to Do & Where to Do It   175
Ballooning 175, Bird Watching 176, Boardsailing & Sailing 178, Caving 179, Climbing 180, Fishing 180, Hikes & Backpack Trips 181, Horseback Riding 187, Mountain Biking 189, Road Biking 192, Sea Kayaking & Rafting 192, Swimming 192, Walks & Rambles 192, Wildlife Viewing 194

Campgrounds & Other Accommodations   195

FEATURES

The Saguaro Cactus & Other Desert Denizens   173
Elegant Trogon   179

8 New Mexico Indian Country 199

The Lay of the Land 200

Orientation 202

Parks & Other Hot Spots 202

Chaco Culture National Historic Park 211

El Malpais National Monument 214

What to Do & Where to Do It 216

Ballooning 216, Bird Watching 216, Caving 216, Fishing 216, Hikes & Backpack Trips 217, Horseback Riding 222, Mountain Biking 222, Road Biking 225, Swimming 226, Walks & Rambles 226, White-Water Kayaking 228, Wildlife Viewing 228

Campgrounds & Other Accommodations 228

FEATURE
Indian Country Pawn 227

9 New Mexico's Rocky Mountains 232

The Lay of the Land 234

Orientation 236

Parks & Other Hot Spots 236

What to Do & Where to Do It 238

Ballooning 238, Bird Watching 239, Boardsailing 240, Climbing 240, Cross-Country Skiing 243, Downhill Skiing & Snowboarding 248, Fishing 252, Hikes & Backpack Trips 256, Horseback Riding 267, Mountain Biking 268, Road Biking 274, Snowshoeing 277, Swimming & Tubing 278, Walks & Rambles 278, White-Water Kayaking 280, White-Water Rafting 282, Wildlife Viewing 283

Campgrounds & Other Accommodations 284

FEATURES
Shredders Unite! 249
Los Alamos: The A-Bomb's Birthplace 266

10 New Mexico High Plains 290

The Lay of the Land 292

Orientation 292

Parks & Other Hot Spots 292

What to Do & Where to Do It   299
  Bird Watching 299, Boardsailing & Sailing 300, Climbing 300, Fishing 300, Hikes & Backpack Trips 302, Horseback Riding 304, Mountain Biking 304, Road Biking 305, Scuba Diving 306, Snowshoeing 306, Swimming 307, Walks & Rambles 307, Wildlife Viewing 309

Campgrounds & Other Accommodations   310

FEATURES
Route 66 Revisited: Rediscovering the Mother Road   293
Cimarron: The Wild Wild West   299
Boy Scouts of America   304
Folsom Man   306
Peace College   309

11 New Mexico Gila Country 314

The Lay of the Land   316

Orientation   317

Parks & Other Hot Spots   319

Gila Cliff Dwellings National Monument   320

What to Do & Where to Do It   323
  Bird Watching 323, Boardsailing & Sailing 324, Climbing 324, Fishing 325, Hikes & Backpack Trips 326, Horseback Riding 330, Mountain Biking 331, Road Biking 333, Swimming 334, Walks & Rambles 335, Wildlife Viewing 338

Campgrounds & Other Accommodations   339

FEATURES
Aldo Leopold & the Gila Wilderness   318
Hatch Chile: You Say Chili, We Say Chile   330
Gold, Silver & Copper in Them Thar Hills   336

12 New Mexico Cave Country 343

The Lay of the Land   346

Orientation   347

Parks & Other Hot Spots   347

What to Do & Where to Do It   352
  Bird Watching 352, Boardsailing 352, Caving 352, Climbing 355, Downhill Skiing & Snowboarding 355, Fishing 356, Hikes & Backpack Trips 357, Horseback Riding & Pack Trips 361, Mountain Biking 362, Road Biking 364, Swimming 364, Walks & Rambles 364, Wildlife Viewing 367

Campgrounds & Other Accommodations 368

FEATURES

Atomic Bombs & Radioactive Waste 344
The Incident at Roswell 353
Billy the Kid 367

Index 374

List of Maps

Outdoors in Arizona & New Mexico	2
Arizona Grand Canyon Country	27
Grand Canyon National Park	32
Arizona Indian Country	63
Arizona's West Coast	89
Arizona Red Rock Country	111
Sedona	112
Eastern Arizona	141
Arizona's White Mountains	142
Arizona's Sky Islands	167
The Arizona Birding Trail	169
Chiricahua National Monument	175
New Mexico Indian Country	201
Chaco Culture National Historic Park	212
El Malpais	215
New Mexico's Rocky Mountains	233
Santa Fe National Forest	235
New Mexico High Plains	291
Capulin Volcano National Monument	294
New Mexico Gila Country	315
New Mexico Cave Country	345
Carlsbad Caverns National Park	348
Carlsbad Caverns Underground	354

Map Legend

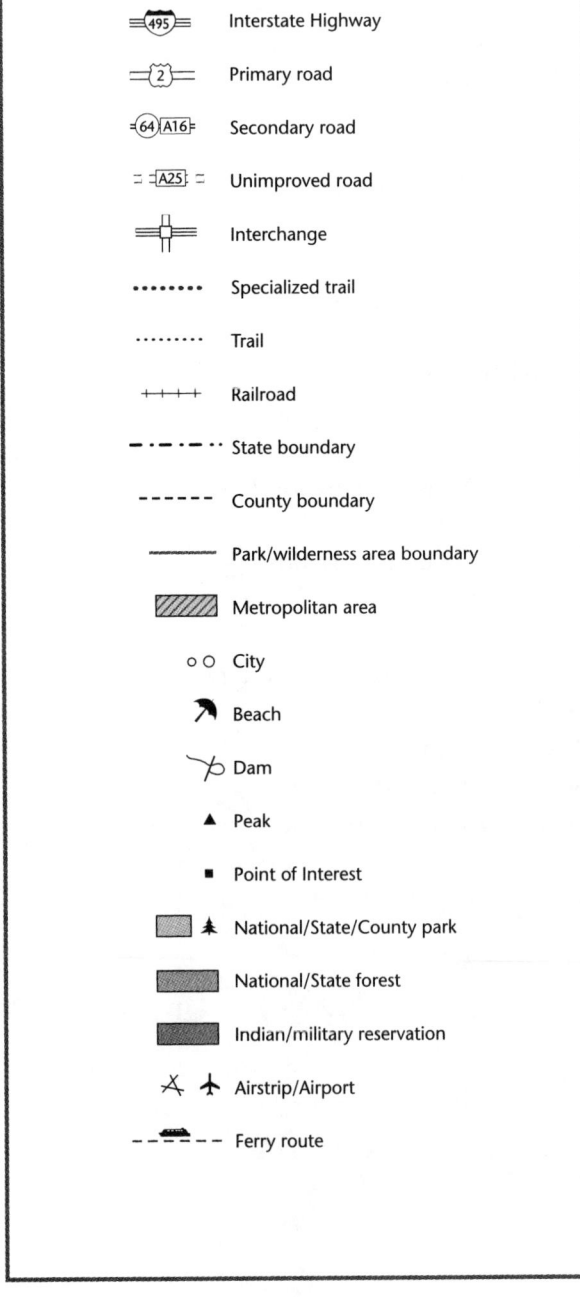

Acknowledgments

To Ann and Barbara, who showed me what an adventure life can be.

Many people helped in completing this project. First I'd like to thank Garji, who reminded me again and again that freedom is now. My assistant, Ki Bassett, helped with fact checking and writing. My mother, Barbara Doolittle, listened to my fears and frustrations and always responded with encouragement, as did my friends, Julie Zimber, Claire Romero, Robert Stivers, Memphis Barbree, and Lex Weimer. I also offer thanks to my father, Eb King, for taking me on my first hike, and to my brother, Brian, who taught me to bend my knees and other critical life lessons, to his wife Nicole, for looking after the ranch, and to Brenda and Amy, who constantly remind me what's important. Kurt Vollbrecht graciously taught me to climb and provided keen geological insight for the book. Dennis McMahon also helped with the geology, especially explaining the stories the landscape tells. Great thanks goes to my editor, Myka Carroll, who was patient about deadlines and occasional clumsy prose, and who was always cheerful and encouraging. Also thanks to my previous Frommer's editor Neil E. Schlecht for recommending me for this project. A long overdue thanks to Jay Neugeboren and Ava Heinrichsdorf, who believed in my writing. And finally, though she can't yet read the acknowledgment, thanks to my dog, Alma, who traveled every mile with me, barked at bears and strangers, and chased away imaginary ghosts in the night.

An Invitation to the Reader

In researching this book, we crisscrossed Arizona and New Mexico in search of the very best places to get outside. We're sure you have your own favorite spots, or at least will find new ones as you explore. Please share your recommendations with us, so we can pass them on in upcoming editions. If you were disappointed with a recommendation, We'd love to know that, too. Please write to:

Frommer's Great Outdoor Guide to Arizona & New Mexico, 1st Edition
Hungry Minds, Inc.
909 Third Avenue
New York, NY 10022

An Additional Note

Please be advised that travel information is subject to change at any time. Every effort has been made to ensure the accuracy of the information provided in this book, but we suggest that you write or call ahead for confirmation when making your travel plans. The author, editors, and Publisher cannot be held responsible for the experiences of readers while traveling. Outdoor sports are, by their very nature, potentially hazardous activities. In doing any of the activities described herein, readers assume all risk of injury or loss that may accompany such activities. The Publisher disavows all responsibility for injury, death, loss, or property damage which may arise from a reader's participation in any of the activities described herein, and the Publisher makes no warranties regarding the competence, safety, and reliability of outfitters, tour companies, or training centers described in this book.

Abbreviations

The following abbreviations are used for credit cards
- AE   American Express
- CB   Carte Blanche
- DC   Diners Club
- DISC   Discover
- ER   enRoute
- EC   Eurocard
- JCB   Japan Credit Bank
- MC   MasterCard
- V   Visa

Find Frommer's Online

www.frommers.com offers up-to-the-minute listings on almost 200 cities around the globe—including the latest bargains and candid, personal articles updated daily by Arthur Frommer himself. No other Web site offers such comprehensive and timely coverage of the world of travel.

Introduction

When I was 23 years old, I left my home state New Mexico to see the world. I wanted to get away from the provincialism I'd grown up with here. After spending much of my life on a cattle ranch, I was tired of cowboys and smoky bars and flat plains. I wanted green lushness, intellectual prowess, and political enlightenment. I traveled from the Berkshire Mountains in Massachusetts to Mount Kinabalu in Borneo to the Himalayas in Nepal and the great savannas of Africa, and then one day, I decided to come home. I'd searched and found all the things I'd hoped to find, and many more, except one, and I now know it was in the Desert Southwest.

I've come to call it soul.

If there is a quality that most defines Arizona and New Mexico, it is that. These southwestern states are like a creative, somewhat tortured child who grows up to be an amazing artist. They are windswept, flooded, cracked, trampled by history, burnt by the sun, and left to lie in their own ashes. They've seen massive volcanic eruptions, tearing apart at the seams, and bold uplifts of great mountain ranges. They've been home to Native Americans for thousands of years, descendants of whom still walk the ground here. They've seen great conquests and natural abuses, and through it all a tender strength has developed, a richness of character, a fathomless depth.

To the outdoor adventurer this means experiencing an intense natural beauty, from the labyrinths of Carlsbad Caverns, one of the world's great wonders, to the thousands of acres of stark dunes at White Sands National Monument. You'll see nature's transformative power when you touch a log with an amethyst core at Petrified Forest National Park or watch the sunset across the Painted Desert, a land of rainbow-colored earth. Even more brilliant colors await you in southeastern Arizona, the land the Chiricahua Apache once roamed, where millions of birds pass through, from vermilion flycatchers to purple-throated hummingbirds to the fabled elegant trogon.

As well as the physical beauty here, you'll experience incredible cultural wealth. Traveling to the Grand Canyon, one of the world's seven wonders, you may traverse the place where the Hopi people believe they were born into this world, or you may visit the villages of the Hualapai tribes, who still live within the canyon's depth. While hiking, biking, or driving through the amazing chiseled formations of Monument Valley, you'll undoubtedly experience some of the culture of the great nomads, the Navajo. While exploring the Sangre de Cristo Mountains, the lower end of the Rocky Mountain chain, you'll walk where the great conquistadors did, and you can even drink wine grown from grapes that the first priests brought from Spain.

Within it all you'll likely be exposed to a pace of life like nothing you've known before. Many of the area's Native Americans and Hispanics are less concerned with time than the rest of us, and that lack of concern resonates through the area, allowing for a relaxed "mañana" attitude. You'll hear a variety of languages spoken, from the Tewa and Tiwa of the Pueblo tribes in New Mexico, to the Navajo language, to the Spanish that in places is more prevalent than English. You'll eat food that will expand your palate, including such treats as the delicate Zuni piki bread or the rich, pork-infused hominy called posole. You'll have to sample a Navajo taco, fried bread smothered with chile, and best of all a New Mexican enchilada, better than any you will have had anywhere, I guarantee.

What all this diverse experience will bring to you is an altered sense of time and space much like what you may have experienced while traveling abroad. The land's myths and mysteries will likely play on you, maybe even bringing you odd visions and dreams, that, when you leave, will impress you forever.

—*Lesley S. King*

1
The Basics

Frommer's Great Outdoor Guide to Arizona & New Mexico remains faithful to the user-friendly template of the *Frommer's Great Outdoor Guide* series by covering every cool outdoor sport available in a clear, concise format. The book is divided into 11 regional chapters, 6 in Arizona and 5 in New Mexico, which are mostly determined by natural boundaries. You don't have to wade through a lot of extraneous information to find your adventure's vital statistics; just turn right to the page and know immediately how to get to a trailhead or a put-in or how many hours a hike or ride will take.

The core of each chapter is the "What to Do & Where to Do It" section, which contains an A to Z list of activities ranging from bird watching to wildlife viewing, with fun sports such as biking, hiking, horseback riding, and white-water rafting, among many others. Most sections also have other helpful bits of information, such as recommended outfitters, guidebooks, and shops.

There are many ways you can use this book. If you're planning a visit to the Southwest, you can read this introductory chapter to find the best places to go to do the sports you enjoy, and plot your journey accordingly. Or, if you're already in Arizona or New Mexico, you can simply look up a sport such as mountain biking and pinpoint the best trails. Maybe you're one of those "endless-summer" types, cruising the blue highways of the West. If so, you can plan weeks of wandering from mountain to canyon to desert to river, using this book as your guide.

I've done my best to find the most awesome trails, routes, waterways, and activities, and give specifics about them so that they're accessible to you. Distance, time, level of difficulty, terrain, location, and availability of maps have been included when appropriate. Be aware that time and level of difficulty are relative terms. I base my ratings for both on the notion that the person performing the sport has done so before. So a 2-hour, moderate hike will take 2 hours and be moderate only to people who hike fairly

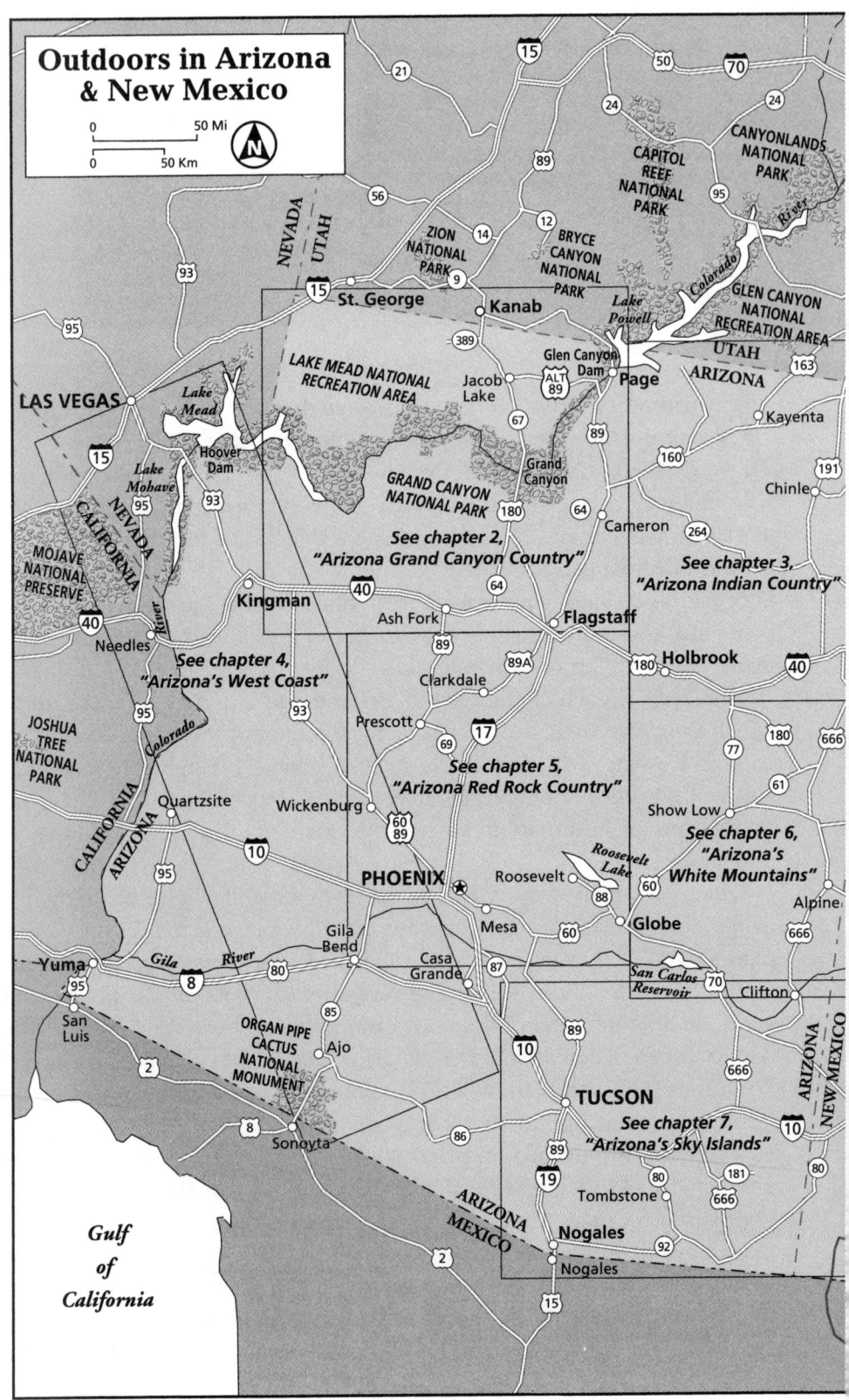

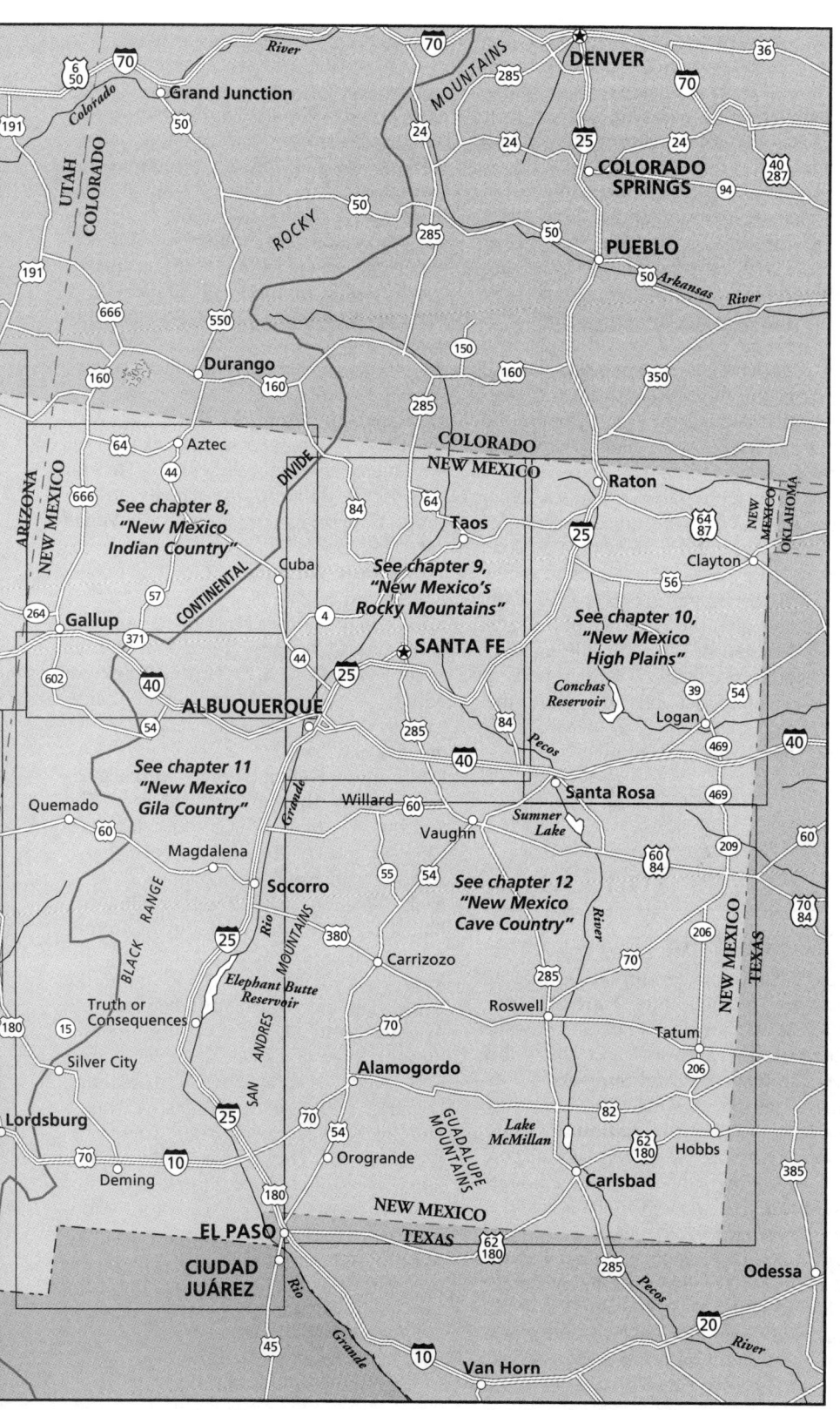

regularly. For those setting out on their first hike, the same journey could take 3 hours and prove difficult.

Preceding the sports and activities in each chapter, I've written an essay introducing the region, describing the flavor of the place, listing what activities are most available there, and explaining how history has played out across the land. Also, early in each chapter, I've given a brief explanation of the region's natural history in the "The Lay of the Land" section, and I've done my best to orient the reader to directions, major towns, and highways in the "Orientation" section.

Next in each chapter is a "Parks & Other Hot Spots" section, which is a listing of important sites, from ancient Puebloan ruins to state parks, from lakes to a few museums that might appeal to outdoors lovers. And, after the rundown of the most primo adventures in each sporting category, you can consult "Campgrounds & Other Accommodations" to ensure that you have a place to lay your tired body down after a day's adventure.

Before You Go

GETTING THERE

There are three major airports in Arizona and New Mexico: **Sky Harbor International Airport** in Phoenix, **Tucson International Airport,** and the **Albuquerque International Sunport.** A secondary airport serving southern New Mexico is **El Paso International Airport** in western Texas. All three major airports are served by the following airlines: **American** (☎ 800/433-7300; www.aa. com), **America West** (☎ 800/235-9292; www.americawest.com), **Continental** (☎ 800/523-3273; www.continental.com), **Delta** (☎ 800/221-1212; www.delta.com), **Northwest** (☎ 800/225-2525; www.nwa. com), and **Southwest** (☎ 800/ 435-9792; www.southwest.com). Additional airlines serving Phoenix and Albuquerque include **TWA** (☎ 800/221-2000; www. twa.com), **United** (☎ 800/241-6522; www.ual.com), **Frontier Airlines** (☎ 800/ 432-1359; www.frontierairlines. com), and **US Airways** (☎ 800/428-4322; www.usairways. com). **Alaska Airlines** (☎ 800/426-0333; www.alaskaair.com) serves Phoenix, but not Albuquerque or Tucson. **Aero México** (☎ 800/237-6639; www.aeromexico.com) serves Phoenix and Tucson, but not Albuquerque. **Mesa Airlines** (☎ 800/ 637-2247; www.mesa-air. com) serves Albuquerque, but not Phoenix or Tucson.

Those wishing to fly directly to the Grand Canyon may do so with **Air Vegas** (☎ 800/255-7474; www.airvegas.com) and **Scenic Airlines** (☎ 800/634-6801; www.scenic.com).

In conjunction with United Airlines, commuter flights are offered to and from Santa Fe via Denver by **United Express,** which is operated by Great Lakes Aviation (☎ 800/241-6522; www. greatlakesav.com).

If you're traveling by train, **Amtrak** has two routes through the region. The Southwest Chief, which runs between Chicago and Los Angeles, passes through Arizona and New Mexico once daily in each direction, with stops in Kingman, Flagstaff, Winslow, Gallup, Grants, Albuquerque, Lamy (for Santa Fe), Las Vegas, and Raton. A second train, the Sunset Limited, which runs between Los Angeles and New Orleans, passes through three times weekly in each direction, with stops in Tucson, Lordsburg, Deming, and El Paso, Texas. A shuttle bus takes passengers from Tucson to Phoenix, and Greyhound/Trailways bus lines provide through-ticketing for Amtrak between El Paso and Albuquerque. You can get a copy of Amtrak's National Timetable from any Amtrak station, from travel agents, or by contacting Amtrak at ☎ **800/USA-RAIL,** or www. amtrak.com.

HANTAVIRUS PULMONARY SYNDROME

News reports regarding the rare, but often fatal, respiratory disease known as Hantavirus have frightened some potential visitors to Arizona and New Mexico. First recognized in 1993, the disease has afflicted just over 100 people, and half of those cases were reported in the Four Corners states of Arizona, New Mexico, Utah, and Colorado. It is believed that the disease is spread through urine and droppings of deer, mice, and other rodents, so outdoor enthusiasts are in one of the highest risk categories. Although there is cause for concern, there are ways (recommended by the Centers for Disease Control) of protecting yourself and your family against Hantavirus:

- ☐ Avoid camping or sleeping in areas with signs of rodent droppings.
- ☐ When using cabins that have been closed for the winter or for an extended period of time, open them and air them out for awhile *before* spending any length of time inside. Check for rodent infestation as well.
- ☐ If you see a rodent burrow or den, do not disturb it, or try to chase the animals out of the area—just set up camp somewhere else.
- ☐ Don't sleep on the bare ground. Use a mat or an elevated cot if possible.
- ☐ Don't set up camp near a woodpile.
- ☐ Keep foods in airtight, rodent-proof containers, and dispose of garbage promptly and efficiently.

If you have some exposure to rodents and begin to exhibit symptoms of the disease (breathing difficulties, headache, flu-like symptoms, fever, abdominal, joint, and lower back pain, and sometimes nausea), see a doctor immediately, and be sure to tell him or her where and when you were in contact with rodents. The sooner you seek medical attention the better your chances for survival.

For bus service, contact **Greyhound** (☎ 800/231-2222; www.greyhound.com), which connects Arizona and New Mexico with the rest of the country. Another more regional bus line is **Texas, New Mexico, and Oklahoma Coaches** (TNM&O; ☎ 505/242-4998). Most visitors to the Grand Canyon fly into Phoenix and then travel to the canyon by car or by bus with **Nava-Hopi Tours** (☎ 800/892-8687 or 520/774-5003; www.navahopitours.com), although there is air service available to Grand Canyon Airport (see above for details). Most visitors to Santa Fe take the bus directly from the Albuquerque airport. **Sandia Shuttle Express** buses (☎ 505/243-3244 in Albuquerque, ☎ 505/474-5696 in Santa Fe) make the 70-minute run between the airport and Santa Fe hotels 10 times daily each way. Reservations are required.

Because distances in Arizona and New Mexico can be long and public transportation is minimal, you'll definitely need a car to get around. All the major car rental agencies are represented in the region, including **Alamo** (☎ 800/327-9633), **Avis** (☎ 800/831-2847), **Budget** (☎ 505/768-5900), **Dollar** (☎ 800/369-4226), **Enterprise** (☎ 800/325-8007), **Hertz** (☎ 800/654-3131), and **Thrifty** (☎ 800/367-2277).

WHEN TO GO

The seasons will certainly determine which parts of Arizona and New Mexico you should visit and when. Know that on the Colorado Plateau, and stretching across the whole northern portion of both states, winters tend to be cold, while in the lowlands of the Great Basin and Range region, particularly in the Sonoran

Desert of Arizona, summers are extremely hot. Fortunately, the transition zone in between gets the best of both. At an elevation averaging 4,500 feet above sea level, much of the region around the area of Sedona, Arizona, and across to Socorro, New Mexico has mild seasons. The higher region around Alpine, Arizona, which cuts through the transition zone I've just indicated across the center of the states, is the exception here, with much cooler temperatures in the summer and winter. Arizona and New Mexico do receive snow, particularly in the higher elevations, as well as sleet and hail. Wherever you are within the two states, you'll likely experience the summer monsoon, which takes place in July, August, and early September. Outdoor enthusiasts should watch out for fast weather changes and beware of thunderstorms.

STAYING HEALTHY

One thing that sets Arizona and New Mexico apart from most other states is the elevation. Most of the region is above 4,000 feet above sea level, and many heavily traveled areas, including Flagstaff and Santa Fe, are at 7,000 feet or above. Visitors should take certain precautions.

The first is to wear appropriate clothing: Don't venture out at any time of year, even in the middle of summer, without at least a warm sweater and rain gear. The second precaution is to protect your health: Don't push yourself too hard during your first few days at higher elevations. The air is thinner, and the sun more direct. If you haven't engaged in physical activity regularly, see your doctor before your trip just to be sure you're in good condition. Under the best of circumstances at these altitudes, you should expect to sunburn more easily and stop to catch your breath more frequently. Getting plenty of rest, avoiding large meals, and drinking lots of nonalcoholic fluids (especially water) can also help make the adjustment easier for flatlanders.

The reduced oxygen and humidity at these altitudes can bring on some unique problems, not the least of which is acute **mountain sickness.** Characterized in its early stages by headaches, shortness of breath, appetite loss and/or nausea, tingling in the fingers or toes, lethargy, and insomnia, it can ordinarily be treated with aspirin and a slower pace. If it persists or worsens, you must descend to a lower altitude.

Another danger of high elevations is **sunburn.** You can burn much faster here than at sea level because the thinner atmosphere offers less protection from the sun. It's wise to wear sunscreen even when riding in a car on a sunny day.

Dehydration is always a concern in the desert. Visitors from humid climates may find the dryness pleasant—dry heat is not as oppressive, and sweat evaporates almost immediately, cooling the skin. This is a mixed blessing, however, because many people don't feel thirsty here until they're already significantly dehydrated. Early symptoms of dehydration include headache and lethargy, and these may progress to impaired concentration and irregular heartbeat. If you feel any of these symptoms, immediately find a cool place to rest and drink plenty of water. Better yet, prevent dehydration by carrying some bottled water with you and sipping it throughout the day, whether or not you feel thirsty.

Rain and thunderstorms are common in Arizona and New Mexico on late-summer afternoons. If you get caught in a fast-developing thunderstorm, seek lower ground immediately. Rain in the region can also cause serious problems. If it begins to rain while you're out hiking, stay out of ditches, narrow canyons, and arroyos (dry creek beds). Flash floods are not uncommon, especially in late summer, and they're very dangerous. If while driving you suddenly find that water is covering part of the roadway, don't try to drive across. It's best to wait it out, since the bulk of the water may be just around the corner upstream. The rain will stop, and the water will recede—more quickly than you might imagine.

It is unfortunate that I have to warn you about **drinking stream water** while partaking in outdoor activities, but I'd be remiss if I didn't. There are still places where it's safe to drink water directly from its source; however, it's easier and more prudent to simply filter all water before you drink it if you're hiking. You can buy mechanical filtration units at outdoors shops, or you can use chemical treatment such as iodine drops or chlorination. If you're going to drink from natural sources, try to get your water from springs located upstream from campgrounds. If you're going hiking or biking only for the day or have a place in mind to stop for the night where you can pick up provisions, it's much better to carry your own drinking water.

Another thing you might be concerned about during outdoor activities is **wildlife.** Basically, you should keep your eyes and ears open, but most wildlife will be more afraid of you than you are of it. No matter what you encounter, be it bear or bighorn sheep, leave it alone. Above all, don't feed it. When camping, it's a good idea to put all food in a bag, tie it to a rope, and hoist it up in a tree. Never sleep with food in your tent.

Always watch out for snakes, especially **rattlers,** and keep a respectful distance if you see one. Like snakes, **scorpions** and **poisonous spiders** are much more rare than their reputations would suggest, but they do live here, too. They're most commonly found in woodpiles, abandoned and decaying buildings, and under rocks. Don't reach into these places without first inspecting them carefully.

Getting Underway

If you're like me, the best vacation possible includes many types of adventures. The list below offers not only an overview of activities within Arizona and New Mexico, but also a list of my favorite adventures and locales within the region to hike, bike, ski, and horseback ride, along with many other outdoor sports to enjoy. Happy trails!

BALLOONING

When I was about 10 years old, my parents went out one night to a party and returned to tell my brother, sister, and me that they had purchased an interest in a hot-air balloon. That was back in the

---

A Few Added Safety Precautions

Before heading out:

Check with the Forest Service for wilderness permits, weather reports, fire regulations, and water conditions.

Get a good topographical map of the area.

Prepare for extreme weather by wearing layers of clothing. Never become chilled; hypothermia can come on quickly.

Let someone know where you're going and how long you'll be gone.

Filter all drinking water.

Build fires away from trees and shrubs.

Don't camp in a flood zone.

1960s when ballooning was unheard of. Their purchase that night, in league with the noted airplane pilot Sid Cutter, brought the first balloon to Albuquerque. By the next year, my brother, sister, and I were the ground crew for the first annual Albuquerque Balloon Fiesta, which then entailed about five balloons chasing after each other in what was called a Coyote-Roadrunner Race. We spent days scrambling across dusty fields in pursuit of balloons and trying to steal sips of champagne from the winners.

Today, the **Kodak Albuquerque International Balloon Fiesta** is the largest balloon rally in the world. Bringing together more than 1,000 colorful globes, the event includes races and contests. There are mass ascensions at sunrise, and "balloon glows" in the evening. Various special events are staged all week.

Balloons lift off at Balloon Fiesta Park (at I-25 and Alameda NE) on Albuquerque's northern city limits during the second week in October. For information call ☎ **800/733-9918** or log on to www.balloonfiesta.com.

Visitors not content to just watch the colorful craft rise into the blue skies have a choice of several hot-air balloon operators in the Albuquerque area, including **Rainbow Ryders** and **World Balloon Corporation** (see chapter 9).

One of the most spectacular places to take a balloon ride is in Sedona, Arizona, where you'll glide over the many red rock formations. I list a number of reliable outfitters in chapter 5.

BIRD WATCHING

The southwestern United States is truly one of the premier birding spots in the world. In fact, while birding along the San Pedro River in southeastern Arizona, I met a man who told me a story that illustrates the fact. An avid birder, he went to a birding conference in Australia. At the beginning of the conference, participants stood to tell where they were from and why they were there. After the introductory ceremony he found himself surrounded by conference-goers from all over the world, who shot question after question at him about places such as **Ramsey Canyon,** the **San Pedro Riparian Area,** and the **Chiricahua Mountains.** If you're a serious birder, head directly to southeastern Arizona (see chapter 7); you won't be disappointed. The "sky islands" of the area, surrounded by deserts and grasslands, represent a convergence for four distinct regions: the Rocky Mountain, Mexico's Sierra Madre, the Sonoran Desert, and the Chihuahuan Desert. The air above these land zones are major flyways, where tropical birds come up from the south, and cold-weather birds fly down from the north; over 500 species have been recorded in the area.

If you're impressed by a number of birds, there's possibly no better place in the United States to experience them than in central New Mexico at **Bosque del Apache National Wildlife Refuge** (see chapter 11). Not only have more than 300 species been spotted upon the 7,000 carefully managed riparian acres, but, in any given winter, there may be as many as 45,000 snow geese, 57,000 ducks of various species, and 18,000 sandhill cranes. One of my more exciting birding experiences was seeing one lone whooping crane feeding on a stubbly field there. People come from all over the world to attend the **Festival of the Cranes** at Bosque del Apache. This bird-watching event is always the weekend before Thanksgiving.

And, if you're into eclectic bird watching, head to the **Vermilion Cliffs** in northern Arizona, where you'll likely catch a glimpse of the noble California condor, which the California Condor Recovery Plan has brought to the area in the hope that it can flourish there (see chapter 2).

BOARDSAILING & SAILING

Because the southwestern United States is mostly desert, it isn't exactly a mecca for board and boat sailors, but there are some amazing intersections of water and air worth experiencing. With its warm, wide-open spaces and strong desert winds, **Lake Powell** is a favorite for many sailors, though the deep canyons can make wind conditions inconsistent (see chapter 3). Arizona's West Coast—**Lake Havasu** and **Lake Mohave**—has thousands of acres of water upon which to ply your sails (see chapter 4). In New Mexico, one of the boarders' favorite spots is **Storrie Lake** in the northeast (see chapter 10). Though it's a small lake, its position on the edge of the plains makes for consistent and strong winds throughout spring, summer, and fall. **Heron Lake** in north central New Mexico is a lovely mountain lake with good steady winds, though the water is always cold (see chapter 9). **Elephant Butte Lake** is also a popular spot for sailors, though it can be overrun with motorboats (see chapter 11).

CAVING

Some of my most memorable experiences researching this book were spent in damp darkness, hundreds of feet below the earth's surface. What most struck me about the caving experiences I had was how varied that underworld can be, from the deep and rough basaltic caves in the northern regions to the smooth and graceful limestone ones in the south. The most notable lava tubes in Arizona and New Mexico are the **Lava River Cave** outside Flagstaff (see chapter 2) and the **Big Tubes** area at El Malpais National Monument near Grants (see chapter 8). You explore both caves on your own. Also in the north are the limestone **Grand Canyon Caverns** west of Flagstaff (see chapter 2), some of the largest dry caverns in the world. These developed caves aren't as lively as the ones I'll mention below, but they do provide a peek into an interesting underground world.

The biggest news in developed caving these days is the newly opened **Kartchner Caverns,** outside Benson, Arizona (see chapter 7). There you'll see rooms larger than football fields and all the exotic elements a live cave presents, from stalactites and stalagmites to shields and bacon, and other interesting formations, to a 58-foot column. The premier developed caving experience in the region is **Carlsbad Caverns** (see chapter 12) in southeastern New Mexico. There you'll travel into a live cave that meanders through limestone to depths of over 850 feet. En route you'll encounter all manner of formations, rooms as large as 14 acres, and a quarter of a million bats.

The most technical caving experience in the region is north of Carlsbad outside Ruidoso. The **Fort Stanton Cave** is the second or third largest in New Mexico. This cave, along with the **Crockett Cave,** forge through limestone similar to what you see at Carlsbad, and both have large rooms and lengthy tunnels. The **Torgac Cave** is considered the premier gypsum cave in the world. All three of these caves

---

Canoeing

Because this is the desert, canoeing isn't a major activity in the region. Some people like to take their flat-water canoes to area lakes, but because of the distances that need to be traversed in places such as Lake Havasu and Lake Powell, most find that sea kayaks are a more expedient option. Still, there are a handful of white-water canoeists, particularly in northern New Mexico. To see the masters of this sport in action is to see sheer poetry; many are capable of rolling their canoes, much the way we kayakers roll our kayaks, but their actions require extensive finesse and power. For those white-water canoeists, I've outlined many runs that will be suitable, from Class I to Class V, in the "White-Water Kayaking & Rafting" section, later in this chapter.

require special permits for which you'll have to apply months in advance (see chapter 12).

CLIMBING

Some of my fondest memories while researching this book were moments when I found myself hanging by my fingertips and toes 60-plus feet up on a new rock face. Similarly, one of my biggest regrets about this book is that I wasn't able to scale all the faces listed here, mostly because of time, but also because of ability—I have quite a ways to go before I'll be heading up any Grade V trad routes laying in my own gear. But that's okay; I like having eternal challenge in a sport.

So now you know where I'm coming from as I wrote this section of the book. I've done my best to list the most notable routes and to give basic directions to get to them. But, a climber certainly couldn't count on just using this book. The scope of it doesn't allow for specific route descriptions, a necessity in most climbing situations. So, the way I suggest you use what I've written here is as an introduction to what's available in a particular region. From there, seek out the texts I mention within the specific sections, and then strap on your shoes and scale the crags.

Two very decent all-purpose resources for the region are *Rock Climbing Arizona* by Stewart M. Green (Falcon Press, 1999), and *Rock Climbing New Mexico and Texas* by Dennis R. Jackson (Falcon Press, 1996). If you'd like some instruction or guide service, **Flagstaff Mountain Guides** (☎ 520/635-0145; e-mail: nazclimb@aol.com) can guide you to climbing spots in the Flagstaff and Sedona areas, including the San Francisco Peaks, while **Southwest Climbing Resource** in Santa Fe (☎ 505/983-8288) and **Mountain Skills** in Taos (☎ 505/776-2037) guide in north central New Mexico as well as in parts of Arizona.

I've used the Yosemite Decimal System (YDS), the usual American grading scale, to identify the technical difficulty of the routes. Be aware that ratings vary from area to area. Use all ratings as a starting point and expect a one- to two-letter grade variation from what you may be accustomed to. Typically, mountain travel is rated as follows:

- **Class 1** Trail hiking.
- **Class 2** Hiking on rough ground; may require use of hands.
- **Class 3** Traveling on rough, often steep ground; may require use of hands and careful foot placement.
- **Class 4** Traveling or scrambling over steep terrain where a fall could result in an injury. May require a rope and belay.
- **Class 5** Climbing on steep terrain where a fall would cause injury or death. Careful placement of hands and feet required. Ropes and belays are needed.

Tacked onto the Class 5 rating is the added difficulty of the pitch, with 5.0 being the easiest and 5.15 the most difficult to date. Other ratings you may encounter are a "+" and "−" symbol, generally used when a consensus hasn't been reached, so you may have a 5.10+, denoting that some believe the route is harder than a 5.10. Also employed are letter subgrades of *a, b,* and *c,* denoting increased difficulty, with a 5.10a easier than a 5.10c. Be aware that routes are rated according to the most difficult move.

Though I'm not going into the subject in detail, know that Class 6 climbing, aid climbing, has a whole set of ratings of its own.

Also, some longer, usually traditional, routes are rated with Roman numerals I through VI to refer to the level of commitment in terms of length and time necessary for the climb.

- **Grade I** Requires a few hours to complete
- **Grade II** Requires up to half a day
- **Grade III** Requires most of the day
- **Grade IV** Requires all day
- **Grade V** Requires a bivouac
- **Grade VI** Requires 2 or more days

Favorite Climbs

As for my favorite climbing spots (and those of friends who have stronger criteria), they are as follows:

- Paradise Fork (chapter 2)
- Granite Mountain (chapter 5)
- Cochise Stronghold (chapter 7)
- Cochiti Mesa (chapter 9)
- Enchanted Tower (chapter 11)

CROSS-COUNTRY SKIING

During wet years, parts of Arizona and New Mexico provide excellent cross-country and backcountry skiing, on terrain ranging from open meadows with little climbing to steep mountains with intense ascents and fast descents. In Arizona, your best bet for skiing is in the **San Francisco Peaks** in the Flagstaff and Grand Canyon areas (see chapter 2) and the **White Mountains** in eastern Arizona (see chapter 6). In New Mexico, look to the **Sangre de Cristo Mountains** in the Red River and Santa Fe areas and to the **Jemez Mountains** in the area around Los Alamos (see chapter 9).

For those who enjoy hut skiing, there are yurts (Mongolian huts) in the **Chama** region and another outside **Taos** both in north central New Mexico (see chapter 9). Both options are great for touring, with plenty of nice, smooth kick-and-glide areas, and for telemark skiing, with lots of wide-open bowls in which to carve turns.

Seasons range broadly: I've found myself skiing near Santa Fe on Halloween and even a little in early June. But, those blessed years aren't the norm. Generally, enough snow will accumulate by early December and remain on the ground through late March. If you do head out, be prepared. Always carry plenty of water, food, sunscreen, layers of clothes, a compass, and duck tape to repair bindings.

DOWNHILL SKIING & SNOWBOARDING

Though Arizona and New Mexico aren't immediately notable as downhill skiing and snowboarding destinations, they should be for a few good reasons: Taos Ski Valley in New Mexico, though smaller than resorts such as Aspen and Vail, is a world-class destination. The region is also a less expensive place to ski than many Colorado and Utah resorts. Following is a rundown of what you'll find.

Taos Ski Valley is consistently ranked by industry magazines as one of the top ski areas in the world, but its appeal is somewhat narrow. It does not allow snowboarders, and many of the runs intimidate beginning skiers. But, it also has one of the best ski schools in the world, so those who want to learn to have fun on this mountain definitely can do so (see chapter 9).

The ski areas surrounding Taos draw many people, especially those from nearby Texas and other southern locales. **Angel Fire** and **Red River** (see chapter 9), in particular, provide good family skiing experiences, but crowds can be immense during holidays. The same applies for southern New Mexico's **Ski Apache** (see chapter 12).

Those looking to ski in Arizona may be surprised to find the variety of terrain available at **Sunrise Park Resort** in the White Mountains, an amazing set of three mountains perched near the edge of the Mogollon Rim which drops off into the Sonoran Desert (see chapter 6). Though I wouldn't build a whole ski vacation around the site, Flagstaff's skiing at **Arizona Snowbowl** has an impressive 2,300-foot drop, with a broad range of runs (see chapter 2).

When planning to ski at any of these southwestern ski areas, be aware that winters can be precarious. I'm writing this on the heels of a few very dry ski seasons. Some fear that the 300-inch snow years that Taos once knew are gone, but that's for Mother Nature and the forces of global warming to determine. As travelers, you may want to keep your plans as flexible as possible.

FISHING

The variety of terrain in Arizona and New Mexico, from deserts to canyons to mountains, makes for a diverse and year-round fishing experience. That variety can be noted without even traveling far. In places such as Lees Ferry and Lake Powell, and the San Juan River and Navajo Lake, cold-water fishing and warm-water fishing are separated by yards rather than miles, thanks to dams set between these and many other rivers and lakes.

The key to fishing the area well is in watching elevation. In winter, look to the lowland lakes and streams. In summer, head to the highlands, where the streams still run cool. Also fish the lower, warm waters during spring runoff (when streams are high) and in late fall, when snow has come to the mountains. The best time of all to fish is in the fall when the days are fair, and the waters are calm and clear.

In the region you'll find mostly rainbow, brown, brook, cutthroat, and Apache trout and arctic grayling in cold waters, while warmer waters hold striped, largemouth, smallmouth, white, and yellow bass, crappie, bluegill, pike, and walleye. Twelve-inch trout are not unusual in streams, with trophies reaching 11 to 26 inches at places such as Navajo Dam.

Practicing catch-and-release techniques is always encouraged. Some areas are designated "Special Trout Waters." Most of them are restricted to the use of artificial flies and lures with single, barbless hooks. All have bag and possession limits. Strong steps are being taken in the region to protect wild trout populations such as the Apache trout in Arizona, the Rio Grande cutthroat in New Mexico, and the Gila trout in both places.

The only native trout in the southern Rockies, the Rio Grande cutthroat, now only live in a few small headwater streams. Their decline is due to destruction of habitat, introduction of non-native species, and hybridization. The Fish and Game Department encourages anglers to return all Rio Grande cutthroats to the water.

In order to fish in either state you will need a license. Contact the **Arizona Department of Game and Fish (☎ 602/942-3000;** www.gmfish.state.az.us) and the **New Mexico Depart-ment of Game and Fish (☎ 800/275-3434;** www.gmfsh.state.nm.us). Both agencies will send you documents covering rules and regulations and lists of public fishing waters. Be aware that fishing on reservation land does not require a state license but does require a tribal permit, which runs from $5 to $15 per day for adults and less for children and seniors.

A helpful guide to the area is *Fly-Fishing in Northern New Mexico,* edited by Craig Martin (UNM Press, 1991). Taylor Streit has a guide for each state, titled **Guide to Fly Fishing in Arizona** and **Guide to Fly Fishing New Mexico** (David Communications, 2000).

The two world-class fishing spots in the region are the **San Juan River** outside Farmington in New Mexico Indian Country and **Lees Ferry** on the Colorado River in Arizona Indian Country. The San Juan can be best appreciated by experienced fishers. Very heavily used, its trout are large and wily. This is the place to go for those who get a kick out of trying to outsmart the small-brained critters and who don't mind being stymied in the process (see chapter 3 for Lees Ferry, chapter 8 for the San Juan River). Also worth exploring are the mountains of **north central New Mexico,** where stream and lake fishing abounds (see chapter 9).

As for the Lees Ferry area, it is a premier spot because of the size and quantity of trout. Fish average 16 inches, but 25-inch fish have been caught here, and 50-fish days have been known to happen. Your best bet is to hire a guide; you'll be traveling 15 miles up a river with many complexities (see chapter 3). Another good fishing destination is **eastern Arizona's "Alps,"** where cool water streams and lakes drain from 11,000-foot peaks (see chapter 6).

HIKES & BACKPACK TRIPS

One of the reasons the Southwest is such a great hiking destination is that any time of year you can always find some sort of hiking. Your best tool for deciding when and where to hike is elevation. During the summer months you'll want to stick to the mountainous regions above 7,000 feet, areas that you should avoid during the winter. During those colder months you'll want to stick to the desert lands, but be aware that in winter the desert does get quite cold at night, at times below freezing. Fall and summer are good months to hike almost anywhere in the region, though you'll always want to be prepared with rain and wind gear, as well as good, hearty insulation for nights.

This region doesn't have the weeks-long backpack trips for which the Northwest is so noted, though it's possible to set out for long stretches. That's one reason I've put the hiking and backpacking sections together in this book. Many of the routes listed would make great day hikes or backpacking trips, and often, if a hike isn't long, it can be linked up with other trails to make a strong backpacking trip. My main criteria for selecting hikes in this book were the scenic value and the adventure quotient. I've made an attempt to pick the very best hikes each region has to offer, though that's nearly an impossible task because every hiker has his or her own criteria.

I've also done my best within the text to give fairly specific route directions for each hike, but these listings are by no means exact descriptions. I have not listed every turn in the trail, every stream you will cross, or viewpoint that you'll encounter. I'm assuming the readers of this book will know how to use a map and follow a trail. Especially for those who plan to backpack, I trust you to acquire the necessary maps, route out a hiking plan, locate your water sources, and know how to read a compass. In an ideal world, each route in this book would be accompanied by a map and a mile-by-mile description, but the scope of it doesn't allow for such detail. Part of the fun of setting out is using and sharpening your outdoor skills; this book will allow you to do that, while helping you find your way.

For day hikes you don't generally need a permit, though you may at some points need to pay a fee. To camp overnight, however, you may need a permit and you may need to acquire it months in advance. For example, in the Grand Canyon and Vermilion Cliffs areas in Arizona, you'll need to apply for a permit many months before your departure. Procedures for doing so are listed in the hiking sections.

Good sources for hikes in Arizona are *Hiking Arizona,* by Stewart Aitchison and Bruce Grubbs (Falcon, 1996); *Exploring Arizona's Wild Areas,* by Scott S. Warren (The Mountaineers, 1996); *Canyoneering Arizona,* by Tyler Williams (Funhog Press, 1998); and *Hiking the Grand Canyon,* by Scott Thybony (Grand Canyon Natural History Association, 1994). For hiking in New Mexico, try *New Mexico's Wilderness Areas,* by Bob Julyan (Westcliff Publishers, 1998), and *75 Hikes in New Mexico,* by Craig Martin (The Mountaineers, 1995).

CANYONEERING BASICS

A term coined fairly recently, *canyoneering* describes the process of traveling down into the earth, as opposed to the process of mountaineering in which you climb to its heights. The two share many characteristics. Hikers in either sport need to be prepared with proper gear, have good map- and compass-reading and route-finding skills, be aware of danger and willing to be uncomfortable at times.

PROPER GEAR AND SKILLS

The main characteristic of canyoneering is that the trails are often rough if there are trails at all. Generally the routes traverse boulder-strewn river bottoms, so what trails might exist are washed away. Because it isn't too difficult to follow a canyon, the options for getting lost are minimized; however, the added complexity of side canyons makes getting lost easy. Thus, an important skill to develop for this sport is sure footing and good map- and compass-reading skills.

Another characteristic of canyons is water. Often canyoneering involves crossing pools of it anywhere from ankle deep to over-your-head deep. This requires special tools. Most canyoneers carry an inflatable mattress of some sort, or an inner tube to float their pack, as well as plastic bags to put over the pack so that gear doesn't get wet. It's also a good idea to pack gear in plastic bags within your pack, just in case water seeps through the outer bags.

Finally, falls. Often canyons are characterized by drops or waterfalls that are sometimes wet, and sometimes dry. Negotiating them may require climbing skills and the use of ropes. If you don't know how to use technical climbing gear, go to your local climbing gym get some instruction, and then spend some time out on the rocks before endeavoring some of the more difficult routes listed in this book.

TOOLS

- [ ] Compass
- [ ] Maps
- [ ] Flotation for your pack
- [ ] Plastic bags to cover your pack
- [ ] Plastic bags for gear within your pack
- [ ] Dry clothes for after swimming
- [ ] Good hiking socks that will stay comfortable even when your boots are wet
- [ ] Climbing ropes
- [ ] Carabiners
- [ ] Climbing harness
- [ ] Belaying device

Favorite Hikes

- Buckskin Gultch and the Wire Pass Trail (chapter 2)
- Peralta Trail in Arizona's Superstition Mountains (chapter 5)
- Wilson Mountain (chapter 5)
- Romero Canyon (chapter 7)
- Pecos Baldy and the Truchas Peaks (chapter 9)
- White Mountain Crest Trail (chapter 12)
- Alkali Flats Trail at White Sands National Monument (chapter 12)
- Hermit's Peak (chapter 10)

HORSEBACK RIDING

Adventurers come from all over the world to horseback ride in Arizona and New Mexico. These are the states where some of the most notable Western historic moments took place, and where many Westerns have been filmed. In Tombstone, Wyatt Earp and Doc Holliday

SAFETY

Be aware that like mountaineering, this sport can, at times, be dangerous and uncomfortable. You'll want to beware of setting out into a canyon during the summer monsoon season, which spans from July through mid-September. During that time, flash floods can wash down canyons, taking all that's not locked down. In August 1997 just such a flash flood killed 11 people hiking in Antelope Canyon near the Arizona/Utah border. Another time flooding can occur is during the spring snowmelt in April, May, and early June.

There is also the constant danger of falling. Besides negotiating the falls I discussed above, which can be very real falling hazards, often the trails will follow narrow ledges high above the canyon floor. Hikers need to be especially careful when walking such tightrope situations with a heavy pack. Most canyons have few escape routes, so if a problem arises, it may be miles to safety. Before setting out, be sure to explore what escape routes there are and be careful so you won't need to use them.

As for discomfort, you'll definitely find it in this sport. Often you'll be gaining or losing thousands of feet of elevation within a few miles, which is hard on the body. Another concern is temperature. Within canyons you'll often encounter great extremes, so you'll have to carry a range of warm- and cold-weather clothing. With the added component of water, through which you may be swimming, hypothermia can be a very real concern. Be sure to come prepared with adequate insulation. You'll want to carry plenty of water at all times, as canyon bottoms can be very hot, and dehydration is a reality. Footwear can be a problem while canyoneering. Though your feet may be wet much of the time, it's still a good idea to wear sturdy hiking boots with good socks that will stay warm even when they're wet. Rangers caution against wearing sandals because they can get lost in the muck and leave hikers shoeless.

While everyone needs to be aware of the physical dangers, some of you may have more internal concerns: Some people find this kind of hiking claustrophobic. Be prepared to be submerged in shadow and confined by narrow walls much of the time. If you've never experienced a narrow "slot" canyon, be sure to day hike one before setting out on a backpacking trip.

killed outlaws at the O.K. Corral, and later a movie was made about it in the vicinity. Butch Cassidy hung out in the region, particularly in the area of Cimarron, New Mexico, and years later, *Butch Cassidy and the Sundance Kid* was filmed near that Old West town.

There's a great deal of variety in the types of riding a person can do in the Southwest, so it's good to choose carefully. If you're content with a nose-to-tail kind of ride, you'll be happiest riding in the mountainous regions such as the White Mountains or in more controlled environments such as through Monument Valley. But if you'd prefer to really ride— to trot and canter your horse—you'll want to go to places where the terrain allows for such riding. The Wickenburg area at the **K El Bar Ranch** (see chapter 5) and in Patagonia at the Circle Z Ranch (see chapter 7) in Arizona are two such places, as are the **Double E Guest Ranch** in the Silver City area of southwestern New Mexico (see chapter 11) and **Roadrunner Tours** near Angel Fire listed in the "New Mexico's Rocky Mountains" chapter (see chapter 9).

CHOOSING AN OUTFITTER

If you're one of those people who loves the idea of heading into the mountains or down into a canyon for days or weeks of fun but doesn't have time to plan such a trip, you may be a candidate for a guided tour. These can have many benefits; the most notable is relieving you of the hassle of planning and executing the adventure. However, guided trips are also more expensive than going on your own, and you're restricted to planned activities. Within many of the "What to Do & Where to Do It" sections I've provided a list of outfitters; a good way to find the most up-to-date options is by searching the Internet under "Adventure Tours" for Arizona and New Mexico. Before getting involved in an organized tour—most likely hiking, mountain biking, road biking, or river rafting—there are a few questions you might want to ask the outfitter, or yourself:

1. **What's the cost and what's included in the price?** First and foremost, discuss the type of accommodations and whether all meals are included. Some companies skip lunch or an occasional dinner. If it's important to you, also ask if liquor is included. Generally, when looking you'll find many options, from overnights in elegant country inns with full breakfasts and fancy dinners, to camping trips where guests help with the meals. Ask yourself what suits you most and find that type of trip. Also ask about potential hidden costs, particularly equipment rentals and transportation to and from the airport.

2. **What level of fitness is required?** This is by far the most important question. Get a feeling for the tour. Is the trip an obstacle course suited for Marines, a play-date for 3-year-olds, or something in between? Do you bike 20, 40, or 60 miles a day, or do you have options for each day? Many tours include options. On a typical day of road biking, for example, a tour company might include two or three ride options ranging between 15 to 60 miles. You might not be fit enough to complete the 60-mile route, but if you think you can ride 15 miles, you're good to go. In general, then, you don't have to be a world-class triathlete to participate in tours in Arizona and New Mexico. But if you fall short of minimal fitness requirements, you're going to be miserable.

3. **What is the guide-to-guest ratio?** I'd say that on a cycling or hiking tour, a ratio of 10 guests for each guide is about the acceptable limit. But for other activities, the limit might be much lower. Use your own judgment. For example, would you want to go fly-fishing with a guide and 10 other anglers? I wouldn't.

A new venue in the horseback-riding world that has expanded greatly thanks to Billy Crystal's *City Slickers* is riding in a ranch setting, actually helping to move cattle and perform other cowboy activities. The most notable ranches in New Mexico to date are **Rancho Cañon Ancho,** in the northeast (see chapter 10), and the **Double E Ranch** in the Silver City area (see chapter 11), both where you work on a real cattle ranch. In the Springerville, Arizona area, **K5 High Country Adventures** also offers real ranch riding (see chapter 6).

If you don't have much riding experience, don't fret—most outfits offer lessons on good, reliable horses. **K El Bar** is especially conscientious about helping beginners get comfortable in the saddle, and work on their skills so that by the end of their stay, if they'd like, they can even canter through an arroyo (see chapter 5).

The guest ranch experience may not be for everyone. Though some can be perfectly content to ride horses once or twice a day for 4 or 5 days to a week, others get bored with the redundancy. If you suspect you may be of that type, you may want to select a guest ranch that has broad range of activities such as the **Sunglow Guest Ranch,** where riding is not included in the price of your stay, so you can mix in some hiking, bird

4. **What are the guides' credentials?** Just being a good cyclist or hiker doesn't make a person a good guide. Ask about the guides' experience level and age. Ask about whether he or she is a naturalist; it's a real plus if someone can identify plant life or a birdcall when walking in the woods. Ask about certification by a professional organization. In some sports, such as rock climbing or hot-air ballooning, such certification can be meaningful. Finally, ask about emergency medical training. Any guide lacking basic first-aid and CPR skills is simply not a guide.

5. **What equipment is required?** Bike-tour companies usually have bike and helmet rentals available, but you'll probably have to reserve a rental bike in advance. In most cases, you'll be expected to bring your own clothing and footwear, although there is the occasional outfitter that may have, say, hiking boots or rain gear to rent or borrow. Generally, river outfitters provide flotation for their clients.

6. **What will the weather be like?** No outfitter, of course, can answer this question with precision. But when packing for the trip, you'll need to know what clothing to bring. Even in midsummer, the temperature at the top of Wheeler Peak in the Rockies can drop into the 40s. Wet weather is a possibility at almost any time of year anywhere in Arizona and New Mexico, so rain gear is a must. Trip itineraries might be modified if the weather is uncooperative, but don't expect any rain checks.

7. **How far in advance do I need to book?** Plan on at least seven weeks, possibly more. Some popular tours get filled up months in advance, especially rafting trips down the Colorado River through the Grand Canyon. On the other hand, tours are occasionally cancelled several weeks before the tour date if the bookings are insufficient.

8. **Who else will be in the group?** Some outfitters and tours cater to singles, some to seniors, and some to families. Do your best to find a group that fits your niche. If you're uncomfortable with the people in a group, you're missing out on one of the real advantages—companionship—of joining a group in the first place. I have a theory that a tour company with a good attitude will generally draw customers with good attitudes. Before booking, take time to talk to the main players at the company; if they don't seem like people you'd like to spend time with, find another outfitter.

9. **Can I bring young children?** This will depend greatly on the type of activity. Your best bet if you'd like to bring your children is to find an outfitter that makes accommodations for kids and encourages them to come along. That way you won't be the only adult with children on the trip, and your kids will have companions.

watching, and even painting during your vacation. **Circle Z Ranch** also offers other activities such as hiking and bird watching, and has a lovely pool and tennis courts on-site. Both are in southeastern Arizona (see chapter 7).

If you're particular about the kind of food you eat and the accommodations that surround you, a few gourmet horse ranches will please your sensibilities. The **Circle Z Ranch** and **K El Bar** both have excellent rooms and delicious food. **Rancho de la Osa,** along the U.S. border with Mexico, has especially comfortable rooms and delectable meals (see chapter 4).

And finally, if you're a connoisseur of terrain and want a long-term adventure, hook up with **Don Donnelly Stables,** headquartered in the Superstition Mountains. This outfit runs horse adventures all over Arizona, from five- and seven-day rides through Monument Valley, to Old West cross-country rides in Bisbee and Tombstone. Donnelly prepares all your meals and does all the planning; you just clip on your spurs and ride. Look to chapter 7 for more information.

Llama and Mountain Goat Trekking

For those of you who like to let docile, Andean llamas carry your load, or the less common domestic goats, there are outfitters who run trips in both Arizona and New Mexico. Since there aren't many, I've lumped them in with the "Horseback Riding" section. Two outfits in north central New Mexico provide excellent treks with llamas. **El Paseo Llama Expeditions** and **Wild Earth Llama Adventures** (see chapter 9) offer day hikes year-round, with gourmet meals provided. Both outfits also offer a variety of custom, multi-day wilderness adventures from May to mid-October, tailored to trekkers' needs and fitness levels.

Purple Mountain Pack Goats (see chapter 7) provides custom day hikes, overnight camping, and educational field trips, letting the animals do the work. It also outfits overnight trips into the scenic Dragoon Mountains east of Tucson.

MOUNTAIN BIKING

I have to admit that after mountain biking for some 10 years I've become a bit of a snob. In most instances I'm not satisfied with simple cruising along on dirt roads. I want single track, the narrow trails created by hikers and horseback riders, and I used good single track as my highest criterion for this book. That said, I realize that not everyone is up to riding miles of winding single track, and so I have included many trails that are fun and beautiful, but also wide enough to allow for steering errors.

One of the greatest difficulties in writing this book was attempting to give trail directions for the rides. Many of the trails are unmarked. In fact, many are simply cool routes that local riders have carved out of the earth (hopefully without causing too much damage). On those, I've done my best to give directions, but the onus of not getting lost will have to remain with the rider. Your best bet, whether on marked National Forest trails or on local unmarked routes, is always to find landmarks upon which you can rely to keep you oriented—a mountain, a lake, or a prominent road will work well. If you're deep in the woods, this will present more of a problem, and you may want to get in the habit of carrying a compass so you can at least know in which direction you're riding. Unfortunately, the scope of this book doesn't allow for the printing of maps for each route. In cases in which there are many trails where maps would greatly help, such as the Sedona area, I've directed riders to check in with local shops where hand-drawn maps are available.

It's also a good idea to heed my warnings when I suggest eliciting the help from a particular bike shop to get you through a complicated route such as the Six Shooter Trail in the Globe, Arizona area and the South Boundary Trail in the Taos, New Mexico area. Both are awesome trails but both will prove frustrating and dangerous if you get lost, which you likely will without help.

Riding in Arizona and New Mexico may be different from anywhere you've ridden, because many of the rides traverse very remote areas. Unlike riding in New England, where if you get lost you'll likely come upon a town at some point, here you're more likely to come upon a bear's den or an impassable canyon. For that reason your excursions into the routes in this book need to be fully self-contained. You must be able to fix a flat tire, and it will help if you can also do minor repairs. For that reason I suggest you carry with you the following:

- At least two bottles of water
- Spare tube
- Patch kit
- Tire lever
- Air pump
- Chain rivet tool
- Spoke wrench
- Allen wrenches
- Six-inch adjustable wrench
- Small screwdriver
- First-aid kit

If you're intrigued about the sport and haven't yet invested in the equipment to participate in it, I can offer a little advice. First, get a decent bike. Though Wal-Mart may have a good deal, once on the trail you'll pay heartily for that low price in terms of effort expended in getting up and down trails. If you're under 40, you'll probably be fine with a good hard-tail bike, which is a bike without rear suspension; however, if you're over 40 you'll be much happier with a dual-suspension bike, meaning it has shock absorbers on both the front and the rear wheels. These newer bikes offer excellent cushioning for our aging bodies, and in many ways can provide higher performance, often with a shorter turning radius and better ability to climb over obstacles. Today you can buy a workable dual-suspension bike for around $1,000, though you'll get much more if you pay a little more. What's most important is your fit on the bike. Ride many bikes before deciding which one is for you. They vary greatly in the way they fit; some will extend your body comfortably, some will cramp your neck, and some will feel unbalanced. Tell your local bike shop how you intend to use the bike, and let them help you find one that suits you well.

Most of all, remember to *always* ride wearing a helmet. Also, be aware that riding in the desert presents a unique obstacle—cactus thorns. Though many bikers eschew the use of green slime because they feel it sloshing around within their tires, the stuff does clog holes, preventing you from having flats. If you can't bring yourself to squirt your tires, then try using liners. Though they don't protect as well, they can be lighter and less distracting.

The most exciting news I came upon while researching this book is the growing popularity of the sport, a fact that national and state agencies are noticing. In many communities I found newly opened bike trails, with more planned for the future. So, as you go, use this book as a guide, but also ask around; you'll likely find many new routes to explore. As you do explore keep in mind the "Leave No Trace" ethics, which are discussed later in this chapter. Though on a mountain bike you will likely leave more of a trace than you would, say, hiking, there are ways of minimizing impact. Always stay on the designated trail, avoid sliding your tires down steep slopes and around corners, and, when possible, ride up *and* down. Though in some areas it's popular to take a shuttle to the top and scream downhill for miles, this type of riding damages the terrain and makes all riders seem irresponsible.

I relied on a few important sources while researching this book, and I recommend them to you, too. *Mountain Biking Arizona* and the *Mountain Biker's Guide to New Mexico,* both by Sarah Bennett (Falcon Press, 1996 and 1994, respectively) are good guides that provide helpful maps of each ride. *Fat Tire Tales and Trails* by Cosmic Ray is a self-published book (1999) with excellent rides, though the maps may, as one biker I encountered said, "Make your head hurt."

Favorite Rides

The rides I've selected as my favorites range from easy to difficult. All offer lovely views and fun track, whether it be road or single track.

- Bell Rock Pathway (chapter 5)
- Broken Arrow/Submarine Rock (chapter 5)
- Starr Pass in the Tucson Mountains (chapter 7)
- Road Apple Trail of the Glade Trail System (chapter 8)
- Windsor Trail in the Rockies (chapter 9)
- Rim Trail in Cloudcroft (chapter 12)

ROAD BIKING

As far as scenery and variety go, Arizona and New Mexico are ideal states to explore on a bicycle. Here you'll pedal through spectacular canyons and mountain ranges, historic villages, and Old West gunslinger towns, generally on decent pavement, and often without too much traffic.

However, there are parts of the region that aren't especially friendly to road bikers, if they acknowledge them at all. Most notable among these is north central New Mexico. Though this region is an ideal spot to clip in and cruise, drivers remain fairly naïve about who has the right-of-way.

Another obstacle the whole region has is the number of RVs that cruise the roads, particularly in parts of Arizona where many people live a sort of turtle lifestyle, traveling around with their homes and whole lives attached to them. Those homes and lives take up a lot of highway space. Because of that, I discourage riding a few routes that might seem on a map ideal, such as U.S. 180 from Flagstaff to the Grand Canyon.

In the entire region it's important to be very aware of traffic when you ride. Never assume a driver sees you, and even if you're sure he does, don't assume he'll give you your hard-earned right-of-way.

In this often-remote part of the world, it's important to be self-sufficient when you ride. In the "Mountain Biking" section above I list bike repair necessities. Use that list of tools when preparing to road bike in the region as well. Be aware that with all the rides I list I'm assuming that the reader has a good road map to follow, so pick one up before you hit the road.

Favorite Rides

My favorite rides range greatly in length and difficulty; all provide beautiful scenery, and most have decent pavement with good shoulders.

- Show Low/Springerville Loop (chapter 6)
- AZ 82 from Sonoita East (chapter 7)
- Enchanted Circle (chapter 9)
- Silver City to Glenwood (chapter 11)

SCUBA DIVING

Scuba diving in this landlocked region? Where there's a will, there's a way. The truth is that few people would venture to this part of the world as a scuba destination, but there are still many of us who like to dive in the ocean but need to learn how close to home. That's where the **Blue Hole** (see chapter 10) in northeastern New Mexico comes in. It's an 81-foot-deep artesian well that's a favorite of divers from throughout New Mexico and neighboring states. Fed by a subterranean river that flows 3,000 gallons per minute at a constant 61°F, it's deep enough to merit open-water certification. Almost as popular is **Lake Powell** in Arizona (see chapter 3). It's not like the ocean—you won't see lots of colorful fish, but you will see some nice scenery. A big hit with divers is scavenging the depths of the lake, where they find anything from Oakley sunglasses to walkie-talkies to wallets to coins.

SEA KAYAKING

Like scuba diving, this sport is definitely an oddity to find in this landlocked region, but actually those who choose to adventure into some of the water-soaked canyons in Arizona are greatly rewarded. Though the pastime is just getting underway, there are a few outfitters who rent boats and can direct you to some excellent paddles. The most notable places right now to kayak are on **Lake Powell** to Antelope Island and the lovely Navajo and Antelope Canyons (see chapter 3) and on **Lake Havasu** and **Lake Mohave,** particularly through the Black Canyon (see chapter 4). The one big drawback of this sport is that kayakers have to share these waters with powerboaters, which may mean miles of paddling in their wakes before you arrive at a quiet can-yon or cove to explore. In order to avoid the noise and commotion, outfitters recommend kayakers plan very early departures.

SNOWSHOEING

This fast-growing sport is just gaining a grip in the region. Essentially, it is winter hiking. That means you can refer to many of the hikes in the northern Arizona, eastern Arizona, and north central New Mexico chapters and find endless miles on which to trod with your big woven feet. In those sections I've listed some hikes especially good for snowshoeing, most notably, the **Grand Canyon's North Rim** (see chapter 2) and the **West Fork of the Little Colorado** up to Mount Baldy outside of the village of Greer, **Sunrise Resort,** and the **Tracks** trail system in Pinetop/Lakeside (all three in chapter 6). The **Windsor Trail** in the Sangre de Cristo Mountains (see chapter 9), though quite challenging, will take you to the snow-covered heights of the Rockies.

Before embarking on any of these adventures, be sure you're well prepared with plenty of warm gear, water, food, a map, and compass.

SWIMMING & TUBING

Some of my most incredible moments in the Southwest have been at that crucial crease in time when water and desert meet, when I was dripping with sweat and was able to dive into a cool pool and feel my whole body tingle. The greatest experience I had like that took place in Sedona, where there's a surprising amount of swimming. It was at the premier swimming hole in the area, **Wet Beaver Creek,** but it's a good 8-mile round-trip hike through lovely Sonoran Desert to get there (see "Hikes & Backpack Trips" earlier in this chapter). Not quite so elaborate a pool or so distant a hike, the **West Clear Creek Canyon** has lovely water worth dipping into. Also in the area, though much more crowded, is **Slide Rock State Park.** (See chapter 5 for details about all three.)

In New Mexico, a lovely large pool of water occurs on the dammed **Pecos River** in the town of Carlsbad, where there's a beach with changing rooms (see chapter 12). Besides these spots, there are many lakes throughout Arizona and New Mexico that offer a cool respite from the desert heat. Many of them have cliffs that may appear to be safe for diving. Be very careful about where you attempt this. A good rule of thumb is, if you can't see the bottom, don't attempt diving or jumping.

There isn't a lot of tubing in Arizona and New Mexico. What waterways there are tend to be rocky and have too much grade or not enough water to make the sport safe. One primo place to go, however, is outside Phoenix on the lower **Salt River** with Salt River Recreation (see chapter 5).

WALKS & RAMBLES

The best aspect of this category is that it's available to everyone. It requires no real skill (though maybe we take for granted what a phenomenon it is to walk upright), little gear (a good pair of running shoes or light hiking boots and a bottle of water), and little time (the bulk of which will be spent taking in the scenery). Mostly, my criterion for the best walks and rambles is their beauty, and there's so much of it within these two states that it's difficult to choose, but here goes:

- Bright Angel Point Trail (chapter 2)
- Antelope Canyon (chapter 3)
- Devil's Bridge Trail (chapter 5)
- Blue Vista (chapter 6)
- Massai Point (chapter 7)

- Main Ruins Trail and Ceremonial Cave at Bandelier National Monument (chapter 9)
- Capulin Volcano (chapter 10)
- Gila Cliff Dwellings National Monument (chapter 11)
- Big Dunes Trail at White Sands National Monument (chapter 12)
- Valley of Fires Loop (chapter 12)

WHITE-WATER KAYAKING & RAFTING

White-water kayaking, I have to admit, is my greatest passion in the book. Unfortunately, it's one of the least-represented sports within the Southwest simply because this is the desert. What there is, though, is high quality. In most instances, I've lumped together white-water kayaking with white-water rafting in this book because the two sports share the same waterways.

As with all of the sports mentioned in this book, be sure your skills are commensurate with the level of water you're running and that you have proper gear. I've used the standard rating system for defining river difficulty. It goes as follows:

- **Class I** Easy. Small waves, clear passages, no serious obstacles.
- **Class II** Moderate. Rapids with waves; passages clear so generally no technical maneuvering required.
- **Class III** Difficult. Rapids with many waves; passages blocked so technical maneuvering required. Eddies. Scouting generally required.
- **Class IV** Very difficult. Long rapids with many waves and many obstacles; passages blocked so technical maneuvering required and consequences are life-threatening; boiling eddies; scouting mandatory first time.
- **Class V** Extremely difficult. Exceedingly long, violent and treacherous rapids. Passages blocked so technical maneuvering required and consequences are life-threatening; often little interruption between such passages; big drops; violent currents; scouting is mandatory first time.
- **Class VI** Almost unrunnable. Navigable by experts only; very life-threatening circumstances.

Of course, the lifetime experience of many boaters, whether kayakers or rafters, is a trip down the Colorado River through the **Grand Canyon.** This trip is so prized for a number of reasons. One is the incredible beauty of floating for up to three weeks through one of the grandest canyons in the world. Another is the sheer volume of water that flows through it—thousands of cubic feet per second; this type of boating defines the term "big water." With monster holes and tough eddy lines, this is not a trip for amateurs, though a number of outfitters buffer the consequences enough so that nearly anyone can partake. In chapter 2, I give fairly detailed information about the types of trips available, how to choose a guide that works for you, and how to apply for your own permit.

The other two major white-water experiences in the desert southwest are the **Taos Box Canyon** on the Rio Grande, a Class IV jaunt through an incredible basaltic canyon (see chapter 9). The second is the **Salt River Canyon,** another scenic and action-packed float on Class III and IV white water in eastern Arizona (see chapter 6).

For those who like to keep their hearts in their chests, I've included nice flat-water floats that are especially good for families. These occur on the **Gila River** not far from Tucson (see chapter 7) and on the **Rio Grande River** in the Embudo, New Mexico area (see chapter 9). If you'd like a trip that has a little white water but won't scare you too much, head to New Mexico's **Chama River,** a Class II run through layers of painted sandstone (see chapter 9). Two good resources for boating in the area are *New Mexico Whitewater,* published by the New Mexico State Parks (1983), and *Western Whitewater,* by Jim Cassady, Bill Cross, and Fryar Caloun (North Fork Press, 1994).

WILDLIFE VIEWING

One of the most spectacular experiences in Arizona and New Mexico is seeing a wisp of brown and gray pass through the woods, or at night hearing a lonesome howl, both signs of the presence of the Mexican gray wolf. This endangered species is gaining rather than falling in numbers today thanks to the Mexican Wolf Reintroduction program, a cooperative effort led by the U.S. Fish and Wildlife Service. Though the wolves are wily, many people have seen them roaming the **White Mountains** in eastern Arizona and the **Gila Wilderness** in southwestern New Mexico (see chapters 6 and 11).

If it's numbers you're after, you'll love the sight at the mouth of **Carlsbad Caverns** in southeastern New Mexico, where in the summer, a quarter of a million Mexican freetail bats take flight for a night of insect feasting (see chapter 12). If you like the sight of wild turkey and mule deer, there's no better place to see them in quantity than on **AZ 64** en route to the North Rim of the Grand Canyon or on many of the trails and forest roads in that region. One denizen of the **Kaibab Plateau** is the Kaibab squirrel (see chapter 2). Bobcat, javelina, desert bighorn sheep, and mule deer are just a few of the many varied inhabitants at the 860,010-acre **Cabeza Prieta National Wildlife Refuge** in southwestern Arizona, but the endangered Sonoran pronghorn may be your most prized sighting there (see chapter 4).

Where to Stay

At the end of each chapter I've listed some of my favorite campsites, inns, and lodges. The lists are by no means exhaustive. In fact, many state parks have camping facilities that I haven't listed in the camping section, so use the book with flexibility, working from the "Parks & Other Hot Spots" section as well as from the "Campgrounds & Other Accommodations" section.

I've tried to list an inn or lodge in each major locale within a regional chapter. Some of them are expensive, some are cheap, but most are average priced. You can always expect to pay extra for a room in tourist centers such as Sedona and Santa Fe, and you may be relegated to a somewhat standard motel in out-of-the-way places such as Yuma and Grants. Except for those more remote locales I've tried to include only inns and lodges that hold some unique quality that I think would appeal to the outdoor adventurer. I assume that any of us are capable of tracking down a Motel 6 or a Best Western.

Favorite Inns & Lodge

Though I have many favorite inns and lodges, I'll do my best to pick out a few here and leave you to find which you like best on your own unique adventure.

- **Inn at 410,** Flagstaff, AZ (chapter 2)
- **Rocamadour,** Prescott, AZ (chapter 5)
- **Red Setter Inn,** Greer, AZ (chapter 6)
- **Casa Tierra,** Tucson, AZ (chapter 7)
- **Aravaipa Farms,** Winkleman, AZ (chapter 7)
- **Skywatcher's Inn,** Benson, AZ (chapter 7)

- **Kokopelli's Cave,** Farmington, NM (chapter 8)
- **Little Tree,** Taos, NM (chapter 9)
- **Hacienda Antigua,** Albuquerque, NM (chapter 9)
- **Bear Mountain Lodge,** Silver City, NM (chapter 11)
- **Casa de Patrón Bed & Breakfast,** Lincoln, NM (chapter 12)
- **Ellis Store & Co. Country Inn,** Lincoln, NM (chapter 12)

Leave No Trace: A Final Note About Preservation

One day while I was hiking Hermit's Peak in northeastern New Mexico with one of my best friends, we had a heated argument. I told her I was going to include a fairly remote locale in Arizona, one that she loved dearly, in this book. She was enraged by the fact that I was going to expose "her" place. Throughout the process of researching this book, I had similar reactions from people—many thought that writing such a book was unethical. A part of me would slink away, agreeing with them, but left with the task nonetheless. Another part of me would feel righteous—I'm helping more people experience the magic of nature. Of course, there's truth to both arguments. But one thing I've come to see is that it's less a question of how *many* people go to these places as it is what they do when they're there. In fact, many wild places are wild because nature lovers took the time and energy to preserve them. That said, my greatest hope is that the readers of this book will act responsibly while using it. In order to help you do just that, I've compiled some of my favorite "Leave No Trace" literature into a list that I hope you'll follow:

1. Be prepared. Know the route and area in which you're planning to hike.
2. Select a campsite where you don't have to disturb the vegetation.
3. Stay on main trails; do not shortcut switchbacks.
4. Pack out what you bring in, including used toilet paper and all trash.
5. Abide by fire rules; pack a gas stove to help conserve firewood.
6. Make sure your fire is cold before leaving a campsite. Scatter cool ash, but never put ash in a water source.
7. Bury solid human waste at least 200 feet from water in a hole 4 to 6 inches deep and 4 to 6 inches in diameter.
8. When washing yourself or your dishes, carry water 200 feet away from creeks and rivers. Scatter strained dishwater.
9. Be quiet so that nature isn't disturbed.
10. Leave what you find. This includes cultural resources of any kind, including artifacts and archeological remains.
11. Don't pick plants or flowers. Leave them for the next visitor to enjoy.

2

Arizona Grand Canyon Country

Though most people come to northern Arizona to see the Grand Canyon, many don't realize that the Grand is but one of many spectacular canyons carving through the region. Each, like the Grand, is a whole world within itself, with sandstone stories laid out across vast walls, their plots twisting and turning with the whim of the long-since-passed waters and winds that formed them. But still, there's no doubt that the most awesome canyon in the world, the Grand Canyon, is incredible.

Usually, when people encounter the Grand they find much more beauty than they'd imagined, but they also find frustration. At a mile deep, 277 miles long, and up to 18 miles wide, this canyon is so immense that a visitor can only experience a small portion of it. Most people satisfy themselves with what they are capable of doing during their short visit to one of the seven natural wonders of the world, but many others return to the canyon again and again. In either case, they usually find in the end that its overwhelming nature only adds to its beauty.

For centuries, the Grand Canyon has proven to be both refuge and rival to humans. Prehistoric hunter-gatherers lived in the area as early as 2000 B.C. Later, around A.D. 500, it was the home and sacred place of Native American tribes such as the Puebloan ancestors (also known as the "Anasazi," though they shun that term), who built homes in caves along the sheer cliffs. Meanwhile, the Cohonina people led a hunter-gatherer existence on the canyon's western portion. In 1300 the Cerbat tribes moved into the South Rim area; their descendants, the Hualapai and Havasupai tribes, still live in and near the canyon today.

In 1540 Spanish explorer Garcia Lopez de Cardenás and his troops were making their way across the Colorado Plateau when they hit a snag in their travel plans: A chasm so deep and broad that even today it presents a formidable obstacle in getting to the very northern belt of Arizona. Not until 1869 would someone actually penetrate the canyon's depths from end to end. In that year, a one-armed Civil War veteran, Major John Wesley

Powell, led an expedition into the area. He and a small contingent set out in wooden boats to navigate the 1,000 miles down the Green and Colorado Rivers, a trip that took 98 days. In the process, rapids smashed boats, and fear drove some of the men to escape the river on foot. They likely died in the process.

But northern Arizona isn't just a land of windswept canyons—there are also peaks. In the Flagstaff area, the San Francisco Peaks rise to a height of 12,643 feet at **Humphreys Peak,** Arizona's highest, below which skiers take to the slopes. There are also mountains in the Williams area, and up in the far northwestern corner of the state, a most undiscovered place, the **Virgins.**

The word in this part of the world is canyoneering, an odd and elegant experience of moving down into the earth's crust and exploring the strangeness there. For hikers and backpackers, northern Arizona offers a glimpse into these underground worlds, whether they're traversing the immensely deep ones at the Grand Canyon or the twisting and narrow ones of **Buckskin** and **Paria.** What's important to remember is that canyoneering is much like mountaineering, but in reverse. Rather than climbing up, you're climbing down what could be seen as mountains; the unfortunate part of the picture is that the way home is always a grind, but by then you're rested, right? This area is also a mountain biker's dream. Ask any avid biker in the southwestern United States where he likes to ride, and he'll likely rank the area around Flagstaff at the very top of his list. The volcanic formations of the San Francisco Peaks offer limitless miles of single track, some fast and smooth, some gnarled with rocks and steep as hell. And, of course, I must mention what for many people is their lifetime experience in the world: rafting or kayaking the Colorado River through the Grand Canyon, a 7- to 18-day trip from which no one returns unchanged.

The Lay of the Land

Tectonically, the **Colorado Plateau,** which stretches across northern Arizona and into Utah, is a large stable landmass. It contrasts with the Basin and Range Province to the south, which is an extending mass, creating great volcanic uplifts. If you haven't seen this landscape you might expect it to be dull, with so little recent action. However, the action that has occurred has happened on the surface. Winds, rain, snow, and hail have gone to work on this land, molding sky-piercing volcanic peaks and carving mile-deep canyons into the earth, a masterful act of chiseling away the unnecessary.

When this area was an ancient seabed, sediments were gradually deposited and turned into limestone and sandstone. Waterways, including what's now known as the Colorado River, washed over this landscape creating great meanders. They worked their way along slowly, and then one day 8 to 10 million years ago, the plateau uplifted, and the rivers that had meandered along suddenly had more grade and began cutting swiftly, deeply, but kept their intricate courses, forming layers of winding canyons. The result for visitors to see along the Colorado River through the Grand Canyon are 21 sedimentary layers, beginning with the youngest (closest to the rim), the Kaibab sandstone, and moving down through the Toroweap and Coconino to the oldest, called Vishnu Schist, dating back 2 billion years. This dark, metamorphic rock is thought to be the remains of a Precambrian mountain range.

Carving through the center of all this exciting topography is what must rate as one of the most tortured rivers in the world—the Colorado. Over 90% of the land area of Arizona is believed to drain into this river. Named by early explorers for the pink color of its muddy waters, the river was once the force responsible for scouring these desert lands, with its powerful spring flooding washing away all that couldn't sustain itself on its shores.

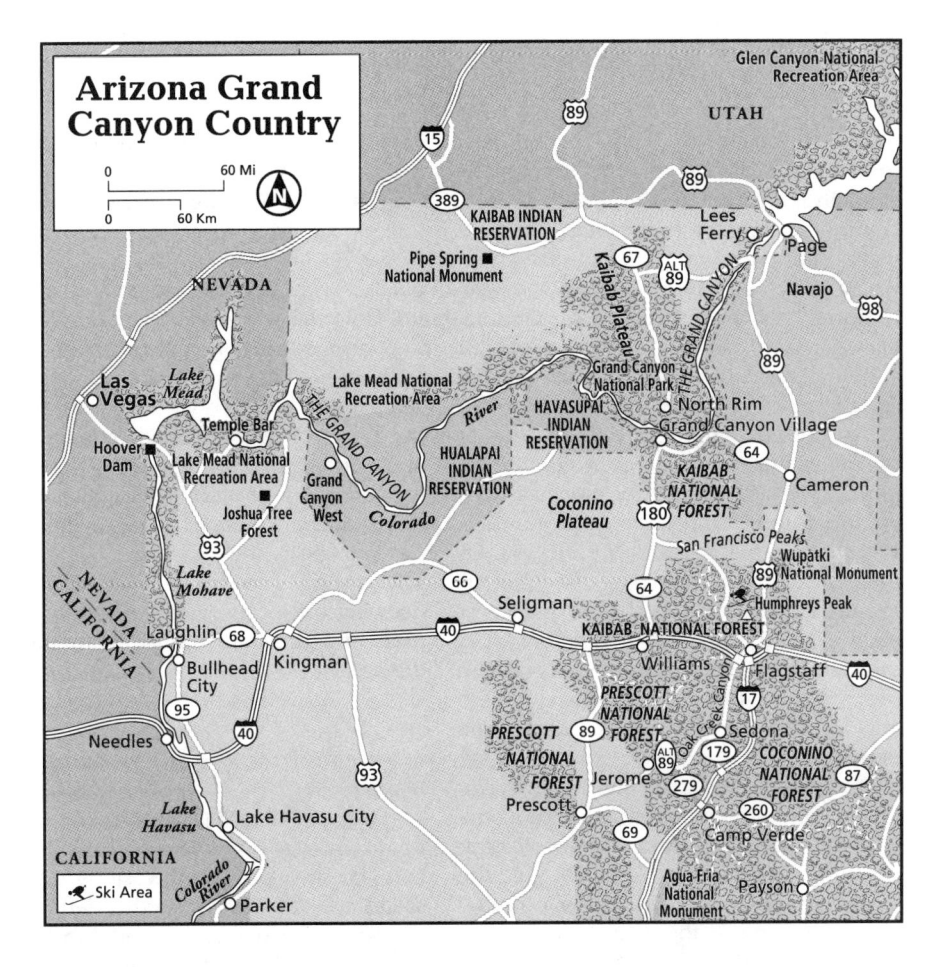

Today, the water of this mighty river runs clean, clear, and cold, the product of damming. In the northeastern part of the region, Glen Canyon Dam stopped the Colorado's flow, flooding canyons much like those you see in parts of the Grand Canyon, deep ruts that developers considered useless. The result was Lake Powell, now a powerboat haven for sunseekers. The silt that once flowed down the river is now building up upon vast arches and striated walls at the bottom of the lake. Meanwhile, downstream of the Grand Canyon stands Hoover Dam, which is an astonishing piece of architecture, even for all the canyon land it destroys.

Leading into the Grand Canyon are hundreds of tributary canyons well worth exploring. The area of Page is known for its wind and rain-washed narrow canyons that create undulating walls of layered sandstone (see chapter 3). This is also the area of the Vermilion Cliffs, an aptly named escarpment running for miles along the northern part of the region; and the **Kaibab Plateau,** a high-forested area that borders Grand Canyon to the north. Upon this plateau rise a number of peaks from the tops of which one can glimpse unsurpassed views of the chasm-filled Colorado Plateau. And to the south lies a land of craters. In fact, Arizona's highest peak, Humphreys, was once an active volcano whose explosions laid out lava beds and lava tubes over many miles.

The **Grand Canyon** has several distinct characters depending upon which part you access. Of course, the most popular and visited is the **South Rim,** an area that receives approximately 5 million visitors annually. The impact is taking its toll. During the summer, traffic clogs the highways, and parking spaces are rare. Fortunately, in 1995, Grand Canyon National Park instituted a General Management Plan that includes plans for a new light-rail system and alternative-fuel buses in order to alleviate not only the congestion problems but also the air pollution. For now, however, you'll have to plan well in advance for much of what you do at the Grand Canyon. If you must visit the South Rim—and the views from there make it very enticing—try to go during the off-season (October to April), or early in the morning. Some notable hikes originate off the South Rim, and on them you will leave most of the crowds behind and be able to enjoy the canyon's true personality.

The **North Rim,** a higher and less accessible place, is much more peaceful. It's open only from mid-May to October or early November. Located on the Kaibab Plateau at an elevation of 8,000 feet, the terrain there includes dense forests of ponderosa pines, Douglas firs, and aspens interspersed with meadows. Hikes originating from the North Rim are often rugged and serene.

The weather in and around the Grand Canyon varies, mostly due to elevation. The South Rim of the Grand Canyon sits at 7,000 feet, and so it gets very cold in the winter. Anytime between November and May you can expect snow, and winter temperatures can be below 0°F at night, with daytime highs in the 20s or 30s. In the summer the rim temperatures generally run in the high 80s, but nights can get chilly. A slightly higher area, the North Rim, is cooler throughout the year and receives as much as 140 inches of snow.

On the canyon floor temperatures are higher. In summer, temperatures of 100°F are not uncommon with lows in the 70s. In winter, you might encounter highs in the 50s and lows in the 30s. In the Flagstaff and Williams area, summers are generally mild, with daytime temperatures in the 70s and low 80s. Winters are much colder, with daytime temperatures ranging from the 30s to the 60s.

Your greatest concern in canyon country is the summer monsoon. During July, August, and early September, thunderheads build over the higher landmasses and can dump rain that races down the canyons. In August 1997, just such a flash flood killed 11 people hiking in Antelope Canyon near the Arizona/Utah border. The spring snowmelt is another time flooding can occur, while generally April, May, and June are the driest months in the area.

Orientation

U.S. 93, stretching northwesterly to **Lake Mead** and the Nevada border, defines this region to the west. The northern border is, of course, Utah. (I have included some hikes that straddle that border. And, I also recommend if you're in the vicinity to take a jaunt up to **Zion and Bryce Canyon National Parks.**) The southern border of the region runs about 20 miles south of I-40, along the upper part of the **Mogollon Rim.** To the east runs U.S. 89, a north-south route leading from Page (pop. 10,000) to Flagstaff, the largest city in the region with a population of 54,000. Other important routes of note are NM 64 and U.S. 180, which head north from I-40 to the Grand Canyon. Cutting through the center of the region is the Grand Canyon, which has proven an obstacle to travelers throughout recorded history, and even today necessitates hours of driving to circumnavigate it.

Parks & Other Hot Spots

Lowell Observatory
1400 W. Mars Hill Rd. ☎ 520/774-2096. www.lowell.edu. Visitor center and exhibits open daily Mar–Oct 9am–5pm; Nov–Feb daily noon–5pm. For evening telescope viewing, call for hours. Admission $4 adults, $3.50 students, seniors and AAA members, and $2 children ages 5–17; free for children under age 5.

Even though the intensive stargazing for which the Lowell Observatory is so noted has been moved 10 miles out of Flagstaff to Anderson Mesa, important observations still take place here, and visitors can still do some gazing, as well as see some interesting exhibits. The original observatory, founded in 1894 by Percival Lowell, was where Lowell intently studied the planet Mars. Most notably, though, through his own calculations, he predicted the discovery of Pluto. He died before his theory was proven correct—Pluto was located almost exactly where he said it would be. The facility includes several observatories, educational exhibits, outdoor displays, and a large visitor center. *Note:* Because heat damages observatory accoutrements, the domes are not heated. Wear warm clothing in winter.

The Arboretum at Flagstaff
Woody Mountain Rd. ☎ 520/774-1442. www.thearb.org. E-mail: steve.yoder@nau.edu. Open Apr 1–Dec 15. Gardens close Dec 15, gift shop closes Dec 22. Guided tours at 11am and 1pm. Admission $4 adults, $3 seniors, $1 children ages 6–12, and free for children 6 and under.

Spanning 200 acres, this research garden contains 11 cultivated gardens including an herb garden and an alpine tundra rock garden, all highlighting the flora found in the Flagstaff area. The arboretum is beginning to become known for its fall colors—aspen, maple, sumac, gooseberry, and wild current bushes all blush with shades of lemony yellow to sunset reds and every color in between.

Lake Mead National Recreation Area
Off U.S. 93 northwest of Kingman. ☎ 702/293-8907. www.desertusa.com/colorado/lm_nra/lake_mead/du_lakemead.html. 2 lakes, 8 campgrounds, 5 motels, 6 RV campgrounds with hookups. Concession-run stores, boat rentals, fishing equipment, 5 picnic areas, paddle-wheel tour boat to Hoover Dam, ranger-led programs, and winter lecture series. Bird watching, boardsailing, camping, canoeing, fishing, hiking, horseback riding, kayaking, mountain biking, powerboating, sailing, swimming, and wildlife viewing. Open year-round 24 hours per day. $5 per vehicle entrance fee, with extra charges for use of motorcraft.

Covering an area twice the size of Rhode Island, Lake Mead National Recreation Area is enormous, encompassing almost 1.5 million acres that include Lake Mead and Lake Mohave. Anglers, wranglers, hikers, swimmers, photographers, and others come in search of outdoor adventure. These outdoor enthusiasts have to share their love of this land with the wild creatures that inhabit the area, such as bighorn sheep, mule deer, ringtail cats, kit foxes, bobcats, desert tortoise, and many others. Because three of America's four desert ecosystems—the Mojave, Great Basin, and the Sonoran Desert—converge here, much of the flora and fauna found here are unique to this area. Taking scenic drives through this country is a great way to see this dramatic landscape. The **Lakeshore and Northshore Scenic Drives** along the edge of Lake Mead will take you through vertical-walled canyons, fields of cactus, and the foothills of the majestic mountains. For the more actively inclined, hiking is another option. One hike that will lead you to colorful sandstone formations is near **Redstone Picnic Area** along

Northshore Road. Park naturalists can lead you on any of these hikes. If you've come to fish Lake Mead and Mohave, you're in luck because the fish are striking. Largemouth bass, striped bass, rainbow, channel catfish, crappie, and bluegill all swim in both lakes. The park is open year-round.

If feats of humankind inspire you, few are as spectacular as **Hoover Dam** (☎ **702/293-8321**), 67 miles northwest of Kingman via U.S. 93. This $175 million dam, completed in 1935, is 727 feet high (think 70-story building) and 660 feet thick at the base (think two football fields). A 45-minute guided tour deep inside the structure leaves every 10 minutes from the exhibit building at the top of the dam; tours daily 9am to 4:15pm. Cost for adults is $8, seniors $7, $2 juniors ages 6 to 16, free for children ages 5 and under. The structure is accessible to people with disabilities.

Grand Canyon National Park

For years on my refrigerator I've had a photograph of my mother and me standing on the very lip of the North Rim of the Grand Canyon. We're facing into the sun with broad smiles on our faces, the temples and canyons of the Grand spread out behind us like a fairyland. My mother and I have stood in other lovely places since that trip—the mountaintops of Machu Picchu, the white beaches of the Yucatán—and yet it is that photo of the Grand that maintains a place on my refrigerator. I think the reason is that it represents a time and place for us that is beyond time and space. The place itself is timeless, so dwarfed are we by the passed years revealed on the canyon walls, from the 2 billion-year-old Vishnu Schist to the 250 million-year-old Kaibab limestone.

We're also dwarfed by the scale of the Grand itself, a park encompassing 1,904 square miles of land, with a canyon stretching 277 miles, and ranging in elevation from 2,400 feet to over 8,000 feet above sea level. At points the canyon is 18 miles wide and 1 mile deep. The park is home to 1,500 types of plants, 305 species birds, 88 types of animals, 26 types of fish, and 58 types of amphibians and reptiles.

GETTING THERE

Daily commuter lines fly from Los Angeles and Las Vegas to the **Grand Canyon Airport** in Tusayan, which is 4 miles from the park. Shuttles run hourly from the airport to Grand Canyon Village.

Grand Canyon Village (South Rim) is located 60 miles north of I-40 (turn at Williams) via AZ 64, and 80 miles northwest of Flagstaff via U.S. 180. Only 10 miles from rim to rim as a raven flies, the North Rim is 215 miles (about 4½ hours) from the South Rim by car. The North Rim is 44 miles south of Jacob Lake, Arizona, via AZ 67; however, the highway is usually closed late November to mid-May. All entrances are open 24 hours a day, but the visitor contact stations typically run from 8am to 5pm daily (often longer hours in the summer).

INFORMATION

For general information, call ☎ **520/ 638-7888** or log on to www.nps.gov/ grca/. The **South Rim** stays open year-round, though the greatest concentration of people is from April to August. The **North Rim** facilities are open mid-May to mid-October. The **Canyon View Center** at Canyon View Information Plaza has informative exhibits about the Grand Canyon. For current road conditions and construction, call ☎ **888/411-ROAD.**

FEES

The entrance fee is $20 per vehicle, or $10 per person if you arrive by bus or taxi. Entrance permits are good for 7

ON THE HORIZON: NEW WAYS TO ENJOY THE GRAND CANYON

With about 5 million visitors to the Grand Canyon each year, the park has decided that it's time to revamp the transportation system. Park representatives have chosen a system that involves a combination of light-rail and alternative-fuel buses. Day-use visitors will have to leave their cars at Tusayan and board a light-rail car for a 6-mile ride to Canyon View Information Plaza, from which they'll hook up with other available transportation. The system will be open year-round, with many departures per day. Overnight visitors will have their own designated parking area, from which they take public transportation to their accommodations. It is anticipated that the light-rail will begin operating sometime in 2004.

Another addition to the park is the **Greenway,** which will follow the rim east and west from Mather Point. Plans call for the trail to be partly paved and partly unpaved, eventually extending 70 miles along the South and North Rims, though these plans stretch well into the future. Contact the park for updates.

consecutive days in the park. Entrance fees are waived for those with an annual Grand Canyon Passport Golden Eagle, Golden Age, or Golden Access Passports, or a National Parks Pass. You can obtain these passes (except the Grand Canyon Passport, which must be purchased at the Grand Canyon) at any national park, monument, or recreation area, including any Grand Canyon Park entrance.

LODGING

If you're interested in staying near the canyon, there are nearly 1,000 rooms, cabins, and suites, including three historic lodging establishments and four motel-type lodges in the area, as well some good campsites. Be aware that you'll want to make reservations as far ahead of time as possible. Reservations may be made up to 23 months in advance. Contact **Amfac Parks & Resorts** at ☎ **303/297-2757** for more information or log on to www.amfac.com. See "Campgrounds & Other Accommodations" at the end of this chapter for additional details.

EXPLORING THE CANYON

The biggest dilemma most people face here is where to begin and where to end their exploration. To get a feel for the canyon, many people do one of the rim drives or hike one of the rim trails, which provide incredible views. The **South Rim** has a few driving options, but due to overcrowding the park is switching over to a mass transit system, so these may change in upcoming years.

One of the drives is the **Desert View Drive,** which follows AZ 64 along the canyon rim for 26 miles east of Grand Canyon Village to the east entrance of the park at Desert View. This is also a great way to get to the park. The road is open year-round. It features canyon vistas, the Tusayan Ruin and Museum, views of the Painted Desert, the Colorado River, the San Francisco Peaks, and the Vermilion Cliffs from the Watchtower at Desert View. The **Hermit Road** follows the rim for 8 miles west from Grand Canyon Village to Hermits Rest, accessing eight main viewpoints along Hermit Road. This drive is closed to private automobiles from March 1 through November 30; however, during those months the park runs a free shuttle bus along this route, and bicyclers can also ride it.

Though the **North Rim** doesn't have a rim drive per se, it's still a great destination for private automobiles. A trip there will likely take you along the stunning Vermilion Cliffs, then through the Kaibab National Forest (where deer are so plentiful you'll have to drive slowly to avoid hitting them), to the canyon rim. Because

Grand Canyon National Park

Unpaved roads are impassable when wet.

Map features:
- Mt. Trumball
- Kanab Plateau
- Kanab Canyon
- Granite Narrow
- Tuckup Point
- Tuckup Canyon
- Chikapanagi Point
- Great Thumb Mesa
- Great Thumb Point
- Fossil Bay
- Mt. Emma
- Tuweep
- Toroweap Valley
- The Dome
- Colorado River
- Flatiron Butte
- Mt. Sinyala
- Towago Point
- Havasu Canyon
- Supai (Reservations required)
- Apache Point
- Vulcans Throne
- Havasupai Indian Reservation
- Havasu Creek
- Hualapai Hilltop
- Hualapai Indian Reservation
- Aubrey Cliffs
- Coconino Plateau
- To 66 & Kingman

Legend: Campground, Gas station, Picnic area, Ranger Station, Unpaved road

---

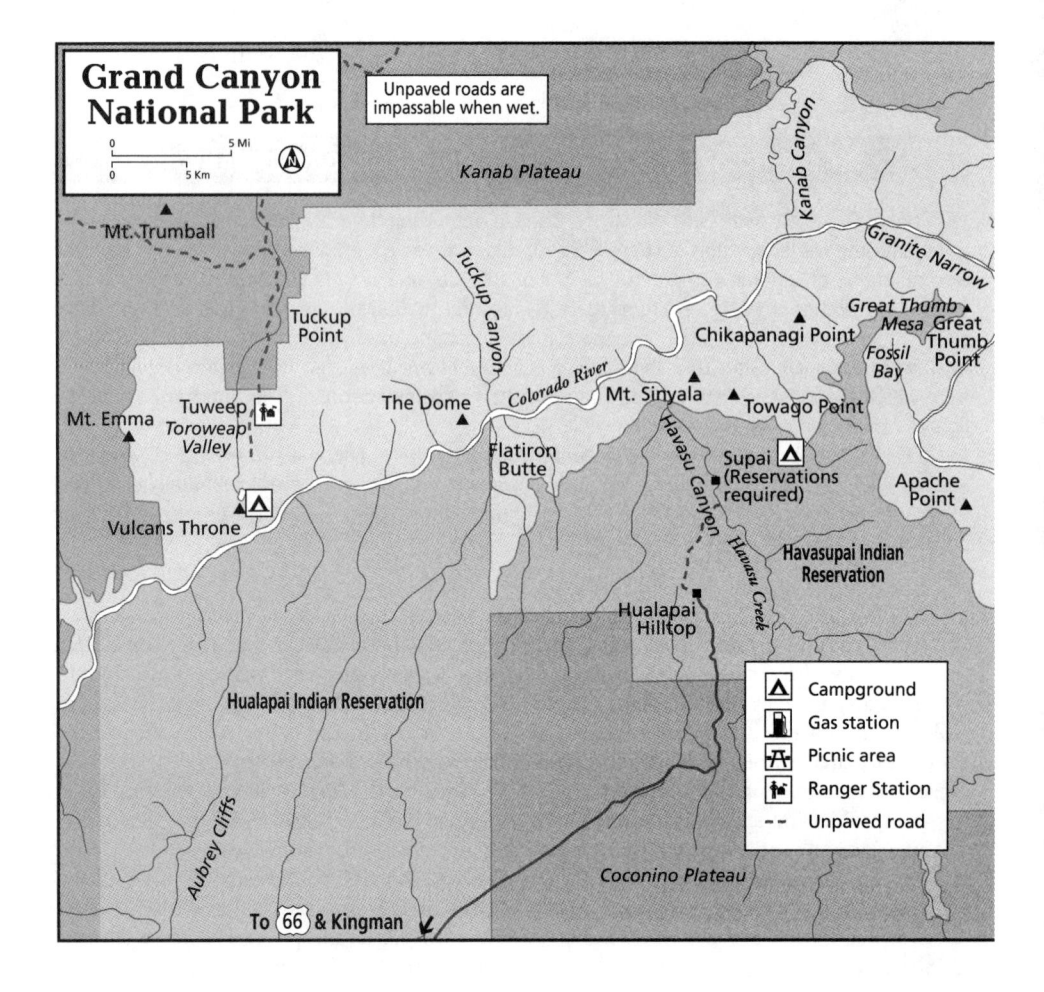

the area can receive up to 140 inches of snow per year, it is not accessible by automobile for most of the period between November and May. There are three main overlooks in the North Rim developed area: Point Imperial, Cape Royal, and Bright Angel Point. From some viewpoints you'll see the Colorado River, more than 5,000 feet below the rim. Many of the extended hikes into the canyon make their way to the shores of this glistening blue-green flow, but you can also drive there by taking the road from Marble Canyon to Lees Ferry.

If you'd rather not deal with your automobile, **Grand Canyon National Park Lodges** has some interesting bus tours of the South Rim. Call ☎ **303/297-2757,** log on to www.grandcanyonlodges.com, or go to the Bright Angel Lodge Transportation Desk to make reservations. Tours run year-round and range in price from $11 to $31.40 for adults and are free for children under 16. The park itself also operates a free shuttle bus system, available daily year-round. Three different routes provide transportation anywhere you want to go on the South Rim. Additionally, **Trans Canyon** (☎ **520/ 638-2820**) offers shuttle bus service between the South Rim and the North Rim. The bus runs one daily round-trip from May 15 to October: It departs from the North Rim at 7am and arrives at the South Rim at noon; it departs from the South Rim at 1:30pm and arrives at the North Rim at 6:30pm. Reservations are required.

Another way to see the canyon not under your own steam is by mule ride; see the "Horseback Riding" section of this chapter. Otherwise, those who want to penetrate the canyon may select from a variety of day or multi-day hikes. However, if you want to backpack here, you'll need to apply for a permit many months in advance. Some on-site permits are issued, but it's difficult to count on them. See the "Hikes & Backpack Trips" and the "Walks & Rambles" sections of this chapter for more information.

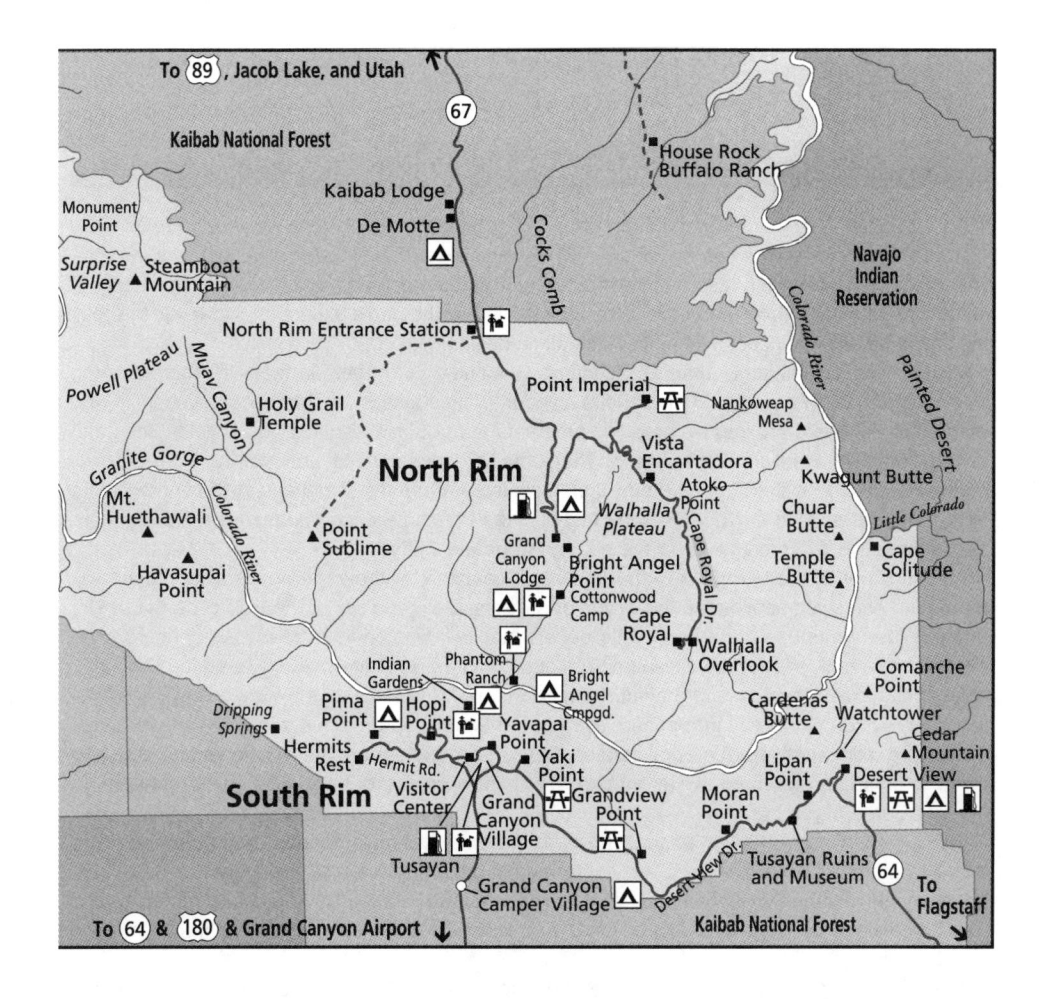

If all these transportation headaches have left you stymied, maybe you should simply experience the virtual canyon by visiting the **Grand Canyon National Geographic Theater** on AZ 64 and U.S. 180 in Tusayan (☎ **520/638-2203**). A 34-minute IMAX theater presentation about the canyon covers John Wesley Powell's pioneer trip down the Colorado River, and the geology, ancient history, and cultural and natural history of the Grand Canyon. The photography is stunning, but doesn't quite compare to what you'll see 6 miles down the road.

What to Do & Where to Do It

BIRD WATCHING

While in the **Vermilion Cliffs** area watch the skies and the ridge tops for California condors. Identify these massive birds by their white or mottled wing lining and featherless, dusky black (immature) or orange (adult) heads. The best spot to see them is from House Rock Valley Road, off U.S. 89A between Fredonia and Marble

CALIFORNIA CONDOR

In April 1987, biologists captured the last free-flying California condor. His wings were folded and he was transported to the Los Angeles Zoo. The tragic loss of this great scavenger whose broad shadow once cast across much of North America was due to many factors. Climactic changes, human overhunting, along with other forces nearly led to the bird's extinction. However, the folding of the last free condor's wings was actually a beginning.

Over a decade later, more than 150 condors live, one-third of them in the wild. Thanks to the California Condor Recovery Plan, various condor populations have been established in the United States. There are captive breeding programs at the San Diego and Los Angeles Zoos and at the Peregrine Fund in Boise, Idaho. There are wild populations are growing from captive-produced condors at the Sespe Condor Sanctuary in southern California and at the Ventana Site in the Big Sur area. In northern Arizona in 1996 the Peregrine Fund released the first condors at the **Vermilion Cliffs** and later at the nearby **Hurricane Cliffs.**

As you travel in the Vermilion Cliffs area you'll hear talk of these scavengers. Someone will have seen one flying above Marble Canyon or strutting along the rim of the Hurricane Cliffs. The story of their tenuous habitation in this desert land will wrench your heart. Six condors were introduced initially, all with radio transmitters and numbers on their wings so Peregrine Fund biologists could track them, which they do from sunrise to sunset, 7 days a week. Slowly over the years more birds have been introduced, a few have been re-captured due to behavioral problems, a few have died mostly from natural causes, though, one condor was shot. One condor flew 180 miles to Moab and returned, while another set a distance record, flying 600 miles round-trip to Flaming Gorge, Wyoming.

The project is new enough so that the birds haven't yet had a chance to demonstrate that they can mate in the wild. "There are some mating displays currently," says Gretchen Druliner, field biologist for the Peregrine Fund. "But the birds don't reach sexual maturity until 5 or 6 and won't produce fertile eggs until 7 or beyond." At this writing the birds range in age from 6 months to 4.5 years.

One of the biggest questions about the birds' ability to survive was whether or not there were enough large mammal carcasses in the wild for them to forage upon. Since the Pleistocene era these birds have foraged on carcasses of large mammals. "This summer the birds fed on their own for almost 5 months, even while being provided carcasses," says Chris Parish, Wildlife specialist for the Arizona Game and Fish Department. "During that time they did not touch a carcass we provided, and yet they came back with full crops, so we know they'd been foraging on their own. They preferred to feed on natural carcasses. It's a small sample; this winter we might see changes, but you have to also keep in mind that birds forage up to 200 miles a day, so at that distance they can find food."

Of course the mass media has jumped on opportunities to show that the birds are desperate and can't make it on their own. A few incidents were reported in which the birds interacted with humans on the South Rim of the Grand Canyon. "It's a big leap saying they approached humans for food," says Parish. "They're attracted to areas of activity; these are juvenile condors with lots of spare time; if you had a few coyotes and a few humans, we don't know which they would approach."

The good news is that at this writing there are more California condors in Arizona than there were in the world in 1987. To find out where to view the condors, see the "Bird Watching" section of this chapter.

Canyon. Travel 2.7 miles north from U.S. 89A. There you'll see a small station with a shade hutch and an information plaque explaining the condor introduction program. Often biologists will be there with a telescope trained on the birds, which may be perched on the rim of the Vermilion Cliffs or flying above them. (See the "California Condor" box in this chapter for more information.)

I've seen innumerable wild turkeys on the **Kaibab Plateau** on the North Rim of the Grand Canyon. They are less skittish here than those I've viewed in other places—at times you can really watch them move through the forest. Any of the Forest Service roads leaving off AZ 67 to the North Rim will likely yield views of these straggly, long-necked fowl. Also in the vicinity of AZ 67 on the North Rim are countless mule deer—so many, in fact, that cars collide with them almost daily. To avoid this tragic sight, please drive slowly as you enjoy their presence.

CAVING

Summer temperatures in Arizona can be extreme. To escape the heat, head down into the state's largest natural icebox, the **Lava River Cave.** Discovered in 1915 by lumbermen, the ice from this cave was collected by homesteaders to be used in their iceboxes. Today, one can tour the lava tube, where lava at one time flowed in an underground river, hollowing out the cave. It's rare, but you also might be lucky enough to see a porcupine, squirrel, or bat. *Note:* The temperature is 35°F, and the floor of the cave is uneven and slick, so dress warmly and wear sturdy shoes. Most importantly, each person should carry two sources of light. Headlamps work best, allowing your hands to be free in case you trip. Visitors may want to wear helmets as well; the ceiling and walls are rough basalt. For more information, call ☎ **520/527-3630.**

Grand Canyon Caverns (☎ **520/422-3223**) are some of the largest dry caverns in the world. Though these multiple caves were originally formed by a raging underground river, today they have no moisture whatsoever. You won't see dripping stalactites and stalagmites here, yet you will see other strange, colorful rock formations. This "dead" cave is not home to critters and insects like wet caves tend to be. Temperatures hover around 56°F throughout the year. The 45-minute tour follows a paved and lit walkway and costs $9.50 for adults and $6.75 children ages 4 to 12. The caverns are open daily from 8am to 6pm in summer, and 9am to 5pm in winter. They're located west of Flagstaff just outside of Peach Springs.

CLIMBING

There's so much climbing in northern Arizona it's difficult to make a complete list of climbing spots here. The area is rich in dacite, granite, limestone, basalt, and sandstone, making for many routes ranging from gnarly to ninny. For detailed accounts of many of the climbs in this section, refer to *A Cheap Way to Fly,* self-published by Tim Toula in 1991 and available at most area climbing stores. The book lists routes and gives details about exactly what hardware is needed. Your climbing contacts for northern Arizona are in Flagstaff at **Mountain Sports,** 1800 S. Milton Rd. (☎ **520/779-5156**) and **Aspen Sports,** 15 North San Francisco St. (☎ **800/771-1935** or 520/779-1935). **Flagstaff Mountain Guides** (☎ **520/635-0145;** e-mail: nazclimb@aol.com) can guide you to climbing spots in the Flagstaff and Sedona area, including the San Francisco Peaks.

Most climbing in the Grand Canyon area is reserved for those with real mountaineering skills, and I'll discuss those below. However, there are a few less extreme areas like the Bright Angel Walls, which have both bolted and trad routes. At this location you'll find the Wailing Wall and Lower Wailing Wall, Flailing Wall, Medivac Wall, and Crumblin' Wall, with routes ranging from 5.6 to 5.12. These crags are easily reached from the South Rim below the West Rim Trail between the Bright Angel Trailhead and Trailview Overlook.

For more serious climbers, Diamond Peak, a 3,512-foot-high tower in the Lower Granite Gorge, is a popular climb during late fall through early spring. A permit must be acquired from the **Hualapai River Runners,** P.O. Box 168, Peach Springs, AZ 86434 (☎ **602/ 769-2216**). You might also try the Brahma, Zoroaster, and Shiva Temples. The **Brahma and Zoroaster Temples** are accessed from the South Rim. At 7,551 and 7,123 feet, respectively, these massive stands of Coconino sandstone and Kaibab limestone offer exciting climbing opportunities. Access is on the **Bright Angel Trail** or the **South Kaibab Trail** through **Phantom Ranch.** Both of these temples require an over 30-mile round-trip trek, and permits from the backcountry office of the Grand Canyon. **Shiva Temple** offers a more moderate chance to ascend one of the Grand Canyon's major temples. This 7,646-foot-high massif juts up from the edge of the North Rim. It's accessed from the Point Sublime and Tiyo Point area and requires some bushwhacking. All three ascents are discussed in detail in John Annerino's *Adventuring in Arizona* (Sierra Club Books, 1996). For details about the Bright Angel Walls and Zoroaster Temple, as well as most of the areas listed below, pick up a copy of *Rock Climbing Arizona* by Stewart M. Green (Falcon, 1999).

The Sycamore Canyon area has some primo rock, including an area known as Paradise Fork, which has earned the moniker of the premier traditional climbing area of northern Arizona. With over 125 routes ranging from 5.10 and up, and varying between 40 and 100 feet, this place is a climber's heaven. Two good climbing areas nearby are Volunteer Canyon and Sycamore Point. Volunteer Canyon has two-pitch routes that vary in difficulty from 5.7 to 5.10. In order to climb it you rappel in and climb out. You'll need a four-wheel drive to get there. Sycamore Point, like Paradise Fork, has innumerable climbs both in the lead and top-roping categories. Climbs here average about 40 feet and run the gamut in range of difficulty from beginner to advanced. Paradise Fork, Volunteer Canyon, and Sycamore Point can be accessed via I-40 west of Flagstaff and FS 141. Also in the Sycamore Canyon area is East Pocket, known for its seclusion, sunshine, and awesome views of Oak Creek Canyon area sandstone cliffs. Climbs here range in difficulty from 5.6 to 5.11. Access is via Woody Mountain Road, off I-40 west of Flagstaff.

Within the Flagstaff area there's some awesome climbing as well. **Le Petit Verdon,** also known as the Pit, offers steep Kaibab limestone routes on walls so south-facing they're even climbable in winter. There are over 80 routes here ranging from 5.8 to 5.13d. Also within Flagstaff is **Priest Draw,** which offers high-quality bouldering and top-roping on limestone. Secret Canyon, a cliff band on the east flank of **Mt. Elden,** has 60 routes both traditional and bolted, which range up to 5.12 in difficulty. Most Flagstaff area climbers will direct you to West Elden for bouldering, short top-rope problems, and leads. Here on a dacite face exist nearly 50 routes in a full range of difficulties. At 8,000 feet, it can get cold up there, so it's a good place to go in the summer. And then there's the old standby **Buffalo Park.** Here you'll find basalt bouldering in a full range of difficulty. Some of the more difficult problems will require a top-rope or a good spotter.

CROSS-COUNTRY SKIING & SNOWSHOEING

On a good snow year, northern Arizona can provide miles and miles of skiing pleasure, whether you're out to kick and glide, cut some tele turns, or slog up and down with snowshoes. If you want to head off into the hinterland but would like some direction, **Flagstaff Mountain Guides** (☎ **520/635-0145;** e-mail: nazclimb@aol.com) will take you into the backcountry.

The Grand Canyon North Rim has innumerable dirt roads and trails to explore in winter (access via automobile to this area is not possible most winters). Since the area can receive as much as 140 inches of snow per year, it can be a great place to cross-country ski and snowshoe. Be aware that the facilities on the North Rim are closed during the winter season (approximately late October through mid-May), but visitors can get in if roads are passable. All concessions are closed, however, and a Backcountry Use Permit is required for overnight use of the area from the park's northern boundary to Bright Angel Point on the canyon rim. For more information about visiting the North Rim in winter, call the **Backcountry Information Center** at ☎ 520/638-7875, answered Monday through Friday between 1 and 5pm MST, or log on to www.thecanyon.com/nps/.

For those who like a little more structure to their skiing, there are a few areas in northern Arizona.

Flagstaff Nordic Center
Located outside Flagstaff in the Coconino National Forest, 7 miles north of Snowbowl Rd. on U.S. 180. ☎ **520/779-1951.** www.arizonsnowbowl.com. Open mid-Dec–Mar daily 9am–4pm, snow permitting. Lift ticket $10; children ages 7 and under and seniors ages 70 and over ski free. 40 kilometers (25 miles) of groomed trails, equipment rentals, ski packages, and group and private lessons. Trail pass $10 for the day, snowshoe pass $5.

These trails wind through the thick stands of ponderosa and Douglas fir as well as high mountain meadows. The center offers professional instruction and equipment rentals. Also check out the novelty of "skijoring," the combination of mushing or dog sledding and cross-country skiing.

Mormon Lake Ski Center
28 miles south of Flagstaff via Lake Mary Rd. ☎ **520/779-1951** or 520/774-0462. www.gorp.com/gorp/resource/US_National_Forest/az/ski_coco.htm. Open mid-Dec–April daily 8am–5pm, snow permitting (call before setting out to be sure it's open). $5 full day, $10 for family. 21 miles of groomed ski trails. Cross-country ski rentals and lessons available. Trail pass $5 for the day.

This ski center at 7,000-feet elevation traverses part of the Coconino National Forest, providing a mix of pine forest and open meadows to ski through and several lakes to ski around. The trails range from beginner to advanced. Moonlight tours on full-moon weekends are a highlight of the area.

DOWNHILL SKIING
Arizona Snowbowl
Take U.S. 180 north of Flagstaff and turn on Snowbowl Rd.; drive 7 miles to the skyride entrance. ☎ **520/779-1951.** www.arizonsnowbowl.com. Open mid-Dec–mid-April daily 9am–4pm, snow permitting. Rental equipment and lessons are available. 32 trails (37% beginner, 42% intermediate, 21% advanced); 5 lifts including two triples, two doubles, and one surface. Full-day tickets $37 weekends/holidays, $37 weekdays.

While other parts of Arizona receive little precipitation, the Flagstaff area gets good snow cover in most years. This mountain reaches up to 11,500 feet at the top of the Agassiz Chairlift and has a 2,300-foot vertical drop. Though the runs aren't long (the longest is 2 miles), they do vary, from some wide-open ones to narrows. Snowboarders like the terrain park at Northstar Trail with its obstacles, half pipe, and spines. There are two lodges, equipment rentals, and a repair shop.

Williams Ski Area
In Williams, south on Fourth St. and continue for 1.5 miles. ☎ **520/635-2626.** www.mwsoftware.com/ski/AZ/Williams_Ski_Area.html. Open mid-Dec–Mar Thurs–Mon 9:30 am–4:30pm, snow permitting. Hours vary: Always call first. Adult lift tickets weekends and holidays $21: juniors ages 12 and under and seniors $16. Midweek adult lift tickets $16: juniors ages 12 and under and seniors $13.

Williams is predominantly a downhill ski area but also has some ungroomed, unmarked cross-country trails. The ski area has six runs (beginner and intermediate) and several offshoots on 600 vertical feet. Lifts include one poma lift and a rope tow. A small day-lodge offers lunch items, ski rentals, and tune-ups. Private and group lessons are available.

FISHING

Some of the best fishing in the southwestern United States is in the Lees Ferry area on the Colorado River. For details, see chapter 3. The section of the Colorado River downstream of **Lees Ferry** through the Grand Canyon is also premier trout-fishing water, though access is quite limited. The area can only be reached by boat or by hiking down the various trails into the canyon. When camping in **Soap Creek Canyon** we had a lavish trout dinner, but that required a full day of intense canyoneering to arrive at the river. Your best bet for fishing in the Grand Canyon is to carry a rod while backpacking. You can almost always count on a dinner or two. Tributaries such as **Bright Angel Creek,** accessible from the North Kaibab Trail off the North Rim, can sometimes yield large rainbow trout. **Clear, Deer, and Tapeats Creeks,** which feed into the Colorado River, are spawning areas for trout during the winter and early spring.

Lake Mead National Recreation Area, off U.S. 93 northwest of Kingman (☎ 702/293-8907), encompasses two giant lakes, Lake Mead and Lake Mohave, with boat rentals and fishing equipment suppliers. Largemouth bass, striped bass, rainbow, channel catfish, crappie, and bluegill are all found in both lakes. The park is open year-round.

About 5 miles southwest of Williams, **Dogtown Lake** spans 50 acres and teems with rainbows and browns, and some crappie. The best way to fish here is by float tubing. During the warmer months fishers can camp at the campground here, but in winter the lake freezes over. There are many more lakes and streams near this region, mostly to the south, so they're covered in chapter 5.

HIKES & BACKPACK TRIPS

In many respects, northern Arizona is *the* place to hike in the southwestern United States. If you gauge your hikes based on beautiful views (which has become my highest criteria), you'll find them here—but in many cases you'll also find challenge. The canyons and mountains of this region are steep. Fortunately for those who would rather meander, there are some nice rim and lowland hikes, which still offer views. Be aware that this is remote territory. The only real city is Flagstaff, to the south. Once you're in the area of the North Rim, you'll be hard pressed to find any real gear, so come prepared. Your hiking contacts for northern Arizona, both in Flagstaff, are **Mountain Sports,** 1800 S. Milton Rd. (☎ **520/779-5156**) and **Aspen Sports,** 15 N. San Francisco St. (☎ **800/771-1935** or 520/779-1935).

Grand Canyon

In order to do any overnight hiking in the Grand Canyon area, you'd best make your plans 4 months in advance (there is a slight exception discussed below). The current non-refundable fee is $10 per permit plus $5 per person per night. Frequent users may purchase a one-year Frequent Hiker membership for $25. This membership will waive the initial $10 fee for each permit obtained by the member trip leader. This membership is valid for 12 months from the date of purchase.

An important note about hiking conditions: Each year park rangers handle hundreds of emergencies in the canyon. Visitors encounter problems varying from heatstroke and dehydration to injuries or death incurred by falling off ledges or drowning in the river. Be aware of the dangers of heat and cold extremes, dehydration, and extreme storm conditions. A good rule of thumb is that it will likely take more than twice the time to climb out of the canyon that it takes to hike in. No pets or bicycles are allowed in the canyon. While hiking, always watch for mule trains carrying heavy loads. Be sure to follow the instructions given by the wrangler while they pass.

A good source for hiking trails in the Grand Canyon is the *Official Guide to Hiking the Grand Canyon* by Scott Thybony (Grand Canyon Assn., 1996). As for maps, I suggest the Grand Canyon National Park Trails Illustrated Topo Maps. These are full-color, with trail designations, covering North and South Rim trails from Lees Ferry to Havasu Canyon, printed on waterproof, tear-proof plastic, available in many outdoor stores as well as at Grand Canyon visitor centers. With longer hikes listed in this section, you may want to hire someone to shuttle your vehicle. Contact **Betty Price** (☎ **520/ 355-2252**).

Availability of Permits

Because the demand for permits exceeds supply, you will have to plan ahead. You'll improve your chances of getting a permit by sending it in on the first day of the month, 4 months prior to the proposed start date. This is the earliest allowable time.

To apply you can go to the **Backcountry Information Center** (☎ **520/ 638-7875,** answered Monday through Friday, only between 1 and 5pm MST). You can request a Backcountry Use Permit application packet from the 24-hour recorded information line at ☎ **520/ 638-7888;** or, log on to the official Grand Canyon Web page at www.nps.gov/grca to print out a permit, which you may then fax to the Backcountry Information Center (fax 520/638-2125), or mail to the Backcountry Information Center, P.O. Box 129, Grand Canyon, AZ 86023-0129, postmarked no earlier than the dates indicated above. The Backcountry Information Center treats all permit requests on a first-come, first-served basis; however, immediate assistance is given to walk-in visitors, essentially moving them ahead of unprocessed written requests. Be aware that all written requests received on the first allowable day are processed randomly regardless of the time of day the request was received.

South Rim Trails

Rim Trail

2–18 miles round-trip. Easy. Allow 1–10 hrs. Access: The trail can be reached from major viewpoints along Hermit Rd. and Village Loop Rd. Maps: See introductory text above.

This trail follows the rim from Hermits Rest to Yavapai Observation Station and Mather Point. It will take you to all the usual South Rim attractions and offers jaunts through piñon pine, juniper, and Gambel oak forests. Unpaved portions of the trail are narrow and close to the edge, including the one at Pima Point where it comes to the 3,000-foot precipice called the Abyss. The trail also leads to Mohave and Hopi points, where amazing views are available, and to the Powell Memorial. The trail is paved from Maricopa Point east to the Yavapai Observation Station. There are interpretive brochures available from boxes along the way, and at any of the major points you can catch a shuttle bus back the way you came.

Bright Angel Trail

7.7 miles one-way. Difficult. 4,420-ft. elevation loss. Allow 4 hrs. down; 2 days for round-trip. (Remember that at twice the time to get back up, that's a total time of 12 hiking hours.) Be aware that the park discourages visitors from attempting to hike to the river and back in one day. On this trail Three-Mile House, Indian Garden, or Plateau Point are appropriate day-hike destinations. Access: The trail starts next to Kolb Studio in Grand Canyon Village. Maps: See introductory text above.

This is the most popular trail in the canyon for many reasons. For one, it is very well maintained, so hikers of many levels can attempt it. It's also quite scenic and is a good route to the cool waters of the Colorado River. It's also a good way for hikers to get a feel for what's below the rim, especially if they plan to do some backcountry hiking later.

You'll begin through a break in the upper cliffs and quickly find yourself in a series of switchbacks called Jacobs Ladder. At mile 1.5 and mile 3, the trail comes to rest houses, where water can be found from May through September. More water is available at Indian Garden. After that stop the trail makes its way through Tapeats Narrows. It then leaves the creek, descending through the Vishnu Schist at switchbacks called Devils Corkscrew. A welcome sight awaits you—the Colorado River. If you'd like, or if you're continuing on up to the North Rim, turn right and follow the river 1.7 miles to the Bright Angel Suspension Bridge, which leads to Bright Angel Campground and Phantom Ranch.

South Kaibab Trail
1.5–6.3 miles one-way. Difficult. 4,620-ft. elevation loss. Allow 2 hrs. for a day hike, 4 hrs. to canyon bottom; 2 days for round-trip (Remember that at twice the time to get back up, that's a total time of 12 hiking hours.) Be aware that park rangers discourage hiking to the river and back in one day. Access: From the Desert View Drive, take the Yaki Point turnoff, then turn onto the first paved road to the left (west). (Much of the year visitors cannot drive to the trailhead, but must take a shuttle bus.) Maps: See introductory text above.

This is one of the shorter ways to the river, and since it's not quite as popular as the Bright Angel Trail, you'll find a little more solitude here (except in the first 1.5 miles). Many people choose to hike down this trail, spend the night in the canyon, and hike back up the Bright Angel, particularly because there's no water available here, while there is water at various points on the Bright Angel from May to September. At 1.5 miles, the trail reaches Cedar Ridge, a good turn-around spot for day hikers. The trail makes its way past O'Neill Butte then switchbacks through Redwall Limestone down to the Tonto platform. When the trail reaches the Colorado River, you may cross on the Kaibab Suspension Bridge, which will take you to Bright Angel Campground and Phantom Ranch, where you'll probably spend the night before heading up the Bright Angel or other trails the following day.

North Rim
North Kaibab Trail
14.2 miles one-way. Moderate to difficult. 5,841-ft. elevation loss. 7 hrs. to the Colorado River. Access: About 2 miles north of Grand Canyon Lodge on the North Entrance Rd. Maps: See introductory text above.

This is an excellent trail from which to explore the North Rim. It's also a good starting point if you plan to do a rim-to-rim hike, connecting with the Bright Angel Trail. It begins at the head of Roaring Springs Canyon, descending quickly for the first 5 miles until it reaches the junction with Bright Angel Creek. At an easier pace it makes its way to Cottonwood Campground, continuing down Bright Angel Canyon through the Box, a 1,200-foot-deep gorge. Finally it arrives at Phantom Ranch, and below, at Bright Angel Campground and the Colorado River.

Widforss Trail
10 miles round-trip. Easy. 200-ft. elevation loss. Allow 5–6 hrs. Access: 2 miles north of Grand Canyon Lodge is the North Kaibab Trail parking area. From there, take a gravel road for 0.25 miles to the trailhead. You can pick up an interpretive brochure at the trailhead. Map: See introductory text above.

This is an ideal way to get a feel for the mixed spruce-fir forests of the Kaibab Plateau, as well as the spectacular views of the North Rim. The well-marked trail follows the canyon rim, from which you can view The Transept, a large tributary gorge of Bright Angel Canyon. The trail is named for Gunnar M. Widforss who painted landscapes in the national parks of the West during the 1920s and 30s. It culminates at a picnic area near Widforss Point overlooking Haunted Canyon. Return the way you came.

Thunder River Trail
30 miles round-trip. Difficult. (*Note:* This is a hike for experienced Grand Canyon backcountry users only.) 4,400-ft. elevation loss. Allow 4–5 days. Access: The trailhead is at Indian Hollow. Go south on AZ 67 from Jacob Lake Center for 27 miles to Forest Development Rd. A permit is required. Travel for 10.5 miles to FS 206, where you'll turn left. Drive 1 mile to FS 425. Follow FS 425 to FS 232, which leads to the trailhead. Maps: USGS Powell Plateau, Tapeats Amphitheater, Fishtail Mesa, and Powell Plateau.

This trail traverses down into the Grand Canyon through some of its most spectacular scenery in the canyon, culminating at a waterfall that blasts like thunder from the canyon wall. Be aware that this route is designated as a Wilderness Trail, which means it is not well maintained and may require some route-finding ability. It is extremely hot and dry in summer. You'll want to stash water on your way in for use on the way out. Again, I want to reiterate that *this trail is for experienced backpackers only.*

The trail descends to the broad Esplanade Terrace. There it runs east and travels about 4 miles until it joins the Monument Point route. This is another way in on the Bill Hall Trail originating at Monument Point. The Thunder River trail then passes several drainages and descends the Redwall Limestone into Surprise Valley. From there you may want to vary your route by taking the Deer Creek Trail into Deer Creek Valley. However, beware of traversing this slot canyon in the late summer when monsoon rains can prove dangerous. The Thunder River Trail crosses several washes and heads down some steep switchbacks until it encounters Thunder River, a spectacular 100-foot waterfall. This is one of the world's shortest rivers, flowing for only a half-mile. Soon the trail and the river reach the confluence with Tapeats Creek, which the trail follows downstream, crossing the creek twice. The trail bypasses the deep lower gorge on the west and soon reaches the Colorado River. Water sources are Thunder River, Tapeats Creek, the Colorado River, and Deer Creek (accessed through Surprise Valley).

In the Northeastern Grand Canyon
Soap Creek Canyon
9 miles round-trip. Difficult. (*Note:* This is a hike for experienced Grand Canyon backcountry users only.) 980-ft. elevation loss. 8 hrs.–2 days. Access: Drive southwest from Marble Canyon on U.S. 89A towards Jacob Lake for 9.5 miles until you see mile marker 548. Just 0.2 mile after the marker, turn east (left) onto a dirt road and follow it through a gate. From there BLM signs will guide you the 0.6 mile to the trailhead. For a permit contact Grand Canyon National Park. See above for phone numbers and Web sites for acquiring a permit. Maps: See introductory text above.

Though not as spectacular as Buckskin Gulch or Paria Canyon, this hike through many layers of sandstone, with the Vermilion Cliffs above and the blue Marble Canyon below, is a challenge and, especially at its end, a treat. At the bottom you'll meet a broad band of sand on the banks of the blue-green Colorado—an awesome place to cool off before you head back out. This hike is a bit of a dilemma. It's almost too long and arduous for a day hike, and yet it's very difficult to maneuver through with a backpack. Make your decisions accordingly, but know that you need a permit in order to stay overnight. The trail begins in a sandy wash, at times dropping quickly off sandstone shelves. The walls, too, are a series of shelves that appear to build as the trail descends, layers of yellow and brown stone. The color contrasts against the blue of Marble Canyon visible in the distance, and, at times, to the north, against the Vermilion Cliffs.

Within the first 45 minutes of the hike the trail hits the first substantial drop. Shortly after that, I encountered on the trail a hiker I'd met in the parking lot while I geared up. The trail continued to be beautiful, he explained, but he'd decided to turn back because it had gotten too hairy for him. He'd balked at a 6-inch wide ledge the trail followed for awhile hundreds of feet above the canyon floor—so if you have acrophobia or are not sure-footed, you'll want to avoid this hike. But before it reaches that point it crosses over a large boulder field—by that I mean a large field with large boulders. There are some cairns placed about, but don't always trust them. Footprints can be as helpful. The route we followed passed very close to the center of the canyon, a little to the left of center. Then the trail very quickly leaves the canyon floor along the right wall, and within moments it narrows to 6 inches. Walk gingerly here, especially if you're wearing a backpack. The next obstacle is a window-like hole with a 15-foot drop. Fortunately, to one side is a boulder. You'll want to lower packs down and then turn on your belly, find the boulder with your foot, and hop down. The rest of the way is less technical. Where the trail meets the river, there's a nice white-sand beach with some primo campsites. You may not find yourself in solitude, however, because rafters often stop for the night at this spot. If you're lucky like I was, you'll get to feast on their food and beer. The trip out is a little easier because the technical climbing is up rather than down. Within the first half-hour you'll come to a side canyon. Take the left fork. The rest of the way is self-explanatory.

Trails Outside Grand Canyon National Park

Nankoweap Trail #57

3–14 miles one-way. Difficult. 1,340-ft. elevation loss. Allow 2–7 hrs., one-way. Access: From Jacob Lake head south on AZ 67 for 27.5 miles and turn left onto FS 611. Drive for 1.4 miles, and turn right onto FS 610. Travel this road for 12.3 miles to its end where you'll find the trailhead. Both 611 and 610 are fine for passenger cars. Note that as a day hike you do not need a permit; however, if you choose to hike down to the Colorado River, you must contact Grand Canyon National Park in order to get one. See above for phone numbers and Web sites. Maps: See introductory text above.

This hike travels up onto Nankoweap Saddle in the Saddle Mountain Wilderness. It's very scenic, winding along a ridge top with views of Marble Canyon with its jagged buttes and deep drainages. Marble Canyon is the upper 60-mile portion of the Grand Canyon. Climbing to 500 feet in height, its walls are so stunning they appear to be made of marble, but actually they are of Redwall limestone. From this trail, hikers can then enter the Grand Canyon National Park or continue to the upper trailhead, which is accessed from FS 8910. The route is pretty straightforward and easy to follow, though it can be brushy in places. This is actually part of a longer hike down to the Colorado River, a difficult trip with many narrow ledges and some difficult downclimbs and for which hikers need a permit.

In Grand Canyon West

Havasu Canyon

20 miles round trip. Moderate. 2,000-ft. elevation gain. Allow 2–3 days, possibly more. Access: Drive I-40 west of Flagstaff to Seligman, where you turn northwest onto AZ 66. Follow this to Indian Route 18, turn right, and drive 60 miles north to the trailhead. (Be sure to have a full tank of gas before you leave Seligman.) For

camping reservations and a permit to enter the canyon, call Havasupai Tourist Enterprise ☎ **520/448-2121,** or write to P.O. Box 160, Supai, AZ 86435. I recommend camping, but if you must have a bed, try the Havasupai Lodge (☎ **520/448-2111**). Rooms are basic, and a restaurant serves three meals daily. The quickest way into the canyon is to fly in by helicopter provided by Papillon Helicopters (☎ **800/528-2418**). Maps: See introductory text above.

There's a definite otherworldly tension to a visit to Havasu Falls. You begin the trek in a world of dusty browns, but eventually they give way to green trees and finally metallic blue pools of clear water, surrounded by lush, nearly tropical vines. This is the land of the Havasupai (the people of the blue water) truly one of the most beautiful places in the southwestern United States. It is the foreignness of the place that makes this trip. After you've traveled across so much dry desert, you can sit within a blue pool, with the cold mist of a waterfall brushing across your skin. At times the place disoriented me, so that I thought I was in the tropics, like Costa Rica or the Cayman Islands.

The hike in is an easy 10-miler (though you'll want to start before the morning heat), descending quickly for 2 miles then leveling out along sandy streambed. Be sure you plan to stay at least one night in the canyon. In order to really enjoy the place, plan on at least 2 nights. You'll travel through canyons layered with spectacularly colored sandstone, deeper and deeper until you come to groves of cottonwoods and then the Havasu Creek, which you follow into Supai village.

This village has charms you may have to search for. The first you'll note is a sign, which reads "No running horses—speed limit 5 mph." You'll find more in the small museum housed in the same building as the tourist office on the main street in the middle of town. There you'll get some sense of these people who have inhabited the canyon for thousands of years. You'll see crafts such as basket weaving, and visit the history of the tribe's struggle to stop a proposed uranium mine at the headwaters of the Havasu Canyon.

The village is made up of scattered government-issue houses, many with small satellite dishes on the roofs and swamp coolers hanging from windows. In the village there is a cafe with a fast-food restaurant sterility that serves burgers, breakfast burritos, and Indian tacos. Prices range from $3 to $7, and it's open until 6pm except on holidays. Across the plaza is a store, which sells batteries and film (no slides) as well as a few fruits and vegetables.

Less than a mile beyond the village you'll come to the first waterfall. We were so enchanted by the sight of it that we immediately threw down our packs and swam in the blue pool at its base. The water is rich in travertine, which gives it an unearthly blue color. These minerals form incredibly intricate rock formations along the edges of the falls. If you like seclusion, this fall is your best bet, but its beauty pales in comparison to the other two. *Also beware:* While we were swimming, a squirrel ate through one pack to our food supply.

The next fall about a half-mile below has two major pours down 70 feet into a perfect blue pool, with smaller terraced pools below. Just below this are the campsites. There are 250 campsites here, most set close together, but all near the river and shaded by cottonwoods. The farther back you go in the camp, the more secluded you're likely to be. Each site has a picnic table.

The third fall is the most spectacular—200 feet pouring off a cliff into a blue pool with a quarter-mile of pools dotting the canyon floor below. The climb down to the base is challenging, but interesting. You'll travel through tunnels and then use chains as support for the last 40 feet or so. The pool at the base of this fall is fun to swim in, or if you'd like to escape the roar of the fall, there's a beach farther below. Over time the fall has shifted its course, and the places where it once flowed have become petrified into beautiful draping overhangs of brown stone. Part of the construction of the curtain-like rocks is the moss, which hangs where the water flows.

This is the route you'll take to hike down to the Colorado River. It's a good 16-mile round-trip hike that can be accomplished in no less than 6 hours, according to most. You'll encounter three river crossings, but spectacular scenery along the way makes the trip worth it for those who really like their exercise. Many, however, opt to simply lounge by the falls or explore some of the side canyons. Camping is allowed only at the campsite.

Be prepared for the hike out. The last 2 miles are a hard grunt up. In fact, if you don't want to carry your pack out, you can arrange its transport through Havasupai Tourist Enterprise. While hiking, always watch for mule trains carrying heavy loads. Be sure to step to the *inside* of the trail while they pass. Be aware that alcohol is not allowed on the reservation, and you may take your dog down in the canyon but he or she must be kept on a leash. Fortunately there is potable water available from a spring at the campground.

Vermilion Cliffs Area
Buckskin Gulch and Wire Pass Trail
2–21 miles one-way. Moderate to difficult. 100–800-ft. elevation loss. Allow 2 hrs.–3 days. Access: From U.S. 89, about 35 miles west of Page, turn south onto House Rock Valley Rd. and drive 8 miles to the Wirepass Trailhead. Or from Jacob Lake, take U.S. 89A 14 miles to House Rock Valley Rd., turn north (left) and travel 21 miles to the Wire Pass Trailhead. (*Note:* The House Rock Valley Rd. isn't well marked, but you can't miss it geographically. It runs in a basin between the high Kaibab Plateau and the Vermilion Cliffs.) Maps: USGS Pine Hollow Canyon, West Clark Bench, and Bridger Pt. Reservation and permit required for overnight trip. $5 fee paid at trailhead for day use. Contact the BLM in Kanab, UT (☎ **435/644-4600**).

Called the premier slot canyon in the world, Buckskin Gulch will open you into an *Alice in Wonderland* type of hiking. I had never hiked a real slot canyon when I came upon this one. Within 1 mile I found myself in a slot that was no narrower than my shoulders and some 50 feet above my head. I was sold. The thrill of such an experience is matched only by its danger. Canyons such as Buckskin have few escape routes, so if water rushes through—and it does, in spring and during the monsoon season in July, August, and early September—there's no escape. While we all need to be aware of that very physical danger, others have more internal concerns: Some people find this kind of hiking claustrophobic. Be prepared to be submerged in shadow and confined by narrow walls much of the time. The only place en route to exit the canyon is about halfway between Wire Pass and the Paria Canyon. *Important note:* Reliable water for drinking can only be found in the last mile before the confluence with Paria Canyon, seeping in the bottom of the wash and building slowly. Treatment is necessary.

For the first mile along the Wire Pass Trail, you hike through an arroyo. Then suddenly you'll drop into the first narrow slot. Within the Wire Pass slot there are four drops. The highest is about 7 feet, while the others vary from 3 to 6 feet. A couple hiking ahead of me with their dog turned back at the 7-foot drop. It's good to have a leash or piece of rope with which to lower your pack; tossing it down can break your valuable water bottle, which you'll need on this hike, as the water you'll be wading through can be murky, and may be difficult to treat. At mile 1.7 the trail comes to the confluence with Buckskin Gulch, with narrow doorways leading either direction. The north route leads to the Buckskin Trailhead, which, if you leave a shuttle vehicle there, can make for a good overnight. The south leads eventually to Paria Canyon. I took the south route, watching while the canyon walls built higher and higher above me. The trail immediately encounters pools. At times these can be waist-deep; in the late fall (October is an ideal time for this hike) they were, at most, thigh-deep. However, these conditions can range from easy, with sometimes knee-deep water, to difficult, with pools so deep that hikers must swim. This water is usually cold, even in the heat of summer. Hikers need to have available dry clothes after going through pools all day in order to avoid hypothermia; campfires are not allowed. The water is also muddy. If you're backpacking, you may want to wear hiking boots with good socks, or good tennis shoes. Rangers caution against wearing sandals because they can get lost in the muck and leave hikers shoeless.

Along the way you'll see giant walls black with desert varnish and circular print rings resounding as though a stone were tossed on the surface of a pond, and miles of crimson canyon walls. You'll encounter rushes of frigid winds followed by lilts of warms ones. Then the darkness opens out to a sunny grotto with trees and, if you look closely, bull snakes. (I also spotted a rattler.) At some point giant boulders will block the trail necessitating some climbing, which my dog had particular trouble with. As a day hike you can turn back at any point. Some people also choose to simply camp within the canyon and hike up and down it, rather than going from one end to the other.

Later, there is also a fall in the canyon, about 1.8 miles above the confluence of Paria Canyon. It is about a 12-foot drop. It is a good idea if you are backpacking to have a short rope or piece of webbing with which to lower your pack. Beware of using the hand and foot holes on the side of the drop—these are unsafe due to a large drop at the bottom onto a slanted boulder. To complete the canyon, continue on until the confluence with Paria Canyon. Hang a left and travel upstream about 7 miles to the Whitehouse trailhead. Or, continue down Paria Canyon to Lees Ferry, a 43-mile hike.

Paria Canyon
10-mile day hike; 38-mile one-way backpack. Easy to moderate. Little elevation gain. Allow 1 full day for day hike; 4–6 days for backpacking trip. Access: Head west from Page on U.S. 89 for 30 miles to the Paria Ranger Station (between mileposts 20 and 21). Turn south onto the road there. Travel this road south for 2 miles to the Whitehouse trailhead. For the lower end, from Marble Canyon, follow the road to Lees Ferry where you'll find the trailhead and parking area. With this long hike, it may be best to hire someone to shuttle your vehicle to Lees Ferry. Contact Betty Price, ☎ **520/355-2252.** Be aware that for a day hike you don't need a permit but for an overnight you do, and you'll need to make arrangements as far in advance as possible (up to 6 months) because only 20 overnight hikers per day are allowed in the canyon. May and Oct are the busiest months. Contact ☎ **435/644-4600** or 435/644-2672 or http://paria.az.blm.gov. At this Web site you may check the calendar for available permit dates. Maps: USGS Lees Ferry, Wrather Arch, Water Pockets, Bridger Pt., West Clark Bench, and Ferry Swale.

If you like your canyons narrow, deep, and long, Paria is one of the primo adventures in the Southwest. Sandstone walls painted with desert varnish rise high above your head, while the channels you walk twist and turn for miles. This canyon is especially popular because it doesn't involve up and down climbing. If you do this as a day hike be aware that the real slot canyon experience doesn't begin until about 4 miles in. At that point you'll enter deep within narrows that twist and turn upward and continue to mile 16.

At about mile 7 Buckskin Gulch enters on the right. Below Buckskin, the usually dry Paria River begins to show signs of water (in fall and winter only), and this means you will cross the stream many times, but the water is rarely over knee-deep. The Paria is mainly dry from mid-May until the end of September, with summer thunderstorms causing floods that last about a day and result in muddy flow for a week or so after (although very little volume). Be aware that at certain times of year this water can be very cold—each dip in the water can create a major rush, leaving your feet numb for many minutes. It's debatable what types of shoes are best for such trips. Rangers caution against wearing river sandals. Hiking boots should be worn with good hiking socks that will stay comfortable despite the moisture. With some 300 river crossings, some over 100 feet long, you'll definitely spend much of the time with wet feet. This canyon also has patches of quicksand that won't exactly swallow you but can trip you up if you're carrying a heavy pack. It's a good idea to carry a walking stick. When the narrows end, campsites become more abundant. Many of the campsites are on terraces above the riverbed. You shouldn't have trouble finding them. Be sure to camp as far away from the river as possible, in case it floods.

You'll be entertained with many spectacular landforms. At mile 20.5 you'll come to Wrather Canyon and at mile 26.5 to Bushhead Canyon. Through this section until mile 28 the riverbed becomes choked with boulders, which will require some climbing. You can avoid boulder-hopping by taking a bypass on a bench above. Much of the last 7 miles you'll also follow a bench. Watch for a trail on river right that leads past the old Wilson Ranch at mile 33.4 and travels along benches, criss-crossing the river at bends, finally leading you to Lees Ferry.

You'll find springs from about mile 10 to 25. The last good spring before the lower 13 miles of the canyon is the one at mile 25, so you won't want to miss it. Before embarking on your hike, pick up the Paria Hikers Guide at the Ranger Station. Treat all water before drinking it. For weather condition information, contact the **BLM** information station or the office in St. George, Utah (☎ **435/688-3230**).

Flagstaff Area

Mount Elden

6 miles round-trip. Moderate. 2,300-ft. elevation gain. Allow 4 hrs. Access: From Flagstaff, follow Santa Fe Ave., which turns to AZ 89 north. Pass Peaks Ranger Station and drive 0.25 miles to the trailhead on your left. Maps: USGS Coconino National Forest; USGS Flagstaff West.

Viewing this antennae-topped peak from the base, I didn't imagine the beauty I would find on the hike. In fact, this trail takes you up a staircase of petrified lava to the peak's 9,295-foot summit. It passes through forests of ponderosa, oak, and mountain mahogany, with spectacular views en route. The trail begins as an easy grade following Fatman's Loop, then intersects with the Elden Lookout Trail. Gradually it grows steeper. Near the top it passes through an area devastated by a 1977 wildfire that is filling in with aspen groves and other colorful flora. The peak delivers 360° views.

Mount Humphreys

9 miles round-trip. Difficult. 3,843-ft. elevation gain. Allow 5 hrs.–2 days. Access: Drive 7 miles north of Flagstaff on U.S. 180 to FS 516. Turn right and follow this paved road 7.4 miles to the Snow Bowl Ski Area and the trailhead. Maps: USGS Humphreys Peak.

For those into bagging peaks, this hike will take you to the top of an extinct volcano that exploded about 2 million years ago, which happens to be the highest point in Arizona at 12,643 feet. The hike is strenuous, made more so because it begins above 8,000 feet, but the views from the top make the effort worthwhile.

While high on its baldness you'll also get a peek at the Arctic-Alpine Life Zone, and you may even see the small *Senecio franciscanus,* a plant that grows nowhere else in the world. The peak is also sacred to the Navajo and Hopi tribes. The Hopi believe it is home of benevolent spirits they call **kachinas.**

The trail travels through spruce, fir, and aspen forests for 3 miles until it reaches the 11,800-foot saddle, which connects Humphreys Peak with Agassiz Peak to the south. Head north on the Humphreys Trail for another mile, along the rocky treeless slopes of the peak. Camping is prohibited in this area because of the fragile environment. From the top you'll have a view of the entire area, including the Grand Canyon.

Sunset Trail

8 miles round-trip. Easy. 1,275-ft. elevation gain. Allow 4 hrs. Access: Drive north from Flagstaff on U.S. 180 to RS 420 (Schultz pass Road), where you'll turn right (north). Drive 6 miles to the trailhead. Map: USGS Sunset East.

This is an excellent hike to take at the end of the day when, as the name implies, you can watch the sun set from on high. En route you'll catch views of the San Francisco Peaks, Sunset Crater, and the Painted Desert. The trail climbs gradually to a high ridge where you can view Humphreys Peak, Arizona's tallest. You'll pass through an area that burned in 1977 and is now recovering nicely with stands of aspen and Gambel oak. Then it continues to the east edge of Mount Elden's summit plateau, from which views abound. Return the way you came.

Kendrick Mountain

7 miles round-trip. Moderate. 2,700-ft. elevation gain. Allow 4 hrs. Access: On U.S. 180 from Flagstaff, drive 15 miles north to mile marker 230. Turn left (west) on FS 245 and drive for just over 3 miles to FS 171. Turn right and drive just over 3 miles to FS 171A. Follow it for 0.5 miles to the trailhead. Map: USGS Kendrick Peak.

This trail winds through old-growth forests and high meadows leading to a summit, which offers 360° views of northern Arizona. Though this route climbs 2,700 feet, its layout is so good it doesn't seem strenuous. It makes its way up the south slopes, first along a former jeep trail, then on switchbacks through stands of limber pine and aspen. Near the top it moves into Engelmann spruce and Arizona corkbark fir. You may see mule deer and elk, as well as black bears and Mexican spotted owls. A quarter-mile from the summit, the trail passes a small cabin that dates back to 1912. It housed fire lookout crews until the 1930s and is listed on the National Register of Historic Places.

Williams Area

Sycamore Rim Trail

11 miles. Easy to moderate. 200-ft. elevation gain. Allow 4 hrs. Access: From I-40 take the Garland Prairie exit (#167) and head south on FS 141. Continue south about 12 miles until you reach FS 56. Turn right and drive for about 1.5 miles to the trail parking lot. If you'd like get to the views immediately, continue for another 2 miles to the end of FS 56. Park and walk south for about 0.25 mile to the clearly marked trail. Maps: USGS Bill Williams Mountains and Sycamore Point.

Traversing an area of ponds, streams, cliffs, and deep canyons, this trail is an ideal way to see Sycamore Canyon without delving into its difficult, and in the summer heat, hostile interior. Originally cleared and marked in 1979, the trail forms a loop with access at several points. The southern and eastern portions follow part of the rim of this 21-mile-long canyon, providing views of amazing red rock formations. In places this canyon spans as much as 7 miles from rim to rim. The northern and western sections travel through ponderosa pine forests. Though the trail is well marked, you'll want to watch for rock cairns and small signs. En route you'll come to Sycamore Falls, a popular rock climbing area.

Virgin Mountains

This little-explored range is ideal for those who like to get off the beaten path. It contains many miles of Bureau of Land Management (BLM) land, much of it ponderosa forest and much desert scrub. From the top of Mount Bangs the views are expansive, crashing 6,000 feet down to the Virgin River, westward toward the Mohave Desert, and northward toward the red cliffs of Zion. But the trek there isn't easy. It's some 50 dirt miles from St. George, and less from Mesquite but on a much rougher road; you have to want this trip.

When I decided to explore the Virgin Mountain in the very northwestern corner of Arizona, I thought the task would be simple. I drove into Mesquite, Nevada (the closest town), and inquired at the visitor center about Mount Bangs, the tallest point in the Arizona part of the range, and about the Paiute Wilderness. The helpful agent had never heard of either, and even as I pointed out the window at them he shrugged and directed me down the street to a sports store. The most knowledgeable person at the sports store hadn't heard about either of them, and I began to think that I suffered from some kind of misinformation. But slowly I realized that the man was an ATV driver, and though he spent a lot of time in the Virgins, he would never be near any wilderness with his all-terrain vehicle (which, the day before, he informed me he had ridden 100 miles through the Virgins).

I did get him to direct me to Elbow Canyon, the route I'd read would take me into the mountains. For those who like to do the Ford Ranger TV commercial thing on jeep trails, this is the route you'll want to take. I used my four-wheel high gear and even a few times the low gear to get in, and the trip was long and I had to explore my way to the canyon. As a result, I'm listing this hike in a slightly unusual way with the best directions I can, but beware—these are unmarked dirt roads.

To get to Elbow Canyon from Mesquite, take the Riverside Drive road toward Bunkerville west. Immediately after crossing the Virgin River, turn north and follow the signs to Elbow Canyon. Eventually you'll reach a sign directing you to Cougar Springs 7 miles, which you'll follow. Here the road begins to climb, and continues for all those 7 miles. An easier route comes down from St. George, Utah.

When I'd almost reached Cougar Springs, I took a small side road where I'd glimpsed some men. I climbed out of my car and was immediately surround by four growling Chihuahuas. An old gringo and an old Navajo man sat drinking Budweiser, already quite drunk at about 10am. Their beat Toyota truck's hood stood open, but they seemed unconcerned about their mechanical dilemma. They were very happy to see me and even happier to give me directions. They suggested that I could drive all the way to St. George on that road, and I decided that's what I'd do when I finished my hike.

A mile farther up the road I reached the stone house at Cougar Springs, a pretty old dwelling made of cut sandstone. The road that goes by this dwelling will eventually take you back to Mesquite, and it is a much easier drive. If you'd rather come in that way, you'll want to take the Lime Kiln Canyon Road out of Mesquite.

Backtracking a bit, I took the road toward Black Rock Mountain and then a side road to the trailhead for Mount Bangs, which went about a half mile and stopped at the trailhead and the beginning of the Paiute Wilderness.

I hiked for about 1.5 miles along road track, which came to a small pond—Littlefield Reservoir—and then turned up toward the peak. Be aware that nothing is signed in the Paiute Wilderness area. The track becomes small trails leading through the scrub, and finally to a scramble track up to the ridge. Even this track is marked by cairns, so be sure to stay on it. Trying to make your way up on your own route will prove frustrating. Another few miles took me to the top. The views from there were spectacular, and not a human footprint to be found. I returned the way I came.

Once back at my car, I decided to drive to St. George through the wilderness, a lovely drive across some 50 miles of mountains and high meadows. The road is good, but if it has rained recently, it will be slick and boggy.

If leaving from St. George, you'll head out Black Rock Canyon toward Black Rock Mountain, and continue on. In either direction—going from say, Utah, into Arizona, and coming out in Nevada, or vice versa—the trip makes a nice adventure.

If you'd like to explore the area more, you can backpack into Sullivans Canyon, from either the top or bottom. Or you can trek up Mount Bangs along the crest of the Virgin Ridge from the Virgin River Gorge. Maps for this area include USGS Mount Bangs and Elbow Canyon, as well as Mountain Sheep Spring, Purgatory Canyon, Littlefield, Wolf Mountain West, Mustang Knoll, Canes Spring, and Jacobs Well.

HORSEBACK RIDING

The Grand Canyon has a few riding options. The most renowned are the **Grand Canyon Mule Rides.** By stepping gingerly and carefully with their small hoofed feet, mules have been transporting visitors down the Grand Canyon since the turn of the century. Grand Canyon National Park Lodges, which operates the mule rides, is proud to say that the company has never lost a rider. Perhaps that's because an orientation is required before saddling up. The one-day trip descends to Plateau Point, where there's a view of the Colorado River. Riders are in the saddle for approximately 7 hours. The overnight trip goes to Phantom Ranch, where cabins and dormitories are available as well as three meals, including a steak dinner. From mid-November through March, there's also a 3-day/2-night trip to Phantom Ranch. Mule trips range in price from $112.94 for a 1-day ride to Plateau Point (lunch provided) to $325.94 for an overnight to Phantom Ranch to $444.88 for a 2-night ride to Phantom Ranch.

Riders must weigh less than 200 pounds fully dressed and stand at least 4 feet 7 inches tall. Pregnant women are not allowed on mule trips, and riders must be able to speak and understand English fluently in order to follow the wranglers' directions. Kids 15 and under must be accompanied by adult. For reservations, call ☎ **303/297-2757** or log on to www.grandcanyonlodges.com. Be advised that mule rides fill up early, particularly during months when temperatures within the canyon are relatively cool; March to June and September to November you'll want to book as far in advance as possible, such as one year or more, and you can book up to 23 months in advance. During the rest of the year, mule rides are more available, but you'll still want to book 3 months in advance. However, the concessionaire stresses that people do cancel quite often, so if your travel plans are somewhat flexible, you may be able to book with little or no advance notice.

Located on the South Rim, by Moqui Lodge, **Apache Stables** (☎ **520/638-2891**) leads riders into the beautiful Kaibab National Forest where they ride along the rim of, but don't go into, the Grand Canyon. Prices range from $30.50 for a 1-hour ride to $95.50 for a 4-hour ride (lunch is not included). The twilight campfire ride is $40.50. Riders are encouraged to bring their own marshmallows or wieners to roast. Round-trip wagon rides are $12.50 for 1 hour. Apache Stables is open from March to early December (depending on weather).

There are many trails in the Coconino National Forest in the Flagstaff area suitable for riding. Those who have their own horses might want to try the Sunset Trail listed in the "Hiking" section above or the Rocky Ridge Trail listed in the "Mountain Biking" section later in this chapter. If you're looking for a guided riding experience, **McDonalds Ranch** (☎ 520/774-4481) offers a variety of trail rides through the Coconino. They last from 1 to 2 hours and begin and end at the corral located at the Fort Valley Barn on the corner of U.S. 180 and Snowbowl Road. Rides start at 9am, and the last one leaves at 5pm for the sunset/moonlight ride. On the first and third Thursdays of each month, McDonalds Ranch offers a hayride through the woods to a cowboy cookout barbeque.

Wranglers at **Hitchin' Post Stables,** in that sexy southern drawl of theirs, will get you saddled up and on the trail for guided trail rides including sunset steak rides and cowboy breakfast rides. Their most famous ride, however, is through Walnut Canyon where ancient cliff dwellings still remain. Petroglyphs can also be seen from the trail. Ride prices range from $25 for a 1-hour ride to $95 for the Walnut Canyon ride. Sleigh rides are available in winter. It's located at 4848 Lake Mary Road (☎ 520/774-1719).

At **Flying Heart at Flagstaff** (☎ 520/526-2788), located 3.5 miles north of Flagstaff Mall on U.S. 89, seasoned wranglers take riders up into the ponderosa pine forest of the San Francisco Peaks to approximately 9,000 feet. During summer, temperatures are considerably cooler at that elevation, making the ride quite pleasant. It's possible you'll see deer, coyote, and jackrabbits. The first ride is at 9am, the last ride at 3pm. Rides start at $35 for 1½ hours.

Mountain Ranch Stables, located 6 miles east of Williams at Exit 171 off I-40, at the Quality Inn Mountain Ranch (☎ 520/635-0706) allows riders to walk, trot, and canter into the Kaibab National Forest and take in the tremendous views of the San Francisco Peaks, the tallest mountains in Arizona. Temperatures hover around 85°F in summer, but ponderosa pine forest periodically shades riders from the brilliant sun. Riders of all levels are welcome. Trail rides are $22 for a 1-hour ride, $40 for a 2-hour ride and $85 for a 4-hour ride, with sack lunch included for the 4-hour ride.

MOUNTAIN BIKING

There are many mountain biking options in northern Arizona. Most are on the Grand Canyon North Rim and in the Flagstaff areas. Those who wish to bike the South Rim will have to be satisfied with paved roads. Be aware that there are no bike shops anywhere near the North Rim, so you'll want to have spare tubes and your own tools if you plan to spend time biking in the area. Your biking contact for northern Arizona is in Flagstaff at **Mountain Sports,** 1800 S. Milton Rd. (☎ **520/779-5156**).

Grand Canyon North Rim
Rainbow Rim Trail
18 miles one-way. Moderate to difficult. 500-ft. elevation gain. Allow 2 hrs.–a full day. Access: Drive 27 miles south of Jacob Lake on AZ 67. Turn right on Forest Development Rd. (FDR) 22 and travel 10.5 miles to FDR 206. Turn left and continue on FDR 206 for 3.5 miles. Turn right on FDR 214 and follow it for 8 miles to Parissawampitts Viewpoint, the northern end of the trail. This trail is open mid-May through mid-Oct.

Imagine a single-track trail winding along the edge of one of the seven natural wonders of the world. Sound like paradise? You found it. Add to the equation plenty of not-so-tough climbs and descents through pine forests and the changing sense of Tapeats Amphitheater, Steamboat Mountain, and Great Thumb Mesa as you go, and your biggest problem in life will be crashing because you're so mesmerized by the beauty. A recent addition to the Grand Canyon area, this 18-mile trail constructed by Kaibab National Forest links the ends of a number of dirt roads, which lead out to rim vantage points. The trail begins either at Parissawampitts Point to the north or at Timp Point to the south, but it can be accessed at any of five points along the way. The roads can be rough, but most will not bother your 2WD vehicle. Camping is free at any of the points. There's no water or food. During August through September, come prepared with rain gear. This trail is so great that I've heard of people spending days doing different sections of it. The worst thing about it is that it puts most other North Rim trails, which merely wind along Forest Service roads through woods to a single lookout point, to shame. If you do any ride here, do this one. Do it many times. Another thing: There's no problem with doing an out-and-back on this trail because the view alters completely when you change directions.

Point Sublime and Tiyo Point
35 miles round-trip. Easy to moderate. 1,180-ft. elevation gain. Allow 4 hrs. Access: On the North Rim, travel 2.5 miles north of Grand Canyon Lodge on AZ 67 and turn west at the road marked Widforss Trailhead. Travel 1 mile to the parking area and start there. Map: Kaibab National Forest map for the North Kaibab Ranger District or the USGS De Motte Park and Powell Plateau. This area is open only from mid-May through mid-Oct.

The full-day ride to Point Sublime follows a rough jeep road, which climbs and descends through old-growth pine forest and high meadows to amazing views of the Grand Canyon. The route to Tiyo Point begins on the same trail and offers awesome views but is only 22 miles round-trip. Both routes are great ways to get a sense of the North Rim's alpine forests and sunny meadows as well as its striking vistas. While pedaling, you're likely to see Kaibab squirrels (found only here; look for black and white markings and tasseled or tufted ears), mule deer, and if you're lucky, mountain lions. Be aware that this route can get saturated from snowmelt in spring and can be attacked by thunderstorms during the late summer monsoon. Check with park rangers for trail and weather conditions at the Grand Canyon Lodge. You'll also need to get a backcountry camping permit if you plan to spend the night at Point Sublime.

The trail rolls through dense forest emerging at times onto open meadows. Just past mile 8 it comes to Crystal Drainage, where a short road heads off to the left to a spot with a sweet panorama. After this point the trail loses elevation, ponderosas giving way to piñon/juniper forest. When it arrives at Point Sublime 8.5 miles later, the vegetation has become even scarcer. If you choose the shorter ride to Tiyo Point and back, take the left fork (south) in a large meadow called The Basin at mile 4 and follow the trail 6 miles to the edge of the canyon.

Crazy Jug Point
22.5 miles round-trip. Moderate to strenuous. Allow 4 hrs. 1,074-ft. elevation gain. Access: Go south on AZ 67 from Jacob Lake Center for 27 miles to Forest Development Rd. 22. Travel for 10.5 miles to FS 206, where you'll turn left. Drive 1 mile to FS 425. Open when snow isn't present, generally May to Oct. You can park at the intersection, or shorten the ride by driving in as far as you'd like on FS 425.

If you like biking through stands of ponderosa, aspen, and oak, which break out into upland meadows, you'll love this ride. However, if you're like me and the only deferred gratification you can really stand is waiting for dessert, you'd better head to the Rainbow Rim trail. This ride pales in comparison to the Rainbow Rim single track and frequent views. It will provide a relaxing jaunt through the woods with a big payoff at the end when you reach Crazy Jug, which looks out on Crazy Jug Canyon, Tapeats Amphitheater, Steamboat Mountain, and Great Thumb Mesa. The ride follows FS 425, a sparsely traveled, primitive road along which you're likely to see wildlife, especially deer and turkey. Follow FS 425 for about

10 miles until it connects with FS 292 on which you'll bear right. This road will take you down through a shallow canyon and back up to Crazy Jug Point, one of the North Rim's most spectacular vantage points. If you're daring, you might even want to camp there, along the rim (no permit required). For an extension to this ride follow FS 292-A west 1.5 miles to Monument Point, which will provide even more stunning views.

Buck Ridge Point
5 miles round trip. Easy. 265-ft. elevation gain. Allow 1.5 hrs. Access: From Jacob Lake center drive 0.25 miles south on AZ 67 to FS 461. Check your odometer and drive 3 miles to the point where FS 461 turns sharply to the left. Going straight will put you on FS 264, which at this writing isn't marked, but does have a gate, which is usually open. Begin the ride here. Open when snow isn't present, generally May to Oct.

I took this ride in the evening upon arriving in the Jacob Lake area, and it served as a short, easy introduction to Kaibab Plateau riding. The trail begins in ponderosa pine stands and follows a fairly smooth forest road through meadows and over hills with only a few technical climbs and descents, made so by rocks. Slowly it drops down into piñon/juniper forest to a sign that reads END 264. Stop here where the views open out to the north and northwest. You'll be standing on the very northwest ridge of the Kaibab Plateau, looking off across what's known as the Arizona Strip, a vast and wild desert land bordered to the north by the Vermilion Cliffs, Zion, and farther still, Bryce Canyon, all faintly visible from this point. The route offers several side roads worth exploring to lengthen it.

South Rim of the Grand Canyon
Hermit Road & Desert View Drive
16 miles and 52 miles round-trip, respectively. Easy. Allow 1.5 hrs., 3.5 hrs., respectively. Access: Head west from Grand Canyon Village or head east from Grand Canyon Village. (Hermit Rd. is closed to private vehicles 9 months each year—see "Exploring the Canyon" section in this chapter.)

If you'd like to ride your bike on the South Rim, these are the only real options, and they can be lovely ones. Hermit Road follows the rim for 8 miles west from Grand Canyon Village to Hermits Rest, accessing 8 main viewpoints along the rim. This drive is closed to private automobiles from March through November, so it can be a relatively quiet place; however, during those months the park runs a free shuttle bus touring this route, so there will still be people.

You can also take a longer ride along the **Desert View Drive,** though it can be very busy in summer. It follows AZ 64 along the canyon rim for 26 miles east of Grand Canyon Village to the east entrance of the park at Desert View. This is also a great way to get *to* the park. This road is open year-round. It features canyon vistas, the Tusayan Ruin and Museum, views of Painted Desert, the Colorado River, the San Francisco Peaks, and the Vermilion Cliffs from the Watchtower at Desert View.

Flagstaff Area
The Mount Elden Trail system winds throughout northern Flagstaff. If you want unlimited exploration of the area, head to the Peaks Ranger Station on N. U.S. 89, where they have 20-something flyers guiding bikers on many rides, a few of which I've listed below.

Schultz Creek Trail
7 miles round-trip. Moderate. 600-ft. elevation gain. Allow 2 hrs. Access: Drive northwest from Flagstaff 2 miles on U.S. 180 to FS 420 (Schultz Pass Rd.), where you'll turn right (north). Follow it about 1 mile, passing through a gate. Turn right (east) and you'll see the trailhead marker.

This is one of many fun trails that snake through the ponderosa forests in the Mount Elden area. The trail parallels an intermittent drainage that carries water down from the San Francisco Peaks. Though the stream only runs in the spring and late summer, the presence of the streambed gives a soothing feel to this ride. With a moderate gradient, this trail won't test your lungs, but it will give you a chance to maneuver over and around some of the basaltic rock that forms these peaks. Be aware that hikers, horseback riders, and motorcycles use this trail. When you reach the end of the trail, turn back or link up with other trails in the system.

Dry Lake Hills Loop

9.3-mile loop. Difficult. 1,500-ft. elevation gain. Allow 2–3 hrs. Access: See instructions for Schultz Creek Trail above.

Some say this is the best single-track loop in the state. It has it all, from views to real technical riding. It begins on the Rocky Ridge Trail, a maze of stones that makes its way to a cattle guard at Elden Lookout Road. En route it leads over rolling terrain through a forest of ponderosa interspersed with Gambel oak and alligator junipers. The terrain is arid here, making this a good early spring and late fall ride. The trail roller coasters over dry washes and offers good views of Flagstaff, Oak Creek Canyon, and even Mormon Lake. From the cattle guard it follows the Brookbank Trail. This section climbs along a forested wash and alternates areas of forest and meadows. It connects with the Sunset Trail, where you'll want to turn left. You'll descend fast to Schultz Creek Trail, where you'll take another left (see above). This trail will lead you back to the beginning. Watch out for hikers, horseback riders, and motorcyclists.

Lower Oldham Trail

6 miles round-trip. Moderate. 460-ft. elevation gain. Allow 1.5 hrs. Access: From downtown, take San Francisco St. north to Forest Ave. Turn right (east) and drive a few miles to the Buffalo Park turn off on the left. Ride straight through the Buffalo Park entryway and follow the road to a green pumping station, next to which stands the trailhead sign.

This fun trail winds through forests and rises and falls over not-too-strenuous hills. It does traverse some rocky terrain in places, giving riders a chance to exercise their technical skills. Since it begins only a few miles from downtown, it provides great access to all the Mt. Elden trails. It begins in Buffalo Park, along an easy road. Once this road reaches the trailhead, the route turns to single track that descends into ponderosa forest. The trail climbs up and down through a variety of terrain that's mostly ponderosa, but also includes some Gambel oak and an occasional fir tree. At mile 3 the trail connects with Rocky Ridge Trail, a good place to hook onto the Dry Lake Hills Loop mentioned above. Or, you can simply turn around and head back the way you came.

ROAD BIKING

There are a few good rides in the Flagstaff area. Some people like to simply head out I-40 west to Williams. On the way back, the views of the San Francisco Peaks will keep you occupied for miles. Although by map the ride up U.S. 180 looks like an appealing way to ride to the Grand Canyon, local cyclists caution against it. The highway has no shoulder and runs rampant with RVs. If you'd like to bike in the Grand Canyon area see the "Mountain Biking" section of this chapter.

Lake Mary Road

55 miles round-trip. Moderate. Allow 4 hrs. Access: Head south of Flagstaff on I-17. Take exit 339 to Lake Mary Rd. Drive to the second cattle guard and begin there.

This ride south of Flagstaff provides a broad shoulder with a good surface and great views. It's an out-and-back with a loop around Mormon Lake. The lake can be lovely, and a great place to spot birds while you ride. Look for hawks, cranes, ospreys, northern harriers, ducks and an occasional bald eagle.

North Rim Drive
50 miles one-way. Easy. Allow 4 hrs. Access: Begin riding at Jacob Lake at the intersection of U.S. 89A and AZ 67. Fee to enter Grand Canyon National Park: $10. This ride is open only from mid-May–mid-Oct.

This is a ride along smooth pavement from Jacob Lake into Grand Canyon National Park. The road has broad shoulders and little traffic except during the height of summer, when it can be a bit busy (but *nothing* like the South Rim). The highway travels through thick ponderosa stands as well as across broad meadows. Unfortunately, you'll have to pay $20 to enter the park, but remember the permit lasts seven days. Once in the park, bikers can make their way to Point Imperial, Cape Royal, and Bright Angel Point. Along the way you'll likely see many deer and possibly wild turkeys.

SWIMMING

Since this is high desert, there aren't a lot of places to swim. But there are a few key ones. The first is **Lake Powell,** discussed in detail in chapter 3. Another is the **Colorado River,** though be aware that access is limited. There are beaches at **Lees Ferry,** and plenty of them along the Colorado River at the bottom of the Grand Canyon. Any of the hikes into the canyon listed above will eventually get you to the river, but in most cases these are multi-day trips. Also be aware that the water runs 48°F, which is very cold. Beware of diving straight in when you're overheated from hiking. Those with heart conditions or other medical conditions might have to enjoy wading only. If you take the trek or helicopter ride into **Havasu Falls,** you'll find abundant swimming, and it's warm enough there from about March through October to make for a long season, though the water is generally cold there as well. The canyon provides blue pools, huge waterfalls, and a lush tropical environment.

WALKS & RAMBLES

Tusayan Ruin Walk
0.2 mile one-way. Easy. Allow 30 min. Access: Along the Desert View Drive 3 miles south of Moran Point on the South Rim. Open year-round.

This paved trail meanders through ruins of ancestral Puebloan people who inhabited the site for a short time around A.D. 1200. The setting has lovely views, so it's no wonder the Hopi word Tusayan means "land of isolated buttes." The nearby Tusayan Museum has artifacts on display and runs guided tours through the ruins. This trail is wheelchair accessible with assistance.

Bright Angel Point Trail
1 mile round-trip. Easy. Allow 30 min. Access: On the grounds of the Grand Canyon Lodge on the North Rim. Open year-round.

This meander takes you to one of the most spectacular vistas on either rim. A well-paved trail makes its way out to a point separating Roaring Springs Canyon and the Transept, from which you have views in many directions, with the canyon laid out in seemingly endless layers of blue and mauve. Be sure to pick up a trail brochure, which will help orient you.

Grand Canyon Railway
Allow 8 hrs., including a 3½-hr. layover at the Grand Canyon. Runs from Williams to the South Rim of the Grand Canyon at Grand Canyon Village. ☎ 800/843-8724 or 520/773-1976. www.grandcanyonlodge.com. Open year-round.

If you're looking for a different way of getting to the canyon, this rail ride may be it, though some people find it isn't worth the time, since the trip itself doesn't offer views of the canyon. The Grand Canyon Railway offers the choice of five classes of service: coach, club with full bar,

Coconino main (downstairs in dome car), Coconino dome (upstairs with the dome windows), and Chief car (a parlor car with luxurious sofas). Prices range from $62.35 for an adult ticket in coach ($27.15 for children ages 2 to 16) to $138.51 for an adult ticket in the Chief car ($103.31 for children). A continental breakfast is served in the Chief car on the way to the Grand Canyon and appetizers, champagne, sparkling cider, and other cold drinks are served on the way back. This is a scenic, steady ride though high grasslands, with some hairpin turns. In summer the railway uses steam engines.

WHITE-WATER KAYAKING & RAFTING

Running the Colorado River through the Grand Canyon ranks as one of life's most fun, accessible, and challenging adventures. The 140-mile trip from Lees Ferry to Lake Mead takes rafters and kayakers on big water through ominous rapids, with limitless scenery to view along the way. Because there are a number of ways to do this run, it's available to people of many ages and fitness levels. Since this is one of the most highly regulated river runs in the world, the trips are relatively safe. Due to Grand Canyon National Park regulations, it's likely that any of the outfitters who run the river will be reliable and safe.

Still, be aware that because of the dynamics of people, any long-term river trip could provide you with challenges. In fact, for me, some of life's most interesting dramas play out on extended kayak/raft trips in which participants vie for power. Look at such notable books as *Into Thin Air* and *Running the Amazon* and you'll find at their very core the tensions caused when bringing people together in life-threatening adventures. I say that only as a way to help you envision your trip down the Grand Canyon. See the whole of it, not just the white water, but the dynamics—the helping each other, the fixing meals and pitching tents—all as a part of the beauty of it. Some of it will be difficult, some will be easy, and most will be a mixture of the two. All of it, every moment, will no doubt be an adventure.

When selecting which outfitter to go with, I suggest looking at Web sites when you can, and then calling and talking to them. Ask questions to find out if the kind of trip they're offering appeals to you. Trips range in length from 3 to 18 days, some of the shorter ones with options of hiking in or out of the canyon. One of the most important decisions involves the type of craft you'll be using. These range from small "paddle rafts" in which rafters get to participate in the adventure by paddling, which I highly recommend, to medium to large oar-craft, upon which rafters sit and simply enjoy the experience. The quickest trips are on large motor-driven rafts. If you have time for a longer trip, and are physically fit, definitely choose a paddle-raft trip. Other options are wooden dories, a method of travel favored by purists, those who like to re-live the kind of experience John Wesley Powell had when he ran the Grand in 1869. But even these are oar craft, so you won't participate in maneuvering the craft.

One of the best online resources to help answer questions about what kind of trip to choose and what you'll need to bring on a trip is at www.azstarnet.com/grandcanyonriver/FAQcom.html. The following outfitters aren't necessarily the best, but they are reliable and do cover a broad range of trips. In order to find the best guide for you, check them out personally, or refer to the Grand Canyon Web page, **www.thecanyon.com/nps**, for a more extensive list.

- **Arizona River Runners,** P.O. Box 47788, Phoenix, AZ 85068-7788 (☎ **800/477-7238** or 602/867-4866; www.adventuresports.com/asap/wwraft/arizona/welcome.htm; e-mail: info@raftarizona.com) offers motor-powered trips (from 5 to 9 days) and 13-day oar trips. Prices range from $1,490 to 2,335.

- **Grand Canyon Expeditions Co.,** P.O. Box 0, Kanab, UT 84741 (☎ **800/544-2691** or 435/644-2691; www.gcex.com; e-mail gcec@xpressweb.com) offers 8-day motorized raft trips and 14-day oar trips in wooden dories and $1,933 to $2705, respectively.

- **Moki Mac River Expeditions,** P.O. Box 71242, Salt Lake City, UT 84171 (☎ **800/284-7280;** www.mokimac.com) offers a variety of trips from 6 to 9 days, using motorized craft, as well as 14-day oar trips. Prices range from $1,260 to $2,490.

- **Canyon Explorations,** PO Box 310, Flagstaff, AZ 86002 (☎ **800/654-0723** or 520/774-4559; www.canyonx.com) offers 6- to 9- and 13- to 14-day oar and paddle trips. It also has such novelties as a 15-day string quartet trip, during which paddlers are serenaded at stops along the way, and a hiker's special trip, during which time is allowed to hike side canyons. It also allows kayakers to come along on certain trips. Prices range from $1,345 to $3,550.

- **Tour West,** P.O. Box 333, Orem, UT 84059 (☎ **800/453-9107** or 801/225-0755; www.twriver.com) offers 3- and 6-night motorized trips and 12-night oar trips at prices ranging from $830 (3-night trip) to $2,363 (12-night oar trip). Its most popular trip is the 6-night trip for $1,695 per person.

- **Outdoors Unlimited,** 6900 Townsend Winona Rd., Flagstaff, AZ 86004 (☎ **800/637-RAFT** or 520/526-2852; www.outdoorsunlimited.com or e-mail: raft@outdoorsunlimited.com) offers a variety of motorized and oar trips, as well as paddle trips, ranging from 5 to 15 days. It also allows kayakers on some trips. Prices range from $1,220 to $2,555.

- **Hualapai River Runners** (☎ **520/769-2219**), a tribal rafting company takes its rafters on a 1- or 2-day rafting trip through the lower portion of the Grand Canyon. The river is ranked as a Class III or IV but can go up to a Class V if the dam has let water out or there have been floods. White-water rapids start about 10 miles into the trip, but there are also long stretches of flat water as well. The river guides will stop for lunch on a sandy beach and at a couple of side canyons where you can get out and hike about. One of the hikes is to a waterfall that falls from a hole in the top of a cave. One-day trips cost $250 plus 5% tax per person, and the 2-day trips are charter only for 8 persons or more at $4,000. The one-day trip includes lunch, cold beverages, and snacks; the 2-day trip includes a breakfast, two lunches, and a steak dinner. Water temperatures are a very chilly 45°F and you will inevitably get wet, so dress warmly. Located in Peach Springs on the Hualapai Indian Reservation.

Non-Commercial Rafting

If you're interested in taking your own boat through the Grand Canyon you'll begin by contacting the **River Permits Office,** P.O. Box 129, Grand Canyon, AZ 86023 (☎ **800/959-9164** or outside the United States at 520/638-7843; fax 520/638-7844). Log on to www.thecanyon.com/nps for detailed information about obtaining a permit. The wait for a permit is currently more than 12 years, though the park is currently reviewing the permitting process. River enthusiasts hope this review will improve the prospects for non-commercial users.

In order to join the waiting list, you must complete a New Additions Application, pay $100, and send it postmarked in the month of February. To stay on the waiting list every year you must submit a Continuing Interest Form postmarked between December 15 and January 31. You are allowed to miss only one year before you'll be removed from the waiting list. There is no fee for this form. Those boaters with flexible schedules can sometimes acquire a permit from a cancelled trip. You must be on the waiting list in order to claim such a permit. For details about the cost of the trip after receiving a permit and for procedures while on the river, log on to the Web page above or contact the River Permits Office. Understand that this is one of the most challenging stretches of water in the West, and those desiring to run it should have many years of river experience.

WILDLIFE VIEWING

Grand Canyon National Park is home to 1,500 types of plants, 305 species birds, 88 types of animals, 26 types of fish, and 58 types of amphibians and reptiles, so it's the place to go looking for animals. Unfortunately, you won't likely see many along the top of the South Rim because there are just too many visitors. A trip down into the canyon will likely yield sightings, particularly of deer and reptiles.

Your best bet for wildlife viewing is the **North Rim,** where mule deer are so abundant you'll have to watch your speed while driving in the area so you don't hit one. Sadly, deer are killed daily on AZ 64 from Jacob Lake to the North Rim. A very unique denizen of the area is the Kaibab squirrel (found only here, some say, though I saw some in the White Mountains near Pinetop). They're distinguished by their nearly black color; look also for white markings and tasseled or tufted ears. Other animals to watch for in this area, the **Kaibab Plateau,** are wild turkey (lots of them!) mountain lion, bobcat, and big horn sheep.

Campgrounds & Other Accommodations

CAMPING

Mather Campground

Located on the South Rim of the Grand Canyon in Grand Canyon Village. ☎ **800/ 365-2267.** RV sites with no hookups, visitor center, interpretive programs, store, rest rooms, pay hot showers, flush toilets, drinking water, laundry, pay phones, and dump station. Campsite fees range from $12–$15. Open year-round.

This 350-site campground has all the amenities of a luxury hotel. For those who like to get back to nature and rough it a little, this may be too busy of a place but it's great for families. Open all year. Reservations required up until November 30, and then it's on a first-come, first-served basis, until spring.

Trailer Village RV Park

Located at the South Rim entrance of Grand Canyon. Follow the main road, past the visitor center and take the first left. ☎ **303/29-PARKS.** 80 sites. Full hook-ups, picnic table and grill at each site, drinking water, flush toilets, pay hot showers (75¢ per minute), laundry services, vending machines, general store, and dump station. $20 plus tax per night for double adult occupancy. Children 16 and under are free. Open year-round.

This cushy trailer park offers so many amenities that you may forget you're camping in the great outdoors. A shuttle runs every 10 minutes from the trailer park to the business center where the general store is located. There is a campground for tent camping here as well.

Ten-X Campground
Located 2 to 3 miles south of Tusayan on the South Rim. ☎ **520/638-2443.** RV and tent sites, drinking water, vault toilets, fire rings, picnic tables, and ranger talks.

You may actually feel alone at this secluded little campground tucked away in a dense ponderosa forest. From Memorial Day to Labor Day weekend, ranger talks are given every Thursday, Friday, and Saturday evening on subjects ranging from the local birds of prey to Kaibab National Forest history and environmental issues. One ranger plays an educational version of Bingo, which teaches kids about the forest around them.

Jacob Lake Campground
Located in Jacob Lake village at the intersection of U.S. 89A and AZ 67 in the vicinity of the North Rim. ☎ **520/643-7770.** 56 RV and tent sites. Interpretive programs, picnic tables and grills, drinking water, and flush toilets. $12 per night. Open mid-April to the end of September.

The Jacob Lake Campground, nestled within tall ponderosa forest, sits at the edge of Jacob Lake village. The actual lake for which the area is named—a pond, really—is located on the other side of the village. Though it doesn't have a lake, one of this campground's selling points is that it's the gateway to the North Rim of the Grand Canyon (about 60 miles away), and it's quite quiet and has a secluded feel.

Kaibab Camper Village
Take 89A south from Fredonia to Jacob Lake. Head through what town there is there, watching for the campground on the right. ☎ **800/525-0924.** www.canyoneers.com. 62 motor home and trailer sites, 34 tenting sites, drinking water, electric hookups, 70 picnic tables. Full hook-up $22; tent $12. Open May–Oct.

Situated about an hour north of Grand Canyon's North Rim, Kaibab Camper Village is a good stop-off point for exploring the area. Sites are among lovely ponderosa pine forest near Jacob Lake, which is really just a little pond. The original North Kaibab forest ranger's cabin, circa 1910, has been restored to its original form.

Demotte Campground
Located 29 miles south of the town of Jacob Lake. ☎ **520/643-7770.** 25 single-unit RV or tent sites, interpretive programs, picnic tables and grills, drinking water, and flush toilets. $12 per night. Open from late May or early June through Oct.

Demotte Campground has excellent access to biking and hiking trails. During the summer months rangers offer interpretive campfire programs on the environment of the area. One creature unique only to the Kaibab National Forest is the Kaibab squirrel. It's the size of a cottontail rabbit, with a white tail and tufted ears, and it eats the bark off ponderosa pines.

North Rim Campground
Located just north of Grand Canyon Lodge. ☎ **800/365-2267.** 83 sites. RV and tent sites (no hookups), interpretive programs, picnic tables and grills, drinking water, and flush toilets. $15 per night. Open mid-May to mid-Oct, it receives reservations up to 3 months in advance.

This is the only designated campground at the North Rim of Grand Canyon. Literally 20 feet from the edge of the canyon, the campground sits in a shady ponderosa pine forest. Parents will want to keep an eye on your kids since there's no fence at the canyon edge. After October 15, visitors can still use the site, and at no cost, but then there are no amenities except for pit toilets, and a permit from the backcountry office is required. *Note:* If Demotte, Jacob Lake, and the North Rim campgrounds are full, visitors can camp anywhere off the AZ 67 in the Kaibab National Forest so long as they're more than a 0.25 miles from a paved road or water source.

In the Williams Area

Kaibab National Forest operates several campsites. All run based on a first-come, first-served basis. Call the Ranger District at ☎ **520/635-2633.** You'll find the campsites at Whitehorse Lake (15 miles south of Williams off Fourth Street/County Road 73); Cataract Lake (2 miles northwest of Williams on Cataract Lake Road); Dogtown Lake (8 miles south of Williams off Fourth Street/Country Road 73); and Kaibab Lake (4 miles northeast of Williams of AZ 64).

Dairy Springs & Double Springs National Forest Campgrounds, Mormon Lake

Drive south from Flagstaff 25 miles on Lake Mary Rd. to the FS 90 intersection. Turn west (right) on FS 90 and drive about 4 miles to the lake. ☎ **520/774-1147.** 45 sites with picnic tables; drinking water, vault toilets; no utilities hookups. $10 per night per vehicle; $5 per vehicle for day use. Open early May–late Sept.

These two campgrounds are near but not on Mormon Lake; however two hikes, Ledges and Mormon Mountain Trails, originate in the campgrounds and lead to panoramic overlooks of the lake. During drought periods, the lake shrinks to the size of a puddle. But when the water is back up, the fishing and windsurfing are excellent. Many like to bring binoculars and catch some birding action. Birds sighted in the area include hawks, cranes, ospreys, northern harriers, ducks and an occasional bald eagle. At the lake there's fishing, water sports, biking, and wildlife viewing.

INNS & LODGES

Bright Angel Lodge & Cabins

Amfac Parks & Resorts, 14001 E. Iliff Ave., Suite 600, Aurora, CO 80014. ☎ **303/297-2757.** www.amfac.com. 89 units (10 with sink only, 10 with sink and toilet, 14 with bathroom), including 55 cabins with bathrooms. Prices range from $44 double (without bathroom)–$116 double; suite $234 double. AE, DC, DISC, MC, V.

Founded in 1896 as a tent and cabin camp on the very edge of the canyon, then built as a lodge in 1935, this inn offers affordable rooms in a variety of types. The lobby is rustic, with a huge fireplace and log walls. The rusticness follows into the rooms, all medium-sized, some with baths, others only with sinks. The cabins vary in their juxtaposition to the canyon, but some sit on the rim; these must be booked a year in advance. The others should be booked 6 months in advance. A coffee shop and steakhouse provide decent food. If you'd like more luxurious rim-side accommodations check into **El Tovar Hotel,** reachable through the same number above. For accommodations outside the south entrance in Tusayan, you may want to look into the **Holiday Inn Express Grand Canyon** (☎ 800/HOLIDAY or 520/638-3000).

Phantom Ranch

Amfac Parks & Resorts, 14001 E. Iliff Ave., Suite 600, Aurora, CO 80014. ☎ **303/297-2757;** reconfirmations ☎ **520/638-3283** or 520/638-2631, ext. 6015. www.amfac.com. 11 cabins, 40 dorm beds. $23 per bed; cabin $69 double. AE, DISC, MC, V. Reservations require full pre-payment.

With a name like Phantom Ranch, who wouldn't want to stay here? Actually, campers probably enjoy the beauty of the canyon more than guests here, but if you're partial to a bed, this is your only option at the very bottom of the Grand Canyon. Built in 1922, the inn has an Old West ranch atmosphere, with stone-walled cabins and gender-segregated dormitories. Evaporative coolers are a welcome luxury in mid-summer. Reservations must be made as early as possible, which usually means up to a year in advance, and reconfirmation is mandatory. Last-minute cancellations are a reality, so you may want to arrive at the Bright Angel Lodge transportation desk before 6am on the day you want to stay at the ranch. Three meals daily are served family-style with a fixed-price menu, but must be reserved in advance. There's also a public phone and mule-baggage carrying service (in case you just can't get the umph to carry your pack back *up* the canyon).

Grand Canyon North Rim
Kaibab Lodge
P.O. Box 2997, Flagstaff, AZ 86003. ☎ 800/525-0924 or 520/526-0924. www.canyoneers.com. 24 units. Mid-May–mid-Oct $70–$120. DISC, MC, V. Pets accepted.

Begun as the VT Ranch in 1922, later renamed the Kaibab Lodge, this place provides decent accommodations near the boundary of Grand Canyon National Park. The lodge is set on a broad meadow where deer and elk graze, but also just off AZ 64, which tracks you into the park and to many important hiking and biking trailheads. The rooms range in quality from the "chariots," modular log cabins that have boxy feel, to older cabins built in the 1930s and 1940s, which have a more authentic feel but could use some refurbishing. This is not a romantic getaway so much as a practical place to sleep en route to adventure. The restaurant serves tasty meals at Grand Canyon prices.

Jacob Lake Inn
Jacob Lake, AZ 86022. ☎ 520/643-7232. www.jacoblake.com. E-mail: jacob@jacoblake.com. 39 units. Mid-May–Nov $85–$100, double, $74–$105 cabins. Dec–mid-May $85–$100 motel rooms only. AE, DC, DISC, MC, V. Pets accepted.

This lodge is set among the pines about 50 miles from the North Rim, and provides clean, reliable rooms. In fact, if you request one of the newer units you'll find quite a comfortable and romantic retreat here. The motel rooms are standard size with small baths and soft beds. The cabins, though small, are set around a fountain and gazebo. The beds in the new cabins are firm, and the baths tiled and spotless. Most rooms have a porch and forest views. The inn has one of the few restaurants for miles around. The food is decent, though expensive, but the baked goods at the Inn's Country Store are worth stocking up on, especially the chocolate parfait cookies.

Grand Canyon Lodge
Amfac Parks & Resorts, 14001 E. Iliff Ave., Suite 600, Aurora, CO 80014. ☎ 303/297-2757. www.amfac.com. 200 units. $78–$104 double. AE, CB, DC, DISC, MC, V. Open May 15–Oct 15.

Listed on the National Register of Historic Places, this unassuming lodge offers a series of stone cabins scattered along the North Rim among ponderosa pines, some with excellent views. There are also newer cabins and standard motel rooms. Three meals daily are served in a large dining hall, and there's a saloon and snack bar as well.

Flagstaff
Sled Dog Inn
10155 Mountainaire Rd., Flagstaff, AZ 86001. ☎ 800/754-0664 or 520/525-6212. www.sleddoginn.com. E-mail: sleddog@infomagic.com. 10 units. $109–$169 double. MC, V.

Set among the hills in a semi-rural area outside Flagstaff, the Sled Dog is a sanctuary for outdoor enthusiasts. It's an especially good place for those who are just dipping their toes into biking or climbing, because the innkeepers offer introductory packages in which guests can learn in non-threatening environments. For those who already have the skills, the innkeepers can help point you in the direction of some of the best trails. The B&B itself is new (opened in 1997), so it's both comfortable and efficient. Rooms are cozy and have good linens and hand-built pine furnishings. There's a Jacuzzi and sauna, which guests can share. A full breakfast is included. Truly adventurous winter guests can even do the "You mush 'em experience" and get a lesson on driving a dog sled or skijoring, a sport in which dogs pull a cross-country skier.

Note: The innkeepers keep these dog-sled dogs on-site, and they can cause a racket barking in the mornings.

Inn at 410
410 N. Leroux St., Flagstaff, AZ 86001.
☎ **800/774-2008** or 520/774-0088. www.inn410.com. E-mail: info@inn410.com. 9 units. $125–$175 double. Rates include full breakfast. MC, V.

Refashioned from an 1894 residence, this inn is a model for how a bed-and-breakfast should be run. The ambiance is comfortable while finely tuned. All the furnishings are unique and accent the particular room's theme. If you get a chance, take a look at the sculpted pine bed in the Dakota suite—a good bet if you're traveling with kids. Some rooms have Jacuzzis and fireplaces. Best of all the innkeepers are skilled guides and will direct you on tours that fit your time schedule. If you're lucky, you'll get to sample the pumpkin pancakes for breakfast.

3

Arizona Indian Country

A few years ago while in the midst of shooting a television documentary here on the Hopi Indians, one of the photographers, a Hopi, led us south from Kayenta, Arizona, to Hopiland. He immediately turned off the main highway, and we followed him for the next three hours on dirt roads, past ruins, wild horses grazing the plains, and small dwellings with no electrical or phone lines in sight. While looking out toward the sunset between two mesas, a line struck me from a David Bowie song: "This is not America." Of course, I realized I was in America, geographically speaking; however, this place was not the United States, so foreign did it seem, with its abrupt mesas and primitive dwellings. For hours, all of the usual landmarks were gone, and we were adrift in an ancient cultural sea.

That wasn't my first experience in losing contact with my home country while stepping across a very thin border demarcating the Native American world. From the time I was a little girl and through much of my life, I have traveled with my mother to this land that she loves beyond words. Before they were tourist destinations, we would climb on foot to the tops of the Hopi mesas to watch dancers float upon what seemed clouds of dust, while drumbeats pulsed in our spines.

Unfortunately, these lands hold the outdoor adventurer somewhat in abeyance. Since the Hopi and Navajo own much of the area, the lands aren't as accessible as areas owned publicly. But there are lovely pockets of immeasurable beauty that will transport you back in time. This vast land of stark mesas, painted deserts, sheer cliffs, and snakelike canyons can be best described as mysterious. If you have any belief whatsoever in the timelessness of history, you may find yourself haunted by the wealth of it here as you climb into ruins abandoned for hundreds of years, squeeze into slot canyons where the wind seems to talk in strange tones, or touch the sparkling amethyst core of an ancient petrified tree.

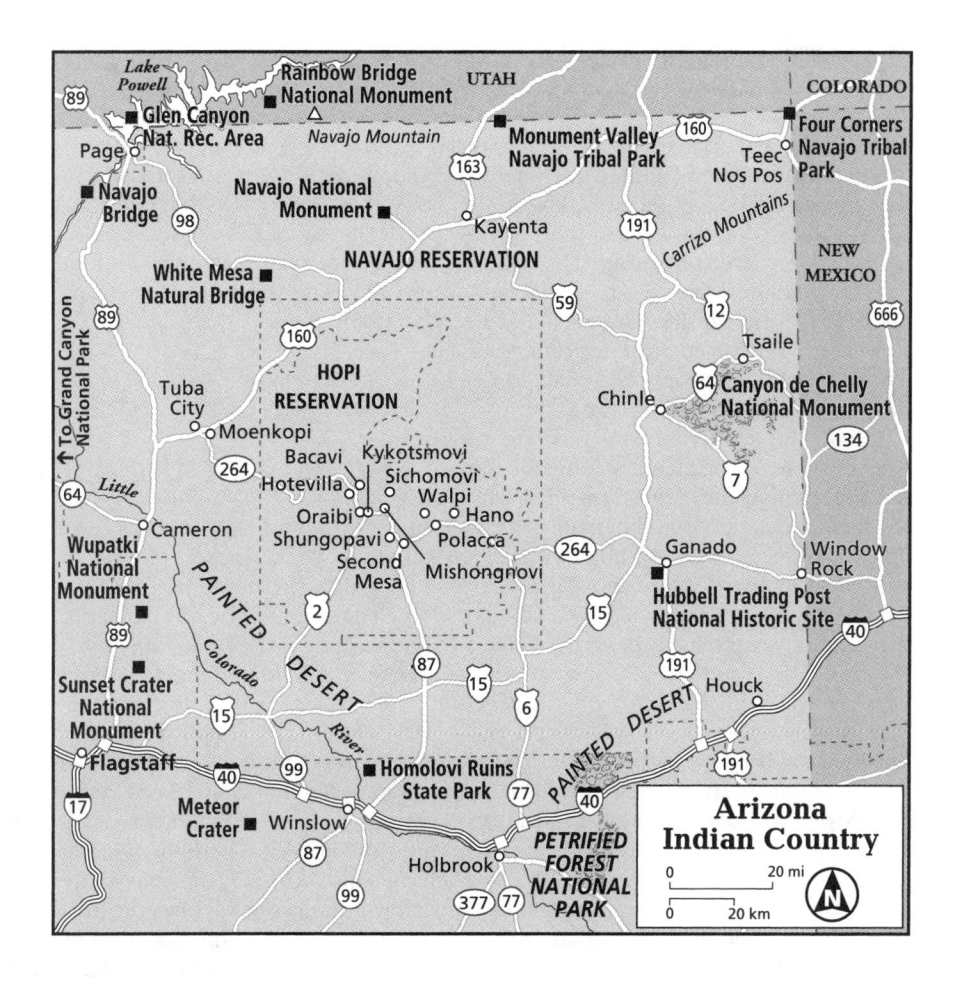

Hikers, particularly those who enjoy pre-Columbian history, will best enjoy this area. Since it's a region with relatively few mountains, many of the hikes are into canyons or along level ground. Though bikers won't find awesome single track here, they will find miles of scenery to occupy them while they pedal. As for swimmers and water lovers, **Lake Powell** can't be beat, and sports such as sea kayaking are becoming increasingly popular there. For fishers, the area between **Lees Ferry** and **Glen Canyon Dam** is world renowned not only for its quantity of fish (on a good day, fishers have been known to hook as many as 50!) but also for amazing scenery, with 1,000-foot cliffs rising along the sides of the river. Above all, Arizona Indian Country is a place to regard physical beauty such as that of the **Petrified Forest** and **Painted Desert**, and to experience new perspectives that the lives of the Navajo and Hopi can bring.

The land in this area is a source of ongoing conflict, particularly between the Navajo and Hopi. The seeds of the conflict were sown hundreds of years ago, before recorded history, probably sometime after 1400, when the Navajo migrated down from what is now northern Canada. The Navajo were nomadic tribes, and they quickly spread out across the area. Meanwhile, for centuries, the Hopi had lived atop the mesas in what is now called Hopiland. Their ancestors, called the *Anasazi* (meaning "ancient ones" or "ancient enemies") by the Navajo, once lived in caves within canyons throughout the region. Unfortunately for the Hopi and other Pueblo tribes, archaeologists were slow in discovering the connections between the Anasazis and the present-day Puebloan tribes. So, when it came time to slice up the land pie of the area, hundreds of thousands of acres went to the Navajo (currently an area covering 17 million acres), while the Hopi, Zuni, Acoma, and the tribes along the Rio Grande River in New Mexico received smaller portions of the land that their people had roamed for the better part of a millennium.

Today, the Hopi are still pushing to recover more of their land. Meanwhile the Navajo, owning the largest parcel of any Native American tribe in the country, continue to prosper. With goldmine holdings such as Monument Valley and Canyon de Chelly, as well as mining and oil holdings, they are the wealthiest tribe in the United States.

Your trip through Arizona Indian Country will undoubtedly weave you into the lives of both tribes, whether you're hiking through the spectacular slot at **Antelope Canyon** or touring **First Mesa** in Hopiland. You'll see Navajo hexagonal log homes, called *hogans,* with their doorways facing east to greet the new day; women in long skirts herding sheep on foot; and cowboys on horseback riding to what appears to be nowhere. You may note a warrior nomad spirit in the Navajo; they are proud people who are at times quiet, but who also can be quite boisterous and outspoken.

Their demeanor contrasts greatly with the Hopis, who still cling tightly to their traditional religion. The mere fact that these people have lived for centuries upon high, dry mesa tops may give you some sense of not only their proud sensibility, but also the depth of their faith in their gods, most of whom are tied to nature and the elements. These are a quiet and solemn people who have a keen sense of humor, often expressed with just a hint of a smile that seems to contain centuries worth of knowledge. To wit, **Third Mesa** in Hopiland is believed to be the oldest continuously inhabited community in the United States.

Both groups are deeply linked to the land, and it's important for visitors to realize while traversing the deserts, buttes, and canyons of the region, that for these Native Americans, every bit of the land and sky, and all the forces acting upon them, are sacred.

The Lay of the Land

This portion of Arizona sits on what's known as the **Colorado Plateau,** a giant, high stable landmass that over the years has been sculpted by the elements, forming stunning buttes and canyons. At first glance, you'll think the place is an impenetrable desert, with little foliage growing and lots of long roads between towns. But closer scrutiny reveals vast hidden canyons, Technicolor deserts, and hidden oases full of life. Monument Valley along the Utah border, where the wind and rain have chiseled eerily familiar shapes into colorful sandstone, defines the area to the north. Here and within the canyons of the regions, you can begin to glimpse the forces that have worked upon the land for millions of years.

What's important to understand about the geology of this area is that the first layers of sandstone, limestone, and shale were laid down through the workings of ancient deserts, oceans, lakes, swamps, deltas, and floodplains. Within the last 8 to 10 million years, great uplifting of the plateau caused the Colorado River and its tributaries to dramatically reshape the land. Where the Colorado had once been a sluggish river, its waters now moved with force, cutting through the layers, exposing the history. Rushing water also cut away vast swatches of land leaving mesas and buttes. Precipitation and freezing and cooling made additional contributions. And, this whole erosional process continues apace: Geologists estimate that the Colorado River erodes and washes away more than 1 million tons of sand and silt every day. Much of it is deposited in Lake Powell and Lake Mead, areas that millions of years from now will be cemented into new sedimentary layers that scientists (if such creatures still exist) will likely name the way they've named the layers we see today.

Also along the northern border of the region is the flat area known as Four Corners, the only place where four states adjoin. Kids and adults love to stand on the concrete slab and occupy four states at once. To the west is Lake Powell, the massive lake created by the damming of the Colorado River, now a pleasure spot for thousands of sun worshippers. If you've had a good look at the Grand Canyon or Utah's Canyonlands, you can begin to imagine what lies beneath the glimmering waters of the desert lake. For a peek into the sentiments of some of those opposed to the building of the dam, you might want to read Edward Abbey's *The Monkey Wrench Gang* (Harperperennial Library, 2000) while you travel this area. Above all, the book illustrates the desperate loss many felt with the building of Glen Canyon Dam. It will also give you some background on the current push to tear down Glen Canyon Dam, an idea that has formed into a fairly strong movement, with proponents around the United States.

To the south of Lake Powell is Navajo National Monument and the spectacular ruins of Keet Seel and Betatakin, both made even more interesting because you must hike to reach them. These ruins lie within Tsegi Canyon and near Canyon de Chelly, which stretches along the region's eastern border, and which some believe is so spectacular they call it the "Baby Grand Canyon." Both the Tsegi Canyon and Canyon de Chelly offer glimpses not only into incredible rock layers exposed on the canyon walls, but also into the lives of the Anasazi, more currently known as the Puebloan ancestors. These people hunted and farmed in this region at least as far back as A.D. 200. Along the high sheer cliffs you'll find their dwellings, featuring layers of stone mortared together with mud, with doorways that open into a mysterious past. Other ruins in the region, each with some kind of minor hiking available, are the Wupatki National Monument and the Homolovi Ruins State Park.

The volcanic San Francisco Mountains define the southwestern corner of the region, with Humphreys Peak the highest in Arizona at 12,633 feet (see chapter 2). At the southern boundary are the subtle but strikingly beautiful Painted Desert and the Petrified Forest National Park. The rocks and sands in the area tell a vivid story that began during Triassic times, when this region was a vast floodplain, and culminated in more recent times as an area rich with minerals, a brilliant desert of fossilized trees and multicolored sands.

Spring and fall are the most comfortable times to visit this part of the world; however, if you plan on hiking slot canyons, spring and fall are the most treacherous times to come, due to flash floods that can be deadly. People still hike the slots in the spring and fall; if you do, check with the rangers first to find out about weather patterns, snowmelt patterns, and escape routes. Hiking elsewhere besides the slot canyons, biking, and even swimming in Lake Powell will be safe and enjoyable during these seasons. Summer and winter are a little trickier. Little shade, combined with high intensity sun means summers can get hot, with average temperatures around 87°F, and hotter in canyon bottoms where temperatures can exceed 100°F. Of course, Lake Powell sun worshippers hit the water during the summer time, but if you don't like crowds and lots of whining boat motors, you'll want to come during spring or fall.

With elevations averaging in the 6,500-foot range, Arizona Indian Country can get very cold in winter, often below freezing.

Anytime between November and May you can expect snow, and winter temperatures can be below zero at night, with daytime temperatures ranging from the 30s to the 60s. Unlike eastern Arizona and the Flagstaff area where mountains play a big role, here we're dealing with a bit more consistent elevation. The coldest area will likely be along the New Mexico border, where the Chuska Mountains reach an elevation of nearly 10,000 feet. That said, I've still had wonderful hikes to Keet Seel in August, and I've camped comfortably near Lake Powell in November.

Your greatest concern in canyon country is the summer monsoon. During July, August, and September, thunderheads build over the higher landmasses and can dump rain that races down the canyons. In August 1996, just such a flash flood killed 11 people hiking in Antelope Canyon in this region. During the spring snowmelt is another time flooding can occur, while generally April, May, and June are the driest months in the area.

A note about time: Though the rest of Arizona doesn't observe daylight savings time, the Navajo reservation does. So, from April to October, it's an hour later in Navajoland than elsewhere in the state.

Orientation

The northeastern corner of Arizona is defined to the west by U.S. 89, which runs north from Flagstaff (pop. 50,000), to the town of Page (pop. 10,000), a city that's grown up around Lake Powell, so it offers the basics in dining and lodging at elaborate prices. The southern boundary for the region parallels I-40 about 30 miles to the south. Along that route you'll find Winslow and Holbrook, two decent towns to get groceries and a cheap motel room, but not much else. U.S. 191 runs near the eastern border of the region, straight through the heart of Navajoland.

Two other highways of interest: U.S. 160 cuts diagonally from west to east toward Four Corners, and features key jumping-off spots for adventure such as Tuba City, the doorway to Hopiland, and Kayenta, the gateway to the Navajo National Monument and Monument Valley. Also of note is U.S. 264, a lonely road that winds along the bases of the three major Hopi mesas; through Ganado, where Ganado Trading Post acts as a central stopover point; and into Window Rock, capital of the Navajo Nation.

Parks & Other Hot Spots

Lake Powell and the Glen Canyon National Recreation Area

2 miles west of Page on U.S. 89. ☎ **520/ 608-6200.** Open year-round, 24 hours per day. Entrance fee for either the lake or the recreation is $5 per vehicle. Bird watching, boardsailing, camping, canoeing, fishing, hiking, kayaking, powerboating, sailing, swimming, wildlife viewing.

Who needs another big old empty canyon anyway? A notion like that must have gone through the minds of those who first thought to take an incredible canyon and fill it with water to form **Lake Powell.** Whatever the rationale, the Glen Canyon Dam was completed in 1963, and the lake took 17 years to fill to capacity, or to become what Edward Abbey calls a "storage pond, silt trap, evaporation tank, and garbage dispose-all, 180-mile-long national sewage lagoon." Even though my own sentiments mirror Abbey's, I must admit that the sight of Lake Powell is awesome, mostly because of its improbability. There, amidst hundreds of miles of red and yellow windswept sandstone where desert creatures scramble to survive, a giant pool of blue reflects the buttes and clouds, and quenches that most insatiable desert thirst. This is the place for those other outdoor enthusiasts, the ones propelled by motors, but there are also a few ways of exploring the 2,000 miles of shoreline and the water within by self-propulsion. Many people like to rent a houseboat and head out to the many secluded coves on this lake to swim and hike the canyons. Be aware, however, that you'll want to reserve far in advance, as summer months book up quickly.

If you don't mind a little motor boating (and you don't care to do the 13-mile hike there), you might want to take a boat cruise to see **Rainbow Bridge,** the world's largest natural bridge. This natural arch carved by wind and water stands 290 feet high and spans 275 feet. You can arrange tours to the bridge as well as houseboat and motorboat rentals through **ARA Leisure Services (☎ 800/528-6154** or 602/278-8888). This company also offers a number of other lake tours worth inquiring about.

A little-known way to see the lake is by sea kayak. Best in the fall through spring when the motor yahoos are off snowmobiling somewhere, this means of travel can take you into mazes of narrow canyons, and out across open expanses of the water. And though the lake is not known for its clarity, some choose to scuba dive there. To rent sea kayaks and arrange scuba trips, see those sections below. Powell is also renowned for its fishing. Smallmouth, largemouth, and striped bass, walleye, catfish, and crappie swim these waters, but you'll need a boat to get to them. Within the area of Lake Powell are some spectacular hikes, some such as Antelope Canyon will take you into a slot canyon so narrow you can touch both walls simultaneously. Others such as Paria Canyon take days of canyoneering, with some technical climbing and swimming involved (see chapter 2). If you're awed by engineering feats, you may want to tour **Glen Canyon Dam,** which is made from 5 million cubic yards of concrete and rises 710 feet off the bedrock.

Petrified Forest National Monument and the Painted Desert
Access from I-40 or U.S. 180 approximately 25 miles east of Holbrook. ☎ **520/524-6228.** Visitor centers are open daily 8am–5pm (with longer hours in summer). $10 per vehicle, $5 walk-in. Backpacking, bird watching, camping, hiking, wildlife viewing.

The rocks in this park tell an intense and vivid story, all through the rich words of brightly painted petrified stone. During the Triassic times, this region was a vast floodplain where dinosaurs and huge amphibians roamed about, and trees grew tall and thick. At times floods would wash tree trunks down to the floodplain, where they were entombed by deposits of silt, mud, and volcanic ash. Eventually these elements were washed away and replaced by silicon, which, in turn, turned to quartz. Some 225 million years later, wind and water eroded the landscape exposing treasures of fossilized trees and animal bones. These treasures rest on the colorful Chinle Formation, a multilayered rock full of minerals dissolved in the sandstone and clay soils deposited during various geologic periods.

As seems fitting for such an outlandish landscape, there are only a few hiking trails; in order to get into the wilderness here, you need to set out on foot sans trail. Most people experience the park by driving a 27-mile-long road, ideally from south to north. In the south you'll see the most impressive petrified wood displayed, and in the north you'll see vast expanses of the Painted Desert. At both the north and south entrances are visitor centers where backpackers can obtain free permits necessary to trek and camp in the park's wilderness areas.

If you don't intend to backpack, but would still like to take in the sights, there are some scenic self-guided trails at some of the 20 stopping points within the park. Most notable is the **Giant Logs** self-guided trail, which begins behind the Rainbow Forest Museum, where you can

DRAINING LAKE POWELL?

Those who know the canyon country of southern Utah and Northern Arizona know of the sacredness of the snakelike gorges and temples of stone, and lament the loss of hundreds of miles of them to Lake Powell. They also lament the imprisonment of the mighty Colorado River. This amazing waterway begins in the high Rockies and drops 14,000 feet in a wild 1,700-mile torrent to the Pacific Ocean. In 1956 when dam construction began (completed in 1963), a 300-foot-deep artificial reservoir was created, covering the ancient riverbed, lands sacred to the Puebloan ancestors and their descendants as well as the Navajo and Ute tribes. In the 40 years of the dam's existence, piles of silt—perhaps 100 feet or more—have settled on the lake floor and in the side canyons and on the rocks.

Currently, a movement is underway to return those canyons to their pristine beauty—and this isn't just a fictional dam-exploding tale along the lines of Edward Abbey's *The Monkey Wrench Gang*. In December 1999, a group of activists calling themselves the Glen Canyon Action Network (www.drainit.org) set up camp in Moab, Utah. Made up of rafters, small business owners, and traditional Navajos, the group's goal is to tear down the dam. This isn't the first public acknowledgement of the damage the dam has done. In 1996, federal officials opened up four floodgates at the dam and released a torrent of water in the Colorado River in an attempt to mimic the spring flood conditions so vital to all rivers' ecosystems. Interior Secretary Bruce Babbitt declared it "a new beginning for the Colorado River, a new beginning for the Grand Canyon ecosystem and a new beginning in dam management." But the move is far from meeting activists' expectations.

At first glance the prospect seems impossible, and considering it concerns the second largest reservoir in the United States, it very well may be, but there is a precedent. Currently the federal government is considering decommissioning three dams on the Snake River. Even conservative Arizona Senator Barry Goldwater regrets the Lake Powell dam. Before he died he was asked which vote he regretted most. "I wish I could take back the vote to put up the Glen Canyon Dam," he said, "and let that river run free."

---

also obtain a booklet explaining the numbered stops along the way. Starting in the same proximity are the **Long Logs** and **Agate House** areas. The Long Logs trail has more impressive trees, while the Agate House area has the ruins of a pueblo built from wood that was turned into agate. North of there is the **Crystal Forest,** and the **Crystal Forest Trail,** a 0.8-mile loop through an area of logs filled with amethyst and quartz crystals. **Jasper Forest Overlook** offers glimpses of logs with petrified roots. At **Agate Bridge** a massive log spans across an arroyo.

Farther north still, the road comes to some interesting erosional features known as the **Teepees,** and then to petroglyphs left by Native Americans at **Newspaper Rock** and ruins at **Puerco Indian Ruins.** Human habitation of the area dates from more than 2,000 years ago. The road then crosses I-40 and leads to the Painted Desert Visitor Center, where there are eight overlooks onto the southern-most edge of the Painted Desert. There, dissolved minerals in sandstone and clay soils create a bizarre landscape, with the full spectrum of colors melding together like a rainbow. If you'd like to backpack in the southern end of the park, inquire about Puerco Ridge. If you'd like to backpack in the north, begin at Kachina Point trailhead located behind Painted Desert Inn. Be aware that water is not available in the backcountry, and shade is scarce. Late fall and spring are the best times to hike in the area. Taking rocks or artifacts from the park is strictly prohibited. If you want souvenirs, you'll find them in area rock shops.

Monument Valley
From U.S. 160, turn north on U.S. 163 toward Kayenta and drive 24 miles. ☎ **435/727-3287** or **435/727-3353**. Open year-round. The visitor center is open May–Sept daily 7am–8pm and Oct–Apr daily 8am–5pm. Entrance fee $2.50. Biking, guided hiking, wildlife viewing.

Straddling the border of Arizona and Utah, Monument Valley is a wonderland of mythically shaped spires and buttes sculpted from red and yellow sandstone. Most people have seen these exotic lands via films such as *How the West Was Won* and *Thelma and Louise*, but the experience of actually moving about within their presence, of watching the sun rise and set upon them, changing their shapes, colors and characters, is far beyond film's capacity to fully capture. Within the area are also more than 100 ancient archaeological sites and petroglyphs dating from before 1300. And Native American life continues in the area today, where Navajo families live in hogans among the sagebrush, many ranching sheep.

Unfortunately for outdoor enthusiasts, much of the park is off-limits for hiking, except if a guide accompanies you. Mountain bikers are fortunate enough to be able to ride a 17-mile loop through the valley, and horseback riders can do the Old-West thing with the help of a Navajo guide. You can also travel the 17-mile loop in your own car, passing by the memorable Mittens and Totem Pole formations. Be sure to take the 15-minute round-trip walk from North Window around the end of Cly Butte. Jeep tours are the most common way to see the valley. Contact **Goulding's Lodge** (☎ **435/727-3231**) or **Sacred Monument Tours** (☎ **435/727-3218**; www.sacredtoursmv.com; e-mail: sacredmv@infomagic.com). Tours cost from $25 to $100. The Monument Valley Visitor Center has displays of ancient and modern history. You can generally find Native American guides there.

Navajo National Monument
On AZ 564 north of U.S. 160. ☎ **520/672-2366**. The visitor center is open year-round daily 8am–5pm, except Thanksgiving, Dec 25, and Jan 1. The campground and two overlook trails are open year-round, weather permitting. The hikes to Betatakin and Keet Seel are generally available from Memorial Day to Labor Day. No fee. Bird watching, hiking, wildlife viewing.

At this monument, operated jointly with the National Parks Service, are three of the best-preserved ancestral Puebloan (Anasazi) cliff dwellings in the region. Betatakin, Keet Seel, and Inscription House were homes to the Kayenta Anasazi who lived in, departed from, and reinhabited the area a few times from 950 to 1300, finally leaving it completely to settle in Hopiland and other areas. Their

---

Trading Posts

Some of the most intriguing places to shop in the Southwest are trading posts and pawnshops, which allow a glimpse into the unique history of this area. Most businesses, such as **Hubbell Trading Post** in Ganado near the intersection of U.S. 191 and AZ 264, have served as lifelines to Native Americans in this area since the mid-1800s. In particular, Hubbell, now a National Historic Site, was vital to helping the Navajos re-establish themselves following the "Long Walk" of 1864. It and others such as **Gouldings Trading Post** in Monument Valley were places for Native Americans to meet and socialize, and served as a base for visitors to the area. Today most trading posts still sell some groceries and dry goods, and they also have lovely jewelry, rugs, and pottery available.

reason for abandoning this lush canyon environment for their starker abode atop the mesas at Hopi is widely debated. Archaeologists believe that drought may have played a part, as well as a phenomenon called arroyo cutting, an erosional process that lowered the water table and made farming difficult. The Inscription House ruin has been shut off from public viewing, however Betatakin and Keet Seel can be accessed, the former on a guided tour, and the latter on a trek through Tsegi Canyon. Both require advance reservations. See the "Hikes and Backpack Trips" section below.

Canyon de Chelly National Monument
From I-40 follow U.S. 91 north through Ganado to Chinle. ☎ 520/674-5500. www.nps.gov/cach. Open year-round, but some of the inner canyons are impassable in winter and during spring run-off. The visitor center open Oct–Apr daily 8am–5pm, May–Sept daily 8am–6mp. No fee. Biking, hiking, wildlife viewing.

This 1,000-foot deep canyon presents museum-quality views of red and yellow sandstone walls intricately painted with desert varnish. The canyon and its three branches measure over 100 miles long and reveal 11 million years of geologic history. Besides the exotic notion of over 100 prehistory dwelling sites in Canyon de Chelly and its neighbor Canyon del Muerto, this National Monument is a tribute to the conflicting interests in the desert southwest. The conflict lies in the fact that the Navajo own the monument, while the ruins they are selling visits to are ancient homes of their enemies the Hopi and other Pueblo tribes. If you're like me and find such conflicts one of the most interesting parts of travel, keep your eyes open while you're in the area, and ask questions of the Navajo about the Anasazi. You may find that to the Navajo the very sights they are guiding visitors to are considered taboo, one reason the ruins all over the Navajo Nation have remained relatively undisturbed for years.

A visit to this canyon will allow you a glimpse of pastoral Navajo life. At the visitor center, you'll see an example of a traditional crib-style hogan, a hexagonal structure of logs and earth that the Navajo use both as a home and as a ceremonial center. When you enter the canyon, you're likely to see other such homes, inhabited during the summer when families move into the canyon to grow corn and beans. But the real treat here is the ruins. Some of them are barely discernible decayed adobe walls, while others, protected within deep amphitheaters, appear untouched by the elements. Unfortunately for the outdoor adventurer, only the **White House Ruin** is accessible without a guide, but with a little planning you can get into the canyon in other ways besides the "shake n' bake" jeep tours booked through the **Thunderbird Lodge** (☎ 800/679-2473 or 520/674-5841). These tours are an expedient way to see the ruins from within the canyon, but while you bounce along in the open-air jeep you might find yourself envying those on guided walks organized by the visitor center and those on horseback. Another option is to take either the North or South Rim drive, either of which will take you through thick piñon/juniper forest to various points along the rim where you can see ruins and natural formations from above. Most astonishing at the end of the drive along the South Rim (22 miles) is the **Spider Rock Overlook,** a remnant of downcutting that occurred where Canyon de Chelly meets Monument Canyon. The 800-foot high pinnacle stands freely on the canyon floor. The rock is home to the Navajo deity *Na'ashje'ii Asdzau,* or "Spider Woman," who is believed to live at the top of the tallest pinnacle. Bring your binoculars.

Homolovi Ruins State Park
On I-40 just east of Winslow. Take exit 257 and drive 1.3 miles north to the park entrance. ☎ 520/289-4106. Picnic area with grills, 53 campsites with or without

hookups, rest rooms, showers, trails, and a visitor center with gift shop. Open daily year-round. Visitor center open year-round daily 8am–5pm. $4 per vehicle. Camping, fishing, hiking, wildlife viewing.

On their long and meandering migration across the southwestern United States, the Hopi made many stops, inhabiting different areas for many years before finally settling in what is the center of their universe, the Hopilands. Homolovi or "place of little hills" was one of their settlements and they occupied it until about 600 years ago. Today, it is a research site, where archaeologists work to unravel the history of the ancient Anasazi (or, as the Hopi call them, the *Hisat'sinom*), who inhabited this valley from the 1200s to the late 1300s. Since 1993, it has been a state park, but archaeological excavations have been taking place there since 1896. Visitors to the site can watch archaeologists work, while enjoying the labyrinth of ruins as well as many panels of petroglyphs. Highlights include a 1,000-room pueblo that is currently the most accessible archaeological site in the park. There are also a museum and a campground. The 0.5-mile Tsu'vo Loop will take you past examples of petrified wood and petroglyphs, including one that is thought to depict a migration story. The Hopi people are working with archaeologists to decipher these messages left on stone and in the form of artifacts. Be sure you don't disturb this process by taking any relics with you; a large fine and countless bad blessings will be your penance. Running through the park is the Little Colorado River, which provides opportunities for wildlife viewing and for spreading out a checkered tablecloth and having a picnic.

Wupatki National Monument
Head north from Flagstaff on U.S. 89 for about 29 miles to FS 545. Turn right and travel 14 miles to the Wupatki Visitor Center. ☎ **520/679-2365**. www.nps.gov/wupa. Open year-round daily 8am–5pm; closed Christmas. $3 entrance fee. There are cultural and historic exhibits, educational programs at the amphitheater, a visitor center, small campground, running water, and rest rooms. Bird watching, camping, hiking, wildlife viewing. Pets are not allowed on trails.

In the winter of 1064–65, debris exploded out of the ground and rained down on the Sinagua Indians' pithouses northeast of Flagstaff, forcing them to vacate the rocky land they had cultivated for 400 years. Lava flows and several feet of cinder destroyed their farmland and homes in the immediate vicinity of Sunset Crater, but just a few decades following the eruption, the Sinagua migrated to the Wupatki area and rebuilt their homes because they had discovered there was more water and fertile land after the eruption. A short self-guided tour of the main Wupatki pueblo begins behind the visitor center. Most notable is an amphitheater, about 50 feet in diameter, which most likely served as a ceremonial gathering place. Visitors can also take a more extended hike with a guide into backcountry on Saturdays at 8:30am. The forest service operates Bonito Campground across from the visitor center at Sunset Crater Volcano. It is open from late spring through early fall. Backcountry hiking at Wupatki is allowed by permit only. Summer temperatures at Wupatki often exceed 100°F, so pack at least 2 liters of water per person for a day hike.

Sunset Crater Volcano National Monument
Head north from Flagstaff on U.S. 89 for about 16 miles to FS 545; turn right. This paved loop road connects at both ends with U.S. 89. Sunset Crater Visitor Center is 2 miles from the southern entrance to the loop road off U.S. 89. ☎ **520/526-0502**. www.nps.gov/sucr. Open daily year-round except Christmas, from 8am–5pm. $3 entrance fee. A brief film, exhibits, and a seismograph station are available. Bird watching, camping, hiking, wildlife viewing. Pets are not allowed on trails.

This cinder cone began forming in a relatively recent eruption in 1064–65, spewed a mixture of molten rock and highly compressed gases into the air. As periodic eruptions continued over the next 200 years, debris accumulated and created the 1,000-foot cone. The result is this highly scenic crater, red-hued from oxidized iron particles. Though the Sunset Crater cinder cone is closed to hikers and climbers, there is a 1-mile self-guided loop trail, the Lava Flow Nature Trail, at the base of the volcano that allows visitors to examine the volcanic features. For a more cardiovascular workout, there are hikes around other cinder cones in the nearby area such as Lenox Crater and Doney Mountain. Visitors can take a lunch break at one of the many picnic areas in natural settings along the loop road. When hiking in the vicinity of Sunset Crater, be sure to wear thick-soled hiking boots since sharp lava can puncture shoes and cause scrapes and cuts. The forest service operates Bonito Campground across from the visitor center at Sunset Crater Volcano. It is open from late spring through early fall.

What to Do & Where to Do It

BIRD WATCHING

If you're in the Lake Powell region, you'll definitely want to travel to the Vermilion Cliffs area to see the California condors that have been transplanted there and seem to be thriving (see the "California Condor" feature in chapter 2). Though they live west of this region, you may very well see their large shadows cross your path as you hike in Indian country. Other birds of prey are also prevalent in the canyons and deserts of the region. Watch for red-tailed hawks and Cooper's hawks, which are year-round residents and Swainson's hawks, which breed here. Watch for snowy egrets and blue herons at some of the lakes in Navajo country as well as the quieter canyons of Lake Powell. Bald eagles winter in the region, and golden eagles are year-round residents.

CLIMBING

Jacks Canyon

From I-40 in Winslow, take AZ 87 30 miles south just past mile marker 314. Turn west passing through a gate onto a dirt road. Close the gate and drive 0.1 miles and turn right, then 0.2 miles and turn left, and then 0.2 miles and turn right. Continue 0.7 miles to the campground and trailhead on the east rim of the canyon.

One of my fondest climbing memories is of a weekend spent at this amazing canyon south of Winslow. This is sport climbing heaven—a winding canyon with faces pointing every which way so you can plan your day around sun exposure, allowing for toasty climbing days even in winter. This is the place where I led my first 5.10a and top roped my first 5.11a. But in order to get comfortable here, I did some sweet leading of some 5.8s and 5.9s on a slab. While I gradually worked my way up those lower numbers, other climbers were pushing up under roofs and other gnarly overhang type situations with no problem. The place can get a little crowded, but some pretty tough climbs are mixed right in with the easy ones, so we novices can pick up a few pointers from watching the big boys and girls play. The rock is limestone ("like a limestone cowboy," my climbing buddy was known to sing), which makes for lots of nice pockets, but can really rip into your fingers and clothes, especially on long lead falls.

You'll camp on the rim of the canyon, which is not generally a quiet place on weekends because it fills up with climbers who may party into the night. I wore earplugs and got a good night's sleep, so in the early morning when we headed down into the canyon I was rested and ready. With almost 300 bolted routes in a range of grades from 5.6 to 5.13c, most any level climber will have a blast here. Best of all, because the canyon is so protected, it's warm even in the dead of winter. *Beware:* Summer can be extremely hot here, but some cottonwoods at the base of the canyon provide shade, and plenty of shady routes to climb.

To help you find your way around, pick up *Jacks Canyon Sport Climbing,* written and published by Dierdre Burton and Jim Steagall (1997).

FISHING

The 16-mile section of the Colorado River below Glen Canyon Dam down to **Lees Ferry** contains probably the best trout fishing in Arizona and is well-known throughout the world. The area is simply spectacular, with grand temples and sheer cliffs rising some 1,000 feet and reflecting on the water's surface. Water temperatures in the river remain in the 48 to 52°F range throughout the year, making it ideal for trout fishing. A boat is required to get to the gravel bars upstream of the put-in point at Lees Ferry. More stable flows out of the dam during the past couple of years have caused a vast improvement in the quantity and health of the rainbows. Fish average 16 inches, but 25-inch fish have been caught here. Wet and dry flies work well. On a good day, a skilled fly fisher may catch 50 fish. To reach Lees Ferry, drive north through Flagstaff on U.S. 89 and take the turnoff at Bitter Springs and stay on 89A. The Marble Canyon Bridge signals the turnoff is near. Turn down Lees Ferry road and drive to the boat ramp at road's end. To fish the walk-in area, park just beyond the small bridge that crosses Paria Creek.

The section of the Colorado River downstream of Lees Ferry through the **Grand Canyon** is home to trout that can only be reached by boat or by hiking down the various trails into the canyon.

Tributaries such as Bright Angel, Clear, Deer, and Tapeats Creeks, which feed into the Colorado River, are spawning areas for trout during the winter and early spring.

Arizona Reel Time (☎ **520/ 355-2222**) runs guided fishing trips below the Glen Canyon Dam at Lees Ferry. You can also arrange for guides through the **Marble Canyon Lodge** in Marble Canyon (☎ **800/726-1789** or 520/ 355-2225).

HIKES & BACKPACK TRIPS
Rainbow Bridge

24 miles round-trip. Moderate. 2,660-ft. elevation loss. Allow 2–3 days. Access: Take U.S. 160 northeast out of Tuba City to AZ 98. Travel east/northeast on 98 for just over 12 miles to Indian Route 16, Navajo Mountain Rd. Turn north and travel this paved-turning-to-sand road for 32 miles. At a major junction take the left fork, which should be marked Rainbow Bridge. Travel about 6.5 miles until the road ends at the ruins of the Rainbow Lodge. Map: USGS Rainbow Bridge and Chaiyahi Flat. You must obtain a permit from the Navajo Reservation desk at the visitor center/ranger station at the junction of highways U.S. 89 and A64 in Cameron, or call the Navajo Parks and Recreation Department in Window Rock. (☎ **520/679-2303**). $10 per person per day for the first day and $5 per person per day for each subsequent day. Call to obtain a permit at least 3 weeks in advance.

This panoramic hike travels around 10,388-foot Navajo Mountain, across the border into Utah, to Rainbow Bridge, one of the most spectacular natural bridges in the world. It's possible to complete the hike in 2 days, but you'll want to allow at least 3 in order to really take in the sandstone stories, which the canyons tell along the way. As with most hikes in this region it's best done from September through November and April through May. From Rainbow Lodge, follow the cairns along an old jeep road northwest about 100 yards; then head west along a piñon/juniper slope. The trail will cross a few canyons (the first called First Canyon) while skirting the slopes of Navajo Mountain. At mile 4 the trail goes through a pass at the head of Cliff Canyon, then descends 1,600 feet into the canyon. Two miles down Cliff Canyon, a modest spring trickles up, the first water you'll encounter on the trip. After a mile or so in the canyon, the trail turns northeast and pierces through a slot in the sandstone at Redbud Pass. The trail follows Redbud Creek to Bridge Canyon, with its clear stream and overhanging walls of Navajo sandstone. After a left turn, Rainbow Bridge comes into view, beyond which are the waters of Lake Powell, a glimpse of desert beauty and tragedy unparalleled. Ideally, you won't have to share the sight with waterborne tourists.

White House Ruin at Canyon de Chelly
2.5 miles round-trip. Easy. 500-ft. elevation loss. Allow 3–4 hrs. Access: From Canyon de Chelly visitor center, take the South Rim Drive. Travel 6.4 miles, and turn left into the White House Overlook parking lot. Maps: USGS Three Turkey Canyon and Del Muerto.

This hike takes you down through layers of crossbedded de Chelly sandstone to one of the most stunning cliff dwellings in the Southwest. It is the only trail within the canyon for which you won't have to be accompanied by a local guide. You can do the hike any time of year except during spring run-off when Chinle Creek is flooding (check with the visitor center). The trail switchbacks down the side of the canyon to the sandy floor just upstream from White House Ruin, named for the white plaster walls that appear like porcelain in the upper part of the cliff. As well as this ruin built within an amphitheater, there are substantial structures on the canyon floor. Fifty or more people inhabited the White House Ruin from approximately 1040 to 1275. The Puebloan ancestors farmed the bottom of the canyon, growing corn, squash, and beans, much the way the Navajo people do seasonally today, some of whom you may see making their way up and down the canyon.

Other Hikes in the Canyon
In order to hike in Canyon de Chelly you must hire a guide, which is easy to do. Simply show up at the **visitor center,** where some of its 150 guides check in each day. Day hikes in the canyon are from 3 to 8 hours in duration and go into any of 11 hiking areas, depending on your desires. Because these trails travel through what they call "people's backyards," which means by their hogans and possibly through their cornfields, the visitor center does not post where these hiking areas are. All of the hikes do go to ruins and to petroglyphs. Cost for day hiking is $15 per hour. During the summer, the visitor center also offers guided overnight trips, which will take you to more ruins and to a campsite in the canyon. Overnights cost $60, and you must bring your own equipment and food. To arrange any of these options, show up at the visitor center from 8am to 6pm in summer or 8am to 5pm in winter, or call ☎ 520/674-5500.

Navajo National Monument—Keet Seel
18 miles round-trip. Moderate. 700-ft. elevation loss. Allow 2 days. Access: From U.S. 160, about 20 miles southeast of Kayenta, turn north on AZ 564 and drive 10 miles to Navajo National Monument. There you'll pick up your permit, and rangers will direct you to the trailhead. It's wise to make reservations in advance; call ☎ 520/672-2366. Maps: USGS Marsh Pass, Keet Seel Ruin, Betatakin Ruin. Available from Memorial Day–Labor Day. No fee.

One of my favorite places in the world, Keet Seel, is one of the largest and best-preserved ancestral Puebloan ruins in Arizona. Few people visit it because it's very remote, necessitating a long, dry trek through sand. The journey begins at 7,268 feet on the rim of the spectacular Tsegi Canyon. The first mile the trail switchbacks 700 feet down, with views out across the Colorado Plateau and toward Laguna Creek, which curves a lazy S below. Once on the canyon floor, the route passes over miles of sand as the canyon snakes deeper and deeper into Indian country. You'll want to have your river sandals for most of this portion of the trip because there are many stream crossings. *And beware:* Some of them have quicksand. On one of my trips in here, a packhorse sunk to his belly in the muck and had trouble extricating himself.

As you hike you can picture the Pueblo ancestral people who grew corn, beans, and squash and tended turkeys in the canyon. Also watch for handholds on the canyon walls where they once climbed up to the mesas above and made their way down into neighboring canyons. About halfway the trail comes to a waterfall, murky from all the cattle that graze the canyon bottom but wet and lovely just the same. It's not a good water source; be sure to carry plenty of your own water.

Nearing Keet Seel, the trail leaves the canyon floor and passes through oak forest. Then, suddenly you'll come to an opening, and there it stands before you. It sits high within a giant amphitheater, completely protected on three sides. The buildings are made of golden stone and mud, a labyrinth of living rooms, granaries, and kivas, their doorways appearing as black tunnels into a mystical past. The trail dives down through brush and then comes to the base of the cliff, where a sturdy pueblo-style ladder leads up. These are the ruins of the Kayenta people who occupied primarily the Betatakin and Keet Seel cliff dwellings from around A.D. 950 intermittently until around 1300. The primitive camping facilities are set within elm forest and are quite comfortable. The site was discovered in 1895 by amateur archaeologist Richard Wetherill. There were tens of thousands of pottery pieces, and they've come to be the Keet Seel trademark, carefully decorated in bold black, red, yellow, and orange. Be sure to leave any artifacts where you found them. Some believe a curse is cast upon those who take them away, and I wouldn't deny it.

Betatakin

5 miles round-trip. Moderate. 700-ft. elevation loss. Allow 4 hrs. Access: From U.S. 160, about 20 miles southeast of Kayenta, turn north on AZ 564 and drive 10 miles to Navajo National Monument. There you'll meet the ranger who will take you on this guided tour/hike. It's wise to make a reservation for the trip; call ☎ 520/672-2366. Map: USGS Betatakin Ruin. Offered May–Sept. No fee.

This day-long tour takes visitors into a large and stunning cliff-perched ancestral Puebloan ruin within the vast and colorful Tsegi Canyon. The tour begins at the visitor center, where a museum tells the story of the Pueblo ancestors' migration from place to place and links the Betatakin people to the Hopi. (Be aware that though this area is the property of the Navajo, who run the monument, they are not related to the people who once inhabited the canyon.)

The hike begins on the canyon's edge with views across toward Navajo Mountain. From here you can glimpse thousands of years of geologic history laid out in bands of color, from the cross-bedded Navajo sandstone to the purple-red of the Kayenta strata. Quickly the trail descends. As you make your way through a slot between two rocks, you may feel as though you're passing through a Puebloan *sipapu,* the hole at the bottom of the sacred kiva, which is the passageway to the Puebloan underworld. At the bottom of the trail you'll likely take a break in the shade while the ranger tells about the ruin.

Betatakin was the home of the Kayenta people, who lived there about 1260. They built and abandoned the village before departing around 1300. The trail passes over a small rise, and the alcove comes into view. It's a massive amphitheater sitting some 500 feet above the canyon floor, its depth providing excellent protection for the ruin. As you continue to hike toward it you'll see the small dwellings, some several stories high and on various platforms of different levels. The path rounds a bend and ascends a path, which enters the village. There are six tiers of rooms and a balcony toward the back. Originally this site had 135 rooms, and it's estimated that 150 people lived here, farming the land below the ruin. Note the timbers used in construction. Their concentric rings reveal that they were living trees sometime around 1100. The ascent out of the canyon is hot and steep, so save water for it.

Water Holes Canyon
2–8 miles round-trip. Moderate–difficult. 400-ft. elevation loss. Allow 2–6 hrs. Access: Take U.S. 89 south from Page for about 5 miles. Note where the highway crosses over the canyon. Park near the bridge. An entrance fee is required and must be purchased at Antelope Canyon (see "Walks and Rambles" below for directions). ☎ 520/698-2808. Maps: USGS Lees Ferry.

This slot canyon has miles of sculpted sandstone twisting and turning toward Glen Canyon. It has easy access to the highway, and both upstream and downstream routes make for good treks. The upstream side is easier but not as long. You'll see the route into the canyon about 50 yards from the bridge. The sandy wash brings you to narrows immediately. Then the canyon widens and narrows again at about 0.7 mile, leading you into the tight, labyrinthine slot. Some shallow, muddy pools may require wading. When you come to a rock slide, blocking passage, you'll want to turn around.

The downstream slot is even more photogenic, but also more technical. In order to avoid having to climb over an old car wedged within the narrows, you'll want to hike along the north side of the canyon for about 20 yards. Then make your way down a 5.0 climb to the base of the canyon. The canyon is lovely, the narrow walls continuous. After a few hundred yards, you'll come to a fall with a moderate down climb. If there is a rope hanging, you may not want to trust it. Below you'll find another mile of canyon that narrows and widens in a lovely rhythm that will keep you constantly entertained. When you reach a 30-foot fall, you'll want to turn around. There are several routes out of the canyon, and you may want to take one of them and walk back toward the highway through the desert. The best time to do this hike is from October through June.

Monument Valley
If you're not satisfied with taking a jeep tour through this land of amazing monuments, you might consider a horseback or hiking tour. **Totem Pole Tours** offers both. The 4-hour hiking tour ($50) goes to the top of Mitchell Mesa, for amazing views across the valley. A better buy, the full-day hike (6 to 8 hours for $65) takes you to the top of Hunts Mesa. This is the point from which many of the most famous Monument Valley photographs have been taken. Inaccessible by car, it's a real treat to be able to access this land that is off-limits to most visitors. For reservations, call ☎ 800/345-8687 or 435/727-3313.

Sacred Monument Tours offers similar hiking packages. A fun, short outing is its Teardrop Trail Walk, a 2½-hour hike to an ancestral Pueblo ruin and a natural arch through which you can see Monument Valley ($25). It also offers a Mitchell Mesa hike ($45) and Hunts Mesa 4-hour ($45) or overnight ($125). The overnight hike is timed to take advantage of sunrise and sunset on the valley. For reservations and information, contact ☎ 435/727-3218; www.sacredtoursmv.com or e-mail: sacredmv@infomagic.com.

ANCIENT ANASAZI

The question of what happened to the ancient Anasazi, more correctly known as the ancestral Pueblo people, is a hotly debated subject. Some still like the notion that they "disappeared," mostly because their culture did disperse at its apex. At that time, from about 1000 to 1125, their culture formed a vast network of pueblos, connected by elaborate road systems and rooted in giant kivas, at the center of which was Chaco Canyon in northwestern New Mexico. They had developed amazing means of deflecting sound from their kivas. They'd also developed solstice markers, windows or openings through which the sun shone only on June 21st, the longest day of the year, and December 21, the shortest day of the year. By the 1300s, the civilization's center at Chaco was deserted.

For years archaeologists blamed drought for the dispersement, but more recently cultural strife has arisen as a possibility. Likely, it was a combination of many factors. Around the time of the culture's collapse, Macaw feathers had been brought into the area by traders. The brightly feathered parrots from Mexico and Central America were used in kachina cult ceremonies. This new ideology introduced new spirit forms into a belief system that had previously been tied more to architecture. It appears that many tribal members remained with their old religion, while others embraced the "cult."

Newer, more controversial evidence ties the 2,000-room Mexican ruin site Casas Grandes to Chaco Canyon. With the use of a Global Positioning Device, Stephen Lekson, curator of anthropology at the University of Colorado at Boulder, noted that a meridian runs 390 miles straight south to Casas Grandes. Lekson also looked at the Pueblo tribes' legends for clues. He found one story that told of some clans staying at Acoma in New Mexico, while others left to the south.

Archaeologists continue to debate the subject, while the Pueblo people still cling tightly to their own beliefs about what happened. The Hopis I've spoken to, who are ancestors of the Kayenta people, say the desertion of their early home in the Tsegi Canyon was all part of a lengthy migration that led them to the Hopi mesas and to the Pueblo lands along the Rio Grande, part of a large plan that involves covering and claiming the land as a part of their cosmos.

HORSEBACK RIDING

Monument Valley

If you long for the feeling of being out in the elements while seeing the stunning monuments in this valley, you might opt for a horseback ride. Be aware, however, that you won't likely be riding a show horse. Most of the horses I've ridden in the area are trail horses with a strong penchant to return to the barn. Still, they do tend to be gentle, and the Navajo guides who run the tours are often interesting characters.

Totem Pole Tours offers 1½-hour tours for $30 around one of the Mittens, and 2½-hour tours for $40 around two Mittens. Half-day tours cost $55 and take you around more monuments, while the full-day tour, at a cost of $75, will take you 6 miles down into the valley where you'll see the Three Sisters and Totem Pole, eat lunch and return. **Sacred Monument Tours** offers horseback trips ranging from one hour to overnight. This company will provide a horse to meet your riding needs. The shorter tours (from 1 to 3 hours) travel around the Mittens and around the Merick Butte and range in price from $25 to $45, with a $10 guide fee. The Mystery Valley Trail ride lasts all day and takes riders around more monuments as well as to natural stone arches, ancestral Puebloan ruins, and petroglyphs. A 6-hour ride costs $90 and an 8-hour ride $120. The Overnight Trail ride includes a Navajo-style dinner and more touring through the valley, as well as camping within the valley and Navajo story-telling. For reservations and information, contact ☎ 435/727-3218 or www.sacredtoursmv.com.

Another outfit, **Don Donnelly Horseback Vacations,** offers 7- and 5-day rides through Monument Valley, as well as other areas of Arizona, on good horses (they're more energetic and better-trained than your average rental horse) and with good food, too. The Monument Valley rides, guided by a Navajo, take riders by the Mittens, Three Sisters, and the Totem, and explore the Ear of the Wind and the Sun's Eye. Riders camp at the base of Thunderbird Mesa on a Navajo's land, who shares stories, music, and crafts. The ride also explores ancestral Puebloan ruins and petroglyphs. This ride was featured in *Modern Maturity* as one of the 50 greatest adventures in the world, and *National Geographic Adventure* ran an article about the trip as well. Prices run from $1,200 for a 5-day to $1,600 for a 7-day ride, double occupancy. Call ☎ 800/346-4403 or 480/982-7822, or log on to www.dondonnelly.com for a schedule and more information.

Canyon de Chelly

Totsonii Ranch offers a number of rides that are unique because they enter on the Bat Trail many miles down Canyon de Chelly. The area is especially interesting because the only access is on foot or by horseback. These rides are moderate in difficulty. The shortest ride lasts 4 hours. It goes to Spider Rock and some unnamed ruins, as well as to petroglyphs. A longer all-day (9-hour) ride traverses Canyon de Chelly, visiting White House and other ruins, with a shuttle waiting at the end. These rides cost $10 per hour per person, plus a $10 per hour guide fee (which is paid only once, so the more people, the lower the cost).

Totsonii Ranch also offers overnight trips. The 1-night trip goes by Spider Rock and through Canyon de Chelly to a campsite close to the White House ruins. The next morning you return the way you came. It costs $320 per person for one person or $480 for two people. The 2-night ride follows the same route as the 1-night, except on the second day you go to the junction of Canyon del Muerto and then follow that canyon past Antelope House and stay at a campsite close to Standing Cow ruin. The next morning, you leave through the mouth of Canyon de Chelly and are picked up and trucked back to the ranch. The cost is $480 for one person; $720 for two people. Totsonii Ranch can also arrange longer tours. For reservations, call ☎ 520/755-6209.

MOUNTAIN BIKING

Since there isn't any public land in this part of the world, you won't find much in the way of single-track riding. However, biking is still one of the best ways to experience some of the sites in the area, especially Monument Valley. Experiencing Canyon de Chelly on a bike can be a spectacular experience, though the roads are paved; for information, see the "Road Biking" section below.

Valley Drive at Monument Valley

17-mile loop. Easy. 200-ft. elevation gain. Allow 2½ hrs. Access: Take U.S. 163 north from Kayenta for 24 miles to the Monument Valley Tribal Park. Map: Obtain one with marked points of interest at the visitor's center.

This graded dirt road tours through a land of mythical giants—spires, buttes, pinnacles, and mesas shaped by millions of years of action from wind and rain. Since no unguided hiking is allowed in Monument Valley, this is the best way to see many of the monuments without having to share a jeep with a bunch of strangers or look through a windshield. Starting at the visitor center, follow the map to 11 points of interest. The road begins by heading toward Camel Butte; then it skirts around Rain God Mesa to Artist's Point and North Window before reconnecting with the inbound trail near Camel Butte. Along the way you'll enjoy views of both Mittens Buttes, Elephant Butte, and the Three Sisters, among others.

ROAD BIKING
Sunset-Wupatki Loop Road
50-mile loop or other variations. Moderate to difficult. Allow 4–5 hrs. Access: Head from Flagstaff on U.S. 89 for about 29 miles to FS 545, which leads to Wupatki National Monument. Begin at the beginning of 545, which connects to U.S. 89 at two points. The description below starts at the northern point.

This road has some hearty climbs and lovely descents through a painted desert-like landscape carpeted with volcanic ash deposited in the 11th century. You may want to stop at Wupatki National Monument to see the ruins of the Sinagua people who inhabited this area from around 1100 until shortly after 1200. Most interesting here is a blow hole, which may have been the reason this pueblo was constructed here. On hot days, cool air rushes out of the hole with astonishing force. Next the road passes through the Strawberry Crater Wilderness, then it comes to the Bonito Lava Flow. You may want to take the time to visit Sunset Crater Volcano National Monument. Here rest the remains of more than 400 volcanic craters, of which Sunset is the youngest. A mile-long interpretive trail passes through the desolate landscape of the lava flows and skirts the base of this 1,000-foot-tall volcano. FS 545 meets up with U.S. 89, which you can follow north back to your car. However, be aware that U.S. 89 has heavy traffic, and many RVs. Locals prefer to turn around and ride back on FS 545.

Leupp Road on the Navajo Indian Reservation
10–64 miles one-way. Easy to moderate. Allow 2–5 hrs. Access: Take I-40 east from Flagstaff for about 10 miles to Winona. Turn northwest on Winona Rd. (FS 510) and drive for a short distance to Leupp Rd., which heads off to the northeast. You can start your ride here. More preferable is to drive about 7 miles to the border of the Navajo Reservation, where the pavement is very smooth, and begin there.

If you're looking for good pavement and no traffic with long views out across Navajo Nation land, this is your ride. Begin at the boundary of the reservation, where suddenly the pavement becomes excellent. This becomes Indian Reservation Route 15, which continues east for as long as you care to ride. This is pretty desolate country, but the colors here can be of the Painted Desert nature, and buttes can stand out like eerie sentinels in the distance. If you ride Leupp Road from its beginning all the way to Indian Wells, you'll have covered about 64 miles.

Petrified Forest National Monument
27 miles one-way. Easy. 300-ft. elevation gain. Allow 4 hrs. Access: For the best ride you'll want to start at the southern end, though either direction will prove exciting. Access: From I-40 or U.S. 180 approximately 25 miles east of Holbrook. ☎ 520/524-6228.

On this relaxing road, you'll ride through rocks that tell an intense and vivid story, all through the rich words of brightly painted petrified stone. (See the "Parks & Other Hot Spots" section earlier in this chapter for a geologic primer of this area.) In the south you'll see the most impressive petrified wood displayed, and in the north you'll see vast expanses of the Painted Desert. At both the south and north entrances are visitor centers. Both centers are open 8am to 5pm (with longer hours in summer). You may even want to stop and walk along some of the self-guided trails. Even if you don't, you'll pass by 20 stopping points within the park. Most notable are the **Giant Log, Long Logs,** and **Agate House** areas. The Long Logs trail has more impressive trees, while the Agate House area has the ruins of a pueblo built from wood that was turned into agate.

North of there is the **Crystal Forest,** and the **Crystal Forest Trail,** a 0.8-mile loop through logs filled with amethyst and quartz crystals. **Jasper Forest Overlook** offers glimpses of logs with petrified roots. At **Agate Bridge** a massive log spans across an arroyo. Farther north still the road comes to some interesting erosional features known as the **Teepees,** and then to petroglyphs left by Native Americans at **Newspaper Rock** and ruins at **Puerco Indian Ruins.** Human habitation of the area dates from more than 2,000 years ago. The road then crosses I-40 and leads to the Painted Desert Visitor Center, where eight overlooks open onto the southernmost edge of the Painted Desert. There, minerals dissolved in the sandstone and clay soils to create a bizarre landscape with the full spectrum of colors melding together like a rainbow.

Be aware that this ride can be very hot, so take plenty of water. At high tourist season (summer), you may be battling with more RVs than you'd like, but the rest of the year should be calm. Late fall and spring are the best times to ride in the area. Taking rocks or artifacts from the park is strictly prohibited. If you want souvenirs, you'll find them in area rock shops.

Canyon de Chelly Rim Rides

30 miles round-trip for each ride. Easy. 400-ft. elevation gain. Allow 3 hrs. Access: From I-40 follow U.S. 91 north through Ganado to Chinle. Follow the signs to the visitor center.

Either of these two rim rides will take you along the edge of the spectacular Canyon de Chelly and its neighbor Canyon del Muerto, with sights of ancient ancestral Puebloan ruins as well as over 11 million years of geologic history. (For more information about the canyons, see the "Parks & Other Hot Spots" section earlier in this chapter.) You'll be traveling the land of the contemporary Navajo, who still farm the canyon and its rims, as did the ancient Puebloan ancestors. At the visitor center, you'll see an example of a traditional crib–style hogan. But the real treat here is the ruins. Some of them are barely discernible decayed adobe walls, while others, protected within deep amphitheaters, appear untouched by the elements.

You'll be on either the North or South Rim Drive, either of which will take you through thick piñon/juniper forest to various points along the rim where you can see ruins and natural formations from above. The **North Rim Drive** overlooks Canyon del Muerto. Its most notable views are the **Antelope House Overlook,** its name taken from paintings of antelopes on a nearby cliff wall. You'll also pass **Mummy Cave Overlook,** named for two mummies found in burial urns below the ruins. At **Massacre Cave Overlook,** you'll see the cave where in 1805 Spaniards massacred more than 115 Navajo. The **South Rim Drive** climbs slowly but steadily along the rim of Canyon de Chelly. Most notable along the way is **Tsegi Overlook,** a view of the beginning of this canyon, which at one point will be 1,000 feet in depth. You'll come to **Junction Overlook,** at the confluence of Canyon del Muerto and Canyon de Chelly. **White House Overlook** has a trail that descends 600 feet to the canyon floor to the White House Ruin, an impressive dwelling built in a cave. **Sliding House Overlook** allows views of ruins built on a narrow shelf. Most astonishing at the end of the ride is the **Spider Rock Overlook,** a remnant of downcutting that occurred where Canyon de Chelly meets Monument Canyon. The 800-foot high pinnacle stands freely on the canyon floor. The rock is home to the Navajo deity Na'ashje'ii Asdzau, or Spider Woman, who is believed to live at the top of the tallest pinnacle. Bring your binoculars.

SCUBA DIVING

Though Lake Powell is not known for its clarity, some people choose to scuba dive there. Many guidebooks tout trips to eerie water-buried Anasazi ruins, but that's basically myth. Run water over sandstone and you'll understand why—it dissolves! However, many divers still like to explore the vast underwater canyons where visibility can vary greatly. It's not like the ocean—you won't see lots of colorful fish, but you will see some nice scenery. A big hit with divers is scavenging the deeps of the lake (something that makes my skin crawl—remember the film *Deliverance?*). Anyway, you might find anything from Oakley sunglasses to walkie-talkies to wallets to coins. On a recent trip, a group scavenged $258 out of the lake. To arrange scuba trips, contact **Twin Finn Diving Center,** 811 Vista Ave. (☎ **520/645-3114**) in Page. It offers full rentals, sales, and service, and links to dive masters, as well as plenty of good advice. Log on to its Web site, www.twinfinn.com, for up-to-date water temperatures and other information. Be aware that this is the only place to fill tanks in the whole Lake Powell area. The most comfortable seasons to dive in the lake are spring, summer, and fall.

SEA KAYAKING

If you're interested in kayaking what's known throughout kayak circles as "The Grand," meaning the Grand Canyon, see chapter 2. However, if you're up for some sea kayaking, you can travel into mazes of some of the 96 canyons at **Lake Powell,** and out across open expanses of the desert's mercy, water. To rent sea kayaks and arrange a boat shuttle, contact **Twin Finn Diving Center,** 811 Vista Ave. (☎ **520/645-3114;** www.twinfinn.com) in Page. Sit-on-tops run $35 to $49 per day, while sea touring boats cost $45 to $55 per day. Twin Finn plans to have canoes in the future. The most comfortable seasons to sea kayak on the lake are spring, summer, and fall, though during summer the lake will be crowded with motorcraft. Twin Finn will rent you the boat as well as pads that mount on top of your vehicle so you can carry it. The sea touring kayaks are offered in singles and tandems, and can be used on Lake Powell or the Colorado River (flat-water sections). On Lake Powell, boaters can park at Antelope Marina and paddle to Antelope Island and to lovely Navajo and Antelope Canyons. Other trips are available as well, such as Wahweap Bay and Crosby Canyon. Details of these trips can be found on **www.gorp.com**. An interesting river float starts at Lees Ferry, where you tip the blue-raft boat pilots $5 to haul you up to the dam so you can drift as many as 15 miles back down through the awesome sandstone canyons. Twin Finn can give you more details.

WALKS & RAMBLES

Getting around in Indian country isn't always a solo experience. Often you'll have to be accompanied by a guide, but that's not all bad, as the tours can reward you with rich historical information. If you're interested in exploring **Hopilands,** you might want to try the 45-minute guided walk through Walpi on First Mesa. It's an easy walk, with no climbing necessary. It starts from the visitor center, and explores kivas, the plaza, and the history of the Hopi people. The fee is $8 for adults, and the tour is offered daily every 20 minutes starting at 9am and ending at 5pm from June to September, and staring at 9:30am and ending at 3pm from October to May. (The schedule is often irregular; call in advance to check.) Tours are not offered Christmas, New Year's, Thanksgiving, and on some ceremonial days. To find the visitor center from AZ 264, turn north at mile marker 392, where signs point to First Mesa. You'll immediately come to a three-way intersection. Turn right and follow this road as it winds to the top of the mesa. Once on top, you'll come to a Y intersection. Go right and look for Ponsi Hall. For information, call ☎ **520/737-2262.**

Meteor Crater

1 mile round-trip. Easy. 100-ft. elevation gain. Allow 1 hr. Access: Take exit 233 off I-40, 35 miles east of Flagstaff or 20

miles west of Winslow, then drive 5 miles to the site. ☎ **800/289-5898.** Open daily 6am–6pm in summer, daily 8am–5pm in winter. Admission fee $10 adults, $9 seniors, and $5 juniors ages 6–17, free for children 5 and under. Hours: Summer 6am–6pm; winter 8am–5pm.

This would be a very worthwhile attraction if it were run by a national or state park system. Then visitors would probably be able to enter and explore this crater, which is 570 feet deep and nearly a mile across. However, it's owned by private enterprise, and access is limited to two observation platforms and a rim trail that can only be hiked on a guided tour, which leaves every hour. The proprietors have built an enormous museum and gift shop right on the rim. Say what you will about our National Parks Service, but it wouldn't do this! Still, the site tells an amazing story of a 1,406-pound meteorite approximately 150 feet in diameter that smashed into the earth about 49,000 years ago. For more information, contact ☎ **520/289-2362** or www.meteorcrater.com.

Antelope Canyon

2 miles round-trip. Easy. 100-ft. elevation loss. Allow 1½–3 hrs. Access: 2.5 miles outside Page on AZ 98 (at milepost 299). ☎ **520/698-2808.** $17 fee is required; since this canyon is on Navajo Land, you must pay an entrance fee of $5 plus $12 for either a shuttle into the upper canyon or for use of ladders into the lower. $17.50 fee required; since this canyon is on Navajo Land, you must pay an entrance fee of $5 plus $12.50 for either a shuttle into the upper canyon or for use of ladders into the lower. For children ages 6–12 the combined fee is $14.50; children under age 5 are free. Open daily 8am–5pm.

This is truly one of the most stunning slot canyons in the world. It has been photographed widely, its walls shimmering red and gold, undulating and twisting poetically in their narrowness. Since it's on the Navajo Indian Reservation, you'll have to hire a guide to take you in to see the upper section, and the cost is mighty. But if you have little time to hike into one of the other, less expensive slot canyons in northern Arizona, this is the espresso run and will allow you excellent photo ops, as well as some amazing mind imprints. The shuttle tour works as follows: After you pay at the entrance, the guide will pick you up and drive 3.5 miles to the mouth of the canyon and let you off. There you'll have one hour to hike the 0.25-mile section of the canyon. The best time to catch the glowing sun within the canyon is from 11am to 1pm, and guides recommend that you arrive at 10:30am. Another option is to hike the lower canyon, which gets its best light in the morning. To hike this, you'll walk about 500 yards from the entrance booth to a series of ladders and stairs stationed below the rim, which you climb down. From there you're on your own, and there's no time limit. This lower section of the canyon is more narrow than the upper. If you choose to see both parts in a single day, you'll have to pay for both the shuttle and use of the ladders, but you'll only have to pay the entrance fee once. Be aware that this is the canyon where, in August 1997, a flash flood killed 11 of 12 people. Remember that the risk of this kind of flooding is always high during the monsoon season (July through September), even if there are no clouds in the immediate vicinity. Other times of year can be risky as well.

Horseshoe Bend Viewpoint

1 mile round-trip. Easy, with no discernible elevation gain. Allow 1 hr. Access: Head south from Page on U.S. 89 to the Carl Yahden Visitor Center. Then continue 5 more miles south to just beyond milepost 545 where you'll see the trailhead.

This viewpoint overlooks a huge loop of the Colorado River. It sits hundreds of feet above the water on the edge of a sheer cliff. Below, rafters and kayakers may be camped at the riverside campsite as they head down to boat the mighty Grand Canyon run.

Walnut Canyon Monument
Up to 2 miles. Moderate. 185-ft. elevation loss. Allow 2 hrs. Access: Head east of Flagstaff on I-40 for 7 miles. Take Exit 204. ☎ **520/526-3367**. Open Dec–Feb daily 9am–5pm; Mar–May and Sept–Oct daily 8am–5pm; June–Aug daily 8am–6pm. Closed Dec 25. Admission $3 per person. Pets are not allowed.

This is a lovely spot within pine stands to stretch your legs and walk through history. Within this 400-foot-deep canyon are dwellings built into cliffsides. The Sinagua inhabited the area from A.D. 600 to 1250. It's believed that they moved down from the Wapatki area to the north after the land there lost its fertility. The Island Trail, a 0.9-mile loop, offers the best views of the ruins. Allow 45 minutes to an hour to climb down and back the 240 steps that lead to the cliff ruins. The Rim Trail at 0.75 miles is level and travels to viewpoints with overlooks of the canyon and some smaller ruins. Allow 20 to 25 minutes. Be aware that entrance to the trails is closed 1 hour before the actual closing hour of the park.

Four Corners Monument Navajo Tribal Park
Easy. No elevation change. Allow ½ hrs. Access: Take U.S. 160 northeast from Teec Nos Pos about 6 miles to the very northeast corner of Arizona. ☎ **520/871-6647**. The park is open daily from 7am–8pm May–late August; from 8am–5pm late August–April. Admission $2.50 for adults, $1 for seniors, and free for children 7 and under.

For map hounds this is an interesting place. It's the only place in the United States where the corners of four states come together. You can stand in Arizona, Colorado, Utah, and New Mexico at the same time. There's not much else here, which is part of the wonder of the place for me—a good reminder that boundaries are simply imaginary imposed lines, but what weight they hold. There is a cement pad surrounded by flags as well as a picnic ground and crafts vendors.

Strawberry Crater
0.5 miles. Easy. 500-ft. elevation gain. Allow 1 hr. Access: Drive north of Flagstaff on U.S. 89 for 22 miles. Turn right (east) onto FS 546 and drive 3.5 miles to where the road veers to the right. Continue straight, following FS 779 for a few miles until it crosses under powerlines that form the western border of the Strawberry Crater Wilderness. Park here and follow the two-track road to the volcano. Seasons: Spring to fall.

This short hike to the top of a cinder cone will transport you into some of northern Arizona's most fascinating and recent geologic history. From the road's end you'll note the established route, which climbs the north side of the crater. Stay on the route to avoid leaving scars on the cinders. This crater was born of volcanic explosions that occurred only about 700 years ago. In addition to the crater, the wilderness holds a large lava flow that fans out to the northwest and miles of cinder terrain. It's also speckled with piñon/juniper, ponderosa pine, and Gambel oak. Sinagua ruins can be found hidden here and there, and coyotes, bobcats, and many birds of prey may peek at you from their hiding places. From the rim, you'll enjoy views of the San Francisco Peaks to the southwest and the Painted Desert to the east.

Grand Falls
1.35 miles. Easy. 210-ft. elevation loss. Allow 1½ hrs. including driving time from I-40. Access: From I-40 east of Flagstaff, take exit 207 and go northwest on Indian Rte. 15 for about 12 miles to Indian Rte. 70. Turn north and travel this rough dirt road about 9 miles to Grand Falls (impassable when wet). Open year-round.

This is one of those amazing experiences that's all the more special because it is so ephemeral. During the spring run-off and at times during the late summer, monsoon water pours over slabs of rock and forms a torrential waterfall that can be heard hundreds of yards away. During the rest of the year, this is simply a quiet spot where water trickles down into pools. Formed by the Little Colorado River and run-off from the San Francisco Peaks, the falls resulted when a part of the Colorado River was blocked by a volcanic eruption a half-million years ago. The river flow diverted and in so doing the falls were created. Owned and managed by the Navajo, the site has picnic tables and grills at the rim. There's also a hiking trail, down past several dinosaur tracks, to the bottom of the falls where temperatures are cooler and swimming is allowed.

Window Rock Tribal Park
50 yards. Easy. Allow ½ hrs. Access: From AZ 264, near the New Mexico border, turn north on Indian Rte. 12, drive about 2 miles, and turn east. Open year-round.

An important symbol and religious place for the Navajo, Window Rock is just that, a lovely window chiseled through pink sandstone, with blue sky behind. It is at the center of the Navajo Nation Capital, and now is home to their tribal park, a place where religious ceremonies are held. Here you'll find a circular path outlining the four cardinal directions, as well as a monument in honor of Navajo war veterans, all set among shade trees with picnic tables. There was once a spring at the base of the formation where medicine men performed the Tohee Ceremony, intended to bring rain.

WHITE-WATER RAFTING

If you're interested in the epic journey down the Grand Canyon on a raft, see chapter 2. However, if you'd like to take a scenic float on a flat-water portion of the Colorado River, which includes spectacular views of multicolored sandstone cliffs and Native American petroglyphs, contact **Wilderness River Adventures** (☎ **800/528-6154** or 520/645-3279). Trips run daily from March to October, and on a limited schedule from November to February (at press time the company was trying out the winter schedule to see if trips would fill). Prices run $55 for half-day and $77 for full-day. This is an especially good adventure for families.

WILDLIFE VIEWING

On these broad desert lands you'll very likely see pronghorn antelope leaping into the distance. Watch for them while you drive highways throughout the region. As you hike the canyons and buttes in the region also watch for mule deer, coyotes, bobcats, jackrabbits, and prairie dogs. Rattlesnakes and bull snakes inhabit many of the canyon areas; they are lovely companions in the wild, but let them be, especially the rattlers.

Campgrounds & Other Accommodations

CAMPING

Wahweap Campground
5 miles north of Page on U.S. 89 near the shore of Lake Powell. ☎ **520/645-1059.** 208 sites above the shores of Lake Powell, flush toilets, water. Coin laundry and showers available at adjacent RV Park. $15 tent site, $25 for full hook-up. Open early May–Oct.

Unfortunately, a person can't just drive up to a sandy beach and lay out a sleeping bag on Lake Powell—the camping is carefully controlled. This site does provide a view of the lake, but it's a big campground and has only a few scrubby trees so it can get murderously hot in summer. Still, it fills up, and reservations aren't accepted, so you may want to arrive early. Campsites are well spaced, but the place can get noisy, with partiers reveling into the night.

Cottonwood Campground
Located 3 miles east of Hwy. 191 in the village of Chinle (adjacent to the Thunderbird Lodge). ☎ **520/674-5500**. 52 RV sites; 95 tent sites, free on a first-come, first-served basis. Flush toilets and water available April–September. Open year-round.

A few cottonwood trees shade the sites at this campground, but generally speaking, it's a hot place to be during the summer months. But it's very close to the canyon and to the cafeteria at Thunderbird Lodge, so it's a convenient spot to stop briefly. There are three comfort stations (rest rooms) and a dump station. For a longer and more scenic stay, try the campgrounds at Tsaile Lake and Wheatfields Lake.

Mitten View Campground
From Kayenta, head northeast on U.S. 160 until it intersects with U.S. 163. Turn left and drive north for 22 miles. Turn right at the signed Monument Valley Navajo Tribal Park. Drive 4 miles to the campground on right side of road. ☎ **435/727-3287**. 99 sites. Showers, rest rooms, drinking water, picnic tables, grills, and decks. $10 camping fee; $5 additional charge for showers in winter. Camping, hiking.

This campground is not a place to seek solace and seclusion. It gets busy and loud on weekends throughout the summer months. Since the campground only accepts reservations for groups of 10 or more, you'll want to arrive early in order to get a choice site. Still, you can't beat the spectacular views from your tent overlooking the spacious valley, West Mitten Butte, Merrick Butte, East Mitten Butte, and Sentinel Mesa. Guided hikes up to Hunts Mesa and Mystery Valley can be booked at the Monument Valley Visitor Center.

Navajo National Monument Campground
On AZ 564 north of U.S. 160. ☎ **520/672-2366**. 30 sites. Drinking water and rest rooms. No fee. Camping.

This is a lovely campground within piñon/juniper forest near the Navajo National Monument Visitor Center. Unlike busy Mitten View Campground, due to the remote locale of Navajo National Monument Campground, all 30 sites here rarely fill. There are RV, tent, and large group sites available. The park is generally closed in winter due to snow-blocked roads.

LODGES & RESORTS
Canyon de Chelly
Thunderbird Lodge
Located 3 miles east of Hwy. 191, on Route 7 in Chinle. ☎ **520/674-5841**. www.tbirdchelly.com. 72 units. April–Oct $96–$101 double; $166 suite. Nov–Mar $65–$77 double, $90.50 suite. AE, DC, DISC, MC, V. Pets not accepted.

The location of this lodge is ideal—right at the mouth of Canyon de Chelly. Built on the site of an early trading post, it's a pleasant establishment of stone and pink adobe units, reminiscent of ancient pueblos. The guest rooms have rustic furniture and Navajo sandpaintings on the walls. Inexpensive cafeteria-style Navajo and American meals are served in the original trading post building. (This is a good place to get a Navajo taco.) The lodge also offers truck tours of Canyon de Chelly.

Coyote Pass Hospitality
Contact Will Tsosie, Box 91-B, Tsaile, NM 86556. ☎ **520/724-3383**. www.navajocentral.org. About $90 for first person and $15 for each additional person; includes full breakfast. No credit cards accepted.

This is lodging for the adventurous traveler. Will Tsosie sets visitors up for short stays in Navajo homes. You'll sleep on bedding on the floor of a traditional hogan, eat a homemade traditional Navajo breakfast such as blue-corn pancakes and herbal tea, and use an outhouse. The stay also includes presentations on Navajo life. Guided hikes and nature programs can be arranged at an additional cost. Tsosie has been arranging these accommodations for 15 years and says he tries to keep a low profile because he doesn't want visitors to infringe on the Navajo culture. He cautions that this experience is only for people who are willing to rough it and who can be open to other cultures. He suggests that visitors read up on Navajo culture before arriving in order to enrich their experience.

Along I-40
La Posada Hotel
303 E. 2nd St., Historic U.S. Route 66, Winslow, AZ 86047. ☎ **520/289-4366.** www.laposada.org. 20 units. $79–$99 double. AE, DC, DISC, MC, V.

Built in the 1930s, La Posada was the last and most elegant of the great Fred Harvey hotels built by the Santa Fe Railroad. It was designed by Mary Colter—one of the great architects of the Southwest—as a Spanish hacienda. Re-opened in 1997 after almost 40 years of being occupied by railroad offices, La Posada is returning to its grand days. It has 20 guest rooms, a private sunken terrace, a soon-to-open restaurant, a martini bar, a ballroom, and reading nooks. The hotel sits on 16 acres of land dotted with groves of aspen. Most of the original furniture was auctioned off when the hotel closed its doors in 1959, but many of those auctioned pieces are slowly being donated back to the hotel.

Near Lake Powell
Marble Canyon Lodge
U.S. 89A at the Navajo Bridge, Marble Canyon, AZ 86036. ☎ **800/726-1789** or 520/355-2225. 60 units. Mid-May–mid-Nov $60–$125 double. Mid-Nov–mid-May $54–$100 double. DISC, MC, V. Pets accepted.

This lodge at the base of the Vermilion Cliffs operates mostly as a last night's respite before rafters and kayakers take to the waters—sometimes for a month—of the mighty Colorado. It reflects that practical purpose. The rooms are spacious, many with kitchenettes (stove and refrigerator). The beds are firm, and the bathrooms are clean. There are televisions, though reception isn't great. Ask for a room in the 100 block to be assured of the most recent remodel. The lodge also has a sundries store where you can buy such pre-river necessities as water bottles and Dr. Bronner's castile soap, as well as a restaurant that serves okay food and has a salad bar at dinner. There's also a fishing shop where you can gear up and get pointed in the right direction to fish the Colorado.

Lees Ferry Lodge
U.S. 89A (HC67-Box1), Marble Canyon, AZ 86036. ☎ **520/355-2231.** 11 units. $50–$75 double. MC, V. Pets accepted.

When you drive up to this lodge at the base of the Vermilion Cliffs, you might just wish you'd strapped on your six-gun. Not that it's a dangerous place—it just exudes an Old West feel that may transport you to times past. The original section was built in 1929 of native stone and rough-hewn timber, but recently the rooms have been refurbished into theme rooms that have a real bed and breakfast atmosphere. You might stay in the cowboy or the condor room. All have comfortably firm beds and clean bathrooms. Behind the original building are some two-bedroom facilities with less character. The lodge has a bar/restaurant that you might not want to leave. With lots of pine and comfy booths, it also has an extensive microbrew menu with offerings such as Avalanche brew and Cave Creek Chili Beer, and some of the best food in probably 100 square miles.

Monument Valley
Gouldings Lodge
2 miles east of U.S. 163, just north of the Utah border. Box 360001, Monument Valley, UT 84536. ☎ **435/727-3231.** 62

> **Navajo Taco**
>
> You simply can't spend time in this region without sampling a Navajo taco. Made with traditional "Indian Fry" bread, a flat deep-fried concoction used almost as a plate, it's smothered with chili and beans and then topped with onions and cheese. The best place to sample one of these is the **Tuba City Truck Stop and Cafe** at the junction of U.S. 160 and AZ 264.

units. AC TV TEL. $62–$162 double, depending on the season and type of room. AE, DISC, DC, JCB, MC, V. Pet accepted.

One of my fondest memories is waking before sunrise at this notable hotel right on the edge of Monument Valley and watching the morning light paint the monuments in a palate of pinks and purples that boggled my imagination. As the sun came up fully, the figures seemed to burn their way into the daylight. Each of the rooms in this Pueblo-style adobe inn comes equipped with a private balcony and is furnished in a contemporary style. The on-site restaurant, decorated with Western movie memorabilia, serves good American food. Gouldings also arranges tours of Monument Valley.

Hopilands

Hopi Cultural Center Restaurant and Inn
On AZ 264. P.O. Box 67, Second Mesa, AZ 86043. ☎ **520/734-2401.** 33 units. A/C TV TEL. Summer $95–$100 double, winter $65–$70 double. AE, DISC, DC, MC, V. Pets accepted with a $50 refundable deposit.

This is the only game in Hopiland. Fortunately it's not a bad one. Be sure to call for reservations before planning to spend the night here, because it's a long way to the next inn. The rooms are clean, quiet, comfortable, and modern, though I found the beds to be oddly short. There's an on-site restaurant serving some Hopi dishes as well as American food.

4

Arizona's West Coast

I have to confess that my loneliest travels in all of Arizona took place in its western region. That's not necessarily a bad thing. In fact, my favorite quote from naturalist writer Terry Tempest Williams goes like this: "Every pilgrimage to the desert is a pilgrimage to the self. There is no place to hide, and so we are found." Such a process can easily take place in this land of almost infinite vastness. This is desert in its truest sense, not the pansy saguaro-filled lushness of the Sonoran (though you'll find that in the south at Organ Pipe National Monument). Much of this region is desert of almost pure blankness, where the few mountains and waterways in sight stand out as immense landforms, their presence and power exaggerated by the law of relativity.

That's what I think of when I remember the Kofa National Wildlife Refuge or the lakes of the region's "West Coast." The Kofa Mountains, which seem to jut up out of nothing, are so startling that when I was there I could barely stand to leave them. I stood around in the parking lot after hiking for days there, looked at the dirt road before me, and listened to a group who had brought primitive drums to the area. As the beats resonated up the canyon, I could hardly bring myself to get in my truck and drive away. Similarly, the lakes in the region can provide such a cool relief from the desert that you won't want to leave them.

But the area is not without its comic relief. The town of Quartzite, located north of the Kofa, is the oddest place I've ever been. Sincerely, Quartzite is a stand-up comic's dream, with endless possibilities for ridicule. One could never tire of making fun of this city in the sun, where over 250,000 people come in RVs to spend the warm months and possibly the rest of their lives. I'm not ridiculing them, really; it's the culture that's grown up around them that is so amazing. This town with a fast-food backbone is possibly the largest, most active flea market in the United States. It's a place of canvas booths selling everything from snowcones to underwear to cow skulls to medjool dates, and, of course, gems. (In fact, this is

Arizona's West Coast

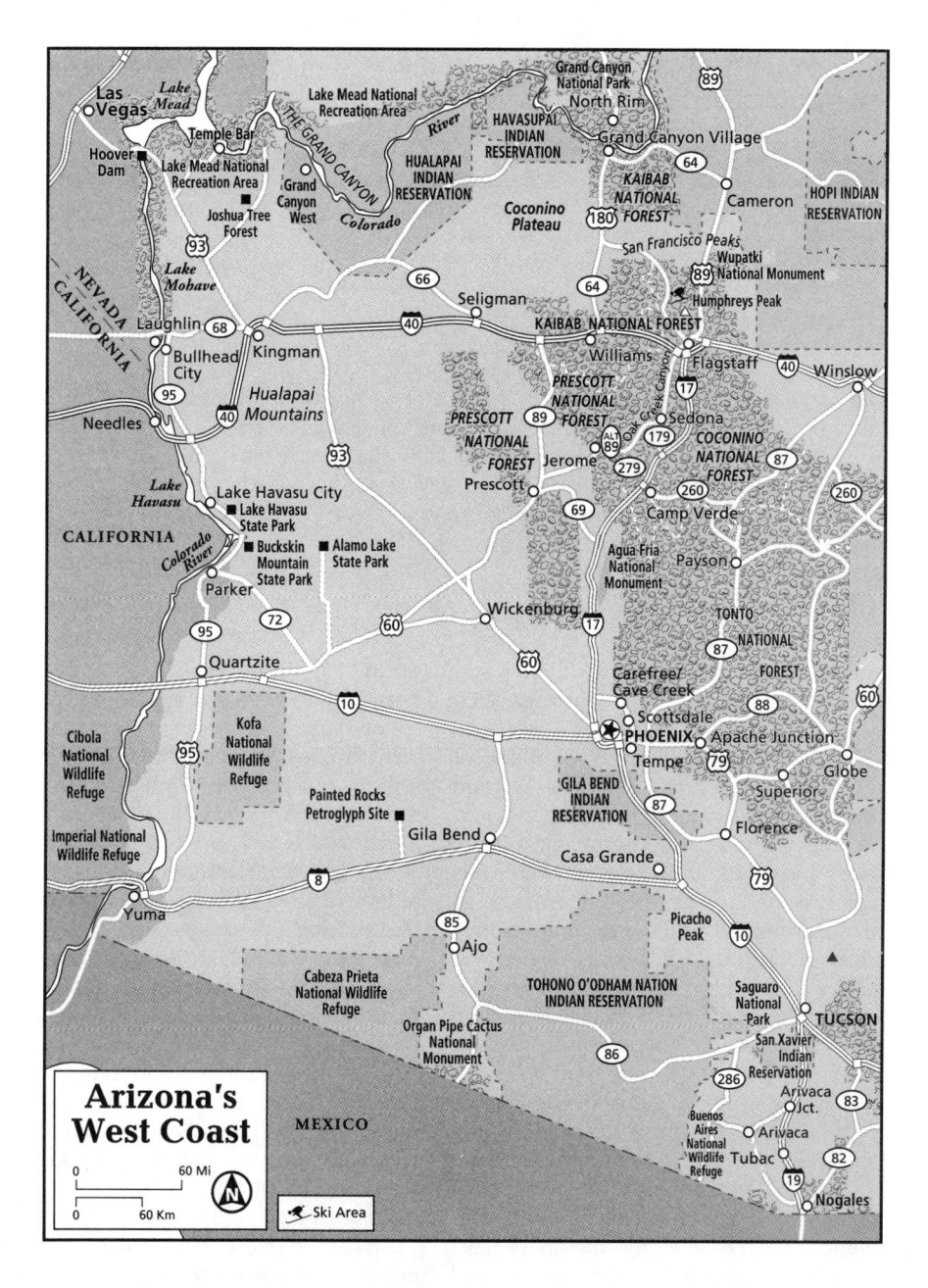

one of the largest gem and mineral marts in the country.) A sparkly kind of prurience pervades the place, with young girls and boys dressed in tiny swimsuits and too-short shorts strutting along the miles of backed-up traffic, with some drivers cruising and checking out the scene, while others like me just try to get through the town before choking on its glare and exhaust.

North of Quartzite, another of the state's great ironies plays out: In spite of being one of the nation's driest states, Arizona has the highest number of boats per capita in the country. And, the "West Coast" is where (besides Lake Powell and Lake Mead) many of those powerboaters and Jet skiers congregate. With 340 miles of Colorado River water separating Arizona from California and Nevada—

THE LONDON BRIDGE

"London Bridge is falling down,
Falling down,
Falling down,
London Bridge is falling down,
My fair lady."

And so the old nursery rhyme goes. Well, long after the nursery rhyme became popular, a bridge did begin to sag toward the Thames River, and the British government put it on the auction block in 1967. The taker? Developer Robert McCulloch, who purchased the dilapidated bridge for $2.5 million and had it shipped to California, and then trucked to Havasu City, stone by stone. The 900-foot bridge spans across a mile-long channel. Drawing curiosity seekers from around the world, it has put Lake Havasu City on the map. The bridge is located 60 miles southwest of Kingman.

---

much of which is impounded in reservoirs to provide electricity to cities such as Phoenix and Las Vegas—this is a land of water. It has thousands of miles of shoreline, with both busy and barren beaches, quiet coves and open-water stretches buzzing with motors, and azure water and basalt cliffs. In some ways this region is superior to the California coast because both air and water temperatures are warmer. It also has some of the best fishing in the country, and, of course, it has the London Bridge, which is second only to the Grand Canyon as the most visited tourist site in the state.

The southern part of this region is home to the Tohono O'odham Reservation (the largest in the country after the Navajo Nation's). O'odham tribe members have inhabited the area for centuries, but contemporary O'odham tribe members have struggled to regain water rights stripped from the over the years. The passage of the 1982 Southern Arizona Water Rights Settlement Act showed some promise, but subsequent years proved discouraging as the rights still didn't come. The battle for water in this arid land continues.

About a century ago prospectors came to western Arizona in search of gold. They found it, and mining towns sprang up in remote desert regions, only to die out a few years later after the gold was spent. Today the town of Oatman is the most famous remaining boomtown in the region, a place that is most known for the wild burrows that roam its once-bustling streets.

Visitors still venture to the area in search of gold, though today their gambling takes place at the tables and machines in Laughlin, Nevada, just across the Colorado River from Bullhead City, Arizona. A miniature Las Vegas perched on the shores of Lake Mohave, Laughlin and the Bullhead City and Lake Havasu City areas are extensive resorts. They offer miles of hotels, RV parks, and campgrounds, but not the swanky kind you'd find in Phoenix or Sedona; this area is less refined.

Arizona's West Coast can best be enjoyed by powerboaters and Jet skiers, but those into quieter pursuits will find plenty to do here as well. Sea kayaking on Lake Havasu and Lake Mohave can provide a peaceful sojourn through great basalt canyons, and houseboating to quiet coves on the lake can offer up great swimming opportunities. Lake fishing is abundant throughout the area, as is bird watching. But the best part of the region, the Organ Pipe Cactus National Monument, provides some of the best hiking in the state in an environment completely unique to the United States.

The Lay of the Land

This region of Arizona is part of the Basin and Range Province, which stretches all the way from southern Oregon to western Texas and covers most of southern Arizona. It is characterized by rugged, northwest-trending mountain ranges connected by low-lying deserts. For the past 75 million years these deserts have been tectonically mobile, with landmass collisions and separations that have frequently changed the tenor of the land. The Basin and Range Province is most characterized by the "sky islands" that stick up from it. Most notable in this region are those on the Kofa National Wildlife Refuge. These, like the many other sky islands, were formed as a result of the extending nature of the province, which creates fissures and breaks, the volcanic mountains rising to the surface.

The Colorado River cuts through the region as part of its 1,700-mile trek from the Rocky Mountains to the Sea of Cortez. With the building of the Hoover Dam and subsequent damming, this waterway is hardly recognizable as a river at all. Now, it is basically an endless lake, the more northern parts of which form a desert-like environment often with beaches, while the southern region around Yuma is more farm-like, with great green swatches and reed-filled waterways.

To the south, the desert takes on more character around the area of Ajo and Organ Pipe Cactus National Monument. This is Sonoran Desert at its lushest. The monument is named for the organ pipe cactus, the finest gathering of this type of cactus in the United States. A many-stemmed plant without any apparent trunk, some grow as tall as 25 feet and have 100 arms. In May or June the cactus blooms; lavender-white flowers grow on its spiny arms, creating a wondrous spectacle. In the Nogales vicinity at the southern end of the region, the Coronado National Forest stretches westward. There, some of Arizona's more remote hikes touch upon the Mexican border.

The weather in the north of the region around Kingman, at about 3,300 feet, is colder than the rest of the region. There, average daytime summer temperatures run in the high 80s and low 90s, while winter daytime temperatures run in the high 40s and low 50s. At a considerably lower elevation of around 1,500 feet, the West Coast daytime summer temperatures will run around and often well above 100°F in summer, and in the 60s and 70s in winter.

Orientation

Arizona's West Coast region is defined to the west by the Colorado River, running some 340 miles separating Arizona from California and Nevada. Its northern border is U.S. 93 cutting southeast through Kingman, meeting up with I-40. The eastern border follows U.S. 93 as it continues to make its way south, meeting up with U.S. 60 and finally I-10 into Casa Grande, which then meets up with I-19 down to Nogales. The southern border is, of course, the United States border with Mexico. The major highways in the region both run east-west. In the north, I-40 dashes across the state en route to California. To the south I-10 makes a similar trek.

In between these major routes are miles of little-used highway, connecting the few cities in the area, including Kingman to the north, with a population of 20,000, and Yuma to the south with 72,000 people in summer, growing to a whopping

> ### Beware of the Borderland
>
> While traveling in southern Arizona, be aware that thousands of Mexicans cross over the 2,000-mile Mexican border into the United States illegally each day. Especially in recent years with crackdowns in areas such as Tijuana and El Paso, as well as increased staffing of the U.S. Border Patrol (in the past six years the staff has grown 122%), the more remote border regions are seeing more traffic. Ten years ago in the small town of Naco, 1,600 people were detained in a year. In the first month and a half of 2000, 2,600 were detained.
>
> You will almost certainly see these travelers making their way across the desert on foot. While in the region, I saw the border patrol rounding up a group just north of Ajo. I also saw others hiding in washes. Most people who live on the border are sensitive to the Mexican's plight. Oscar Ayoub, the police chief in the small town of Naco, has been known to let them sleep in the jail. He and others are aware that these travelers are only seeking the promise that so many of us in the United States were born into. Rangers at some of the border parks such as Organ Pipe have been known to allow them to stop in at the visitor areas for water, simply so they don't die en route. The rangers leave it to the border patrol to fight the battle, and my advice is so should we travelers.
>
> No matter what your sentiments toward illegal immigration to the United States are, be aware that many of the people are desperate. In general they are not thieves, nor murderers. They don't intend to harm people. But desperation can lead people to act outside of their morals and intentions, and so this area isn't exactly safe. Avoid leaving valuables in your automobile. If you encounter these travelers, avoid them as best you can. It's probably not a good idea to offer a ride or other help. I generally give them a silent blessing for their journey and head on my own way.

160,000 in winter. Both towns are decent places to get a meal, but neither is a good place to stock up on hiking or biking necessities. For those items you'll have to go to Flagstaff, Phoenix, or Tucson. The most charming town in the region is Ajo, about 50 miles north of Organ Pipe Cactus National Monument. Built around a Mexican-style plaza, it has a white adobe mission-style church and palm trees. Its pace is slower than slow, lending a sense of the mañana attitude that gives Mexico such a seductive flavor.

Parks & Other Hot Spots

Lake Havasu State Park
On London Bridge Rd. off AZ 95. ☎ **520/855-9394.** Campground, beach, launch ramps, docks, group use area, picnic area with grills, rest rooms, and showers. Open daily year-round with day use hours ending at 10pm. Boating, camping, fishing, hiking, powerboating, swimming.

This 45-mile-long lake was created from the damming of the Colorado River at Parker in 1938. But it wasn't until 1963 that the town of Lake Havasu City was founded and, with the help of the London Bridge, became a happening place. Quickly, its open waters and quiet coves drew boating, jet skiing, and fishing enthusiasts, many of them the college crowd variety, to party it up in temperatures that often exceed 110°F. Especially during spring break, this area is a Fort Lauderdale in the desert, and the businesses in the area cater to them, so you won't find much of real quality here. Also be prepared for a lot of noise if you're in the area on weekends or holidays. For those who like to get away from the bustle, serenity can be found in coves and beaches. Rock hobbyists will have a blast here, searching for rare and riveting rocks outside the park, including geodes, jaspers, obsidian, turquoise, and agate. Campers enjoy great sunsets from most of the 200 boat-in campsites along the lake's shores.

One of the best ways to experience the lake is by houseboat. **H2O Houseboats** (☎ **520/505-4337**) charters 52-foot houseboats for weekend-long or week-long trips. You must be 21 years of age or older to operate the boat. These houseboats come equipped with air-conditioning, a kitchen (including microwave, fridge, range oven, and stove top), a waterslide, a swim platform, custom-built sofas, double beds, a radio, and wardrobe closet. H2O Houseboats offers a linen package, which contains towels, sheets, pillows, blankets, and washcloths for $75. They ask that you give them three weeks' notice when ordering. Prices change depending on the month. In January, a weekend costs $840; in August, the weekend rate is $1,449. Weekly rates run higher. For more information, log on to www.H2Ohouseboats.com.

Alamo Lake State Park
(West of Phoenix) 38 miles north of Wenden and U.S. 60. Salome Exit #53. ☎ **520/669-2088**. Campgrounds, launch ramp, fish-cleaning station, camp store, and playground. Open daily year-round. $4 per vehicle, $8 for underdeveloped campsite, $10 developed campsite, $15 full hook-up. Bird watching, camping, canoeing, fishing, rowing.

This large park covers some 5,642 acres with terrain ranging from a desert floor dotted with saguaros, to rugged mountains and a lake, which seems to suddenly appear out of the desert like an oasis. It's a very popular angling spot, touting some of the best bass fishing in the state. The park is home to great blue herons, cattle egrets, brown pelicans and even bald eagles. Wild burros are also a common sight here. They may seem cute, but beware—these burros are worse than raccoons when it comes to getting into your cooler. Keep all food sealed and out of the burros' kicking range. With its 250+ RV lots, this park gets very crowded on the weekends. So if you're a tenter looking for solitude, this may not be the park for you. *A note of caution:* When water is released from the dam the lake can rise at the rate of 3 feet per hour, creating a fluctuating shoreline.

Yuma Crossing State Historic Park
In the Yuma area, at Fourth Ave. exit south from I-8. Cross the Colorado River and enter the park on the east side of Fourth Ave. ☎ **520/329-0471**. Swimming in Pine Creek, historic lodge, picnic area with grills, trails, gift shop, and rest rooms. Open daily year-round (except Dec. 25) 10am–5pm. Admission $3 for visitors 14 and older, $2 for kids 7–13, free for children 6 and under.

If you like mixing your strolls with a glimpse into times passed, this park offers some of the richest history in the Southwest. Pathways wind and weave their way around historic buildings and through nicely landscaped areas. The main attraction here is the Yuma Crossing itself, a 20-acre area along the Colorado River that for centuries was *the* way to get across this mighty river. The area was first inhabited by the prehistoric Patayan culture; later, the Quechan Native American tribe lived here. Spanish explorers used the crossing en route to their settlements in California, as did mountain men, gold seekers, and soldiers. A strategic site, over the years many people have fought over the control of Yuma Crossing.

Hualapai Mountain Park
Located southeast of Kingman on Hualapai Mountain Rd. ☎ **877/757-0915** (for reservations) or 520/757-0915. 14 cabins, 3 group recreation areas, 70 tent sites, 11 RV sites with hookups. Open year-round 24 hours per day. Ranger station open daily 7am–3pm;

closed Dec. 25. No entrance fee. Bird watching, camping, hiking, wildlife viewing.

If you're in the Kingman area and you're looking to get cool, your best bet may be this park with more than 2,200 wooded acres at elevations ranging from 6,000 to 8,400 feet. The park has 6 miles of hiking trails, picnic areas, rustic cabins and RV and tenting areas.

Kitt Peak National Observatory

Located off AZ 86, west of Tucson. ☎ **520/318-8200.** Daily 9am–4pm (1-hour tours at 10am, 11:30am, and 1:30pm) and evening hours (call for a reservation). Closed Thanksgiving, Dec. 25, and Jan. 1. $2 suggested donation. Stargazing program $35 adult, $25 students, seniors, and children under 18.

Astronomers around the world tend to agree that southern Arizona has the best stargazing anywhere. You can take advantage of it at this notable observatory, which is situated atop 6,882-foot Kitt Peak on the Tohono O'odham Reservation, where a 16-inch telescope hones in on planets, binary stars, and distant galaxies. Since it is a national observatory, visiting research scientists come to Kitt Peak to conduct their solar research and observe distant galaxies by using five high-powered telescopes, including the McMath telescope, the world's largest solar telescope, and the powerful 158-inch Mayall telescope, which is used for viewing extremely distant regions of the universe. These telescopes are not open to the public except on guided tour.

Self-guided tours are available during the day. A box lunch is provided during the guided evening tour. But if you can't make it to Kitt Peak, drive down any country dirt road, lie back on the warm car hood, and take in the Arizona night sky. With the right combination of low humidity, little atmospheric interference, and almost no light pollution, the stars here shine brightly.

Organ Pipe Cactus National Monument

This is definitely *the* destination for outdoors lovers in western Arizona. A land of rolling mountains lush with saguaro, ocotillo, and of course the park's namesake, the organ pipe cactus, it is also one of life's true enigmas. That may be why so many people go so far out of their way to come here. After all, the park is en route to nowhere, and that's part of its beauty. The mystery lies in the great question your mind will likely pose again and again upon gazing out across these lands, which receive an average of 9.5 inches of precipitation per year: How can all this life survive on so little water? That question is at the center of research that takes place in the area. Declared an International Biosphere Reserve in 1976, studies are ongoing.

INFORMATION

Organ Pipe Cactus National Monument is located 70 miles south of I-8 between Tucson and Yuma. Call ☎ **520/387-6849** for information. The park is open 24 hours daily. The visitor center is open daily 8am to 5pm, except Christmas Day. The entrance fee is $4 per vehicle, and the camping fee is $8.

WHEN TO GO

Because this is such an extreme place, planning when to go is critical. If you care to do more than simply drive through with your air-conditioning cranked up, you'll want to avoid the months from May through September when temperatures often exceed 105°F. However, even during those months, early morning and late evening hours will provide reduced temperatures. Through the fall, winter, and spring, temperatures run in the comfortable 60s and 70s. Though at times (during holidays, for instance) the park can get a little crowded, its remote location makes crowd-dodging one of your lesser considerations.

CAMPING & PICNICKING

See "Campgrounds & Other Accommodations" later in this chapter for two camping options in the park, one in the developed campsite near the visitor center, and the other in a lovely primitive campsite out in the monument. Picnic sites are located along both drives. Most have tables and pit toilets, some have shade. Water is only available at the visitor center picnic area. Before coming to the park, stock up on all necessary food and supplies at the nearby towns of Lukeville and Why, where you'll find minimal supplies. Better yet, stop in Ajo, where you'll find a wide range. Ajo is also a good place to stay the night, though camping at the park will give you a greater sense of it, night and day.

FLORA & FAUNA

One reason Organ Pipe is so unique is due to the variety of plant life. Certainly, the organ pipe cactus itself is distinctive in that it is rarely found in the United States, and this stand represents the bulk of its U.S. population. But the monument is also exceptional due to the many types of cactus that live there. The reason there's such variety is that two distinctly different Sonoran Desert vegetative zones converge there: The Lower Colorado comes from the west, and the Arizona Upland comes from the east. The Lower Colorado—the hottest, driest part of the Sonoran Desert—is inhabited by creosote bush and mixed scrub, including brittlebush, triangle bursage, and foothill palo verde. It also has members of the saltbush community, whose plants tolerate silty, salty soil. The Arizona Upland zone is a much lusher part of the Sonoran Desert, and it includes communities of mixed cactus such as saguaro, organ pipe, prickly pear, and cholla, as well as palo verde trees. The zone also includes the jojoba/ evergreen scrubland community, appearing in canyons of the Ajo Mountains, where rainfall is most abundant. The plants in that community include jojoba, agave, rosewood, and juniper.

A third vegetative zone, though less represented, also fans into the region. The Central Gulf Coast zone extends up from Mexico, bringing such oddities as the elephant tree, senita cactus, and limber bush.

The organ pipe cactus and other cacti are tuned to the rhythms of the sun and infrequent rains. Generally, you'll find the organ pipe on south-facing slopes where they can absorb the most possible sun. Since desert temperatures can dip below freezing, the location becomes even more strategic during the winter months, when the plants must avoid severe frosts. The organ pipe cacti bloom in the heat of May, June, and July, with its delicate lavender-white flowers opening in the night. Other cacti bloom at varying times, producing a broad range of brilliant color from yellow to red to pink. Alongside the cacti, other desert bloomers that show colors in spring are gold poppies, blue lupines, and pink owl clover.

As well as flora, the desert is full of fauna, though these denizens can prove hard to see. Many of them circulate the desert only during the night, including elf owls, kangaroo rats, jackrabbits, and snakes. They spend their days in cactus holes and underground burrows. Animals such as bighorn sheep, many birds, and lizards do venture out in the day, but even their movement is often restricted to the cooler hours.

EXPLORING THE MONUMENT
Scenic Drives

In order to hike in the area (except for hikes near the visitor center) you'll need to do one of the two available drives through the monument. Before you start your engine, though, be sure to stop in at the visitor center and pick up a map. These interpretive maps, which point out important land formations and flora, will prove invaluable. Both drives penetrate deeply into the monument, and both meander up and down graded dirt roads. They offer easy traveling for passenger cars, but not for motor homes more than 25 feet long or for trailers. When on the drives, carry emergency supplies: food, drinking water, and water for your vehicle. Also, stay out of flooded areas, and do not drive off the road. Both drives are on one-way roads.

The 21-mile **Ajo Mountain Drive** winds along the foothills of the highest range in the area, the Ajo Mountains. All along the way it passes impressive stands of cactus, including large forests of organ pipe sprawling across southern-exposed hills. Plan two hours for this drive. The 53-mile **Puerto Blanco Drive** is a half-day excursion circumnavigating the Puerto Blanco Mountains, a long range that includes the tallest peak in the monument, Pinkley Peak at 3,145 feet. The drive makes its way past the desert oasis of Quitobaquito (see the "Walks & Rambles" section later in this chapter). Meanwhile it passes through a truly unique part of the Sonoran Desert. In a part of the monument, mostly within the Senita Basin area, the Central Gulf Coast vegetative zone (which is found only in Mexico) reaches into the park, bringing such atypical species as the elephant tree, senita cactus, and limber bush, all viewable from this drive.

The monument also has a few unimproved roads that lead into the backcountry, to historic sites, ranch houses, and abandoned gold and silver mines. It's advisable to have a four-wheel-drive vehicle to venture onto these roads. Be sure to check road conditions at the visitor center.

Walks & Hikes

The only way to really get a sense of this desert is to strike out into it, and the monument offers many types of trails upon which to do so. The best months to hike are October through April. If you're traveling with your pet, only two trails are available to your leashed dog—the Campground Perimeter Trail and the Palo Verde Trail, both in the vicinity of the visitor center. Later in this chapter in the "Hikes & Backpack Trips" and "Walks & Rambles" sections, I list other hikes. Be sure to take 1 gallon of water per person per day. While on your hike, beware of touching or bumping against cactus spines, avoid overexertion and overexposure to the sun, and watch out for rattlesnakes. If hiking at night, carry a flashlight. If you intend to do any cross-country hiking, discuss your plans with a park ranger.

What to Do & Where to Do It

BIRD WATCHING

One of the prime birding spots in the region is the **Havasu National Wildlife Refuge** (☎ 760/326-3853). The refuge runs north of Lake Havasu City along the Colorado River for 30 miles. More than 260 species of birds pass through this refuge at one time or another during the course of a year. Look for mallards and pintails, as well as great blue herons and great egrets. This is also home to bald eagles and the rare and endangered southwest willow flycatcher. Bobcats, coyotes, and foxes live within this marshy river habitat as well. Most of the refuge is accessible only by boat, but there are stretches of ground along the marshes in the communities of Golden Shores and Topock where you can catch some action from shore. One area that is particularly nice is the 15-mile stretch along the banks of the Colorado River through Topock Gorge, where colorful, striated cliffs tower above the water (see the "Sea Kayaking" section later in this chapter).

The **Bill Williams National Wildlife Refuge** (☎ 520/661-4144), 40 miles south of Lake Havasu City off AZ 95, preserves the lower reaches of the Bill Williams River. The refuge is open during daylight hours. A small visitor center is open Monday to Friday from 8am to 4pm. There's no entrance fee, and camping and fires are not allowed. Pets are allowed on a leash. Some say this is the best bird watching in western Arizona, and I would have to agree. More than 200 species have been sighted here, including vermilion flycatchers, Yuma clapper rails, soras, Swainson's hawks, and white-faced ibises. Desert bighorn sheep are also resident.

From a naturalist's perspective, the area around Yuma is tragic. Here, where once the Colorado River flowed, there are only channels, irrigated fields, and marshes. The once-mighty river has been dammed, diverted, and directed into a series of lakes and ditches that are most popular with people who like to use motors to get around—boaters and ATV riders. But there's another, less heartbreaking side to this area: All the water attracts lots of birds. Two refuges have been carved out of this very utilitarian area, the **Imperial** (☎ 520/783-3371) and **Cibola National Wildlife Refuges** (☎ 520/857-3253).

The Imperial, the more accessible of the two, protects wildlife habitat along 30 miles of the lower Colorado River in Arizona and California. During the winter the spot is a stop for birds such as Canada geese, cinnamon teal, and northern pintail; during spring and fall, expect to see pelicans and cormorants; and some of the permanent residents are egrets and great blue herons. Sonoran Desert creatures such as desert tortoises, bobcats, and bighorn sheep also live here. One way to see the refuge is by canoe, which can be rented at **Martinez Lake Marina** (☎ 520/783-9589), 3.5 miles southeast of the refuge headquarters. There is also a scenic drive along Red Cloud Mine Road, through the Sonoran Desert landscape, with lookout points along the way. The Painted Desert Trail, a 1.3-mile self-guided hike, traverses through myriad-colored volcanic formations of the Colorado River Valley (see the "Walks & Rambles" section later in this chapter). Mid-October to May is the best season here, when birds are plentiful, and mosquitos are scarce. To get to the refuge take AZ 95 north from Yuma and turn west on Martinez Lake Road. Travel 10.4 miles, then turn north onto the entrance road. Drive another 2.1 miles following signs to the visitor center. At the visitor center there are exhibits and a native plant garden.

Along the banks of the lower Colorado River is **Betty's Kitchen Nature Trail,** a half-mile loop through the marshes. A less attractive place than one might expect, it was once a residential area before a 1983 flood wiped it out, and now the Bureau of Land Management (BLM) is trying to resurrect it as a bird and wildlife sanctuary. Though it's not the most scenic hike, it is a good place to spot cinnamon teal, lesser nighthawks, western kingbirds, and western tanagers. The area has some barren, bulldozed spots and one nice platform that sits out over a marsh where you can see lots of ducks. We saw a coyote disappear into the brush. It's nothing to go very far out of your way for, but for a real birder, it's worthwhile. A $5 fee is charged. (We parked outside the area to avoid the fee, which is steep for what you get.) From Yuma take U.S. 95 east to Avenue 7E (Laguna Dam Rd.). Continue north for 9 miles. One-quarter mile after the road turns to dirt, turn left. If you keep driving on Laguna Dam Road beyond Betty's Kitchen, the terrain opens up so you can see the long fingers of the lake, and there you'll see more birds, particularly larger ones such as herons and hawks. This dirt road is also a decent place to ride a bike.

Buenos Aires National Wildlife Refuge (☎ 520/823-4251), located near the Mexico border, encompasses an unusual Sonoran Desert landscape. Instead of saguaro-studded expanses, this is a land of rolling grasslands, rocky canyons, and cottonwood-lined streams. Some 326 species of birds have been sighted in the refuge. You will now find masked bobwhite, a small quail once native to this area that disappeared around the turn of the century due to drought and overgrazing. Some of these bobwhite were imported from Mexico, and a population has established itself at this refuge. The habitats range from the riparian **Arivaca Creek,** where you'll likely see orioles, tanagers, and warblers, as well as owls, woodpeckers, and sapsuckers; to sycamore-lined **Brown Canyon,** where 12 types of hummingbirds have been spotted, as well as painted redstarts, sulpur-bellied flycatchers, and zone-tailed hawks; to **Aguirre Lake,** where you'll see migrating shorebirds such as white-faced ibis, many species of ducks, as well as green-tailed towhee and crissal thrasher; and to **Sonoran savannah grasslands,** where golden eagles winter, white-tailed kites summer, and loggerhead shrikes, imperiled elsewhere in the west, are plentiful. Gambel's quail, canyon towhee, and curve-billed thrasher feast on shrubs in this area. The Buenos Aires is 28 miles from Tubac. Access it by heading north from Tubac on I-19 to Arivaca Junction and then driving west on the scenic, paved road to the refuge just outside the village of Arivaca. The headquarters is located 38 miles south of Robles Jct. (Three Points) off AZ 286. There are hiking trails and guided tours through the area.

The **Cabeza Prieta National Wildlife Refuge,** outside the village of Ajo, boasts a bird list of some 212 species. This refuge is for those hearty birders who don't mind the rough and rocky road. The refuge includes some of the most arid desert in North America. Most roads require four-wheel-drive vehicles with high ground clearance, and there is no water available. Bird-watchers must obtain a permit from the visitor center in Ajo (☎ **520/387-6483**). Those who do venture out into this land of the Camino del Diablo (Spanish for "Devil's Road"; see the "El Camino del Diablo" feature later in this chapter) will find the most birds along the washes, particularly in areas where there is a permanent water source. The lushest of these areas is in the northeastern region of the refuge near Ajo. The **Papago Well** and **Tule Well** are also good bird habitats. The refuge provides a special home for Neotropical migrants, those species that nest in the United States or Canada and spend the winter primarily south of our border in Mexico, Central or South America, or in the Caribbean. These include many species of hawks, hummingbirds, warblers, and orioles, as well as shorebirds, flycatchers, and thrushes.

BOARDSAILING & SAILING

Lake Mohave and Lake Havasu are the spots to ply your sails in the region. The spots are appealing because during summer water temperatures are warm, and winds can blow consistently. However, the number of motorcraft on both lakes makes the sites less appealing.

FISHING

Lake Havasu State Park, off Arizona 95, offers good lake fishing for largemouth and striped bass, bluegill, and crappie. Because the lake is large, much of the fishing is done by boat; however, some enjoy fishing from shore. Also located on Lake Havasu (but south of Lake Havasu State Park and 15 miles south of Lake Havasu City), **Cattail Cove State Park** also has nice beaches from which to fish. Both areas are known to yield striped bass in the 25-pound range. Boat rentals can be obtained at **Sandpoint Marina** (☎ **520/855-0549**). Both parks are open year-round. Day-use hours end at 10pm.

Due to the diversity of habitat in the **Lake Mead National Recreation Area** (☎ **702/293-8907**), largemouth bass and rainbow trout are plentiful. Many like to fish the cold waters that flow out from Hoover Dam through Black Canyon and into Lake Mohave. Trout are stocked during winter and spring in both Lake Mead and Lake Mohave (for more information on Lake Mead, see chapter 2). In the Yuma Area, fishing is plentiful on the meandering waterways of the **Imperial and Cibola National Wildlife Refuges.** Home base for boat rentals and supplies is Martinez Lake Resort (☎ **520/783-9589**).

Smaller than Patagonia Lake in southeastern Arizona (see chapter 7), **Arivaca Lake** also offers decent warm-water fishing year-round in a pretty setting. Be aware that, with an average depth of 28 feet, this is a fairly shallow lake; the water level fluctuates, and the shoreline can get weedy. Wading is a good bet, but a kickboat or float tube works even better here. Only electric motors are allowed on the lake. Two-pound red-ear sunfish have been caught here. Take I-19 south from Tucson to exit 30 at Arivaca Junction. Then take Arivaca Road west to the town of Arivaca. Go south on FS 39, the Ruby Rd., to the lake.

HIKES & BACKPACK TRIPS

Bill Williams River Canyon

11 miles round-trip. Moderate to difficult. 378-ft. elevation loss. Allow 5–9 hrs. or 2 days. Access: Head west from Wickenburg on U.S. 93 to Wenden; turn north on Alamo Lake Rd. and drive to Alamo Lake State Park. Head west toward the dam and the Bill Williams Overlook Point, where you'll pay a small parking fee. Maps: USGS Alamo Dam and Reid Valley.

This hike, which requires one good swim, explores a lovely desert canyon with 600-foot high walls and abundant wildlife. It traverses part of the Rawhide Mountains Wilderness, a unique park in this part of the state because it contains not only desert foothills and mountains, but also this at-times lush riparian habitat. From the Overlook Point, walk 1.5 miles down a service road to the river, which is downstream from the dam. Shortly the wilderness begins, just beyond a river gauging station. At 0.25 miles you'll come to the stretch of the river banked by vertical cliffs where swimming may be required. Here you'll likely need some kind of flotation for your pack, as well as dry gear to put on after you swim (see "Canyoneering Basics" in chapter 1). You may want to try climbing around the pool to the right. Once past the pool the going is relatively easy, hiking along the flat river bottom, but with many stream crossings. You'll want to wear good socks in your hiking boots so the wetness doesn't injure your feet. Most rangers discourage wearing river sandals because they've been known to get lost in river muck, leaving hikers shoeless. The turn-around point comes at about 5 miles from the dam, where the river enters a wide valley. Because the area is so hot, it's best to hike the canyon from October to April. Be aware that stream flow in the Bill Williams can vary greatly, from 25 cubic feet per second (CFS) to a roaring 7,000 CFS. Since this is a dam-controlled river, park rangers should be able to tell you what the water release plans are, so your hiking will be safe. Also be aware that the canyon may be closed in the spring to protect a nesting pair of bald eagles. Though this makes for a scenic and fun day hike, it is an even better overnight, with plenty of good camping within the canyon. A camping permit is not required.

Palm Canyon

1.5 miles round-trip or much farther if you care to bushwhack. Easy. 400-ft. elevation gain. Allow 45 min.–3 hrs. Access: On AZ 95, drive south from Quartzite 18 miles to a signed dirt road that heads east into the Kofa National Wildlife Refuge. Follow this dirt road for 9 miles to the trailhead.

This hike takes you into a spectacular canyon where rare native palm trees grow. It's a heavily traveled place but worth the visit. As you near the canyon you'll likely be awed by the jagged rhyolite peaks jutting hundreds of feet up out of the ground. The awesome rock formations are really the reason to come here, though the palm trees are interesting too. The California fan palms run a thin line down some of the narrow canyons up above the central canyon. In Arizona, these lush little palms only occur in the Kofa Mountains, though they are sometimes planted as ornamentals in other parts of southern Arizona. In addition to the palms you'll see plenty of cactus tucked into rock formations—saguaros, jumping cholla—and you may even see desert bighorn sheep, if you're lucky. You can't get lost on this hike, but you may slip. The trail is littered with loose rock, so be careful. If the hike isn't enough for you, you can opt to go farther into the canyon where there are connecting canyons and even places where you can do some climbing. (It seems like a totally unexplored technical climbing area.) The 516,300-acre Kofa National Wildlife Refuge is a primo area for those who like to break their own trail; it's full of wildlife and little-explored terrain.

Sycamore Canyon Trail

1–12 miles round-trip. Moderate. 500-ft. elevation loss. Allow 1–5 hrs. Access: Drive 55 miles south of Tucson on I-19 to AZ 289. Travel this paved, then dirt road for 20 miles to the trailhead on your left. Signs say Hank and Yank Spring. There's no trailhead per se, but you'll see where posts have been set to mitigate auto traffic farther down to Hank and Yank Spring. *Note:* Avoid this hike if there is any chance of flooding. Maps: USGS Ruby and/or USFS Coronado National Forest Nogales Ranger District.

The sense that this perennial spring runs down and across the U.S.–Mexico border gives this hike a mysterious quality, which enhances what is already a lovely hike through a little-explored riparian area, rich with plant and bird life and artistic rock formations.

But first a note about the drive to get here: If you can manage to do the drive from Arivaca, it's well worth it (see Ruby Road in the "Walks & Rambles" section later in this chapter). You pass through an area of lovely rolling hills with trees scattered across them. The Sycamore Canyon starts about 20 miles from the Arivaca side.

The trail starts in the midst of the rolling hills and works its way down the canyon to Hank and Yank Spring, a Civil War–era homestead, which was abandoned after a Native American attack in 1886. As the canyon grows deeper and narrower, the trail crisscrosses the creek, finally making its way to some narrow sections, through which you'll have to maneuver carefully. The turn-around point is a barbed-wire fence, which marks the border. En route watch for some of the 625 plant species that have been spotted within the Pajarita Wilderness, some of them rare or endangered, such as the Gooding Ash and a species of fern found only in the Himalayas, Mexico, and this canyon. The Gooding Ash and the Gooding Research Center (which this trail traverses) were named after the notable botanist Leslie N. Gooding, who called Sycamore Canyon a "hidden botanical garden." For those looking for wildlife, watch for vermilion flycatchers and black Phoebes, as well as lovely cardinals flitting about. In the creek look for the tiny Sonoran chub, a rare desert fish protected by law.

Organ Pipe Cactus National Monument

The Bull Pasture and the Estes Canyon Trail

4-mile loop. Moderate. 800-ft. elevation gain. Allow 2½ hrs. Access: 32 miles south of Ajo on AZ 85. From the monument visitor center, take the Ajo Mountain Loop for 8 miles to stop 15 where there's a signed trailhead. Before you head to the trail, be sure to pick the road guide book (75¢) at the visitor center; it explains the numbered stops along the way. You'll also want to pick up a copy of the *Explorer's Guide* ($1.50), which describes many hikes within the monument. Park entrance fee $4.

This loop hike is a perfect way to get acquainted with organ pipe cactus. It traverses rich desert lowlands, then climbs up onto a saddle from which you can view the layers of cactus-covered hills. The Bull Pasture Trail climbs gradually around a long mountain, and then comes up over a pass, whereas the Estes Canyon Trail travels along a wash, and then climbs up to the saddle to meet the Bull Pasture Trail. You can decide which way you'd like to start. Assuming you start in Estes Canyon, you'll find the terrain is immediately beautiful with lots of cactus and growth in the wash. This trail climbs more gradually than the Bull Pasture Trail, meandering up to the saddle where it meets up for the last leg of the Bull Pasture. Once you get into this backcountry, the cacti become more prevalent, and the views of the organ pipe cacti with the Blue Mountains in the distance are unparalleled. Coming down, veer toward the Bull Pasture Trail, which will take you farther along the saddle's back and then in a slow traverse across the side of a hill, with switchbacks taking you downward. On these trails, beware of taking a wrong turn. I did, and somehow got off on something that looked like a trail but diminished and diminished to the point where I was following cairns but breaking trail. Finally, I realized I might not be on the actual route. It took a few scary moments to find my way back. If you find the trail difficult to follow at all, then you're not on it because it is well established. The Bull Pasture Trail is also part of the route to reach Mount Ajo, a notable backcountry destination. If you care to explore this 7-mile round-trip route, you must check in with the park rangers, who can help direct you.

Victoria Mine Trail

4.5 miles round-trip. Easy. 300-ft. elevation gain. Allow 3 hrs. Access: 32 miles south of Ajo on AZ 85. From the monument visitor center, head to the south end of the campground dump station. You may want to pick up a copy of the *Explorer's Guide* ($1.50) from the visitor center. It lists many good hikes in the area. Park entrance fee $4.

This trail travels over rolling terrain covered with numerous types of cacti, including organ pipe, to the monument's richest and oldest gold and silver mine. It begins toward the west, over some hills and down into arroyos, passing interpretive signs along the way. At mile 2 it meets up with an old jeep track. Turn left there and hike .33 miles to arrive at the old mine store. The mine itself had been worked for some years before Cipriano Ortega took it over in the 1880s to mine silver. In 1899, Mikul Levy began mining here and built the store and several other buildings. From the mine area you can either return the way you came or continue on to the **Lost Cabin Mine Trail,** a less-established route that continues on for another 4.4 miles to the remains of an old stone house and abandoned prospectors' holes.

HORSEBACK RIDING

If riding a horse along the U.S.–Mexico border conjures Cormac McCarthy-esque images for you—of uninterrupted miles of saguaro cactus, rickety cedar fence posts, and a boldly colored Mexican hacienda surrounded by eucalyptus trees—then you'll have to go to **Rancho de la Osa.** It's an odd sort of guest ranch; whereas most of these places emphasize the riding, here the emphasis is on a lovely stay, including inventively decorated rooms, with bold sponge-painted walls and original art—a "Frida Kahlo languishing in Santa Fe style" kind of place. The rooms are set in a number of 1800s-era buildings arranged around a quadrangle; one such building was even a church. Never have I seen guests spend so much time photographing their accommodations as they did here. Meals are served at a long, formal table (and guests are asked to dress for dinner). We had such delicacies as grilled tuna for dinner and an elaborate huevos rancheros made with black beans for breakfast.

The riding is enjoyable as well, very personal, with trips available in many directions from the ranch but most taking you along the border. You won't find canter rides here, though, except in the pens, as the terrain is too rough to allow for it. We rode out through a stunning ocotillo forest to ruins of a Native American village, where we hunted for arrowheads and potsherds, which we found, but left in their place. When you're not riding you can mountain bike, swim in the pool, or play croquet. Rates include all meals and activities, and range from the low-end of $310 per day for two people or $2,100 per week, to the high-end of $375 per day for two people or $2,500 per week, with minimum stay requirements. Discounts are available June through August. Contact the ranch at ☎ **800/872-6240** or 520/823-4257, or visit www.guestranches.com/ranchodelaosa or www.bbhost.com/ranchdelaosa or e-mail the ranch at osagal@aol.com.

MOUNTAIN BIKING

Beside the rides listed below there are a few places that have good dirt roads to ride including the **Buenos Aires National Wildlife Refuge (☎ 520/823-4251)**. The headquarters are located 38 miles south of Robles Jct. (Three Points) off AZ 286. Some of the best roads to ride are located near the town of Arivaca.

Ajo Mountain Drive
21-mile loop. Moderate. 1,800-ft. elevation gain. Allow 4–5 hrs. Access: 32 miles south of Ajo on AZ 85. The ride starts near the visitor center. Before you head out, be sure to pick up the road guide book (75¢) at the visitor center; it explains the numbered stops along the way. Park entrance fee $4.

This is primarily a driving road, so you won't encounter pristine automobile-less tracks here, but it's such a lovely place to be on a bicycle it's well worth the trip. The graded dirt, one-way road winds along the foothills of the Ajo Mountains, the highest range in the area. Along the way it traverses impressive stands of many types of cacti, especially organ pipe, often with lovely mountain views in the distance. During peak vacation seasons, this road may have some traffic, but overall the monument is not a very busy place. When I traveled this road I saw only five or six vehicles. Very hearty bikers might want to try the other monument loop, the 53-mile **Puerto Blanco Drive,** which circles the Puerto Blanco Mountains, passing by the desert oasis of Quitobaquito, though that ride would make for a very long day. Be aware that bikes are only allowed on the dirt roads within the park.

Hunter's Access Road to Diablito Mountain
8 miles round-trip. Moderate. 800-ft. elevation gain. Allow 2 hrs. Access: Take the Chavez Siding Rd. (Exit 40) off of I-19, south of Amado. Turn right onto the W. Frontage Rd. (runs west along I-19). At this point you're heading north. After less than 0.5 miles, turn left where the sign reads Hunter's Access Road. Park immediately. No fee required.

This double-track forest service road leads up along the base of the Tumacacori Mountains. The ride doesn't win big marks in my book because it is a jeep road rather than single track, but it does climb gradually toward an interesting desert mountain range. The real reward comes when you turn around and see views across the Santa Cruz Valley toward the Santa Rita Mountains. A couple of Tubac/Amado locals were gracious enough to show me this ride. I have to admit I was disappointed; I thought they'd take me out on some of their best single track, but once we turned around I got a sense of how lovely the area is.

The trail starts heading straight for the Tumacacoris; it ascends slowly. At the top of one rise it passes over a gas line. It continues heading toward the north end of the mountain range. At about mile 2, a road heads to the right down hill; it's marked by a small sign that says Diablito Mountain. Turn right and follow that rougher road down through a wash and up into some ocotillo forest, and up even more through some mesquite forest. The trail is fairly rough, with a few places where you might have to walk through a rocky wash. As you near the mountains, you'll note a small peak sitting out on its own at the end of the string of Tumacacoris. It has a bit of a horn; you'll be making your way toward it. You'll pass a windmill on your left and a little road going to it, which you should ignore. Continue up a hill; taking the next road to your left. It heads between the horned peak and the end of the mountain range. The road stops atop an open area, a great place to sit and gaze out across the valley toward the Santa Rita Mountains and the Rincons. Head back the way you came. The trip back is fast and easy. Forest Service roads spread throughout these foothills—you may want to explore them further.

ROAD BIKING

Arivaca Road

36 miles one-way. Easy. Allow 3 hrs. Begin at Arivaca Junction on I-19.

Though this road doesn't have shoulders and isn't the smoothest of pavement, it is a lovely trek through the Sonoran Desert south of Tucson. It makes its way along the northern edge of the Tumacacori Mountains and south of the Cerro Colorado Mountains, across the Papalote Wash to the village of Arivaca, a good place to stop for lunch. Then it continues along the southern end of the Las Guijas Mountains and through the Buenos Aires National Wildlife Refuge, where bird and wildlife abound. Bikers can stop at the junction of AZ 286, or turn south on that road and ride 12 miles to the border village of Sasabe, an interesting place where the few dwellings and businesses are painted bold yellow, purple, and pink. Return the way you came. Any portion of this route makes for a good ride through very desolate country. Generally there will be little traffic, but on weekends in spring and fall, when bird-watchers are out, you may encounter traffic.

SEA KAYAKING

One of the most notable experiences in the region is sea kayaking on Lake Mohave and Lake Havasu. **Back Bay Canoes and Kayaks** in Bullhead City (☎ **888/KAYAKEN** or 520/758-6242; www.backbaycanoes.com) offers a number of options. Trips include a half-day excursion in the Bullhead City area and a one-day Laughlin trip, which starts at the base of Davis Dam, passes under the Laughlin Bridge and continues by the waters of the Back Bay area and marinas, where kayakers see the many casinos and riverfront homes. Another option is the Topock Gorge trip, during which paddlers make their way through the red rocks of the canyons of the Havasu National Wildlife Refuge, a fairly rigorous journey with many opportunities to see wildlife and migratory birds. This 17-mile currentless paddle that's prone to headwinds is a difficult trip for the average person. The trip ends at Castle Rock Bay. The Black Canyon trip begins at Hoover Dam and travels through a lovely canyon with wildlife and points of historic interest along the way. This trip requires a 30-day advance notice. Kayak rentals for all trips run from $25 for a half day to $35 for a full day. All trips are designed to be accessible to beginning kayakers.

Back Bay can provide pickup service at motels and casinos. Fees include transportation, boat, paddle, floatation and launching fees. Back Bay also supplies a map of the area to help you on these self-guided adventures, and picks you up at the end. The owner of Back Bay says that depending on the time of year you'll see wildlife ranging from beavers to waterfowl to nude sunbathers. During holiday weekends kayakers need to head out early before the powerboaters take over the waters, which happens around 11am. Some people like to fish from the canoes or kayaks.

SWIMMING

Lake Havasu attracts swimmers, paddleboaters, parasailors and other water enthusiasts. The beaches are sandy, the water depths are gradual, and the water itself maintains a very comfortable 80°F throughout the summer months. Lakegoers seem to prefer **London Bridge Beach,** located in a park off West McCulloch Boulevard. Transplanted palm trees create a Caribbean experience, except of course when you look up and see the stark desert mountains. Picnic tables, a snack bar, and the nearby **Fun Center** makes this a good place to spend the day with your family, though the area can be quite crowded. The Fun Center can outfit you with its paddleboats, aquacycles, bumper boats, two-man motorboats, WaveRunners, as well as para- sailing and paragliding gear. Parasailing involves hooking oneself to the back of a long cord behind a motorboat and letting the boat pull you into the air. Paragliding starts off the same, but then the rope is cut, and you and a guide glide back down to the water. Paragliders fly between 1,500 and 2,500 feet above the water. Other beaches on Lake Havasu are **Windsor Beach Unit,** 2 miles north of the London Bridge and **Cattail Cove State Park,** 15 miles south of Lake Havasu City. If you have a boat, you'll find many miles of boat-in beaches on both Havasu and Mohave Lakes.

WALKS & RAMBLES

Desert View Loop at Organ Pipe Cactus National Monument

1.2-mile loop. Easy. 300-ft. elevation gain. Allow 1 hr. Access: 32 miles south of Ajo on AZ 85. The trailhead is at the monument group campground parking area. Park entrance fee $4.

This hike provides a brief introduction to Organ Pipe Cactus by taking you up a hill from which you can see many miles of the monument, Mexico's Sonoyta Valley, and the Cubabi Mountains. The trail climbs fairly steeply, but not for long. Along the way you'll see plenty of organ pipe cactus as well as limber bush, prickly pear, jumping cholla, and birds and rodents. Interpretive signs identify these and other plants and describe the ethnobotany of the local people.

Painted Desert Trail at the Imperial National Wildlife Refuge

1.3-mile loop. Easy. No elevation gain. Allow 1 hr. Access: Take AZ 95 north from Yuma and turn west on Martinez Lake Rd. Travel 10.4 miles, then turn north onto the entrance road. Drive another 2.1 miles following signs to the visitor center where the trail begins.

This scenic trail traverses through multicolored volcanic formations of the Colorado River Valley. Mid-October to May is the best season here, when birds are plentiful, and mosquitos are scarce. While hiking watch for such desert denizens as rattlesnakes, tarantulas, scorpions, and black widows. (After that hearty introduction, I know you'll want to hike here.)

The trail follows a wash, crosses a ridge, and winds its way back to the beginning. Traversing an area of a once-active volcano, the area has sparse Sonoran Desert vegetation. In fact, this area receives only 3.2 inches of precipitation annually. If you catch this hike in the spring you're likely to see wildflowers blooming. Watch for such beauties as scorpion weed (purple flowers), evening primrose (yellow), and chuparosa (red-orange). Also watch for black-tailed jackrabbits and Gambel's quail. As you continue on the trail you'll pass fascinating rock formations produced by water cutting through the red volcanic rock. The volcano that produced the lava and ash flows in the vicinity probably erupted 23 to 30 million years ago. The odd formations were created partly by steam coming up through cracks and fissures, and then completed by running water and the work of other erosional forces. During the next part of the trail a picturesque section of the Colorado River comes into view—Chocolate Mountains on the opposite shore. Next you'll see a jagged ridge of columns and spires. Toward the end of the hike the trail comes to Shady Canyon Wash where iron wood trees grow. Watch for mule deer that feed on the branches of these trees.

Quitobaquito Warm Springs
Organ Pipe Cactus Monument is 32 miles south of Ajo on AZ 85. Reach the spring by traveling to the visitor center, then taking the Puerto Blanco Drive for 12 miles. This drive is a one-way graded 53-mile dirt road. Allow a half day for the very scenic trip. Park entrance fee $4.

This is the quintessential oasis in the desert. Near a canopy of mesquite and Fremont cottonwoods sits this enchanting pool. One of the few sources of water for miles, it's a definite stopping place for birds such as herons and killdeers, and mammals such as coyotes and javalenas. The most notable inhabitant, though, is a special species of pupfish, the *Cyprinodon macularius eremus*. The thumb-sized silvery-blue fish you see at Quitobaquito are the only surviving natural population in Arizona. Unfortunately for humans who like to swim, you're not allowed to frolic with the pupfish. Since this is the only spring within miles, it has been a stopping place for many cultures, including the O'odham people, the Spanish conquistadors, prospectors, and travelers following the dreaded Camino del Diablo (see the sidebar in this chapter) from Sonora to Yuma.

Ruby Road
40-mile drive. Allow 2 hrs. Access: Drive 55 miles south of Tucson on I-19 to AZ 289. Travel this paved, then dirt road for 40 miles to the village of Arivaca. Or from Arivaca, take the Ruby Rd., FS 39, east to I-19.

When I set out on this mostly dirt road into the borderland, I was wary. No one I'd spoken to had driven it, and it skirts the edge of the border, with no towns or any kind of civilization on the way. I was headed to hike Sycamore Canyon (see "Hikes & Backpack Trips" earlier in this chapter), but I also wanted to make my way over to the Nogales area. I set out from Arivaca on a twisting paved road that traversed lovely rolling grasslands and cultivated fields. The road turned to dirt and continued in a southeasterly direction around the base of Black Peak and then over to the spectacular Ruby Peak, a sandstone monument with layers of varying red. Then the road dropped down into the lush Sycamore Canyon area, where I stopped to hike the wildlife-filled canyon. From there the road continued to skirt the border region along the base of Thumb Butte, past Peña Blanca Lake and then through Calabasas Canyon to I-19.

WILDLIFE VIEWING

Bobcat, javalina, desert bighorn sheep, and mule deer are just a few of the many varied inhabitants at the 860,010-acre **Cabeza Prieta National Wildlife Refuge.** Endangered Sonoran pronghorn also live here, as do many species of birds and reptiles, including the desert tortoise and desert iguana. Seven rugged mountain ranges rise within the refuge, which is located west of the village of Ajo and runs south, sharing 53 miles of border with Sonora, Mexico, forming what some say is the loneliest international boundary on the continent. The refuge is a wild place, with only two roads open to travel, no designated trails (except a small nature trail near the visitor center), and no services available out on the refuge. Before heading out, get a permit from the visitor center on the main street in Ajo. Most

EL CAMINO DEL DIABLO

The Camino del Diablo, or Devil's Highway, was once the route that linked the northern frontier of Mexico to the Spanish settlements of California. Though for centuries travelers used the route, as the name implies, the way was never easy. As many as 400 graves provide testament to the difficulty.

It begins at Caborca, Sonora, Mexico, and traverses 250 miles through some of the harshest land known to humans. The first section is tame compared to later ones. It makes stops at Quitovac, Sonoyta, and Quitobaquito, places where water is available, before reaching its most desolate section, the 130-mile stretch between Sonoyta and Yuma. Through this region it crosses severe desert flatlands, nearly impassable malpais, and miles of drifting sand. Water is scarce, if available at all. With temperatures soaring to 120°F, death lurks in the air. The route is still marked by some 65 primitive graves, many in the Tinajas Altas (High Tanks) region, where travelers hoped to find water, but weren't always fortunate. From Tinajas Altas the camino forks, leading either north in the direction of the Gila or Colorado Rivers, or west through Tinajas Pass and the Yuma Desert to Yuma Crossing.

Lack of water wasn't the only treachery on the route. Marauders threatened travelers, sandstorms could obscure the way, and broken equipment could leave travelers stranded. But the camino was used because it shaved 150 miles off the traditional route to California, which went via Tucson. It was also a way to avoid attack by hostile Apaches. Despite the route's difficulty, it was the most propitious, since it skirts along the bases of rugged mountain ranges and on the ground with easy footing relative to surrounding land, which is riddled with sand and malpais.

Native Americans used the trail long before Europeans did. It was part of a vast system used by the Tohono O'odham tribe that still inhabits the area. The first Spaniards used the trail in the 16th century, and it continued to be used until its popularity waned in the 1870s when the railroad reached Yuma.

In 1978, in recognition of its historic significance, El Camino del Diablo was listed on the National Register of Historic places. Visitors can visit El Camino, though they must obtain a permit from **Cabeza Prieta National Wildlife Refuge (☎ 520/387-6483)**. Be aware that this is a self-contained wilderness experience. All gasoline, water, and supplies must be carried. There are no facilities along the way. Four-wheel-drive vehicles are required, and vehicles must remain within 50 feet of the roadway. At times, the road is impassable.

notable here is the **Camino del Diablo,** which was initially an old Native American track, and was later used by early Europeans to travel from Sonora to Yuma. As many as 400 graves line the 130-mile "Highway of the Devil." Traversing this route requires expedition planning for food, water, and disaster contingencies. For more information see the "El Camino del Diablo" feature earlier in this chapter and call ☎ **520/387-6483.**

For a very different type of wildlife viewing experience head east toward the town of Sasabe to the **Buenos Aires National Wildlife Refuge.** This refuge was established in 1985 to restore a grassland ecosystem. As well as the grasslands, the refuge has wetland and riparian habitats. Over 300 species of birds have been recorded on the refuge. Spring and fall migration brings warblers, bitterns, and egrets; summer brings gray hawks and thick-billed kingbirds up from Mexico; while snow geese and vermilion flycatchers may be seen in winter. Eleven species of bats have been spotted here, 11 types of amphibians, and many other mammals including the endangered Mexican wolf, mountain lion, and jaguar. What you're most likely to see are the graceful pronghorn (antelope) as they bound across the grassland. The refuge is a very friendly place offering many ways to view wildlife, including designated drives, mountain biking on jeep roads, horseback riding (bring your own), as well as a number of hikes and nature trails. Primitive camping is also available. For information call ☎ 520/823-4251. The headquarters are located 38 miles south of Robles Jct. (Three Points) off AZ 286. You can also access two trails 2 miles west of the town of Arivaca at the Wildlife Viewing Area.

Campgrounds & Other Accommodations

CAMPING

Lake Havasu State Park's Windsor Beach Unit

Located 2 miles north of the London Bridge on London Bridge Rd. ☎ 520/855-9394. 50 beach campsites, flush toilets, showers, BBQ rings, cabanas, and picnic tables. Open year-round. $12 for tent and RV sites (no hookups available).

Mesquite, cottonwood, and palo verde trees shade these water-edge campsites. A cactus garden here displays the state's indigenous plants and attracts a nice variety of birds and wildlife. There is water to shower and cook with, but due to its alkalinity, it tastes like a rusty nail. It's best to bring bottled water for drinking. These sites can get crowded and a bit raucous during holidays and summer weekends.

Buckskin Mountain State Park

From I-40, turn south AZ 95 and drive approximately 50 miles. ☎ 520/667-3231.

Two campgrounds are located in Buckskin Mountain State Park—Buckskin and River Island—and both reside along the Colorado River. **Buckskin Campground** is the larger of the two, with 68 campsites including tent and RV sites with hookups. There are plenty of amenities at this campground. There's a market, fast food restaurant, playground, arcade, boutique, and, of course, showers, flush toilets, and drinking water. Easy-to-moderate hiking trails start in the campground and head into the Buckskin Mountains. **River Island** has 35 campsites, but none with electric hookups. Like Buckskin, River Island has cabanas located on the river. Jet skis can be rented from a nearby shop and taken to this section of the river. Buckskin sites cost $15 per night, River Island sites $12. Day-use areas are $7 and that includes access to the river and hiking trails.

Hualapai Mountain Park

Located southeast of Kingman on Hualapai Mountain Rd. ☎ 877/757-0915 (for reservations) or 520/757-0915. 14 cabins, 3 group recreation areas, 70 tent sites, 11 RV sites with hookups. Cooktop stove, refrigerator, bathroom, shower, telephone, beds, picnic tables, barbeque grill, and fireplace or woodstove. Open year-round. Camping fee $8 per night for a tent; cabin fees vary from $25 to $65 depending on the cabin size and day of the week.

If you're in the Kingman area and you're looking to spend a few days in the pines, your best bet may be this park with more than 2,200 wooded acres at elevations ranging from 6,000 to 8,400 feet. The park has picnic areas, rustic cabins, and RV and tenting area. The cabins, built by the Civilian Conversation Corp, have changed very little since the 1930s. You must provide your own bedding, towels, and cooking utensils. Reservations for cabins can be made Monday through Friday, 7am to 4pm. Tent and RV sites are on a first-come, first-served basis. This campground fills up early, so get there before the summer weekend rush by arriving on a Thursday if possible.

Kofa National Wildlife Refuge
Located 40 miles north of Yuma on AZ 95. ☎ 520/783-7861. No visitor center or other facilities. Primitive camping, with no designated sites and no water. Open 24 hours per day, year-round. No entrance or camping fees. Camping, hiking, hunting, photography, wildlife viewing.

The closest thing you'll get to shade in this extreme desert is from the shadow of the California fan palm, a tree rare in Arizona. Unfortunately, most of them are short and live high up in little cracks in the canyon walls of Palm Canyon. But palms aside, this refuge, while incredibly beautiful, is wild and unforgiving. There is little to no water here, barely enough for the bighorn sheep, deer, fox and other wild animals. This is primitive camping at its finest. Campers can camp anywhere in the refuge so long as they are more than 0.25 miles from any water source. Cars must stay on dirt roads. Campfires made from dead, down, and detached wood are permitted. However, due to the paucity of wood, removal of it from the refuge is prohibited.

Organ Pipe Cactus National Monument
32 miles south of Ajo on AZ 85. ☎ 520/387-6849. 208 sites, no hookups. Open year-round. $4 park entrance fee, $8 campground fee. Pets allowed only in campground and on a few designated trails.

This monument has two camping options. The first is the campgrounds near the visitor center. You'll find yourself amidst many RVs at this site, which has rest rooms, running water, grills, and tables. A much better bet, though limited in space, are the four primitive campsites available in the backcountry. This site is so lovely you won't want to leave it. You'll need to obtain a permit to use these sites. All camping is on a first-come, first-served basis.

INNS & LODGES
Shilo Inn
1550 S. Castle Dome Rd., Yuma, AZ 85365-1702. ☎ 800/222-2244 or 520/782-9511. 134 units. A/C TV TEL. $109–$250 double; a full breakfast is included in the price. AE, DISC, DC, MC, V.

If for some odd reason you find yourself exploring the outdoors in Yuma, you may want to treat yourself to this four-story resort hotel. Rooms here are large, with contemporary furniture, firm beds, big TVs, small refrigerators, as well as a microwave, hair dryer, and coffeemaker. On the grounds are a Jacuzzi, a large pool, sauna, steam room, and an exercise room. The hotel is located on the outskirts of Yuma with views of lettuce fields, so it offers more quiet than you'll find within town.

Guest House Inn
700 Guest House Rd., Ajo, AZ 85321. ☎ 520/387-6133. 4 units. A/C. $69–$79 double. DC, MC, V.

Just thinking about this inn brings me a sense of comfort. It sits on a hill overlooking the quiet village of Ajo, which in itself is an enchanting place, with one of the loveliest plazas I've seen. The inn was built in 1925 by Phelps Dodge to accommodate company officials visiting the Ajo mines. Now the Queen Ann–style inn is decorated with a combination of early American and Southwestern furniture. My room had a four-poster queen bed and tile in the bathroom. Other rooms have queen and twin beds in a variety of styles from Victorian to Southwestern and tile bathrooms also. All rooms open onto an enclosed veranda. During warm months guests can sit on the patio and bird watch. A full and delicious breakfast is served in the stately dining room.

5

Arizona Red Rock Country

Arizona's central highlands are caught in the middle of two distinct regions. Because of its transitional status, it's a land of contrasts—from high to low, from lush to barren, from soaking wet to bone-dry. To the north is the Colorado Plateau, which stands 4,000 to 9,000 feet above sea level, and to the south the low-lying deserts of the Great Basin and Range Province. In between, rain and other weather forces have carved profound canyons and monumental land formations, many of them from startling black, red, and gray stone. It is a land that snakes along and towers above, where the elements have ground away the unnecessary and left the imperative, an exciting history painted in layers of stone.

It's not surprising that such beauty would draw the devout. All manners of people have come to the center of these central highlands, Sedona, to seek inspiration from the land. Here you'll meet a vast array of characters, from those who worship by hiking canyons and biking up peaks to those who have found "vortexes" or power spots on the landscape where, they believe, they may have closer contact to spirit. At times the visitors can overwhelm the place. In fact, with all the tourists and the Phoenicians who come up to cool off, Sedona, with its resort hotels, T-shirt shops, and traffic jams, has become more a place to avoid than to visit.

But the area has always attracted people. Its history tells tales that begin with the Sinagua people who once lived among the cliffs in the area, farming the river valleys, where they created irrigation systems to run water to their squash, bean, and corn crops. In the 16th century, the Spaniards came in search of gold and souls, and upon failing to find the former, began a lengthy process of subjugating the Native Americans and converting them to Catholicism. During the development of the area as a territory, farmers and ranchers settled the lowlands, setting their cattle and sheep to graze what little there was to eat. Nearby, on Minus Mountain, prospectors found copper ore, and through the late 19th and early 20th centuries they mined it, dancing to the stop-and-go tune of supply and demand. The mining town of Jerome sprang up and to this day remains perched precariously on the edge of a hillside, from which the forces of nature have attempted to dislodge it nearly since its inception.

Fortunately for outdoors people, much of these central highlands are national forest land, allowing for plenty of hiking, biking, swimming, horseback riding, fishing, and even ballooning. Surrounding Sedona is the Coconino National Forest, a massive body of land traversed by forest roads allowing excellent access to the canyons and buttes. Though the mouths of many of the canyons have been explored and overused, deep in their depths lie mysterious wonders that few have seen, since the creeks tend to wash away trails, leaving backpackers bushwhacking, boulder-hopping, and swimming their way through. Those who do make it into their depths find deep clear pools, long waterfalls, and Sonoran Desert plants such as ocotillo and prickly pear cactus bordering a lush riparian habitat of sycamore and walnut, bordered in turn by conifer forest of Douglas fir and ponderosa pine. The wildlife is equally diverse; visitors may encounter desert dwellers such as rattlesnakes and tarantulas and moments later spot more mountain-going creatures such as black bears or mountain lions.

And while some canyon country is just that—a vast land to explore downward—this area also has upward beauty. Peaks and buttes with romantic names such as Secret Mountain and Cathedral Rock jut up out of these desert lands, the tops of which allow for views across bordering states and even down into Mexico. They and their surroundings have made this area a mecca for mountain bikers. Often with bases of slickrock-type stone, which grips tires ceaselessly, the trails wind around through green forest and red stones, creating a kaleidoscopic wonderland for the rider.

The Lay of the Land

As I noted earlier, the central highlands mark a transition from the Colorado Plateau to the north and the Great Basin and Range Province to the south. The Colorado Plateau, which stretches into Utah, Colorado, New Mexico, and Arizona, is a 130,000-square-mile mass that has moved like a large plate, resisting many of the more severe tectonic occurrences that have struck the lower section of the state. Ranging from 4,000 to 9,000 feet above sea level, this landmass has remained relatively stable for 600 to 700 million years. Meanwhile, below, at a lower overall elevation range but with peaks standing up to 9,000 feet high, lies the Great Basin and Range Province, which stretches all the way from southern Oregon to western Texas and covers most of southern Arizona. It is characterized by rugged, northwest-trending mountain ranges connected by low-lying deserts. For the past 75 million years, these deserts have been tectonically mobile, with landmass collisions and separations that have frequently changed the tenor of the land.

Between the Colorado Plateau and the Great Basin and Range Province lies this central highlands transition zone. What characterizes it is the fabled Mogollon Rim (pronounced "MUG-e-own"), a 2,000-foot escarpment from which the high plateau drains onto the Basin and Range Province. Since it's set between two utterly distinct regions, it has the character of a middle child, often rambunctious and definitely adventurous. A place that in so many ways lies naked to the forces of weather, it has been carved and beaten into a chiseled beauty. Here mountains have risen, and canyons have been carved away, a process some 350 million years in the making. It began with years and years of sedimentation laid down that turned to rock. Exposed to uneven uplift, faulting, erosion, and lava flows, it was shaped into the landscape we see today. At this very moment waterways such as Oak Creek and the Verde River, along with the forces of precipitation and freezing, continue to shape this land.

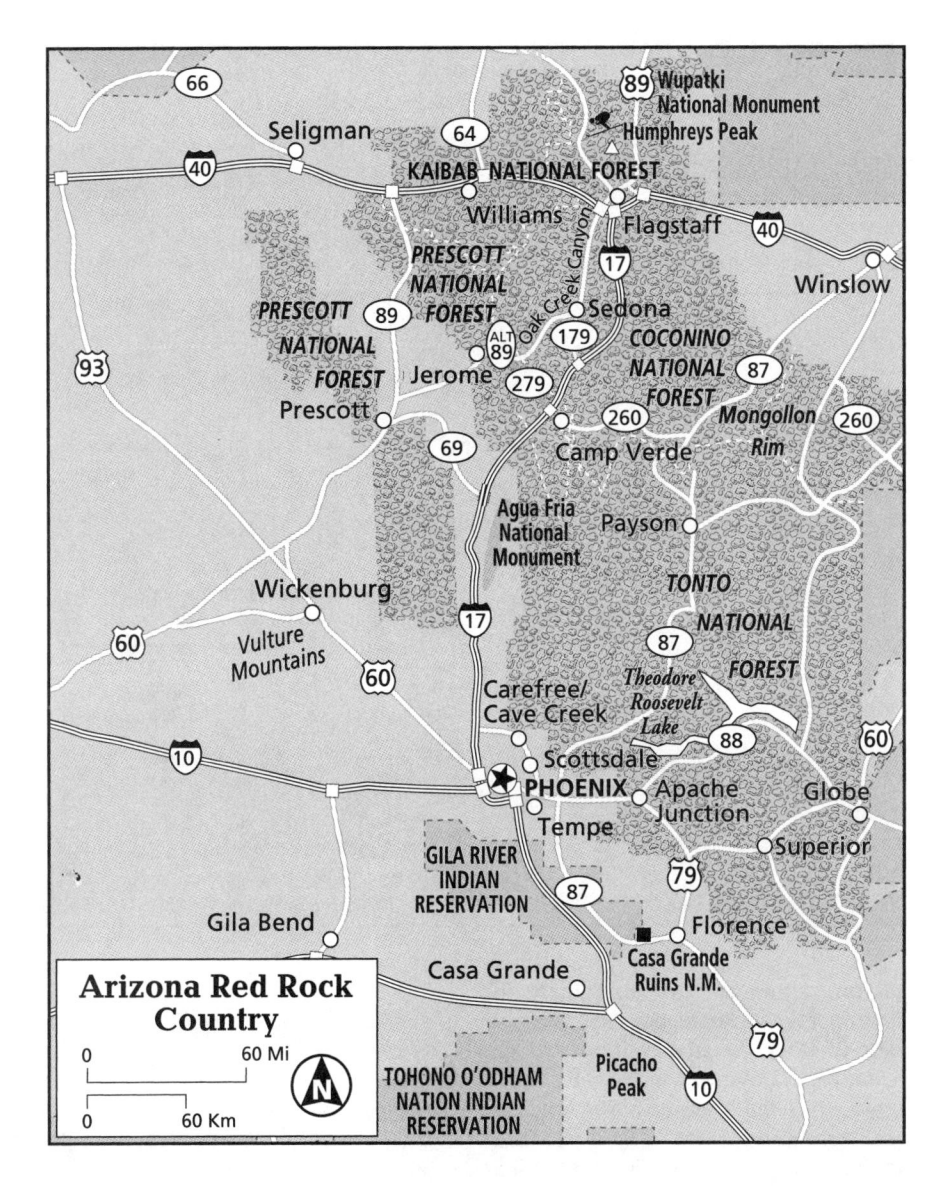

In the area around Sedona the geology is laid out and easy to read. Basalt covers the rims of many of the canyons. The next layer below is Coconino sandstone, a buff- to white-colored stone that often polishes to a pearly finish. Below the Coconino is the Supai sandstone, the red rock that is the signature of Sedona. Bands of red rock light the skies around the city, creating an almost disconcerting passionate heat in the area. Farther to the east the geology of the rim is more complex, with igneous and metamorphic rock bands intruding in places.

The weather here is of an in-between sort as well. On the Colorado Plateau winters tend to be cold, and in the lowlands of the Great Basin and Range region, summers are extremely hot. Fortunately, the transition zone gets the best of both. At an elevation averaging 4,500 feet above sea level, much of the region has mild seasons. Daytime summer temperatures are in the low 90s and in the winter in the low 50s, with fall and spring the ideal times of year. The region does receive snow, particularly in the higher elevations, as well as sleet and hail. During the summer monsoon, which takes place in late July, August, and early September, outdoor enthusiasts must watch for fast weather changes and beware of thunderstorms. You should especially avoid deep, narrow canyons during the monsoon. The southern part of the region is considerably hotter, with Phoenix temperatures often around 100°F in summer, and in the 60s and 70s in winter.

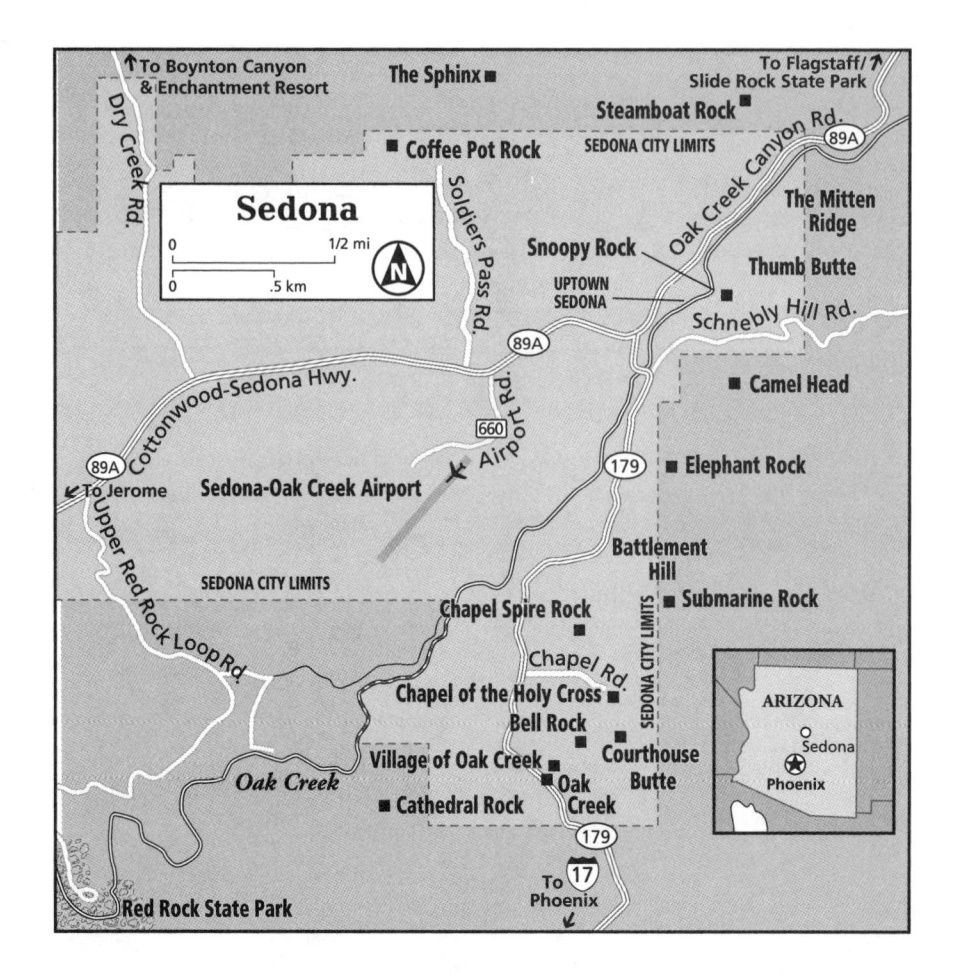

Orientation

I define central Arizona as a circular area at the very center of Arizona. It's bordered to the north by the Mogollon Rim, which cuts a southeasterly slash from the I-40 area south of Williams, south of Flagstaff, and almost to the Show Low area. This includes the pine-covered Oak Creek Canyon, which transitions from the high country down into the red-rock country around Sedona. U.S. 93 defines the western border of the region, so the region includes Wickenburg and Prescott. To the south it stretches south of I-10 to the region of Casa Grande, so it also includes the Phoenix area. To the east it's defined by AZ 77 and AZ 188 running north-south, so it includes the rich Sonoran Desert of the Superstition Mountains east of Phoenix.

Today, the region's biggest threat comes from the south. Phoenix, the fifth largest city in the United States, stretches across the area applying pressure to all that surrounds it. Weekends bring hordes of people to the lower ends of the canyons bent on supping the cool waters and basking in canyon shade. It's not difficult to avoid the city dwellers, though. Just one day into a backpack trip is all it takes to leave them behind, or a turn onto a more difficult mountain-bike route to have the trail to yourself. Still, you will want to avoid the power vortexes like the city of Sedona. I use the city as a stop for water and supplies, and then head to the forests for refuge.

Parks & Other Hot Spots

Red Rock State Park
Red Rock Loop Rd. off Hwy. 89A in Sedona. ☎ 520/282-6907. Visitor center, theater, gift shop, special educational programs, picnic area, developed trails, and rest rooms. Daily 8am–6pm in summer, 8am–5pm in winter. Bird watching, hiking, wildlife viewing.

Though camping is not permitted for the general public, a day's hike through the 286 acres of this park will be enough to satisfy your hunger for the great outdoors. Ten hiking trails lead you through manzanita and juniper to the lush banks of Oak Creek, where bird watching and wildlife viewing will keep you busy for hours. A guided nature walk (daily at 10am) and guided bird walks (Wednesdays and Saturdays at 8am in winter, 7am in summer) explore the ecology of the park. An interesting historical note: Hundreds of years ago, the Sinagua and Yavapai Indians called this area their home, and it was revered as a place of many riches. Today those riches are still abundant, and park rangers ask that visitors respect them.

Dead Horse Ranch State Park
Off 10th Street in Cottonwood. ☎ 520/634-5283. Trails, stocked pond, picnic area with grills, campsites with or without hookups, rest rooms and showers. Open daily year-round. Camping, canoeing, fishing, hiking, swimming.

This park, sitting at 3,300 feet, offers a good introduction to life along the lush Verde River. Sighted wildlife in the park includes bald eagles, river otters, black hawks, coyotes, and mule deer. With mild temperatures, canoeing, fishing, wading, and hiking in and along the river are quite pleasant.

Boyce Thompson Arboretum State Park
3 miles west of Superior off U.S. 60. ☎ 520/689-2811. Demonstration garden, picnic areas, and rest rooms. Daily 8am–5pm. Closed Dec 25.

This 323-acre park features Arizona's oldest and largest botanical garden. Founded in the 1920s by mining magnate Colonel William Boyce Thompson, this park has an abundance of flora including plants from the world's deserts, innumerable types of cacti, and towering trees. Steep mountain cliffs, a streamside forest, a desert lake, and a hidden canyon are additional attractions. The arboretum's mission is "to instill in people an appreciation of plants, through the fostering of educational, recreational and research opportunities associated with arid-land plants." March, which is wildflower month, is a lovely time to tour the botanical gardens. A 1.25-mile nature trail meanders through the arboretum. All plants are labeled with their Latin names and an English translation. The drive alone along U.S. 60 from Globe to Phoenix is enchanting.

Jerome State Historic Park
In Jerome just off AZ 89A, on Douglas Rd. ☎ 520/634-5381. Picnic area, rest rooms, and history exhibit. Daily 8am–5pm. Closed Dec 25.

If you have any interest in history at all you should definitely include a trip to Jerome on your itinerary. A walking tour of this enchanting mining town perched precariously on a hill makes for a great outdoor jaunt. En route, head to this park. Copper mining artifacts, history exhibits, and video presentations on the boom-and-bust history of the town of Jerome are housed in a mansion built in 1882. The mansion was originally built for Eugene Jerome, a New York City attorney and second cousin to England's Winston Churchill.

Lost Dutchman State Park
5 miles north of Apache Junction on AZ 88. ☎ 602/982-4485. Visitor center with maps, picnic area with grills, 35 campsites (no hookups), rest rooms and showers. Open daily year-round. Camping, hiking.

The Superstition Mountains tower over Lost Dutchman State Park, where three-armed saguaros stand tall and motionless. Because of their extensive in-search-of-water root system, saguaros grow a great distance from one another, creating a nice openness to the landscape. The park was named after Jacob "Dutchman" Waltz who hiked these mountains in search of gold. One of the highlights of this park is an educational program, offered to campers in the evenings, on desert creatures, the old Dutchman himself, and other topics. For hiking buffs, there are several rugged trails heading into the Superstition Wilderness. Remember to pack approximately 2 liters of water per person for a day hike.

Picacho Peak State Park
Off I-10, 60 miles south of Phoenix and 40 miles north of Tucson. ☎ 520/466-3183. 100 campsites (first-come, first-served basis) with or without hookups, picnic areas with grills, trails, playground, rest rooms and showers. Open daily year-round. Camping, hiking, wildflower viewing.

Soaring up out of this immense state park of 3,703 acres is Picacho Peak. It rises 2,000 feet above the desert floor, and offers some nice hiking and wildflower viewing. When the skies are clear, Tucson can be seen from the top of the peak. An historical note of interest: War reached the peak when Union troops met the Confederates in the Battle of Picacho Pass, the largest Civil War battle in Arizona.

Tonto Natural Bridge State Park
Off AZ 87, 10 miles north of Payson. Swimming in Pine Creek, historic lodge, picnic area with grills, trails, gift shop and rest rooms. Apr–Oct daily 8am–6pm, Nov–Mar daily 9am–5pm. Hiking, swimming.

The highlight of this park is the 183-foot-high, 400-foot-long travertine bridge, believed to be the largest natural bridge in the world. Within it is a tunnel that measures 150 feet at its widest point. The discovery of the natural bridge was made by David Gowarn, a prospector, who came across this geologic wonder while being chased by Apache Indians. He hid out within the tunnel. Later he claimed squatter's rights and moved his family to the tiny, pine-laden valley near where he first laid eyes on the bridge. You can stand on top of the bridge or hike down below to get a true sense of the size and beauty of this awesome rock formation. Then, cool off in Pine Creek or enjoy a picnic along the river's edge.

What to Do & Where to Do It

BALLOONING

There are few better ways to spot javelenas, deer, and jackrabbits than floating quietly above them and watching them bound away into the Sonoran Desert. **Adventures Out West** (☎ **800/755-0935** or 602/996-6100) has provided such an experience in the Phoenix area since 1973. Another reputable outfit, **BalloonRidesUSA,** has been in business for 25 years and, as do all the others mentioned here, uses only professionally licensed Federal Aviation Administration-certified commercial balloon pilots. Log on to www.balloonridesusa.com, e-mail: info@balloonridesusa.com, or call ☎ **520/299-7744** for more information.

Red Rock Balloon Adventures will take you on a stunning ride over Sedona's red rock country. The adventure begins with the inflation of the balloon and then its lift-off. Views from the basket are stunningly beautiful, especially when the setting sun turns the rock fiery red. Call ☎ **800/258-3754** or e-mail: info@redrockballoons.com.

With over 30 years of piloting experience, **Northern Light Balloon Expeditions** puts safety first. Its trips include information about the history and geography of the region. Flights take off at sunrise, and there's free hotel pickup. Call ☎ **800/230-6222** or 520/282-2274 or e-mail: balloon@sedona.net.

BIRD WATCHING

For most of its 100-mile course, the Hassayampa River flows underground; however, near the town of Wickenburg, it does emerge, creating a wildlife oasis in this desert land. The fragile nature of this river and the *bosque* (Spanish for forest) that surrounds it led the Nature Conservancy to found the **Hassayampa River Preserve** (☎ **520/684-2772**). At this preserve, 3 miles south of Wickenburg on U.S. 60, more than 270 species of birds live, nest, or migrate along the river corridor. Especially in such an arid land as Arizona, this type of habitat is rare and disappearing due to damming of rivers and lowering water tables caused by the large number of wells drilled in the area. While meandering along the River Ramble (a 0.5-mile walk) or the Mesquite Meander (also a 0.5-mile walk), you may see rare raptors, such as the zone-tailed hawk, the black hawk, or the Harris hawk. You also might see a Mississippi kite, yellow-billed cuckoo, or vermilion flycatcher, and desert birds such as the Gila woodpecker and cactus wren. Five different species of hummingbirds also visit or live in the area. During migration, large numbers of migratory land birds use the preserve for "refueling" for flights north and south; you might see 10 to 12 species of western warblers and large numbers of migrating hawks, such as ferruginous hawks and rough-legged hawks. A third trail, the Lake Trail (also a 0.5-mile walk), loops around the 5-acre lake and marsh called Palm Lake, where you might see blue herons, green-backed herons, and white-faced ibis. Other wildlife inhabit the area including Gilbert's skink, a rare type of lizard, as well as mule deer and even mountain lion. Call in advance in order to hook up with guided walks offered on the last Saturday of each month. The preserve is open from mid-September to mid-May, Wednesday through Sunday from 8am to 5pm, and mid-May to mid-September, Wednesday through Sunday from 6am to noon. The visitor center has interactive displays on desert and riparian ecology.

As with much of the red rock area around Sedona, **Red Rock State Park** (on Red Rock Loop Road off Hwy. 89A in Sedona) is a great place to spot hawks and falcons of many types. Cooper's hawks are year-round residents in the area while Swainson's hawks breed here, as do peregrine falcons. This is also a year-round home to golden eagles and American kestrels. A much more remote area to see these birds (and thus more likely) is **Sycamore Canyon** west of Sedona (see "Hikes & Backpack Trips" later in this chapter).

CLIMBING

What could be more alluring than climbing in mountains renowned for hidden treasure and unsolved murders? In the **Superstition Mountains,** 51 people have died since the turn of the century, and that figure doesn't include lost hikers or fallen climbers. Many of them died in conspiracies related to the fabled Lost Dutchman Mine, said to be located in the shadow of the very face upon which climbers cling, **Weaver's Needle.** The mine purportedly contains untold amounts of gold, left in the late 1800s by a German immigrant who for some reason was tagged as a Dutchman. Pitches on the 4,553-foot-high Weaver's Needle are traditional routes that range broadly in difficulty and complexity, and the hiking mileage is 8 round-trip miles of dry, hot desert. Despite that fact, this face can get crowded on weekends in spring and fall. Tonto National Forest policy prohibits use of permanent fixtures such as pitons or bolts. To get there, drive 8 miles east of Apache Junction on U.S. 60; turn left on Peralta Road and drive 8 miles to Peralta Canyon Trailhead. Hike 4 miles to the base of the Needle.

The **Eagletail Mountains,** with their rugged peaks, buttes, and spires also provide excellent climbing opportunities. Most popular are Courthouse Rock and Eagletail Peak, both of which have a variety of traditional routes, which vary in difficulty. From the summits you'll see views of vast desert basins to the west and lush farmlands to the east. The Eagletail Mountains are located 65 miles west of Phoenix. From Phoenix, travel west along Interstate 10 to the Tonopah exit. Travel south from Tonopah to the paved Salome Highway, then west to the Harquahala Valley via the Courthouse Rock Road.

With its dramatic formation of granite outcroppings and cliff faces, **Granite Mountain** is the destination of many rock climbers. The "Swamp Slabs" portion of the southwest face offers beginning climbers a gentle challenge. Meanwhile, the middle section of the southwest face offers more of a challenge. Within the section, "The Classic" is known by many as the best climb on the southwest face. Since this is a nesting area for endangered peregrine falcons, the cliffs are closed from February to July. Granite Mountain is 7 miles west of Prescott. From the Town Square in Prescott, head west on Montequma, which will become Iron Springs Road. Drive 4.5 miles to FS 374. Turn right and drive 4 miles to the Metate Trailhead, where you'll park and where the Granite Mountain Trail begins. Hike 2 miles to the climbing areas.

In the Oak Creek Canyon area there are also several good climbing spots. **Oak Creek Overlook** has over 100 routes. This great basalt flow, located just 20 minutes from Flagstaff, has routes varying from 20 to 80 feet with a broad range of difficulty. Access the overlook from AZ 89A south of Flagstaff. Farther south on AZ 89A at **Grasshopper Point** are some fun bouldering and top-rope problems. Once you're finished on the rock, you can dunk in the water there. Beginner and intermediate climbers will enjoy the rock at **Schnebly Hill.** And between climbs you can sit back and take in the views.

A good additional source for climbs in this area is *Rock Climbing Arizona* by Stewart M. Green (Falcon, 1999). Also look for *A Better Way to Die: Rock Climbers Guide to Sedona and Oak Creek Canyon,* written and self-published by Tim Toula and, as you might have guessed from the title, full of attitude.

FISHING

One of the biggest surprises about central Arizona is the amount of water here. This area between the Colorado Plateau and the Basin and Range Province is scored with many canyons, most of which flow with streams. The only permitted guide in Oak Creek, **Jim McInnis** of **Gon'**

Fishen, (☎ **520/282-0788**), runs half- and full-day trips above Sedona, as well as on the Verde River. Call for rates.

Located southeast of Sedona on Stoneman Lake Road, 9 miles east of I-17, **Stoneman Lake** fills a 170-acre volcanic crater and is the only year-round natural lake in the state. It's stocked with northern pike and yellow perch. Fishers can avoid the frustration of getting their lines hooked into the ring of reeds along the outside of the lake by motoring out to the middle. The launch ramp is on the western end. In winter the lake is usually frozen over.

Along AZ 89A north of Sedona is **Oak Creek,** one of the finest trout streams in the southwestern United States. The paved and winding highway snakes along the edge of the stream, allowing for plenty of good pull-off spots, but there are also plenty of fishers. You may want to head to the upper reaches of the canyon where the waters remain cold and clear and where there's more solitude. Some stretches of the canyon are very narrow, making casting difficult unless you are a skilled fly fisher. At these tight spots, hiking through the water is necessary to get to sandbars. If you're fishing in early spring, the water is extremely cold, so wear wool socks and gators or waders. The creek is stocked year-round with rainbow trout and also has resident brown trout. Fishing is good on Oak Creek year-round, though during January to March the waters are so cold the fish move slowly.

West Clear Creek offers lovely freestone fishing between high canyon walls of basalt and Supai sandstone. In a similar setting, **Wet Beaver Creek** allows fishers a little more casting room. Both are stocked with trout, and both are located in the Sedona area. See the "Hikes & Backpack Trips" section of later in this chapter for details on how to get there.

Starting near Chino Valley and flowing past Sycamore Canyon and through the towns of Cottonwood and Camp Verde is the **Verde River.** Here good-sized catfish swim in the lower portions of the river. During the winter months the river contains stocked trout. The river is located 90 miles north of Phoenix near Cottonwood. From I-17, head west of AZ 260. You'll find good access at Dead Horse Ranch State Park (which charges a fee for parking). You can also access the upper Verde at Tuzigoot National Monument, a couple of miles upriver from Cottonwood.

Only 40 minutes from downtown Phoenix, the **Lower Salt River,** runs through an amazingly pristine canyon where trout fishing is excellent. It's very popular with fly fishers who want to head to this beautiful creek after work. The river is stocked with rainbow trout, and there are bluegill, largemouth, and smallmouth bass as well. The unsightly suckerfish also makes its home here. The river is rich in insect life and other aquatic food sources. If you want to fish this portion of the river, you'll have to share it with recreational tubers, bait fishers, and day users. To get there from Scottsdale, drive through Fountain Hills on Shea Blvd. to AZ 87. Take the Saguaro Lake and Salt River Recreation area exit.

The 120-acre **Kinnikinick Reservoir** contains rainbow and some brown trout. Fly-fishing can be good in this lake, especially in the fall. The lake is located 9 miles east of Lake Mary Road via FS 125 and FS 82.

Two other fishing grounds in northern Arizona include **Upper and Lower Lake Mary** on Lake Mary Road southeast of Flagstaff. The fishing isn't great here, but if this is your only option, it's at least worth a try. Some fishers are especially drawn to Lower Lake Mary to fish for those wily northern pike. Flagstaff built these two lakes as reservoirs for the town, and their close proximity to the city makes them at times quite busy; be aware that your fishing may be disturbed by speedboats and water-skiers. During drought years these lakes tend to dry up, but when it's wet, the fishing can be good. The lakes are surrounded by pines and cedars, and lots of picnic areas. Both have boat access. Be aware that these lakes do freeze in winter.

HIKES & BACKPACK TRIPS

Some of the most exciting hiking and backpacking in the southwestern United States are in this part of Arizona. The hikes vary from high buttes with 360° views to deep canyons with water holes that must be swum, with your backpack floating beside you. Before hiking in this area you'll definitely want to read up on the desert and canyoneering pointers (see chapter 1). Though many of the hikes are simple and gentle, some are for the lionhearted only. Some of them require a shuttle, particularly for canyoneering from one end of a canyon to the other. Though there's no real shuttle service in the region per se; you may want to call **Bob's Taxi** at ☎ **520/282-1234** to help you to and from the trailhead.

Sedona Area

Boynton Canyon

5 miles round-trip. Easy. 600-ft. elevation gain. Allow 3 hrs. Access: Head west on 89A out of Sedona to the well-marked Dry Creek Rd. Turn right (north) and drive 3 miles to the first T intersection, where you'll turn left. In another 1.6 miles at the second "T," go right. The trailhead is on the right.

My introduction to this canyon in some ways typifies the Sedona experience. While I hiked in one autumn evening as the pinks of sunset had just begun to ignite the west, I heard the "om"-like chanting of many voices coming from the direction of a red Supai sandstone pinnacle to the northeast. Meanwhile, from the west came the distinct sound of tennis balls hitting nylon. I had to chuckle at this momentary auditory encounter with the New Age and the resort-age lifestyles in this Arizona town. Though this hike is not of the get-away-from-it-all variety, it still provides spectacular access to the red Supai and gray Coconino sandstone country for which Sedona is so famed. The hike begins by skirting (for longer than you'll like—about 15 minutes) the perimeter of a resort. Once past the resort, the trail passes through shady forest and then thick stands of creosote before breaking out in the open at the center of a massive stone amphitheater. Above you stand 800-foot-high canyon walls that guard Bear Mountain. Look for a 400-year-old ponderosa to add to the marvel.

West Fork of Oak Creek

2–15 miles one-way. Easy to difficult. 1,400-ft. elevation gain for entire canyon. 150-ft. elevation gain for signed trail portion of canyon. Allow 2 hrs.–2 days. Access: Take AZ 89A south out of Flagstaff or north out of Sedona. The parking lot is on the west side of the highway, 1 mile south of Cave Spring Campground and 1 mile north of Don Hoel's Cabins. $3 parking fee. Maps: USGS Dutton Hill, Wilson Mtn., USFS Coconino National Forest.

This trail, though quite populated due to its easy access, is one of the most enjoyable and scenic ones Arizona. It winds through an ever-narrowing canyon of bold red and gray sandstone, always following a stream and sheltered by cool forest. Most people choose to simply hike the lower section, which is 3 miles in, and return; others like to really canyoneer it, beginning at the top and traversing through pools and over rocks for 12 miles to the bottom. If you hike the lower section, the trail starts in wild apple orchards and then, fairly abruptly, turns right into a narrow, steep-walled canyon, through which the slow-flowing perennial creek trickles over red sandstone floor. It pools in spots, creating nice wading, and at times it flows poetically through little chutes and then broadly washes over big slabs. The canyon walls grow more spectacular as you go, with the red Supai sandstone contrasting against the gray Coconino sandstone. The forest is richly diverse, with Douglas fir, white fir, and ponderosa pine, as well as canyon maple and box elder; the endangered and rare Arizona Bugbane even grows here. Fortunately, most of the hikers turn back at about mile 2, leaving the most interesting part of the hike pristine and quiet. In that area, the canyon narrows to a width of about 12 feet, forcing hikers to walk through occasionally thigh-deep water (depending on the season and the time of year). You'll definitely want to wear river sandals for this day hike. At around mile 3, the going gets rougher and becomes a boulder-hop/creek-wade for the remaining 9 miles. The upper section contains a number of pools, some of which must be swum. Campsites are limited in the upper section, and camping is not allowed in the lower 6 miles. To reach the upper section of the canyon, take FS 231 off Old Highway 66 in west Flagstaff for 18 miles. Parking at the lower trailhead is limited to day hours. The lower portion of the canyon is great for family hiking.

Sycamore Canyon
10–25 miles. Moderate to difficult. 2,100-ft. elevation loss. Allow 5 hrs.–3 days. Access: Take AZ 89A southwest out of Sedona for about 6 miles and turn north on FS 525. Follow signs to Sycamore Pass. After 2.7 miles bear left onto FS 525C. In another 3.2 miles bear right on 525C, and follow this road just over 5 miles to the Sycamore Pass and the Dogie trailhead. Maps: USGS Loy Butte, Sycamore Point, Clarkdale; USFS Coconino National Forest.

Rugged and highly scenic terrain are what draw hikers to this canyon. Remote, with a lawless kind of personality, it's a place for those who like to escape the luxuries of groomed trails and available water. One day when we came out of the canyon we ran into some men on ATVs who had been riding the rim and had watched four bears and a javalena patrolling around our camp; we never saw them. As well as wildlife, you'll see bands of red Supai and tan Coconino sandstone laid out across a canyon whose breadth can be measured in miles in the lower reaches and by feet in the upper. Because the canyon is so rough, it's difficult to select the best route to traverse it. Some recommend hiking the 17-mile length of it from top to bottom. This is a good option, though it will require bushwhacking at the top. Others recommend entering through Sycamore Pass, hiking up the canyon, and coming out along the eastern rim. Whichever option you choose, a shuttle is recommended (unless you choose to do an out-and-back trip), and be aware that water will be scarce.

Entering from Sycamore Pass you'll climb down the rocky Dogie Trail from sandstone cliffs into piñon/juniper rolling hills that at mile 5 take you to Sycamore Creek, an oft-dry waterway with a few brown puddles. At the creek you'll intersect with Trail 63 coming from the southwest, which will take you 3 miles northeast to Taylor Cabin, where there will likely be a little more water in the creek. This stone building built in 1931 was once a cowboy line shack; along the front wall are carved brands from four ranches, which used the cabin. From here you have a few options. Most guidebooks suggest continuing upstream on the Taylor Cabin Trail, which climbs 1,800 vertical feet within 2 miles to Bunker Ridge. If you want to do a loop hike, this is a good option except that you either have to hike 7 miles under power lines across Casner Mountain, or take a much longer hike along Mooney Jeep Trail and along 525C back to your car (be sure to stash water). A better option is to leave a shuttle car (or bike) at the canyon rim at the top of the Taylor Cabin Trail or at the top of Winter Cabin Trail. Access to those trailheads is via FS 538B and 538A respectively. These can be reached from Flagstaff by driving Turkey Butte Road (FS 231) 18 miles to FS 538. After approximately 5 miles it intersects 538A and, shortly thereafter, 538B. A bike shuttle would work well for this hike; drop the bike at the Taylor Cabin Trailhead and ride the Mooney Jeep Trail to pick up your vehicle. *Note:* This canyon gets very hot and dry. It is best hiked in spring and fall.

West Clear Creek
2–16 miles one-way. Easy to difficult. 2,280-ft. elevation loss for the backpack trip. Allow 2–4 hrs. for a day hike of the lower sections, 3–4 days to backpack the central section. Lower canyon access: Drive 6 miles southeast from Camp Verde on AZ 260 to FS 618. Turn north and drive 2.2 miles to FS 215. Follow this dirt road 3 miles to the Bull Pen camping area. Central section access: Take AZ 260 east from Camp Verde and then turn left (east) on FS 144. (If you reach A87, you've gone too far.) Follow 144 for 1.8 miles to FS 149. Turn left and follow 149 for 1.2 miles to FS 142. Turn left (west) on 142 and drive 2.8 miles to FS 142B. Follow 142B for 2.5 miles to the canyon rim and Trail 33. To run shuttle for the central section, leave your car at the head for Trail 17. Follow the instructions above to get to FS 618. From 618, turn east on FS 214. From 214, turn right on 214A and follow this jeep road to the trailhead. Maps: USFS Coconino National Forest; USGS Calloway Butte, Buckhorn Mountain, Walker Mountain.

The big draws to this canyon are the awesome walls of basalt and sandstone, and the clear pools of cool water. As a day hike, it offers places to swim and lounge on warm rocks as well as some boulder-hopping adventure. As a backpack trip, it offers the best of canyoneering, with the aforementioned amenities as well as long pools to swim.

The first mile or so into lower West Clear Creek shows its overuse—lots of people signs, mashed grass, "Kleenex flowers" (as Edward Abbey calls them), and a few obvious swimming holes that are overpopulated (including one very cool one with a high rope swing). But the farther along you go, the fewer the people. During this part of the hike you're just getting a taste of the canyon; it's broad here with meadows alongside, the walls black to the south and red to the north. The trail skirts the creek edge; occasionally you'll want to poke your head through the brush to see what the creek is doing. Parts of it are freestone stream great for fly-fishing. As the canyon walls narrow, the path is often obstructed by large pools, around which you'll have to make your way. The boulder-hopping is endless through these sections; if you've never backpacked in this type of terrain, this is a good stretch to try out before you strap on weight. The stones in this canyon are especially lovely, since some fall from the basalt walls and some fall from the Supai and Coconino sandstone. When combined into cairns that mark the way, they form works of art. While in the canyon watch for sycamore and walnut trees, and for deer and even mountain lions in the upper reaches.

To hike the central section, begin on Trail 33 switchbacking 680 feet down into the canyon. Here you'll encounter Coconino sandstone and Douglas fir trees surrounding the creek. Heading downstream, you'll frequently find yourself wading and swimming in pools. Watch for a point where power lines cross the canyon, where you'll find one of few good campsites along this route. Below this section the canyon grows gentler, but soon it revs up again. The canyon narrows and draws you into the longest pool made of white stone and called the White Box. More miles down the canyon you'll note a change from the Coconino sandstone to the black basalt and the red Supai sandstone. One more long swim and then about a mile of hiking and you'll come to Trail 17. Watch your map closely to find this trail, as its entry into the base of the canyon is obscured. Trail 17 will take you up 1,700 feet to the north canyon rim, which is accessed by FS 214 and 214A. Another option is to follow West Clear Creek Canyon 30 miles from the headwaters to Bull Pen.

Wet Beaver Creek
3–24 miles one-way. Easy to difficult. 2,000-ft. elevation loss for entire canyon. Allow 3 hrs.–3 days. Access: From the junction of Interstate 17 and Highway 179 south of Sedona, head onto FS 618 and drive 2 miles to where you'll turn right toward the ranger station and find the trailhead for Bell Trail 13. For the head of Wet Beaver Creek: From Sedona drive 7 miles north on Interstate 17 to Exit 306; take paved FS 213 for 6.5 miles to FS 229. Turn right and drive 5 miles to FS 620. Turn right on 620 and drive 2 miles until you turn left on 620E. Follow this a 0.5 mile to a spur road marked 9288; this four-wheel-drive road goes 1 mile to Waldroup Place Tank at the head of Waldroup Canyon. Maps: USFS Coconino National Forest; USGS Casner Butte, Apache Maid Mountain.

The big reason for dwelling in this canyon—and you will want to dwell here for awhile—is water, clear pools of it, some deep enough to dive into from 30-foot cliffs, much of it warm enough to wallow in. If you're looking for a scenic but rigorous day hike, you'll want to go to Bell Crossing. Though you won't likely find solitude there, you won't find crowds either. Hardcore canyoneers will want to take 2 to 3 days to hike the canyon from end to end, or do a loop on the Apache Maid Trail. If you start from the bottom, the Bell Trail follows the creek, making its way along some lesser pools in which to swim. At about mile 2 the trail enters the Wet Beaver Wilderness area and climbs along the desert canyon wall, where you'll see ocotillo twining their elegant limbs toward the sky. The canyon walls are red Supai sandstone on the north and black basalt on the south. The trail drops down to Bell Crossing at mile 4, a swimming hole with an hour-glass shape, at the center of which swimmers jump some 15 feet into the pool. (*Note:* Always be careful while diving when you can't see the bottom.) The water is warm enough to linger and swim around in, but cool enough to give you those delicious chills when the sun begins evaporating it off your skin. About another 45 minutes of boulder-hopping up the canyon will take you to a much longer pool with a stone island in the center.

If you choose to hike the whole canyon you have two options. One is a loop hike following the Apache Maid Trail. To travel this 24-mile loop you'll begin at the Bell Trailhead and follow that trail to the Apache Maid, then follow it up on the rim for a long, hot, and dry trek to Waldroup Canyon. Waldroup Canyon will channel you to the head of Wet Beaver Creek, which you'll follow back to your car. Due to the heat and dryness, this is not a very popular route. The more popular option is to hike the canyon from top to bottom, in which case you'll run a shuttle and begin at the head of Waldroup Canyon. Either of these latter options involves extensive boulder-hopping and some technical climbing. You'll need a 50-foot rope and flotation for your pack (see "Canyoneering Basics" in chapter 1). This route has 7 drops ranging in difficulty from 20 to 30 feet, some that can be circumnavigated, others that will require downclimbing.

Parsons Trail
2–8 miles round-trip. Easy. 200-ft. elevation gain. Allow 2–5 hrs. Access: Head southwest of Sedona on AZ 89A through Cottonwood and take the Tuzigoot National Monument turnoff. The turnoff will lead you across the Verde River, after which you'll turn left on FS 131 and follow the river onto Duff Flat. Continue on FS 131 to the parking area, about 11 miles from the Tuzigoot Rd.

This hike is a refreshing alternative to the hot red desertscapes of the Sedona area. Here you'll hike along Sycamore Creek, a rich riparian habitat shaded by cottonwoods and sycamores. Initially the trail drops down rather steeply until it comes to the base of the canyon. Then it follows the waterway upstream, crossing twice. These crossings should present no problem except during spring runoff. Because of this flooding, at 2.3 miles the trail may become difficult to follow, requiring some boulder-hopping along the stream bottom. Be aware that camping is prohibited from the trailhead to Parsons Springs (the end of this hike) in order to protect the riparian habitat. North of Parsons Springs the streambed is generally dry. Water from either the springs or the stream should be treated before drinking. The Sinagua people once traveled up and down this canyon, as did the Spaniards.

Wilson Mountain Trail

11.2 miles round-trip. Difficult. 2,400-ft. elevation gain. Allow 1 full day. Access: In Sedona at the junction of AZ 89A and AZ 179, head north on 89A for 1.1 miles across Midgely Bridge. Turn left into the parking area.

This hike will take you to the top of one of the highest points in the Sedona area, with amazing views along the way. It begins in Arizona cypress woodland and ends in ponderosa pine, with views of the San Francisco Peaks, the Sterling and Oak Creek Canyons, and the Verde Valley. The trail begins at the picnic ramada off the old roadway and branches right. It climbs moderately, then flattens out. At 0.5 mile it enters the Red Rock–Secret Mountain Wilderness. It ascends the mountain's southeast face then climbs steeply along a fault canyon face to a bench from which you can catch spectacular views at 2.5 miles. In another 0.5 mile it meets the North Wilson Trail. Bear left and resume the climb. The trail enters the shade of Gambel oak and mixed conifer forest. You'll find good views to the east over Oak Creek and Munds Canyon. At 4.25 miles the trail comes to another junction. Continue to the Canyon Overlook on the north rim of the mountain. Another spur trail will take you 0.5 miles to the Sedona Overlook for views of red rock country. Return by the same route.

Vultee Arch

3.5 miles round-trip. Easy. 400-ft. elevation gain. Allow 2–3 hrs. Access: In Sedona at the junction of AZ 89A and AZ 179, head west on 89A for 3.2 miles to Dry Creek Rd. Turn right and travel 1.9 miles to FS 152. Turn right on this unpaved road and travel for 4.4 miles to the trailhead parking at its end.

This hike takes you through stands of Arizona cypress, oak, pine, and fir, and up red rock terraces to a large natural bridge created by cascading runoff, with lots of views en route. Almost immediately, the trail enters the Red Rock–Secret Mountain Wilderness and climbs in the shade of Arizona cypress along the dry streambed of Sterling Canyon. Wilson Mountain's sheer walls jut up to the right, while views of red rock country spread out to the left. At 0.75 miles the trail enters a forest of ponderosa and oak that was scarred by the 1996 arch fire. Nearing the arch, the trail comes to a marked fork, with the Sterling Pass Trail branching off to the right. If you've had the foresight to park a shuttle car at the Sterling Pass Trailhead in Oak Creek Canyon, you can head up to the arch, and then return and take this fork for 2.4 miles through Sterling Pass and to Oak Creek Canyon. To get to the arch you'll want to bear left and hike 100 yards to a large rock outcropping.

Here you'll find views of Sterling Canyon, mountains in the distance, and the arch itself. It's named for aviation pioneer Gerard Vultee and his wife who died in a 1938 plane crash high on a slope to the north. Head back the way you came.

THE ARIZONA TRAIL

There are those who like to bag peaks, and those who like to explore canyons. Then there are those hearty souls who set out to cross great swatches of land. They travel for months at a time along the Appalachian Trail, which runs from Georgia to Maine in just shy of 2,167 miles, or the Pacific Crest Trail, which runs 2,650 miles from Mexico to Canada. Or they may traverse from Mexico to Canada on the Continental Divide Trail, which runs 3,000 miles through the Rocky Mountain states (including New Mexico). In recent years, Arizona earned a place in the annals of monumental trails, with its new Arizona Trail.

Though it is considerably shorter than the major leagues listed above, the Arizona Trail has much to offer. It stretches the entire length of Arizona, from its border with Mexico to southern Utah. It connects high deserts, low lake valleys, ponderosa pine forests, and plunging canyons. The 790 miles of trail traverse through seven life zones, with terrain ranging from Sonoran Desert to snowcapped peaks. This Southwestern trail, like its big cousins, is attracting its share of "thru hikers," those individuals with a drive to conquer the whole thing, but peak baggers, canyon explorers, and just plain hikers will enjoy it as well, by tackling parts of it.

It begins at the Mexican border. Starting at **Coronado National Memorial** it works its way north through the **Santa Rita Mountains** and **Saguaro National Park**. Next it traverses the **Santa Catalina Mountains** outside of Tucson. The trail continues north through the **Superstition Mountains** near Phoenix and then into lush pine country at **Tonto Natural Bridge State Park** in Tonto National Forest. Next it climbs some 2,000 feet to the top of the **Mogollon Rim**. Farther north it comes to **Walnut Canyon National Monument** near Flagstaff, and then heads through **Grand Canyon National Park**. Nearing the Utah border it traverses the **Kaibab National Forest, Jacob Lake,** and finally **Buckskin Mountain**.

The Arizona Trail Association, a non-profit organization, brought together many interests to make this a reality. For information about traversing all or parts of the route, contact the association by calling ☎ **602/252-4794** or by e-mailing ata@aztrail.org.

Prescott

Granite Mountain

7 miles round-trip. Moderate to strenuous. 2,000-ft. elevation gain. Allow 4 hrs. Access: From the Town Square in Prescott, head west on Montezuma, which will become Iron Springs Rd. Drive 4.5 miles to FS 374. Turn right and drive 4 miles to the Metate Trailhead, where you'll park and where the Granite Mountain Trail begins. Maps: USFS Granite Mountain Wilderness.

This hike traverses stands of piñon/juniper, manzanita, and ponderosa weaving through creature-like stands of 2 billion-year-old granite, then climbs high above the surrounding hills allowing for spectacular views of central Arizona. This primo hike follows a well-marked trail as it meanders easily for the first mile. Then it turns north and climbs switchbacks up to Granite Mountain Saddle, climbing 800 feet in 1.3 miles. From there, the trail heads south for 1.5 miles to a viewpoint along the southern edge of the mountain. The summit is a 0.5 mile to the east. En route you're likely to see technical rock climbers scaling the notorious southern face.

Thumb Butte

3-mile loop. Moderate. 1,200-ft. elevation gain. Allow 2 hrs. Access: From Prescott travel west on Gurley St. for 2.5 miles to Thumb Butte Rd. Continue northwest on this road for 1.5 miles to the parking area on your right. The trailhead is across the road uphill.

This trail offers a great way to get acquainted with the Prescott area. It climbs through ponderosa forest and culminates with views of Mingus and Granite Mountains and the San Francisco Peaks. The very maintained and fairly heavily traveled trail leaves from the parking lot and climbs up rapidly. Along the way you'll encounter spectacular views off to the south and west. It switchbacks here and there, finally reaching a saddle. At this point you'll want to take the spur trail to the Groom Creek Viewpoint, which will give you views in every direction. After taking it all in, head back to the main trail and follow the signs down. You'll climb a little before starting your descent. Watch to your left for a spur path leading up to the granite outcropping. There's some bouldering to be done on top, though even getting to it requires some 5.6 slab climbing. Of course, views from atop this granite thumb are unparalleled. The way down is paved, allowing you to gaze at Granite Mountain without tripping.

Peavine Trail

4.6 miles one-way. Easy. Little elevation change. Allow 2–5 hrs. Access: From Prescott head north on AZ 89 for just over 1 mile to Sun Dog Ranch Rd. Turn right and drive 1.3 miles to the trailhead on your left.

Though this hike starts in an ugly industrial section, it soon takes you into a magical rock land, with plenty of spur trails to enjoy. Traversing the old railroad bed that cuts through the Dells, this trail is completely flat, a good place for those who have trouble with rough surfaces. The hike really begins when you come to the stunning blue of Watson Lake. Watch closely here—I saw a heron take off from the marsh to the right. Beyond the lake are the oddly shaped Granite Dells, like lumps of gold, sticking up in many directions. The trail runs along the shore of the lake, then enters the Dells. As you go, watch for spur trails where you'll want to explore. The trail continues through the strange undulating stones for a number of miles. Farther along it passes close to a rifle range (a bit disconcerting). Turn back at the end or at any other point. The trip back is just as scenic as the trip out. This is an excellent sunset hike.

Phoenix

Camelback Mountain–Echo Canyon Trail

2.4 miles round-trip. Moderate to difficult. 1,300-ft. elevation change. Allow 2 hrs. Access: From U.S. 17 within Phoenix turn east on Camelback Road and follow it to Camelback Mountain.

This hike takes you up the northwestern face of Phoenix's most prominent peak. A heavily traveled trail, it's a favorite daily exercise trek for many Phoenicians—more than 30,000 people hike it each year. The hike climbs to the top of the camel's hump, a mass of Precambrian granite nearly 1.5 billion years old, en route passing by a ceremonial grotto shrine that was sacred to the Hohokum tribe. The trail begins through a wash, then heads through forest of paloverde trees and saguaro cactus, where a sandstone slab rises 100 feet to the left. It climbs up 80 steps to a large boulder, a popular bouldering spot. At 0.25 miles it reaches a saddle where you'll get a view of northern Scottsdale, the McDowell Mountains, the Four Peaks, and the Superstition Mountains, all to the east. The trail flattens out for awhile and comes to a chain-link fence; then it climbs steeply up railroad-tie steps. Next you'll have the option of scrambling up "The Slab" or continuing on the trail. At 0.75 miles the trail gets steep and requires some boulder-hopping, finally reaching the peak at 2,704 feet, where you'll likely see swallows dipping in the breeze.

Superstition Mountains, East of Phoenix

Peralta Trail to Fremont Saddle

4 miles round-trip. Moderate. 1,370-ft. elevation gain. Allow 3 hrs. Access: From Apache Junction head southeast on U.S.

60 for 14 miles. Turn left (north) on the well-marked Peralta Rd. Follow this graded dirt road for 8 miles to the trailhead. Map: USFS Superstition Wilderness.

This amazing hike traverses classic Sonoran Desert on a winding trail that leads through a rhyolite spike-lined canyon to a big payoff. At the top you come to Fremont Saddle, which offers an awe-inspiring view of Weaver's Needle, the often-photographed spire. This route offers stunningly colorful views, especially when hiked at dusk. I arrived at the saddle an hour before sunset, when the trail was submerged in shadows, but the Needle was still brilliantly lit like a giant pottery shard sitting on end. The trail begins in a meandering way, fairly level and traveling across washes that initially seem confounding because the trail becomes obscure, but you can't really get lost here—just follow the most worn path (this is a fairly well-traveled trail). Soon the trail breaks away from the brushy lowlands and begins a gradual ascent up to the saddle. Be sure to look behind you and get a taste of the views you'll enjoy all the way back down—vast expanses of Superstition Wilderness layering out in blue folds to the east. The trail grows even steeper along a series of switchbacks. It comes to a cave under a rock and then makes its last dash to the saddle. Once on top you'll look over the other side at the spectacular Weaver's Needle, a rock spewed from a volcano some 15 to 35 million years ago.

HORSEBACK RIDING

If the red rocks of Sedona call your name with a bit of a western twang, or if you long to ride the range like those in movies such as *Broken Arrow, The Riders of the Purple Sage,* and *The Call of the Canyon,* you won't have trouble hitching up with someone who can help you. Even on the hottest days, riders will want to wear jeans and rugged shoes to protect them from thorny cactus. It's also a good idea to take along a handkerchief to protect your nose and mouth from dust. And bring at least 1 liter of water per person.

Trail Horse Adventures has ranches in Sedona, Scottsdale, Phoenix, Tempe, Cave Creek, and Apache Junction. They have 180 trail horses and professionally trained wranglers as well as event planners who can help you plan a small private outing or a large corporate offsite. Contact them at ☎ **800/723-3538** or e-mail: trails4u@sedona.net.

You can get a taste for what it was like to be a wrangler in the wild Wild West by saddling up for a ride with **A Day in the West** out of Sedona. This outfit will pick you up in town in a 4×4 Jeep, drive you to the ranch in 45 minutes, help you onto a horse for a 1-hour ride, and then drive you back to town. Prices range from $54.95 for the basic to $75 for a ride with a cookout dinner. Call ☎ **800/973-3662.**

For either day riding or a ranch experience in the Prescott area call the **Double D Ranch** (☎ **520/636-0418,** or look it up at www.ranchweb.com). In business for 10 years, the ranch has two guest room suites, with access to the entire ranch house. This is a true Western experience, not a touristy one. Visitors do what the ranch owners call "open ranch cross-country riding," allowing guests to ride to their ability. The ranch also organizes llama treks, fly-fishing trips, and wildlife tours to Sycamore Canyon and the Grand Canyon. This is not a B&B, nor a dude ranch situation. It's an experience for, as one of the proprietors says, "people with a sense of adventure in their souls." Children 12 years and older are invited.

For those who carry their own horses with them to the Prescott area, the **Cayuse Equestrian Area,** near Granite Mountain has lovely trails that wind through piñon/juniper forest and oddly shaped granite formations. For information, contact the Bradshaw Ranger district at ☎ **520/445-7253.**

Horseback riding in the Wickenburg area is a legendary experience. Surrounded by the Bradshaw and Wickenburg Ranges, with the ominous pinnacle Vulture Peak casting its shadow across a desert of saguaro and jumping cholla cactus, the area is so Western, you'll swear John Wayne is just up the next draw. Your best bet for a day of riding is **No Fences on Moonlight Mesa.** Owner and wrangler Dianna Tangen will ensure that you have a reliable steed and get a great tour of the area. She only takes small groups, so you won't be tenth in line on a nose-to-tail train. The cost for 1½- to 2-hour rides is $35; 5-hour rides into the notable Box Canyon run $60; or she'll tailor the experience to meet your needs. Call ☎ **520/684-3308** for reservations, or e-mail: dtangen@primenet.com.

If you're seeking a guest ranch experience, you're in luck—one of the best in Arizona is in Wickenburg. **Kay El Bar** is a model ranch, complete with 1920s adobe buildings and excellent mounts with equally competent wranglers to manage them and your riding experience. Rides take you through both private and public land in the saguaro-speckled hills located just minutes from Wickenburg. Rides range in length from 2 hours to all day, with a range of difficulty from first-time-on-a-steed to rodeo-cowboy. The accommodations are quiet, well renovated and have a dynamic Western theme. The food is superb, and there's a pool and hot tub to relax in—what more could you want? Call ☎ **800/684-7583** or 520/684-7593 or log on to www.kayelbar.com. Kay El Bar is located 2 miles east of Wickenburg on U.S. 89/93, and it's open October through early May. Minimum stay requirements vary from 2 to 4 days, depending on the season. Double occupancy, including meals, riding and other activities, costs $275 per day or $1,825 per week.

MOUNTAIN BIKING

Home base in Sedona for bikers runs in two veins. **Bike & Bean,** 6020 U.S. 179 in the village of Oak Creek (☎ **520/282-3515;** www.bike-bean.com), is where the more yuppie crowd hangs, while **Mountain Bike Heaven,** 1695 W. Highway 89A, Sedona (☎ **520/282-1312;** www.mountainbikeheaven.com), is where the penny-pinching bikers go. Either shop provides excellent trail directions, rentals, and gear for purchase. Bike & Bean will arrange to have someone take you out and show you trails, while Mountain Bike Heaven has scheduled "club rides" leaving the shop on certain days of the week. Both are great ways to get on the best rides for little money. As a courtesy you might want to tip your guide. While biking in this area you'll definitely want to pick up one of the hand-drawn biking maps sold at both stores.

A good home base in Prescott for bikers is **High Gear Bike Shop** (☎ **520/HI5-0636** or 520/HI5-8417) near downtown. The staff will help you find the trailhead and fix you up if your bike is broken. In Phoenix, stop in at **Bicycle Showcase,** at the corner of Shea Blvd. and Scottsdale Rd. (☎ **480/998-2776**). It rents and services all manner of bikes.

Sedona Area
Bell Rock Pathway
3–10 miles round-trip. Easy to moderate. 200-ft. elevation gain. Allow 1–3 hrs. Access: Take U.S. 179 south of Sedona about 10 miles until the village of Oak Creek comes into view; look to the left for the trailhead.

This is a perfect trail to initiate you into Sedona-area riding. It's also perfect for families. Full of amazing views in every direction, the trail will please adults, and it's broad enough so that kids won't get frustrated. Cutting off from it are a number of more challenging single-track routes to explore. Begin at the trailhead and ride north. The trail meanders before Courthouse Butte and then carves along the base of Bell Rock, continuing for 4.5 miles north. It's difficult to get lost if you just follow the cairns. Early on, you'll see the first turnoff for the Courthouse Loop. This will take you many more miles on more challenging single track that climbs somewhat, curves through washes, and zips through piñon/juniper forest. If you head out that direction, use Bell Rock and Courthouse Butte to keep your bearings. It's not easy to get lost on these trails, but local guides have plenty of stories about people who have succeeded in doing so.

Jim Thomspon–Midgley Bridge Trail

6 miles. Moderate to difficult. 500-ft. elevation gain. Allow 2 hrs. Access: Off Highway 89A in the center of Sedona, take Jordan Rd. until you reach a T intersection at Park Ridge Drive. Turn left and follow this road until it turns to dirt. Park here. You will have traveled 1 mile from the beginning of Jordan. You'll see the trailhead at the north end of the dirt parking area.

This is a majorly scenic trip up Mormon Canyon, then along the side of a monument face, and back down through town. The ascent is technical and rocky, as is the descent, but in between are miles of rolling single track. The trail heads east, making its way through an arroyo and then heads upward. People have rated this as a moderate trail, but I found the ascent very difficult. Later I learned that an active monsoon season had made it much more rocky than usual. Be aware that you may have to push your bike through rocky sections. This ascent continues for about 1.5 miles. Then the trail passes through a gate and begins its fast contour below Steamboat Rock. The hardest thing about this section is keeping your eye on the trail, since views scream "Look at me!" as you go. At about 3.5 miles the trail seems to end at a short loop. Look to your left for a way off the loop. This section is steep and rough; the trail crosses through a creek and onto Midgley Bridge, a busy, tourist-filled area. Be careful. If you'd like, you can lock your bike and make your way down to Oak Creek for a dip. Once you're back on your bike, it's a quick downhill back to Sedona. Take the shortcut right on Apple Road onto Jordan, and then it's a short jaunt back up to your car. Another option is to start this ride in town, and end there too!

Broken Arrow/Submarine Rock

10-mile loop. Difficult. 100-ft. elevation gain. Allow 2½–4 hrs. Access: Drive south of Sedona on U.S. 179 until you reach Morgan Rd. Follow it for 0.5 miles to a parking area. The trail begins across the road where the sign directs you to Chicken Point. For a less challenging beginning, you can also follow the jeep road to Chicken Point.

One of the funnest romps in Sedona, this trail leads through piñon/juniper forests, screams around turns, and pauses at some of the most spectacular vantage points in the west. Begin either on the Chicken Point Trail or on the continuation of Morgan Road. The Chicken Point Trail is well marked with basket cairns. It passes around a sinkhole and leads to a little side trail up to Submarine Rock. Then it continues through some rough single track to the Chicken Point vista, a rock you'll want to linger on. From there it heads through 2 miles of full-on, downhill fun until it connects up with the Bell Rock Pathway. Turn north (right) here and follow the pathway back to Morgan Road and your vehicle. You may want to pick up a map for this ride at Bike & Bean or Mountain Bike Heaven.

Cathedral Rock

12-mile loop. Moderate to difficult. 250-ft. elevation gain. Allow 4 hrs. Access: Begin at the Circle K in the village of Oak Creek. Follow Bell Rock Blvd. west for 1.1 miles to Verde Valley School Rd. Turn northwest (right) and travel 2 miles until the pavement ends. Travel 1 more mile to where the trail heads off to the right.

Another of Sedona's primo rides, this trail takes you around the very base of one of the area's most elaborate monuments.

Cathedral Rock is also one of Sedona's big vortices. Some people say being this close to the monument will help strengthen your feminine side (or the parts of you that deal with kindness and compassion), though you'll definitely want that testosterone pumping for the climbs.

You'll see Cathedral Rock to your right. The trail heads through a steep bouldery section to a gate. Then it veers east along Oak Creek at what's called Buddha Beach, and continues to climb, making its way around the very edge of Cathedral Rock. The views from up there are amazing, and you'll want to stop and catch your breath and take them in before beginning the descent back down toward U.S. 179. Continue past a gravel pit to a tunnel that will take you over to the Bell Rock Pathway. Follow the Pathway back to the Trailhead and the Circle K where you left your car. Pick up a map for this ride at Bike & Bean or Mountain Bike Heaven.

Deadman's Pass Loop (and Cockscomb Loop)
6.4-mile loop. Moderate. 150-ft. elevation gain. Allow 2 hrs. Access: From the junction of 89A and U.S. 179 drive 3.2 miles west on 89A to Dry Creek Rd. Turn right and drive 2.9 miles to the T intersection. Turn left (this is all 152C) and follow it to the next T intersection. Turn left and drive to the Fay Canyon Trailhead. The trail begins just across the road from the trailhead parking lot. Pick up a map at Bike & Bean or Mountain Bike Heaven.

This trail has lots of drops and dips along single track and double track. It has some fun downhill romps and leads through the Boynton Canyon Vortex, a place cyclers ought to like because its power supposedly deals with balance, though I find that generally just keeping my pedals horizontal will do the trick on the downhill.

The trail heads southeast through the red dirt and connects with the Powerline double track, which it follows for a ways. Beware of a blind ditch in this section. Watch your left; the trail takes off from there, going east until it connects with the pavement of FS 152C and 152D. It makes its way up to the Long Canyon Trail. From this trail, the route goes left onto Deadman's Pass Trail, a fast and fun single track behind Mescal Mountain. This leads you back to the pavement of Boynton Canyon Road where you'll turn left. The pavement eventually turns to dirt, which leads you back to the Fay Canyon Trailhead.

Also heading off from this spot is the Cockscomb Loop, an intermediate 6-mile trail that begins in the same place, following the Powerline Trail, but turns right (south) and follows mostly jeep roads in a broad circle contouring Doe Mountain. This ride takes you through some of Sedona's most beautiful red rock spires, where you may want to stop and climb to the top for, as northern Arizona biking guru Cosmic Ray calls it, "420° views." Begin as you did the Deadman's Loop, but once on the Powerline Trail and past the blind ditch, turn right on an old jeep road double-track trail. When you reach an area of deciduous trees take the single track right through a gate. The single track crosses a jeep road, but you'll continue straight. Soon you'll come to a good place to stash your bike and find the trail, which will take you to the top of the Cockscomb, a 400-foot-tall spire. Follow the cairns. Once back on your bike, continue on single track along the fence until you reach a gravel road. Go left for 1 mile until you reach Boynton Pass Road. Go right back to the Fay Canyon Parking Lot. You can combine these two rides to form a figure eight.

McDowell Mountains near Phoenix
Pemberton Loop
15-mile loop. Moderate. 800-ft. elevation gain. Allow 3 hrs. Access: Located in the McDowell Mountain Regional Park (15 miles northeast of Scottsdale). Take Shea Blvd. east from Scottsdale; turn left

onto Fountain Hills Blvd and follow this road to the park on your left. You'll find a map to all the trailheads at the park entrance. $3 self-pay fee.

This great desert cruising trail works its way on a slow grade toward McDowell Mountains and follows along their foothills until it drops back down. The grade is gradual; however, the trail descends down into and climbs up out of a few washes. These present some fun, rocky technical sections that are especially interesting when you're coming down from the McDowell Mountains. Though this is a loop ride, you don't have to do the whole loop, since an up-and-back is equally lovely and enjoyable. The trail is well marked and easy to follow. It travels though serious desert, crossing McDowell Mountain Park Drive, then makes its way mountainward, through smooth washes and up a technical section, with views of the McDowell Mountains all the way. It cruises along the base of the foothills, then turns away from them, at which time the descent begins in earnest, and the views become spectacular, with waves upon waves of blue created by the Superstition and other mountains. The trail crosses McDowell Mountain Park Drive again before returning to the parking lot. This is a multiple-use trail; watch for hikers and horseback riders.

McDowell Competitive Track

3–14 miles loops. Easy to advanced. 150-ft. elevation gain. Allow 1–3 hrs. Access: See Pemberton Trail access above. Once you're in McDowell Mountain Regional Park ($3 fee) you'll find this trailhead a short distance from the park entrance on your left. At the park entrance you'll find a map that shows the three rides available here.

These consciously designed trails provide any level rider with the best single track has to offer, in a scenic desert setting. They remind me of a ride we used to do when I was a kid on our little banana-seat bikes out in an area in Albuquerque called "the Boondocks." These trails take you over all kinds of whoop-te-doos, up and down washes, over hills, and around banked corners. It all happens very fast and furiously. Unlike the Pemberton Loop, which is more of a cruiser run, this is all fast action. There are three different trails. The Long Loop runs 6 miles around fast-action single track. The Sports Loop is a shorter version of the Long Loop, though the two tracks don't repeat themselves. The Technical Loop is similar to the others except it has more drops, more technical climbs, and more rocky areas. If you do all three you'll ride 14 miles. The trails are also scenic. They climb and descend through the desert at the base of the McDowell Mountains. All trails are very well marked with road-sign-like commands telling you when to do things such as slow down and merge. From the area you can even see Weaver's Needle sticking up ominously out of the Superstition Mountains.

Desert Classic Trail

10 miles one-way. Moderate. Allow 24 hrs. Access: In Phoenix, take I-10 south to the Baseline Exit and turn west on 48th St. Once you get on 48th St. you go through a residential area over umpteen speed bumps—serious, extreme bumps. After you're through with them, you'll see the turn to your right, marked by a very subtle sign for South Mountain Park. If you come to a major street, which is Guadalupe, you've gone too far.

Finding this trail isn't as easy as the directions make it out to be. Fortunately for me, someone guessed I was lost and stopped and showed me the way to the park. That was Lex, who turned out to be my guide for the day. We ended up biking this fun romp through the South Mountains together. Lex is a crop duster who spends his off-season sunning in Phoenix, so he had plenty of adrenaline to burn onto the trail. Fortunately, he'd already ridden once that day, so we didn't have to spill any blood. Not that this trail would necessarily prompt such an occurrence. The trail is very fun, fast, hard-packed single track, interspersed with some rocky and sandy sections. It weaves and turns and dips up and down for miles and miles, none of it very difficult, all very fun, for up to 10 miles out and then back. This trail doesn't provide the kind of beauty you'll find out in the McDowell Mountains. It's a much more urban setting. In fact, it follows along a residential area for the first 4 miles or so until breaking out into real desert expanses. When you're in close to the residential area it is desert, but you can tell there's a stress on the system. The variety of plants is low, and many of the cacti look as though they're not healthy. Once you get away from the suburban area you can really see the desert flower and grow. There's much more variety—a much more healthy ecosystem. Coming back is even more of a scream than going out because there's a bit of a descent. It's a total riot.

In the same park you'll find the **National Trail** and the **Mormon Loop.** Both head off from a 1.3-mile service road (closed to vehicles), which is a nice chitchat ride if you like to ride side-by-side before hitting single track. The road reaches a saddle from which the two trails depart. The National Trail is very technical with big ledges and boulders to cross, recommended for experts only. The Mormon Trail is gentler. It ascends for awhile and then has a long, very sweet descent along the rest of the loop back to the parking lot.

Prescott

Thumb Butte Loop Trails (also known as White Rock Loop Trails)

12 miles of loop trails. Moderate. 100-ft. elevation gain. Allow 2–3 hrs. Access: From Courthouse Square in downtown Prescott, travel 3.5 miles on Gurley St. (It becomes Thumb Butte Rd.). Park in the Thumb Butte parking area on your right. If you reach a dirt road, you've gone too far. $2 self-pay fee.

These fun trails cruise through ponderosa forest at the base of Thumb Butte. They're a favorite of locals (probably because it's one place where you don't have to climb a rock-strewn peak). To turn this into an interesting loop ride, head west out of the parking lot on Thumb Butte Road. Just before the road turns to dirt, watch to your left for a trail. This trail follows the creek in an easterly direction for about a mile until it makes its way back up onto Thumb Butte Road. Follow the road for over 0.5 miles, watching on your right for Dugan Camp Rd. and a white-painted rock. Look for the trail on the northeast corner of this intersection. Though you won't encounter a marker for awhile, you're on Trail 318. It heads down smooth single track, with some fun rocky technical sections into the woods where it meets up with other trails. A good bet is to follow 318 to 316, where you'll turn left, staying on 316 as it cruises around and becomes 315, which makes its way back to where you parked your car. Other variations make for fun biking, so mix it up and enjoy.

Another option in this area is to follow the many old logging roads that traverse Thumb Butte. To get to them continue east from the parking lot on Thumb Butte Road (a fairly busy dirt road) for a number of miles watching for FS 51 on your left. This double track will wind around and finally reconnect (farther down) with Thumb Butte Road. You'll find many other roads traversing this one—a good chance to explore, though you may want to bring along a compass.

Spruce Mountain

9-mile loop. Difficult. 1,300-ft. elevation gain. Allow 2–3 hrs. Access: From Courthouse Square, travel 6 miles east on E. Gurley. Turn right on S. Mt. Vernon St. (Senator Highway). After 7.6 miles turn into the parking lot for Trail 307 on your left. If the road turns to dirt, you've gone too far.

As I made my way down the last romping mile of this challenging single-track loop, I met up with a hiker. He high-fived me just for having survived this trail. Renowned in this part of the world, this is the kind of ponderosa forest single track that invites bikers from Sedona over the mountain to Prescott. Do this loop clockwise, beginning at the north side (the direction of Prescott) of the parking area. The first few miles follow relatively smooth but steep single track through woods, with some technical, rocky sections thrown in to prepare you for what's to come. You'll pass through a wilderness gate, and then the real grind begins—over a mile of tough, rocky, relentless climbing, which may find you off your bike more than on (excluding you real hair-bikers). Finally the trail reaches the summit. Head to the left to the lookout spot and take in views of the San Francisco Peaks and Mingus Mountain to the north and the Bradshaws to the south. Then clip in for a fast and wild romp down—5.5 miles of non-stop single track that definitely isn't easy; it's full of rocky outcrops that test your skills as well as banked turns and lots of trees to miss. At one point toward the end of the descent you may be confused by a sign that points cryptically between two trails and says 307, which is the one you want to follow; I had to stand at different angles to figure out which direction to go. Bear right, and follow the trail back to your car.

Peavine Trail

4.6 miles one-way. Easy. No elevation change. Allow 1–2 hrs. Access: From Prescott, head north on AZ 89 for just over one mile to Sun Dog Ranch Rd. Turn right and drive 1.3 miles to the trailhead on your left.

For years hikers and bikers have had limited access to the Granite Dells. These truly stupendous rock formations minutes from Prescott are primarily privately owned. Recently, though, a trail was opened that traverses the old railroad bed that cuts through the Dells. This is one of the loveliest places in Arizona. The first 0.5 miles takes you past some industrial sites. Then you come upon the stunning blue of Watson Lake. Beyond it are the oddly shaped Dells, like lumps of gold, sticking up in whatever direction they choose. The trail runs along the shore of the lake, then enters the Dells. As you go, watch for spur trails where you may want to park your bike and skip and jump over the bold rock faces—these Dells will definitely invite you into their folds. The trail continues through the strange undulating stones for a number of miles. It passes close to a rifle range (a bit disconcerting). Turn back at the end or at any other point. The trip back is just as scenic.

ROAD BIKING

Fountain Hills Loop

About 45 miles. Moderate. Allow 3–4 hrs. Access: From Scottsdale Rd. in Phoenix turn east on Shea Blvd. and continue to Pima Rd.

This scenic ride on the outskirts of Phoenix circumnavigates the McDowell Mountains, providing lots of good pavement and some awesome views. Most of it is out of traffic, with nice shoulders and rolling hills to keep your pulse working, but not overworking. Begin at the corner of Shea Boulevard and Pima Road in northeastern Phoenix. Head east on Shea; turn left on Palisades Boulevard, which will take you to Fountain Hills Boulevard, where you'll turn left. This becomes McDowell Mountain Road. Follow it straight into Rio Verde, and turn left on Rio Verde Drive, which you follow to Pima Road. Turn left and return to your car.

Apache Trail

36 miles round-trip. Moderate. Allow 3–5 hrs. Access: Head east from Phoenix on U.S. 60 to Apache Junction; turn left on AZ 88, also known as the Apache Trail.

This lovely highway snakes along the north side of the Superstition Mountains, offering incredibly scenic pedaling with stops at a ghost town and a lake. This is part of a notable auto loop, including some dirt road, connecting Apache Junction, Theodore Roosevelt Lake, and the towns of Globe, and Superior. I'm only recommending the paved section of AZ 88 to Tortilla Flats because much of the rest of the loop is on busy highway and some dirt road. Start riding north from Apache Junction. At mile 3.5 you'll come to Goldfield Ghost Town, 1890s vintage and reconstructed with tourist trappings such as gift and ice cream shops, but there is the Superstition Mountains/Lost Dutchman Museum worth checking out if you're interested in the mysterious gold mine, famous mostly because it has never been found. Nearby is the Lost Dutchman State Park, a good place to hike and camp. AZ 88 continues northeasterly arriving at Canyon Lake, which provides much of Phoenix's drinking water. This is a good place to stop and take a dip, or jump on the Dolly Steamboat for a 90-minute cruise. After the lake, continue pedaling to Tortilla Flat, an old stagecoach stop, with a restaurant, saloon, and general store. Here you'll find walls papered with business cards and more than $50,000 worth of dollar bills pinned to the walls. Many theories circulate as to how the tradition of pinning up bills came about, but one thing is certain—it endures. Every month the restaurant accumulates a 5-gallon bucket full of bills from all over the world, which are then papered onto the walls from floor to ceiling. For a taste-adventure before you head back, try its prickly pear ice cream.

If you're doing this ride on a mountain bike, you may want to continue on after the road turns to dirt and make your way to Apache Lake, Roosevelt Lake, and the Salado ruins at Tonto National Monument. At any point you can turn around and return the way you came.

SWIMMING & TUBING

One of the most pleasant surprises I had while exploring central Arizona is how much water is available for swimming. In fact, of any region in this entire book, you'll find the most swimming holes in this area. Not all are easy to get to, which makes them even more delectable. If you're wanting something very accessible, but don't mind crowds, head to **Slide Rock State Park** (☎ 520/282-3034). Located 6 miles north of Sedona, this park preserves a natural water slide and long lazy pools flowing over algae-covered sandstone. It's open daily, with a small admission fee. Downstream and closer to Sedona at **Grasshopper Point** more swimming is available, with a small fee as well. At many of the pullouts along AZ 89A you'll find cool pools worth dunking into, for free; you can even take your pets to these.

The premier swimming hole in the area is in **Wet Beaver Creek,** but it's a good 8-mile round-trip hike through lovely Sonoran Desert. See "Hikes & Backpack Trips" earlier in this chapter for a full review. Not quite so elaborate a pool, nor so distant a hike, the **West Clear Creek Canyon** has lovely pools worth dipping into; as with Wet Beaver Creek, see "Hikes & Backpack Trips" for details. Outside Phoenix, some like to inner tube down the lower **Salt River.** The activity takes place in northeast Mesa on Power Road, 15 miles north of U.S. 60. Contact **Arizona's Salt River Tubing** (☎ 480/984-3305). Tubes cost $10 per day, and the season runs from May to October.

WALKS & RAMBLES

Sedona Area

Montezuma's Well

1 mile round-trip. Easy. 150-ft. elevation gain. Allow 45 min. Access: Head south of Sedona on I-17 and take Exit 289.

Montezuma's Well is a water-filled sinkhole, unique because it's surrounded by cliff dwellings and, on the outlying hills, mounds from larger dwellings once inhabited by the Sinagua people. The Sinagua built their homes on hills and mesas in this area from about A.D. 700 to the early 1400s. Measuring 365 feet across and 65 feet deep, the well holds water so rich in carbon dioxide that fish can't live there, but algae, amphipods (like shrimp), and leaches fare nicely, as do turtles. Walnut trees and lush vines also inhabit the nearly tropical environment above water-level within the hole. The water leaves the hole through an exit, the beginning of an irrigation ditch that the Sinagua carved along the valley (lower Wet Beaver Creek) below, in order to irrigate squash, corn, and beans. The paved trail leads to an observation platform, along the rim to some mounds, and down to the irrigation canal. If this whets your appetite for more Sinagua history, head south on I-17 and take Exit 289 to **Montezuma Castle National Monument,** one of the best-preserved Sinagua cliff dwellings in Arizona. It consists of two stone pueblos, one set in a cave 100 feet above Beaver Creek.

Red Rocks in Sedona

It's not difficult to see Sedona's red rocks. Just look above you in any direction and there they'll be. However, if you want a closer view of them, here are a few suggestions: Drive south of Sedona on AZ 179 to Bell Rock on the east side of the road. There you'll find a parking area and trails leading up to the top of this monumental formation. From there you'll see the most photographed formation in Sedona, Cathedral Rock, to the west. Adjacent to Bell Rock is Courthouse Butte. After leaving Bell Rock, continue south on A179 to Schnebly Hill Road (a left-hand turn just after you cross the bridge over Oak Creek). This unpaved road suitable for high-clearance vehicles, climbs and winds into the hills, yielding views at every turn, surpassed only by the final vista at the rim overlook.

Oak Creek Canyon Overlook

North of Sedona on AZ 89A. Allow 10 minutes.

To stand on the forested edge of the Mogollon Rim and look down a canyon to the vastness of Sedona's sculpted wonderland is to know some little thing about the contrasts that await you in this transition zone between the Colorado Plateau and the Great Basin and Range Province. Notice that one rim of the canyon is lower than the other. Oak Creek Canyon is on a geologic fault line, so one side of the canyon is moving in a different direction than the other. If you can catch this view between late September and mid-October, the canyon will likely be a fiery spectacle, with red and yellow leaves. Also on AZ 89A through Oak Creek Canyon is **Garlands General Store** in Indian Gardens, about 4 miles north of Sedona. Available here is delicious organic apple juice made from apples grown in the canyon. Still closer to town is **Midgely Bridge** (look for a small parking lot at the north end of the bridge) allows for a precipitous view down into Oak Creek Canyon.

Palatki Ruin

2 miles. Easy. 25-ft. elevation gain. Allow 1½ hrs. Access: From Sedona head west on AZ 89A 9 miles to FS 525. Turn right and continue driving past the intersection with FS 525C. At 5.8 miles you'll veer right onto FS 795. Follow this road 2 miles to the Red Canyon Ranch site.

This ruin is a favorite of many locals because it allows visitors to explore one of the largest ruins in the red rock region without the watchful eye of Big Brother. With that freedom comes the responsibility to care for these fragile ruins by not straying from the path and definitely not climbing upon these walls built over 700 years ago. The ruins sit at the base of the spectacular red sandstone cliffs of Bear Mountain and at the boundary of Red Rock–Secret Mountain Wilderness. They were once the home of the Sinagua culture, a name derived from Spanish and meaning without (*sin*) water (*agua*). The Sinagua lived at this site between 1100 and 1300 in oval-shaped masonry homes that have vestibule entries. The trails meander through what are believed to be two separate pueblos suggesting that two family or kin groups inhabited the site. The smaller, western pueblo has one of the largest accumulations of pictographs in this region. The word *palatki* is derived from the Hopi word meaning "place among the red rocks." Historians trace the Sinagua to the modern Hopi people who live in eastern Arizona.

Devil's Bridge Trail

2 miles round-trip. Easy. 350-ft. elevation gain. Allow 1½ hrs. Access: In Sedona at the junction of AZ 89A and AZ 179, drive west on 89A for 3.2 miles to Dry Creek Rd. Turn right and drive 1.9 miles to FS 152. Turn right on this dirt road and drive 1.4 miles to the trailhead parking area on the right.

This easy route allows you to view one of Sedona's most spectacular natural bridges against the backdrop of Secret and Long Canyons. The trail begins gently climbing an old road. At 0.4 mile the road ends, and the trail turns south, entering the wilderness. Shortly the trail ascends more steeply and the Devil's Bridge comes into view. At 0.7 mile the trail forks. Follow the main trail up rock steps, which climb the cliff face, then behind the top of the arch from which you'll see expansive views. On the way back down, follow the other, narrow trail to the base of the bridge. This bridge was formed after a fracture separated a slab of sandstone from the main wall. Erosion worked on both sides of the slab sluicing away all but the hardest stone creating a hole. This trail had no shade and will be very hot in summer.

Doe Mountain Trail

1.5 miles round-trip. Easy. 400-ft. elevation gain. Allow 1½–2 hrs. Access: In Sedona at the junction of AZ 89A and AZ 179, head west 3.2 miles to Dry Creek Rd. Turn right and travel 2.9 miles to a T intersection. Turn left on Boyton Pass Rd. and travel 1.6 miles to another T. Turn left and drive 1.2 miles on a dirt road to the Bear Mountain Trail parking area. The Doe Mountain Trailhead is across the road.

This is good hike to take when you first arrive in Sedona. From the top of this mesa you'll have 360° views of the area, giving you a strong sense of where each of the monuments stands and where you'll want to go. The trail travels through piñon/juniper forest, crisscrossing the mountain in a gradual ascent. Near the top it passes through a narrow red rock chute that leads to steps. Once on top, you'll be able to see Mingus Mountain and the old mining town of Jerome. You might want to walk around the top of the mesa, a distance of about 1.3 miles, but before you do, take note of where you came up, so you can find your way back down. From the north side you can see Mescal Mountain, Enchantment Resort, and Boynton Canyon. Heading east, you'll see Wilson Mountain, Capitol Butte, Schnebly Hill, and Sedona. From the south edge, you'll see Courthouse, Bell, and Cathedral Rocks and the vast Verde Valley in the distance. Back on the western edge you'll see Robber's Roost and Casner and Black Mountains.

Cathedral Rock

1.5 miles round-trip. Moderate. 600-ft. elevation gain. Allow 2 hrs. Access: In Sedona at the junction of AZ 89A and AZ 179, take AZ 179 south 3.5 miles to Back-O' Beyond Rd. Turn right and travel 0.6 mile to the trailhead parking area on the left.

This hike takes you into the heart of one of Sedona's most prominent monuments, and, for those who are curious about such things, into the center of one of Sedona's most powerful vortices. It's a fairly steep, rocky climb on a trail well marked with basket-cairns. The trail begins by crossing a wash and heading up a moderate slope toward the spires. At 0.25 miles, it comes to a ledge and the first place to stop and take in some views. The climb steepens over slick rock, in a step-like fashion that might remind you of climbing Chichén Itzá or other stone temples in the Mexican Yucatan. It emerges on a small knob, where cairns show the way up and across several ledges toward a drainage, which it climbs to a saddle between two spires. From here you can see Snoopy and Steamboat Rocks, as well as Wilson Mountain and Oak Creek Canyon. An unmaintained path leads south along the base of the spires to two more saddles. This trail has little shade and will be very hot in summer. The energy of this vortex is supposed to strengthen the feminine side, which is said to relate to kindness, compassion, and patience—traits you may need as you leave this incredible spot the way you came and head back into the wearying pace of Sedona itself.

Wilson Canyon Trail

2 miles round-trip. Easy. 380-ft. elevation gain. Allow 1½–2 hrs. Access: In Sedona at the junction of AZ 89A and AZ 179, head north for 1.1 miles across Midgely Bridge. Turn left into the parking area.

This trail winds through Arizona cypress stands, with spectacular views of red-bluff cliffs, then enters a canyon where it snakes along through riparian habitat full of wildlife. The trail begins east of Midgley Bridge on fairly level ground initially following an old jeep road. The hike follows along below Steamboat Rock, then enters the riparian canyon where small pools feed grass and wildflowers. Soon it enters the Red Rock–Secret Mountain Wilderness area. Next the trail crosses to the left side of the wash and moves along a massive boulder field. The trail comes to a natural dam where hummingbirds might be seen. Farther along look high up the canyon wall for a waterfall that tumbles off the top of the mountain during spring runoff and late-summer monsoon. The hike ends at a log and rock jam. The area is named for Richard Wilson, a bear hunter who was killed by a bear in the canyon in 1885.

McDowell Mountains Outside Phoenix

Lousley Hill Trail

1.2 miles round-trip. Easy. 200-ft. elevation gain. Allow 1 hr. Access: In McDowell Mountain Regional Park (15 miles northeast of Scottsdale). Take Shea Blvd. east from Scottsdale; turn left onto Fountain Hills Blvd. The park is on your left.

This hike doesn't look like much—a semi-bald hill with flat desert immediately surrounding it, but that's not the reason you climb it. Once you're on top you have a full 360° view of the McDowell Mountains to west, the Superstition Mountains to east, and even Weaver's Needle. You'll get a sense of the Great Basin area and these wonderful volcanic features that have thrust up from the floor through the extension process. The trail climbs steadily up at a not-too-strenuous grade. You might get lost if you were blindfolded.

WILDLIFE VIEWING

Due to its isolation, **Sycamore Canyon** is a good place to find wild animals, though they are quite wily, so you'll have to be on your toes to see them. Once we spent a few nights camping along the Dogie Trail there; upon departing the wilderness, we ran into a couple of ATV riders who said that from a hill they had observed four black bears circling our camp at dawn and a javelina drinking from a spring a little later, none of which we observed. However, that same day we did have a rattlesnake encounter. The canyon is also home to ring-tailed cat, bobcat, and mountain lion. Similar sightings may be seen in the upper reaches of **West Clear Creek Canyon** and **Wet Beaver Creek.** Mule deer are also plentiful in these areas.

Campgrounds & Other Accommodations

CAMPING

Sedona Area

During much of the time I spent in the Sedona area I camped in the **Coconino National Forest** outside town. I'd spend my day hiking and then find a campsite close to wherever I ended up. Forest roads traverse the area and camping is allowed at large anywhere except in a very well-defined area in the vicinity of Sedona. That area includes all the red rock country to the north of town, Oak Creek Canyon, both east and west of U.S. 179 from Sedona down to Oak Creek Village, and across to the Doe Mountain area to the west. The National Forest Service provides a map that defines the area and also gives campfire restrictions. There are also signs posted around the perimeter of Sedona explaining where you can and can't camp. Good areas to head for are the Sycamore Canyon area west of Sedona and the Beaver Creek area to the east.

Oak Creek Canyon Campgrounds

North of Sedona on AZ 89A along the lovely Oak Creek Canyon, the National Forest Service (☎ **520/282-4119**) maintains five campgrounds. All are nestled within the shady forest that defines this canyon, and all can be crowded during the busy seasons, particularly summer and into October. Manzanita, 6 miles north of Sedona, is my favorite, while Banjo Bill, 8 miles north of town, is also nice, and Bootlegger, 9 miles north of Sedona, is the largest. Reservations can be made at Cave Spring, 12 miles north of town, and Pine Flat, 13 miles north of town, by calling the National Recreation Reservation Service (☎ **877/444-6777**). All campgrounds have toilet facilities, fire rings, and grills, and Cave Springs has shower facilities. None have RV hookups. Some are too small to accommodate RVs at all; for example, no trailers are allowed at Bootlegger or Manzanita. However, Cave Spring and Pine Flat east and west will accommodate larger vehicles. Cost for all campsites is $15 per night. Be aware that 85% of the sites are available on a first-come, first-served basis so arrive as early as possible. On busy weekends reservable spots will be booked months in advance.

Prescott

Yavapai Campground near Granite Mountain
From the Town Square in Prescott, head west on Montezuma, which will become Iron Springs Rd. Drive 4.5 miles to FS 374. Turn right and drive a short distance looking for the campground on your left. ☎ **520/445-7253**. 25 sites, with space for RVs under 40 feet but no hookups. Grill, firepit, toilet facilities, water. $10 per night. Open daily year-round.

The best thing about this campground is its access to the Granite Mountain Wilderness, an awesome land of oddly shaped granite formations interspersed with piñon/juniper and ponderosa pine forest. The campground itself is nestled within pines, a generally quiet place that does get crowded during summer and on holiday weekends. All sites are available on a first-come, first-served basis. Altogether there are six campgrounds within a 10-mile radius of Prescott. Call the number above for locations.

Phoenix Area

Lost Dutchman State Park
5 miles north of Apache Junction on AZ 88. ☎ **602/982-4485**. 35 campsites (no hookups). visitor center with maps, grills, rest rooms, and showers. Open daily year-round.

With the Superstition Mountains towering over this park, it's a lovely place to camp. Nearby there's plenty to explore, from trails in the park to ghost towns along the Apache Trail. The park was named after Jacob "Dutchman" Waltz who hiked these mountains in search of gold. One of the highlights is an educational program offered to campers in the evenings on desert creatures, the old Dutchman himself, and other topics. For hiking buffs, there are several rugged trails heading into the Superstition Wilderness.

Picacho Peak State Park
Off I-10, 60 miles south of Phoenix and 40 miles north of Tucson. ☎ 520/466-3183. 100 campsites (first-come, first-served basis) with or without hookups, grills, trails, playground, rest rooms, and showers. Open daily year-round.

Though a large and often busy campground, if you're looking to camp between Phoenix and Tucson, this is a good place to stop. The campsites sit at the base of Picacho Peak, which rises 2,000 feet above the desert floor.

INNS & LODGES
Sedona
Briar Patch Inn
3190 N. Highway 89A, Sedona, AZ 86336. ☎ 888/809-3030 or 520/282-2342. www.sedona.net/bb/briarpch. 16 units. A/C. $149–$295 double. Rates include full breakfast. MC, V.

Shade. Come mid-summer in central Arizona it's at a premium. As is flowing water. Both can be had in abundance at this inn 3 miles north of Sedona on the shores of Oak Creek. Set on 8.5 acres, this smattering of cottages provides a rustically tranquil stay with hints of lavishness. The cottages—built in the 1930s—have a Western feel, with rough pine walls, but have delicate touches such as fine bedding. Most have fireplaces and kitchenettes. Type A personalities might be a bit unnerved by the fact that the only phone is a communal payphone, but even those sorts will love the deep swimming hole just feet from the cottages and the full breakfast served either fire- or creekside. The innkeepers here can provide good directions about where to hike and bike.

Sky Ranch Lodge
Airport Rd. (P.O. Box 2579), Sedona, AZ 86339. ☎ 888/708-6400 or 520/282-6400. 94 units. A/C TV TEL. $75–$150 double. AE, MC, V. Pets accepted with $10 charge.

With one of the most awesome views in town, this motel atop Airport Mesa is a good, reasonably priced choice. These are fairly standard motel-style rooms, the more expensive ones with private patios and balconies with views. Some have stone fireplaces and some have kitchenettes. Though some of the rooms could use sprucing up, all are very clean. Fountains, meandering pathways, and flower gardens enhance the experience, as does the outdoor swimming pool.

Prescott
Rocamadour Bed & Breakfast for (Rock) Lovers
3386 N Highway 89, Prescott, AZ 86301. ☎ 888/771-1933 or 520/771-1933. 4 units. A/C TV TEL. $95–$195 double. Rates include full breakfast. No credit cards.

This B&B manages to combine cozy and chic in a unique rock landscape. It sits in the heart of the Granite Dells, a formation that's mostly privately owned, so access is limited. From the doorstep you can hike out across the smooth, undulating stone to views across central Arizona. The inn's rooms have a decidedly French feel, with luxurious robes and elaborate furnishings. Two of the units have private Jacuzzis; all have views of the Dells. The hospitality is lavish as well, honed when the innkeepers Mike and Twila Coffey owned a 40-room chateau in France.

Gourmet breakfasts are served in the main room, which looks out upon the Dells.

Phoenix

Hacienda Alta

5750 E. Camelback Rd., Phoenix, AZ 85018. ☎ **602/945-8525.** 3 units. A/C TV. $100–$150 double. No credit cards.

Built in the 1920s at the base of Camelback Mountain, this hacienda-style home maintains a secluded feel, despite the fact that Scottsdale has grown in around it. The property abuts the Phoenician Hotel's golf course so you'll always smell freshly cut grass. The hosts are very accommodating as well as eccentric enough to make your stay memorable. Rooms are homey feeling, decorated in Southwestern style. With a sleeping loft and fold-out couch, the casita is good for families. *Note:* Busy Scottsdale street noise does penetrate through the thickly grown vines and orange trees.

6

Arizona's White Mountains

My first adventure through eastern Arizona's White Mountains (often locally referred to as the "Alps") took place many years ago on a drive from Albuquerque to Tucson with my father. My father is the ideal travel companion; he always brings along fresh apples from his orchards in Albuquerque and fresh oranges from his little grove in Tucson. He carries a cooler full of his own home-grown green chile, basil, cilantro, tomatoes, and bell peppers. Before we set out he has our route planned, always with a stop somewhere lovely to eat lunch. This trip, our stop was to be the Salt River Canyon.

En route to the Salt, we crossed vast lava fields and rolling hills of bleached knee-high grass in the Springerville area and then into the lushness of the White Mountains. We made our way past many mountain lakes; there are some 40 of them in the area, I later learned, making the place ripe for boating, swimming, and fishing. We drove through endless stands of ponderosas—the largest stand in the world, in fact—then south across the 1,664,874-acre Fort Apache Indian Reservation, which also holds some of the state's best fishing and its best ski area, Sunrise Park Resort. We made our way down off the Mogollon Rim (pronounced MUG-e-own), a 2,000-foot-high escarpment that stretches 200 miles across the center of Arizona, making for major climactic differences. Then we dropped down into the domain of the Salt. The river cuts an intent gash through a canyon, and the highway winds poetically down to its base and crosses this river that ranges in character from boisterous to serene depending on the season.

At the base of the canyon we sat on my dad's tailgate and ate all the things he'd grown, along with smoked oysters on good sourdough bread. I was mesmerized. Never had I imagined that Arizona could hold lands such as I'd seen that day. Like its neighbor New Mexico, the state had many more surprises than I knew of, and I was determined to explore them further. Subsequent trips in this region have taken me on hikes across broad meadows and through golden stands of aspen, and to the second highest peak in the state, the 11,590-foot Mount Baldy. I've skied lovely cross-country trails through the woods, and biked some of the smoothest and sweetest single track in the Southwest. These activities—hiking, biking, skiing, and white-water rafting—are the ones to enjoy in the region.

My only complaint about the region is the people pressure it receives from nearby Phoenix. This is the place Phoenicians come in the summer to get cool, and in the winter to ski, and though the pressure lessens as you near the New Mexico border, it is definitely creeping its way across, with places such as Pinetop and Lakeside losing their rural feel and becoming like cities themselves. Still, there are very quiet pockets within this region—Greer, Alpine, and Hannigan Meadow, for instance, are nearly deserted at some times of year, and almost anywhere in these mountains, if you hike a half-day in, you'll likely find yourself alone.

The region has a rich historical background in evidence throughout the area. Along the New Mexico border in the Springerville area, the Mogollon people, a large prehistoric community dating back to around 1300, lived and farmed in the area, leaving a record of their time in the well-preserved archaeological site called Casa Malpais. One of the most scenic drives in the region, the winding Scenic Highway 191, a 120-mile stretch along the edges of the Apache-Sitgreaves National Forest, follows the route Spanish explorer Francisco Vásquez de Coronado used coming north in search of the fabled Seven Cities of Cíbola in 1540. Eastern Arizona is an area that still holds the feel of the trappers, traders, and other Western pioneers who settled it, with century-old log cabins hidden in the woods, and old stone fences marking territory. In fact, this was where cowboy author Zane Grey lived and worked, hunting the mountains to help feed his hungry appetite for writing. Though a forest fire destroyed his cabin, the Zane Grey Museum still commemorates his presence in the Payson area.

The Lay of the Land

A 1,158-square-mile White Mountain Volcanic Field extends from Show Low to Springerville and from Greer to just south of St. Johns. The central point of this field is Mount Baldy, the second highest peak in the state. An extinct volcano that last erupted about 10 million years ago, it is composed of a layer of volcanic rock at least 4,000 feet thick. Its rounded valleys and canyons are evidence of glacial activity as well. The headwaters of the Little Colorado River drain from these mountains into the Grand Canyon more than 200 miles downstream. Sacred to the White Mountain Apaches, who call Baldy *dzil ligai,* its very peak is off-limits to the public.

Extending to the north of Baldy is an open area where the volcanics of the region are more apparent. At the Springerville Volcanic Field, the third largest of its kind in the continental United States, visitors can view a 300,000- to 700,000-year-old lava flow, with all its varying vents and covers spread out across rolling plains.

On the southern portion of the White Mountains is the Mogollon Rim. Though the Rim stretches for 200 miles across central Arizona, its character is nowhere more apparent than in this region, where at various places you're suddenly confronted with driving or hiking up or down this 2,000-foot-high escarpment. In the area east of Payson, AZ 260 makes a quick dash to the top, where views abound. Similarly, on Scenic Highway U.S. 191, the journey is slower, capturing all the varying shades of the contrast between the Colorado Plateau and the Basin and Range Province.

With an elevation averaging around 8,000 feet, this is, overall, a cool area, though be aware that below the rim the elevation is lower, so you'll note a marked difference in temperature. During the summer, daytime temperatures are in the mid-80s, while in the winter they average in the 40s, with nights much colder. I find this region most pleasurable in the off-season, in the spring and fall. It's a great time to hike, to see the vivid wildflowers and glowing autumnal colors, and crowds will be at a minimum. During the summer, the "Alps" fill with city dwellers intent on escaping the desert heat. In the winter, they fill with skiers, out for some snowy fun.

Orientation

At the very center of the region are the White Mountains, jutting up to Arizona's second highest peak, Mount Baldy. The region is mostly defined by this mass of volcanic mountains, but it does also encompass the rolling grasslands of Springerville and as far north as St. Johns. The eastern boundary, is, of course, New Mexico, and AZ 87 and 188 define the western boundary, an area that includes the lush pine country and deep canyons of basalt and Supai sandstone in the area of Payson. To the south, the mountain area gives way to vast tracts of nearly barren land and contemporary mining projects in the Morenci and Safford area.

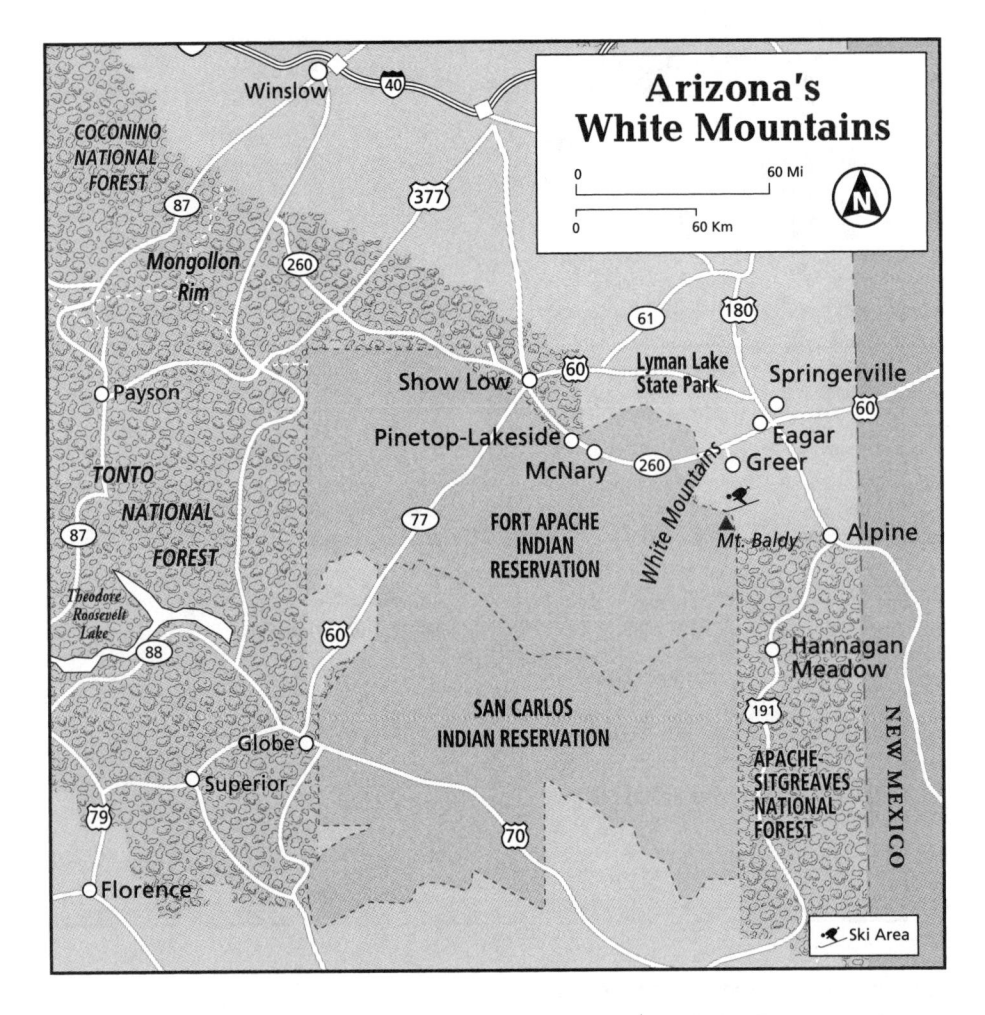

Though I-10 would mark that southern boundary well, the border I've chosen runs north of there, leaving much of the southern Sonoran Desert around Tucson to chapter 7.

It's interesting to note that there is no major city in this region, and that's one of the reasons it's so appealing. Adventurers can spend weeks here, rarely encountering a traffic signal or a honking horn. If you're looking for supplies, though, don't expect anything sophisticated. This is a meat and potatoes kind of region, the kind of place where, when you ask where the rest room is you'll likely get the laconic answer, "Yonder." Springerville, with a whopping population of 2,085, is the largest city to the north, while Globe, an old mining town to the west, is the largest city in the region with 8,024 people. In between, within the White Mountains, are the fast-growing towns of Pinetop and Lakeside. Other places where visitors might find some bacon and eggs are Safford and Superior, both to the south.

Parks & Other Hot Spots

Lyman Lake State Park
11 miles south of St. Johns on U.S. 191. ☎ **520/337-4441.** Beach, boat ramp, camper supply and boat rental store, 61 campsites (more than half with hookups), rest rooms, and showers. Open daily year-round. Camping, fishing, jet skiing, powerboating, swimming.

Set among the rolling hills of eastern Arizona, this small lake provides a good stopover point for those camping, as well as some interesting archaeological treats. Its 1,500 surface acres of water, fed by the Little Colorado River, are protected enough to often provide a glassy surface, which water-skiers love. In fact, a giant slalom water-ski course is set up each summer. Buffalo graze the shores, adding to the ancient feeling of the place where Mogollon people once roamed. Guided tours of the 600-year-old archaeological sites, including a trip across the lake to petroglyphs, are big attractions. *Beware:* Spring winds howl through the area.

Luna Lake
Drive 5 miles east from Alpine on U.S. 180 and turn north at the Luna Lake entrance. ☎ 877/444-6777. Bird watching, boating, camping, fishing.

If you're in the mood to sit by a blue high alpine lake, surrounded by meadows and pines, while you hook a few trout for dinner, head to this sweet spot a few miles outside the hamlet of Alpine. At its fullest this lake at 7,900-foot elevation is 75 acres large and is stocked with brook and cutthroat trout from May to September, except during very hot and dry years when the water becomes too warm to accommodate stocked fish. The lake also has lovely campsites and mountain-biking trails; see those respective sections for details. Small motorboats are allowed on this lake.

Roper Lake State Park
6 miles south of Safford on U.S. 191. ☎ 520/428-6760. Bird watching, boardsailing, boating (small motors), camping, fishing, hiking.

This 339-acre park sits out on the edge of the plains not far from the Pinaleño Mountains. Its 30-acre lake is popular with anglers, but the park is especially desirable to hot spring enthusiasts because of the hot tub there, a lovely stone pool, filled with natural mineral water. While soaking, watch the skies for such birds as the northern cardinal, Albert's touhee, and yellowheaded blackbird. Due to the large number of RVs in the area, tent campers may want to opt for one of the campgrounds in the Pinaleño Mountains.

What to Do & Where to Do It

BIRD WATCHING
This region has a birding list pages long, with some 280 species. Your best bet for spotting them is at any of the 40 some lakes in the region, where you may see pied-bill, horned, Western, and eared grebes; great blue heron, great, snowy and cattle egrets; and tundra swans. Along the **Mogollon Rim,** where fast updrafts come off the floor of the Basin and Range Province, look for birds of prey, of course turkey vultures, but also peregrine falcons, sharp-shinned hawks and even bald and golden eagles. You'll likely encounter in any of the forests in the region wild turkey. **Pintail Lake Wild Game Observation Area,** located 2 miles north of Show Low, is a migration rest area for ducks, geese, and other waterfowl. It boasts unique grasslands and reeds. With a number of observation platforms, the park is quite accessible to nature lovers.

BOARDSAILING & SAILING
Your best bet in the Arizona "Alps" for catching winds is **Lyman Lake State Park** outside of Springerville, a place where boarders once held many contests, and still hold some on July 4th weekend. Because of the canyons in the area the winds can be strange. **Roosevelt Lake** between Globe and Phoenix is popular for some boardsailors but more popular

for boat sailors. A good equipment and information source in the area is **Wind and Water Sports** on the main drag in Pinetop (☎ 520/367-3046).

CROSS-COUNTRY SKIING & SNOWSHOEING

The Arizona "Alps" offer plenty of cross-country options, but only during good snow years, so beware of planning your ski vacation until you have some idea what the winter is going to bring. There are a number of groomed areas where you'll find days of enjoyment. If you prefer to strike out on your own, you might try skiing or snowshoeing the **West Fork of the Little Colorado** up to Mount Baldy outside of the village of Greer. **Sunrise Resort** has a snowshoe area. Another area that's worth checking out is the **Tracks** trail system in Pinetop-Lakeside.

Poll Knoll Recreation Area
Cross-Country Ski Trails

35 miles. Easy to difficult. Access: Off AZ 260 midway between AZ 273 and AZ 373, just east of the 383 mile·marker. The lower portion of the trails is accessed from AZ 373 en route to Greer.

This set of trails has all of life's best: beautiful ponderosa, fir, and aspen forests, alpine meadows, mountain views, and easy through challenging runs—all for free. The trails are groomed by the National Forest Service, Springerville Ranger District. The Poll Knoll Loop is a great way to get acquainted with the area. It runs a broad ring around the outer edge of the northern trail system, and includes both easy and moderate sections, with one difficult bypass for those who choose the route. The southern trail system is open to those who like to ski with their dogs. This is where skiers interested in more challenge will want to go. Trails here are numbered 1 through 6, with 3 through 6 classified as expert. The lower section can be accessed off AZ 373 or you can ski to it from the north system via the Poll Knoll Loop trail. Both areas have information booths, but only the north system has rest rooms.

Williams Valley Winter Sports Area

20 km of trails. Easy to moderate. Allow 1–3 hrs. Access: Drive 1.5 miles north of Alpine on U.S. 191 and turn west on FS 249. Drive 4.5 miles on this gravel road. Map: Pick up a four-color illustrated map from the Alpine Ranger Station. ☎ 520/339-4384.

In the winter this is a wonderful series of groomed trails winding over and around a long narrow meadow surrounded by ponderosa pines; in summer the same routes become bike trails. There are a number of access points to this series of trails. The first is located at a toboggan hill, and is a good way to enter on the easiest trails. The second access is at the Divide Hill Trail; this trail begins with some easy meadow skiing and works its way back into the more challenging terrain, from which you can connect to the Isolation Trail and Half Moon Trail, the longest and most difficult. Another access point is at the junction of FS 249 and 276, marked with a sign that reads "Bike Access." Here you'll find plenty of parking and fast entry to the more challenging terrain. Cross through the gate and head into the forest onto the Isolation Trail. You can either loop back through the Lookout Meadow Loop area or continue farther on the Half Moon Trail. Most of all this is a great place to explore. As you ski, watch for the many elk and deer that graze these meadowlands.

Hannagan Meadow Loop

14 km of groomed trails. Easy to advanced. Allow 1–3 hrs. Access: Drive 23 miles south of Alpine on U.S. 191. The area is on the east side of the highway. Map: Pick up the four-color illustrated trail map from the Alpine Ranger District. ☎ 520/339-4384.

In winter this awesome series of trails treks skiers through lovely meadows and aspen and pine forests; in summer, some of them are open to bikers. Most trails are narrower than those at Williams Valley, with more advanced opportunities. As well as gentle meadowland trails, this area has backcountry trails leading into the upper elevations of the Blue Range Primitive Area. This outlying area is popular for advanced skiers and those with snow-camping skills.

DOWNHILL SKIING
Sunrise Park Resort
McNary, AZ 85930. ☎ 800/772-SNOW or 520/735-7669. 65 trails (40% beginner, 40% intermediate, 20% expert); 10 lifts including 1 high-speed quad, 2 regular quads, 4 triples, 1 double, and 2 surface lifts; 1,800-ft. vertical drop. Full-day tickets $35.

Operated by the White Mountain Apache Tribe, Sunrise is the largest and most popular ski area in Arizona. Though some years the ski area doesn't receive enough snow to open, on a good year over 250 inches can fall there. The runs are spread across three mountains; the longest run, Lonestar, on Cyclone Peak, is 2.75 miles. The best thing about this mountain is that it has something for every level skier, and with the sweet Arizona sun shining much of the time it is a very friendly place. Beginners aren't relegated to one part of the mountain. They'll find some nice skiing off of all three, with most of their trails on the 10,700-foot Sunrise Peak. The top of Apache Peak is also a good bet for beginners. Intermediate skiers will want to head to the top of Sunrise and over the Cyclone Peak as well. Advanced skiers will most appreciate the steep faces of Cyclone Peak where runs such as Thunder and Tempest can provide plenty of bumps. Snowboarders can enjoy their own park on Sunrise Peak between the Pump House and Fairway runs. The mountain has a full-service ski school, with some promising beginner packages, 5 day-lodges, and a 100-room full-service lodge, with a restaurant, spa, and an indoor pool. During holidays this resort gets quite crowded.

FISHING
Because of its extensive mountains feeding many streams and lakes, this region is one of the Southwest's best fishing destinations. Your home base for fishing in the region is in Greer, with **Robert C. Pollock** (☎ 520/735-7293) the most recommended guide. He works with all levels, from extreme novices to experts, not only guiding but also giving some of the best lessons in the Southwest. In the Springerville area, the **Speckled Trout** (☎ 520/333-0852) is an all-purpose fishing store, offering gear, guide service, and lessons. Best of all, it's the only place in the entire region to get a cappuccino or espresso. Be aware that most of the lakes in the region freeze over in winter.

White Mountains
In the town of Greer itself, stream fishers like to ply the waters of the **East Fork of Little Colorado,** which is stocked with Apache trout. Hike from Greer up to Sheep's Crossing. Fly fish all along that trail and continue up into the wilderness on the same creek. You'll likely catch some nice, stream-sized trout, and see elk and deer too.

The main fare at **Greer Lakes** is rainbow trout with a good population of browns and occasional cut-bows. Located off AZ 373 heading into Greer (about 5 miles south of AZ 260), all three Greer Lakes—River Reservoir, Bunch Reservoir, and Tunnel Reservoir—tend to be muddy, but the fish populations are alive and healthy. These are good bait and fly-fishing lakes. The water level tends to be lower in summer because these lakes form a significant part of Springerville's water supply.

The White Mountains are a dynamite area to catch cold-water fish, especially at **Big Lake.** To get there, take AZ 273 south from AZ 260. The last 15 miles are graded dirt, but can be accessed by most cars. Because the lake freezes over in winter, it is not accessible from December to mid-April. High winds sweep into the White Mountains in spring sometimes making casting difficult. More trout are fished out of this lake than any other lake in the state, making it the most heavily fished cold-water fishery in the White Mountains. Most anglers who come here use bait, but flies can be successful.

Just north of Big Lake is **Crescent Lake,** a popular fishing destination up around 9,000 feet in the White Mountains. This 100-acre, crescent moon-shaped lake is known for fast fish growth. Because the lake had been experiencing winter kills, the Arizona Department of Fish and Game installed bubblers during the winter freeze, and it's helping some. Rainbow and brown trout tend to hang out in the weeds and coves, making this a good float-tubing destination. Take AZ 260 to AZ 273. The lake is right along the road.

Another splendid White Mountain fishing hole is **Lee Valley Reservoir.** From FS 260, turn south on the Sunrise Lake Road, AZ 273. Continue on FS 113 when you enter the National Forest. Drive past Sheep's Crossing on the Little Colorado until you see the sign for the lake on the right. This 35-acre lake is a favorite destination for beginner to advanced fly fishers seeking a secluded setting and good trout catching. The Arctic grayling, rarely found in southern states, swims these waters as does the Apache trout. Both fish come into the shallows, so shore wading is a great way to catch fish. Restrictions include using fly and lure only, a two-fish catch limit, and no more than one grayling of a minimum 12-inch length. The coves and points are the best places to fish along the weed banks. Fishing is best during spring, summer, and fall.

By damming the Little Colorado River, the 1,500-acre irrigation reservoir **Lyman Lake** was created. It is located 11 miles south of St. Johns on U.S. 191. Lyman Lake is a common destination for water-skiers as well as fishers. Because of its vastness, there are no size restrictions on boats. Luckily for anglers, the west end of the lake is buoyed off and restricted as a no-wake area. Walleye, channel catfish, crappie, and largemouth bass make their homes here. Though open year-round, summer days, with highs in the 80s to low 90s, are perfect for fishing.

Apache Country

Apache Country in eastern Arizona offers plenty of great cold-water fishing. In order to fish there you'll need to contact the Tribal Game and Fish Department (☎ 520/338-4385).

Christmas Tree Lake is one fine example of the area's cold-water fisheries. Many anglers have described this lake as "in the middle of nowhere" and "unforgettable" due to its remote locale and opportunity to catch large Apache trout. You won't have to vie for a fishing spot since only 20 fishers are allowed on the lake per day. Set in a breathtaking alpine setting, on 41-acres of pristine land, Christmas Tree Lake is a real find. It's best to have a tube or boat to maneuver your way into all the fishing nooks. Many fish have been caught in the 2- to 5-pound range! As well as Apache trout, you'll find brown and rainbow too. From Phoenix, take U.S. 60 east to AZ 260. Take the Hawley Lake turnoff to Rd. 473 and follow the signs. The roads close to the lake are rutted and bumpy.

Located right off AZ 260 about 20 miles east of Pinetop between Hawley Lake turnoff and the Sunrise Lake turnoff, is **Horseshoe Cienega Lake.** One of five White Mountain lakes, Horseshoe Cienega can be fished from shore or by boat. Known for its excellent brown trout fishing, this lake at 8,100 feet offers anglers an opportunity to get away from the other popular White Mountain lakes. Expect to catch Apache, brown, rainbow, and brook trout. The lake is rarely clear, but don't let the muddy or off-color water deter you.

Several species of trout can be caught in **Reservation Lake** including Apache, brown, rainbow, and brook. This 280-acre lake on the eastern edge of the reservation is located at the base of Mount Baldy at about 9,000 feet. The lake has good dry fly-fishing in the evenings during the summer and fall months. Classic lake flies work well in this lake. It holds the state record for trout, a whopping 26 pounds caught there recently. There are a campground and a store, open in summer only. Take the Sunrise Lake turnoff from AZ 260 and drive to FS 116, then turn onto Y20.

Perhaps the most popular lake for fly-fishing, **Sunrise Lake** is touted to have the largest trout of all the White Mountain Apache Reservation lakes. This 800-acre "jewel," as some fishers have coined it, is easy to launch a boat in. The snowmelt from Mounts Ord and Baldy feed the lake and surrounding streams with pure mountain water. Those anglers who seek out Sunrise Lake are serious fishers. You'll see no one using powerbait here! Types of fish include rainbow, brook, Apache trout, and some grayling. The best time is late September through November. There are many facilities here including a campground, gas station, store, and hotel. Take AZ 260 east from Pinetop and follow the signs.

One of the top Arizona fly-fishing waters, the East and West forks of the **Black River** are highly sought-after because of their high production of Apache, rainbow, and brown trout. The river runs through about 60 miles of rugged canyon, which due to its Alpine zone status, will feel more like Colorado than Arizona. The Black River forms the border between the White Mountain and San Carlos Apache tribal lands, so it's wise to have the proper permits from both tribes. Unfortunately, the East Fork gets overrun by anglers. But it's worth seeing in early spring or late fall when the hordes have gone home. Because most of the stream is high in the mountains, the West Fork is not nearly as crowded. You can fish there three seasons out of the year. Access to the East Fork or lower West Fork is via U.S. 191, from Hannagan Meadow or Alpine. Access to the West Fork is easiest from the north, past Sunrise Lake to FS 116.

The cold, clear water of the **White River** is ideal for trout fishing. Yet once the North Fork merges with East Fork, the river becomes too warm for trout to live. The river is heavily stocked with rainbows, browns, and Apaches, and is fishable from major road crossings. The North Fork runs from Sunrise Lake down past the town of Whiteriver. This area is bucolic, with pine, spruce, and willow trees. At Ditch Camp, the river is catch and release only. To reach the North Fork from Pinetop, go south on AZ 73 to the Log Road turnoff or stay on AZ 260 east of Hon Dah to the Hawley Lake turnoff. Cross the river and head west.

Rim Country

In the region around Payson, there are several remote lakes and creeks with excellent big brown and rainbow trout fishing including **Chevelon Canyon Lake.** The steep hike down to the water combined with its remote setting at 6,400 feet in the Apache-Sitgreaves National Forest deter most anglers from fishing this watering hole. It's smart to pack in a float tube or kick-boat to allow you to fish most of the lake. Head east from Payson on AZ 260 and turn north on FS 300; turn right on FS 169B and drive to the parking area.

Beginning near Woods Canyon Lake and running north through a rugged canyon to feed Chevelon Canyon Lake is **Chevelon Creek.** The location of this creek is remote, which is why it's a good small stream to fish.

In addition to Chevelon Canyon Lake, there are two other lakes in close proximity to Phoenix—Willow Spring and Woods Canyon Lakes. The 150-acre **Willow Springs Lake** is one of the heaviest-used cold-water fishing spots in Arizona, but the fishing is decent. You'll have luck catching rainbows, browns, and brookies. Shore angling is popular, but the best way to fish the lake is either by boat or float tube. You may find you've hooked a very big largemouth bass, which was illegally stocked into the lakes several years ago. **Woods Canyon Lake** is the heaviest used cold-water fishing spot in the state. In summertime fishers stand nearly should-to-shoulder at this 50-acre reservoir. The interior of the lake gets congested with boaters too. A store provides snacks and necessities, and a boat rental shop beside the paved launch ramp will help get you onto the water. Both lakes are east of Payson of AZ 260.

One of Arizona's two designated catch-and-release streams (except for the northern section where bait fishing and a six-fish limit are allowed), **Canyon Creek** meanders its way through one of the prettiest grassy valleys in the state. The lower stretch has a good population of naturally reproducing brown trout. Due to its close proximity to Phoenix and Scottsdale, the adjacent campgrounds are filled with Boy Scouts and church groups. To get there, take AZ 260 east out of Payson up onto the rim and turn south on AZ 288 (the road to Young). After a short distance turn left on FS 188. This dirt road can be taken to the south end of the creek. To get to the north end, follow the signs to the fish hatchery up FS 33.

Flowing perpendicular and just a bit south of Chevelon Creek is spring-fed **Christopher Creek,** which gets occasional runoff water that helps increase flows. Unfortunately, due to new housing developments in the area, Christopher Creek's water level has dropped in the past 10 years. The good news is the shallow creek makes wading easy. The creek is home to rainbow and brown trout, 8 to 9 inches in size. There's a campground nearby. From Payson, take AZ 260 east 25 miles to where the creek crosses under the highway. This creek is fishable spring, summer, and fall.

Nearby **Tonto Creek** has received less snowmelt than in years past and has also been ill-affected by developments in the area. Yet the upper, easily accessible portion of this creek near Kohl's Ranch on AZ 260 east of Payson is still a popular destination for fishers and campers due to its close proximity to Phoenix. This small creek is regularly stocked with rainbows. The lower portion of the creek flows into a narrow and deep canyon into the Hellsgate Wilderness area, where it meets up with Haigler Creek. A rugged 7-mile hike from Little Green Valley down Trail 37 will bring you to this confluence. The occasional good-sized rainbow and wild brown trout makes the hiking well worth it.

HIKES & BACKPACK TRIPS
White Mountains
Mount Baldy
14 miles round-trip. Moderate. 2,200-ft. elevation gain. Allow 7 hrs. From AZ 373 in Greer, head west on FS 87 and drive about 6 miles to its junction with FS 113. Turn left and drive about 2 miles to the Sheep's Crossing area, looking for a spur road on the right that leads 0.5 miles to the trailhead. Maps: USGS Mount Baldy or USFS Mount Baldy Wilderness.

This is a relaxing hike along an alpine river and through meadows of aster and penstemmon, and forests of ponderosa pine, white fir and Engelmann spruce, with some mountain views along the way. The well-marked trail begins along the West Fork of the Little Colorado River. You'll want to take your fishing rod to try to hook brook, rainbow, and cutthroat trout en route. At mile 5 the trail reaches the ridge leading to Baldy Peak. Later, about a mile from the peak, the East Fork Trail joins this West Fork route. As the trail climbs toward the summit you'll find awesome views out across the White Mountains. About 0.3 mile from the summit you'll come to the boundary for the Apache Reservation, which must serve as your turn-around point. Baldy is sacred to the tribe, and they will enforce their rules disallowing passage to the summit. You could have your pack confiscated or be arrested. The trip back down is easy, with gravity doing much of the work.

Escudilla Mountain
7 miles round-trip. Moderate. 1,300-ft. elevation gain. Allow 3–4 hrs. Access: Drive on U.S. 191 6 miles north of Alpine and turn right on FS 56. Follow this dirt road 4.7 miles to a sign pointing to Escudilla Mountain Trail 308. Bear left and drive 0.3 mile to the trailhead. Maps: USGS Nutrioso or Escudilla and/or USFS Apache National Forest.

The Zuni Indians call this extinct volcano the "sleeping buffalo," but for others it's known mostly as a premier fall hike, with its acres and acres of aspens showing their bold colors. The trail takes you into the Escudilla Wilderness, a relatively small wilderness area that has much to offer, including this, the third highest peak in Arizona at 10,877 feet, as well as 500 acres of meadow. Remnants of a 1951 fire are visible; the first mile climbs through a portion of that burn area, with thick stands of aspen enclosing the trail. Large Douglas fir stumps along the way provide evidence of the climax forest existing prior to fire and of the salvage logging operation after. Watch the sides of the trail for raspberry and gooseberry thickets.

After the first mile the area opens out to steep wildflower meadows. Then the trail skirts along the uphill side of the saddle of Toolbox Draw, from which you'll have panoramic views to the south and west. Finally, at 0.25 miles from the summit, the trail reaches a fire lookout, the highest in the state. On a clear day you should be able to see the San Francisco Peaks near Flagstaff, the Blue Range to the south, the Gila Wilderness in New Mexico, and Mount Graham near Safford. Naturalist Aldo Leopold mentions Escudilla Mountain in *A Sand County Almanac* as the place where one of the last grizzly bears in Arizona was killed. He wrote: "Escudilla still hangs on the horizon, but when you see it you no longer think of the bear. It's only a mountain now." While hiking, watch for black bear, mule deer, and wild turkeys.

Rose Spring Trail
10 miles round-trip. 2,000-ft. elevation gain. Access: Drive south from Hannagan Meadow 6.5 miles and turn right onto FS 54; drive this dirt road 6 miles to a sign that directs you through a gate to Trail 309; it's another 0.5 miles on a rough road to the trailhead. Map: USGS Baldy Bill.

This trail is on one hand spectacular and on the other hand odd. It's spectacular because it offers one of the few opportunities to traverse on foot the Mogollon Rim, the 2,000-foot drop-off that forms the southern edge of the Colorado Plateau, with its vast views across southern Arizona. It's odd because of the way the trail was built. Rather than putting it right along the rim where the views are, the builders put it about 20 feet in from the rim, forcing you to hike along a fenceline far enough back so that the views are nearly out of your grasp. That's why I recommend this more as a meander through the 11,000-acre Bear Wallow Wilderness than a mileage-conscious hike. What I did was hike the trail on the way out, and on the way back I meandered along the rim where the views are, following little trails that people have cut probably experiencing a similar frustration to what I had.

At the trailhead you'll see that it's 3 miles to Schell Canyon and another 2 miles to Rose Spring. The trail follows the fence line west along the rim, variously climbing and descending. Semi-obstructed views are available through the trees throughout, with larger openings here and there. At various points you'll see Red Mountain, Rose Peak, Maple Mountain and, far in the distance, Mount Graham and the

Pinaleños. Another positive note about this trail is that because of its remoteness you won't find crowds. En route watch for wildlife that is common in this isolated area. The Bear Wallow Wilderness Area was named for many bear wallows, which cattleman Pete Slaughter encountered while driving cattle through the area in 1884. Black bear still roam the area, as do elk and mountain lion. If you're looking for a good overnight trip, you might want to hike the Rose Spring Trail to the Schell Canyon Trail, descend into the south fork of Bear Wallow Creek to the Bear Wallow Trail to campsites along Bear Wallow Creek.

Rim Country

This area is intersected by the Highline Trail, a 51-mile route that parallels the Mogollon Rim. With many creeks and side trails, it's an excellent place for fly-fishing and exploring; however, as an extended backpacking trail it isn't remote enough to merit the effort. If you do traverse it, allow 5 days. The west trailhead is located about 2.5 miles south of Pine on AZ 87, and the east trailhead is on AZ 260 about 4 miles below the top of the Mogollon Rim at the Two-Sixty Trailhead. This historic trail was established in the late 1800s to link various homesteads and ranches under the Mogollon Rim. I've listed three hikes here that cross the Highline. Using a good map you can put together loops connecting trails within Highline Trail system.

See Canyon

7 miles round-trip. Moderate–difficult. 1,760-ft. elevation gain. Allow 4–5 hrs. Access: Follow AZ 260 east of Payson for 21 miles to FS 284, across from a mechanic's shop. Turn right and follow FS 284 for 1.5 miles. Watch for the trailhead on the right; parking is about 50 yards up the road. Map: USGS Promontory Butte.

This trail follows Christopher Creek through forests of ponderosa and aspen, and then makes its way up onto the Mogollon Rim, where views stretch to the east, south, and west. The first 2 miles follow Christopher Creek in a not-so-steep ascent through the forest. Be aware, however, that this is considered a primitive trail; it can be washed away in places. Then the real climb starts for 1.5 miles up onto the rim. The trail continues up to the Rim Road, FS 300. This hike is especially pretty in the fall when maple, aspen, and oaks flash their colors. Return on the same route.

Horton Creek Trail

8 miles round-trip. Easy. 1,180-ft. elevation gain. Allow 4 hrs. Access: Follow AZ 260 15 miles east from Payson to Tonto Creek. Turn north (left) on Tonto Creek Rd. (FS 289), and drive 1 mile to the Horton Creek picnic area. Cross the bridge and head up the campground road to the trailhead. Map: USGS Promontory Butte.

This relaxing hike makes its way along Horton Creek, past waterfalls, and through stands of ponderosa pines. It's most known as a great fly-fishing hike. The trail follows an abandoned logging road, staying within sight of Horton Creek for the first 1.2 miles and farther from it the rest of the way. The trail is rocky and grows more so as the canyon walls narrow. Toward the top, the trail meets up with the Highline Trail, and then continues on to the point where Horton Spring gushes out of the side of the mountain. This interesting geologic occurrence happens due to rainwater collecting on top of the Mogollon Rim. Acting as a giant sponge, the rocks along the rim soak up water and release it below. The trail was named for Mississippian Willis B. Horton, who lived halfway up this canyon.

Pine Canyon Trail

8 miles one-way. Moderate to difficult. 2,200-ft. elevation gain. Allow 4 hrs. Access: Head south of Pine on AZ 87 for 2.5 miles to the Highline Trailhead. Begin hiking on the Highline Trail, which after about 450 ft. will take you to the Pine Canyon trailhead. Map: USGS Pine.

This trail treats the hiker to a variety of scenery including distant views south across the pine-covered hills, closer views down across Pine Canyon, and closer still peeks into the lushness of the riparian banks of Pine Creek. At the end of the first mile the trail turns steep, then it gets gentler for many more miles. At mile 6 it begins to ascend the Mogollon Rim in a series of switchbacks. At mile 8 it tops out on the rim at State Highway 87 about 2 miles north of the Camp Verde turnoff. The trip back is an easy downhill the way you came. For a very scenic and less difficult day hike, leave a shuttle car at the base and hike this from the rim downward.

Tonto Creek in the Hellsgate Wilderness

22 miles one-way. Difficult. 2,350-ft. elevation gain. 3–4 days. Access: You have two options. Northern terminus: Head east from Payson on AZ 260 for about 11 miles to the turnoff for FS 405A. Turn right and drive 5 miles to FS 893, where you'll want to park. Four-wheel-drive vehicles can drive a little farther on FS 893. End of the canyon: From Payson take AZ 87 south for 11.8 miles to FS 417. Turn east and travel through the small community of Gisela. Follow FS 417 past Gisela to a gate that marks private property. Park here. You will have traveled just over 6.5 miles. Maps: USGS Diamond Butte, McDonald Mtn., Payson So.; USFS Tonto National Forest.

In his book *Canyoneering Arizona*, Tyler Williams calls this the "Granddaddy of Mogollon Rim canyons." That's because along its course it becomes a massive gorge with walls 200 feet high and pools through which you have to maneuver that are 20 feet deep. This is not a sissy's canyon. Only the heartiest canyoneers should attempt it. Do so with maps, flotation for your pack, and enough guts to handle some major scrambling and a few substantial drops. That said, this is a very remote canyon, and those seeking solitude will definitely find it here, as well as beauty beyond measure.

This trip begins on the Hellsgate Trail meandering through forests of ponderosa pine and Douglas fir, slowly working its way into alligator juniper and piñon pine along Apache Ridge. Then it switchbacks off the ridge down to the confluence of Tonto and Haigler Creeks. This is a good place to spend the night. Here you'll encounter sheer rock walls and beautiful pools. You can either complete the 11-mile Hellsgate Trail or head downstream on this multi-day canyoneering route. If you continue on the Hellsgate Trail you'll encounter uncertain footing and rocky terrain, climbing more than 1,600 feet in a short distance. If you head downstream you definitely won't stay dry. For 17 miles you'll wade and swim through water that is, even in summer, cold. Avoid doing this hike during spring runoff when as much as 60,000 cubic feet per second (CFS) of flow can rush through. As you go you'll encounter complex geology including a lovely pink granite as well as rhyolite. You can't really get lost as you continue through the canyon. At about mile 12 you'll begin to see Sonoran Desert growth such as saguaros cactus, and soon you'll come to a 100-yard-long pool framed by 200-foot-high canyon walls. Next you'll come to a 12-foot waterfall, at the base of which is another delightful pool. Toward the mouth of the canyon look for a path near the Houston Creek confluence. It will lead you around private property for 0.5 miles to where your car is parked. Another option is to begin at the south end of the Hellsgate Trail. From the community of Young, drive west along FS 129 for 7.5 miles to the four-wheel-drive FS 133. Turn left and travel about 8 miles to the trailhead.

Pinaleño Mountains

Round the Mountain Trail

2–14.5 miles one-way. Moderate. 4,040-ft. elevation gain. Allow 2 hrs.–2 days. Access: From Safford, drive 8 miles south on U.S. 191 to the Swift Trail (AZ 366). Turn right and drive 7.5 miles to the trailhead on the right. Maps: USGS

Webb Peak and Mount Graham or USFS Coronado National Forest Safford District.

This trail is a sweet cross-country jaunt through oak/juniper woodlands and ponderosa pine forest, with mountain and valley views. Be aware that during the course of the trail from end to end there is a substantial elevation gain. The area is known to have a large black bear population, so be prepared for a treat. Also, be sure to stash your food in accordance with the guidelines in chapter 1.

This is a great day hike—you can go for as long as you like and then turn back. Or, if you can arrange a shuttle, it is a good way to traverse the lovely Pinaleños all the way to Columbine. The trail quickly falls down into a creek, and then starts climbing gradually toward the peaks, with beautiful views behind you and before you. Then it comes to a crossroads where you'll turn left toward Noon Creek. It heads through the canyon, across scenic slopes and through several creeks as it passes around the mountain, and ends up at the historic Columbine area on a central plateau. If you're hiking this as an out-and-back, you'll find the most stunning views when you return.

Ladybug Trail 329
5.9 miles. Difficult. 3,580-ft. elevation gain. Allow 3 hrs. Access: From Safford drive south 8 miles on U.S. 191 to the Swift Trail (AZ 366). Turn right and drive about 7 miles to the turn-off for the Ladybug trailhead on your left. Follow this dirt road for 0.5 miles to the trailhead.

Though it's not quite as scenic as the Round the Mountain Trail, this is a good way to get a quick introduction to the Pinaleños. I pulled into these lovely mountains in the evening and tripped my way up the steep, rocky trail high enough to get a good look out across Jacobson Canyon, the town of Safford, and the Gila Mountains in the distance. However, if you don't feel like grunting your way up this climb, you can start at the upper Ladybug Trailhead (17 miles up the Swift Trail) and hike only 0.5 miles to the top of Ladybug Peak. If you start at the lower trailhead, here's what you'll find: The trail heads up a wash and down through a creek bed and then switchbacks up to Ladybug Peak. The only real drawback to the scenery along the way is that the paved Swift Trail often comes into view, but it doesn't have much traffic traveling it, despite the fact that it's an amazing piece of roadway, traversing far back into the depths of this range. If you choose to hike the upper part of the trail, you'll find the signed trailhead but will have to make your way past some false trails. Soon you'll come to switchbacks. Toward the top, turn right at the unsigned junction trail to reach to rocky summit. If you have a game shuttle driver, you may want to hike from the peak *down* to the lower trailhead.

HORSEBACK RIDING

The Springerville area is well-known for its cattle-raising. I remember when I was younger going to Hooper Herefords there for the annual Hereford Field Day to practice judging cattle. One local outfit, **K5 High Country Adventures (☎ 800/814-6451** or 520/333-4323) has capitalized on the beauty of the rolling grasslands and created a unique "shared ranch" experience. Activities include brandings, roundups, and other adventures on a real cattle ranch. Unlike many of the more traditional dude ranches, this is a ranch owned by a local family that runs Reed's Lodge in Springerville, the place guests stay. Guests then go out to the ranch to ride. Trips range from a half-day of riding to more extended ranch experiences, such as a multi-day cattle drive moving the herd up to the high country for the summer or back down from the high country for the winter. K5 also tailors riding trips for those interested in birding, photography, petroglyphs, and wildlife and wildflower viewing.

At **X-Diamond & MLY Ranch** outside Springerville, (☎ **520/333-2286**; www.xdiamondranch.com), Wrangler Sam Udall, a real, working cowboy, will set you up on one of the ranch horses and take you into the wilderness where you'll ride to the top of South Fork Canyon, along the Little Colorado River, through grassy meadows, and into pine forest. The ranch has rides for every level rider. The Brushpopper Ride promises to give its riders "real action," including stories by Sam and a sack lunch with homemade cookies. He'll share poetry, anecdotal facts about the working cattle ranch, and more. The ranch has year-round accommodations in quaint log cabins, a day spa, private fishing, archeological sites, and The Little House Museum.

Lee Valley Outfitters (☎ **520/735-7454**), located on the White Mountain Apache Reservation 27 miles southeast of Pinetop-Lakeside, offers nose-to-tail rides starting at the base of Sunrise Park Resort ski area in open meadows and quickly winding into the mountains. Trotting and cantering are not allowed. One hour costs $20, two hours cost $32; half-day rides run $55 and full-day rides are $100. Hayrides, sleigh rides, photography rides, and cookouts are also available.

MOUNTAIN BIKING
White Mountains
Luna Lake Loop
2.5 or 8 miles. Easy to moderate. 400-ft. elevation gain. Allow 1–2½ hrs., respectively. Access: Drive 5 miles east from Alpine on U.S. 180 and turn north at the Luna Lake entrance. A gravel road leads 1 mile to the trail marked by the international bike symbol near the campground entrance. (*Note:* There is a bike trail marker just before the actual trailhead. Be sure to continue on to the trailhead placard.)

These trails take you through meadows and ponderosa forest in the vicinity of a pretty mountain lake. All junctions are well marked—just follow the blue diamonds.

For the 2.5-mile loop, ride through the gate and follow the blue diamonds north to the junction where a sign that reads "easier" marks the right fork; follow this leg 1 mile to a second signed junction; at this junction, the right fork will return you to the road you drove in on 100 yards south of the trailhead. To ride the 8-mile upper loop, follow the directions above to the first signed junction. Take the left-hand fork marked "more difficult" and continue 1 mile through a gate (watch diamonds); travel across Little Creek, over a cattle guard, and down the main road about 0.25 miles to a signed road and gate on the right; go through this gate and enjoy relatively flat terrain for 2.5 miles. After this, the trail gets a little more technical over a series of short climbs and drops, which lead back to a signed junction. The right fork marked easiest will take you back to the trail system, while the left fork will bring you back to the Luna Lake in a quick 0.25 miles.

Williams Valley Loops
5 miles. Easy to moderate. 700-ft. elevation gain. Allow 1–3 hrs. Access: Drive 1.5 miles north of Alpine on U.S. 191 and turn west on FS 249. Drive 4.5 miles on this gravel road.

In order to take full advantage of this area you may want to pick up an illustrated four-color map from the Alpine Ranger Station. There are two access points to this series of trails built as a cross-country ski area. They traverse a long, narrow meadow and make their way back into forests of ponderosa. The first access point to the trails is the Divide Hill Trail access. Here you'll begin with some easy meadow riding and work your way back into the more challenging terrain, from which you can connect to the Isolation Trail and Half Moon Trail, the longest and most technical. The second access point is at the junction of FS 249 and 276, marked with a sign that reads "Bike Access." Here you'll find plenty of parking and fast access to the more challenging terrain.

Cross through the gate and head into the forest onto the Isolation Trail. You can either loop back through the Lookout Meadow Loop area or continue farther on the Half Moon Trail. Most of all it's a great place to explore. As you pedal, watch for the many elk and deer that graze these meadowlands.

Hannagan Meadow Loop
5.5-mile loop. Easy to moderate. 400-ft. elevation gain. Allow 1½–2 hrs. Access: Drive 23 miles south of Alpine on U.S. 191 to FS 576 (0.25 miles before Hannagan Lodge). The ride begins here and in a short distance turns right along a power line.

These trails meander through meadows and pine and aspen forests where you're likely to see such denizens as wild turkey, elk, and black bear. The route includes some single track and some forest roads. The drawback is that some of it is under power lines.

Begin following FS 576 for 100 yards to the road running under a power line on your right. Follow this road, marked with blue diamonds, 1 mile to a marked junction with a two-track road that bears to the left. Take this primitive road for 1.5 miles to another marked junction where you'll turn right. Ride this well-traveled dirt road for 2 miles to a corral. Turn right to a marked junction once again at a power line. Follow the power line road back to Hannagan Lodge, which is a quarter- mile south of the trailhead. For information, call the Alpine Ranger District (☎ 520/339-4384).

Ackre Lake Trail
7 miles round-trip. Easy. 400-ft. elevation loss. Allow 2 hrs. Access: Drive 23 miles south of Alpine on U.S. 191 to FS 576, Hannagan Meadows Campground. The trailhead starts between campsites #6 and #7.

This trail travels along single track and some forest roads. It begins at Hannagan Meadow and meanders south, through pine and aspen forests, crossing a broad meadow and looping near Acker Lake, then back. When I visited the area, these trails were not well marked. In order to find your way around, you may want to pick up a four-color ski trail map at the Alpine Ranger Station before heading out. If you get confounded, you can get directions at the Hannagan Meadow Lodge, the only real civilization in the area, or call the Alpine Ranger District at ☎ 520/339-4384.

There is abundant flora and fauna along the way; watch for the calypso orchid, elk, deer, and listen for hermit thrushes and evening grosbeaks. The trail begins heading south through mixed conifer forest. At 1.8 miles it reaches a fork; bear right and descend into Butterfly Cienega at 2 miles, a good place to spot elk. At the end of the Cienega, the trail re-enters forest, follows a ridge around the mountains, then enters a valley on the west side of Ackre Lake. Continue a short way to the lake, crossing a log bridge over the spillway, and along the dam to the parking area. At this point you'll want to get onto FS 8312, which will loop you back to Butterfly Cienega in about 1.3 miles. At Butterfly Cienega retrace the Ackre Lake Trail back to Hannagan Meadows Campground.

Rim Country Trails
Horton Creek
8 miles round-trip. Difficult. 1,180-ft. elevation gain. Allow 1½–2 hrs. Access: Follow AZ 260 15 miles east from Payson to Tonto Creek. Turn north (left) on Tonto Creek Rd. (FS 289), and drive 1 mile to the Horton Creek picnic area. Cross the bridge and head up the campground road to the trailhead.

This rigorous ride makes its way along Horton Creek, past waterfalls, and through stands of ponderosa pines. Though it's an easy hike (see "Hikes & Backpack Trips" earlier in this chapter), the rocky nature of the trail makes it a good, technical ride.

The trail follows an abandoned logging road, staying within sight of Horton Creek for the first 1.2 miles and farther from it the rest of the way. This first section is quite rocky. As it climbs, the canyon walls narrow. Toward the top, the trail meets up with the Highline Trail then continues on to the point where Horton Spring gushes out of the side of the mountain. This interesting geologic occurrence happens due to rainwater collecting on top of the Mogollon Rim. Acting as a giant sponge, the rocks along the rim soak up water and release it below. The trip back is a fun downhill romp.

Highline Trail

12 miles. Difficult. Approximately 800-ft. elevation gain. Allow 3 hrs. Access: From Payson drive east on AZ 260 for about 25 miles. At this point the highway begins climbing up on the Mogollon Rim. Shortly after the climb begins watch for the Two-Sixty Trailhead on your left. Start there.

The Highline Trail is a 51-mile route that parallels the Mogollon Rim. With many creeks and side trails, it's an excellent place for fly-fishing and exploring. It's a much more interesting bike ride than it is a hike, taking you down into drainages and up over ridges in what some say is the best single track in the state. However, if you ride this trail be prepared to carry your bike over rough and rocky sections. This historic trail was established in the late 1800s to link various homesteads and ranches under the Mogollon Rim. Once on the trail there are many options. One I've listed here gives you views and fun single track.

Head east on the Military Sinkhole Trail as it traverses through thick ponderosa and Douglas fir forest. At about 1.4 miles it begins a steep climb up onto the rim. After a mile of climbing it comes to the rim, where you'll want to turn left on the partly paved Rim Vista Trail, which parallels the rim. This is an incredible view opportunity. Just don't get carried away with looking off at the layers of blue in the distance and slide right off the side. At 4.1 miles this trail ends. Head over to the General Crook Trail, which parallels the Rim Road. At not quite 6 miles turn left onto a jeep road marked #9350. Follow this road until you come to the Drew Trail 291 where you'll turn left and follow a steep single track for 1 mile. At 7.6 miles this trail meets up with the Highline Trail. Turn left and romp down this awesome single track and back to your car.

Little Green Valley

7 miles round-trip. Easy. 400-ft. elevation gain. Allow 1½ hrs. Access: From Payson, follow AZ 260 east for 13 miles to Ponderosa Campground. Park at the entrance.

Settled in 1876 by William Burch and John Hood, the area was named Little Green Valley in contradistinction to the Payson area, which was called Big Green Valley. This is a good family ride, winding through ponderosa pine stands on a forest road leading to a lush green valley. Begin the route by riding along the main campground road until you get to the far end where the road is blocked to motor vehicles by a gate. Walk under the gate, and turn right on the dirt road just beyond it. Follow this road down through the ponderosa forest. At 2.5 miles you'll pass the trailhead leading to Hellsgate Wilderness. The route then climbs over a small hill and drops into Little Green Valley, where you'll want to turn around and head back.

Rim View Trail

4.8 miles. Easy. 80-ft. elevation gain. Allow 1 hr. Access: From Payson follow AZ 260 east about 30 miles until you come to the top of the Mogollon Rim. Turn left onto Rim Rd. Immediately veer right into the parking area. The General Crook Trail (which leads to the Rim View) leaves from there.

This is a gentle ride through ponderosa pine forest along which you'll find spectacular views from the Mogollon Rim across the vast mountains and deserts of southern Arizona. Begin on the General Crook Trail, an abandoned road that rolls through woods and meadows. At 2.3 miles you'll come to the Woods Canyon Lake entrance road. Turn left and follow it out to Rim Road. Cross the road and head to the viewpoint parking area. From there you'll find a paved trail that contours the edge of the Rim. It's a spectacular ride eastward, but hold your speed—this is a wheelchair- accessible trail. The trail seems to peter out at a small canyon. At this point simply return to Rim Road for a few yards then head back out to the edge to resume riding along the trail that will, at this point, have turned to dirt. Follow this single track to a trail intersection, where you'll turn left, leaving the Rim and heading back to the Rim View Campground and back to your vehicle.

Show Low Area

Los Burros Loop

13.5-mile loop. Moderate. 400-ft. elevation gain. Allow 3–4 hrs. Access: Head east on U.S. 60. At Vernon turn right onto FS 224. Drive 10 miles to the Los Burros Campground and trailhead. Or from Lakeside, travel south on AZ 260 to McNary. Go north (left) on Vernon Rd., FS 224, for just over 7 miles. Turn right into the Los Burros Campground. The trailhead is at the far end. This is a great place to camp, full of lovely cottonwoods and open meadows.

This trail is so fun you'll get bugs in your teeth from smiling so much. It gently cruises through ponderosa and Douglas fir forest and meanders through meadows, all on fast, well-packed single track. The Los Burros is part of the White Mountain Trail System, a dozen or so trails that interconnect. You can obtain a guide to all the trails by contacting the U.S. Forest Service Lakeside Ranger Station.

The trail begins at a lovely meadow at the Los Burros Campground, a place that was once a ranger station, with an antique building to attest to the fact. It meanders up a small hill and down through a gate, then follows a double-track route for a short ways. Heading off to the left of the double-track, it climbs and descends through the forest passing small water holes. The trail is very well marked with blue diamonds. If you go more than 50 yards without seeing one, backtrack until you do. For a while the trail levels off and passes through some large meadows so beautiful that you might want to linger. You'll come to more gentle climbs and descents and then one grind and you'll find yourself back at the gate and your car. I'd rate this the funnest romp in the White Mountains.

Woodland Lakes

2–5 miles. Easy. 100-ft. elevation gain. Allow 1 hr. Access: In the center of Pinetop, on AZ 260, turn west into the Woodland Lake Park entrance; drive 0.3 mile to the Woodland Lake sign and to the lake's pier. Park there.

This is a good family spot to bike. Trails are wide and maintained, with a few options that head into a little trickier single track. All the trails travel through ponderosa forest and circumnavigate Woodland Lake, including one that cruises the very edge, which is paved. I recommend beginning on the Turkey Trot Trail, which heads through the woods in a counter-clockwise direction just beyond the lake's shores. As you go, trail signs will point out new options. If you're up for a little more challenging riding, follow the signs to Big Spring; en route you'll climb a hill, and the trail will get technical for a bit. The Big Spring Environmental Study Area is lovely and has interpretive signs. The spring's banks form a marsh area where you'll likely see many birds. Follow the spring to a pond and from there follow the signs back to Woodland Lake. When you reach the lake you can climb onto the paved trail for an easy cool-down. If you find yourself on another trail, simply enjoy yourself, and keep a sense of where the lake is in your direction finder. It's a gentle area that's fairly populated, with people fishing and families enjoying the water, but makes for a nice outing.

Globe Area
Six Shooter Trail
6 miles one-way. Difficult. 3,000-ft. elevation loss. Allow 2 hrs. Access: It took me many tries to find this trailhead. For the best success with this ride, I recommend going with the **Ride-On Bike Shop**, 430 N. Broad St. in Globe (☎ **520/ 425-8100**) on one of its Saturday rides or hiring someone there to run you to the top, since it's a shuttle ride anyway. If not, try this: Head east from Globe center on Broad St. Turn right and cross over a bridge onto Jess Hayes Rd. Travel less than 1 mile and turn right onto Ice House Canyon Rd. (Just before this turn you'll see to your left the Icehouse C.C.C. up a hill; park your shuttle vehicle there.) Travel less than 2 miles on Ice House Canyon Rd. and turn right where the sign directs you to Kellner Canyon FS 55, following signs to Pinal Peak. Travel just under 3 miles and bear left onto FS 651. Continue on FS 651 for 9 miles. Bear left at a sign that reads Ferndell and follow the signs for the Six Shooter Trail 197.

This ride takes you down 3,000 feet—much of it single track—from the peaks of the Pinal Mountains into the town of Globe. As you travel to the trailhead you'll be awed by views in every direction. The trail itself offers views of the Miami/Globe area and a continual descent though several life zones showing dramatic changes in vegetation. During wet months you'll also see small waterfalls along the trail at several locations. As with many of the trails in the Pinal Mountains, this one is maintained very little. Expect plenty of loose rock and dead branches, as well as erosion-prevention dams. The trail immediately descends through pine forest meeting up with Trail 192. You'll see an old mine shaft and remains of a sawmill and cabin there. Shortly the trail passes along a fence line, around a ridge and through a saddle, and then crosses Pioneer Pass Rd. FS 112. The trail gradually becomes more of a road and ends at the Icehouse C.C.C. parking area.

ROAD BIKING
For those who don't mind a little uphill on their rides, eastern Arizona is a great biking area. Most of the major highways are well maintained and have good shoulders. If you can hit this area during off-season you'll have the road to yourself. Beware, though, the areas around Show Low and Pinetop-Lakeside get busy. One scenic ride that I won't fully recommend is the famous **Coronado Trail, U.S. 191** from Springerville down to Clifton. This 127-mile road winds intensely and descends nearly 5,000 feet, offering incredible views southward off the Mogollon Rim. However, there aren't always shoulders, so it can be a dangerous stretch. If you want to ride it, I suggest doing it in the spring or fall when very few cars travel it. My last time on it in a car was in the early spring, and I only saw one or two cars the entire way.

Show Low/Springerville Loop
102 miles. Moderate to difficult. Allow 8 hrs. (a good stopover point for an overnight is Greer). Access: Start at the junction of U.S. 60 and AZ 77 in Show Low or at AZ 260 and U.S. 60 in Springerville.

Beginning in Show Low, this ride heads south through the busy towns of Lakeside and Pinetop, then breaks into nice riding through ponderosa forest into the Apache country at Hon Day and McNary. Soon the views open out and the road, at this point lovely highway with broad shoulders, crosses a series of long, rolling hills, with wide meadows stretching south toward 11,590-foot Baldy Peak. Riding becomes tougher as you make your way through the more mountainous area around Greer. Then you'll come to plains-like terrain in the area around Springerville. Here AZ 260 meets up with U.S. 60. Turn left on U.S. 60 and head back through the pines on a highway that will likely be busier much of the way to Show Low.

Swift Trail
42 miles round-trip. Difficult. Allow 4 hrs. Access: Start south of Safford at the intersection of U.S. 191 and AZ 366 (which is the Swift Trail).

This lovely and little-traveled stretch of pavement climbs the north slope into the Pinaleño Mountains, crossing Ladybug pass and making its way farther back to the south slopes of these remote sky islands. The pavement is good throughout. You'll begin heading west on AZ 366 climbing steadily through Jacobson Canyon, the pine forest becoming denser as you gain elevation. At mile 21, the pavement ends. If you're on a mountain bike you might want to continue another 14 miles to the road's terminus at Columbine. Otherwise, return the way you came, enjoying the views across Jacobson Canyon, the town of Safford, and the Gila Mountains in the distance.

SWIMMING

Some of the sweetest swimming in the region is at **Christopher Creek** east of Payson. There water pools and makes its way down small falls in a Japanese garden fashion. Unfortunately, during the warm months it can be overrun with swimmers. In order to get there see the "Walks & Rambles" section below. **Lyman Lake State Park** has a few nice beaches and cool water to dunk in on a hot summer day.

WALKS & RAMBLES
Springerville
Raven Site Ruin
0.5 miles. Easy. Allow 1 hr. Access: Between Springerville and St. Johns on U.S. 191. ☎ 520/333-5857.

Out on the rolling grasslands of eastern Arizona, this meander allows not only glimpses back in time but also into the process of uncovering ancient mysteries. While you walk you'll get to watch archaeologists at work, and, if you'd like and you make advance reservations, you too can participate. The self-guided ruin tour makes its way around and through 800 rooms covering a span of 3 acres. You'll see living quarters, grain storage areas, and ceremonial kivas left by the Mogollon people who inhabited the area around 1300. You can also explore a village re-creation, where you can see what the buildings may have looked like when they were inhabited. A guided site tour is also available for a nominal fee, but you must reserve in advance. If you'd like to spend a day participating in the work, you'll begin with excavating, then do lab work, and then go on a tour of nearby petroglyphs. Prices for the workday range from $35 for children to $55 for adults, and multiple days can also be arranged. Camping is also available at the site.

Rim Country
Rim Lakes Vista Point Trail
3 miles. Easy. No elevation gain. Allow 1–2 hrs. Access: From Payson follow AZ 260 east about 30 miles until you come to the top of the Mogollon rim. Turn left onto Rim Rd., FS 300. Follow it a few miles to the trailhead on the left.

If you're like me and you keep hearing about the notorious Mogollon Rim, that giant escarpment that runs from western Arizona all the way into New Mexico, you'll probably want to really *see* what the rim is. This is the best place to do it. This trail, paved toward the west and gravel toward the east, meanders along the rim, with stops at key rocky outcroppings where you can sit and ponder the vastness. It's a great place for a picnic. In the fall you'll see patches of oak and aspen exhibiting their orange and yellow hues, and beyond, in any season, you'll look across hundreds of miles of mountainous terrain down toward the Sonoran Desert lands.

Christopher Creek

1–3 miles. Easy. 840-ft. elevation loss. Allow 30 min.–3 hrs. Access: From Payson, head east on AZ 260 for about 19 miles. Just past milepost 271, turn right (south) into the trailhead parking lot. Maps: USGS Promontory Butte; USFS Tonto National Forest.

In about a 10-minute hike from your car, you're at the rim of this awesome gorge, looking down at what appear to be Japanese garden-style waterfall-fed pools large enough to swim in. On weekends this place will be crowded, but weekdays ought to be calmer. On an October day too cool to swim but sunny enough to sit by the creek, I was the only one there. Unfortunately, the site's popularity is apparent by cigarette butts here and there, and fire rings. In an attempt to keep people from driving to the edge of the canyon, the forest service has erected barbed wire fences at the trailhead. At the time of this writing the barbed wire fences had been cut through. As the Forest Service is able to enforce the hiking nature of the place, there will likely be fewer and fewer people visiting this little gem.

The trail heads south through ponderosa pine forest, crosses some campgrounds, and comes to the edge of the canyon. Watch for a sign that says end Trail 298. Walk directly past the sign to the rim of the canyon. At the rim, head down to your left. The descent isn't for ninnies, but if you watch your step you'll make it easily. If you wish to make your way farther downstream, you'll have to climb or find routes around several waterfalls.

Pinetop-Lakeside

This area isn't necessarily a destination. It has become too crowded and busy for that, but if you happen to be in the vicinity there's some nice hiking to be found.

Rim Trail

1 mile. Easy. No elevation gain. Allow 30 min. Access: From Cub Lake Rd. just before you enter actual, drive approximately 1.5 miles to the Rim Trailhead on the right.

Especially for those who like to follow the Mogollon Rim as it transforms en route to the New Mexico border, this is a great place to stop. Here you'll see the rim is less dramatic than it was in the Kohl's Ranch area. The short trail meanders through ponderosa and mansanita to spectacular views. The first 0.3 mile is paved for wheelchair access. All along the way are interpretive signs naming vegetation and the geology of the rim.

Blue Vista

1 mile round-trip. Easy. Allow 30 min. Access: Drive south of Hannagan Meadow on the Coronado Trail, U.S. 191. Watch for the turn-out on your right.

The real reason to stop at Blue Vista is for the views, though it is a nice place to stretch your legs along this 4-hour journey on a winding road that drops off the Mogollon Rim. From this little point on the rim you can see for hundreds of miles toward the east, south, and west. The Coronado Trail–U.S. 191, which you'll drive to get there, runs from Springerville to Clifton, en route descending nearly 5,000 feet in elevation within only 127 miles. You'll pass through as many life zones as you would in driving from Canada to Mexico. The nature trail drops quickly from the parking area and travels a narrow finger ridge to the south, with interpretive signs along the way. You really get a sense of what the rim's like here as it drops from the Colorado Plateau down into the Basin and Range Province. The parking area is a great place to have a picnic.

WHITE-WATER KAYAKING & RAFTING

Arizona doesn't have much in the way of white water (except the Grand Canyon, of course!), and what there is can be chimerical to say the least. But for those who like to catch their water on the fly, the Salt River and its tributaries the Blue and Black Rivers are your tickets to pleasure.

The **Salt River** is a legendary class III-IV run through eastern Arizona. Trips on this route can range from 1 day (about 12 miles) to 5 days (about 53 miles). Not only does it provide fairly continuous white water, it also passes through canyons with walls over 2,000 feet high. Private permits are given out on a lottery system early each year. To apply, contact the Tonto National Forest Globe Ranger Station (☎ **520/402-6200**). Unfortunately, the Salt only runs on years when there's enough run-off to make it safe, and its season is very short, running from mid-March through mid-June with the best flows in a very tight window in March and April.

A number of raft companies run the Salt in every year when there's enough water to do so. **Chandelle River Tours** (☎ 800/242-6335 or 520/577-1824; www.arizonaguide.com) runs a variety of trips. The cost is $99 for a one-day and includes lunch. An overnight is $245 and a 5-day trip is $500+. Prices are subject to change. **Far Flung Adventures** (☎ 800/231-7238; www.farflung.com) offers Apache Whitewater One-Day rafting trips for $79 to $95, which cover 11 miles of white water. Upper Salt Two-Day rafting trips cost $245, and cover 20 river miles. Its Salt River Canyon Wilderness Three-Day trips run $385, and Salt River Canyons Five-Day trips cost $650. The latter covers 53 river miles. Far Flung Adventures provides wet suits and/or rain gear, deliciously prepared meals, eating utensils, tents, and waterproof gear bags.

The **Blue and Black Rivers** have *very* short seasons, generally in March and April, lasting only a day or so. Sometimes these rivers can be runable during the summer monsoons, but that occasion is rare. Both offer incredible scenery and unique challenges. They are a veritable mélange of obstacles, from tight passages to strainers to hydraulics to barbed wire and undercuts. Both are suitable for kayaks, small rafts, or one- or two-person inflatables.

Of the two, the easiest and most accessible is the Blue, with most of its rapids in the class II range, except for within the Blue Box, which should be portaged. Still, there are plenty of hazards, including undercut rocks looming along the big sweeping curves this stream has cut at the base of the high cliffs that border it. The Blue is very accessible; FS 281 runs alongside it. To reach the river, drive south from Alpine 14.5 miles on U.S. 191 to FS 567, which you'll follow about 12 miles to FS 281; turn right and head upstream. You can put in just about anywhere downstream of its origin at the confluence of the Campbell Blue and Dry Blue Rivers. From there the road follows it for 21 miles, so you can take out where you please.

The Black River is mostly tree-lined and flows out of Big Lake and off of Mount Baldy; it is one of the major headwater streams of the Salt River. Rated class IV-V, it drops 400 feet along 13 miles, with a pool/drop configuration. Flows can range as high as 400 CFS, but generally are in the 200 CFS range. The 13-mile segment of the river runs between Buffalo Crossing Bridge on FS 25 and Wildcat Bridge along on FS 25. To reach the put-in, drive south from Alpine 14.5 miles on U.S. 191 to FS 26. Follow FS 26 for 9.5 miles to FS 24. Turn right and drive 3 miles to FS 25 and the put-in at the bridge below Buffalo Crossing. Drive 12.5 miles west on FS 25 to the take-out at Wildcat Bridge. For further information and to check the flows, contact the Alpine Ranger District (☎ **520/339-4384**).

THE RETURN OF THE WOLF

Sometime, a half century ago, the rich and hollow howl of the Mexican gray wolf disappeared from the southwestern United States. His large paws ceased to crease the mud along stream shores, and his quick golden eyes ceased to peer at prey in the night. Ranchers and progress ruled, and the wolf disappeared. But in March 1998, the call of the wild returned to the Southwest, specifically to eastern Arizona, the Apache Mountains, and later to western New Mexico, the Gila Wilderness.

The Mexican Wolf Reintroduction program, a cooperative effort led by the U.S. Fish and Wildlife Service, set about reestablishing about 100 wolves in the area. At the program's inception, only 200 Mexican wolves were known to exist, most of them born in zoos and wildlife sanctuaries in the United States and Mexico. These lovely and powerful creatures that weigh 50 to 85 pounds and measure about 5 feet long, with a richly colored coat of buff, gray, rust, and black, now roam the area and are often spotted by visitors.

The process of releasing the wolves is carefully calculated. They are raised in pens with little human contact at the Sevilleta National Wildlife Refuge in central New Mexico. Using a "soft release" approach, the wolves are taken to the release area and held in acclimation pens for several months before release so that they can become familiar with the area and will hopefully stay there. All adult wolves are fitted with radio collars to monitor their movements. Any wolves leaving the established release area are moved back in, unless they are on private or tribal land and the owner approves.

The story since their release into the 5,000-square-mile area has been a mixture of tragedy and success. Early on in the program a few of the wolves were found shot, a symbol of the opposition area ranchers have to the program. Many sensed failure in the wind. But a few packs succeeded, and soon the Gila was opened to the wolves as well. Latest reports show that 22 are surviving in the wild.

If you see a wolf, keep your distance and restrain your pets. If you must, frighten the wolf away. Don't feed him. If you're camping, dispose of gray water at least 100 yards from camp. It is against the law to kill or injure a wolf just because it is near you or your property, because it attacks your pet, or because you thought it was a coyote or another animal. The penalty for killing or injuring a wolf is up to one year in jail and a fine of up to $100,000.

WILDLIFE VIEWING

The primo wildlife sighting in the region is, of course, the Mexican gray wolf, whose hollow call has only recently returned to the area (see "The Return of the Wolf" feature in this chapter). If you're fortunate enough to see one—and many locals to the area have been—it will happen in the **White Mountains.** Especially watch for them in the remote regions around Mount Baldy and Escudilla Mountain. The White Mountains as well as the **Pinaleño Mountains** to the south are also home to black bears, mule deer, and elk. **Big Springs Environmental Study Area** off Woodland Road in Pinetop-Lakeside attracts mule deer as well, and many smaller creatures such as raccoon, skunk, and Kaibab squirrels.

A trail with interpretive signs leads around some marshes abundant with bird life. **Jacques Marsh Wildlife Area,** located 2 miles north of Pinetop-Lakeside, consists of 130 acres of national forest land and has a 7 ponds and 18 islands, which provide perfect sustenance for such creatures as ducks and geese as well as coyote, fox, bobcat, and elk. **Pintail Lake Wild Game Observation Area,** located 2 miles north of Show Low, is a migration rest area for ducks, geese, and other waterfowl. Their presence enhances the game in the area, both big and small, often visible from observation platforms.

Campgrounds & Other Accommodations

CAMPING

Luna Lake Campground
Drive 5 miles east from Alpine on U.S. 180 and turn north (left) on FS 570 just east of Luna Lake. ☎ **877/444-6777.** 50 single-unit sites, 1 group site. Fire rings, cooking grills, drinking water, tackle shop and boat rental concessionaire at lake, trash dumpsters in season, vault toilets. Pets on leash accepted. $8 per night.

Located within an open stand of large vanilla-scented ponderosa pines, Luna Lake sits on this campground. Beyond the lake is open grassland where some 80 species of wildflowers bloom. Fishing is best in early season—from ice-out in March until late June. Just a short ride from the camp is a system of mountain-biking trails. The nearby Blue Range Primitive Area offers access to dozens of hiking trails.

Alpine Divide Campground
Drive 4 miles north of Alpine on paved U.S. 191. ☎ **520/339-4384.** 12 single unit sites. Tables, fire rings, cooking grills, spring-fed water supply, vault toilets, trash dumpsters in season. $5 per night.

This small, intimate campsite sits in a cool forest of ponderosa pines at the foot of Escudilla Mountain. There's not a whole lot to do at this campground except eat and sleep, but its convenient location makes it an attractive place to spend the night. Fishing and boating at Luna Lake is just a short drive away; mountain biking in Williams Valley is approximately 6 miles away; and trout fishing at the Black River is about 10 miles from the campground.

Rolfe C. Hoyer Campgrounds
Located near Greer on AZ 373 directly south of AZ 260. ☎ **520/735-7313;** for reservations, call 877/444-6777. 100 campsites (RV and tent), showers, flush toilets, picnic tables, firepits, Butterfly Museum. No electric hookups available. $12 per night plus an $8.65 one-time surcharge; $5 for a bundle of firewood.

Set in a grove of ponderosa pine, this 8,500-foot elevation campground is a lovely spot. Unfortunately it fills up with urban folks, many from Phoenix, who come to fish in nearby Greer Lakes. Due to the mucky bottom, these lakes are not suitable for swimming. A century ago this spot was most renowned for its butterflies, but today the numbers are few. A museum, named in honor of the once abundant population, houses information on the history of the area, including its colorful, fluttery friends. Campers can also enjoy hiking trails nearby. You can find decent, upscale eateries in Greer.

Los Burros Campground
Located in the Apache-Sitgreaves National Forest 7 miles north of McNary on FS 224. ☎ **520/368-5111.** 5 primitive campsites, fire rings, picnic tables, and 1 vault toilet.

This is one of the prettiest campgrounds I've experienced. Set at 7,900 feet, within a lovely meadow bordered by cottonwoods and ponderosa pines, it's a great place to cool your heels before heading out on the bike trail of the same name (see the "Mountain Biking" section earlier in this chapter). This is a pack-it-in, pack-it-out campground. It is open from May to October. Twenty-two foot trailers are allowed, but not advised since the dirt road leading into the campground can get rough.

Christopher Creek Campground

Located 19 miles east of Payson off AZ 260. 43 campsites (tent and RV), drinking water, vault toilets, picnic tables and grills, and amphitheater.

Set in a canyon along Christopher Creek, this campground is shaded by ponderosa pine forest. Unfortunately, it gets very busy on summer weekends. When all 43 sites are full, it becomes a rowdy place. I recommend visiting this campground only during the off-seasons, fall and spring. The swimming holes along the creek are perfect for all ages to access, but during a drought, the creek becomes a trickle. During summer months, educational programs are periodically held in the amphitheater.

INNS & LODGES

Rawhide & Roses

From the hospital on AZ 260 west of Pinetop-Lakeside, go south on Cub Lake Rd., turn left on Flores Dr. and left again on S. Flores Dr. 5130 South Flores Dr. (P.O. Box 1153), Lakeside, AZ 85929. ☎ 520/537-0216; www.rawhide-roses.com/index.htm. E-mail: rawhideroses@wmonline.com. 3 units. $95–$215 double. Price includes full breakfast. DISC, MC, V.

The first word that comes to mind regarding this inn is imagination. Each of its three rooms has a theme played out fully, from the John Wayne Room, with its log canopy bed and clawfoot tub, to the Geronimo Room, with a painted elkskin headboard and a spa. These rooms fulfill fantasies you might not know you have. A romantic path leading out back through the woods to the hot tub fuels even more. After a breakfast such as chuckwagon quiche with praline scones, you may want to feed the Kaibab squirrels that scurry around outside the glass door. The only complaint here is the place may be a little too precious. If you don't like being careful with lovely art, you might want to pick an inn where you can kick off your shoes.

Red Setter Inn

8 Main St. (P.O. Box 133), Greer, AZ 85927. ☎ 888-994-7337 or 520/735-7441. Fax 520/735-7425. www.redsetterinn.com. 10 units. $130–$195 double. Room rates include full breakfast. AE, MC, V.

This is one of the few B&Bs I've stayed in where people really use the shared spaces, where couples sit reading and playing chess near the fire. That's because this modern Adirondack-style log inn has such a cozy, homey feeling. Set steps away from the Little Colorado River, it's a bright, airy space. The rooms are decorated in early American antiques, the beds with down comforters and fine linens. A Godiva chocolate on your pillow bids you good night. Some rooms have their own fireplaces and whirlpool tubs. Breakfast will carry you through the day. During my stay we had eggs Benedict, potato pancakes, asparagus, and freshly baked apricot Danish pastries. If you stay for more than 2 nights you'll get a complimentary lunch to take along on your outing. The very conscientious innkeepers will help direct you to the best trails in the area.

Noftsiger Hill Inn

425 North St., Globe, AZ 85501. ☎ 520/425-2260. 5 units. $55–$75 double, includes full breakfast. MC, V.

This semi-restored 1907 schoolhouse sits atop a hill overlooking Globe and the surrounding area, and provides a strangely unique stay. Since most of the rooms are fashioned from classrooms, they lack coziness, but they are very spacious, with blackboards on the walls and large banks of windows letting in lots of light. Hardwood floors and antique furnishings lend atmosphere to rooms with subtle themes such as one with an Old Mexico feel and another decorated with mission-style furniture. At press time ownership of the inn was shifting hands, so changes may be made.

Hannagan Meadows Lodge

23 miles south of Alpine on U.S. 191. HC 61, Box 335, Alpine, AZ 85920. ☎ **520/339-4370.** 8 units, 8 cabins. $60–$110 double. AE, DISC, DC, MC, V.

Ever wonder what people do when they win the lottery? Here's your chance to see. Owners of this inn did just that and they took their winnings, skipped town, and opened up this inn nearly in the middle of nowhere and now run it with the help of all family members from grandparents to children. With that background, the service ranges broadly from the friendly and conscientious grands and kids to the less-concerned main proprietors. Originally built in 1926 after the dedication of the "Clifton to Springerville" Highway, part of the lodge is comprised of rustic cabins. The main lodge, though, is modern, built in 1996. Decorated in a Victorian style, the rooms range broadly in size, from ones almost too small for one, to expansive bridal-suite-like ones. A dining room with hewn-log beams serves three meals. During summer the lodge offers horseback riding and good access to mountain biking; during snowy winters it has access to cross-country skiing and snowmobiling.

Kohl's Ranch

17 miles east of Payson on AZ 260. ☎ **800/331-5645** or 520/478-4211. www.ilxresorts.com. 46 units. $75–$250 double. AE, DISC, MC, V.

This is an interesting family-style hotel within the ponderosa-filled rim country. For years it has served as a summer retreat for Phoenicians, and so it hasn't had to try very hard. Thus, you could count on the basics: a decent bed, a nice swimming pool, and fair, Denny's-style food in the dining room. At this writing, the owners were working to upgrade the place to appeal more to sports enthusiasts and the fast-spending yuppie crowd, but they weren't fully succeeding. Many of the cabins have been redecorated with a lovely style and have their own hot tubs on private porches, but the hotel rooms at this writing were still ordinary, though quite spacious, many with refrigerators, microwaves, and stoves. The cafe still serves basic food, but some travelers will really like what they call "Western" cuisine—barbequed ribs and such. On-site, guests can enjoy horseback riding, trout fishing, an outdoor pool, whirlpool, sport court, jogging track, fitness room, volleyball, and children's playground and petting zoo.

7

Arizona's Sky Islands

Even before I first set foot in southeastern Arizona, I was enchanted by it. With mountain names such as the Chiricahuas and Dragoons and place names such as Dos Cabezas (Spanish for "two heads") and Tombstone, my skin tingled simply because of the sounds of the words. They conjured up a kind of renegade lawlessness that I found completely enticing. And after traversing the region up and down, and back and forth, I've found that the word "lawless" may be the best description of this area yet. Its nature is anarchic, with extremes that defy convention. The most notable extremes are the stark desert lands from which jut up spectacular blue "sky islands," rich and varied mountain ranges, each with a character of its own. Other extremes come within the habitat of those mountains, which range from dry desert to lush riparian habitat. The creatures that inhabit the mountains are extreme as well: You may see ominous, ground-bound Gila monsters and scorpions, or flitting, skyborne vermilion flycatchers and violet-crowned hummingbirds.

For centuries, southeastern Arizona has been a region for renegades. The Chiricahua Mountains were once the homeland of the Chiricahua Apaches. During the mid-19th century, famed leader Geronimo led the Apaches on attacks against encroaching pioneers in the area for more than 25 years. The Apaches' resistance was unable to stop the settlement, and U.S. troops fought to vanquish them. In 1886 Geronimo and his band surrendered and were removed to Florida. Meanwhile, in the nearby Dragoon Mountains, other Apaches hid out within what turned out to be a natural fortress at Cochise Stronghold, named for their leader, Cochise. He was born around 1815 in the Dragoon Mountains. From 1860 to 1872, he and his band battled the U.S. Cavalry because of the handling of an incident at Apache Pass about 30 miles east. Cochise died in the area of his homeland and is believed to be buried within the stronghold.

This is also the region Francisco Vásquez de Coronado traversed in his 1540 expedition in search of the fabled Seven Cities of Cíbola, cities that were rumored to be made of gold. He marched up the San Pedro River Valley past present-day Sierra Vista. Within the area, a monument commemorates his trip. Nearly 150 years later a Jesuit priest, Father Eusebio Francisco Kino founded a series of mission churches in the area, two of which (San Xavier del Bac and San José de Tumacacori) still stand.

Sprawling below the notable mountain ranges in the region are miles of rolling hills that for over a century have proven prime cattle ranching country, and from that tradition arose the Old West character of this region. This is where Wyatt Earp, his brothers Virgil and Morgan, and Doc Holliday fought the outlaws Ike Clanton and Frank and Tom McLaury on October 26, 1881, at a livery stable known as the O.K. Corral. The outlaws' graves now rest in the town's Boot Hill Graveyard. "The town too tough to die" was born and hit its peak as a mining town. In fact, in the late 1800s Tombstone and Bisbee were the wildest stops in the region between New Orleans and San Francisco, infamous for their gambling halls, bordellos, saloons, and shoot-outs in the streets.

It's ironic that a place with such a raucous history would be home to one of the world's most serene pastimes: bird watching. The reason the area is so prime for this pursuit is that four distinct regions and their plants and animals come together here. The Rocky Mountains, Mexico's Sierra Madre, the Sonoran Desert, and the Chihuahuan Desert converge to create a broad range of habitats for birds and other wildlife. Southeastern Arizona also lies along a major flyway connecting points as far south as Costa Rica with points as far north as Canada, which means you'll find not only tropical birds rare to the United States such as the hepatic tanager and elegant trogon, but also masses of northern birds such as snow geese and sandhill cranes.

For those whose pace is a little faster, there's plenty of hiking and mountain biking in the region, as well as some of the most interesting horseback riding in the United States. Another pastime rarely mentioned in this book but very popular here is "sky watching." Southern Arizona is one of the prime stargazing spots in the world, especially in the area around Benson at the Skywatcher Inn and the Vega-Bray Observatory (see the "Stargazing" note later in this chapter).

The Lay of the Land

Nowhere in the Great Basin and Range Province are its characteristics more pronounced than in southeastern Arizona. The Basin and Range Province, which stretches all the way from southern Oregon to western Texas and covers most of southern Arizona, is characterized by rugged, northwest-trending mountain ranges connected by low-lying deserts. These deserts have for the past 75 million years been tectonically mobile, with relatively frequent landmass collisions and separations that create "sky islands" that stick up from the rolling grassland. These range from the Santa Catalinas and Santa Ritas and Patagonias to the west, to the Dragoons and Chiricahuas to the east, with many others in between. Like the many other sky islands of the Basin and Range Province, these were formed as a result of the extending nature of the province, which creates fissures and breaks, the volcanic mountains rising to the surface.

Though some would be tempted to simply call southeastern Arizona a dry desert, the type of desert ranges here, from the very exemplary Sonoran Desert represented by Saguaro National Monument in the Tucson area, to the dry and scrubby Chihuahuan Desert along the border, to the high piñon/juniper desert represented by the mountain regions.

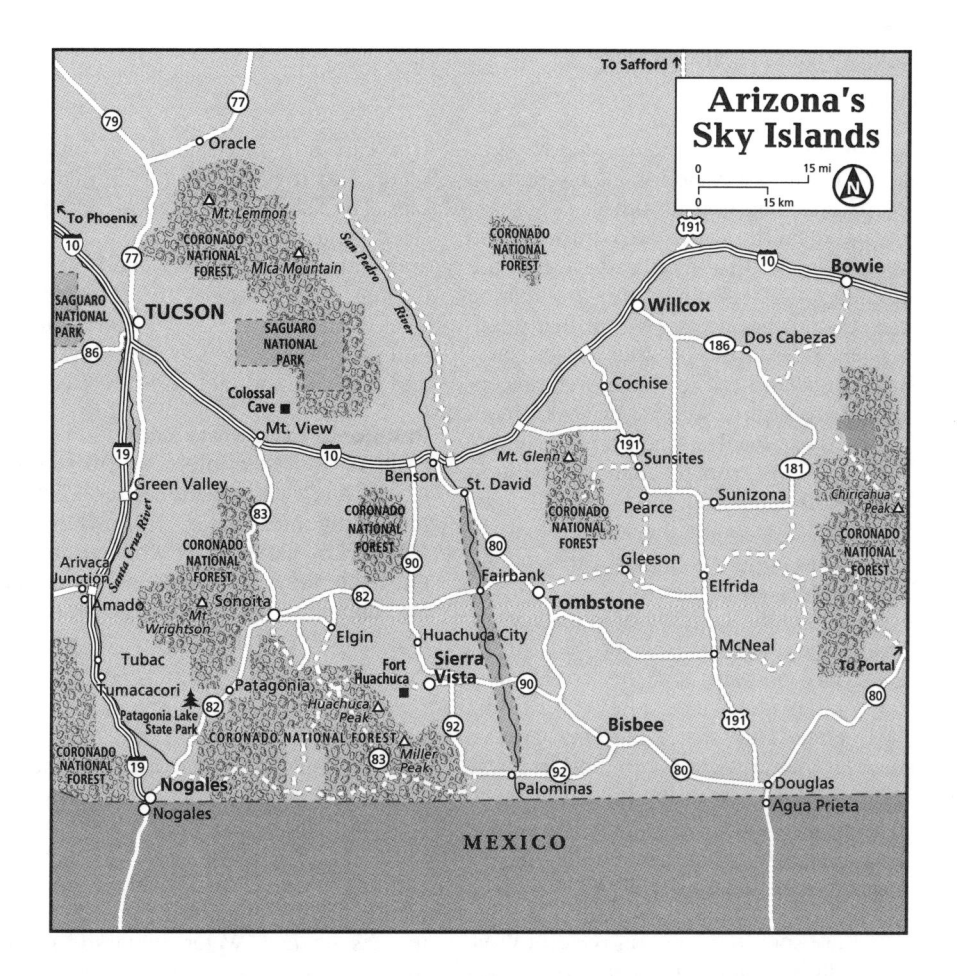

The San Pedro River, an amazing waterway that makes its way through the often-brown desertscape, cuts through the middle of the region. Within its narrow border are century-old cottonwoods and other lush riparian habitat. Some 380 bird species have been reported along its banks, including green kingfisher, crissal thrasher, and vermilion flycatcher.

The best time to visit this region is in the spring and fall, when the weather is mild and the birds are plentiful. During that time temperatures in the desert will be in the 60s and 70s, while in the mountains they'll be in the 50s and 60s. In the summer, temperatures in the desert will often be in the 90s and at times above 100°F, while in the mountains they'll be in the 80s. Winter temperatures can get chilly in the desert, but within this region will likely be in the 50s and 60s, while in the mountains they may get down to the 30s and 40s. The region receives little snow and rain, though during monsoon season the sky islands will at times get abundant afternoon thundershowers. During those months it's a good idea to hike early in the day to avoid the lightning that accompanies the showers.

Orientation

The region's northern border is north of Tucson, so it encompasses the Santa Catalina Mountains and Saguaro National Park East and West. The northern border continues east paralleling I-10 to the New Mexico border, which forms the eastern border of the region. The southern border is defined by the boundary with Mexico, and the western region is mainly defined by I-19 running north-south.

The main thoroughfares through the region are I-10 running east-west to the north and I-19 running north-south along the western boundary. Within that quadrangle there are no other major thoroughfares, and traffic in the area, except in and around Tucson, Sierra Vista, Green Valley, and Nogales, will be minimal. AZ 82 and AZ 83 run through the western part of the region, and U.S. 191 runs north-south through the eastern part of the region connecting I-10 with Douglas on the Mexican border.

Tucson is the largest city in the region, with a population of about 900,000. Its size puts pressure on the entire area, though places like the Chiricahua Mountains and the Dragoons are so remote that a visitor can find solitude there. The I-19 corridor from Tucson to Nogales is fairly developed the whole way, but the Santa Rita Mountains are vast enough to provide plenty of opportunities to escape the crowds. The only other hot spot in the region is Sierra Vista, a rapidly growing retirement community that is sprawling across the grasslands at the base of the Huachuca Mountains.

Parks & Other Hot Spots

Parker Canyon Lake
South of Sonoita via AZ 83. ☎ **505/455-5847.** Bird watching, boardsailing, boating (small motor), camping, fishing, hiking.

Set within a little valley surrounded by hills, this lake's biggest draw is the 5-mile trail that circumnavigates it. It is also a stop-off point on the famed Arizona Trail (see the feature in chapter 1). While visiting the area, I met some birders who said you can find three kinds of bluebirds there, and they had just seen some orioles. The fishing can be good, with giant-sized largemouth bass, channel catfish, and rainbow trout stocked October through March. There are 64 campsites. The Parker Canyon Lake Store can set you up with fishing gear, including a boat and that all-important cup of coffee.

Patagonia Lake State Park
From Tucson, take Interstate 19 south to AZ 82 and head northeast for 12 miles to Patagonia Lake Rd. ☎ **520/287-6965.** Open daily 4am–10pm. $5 entrance fee. Bird watching, boardsailing, camping, fishing, hiking, powerboating, sailing, swimming.

One day when I visited this lake to swim, rangers stood at the entrance turning people away because it was full. That's how popular this 640-acre spread of water can be on a hot spring day. I'm sure that summer is even worse. On-site there's a beach that's comfortable, but can fill up with kids. The lake is good for fishing and has a no-wake speed limit on the eastern half. Water-skiing and jet skiing are limited to weekdays and non-holidays. Look for white-tailed deer roaming the hills and great blue herons walking the shoreline.

Arizona-Sonora Desert Museum
Located 14 miles west of Tucson. Take Speedway west to Gates Pass Rd., then to Kinney Rd. ☎ **520/883-2702.** www.desertmuseum.org. Daily Oct–Feb 8:30am–5pm and Mar–Sept 7:30am–5pm. Admission: $9.95 Nov–April for adults 13 and older; $8.95 May–Oct for adults 13 and older; $1.75 year-round for children ages 6–12.

Don't be fooled by the name "museum," because you won't be roaming the halls of any stuffy establishment here. Rather, this "museum" is home to many of Arizona's indigenous plants and animals, and you'll view them outdoors in designed habitats. A wide range of

The Arizona Birding Trail

Arizona-Sonora Desert Museum **4**
Carr Canyon **12**
Catalina State Park **1**
Chiricahua National Monument **16**
Cochise Stronghold Recreation Area **15**
Coronado National Memorial **13**
Empire Cienega Wildlife Preserve **9**
Madera Canyon **6**
Mount Lemmon **2**
Parker Canyon Lake **10**
Patagonia Lake State Park **7**
Patagonia-Sonoita Creek Preserve **8**
Ramsey Canyon Preserve **11**
Rucker Canyon **19**
Rustler Park **17**
Saguaro National Park East **5**
Saguaro National Park West **3**
San Pedro Riparian Preserve **14**
South Fork Cave Creek **18**

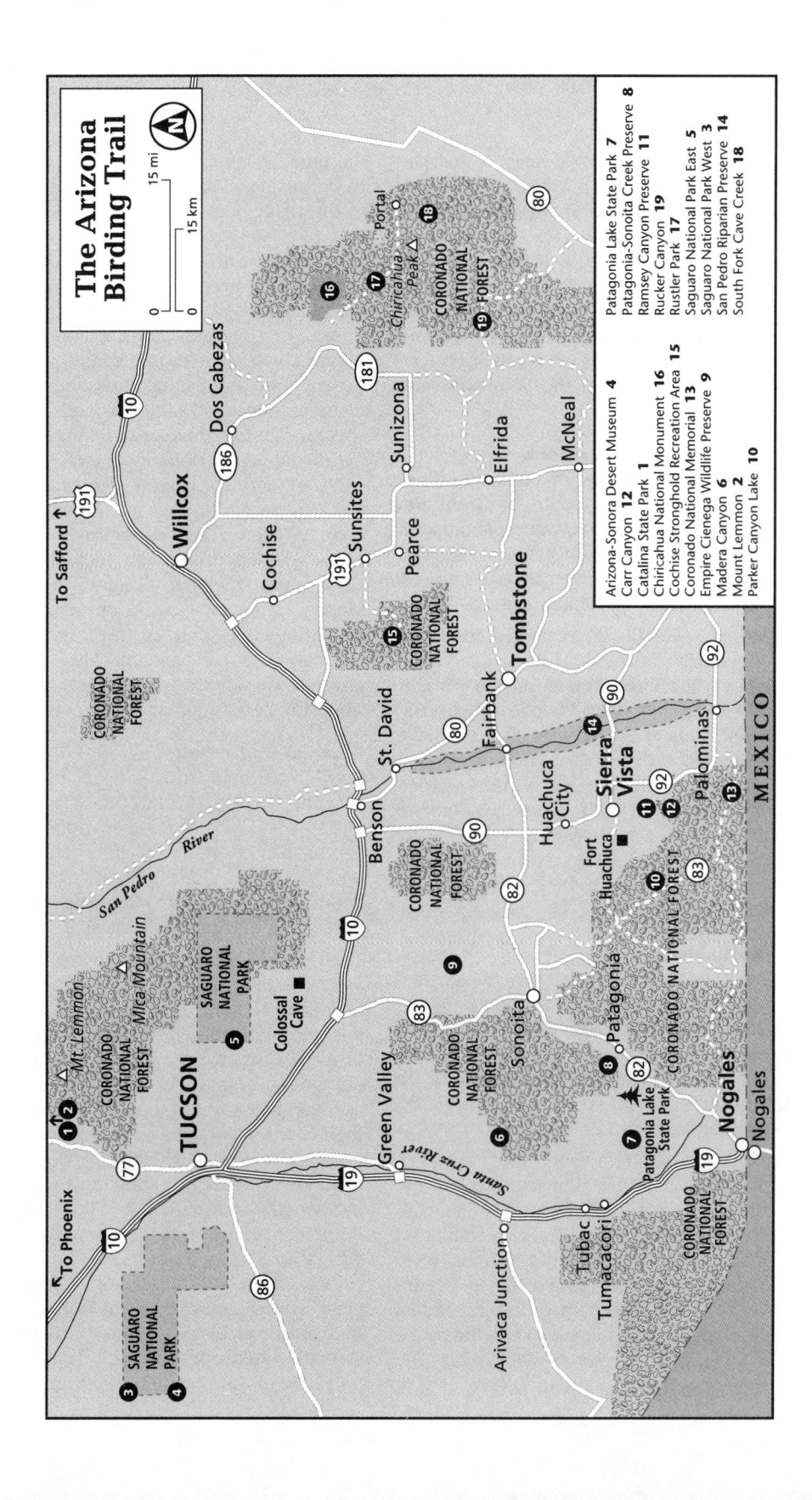

animals, including coatimundis (similar to a raccoon, but with a longer body, a tail, and a long flexible snout), rattlers, and desert rodents, live at the museum. Special features include a fake limestone cave where bats sleep the day away upside down and a coyote exhibit that has an invisible barrier between the animals and the spectators. A gift shop specializes in books on the Southwest and jewelry.

Tucson Botanical Gardens
Located in the center of Tucson, north of Alvernon Way, just south of Grant Rd. ☎ **520/326-9686.** www.tucsonbotanical.org. Daily 8:30am–4:30pm. Admission $4 for adults; $3 for seniors ages 62 and older, and $1 for children ages 6–11.

This 5.5-acre botanical garden maintains 17 specialty gardens including a succulent garden, an herb garden, and an iris garden. Other highlights include a Mediterranean landscape that was planted in the 1930s by the original owners; a verdant tropical greenhouse; and sensory garden where you can sniff, touch, and admire the native Southwestern plants. The newest garden here is the Children's Discovery Garden, which is designed to their scale.

Biosphere 2
Take Oracle Rd. north from Tucson and continue north on AZ 77 to mile marker 96.5. ☎ **800/828-2462** or **520/896-6200.** www.bio2.edu. Daily 8:30am–6pm. Closed Dec 25. Admission $12.95 for adults, $8.95 youth ages 13–17, $6 children ages 6–12.

Many people remember the swarm of media stories that buzzed around the Biosphere 2 project (Earth was considered Biosphere 1) that took place around 1991. Four men and four women were locked inside this airtight, 3-acre greenhouse in the desert in order to conduct experiments, the biggest one being to see if they could survive on their own. The project was shrouded in controversy at the time, and the outcome of the experiment was never really clear, though some of the participants walked out before the end date. What's left is a science project/tourist attraction sponsored by Columbia University. It is a sight to behold—a series of complex greenhouses that support tropical rain forest, savanna, desert, thorn scrub, marsh, ocean, and agricultural areas, and that includes almost 4,000 plant and animal species. Though there are no longer people living in Biosphere 2, experiments continue and, for a fairly steep fee, visitors can take a 2-hour tour of part of the project. There's an orientation followed by a guided tour that includes the Underwater Viewing Gallery, the Test Module, and multimedia presentations. An interactive display area provides entertainment for children. Also on the grounds are a hotel, a restaurant, cafes, a bookstore, and a gift shop.

Catalina State Park
Hwy. 77 (Oracle Rd.), 9 miles north of Tucson. ☎ **520/628-5798.** 48 campsites—half with hookups, equestrian center, picnic area with grills, showers, and gift shop. Open daily with day-use hours ending at 10pm. Camping, hiking, horseback riding, wildlife viewing.

This scenic park shoulders up against the Santa Catalina Mountains within the Coronado National Forest offering incredible mountain desert terrain as well as history. A wash here called the Cañada del Oro (or Canyon of Gold) was a mining site first for Jesuit missionaries and then later for Tucsonans who scoured the banks for gold. Highlights of the park include seven hiking/riding trails of varying length and difficulty. The Romero Ruin Interpretive Trail gently weaves its way through saguaro cactus and past Hohokam Indian ruins. For a tougher climb, the Romero Canyon Trail climbs high into the lush desert to cool pools (see the "Hikes & Backpack Trips" section later in this chapter). The Sutherland

Trail gains more in elevation, climbing toward the top of the Catalinas and Mount Lemmon. Over 20 years ago this was an important breeding ground for desert bighorn sheep. Unfortunately, the herd of 75 to 80 has dwindled to nothing. With pressure from Tucson and an inability to range, inbreeding may have set in. That factor along with predation has either killed the herd or driven them into bordering national forest lands.

Garden Canyon
Located 2 miles from Sierra Vista, on the Fort Huachuca military reservation. ☎ 520/533-7083. Bird watching, hiking, mountain biking, wildlife viewing.

If you're willing to submit to Fort Huachuca's strict regulations, this canyon in the Huachuca Mountains is worth exploring. It has 8 miles of hiking trails through desert and riparian canyon. Some 350 species of birds have been sighted, including the famed elegant trogon and the Mexican spotted owl. There are also Native American petroglyphs. Wildflowers and butterflies are also plentiful. Before entering the main gate of Fort Huachuca, visitors must show a driver's license, registration, and proof of auto insurance. Picnickers must obtain a permit from the Sportsman Center before using facilities.

Saguaro National Park

Saguaro National Park, encompassing 91,327 acres, contains one of the most expansive and best-preserved parts of the Sonoran Desert. It offers visitors to the southwestern United States a prime chance to become immersed in the image that has come to be synonymous with the word desert: the great saguaro cactus. What you'll find here are rolling hills with literal forests of saguaro, surrounded by the rich and varied flora and fauna for which the Sonoran is so renowned. The park has two districts, West and East, separated by the city of Tucson. Each has a distinct character. Some say Saguaro West is prettier, with more rich stands of cactus; it is definitely the more intimate of the two. Saguaro East is larger and sits closer to the city; it spreads through the Rincon Mountains, so the terrain is more varied than Saguaro West. For information about the saguaro, see the "The Saguaro Cactus & Other Desert Denizens" feature later in this chapter.

GETTING THERE

Both Saguaro West and Saguaro East are located in Tucson. To reach Saguaro West, take Gates Pass Road west through the Tucson Mountains to Kinney Road, which leads to the visitor center, about a 25-minute drive from Tucson. To visit Saguaro East, head east on Speedway Boulevard. Turn right on Old Spanish Trail, which will lead to the visitor center, about a 15-minute drive from Tucson.

INFORMATION

You can reach the Saguaro West visitor center at ☎ 520/733-5158; contact the Saguaro East visitor center at ☎ 520/733-5153. The visitor centers are open daily from 8:30am to 5pm. Saguaro West Park itself is open 24 hours; Saguaro East Park is open from 7:30am to sunset. The entrance fee is $6. Popular activities in the park include backpacking (in Saguaro East only), biking (Saguaro East only), bird watching, camping, hiking, horseback riding, mountain biking, and wildlife viewing.

CLIMATE

Planning when to visit the park is key. Generally the best season is from October to April, when temperatures are in the 60s and 70s. Nighttime temperatures during the winter can dip below freezing. During the hottest period, from May to September, temperatures often hover around 100°F.

However nighttime temperatures can drop by as many as 30°F, and even more in the heights of the Rincon Mountains. Hikers and horseback riders should beware of the monsoon season from July to September when thunderstorms and floods can prove dangerous. Avoid open and low-lying areas and washes.

PARK RULES

Though both districts have visitor centers, neither has a campground, though backcountry camping is possible in Saguaro East. Since temperatures run so high within the park, be sure to carry at least 1 gallon of water per person per day while hiking. There is no water available at picnic areas or along trails.

Beware of the spiny nature of the desert's flora. Especially beware of the cholla cactus spines that, with the slightest touch, can become embedded in skin.

Leave all plants and animals undisturbed. Beware of such desert denizens as rattlesnakes, scorpions, and Gila monsters. If you plan to hike at night, carry a flashlight. Never put your fingers anywhere you can't first see. Obey park speed limits; driving off roads is prohibited. Pets must be leashed at all times and are not allowed on the trails.

PARK PROGRAMS

Both parks have visitor centers with expansive exhibits, audiovisual programs, brochures, maps, and driving guides. Activities include guided hikes, nature walks, and talks, generally from December to April.

SCENIC DRIVES

The 9-mile **Bajada Loop Drive** in Saguaro West begins at the visitor center and passes through thick stands of saguaro forest. The road is graded dirt and suitable for most vehicles, though people driving motor homes or pulling trailers should check road conditions before setting out. The paved 8-mile **Cactus Forest Drive** in Saguaro East winds over hills of rich Sonoran Desert and through large stands of saguaro. Be sure to pick up a guidebook before embarking on either drive. The drive at Saguaro East has picnic areas along the way, each with picnic tables, fire grills, and pit toilets. There is no drinking water.

HIKING & HORSEBACK RIDING TRAILS

Both parks combined have well over 100 miles of trails winding through the desert and, at Saguaro East, mountain country. Within 1 mile of the Saguaro West visitor center are two nature trails. A number of other trails in the area are under 2 miles round-trip. Longer trails make their way farther into the park and even connect with trails outside the park in the Tucson Mountains. Similarly, Saguaro East has short hikes with interpretive signs near the visitor center. Longer hikes penetrate the wilderness of the Rincon Mountains and their foothills. In the mountains the terrain changes measurably, from the Sonoran Desert to woodlands of scrub oak to forests of ponderosa pine and Douglas fir. In order to camp in the backcountry at Saguaro East you must obtain a permit at the visitor center in advance. Those who'd like to bike the parks have only a few options. Road bikers can ride the paved 8-mile Cactus Forest Drive at Saguaro East. Mountain bikers can also enjoy that drive as well as the 9-mile Bajada Loop Drive in Saguaro West. Also at Saguaro East is the Cactus Forest Trail, a 2.5-mile section of single track located on the drive. (See the "Mountain Biking" section later in this chapter.)

Chiricahua National Monument

This "Land of Standing Up Rocks," as named by the Chiricahua Apaches, is a Dr. Seuss storybook place of magical

THE SAGUARO CACTUS & OTHER DESERT DENIZENS

The supreme symbol of the American Southwest, the multiarmed saguaro cactus is not only lovely, but it's also at the center of a complex desert ecosystem. Many species rely on it as a source of food and shelter.

Much of the cactus's power is due to its ability to acquire and store water. The saguaro collects water with roots that lie about 3 inches below the surface and generally stretch as far out as the saguaro is tall. During a single rainfall, the cactus's roots and the thin fibers along them can collect as much as 200 gallons of water, enough to sustain the plant for a year. Accordion-like pleats allow the saguaro to expand and hold the water in a gelatin-like substance within its spongy trunk and branches. Unlike most plants, where leaves perform the photosynthetic process of food-making, in the saguaro it is performed in the trunk and branches. Waxy skin further reduces moisture loss.

The saguaro begins as a pinhead-sized seed. Often finding a home under such shelter as paloverde and mesquite, its seedlings are shaded from the desert's intense sunlight, protected from the cold, and hidden from animals that might eat them. The saguaro's growth is very slow and comes in spurts, with most of it taking place in the summer rainy season. After 15 years the saguaro may be barely a foot tall. At 30 years it may begin to flower and produce fruit. By the time it's 50 years old, it can be as tall as 7 feet. Its first branches may sprout at 75 years. After 100 years, it may measure 25 feet tall. The grandest saguaros—the largest cacti in the United States—can be a high as 50 feet, weigh 8 tons, and have lived 150 years.

The saguaro blooms in spring; big bold flowers open in the night, wilting by the next afternoon. During this short time many flying animals succeed in pollinating the cactus. White-winged doves, long-nosed bats, honeybees, and moths become powdered with sticky pollen as they feed on the nectar inside the flower. They travel, transporting the pollen, fertilizing as they go.

In summer the fruit of the saguaro ripens, creating a sugary pulp with as many as 2,000 seeds. Coyotes, foxes, javalenas and other animals feast on the fruit. As well as providing food for many desert denizens, the saguaro also serves as a home to many. The Gila woodpecker and the gilded flicker bore holes and make their nests in the trunk and in larger branches. Once those holes are abandoned, other animals move in, including many birds and honeybees that appreciate a temperature as much as 20°F cooler than the outer air in summer and 20°F warmer in winter.

Unfortunately, the numbers of saguaros in Saguaro National Park are declining. Killing freezes seem to be the major cause. Human encroachment on the land, including grazing that took place from the 1880s to 1979, may also contribute to the decline in numbers. However, biologists are noting a recovery, with many young saguaros thriving, though the cactus is still in danger. Natural forces, vandalism, and cactus rustling—the theft of them for use in landscaping—are very real threats to these giants, as well as to the many lives that depend on them.

---

landforms. Its history stretches back 27 million years to a time when violent volcanic eruptions from the nearby Turkey Creek caldera spewed white-hot ash. Once the ash had cooled and fused, it became a 2,000-foot-thick layer of dark volcanic rock known as rhyolite, which over time heaved up to form the Chiricahua Mountains. The forces of erosion eventually sculpted the rock into odd formations. Weak vertical cracks let in moisture allowing for still more erosion, which created the fascinating forms the monument preserves today. These forms have wildly vivid characters with descriptive names such as Duck on a Rock and Totem Pole Rock. When viewed from a distance the many rock forms appear as a stone army marching down toward the desert lands below.

INFORMATION

To reach Chiricahua National Monument, drive on AZ 86; the park is located 30 miles southwest of Wilcox. For information, call ☎ **520/824-3560.** The visitor center is open daily 8am to 5pm; the park itself is open year-round 24 hours a day. The entrance fee is $6, and there's an $8 camping fee. The most popular activities in the park are bird watching, camping, and hiking.

HISTORY

Named for the Chiricahua Apache who for centuries lived in these hills, this monument is the place where Apache leader Geronimo finally, after 25 years of battling settlement of the area, surrendered his fighters in 1886. He and his tribe members were sent to Florida. With the resistance gone, the region was more hospitable to settlers. Among the first were Neil and Emma Erickson, a Swedish immigrant couple that built a home in Bonita Canyon where they farmed and ranched. One of their daughters, Lillian, and her husband, Ed Riggs, turned the homestead into a guest ranch in 1920 and named it Faraway Ranch because of its remote location. The Riggs explored the Chiricahuas extensively, building trails and touring guests through the formations. They promoted the idea of creating a national park. In 1924, Chiricahua National Monument was established. Today, visits to the Faraway Ranch and the Stafford's Cabin (the only neighbor of the Faraway) are available year-round, with tours conducted daily.

FLORA & FAUNA

Due to its close proximity to Mexico, the Chiricahuas are home to a unique ecosystem. In this "sky island" dwell creatures native not only to the Sonoran Desert, but also to the Mexican Sierra Madre. Most conspicuous are the unusual birds, such as hepatic tanager, red-faced warbler, and elegant trogon. Mammal species that have come up from the Sierra include Chiricahua fox squirrels, coatimundis, and peccaries. Mexican influence is apparent in the tree species as well, with such inhabitants as Chihuahua pine and Apache pine dotting the mountainsides. The plant species spectrum is broad here. You'll find cacti in the lowlands; oaks, alligator juniper, and Arizona cypress in the canyon forests; manzanita, buckhorn, and skunkbush chaparral on ridges; and Douglas fir and aspen on the highest slopes.

SCENIC DRIVE

The best way to get acquainted with the monument is on the **Bonita Canyon Drive,** which winds 8 miles to the mountains' crest and Massai Point, the best vantage spot in the monument. From Massai Point much of the monument can be seen, as well as the vast lowland desert below and the landmark peaks of Sugarloaf Mountain and Cochise Head. During your return you can stop en route at roadside pullouts to see formations and other geologic features. This is also the route to follow to get to the hiking trails listed in this chapter.

HIKING

Winding through the magical land are more than 20 miles of trials. They pass formations such as Pinnacle Balanced Rock, Totem Pole, and Duck on a Rock, and they also meander along streams and through deep canyons. The trails lead to a small natural bridge and a ledge of volcanic hailstones, evidence of ancient eruptions. Ranging in length from 0.25 miles to 9 miles round-trip, they offer days of exploring. For specific hiking information, pick up a hiking guide at the visitor center and see the "Hikes & Backpack Trips" and "Walks & Rambles" sections later in this chapter.

CAMPING

The campground in this monument is one of the best in southeastern Arizona. Though it can be crowded, necessitating early arrival, a few of the sites are tucked into the oak trees providing privacy, and quiet hours are enforced so the place is peaceful. All sites are on a first-come, first-served basis. See the "Campgrounds & Other Accommodations" section later in this chapter.

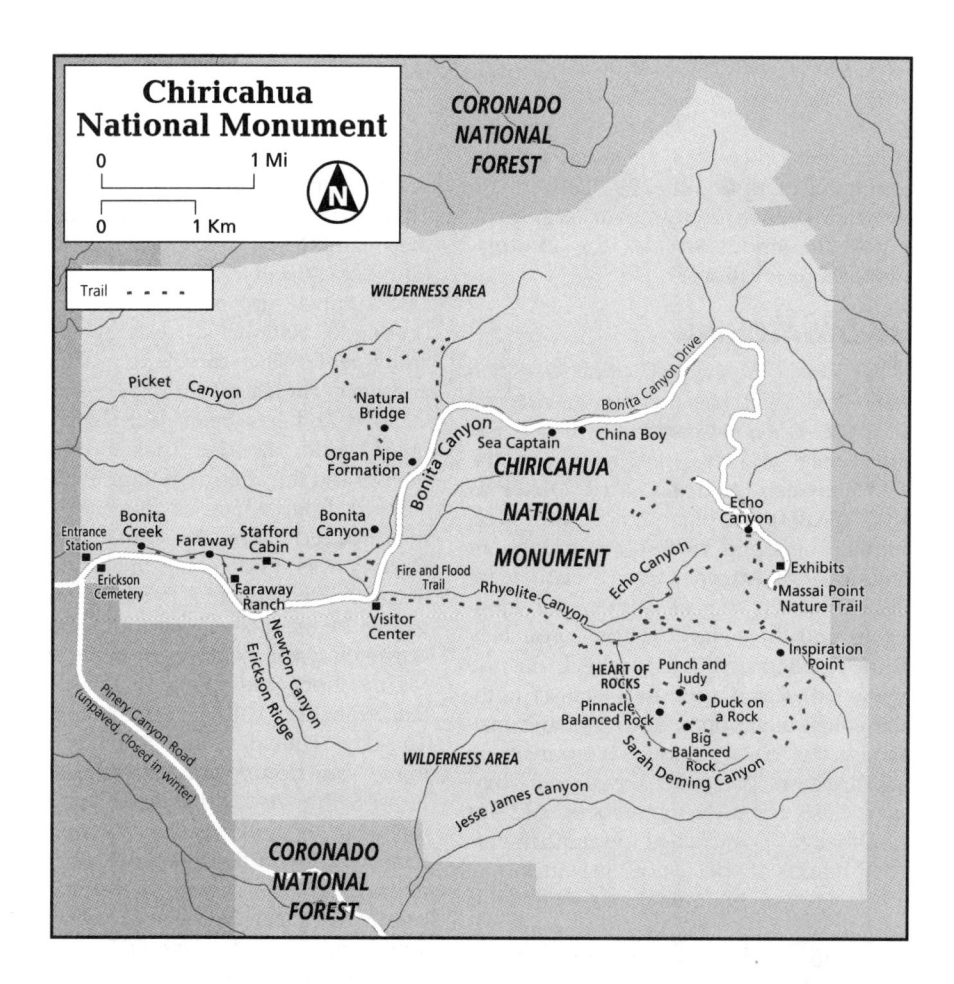

PARK RULES

Park rangers remind visitors that this is a unique landscape. At an elevation of 5,000 to 7,000 feet, the monument provides a hiking challenge for those coming from the lowlands. It is also a dry place that can get very hot in summer. Carry ample water and wear protective gear. During summer monsoon season from July to September watch out for afternoon thundershowers. Also watch for fallen rocks on roads. Do not collect firewood. Pets mush be leashed at all times and are restricted to the trails between the Faraway Ranch campground and the visitor center, and are prohibited from all others. Mountain bikes are restricted to established paved roads and prohibited on monument trials.

What to Do & Where to Do It

BALLOONING

The Sonoran Desert is one of the loveliest places to experience hot air ballooning. One reliable company based in Tucson that does trips here, as well as in other parts of Arizona, is **BalloonRidesUSA.** In business for 25 years, it uses only professionally licensed Federal Aviation

Administration-certified commercial balloon pilots. Call ☎ **520/299-7744,** log on to www.balloonridesusa.com, or e-mail: info@balloonridesusa.com for information and reservations.

BIRD WATCHING

What makes a sharp clicking *tick tick tick*? And what has the bright, cheerful song *tsee-tsee-tsee-tsee-titi-wee*? If you just aren't sure, you may find help from the **Southeastern Arizona Bird Observatory (SABO),** an organization that offers birding tours and workshops throughout southeastern Arizona. Even if you were able to identify the call of the green kingfisher and the yellow warbler, you may want to contact SABO to check out the many projects it sponsors such as hummingbird migration studies and the promotion of conscientious ecotourism in southeastern Arizona. Three-hour bird walks ($8 for SABO members, $12 for non-members) introduce tour participants to hundreds of species of birds including 15 species of hummingbirds. Highlights of fall and winter birding walks are the thousands of sandhill cranes that migrate to the southeast as well as sightings of scaled quail, Bendire's thrasher, and greater roadrunner. Personalized tours headed by a naturalist guide are also available. Contact ☎ **520/432-1388,** or visit www.sabo.org for schedules, reservations, and member information.

Another useful resource for the region is a map called *Southeastern Arizona Birding Trail,* which describes 50 birding hot spots and the birds you might see at each one. It's available at most bookstores, visitor centers, and inns.

World renowned for its hummingbird diversity (14 species have been sighted here), **Ramsey Canyon (**☎ **520/378-2785)** is a feast for the eyes and ears. Most people begin their visits by sitting at benches behind the visitor center. Within the first moments I was there I spotted a broadbilled hummingbird, magnificent hummingbird and blue-throated hummingbird. After you've had your fill, you'll want to hike up the canyon. Though you may go for many miles on the Hamburg Trail, following Ramsey Canyon Creek (first on Nature Conservancy property, later in the Coronado National Forest), you likely won't get far since there's so much to see and hear. The elegant trogon nested here in 1994 and has been seen here since; other rarities are the Strickland's woodpecker and the cherished Ramsey Canyon leopard frog, which is currently being reintroduced here. At press time the canyon was undergoing major restoration, which detracted from the pristine nature of the place; once it's complete, however, it will be an even better habitat for the flora and fauna that live there. Guided nature walks are conducted every Tuesday, Thursday, and Saturday morning at 9am from March through October. From Sierra Vista drive south on AZ 92 for 6 miles and turn west (right) on Ramsey Canyon Road. Follow the road 4 miles to its end. If you stay at the B&B on-site, you can access the property at any hour; alas, if you're a day visitor, hours are limited as follows: from March through October, 8am to 5pm; from November to February, 9am to 5pm. It's closed Thanksgiving, Christmas, and New Year's Day.

At the **San Pedro Riparian Preserve (**☎ **602/458-3559)** just east of Sierra Vista, a brave river cuts through the desert southwest, and bordering it stand ancient cottonwoods harboring thousands of species. I was fortunate enough to stay on the very edge of the preserve and have easy access early in the morning. I headed out before sunup. En route to the river I saw four white-tailed deer and some bobwhite quail skitter away. But by the river little was happening until the sun's rays actually hit the canopy. Suddenly, the world came alive. Vermilion flycatchers flitted in their loopy manner, as bold and bright as any creature I'd ever seen. A purple finch flew by, as did a yellow-throated warbler and a summer tanager with its robin-like call. It all happened fast, with flashes of bold color.

Managed by the Bureau of Land Management, this was the first area in the United States designated a Globally Important Bird Area because of the riparian habitat and its location along a major flyway. It protects over 36 acres of river with seven access sites. Some 380 species have been reported here, including green kingfisher, crissal thrasher, and various flycatchers. A small bookstore and visitor facilities are located 7 miles east of Sierra Vista off AZ 90. This is a decent access point, though it has a hot half-mile walk to the river. A favorite point for locals is the Hereford Bridge on Hereford Road south of Sierra Vista. Whichever access point you select, you'll walk along a meandering trail that at times can be obscured by runoff. You may note trash along the stream; at night this river corridor becomes a freeway for Mexicans traveling illegally up from the border. Locals warn visitors not to be in the river bottom after dark.

Patagonia Sonoita Creek Preserve (☎ 520/394-2400), another Nature Conservancy property, sits within a floodplain valley between the Patagonia and Santa Rita Mountains. Sonoita Creek runs through, providing a rich riparian habitat. The Conservancy purchased the property in 1966 and has worked to preserve a stand of the largest (over 100 feet tall) and oldest (130 years) Fremont cottonwood trees in the United States. The preserve is best known for the 260 bird species observed there. You might see such species as the gray hawk, green kingfisher, thick-billed kingbird, and northern beardless tyrannulet. Other inhabitants of the preserve are bobcat, javalena, desert tortoise, and coatimundi. At the site is a visitor center and interpretative display, where trained volunteers are sometimes on hand to answer questions. From there you can access the Creek, Railroad, Cienega, and Dr. Catherine Locke Berg Trails. The Creek Trail winds through the cottonwoods, while the Railroad Trail makes its way through wetlands and cienegas. Guided tours are offered every Saturday at 9am. The preserve is open Wednesday through Sunday from 7:30am to 4pm. A $5 donation is recommended. Dogs are not allowed. To reach the preserve take AZ 82 to Patagonia. In town turn west on Fourth Avenue. Travel a few blocks and turn left on Pennsylvania, cross the creek, and go about 1 mile to the entrance.

One afternoon after making my way through the Patagonia-Sonoita Preserve, I stopped in at **Hummingbird Haven,** also known as The Patons', a backyard in a retired couple's home that I'd heard about for days. There was a solemn atmosphere in the yard as I entered; it was though I was coming into church late, and I sat down on one of the pews. The eight people there acknowledged me with a little nod. Then suddenly someone said "seven" and everyone trained their field glasses on a hummingbird feeder labeled with that number. I followed suit, while someone whispered, "broadbill" and there was a collective appreciative sign, my own included, at the sight of its scarlet throat and bright green back. Suddenly someone whispered "nine," and everyone trained their binoculars on that feeder, and someone else said "female violet crown." The routine continued like that for hours, punctuated by a sighting in a nearby tree. "Blue bunting," someone whispered, and we searched and found the mass of sea blue feathers. The man next to me leaned over and whispered, "I've waited all day to see the white-eared hummingbird, but it hasn't shown." He explained that it is very rare but visited a few days earlier. He clued me in on the sugar fund, where people donate money. "If it depends on how long you've been here. I'll probably have to use my Visa card to contribute," he said. To reach The Patons', take AZ 82 to Patagonia. In town turn west on 4th

Avenue. Turn south on Pennsylvania. Just before you leave the edge of town, watch for the house on your left.

Another backyard birding experience is available in the Sierra Vista area at **Beatty's Miller Canyon Apiary & Orchard Co. (☎ 520/378-2728)**. Apple groves climb up the hills at the mouth of this canyon in the Huachuca Mountains where the Beatty family has created a birding oasis. Visitors sit in the parking area and watch some of the 14 species of hummingbirds that have been spotted here. The Ramsey Canyon leopard frog has been reintroduced here, and a thriving population lives in little ponds on the property, though viewing them is limited to guests staying in the B&B-style cabins and campsites. The cabins are on the rustic side with full kitchens. The best bet here are the campsites, complete with rest room, shower, and picnic table in a perfect birding setting.

According to one guidebook I used, **Cave Creek Canyon** near the town of Portal on the eastern edge of the Chiricahua range is the most important birding spot in the United States. While hiking the South Fork Trail there, I immediately spotted a bright yellow oriole and an olivaceous flycatcher. Shortly I came upon some bird-watchers making their way through the woods. In the bird-watchers' tradition of sharing, they said that they'd seen an elegant trogon not far up the trail. (This notable bird is the prize of most watchers; see the "Elegant Trogon" feature later in this chapter for details.) The birders remarked on its size, its beauty, and its curdling call, which is so loud they were surprised I didn't hear it. I'm certain if I were a better birder I would have, but I had no time to lament such deficiencies. I traced their tracks in pursuit. I hiked farther up the canyon, crossing the stream again and again, its cool pools quickly warming with the day's heat. What birds that had been flitting about were hidden away, and after awhile the going became senseless. I'd been walking for hours. It was time to turn back. When I got to the parking lot, it was obvious that word had spread. The big guns had arrived, bird-watchers with their cameras and large binoculars. They tromped up the trail in quick pursuit, and I wished them well. If you'd like to see the elegant trogon, this area may be your best bet; I hope you fare better than I.

For a much more secluded trip into birdland, head to **Aravaipa Canyon**, 11 miles south of Winkleman, on the hike described in the "Hikes & Backpack Trips" section later in this chapter. There you may see common black- and zone-tailed hawks nesting in the cottonwoods; yellow-billed cuckoo and northern beardless tyrannulet flitting by; as well as hummingbirds, desert wrens, peregrine falcons, and bald eagles.

Empire Cienega offers a very unique birding and hiking experience. This is a great way to get a sense of the savanna-like rangeland in the area around Sonoita. Look for lark buntings in winter and yellow-billed cuckoos, summer tanagers, and maybe a green kingfisher in summer. A small herd of pronghorn was introduced here in the 1980s. You'll likely bushwhack almost any way you go; I recommend going in the entrance 7 miles north of the village of Sonoita off AZ 83, driving a couple of miles, and finding a wash. Hike the wash onto a hill. Another alternative is to continue on the main road until you come into a riparian area where there's some hiking along the stream, but again even from there you might want to hike onto one of the hilltops, particularly around sunset. This land is not grazed much so it's covered by knee-high golden grass stretching for miles and miles to the mountains.

BOARDSAILING & SAILING

Southeastern Arizona is not known for its large bodies of water, but if you do want to get on a board, head to **Patagonia Lake State Park**, located on AZ 82 south of Patagonia. Though this 640-acre

ELEGANT TROGON

The Chiricahuas and Dragoons are the sky islands for which this region is so noted, and within those islands of blue, which jut up out of an ocean of pale grass, millions upon millions of birds frolic each spring and fall. The most noted of these travelers from the tropics is the elegant trogon.

Trogon elegans, the parrot-like tropical fruit eater that barks like a dog, is something you would never expect to see in the United States. Large and iridescent green, with a striking patch of red on its breast, it comes from as far away as Costa Rica to spend its summers in Arizona. With only some 50 pairs nesting in the area, it is the coveted find of many birders.

Your best bet for spotting the trogon is to look in mountain forests and pine-oak or sycamore canyons. As well as the Chiricahuas and Dragoons, the trogon has been spotted in the Huachucas at Ramsey Canyon, where the bird nested in 1994, and in Madera Canyon in the Santa Rita Mountains.

spread of water can be very busy during the warmer months, it is located in a lovely setting and, particularly in spring, it provides nice winds blowing off the surrounding cienegas. On-site there's a beach with picnic and bathroom facilities. Water-skiing and jet skiing are limited to weekdays and non-holidays. Look for white-tailed deer roaming the hills and great blue herons walking the shoreline. The park is open daily from 4am to 10pm; the entrance fee is $5.

CAVING

Kartchner Caverns

0.75 miles. Easy. Allow about 1 hr. Access: Head west from Benson on I-10 a short distance to AZ 90. Turn south and drive 9 miles to exit 302. ☎ **520/586-4100** for information or 520/586-CAVE for tour reservations. www.pr.state.az.us. Open daily 7:30am–6pm. $10 entrance fee per car for up to 4 people, $1 for each additional person. Cave tour $14 for adults, $6 children ages 7–13, free for children under 6.

I was fortunate enough to be one of the first rounds of visitors at this series of caves that opened in November 1999 not far from Benson. The experience was amazing, as is the story of their discovery. Two young cavers found the caves in 1974. For 4 years they kept them secret, while exploring their depths. The caves had been formed by rainwater seeping into a huge limestone block, slowly dissolving passages in it. Finally, the young cavers disclosed the presence of the caves to the private landowners, who were determined to keep their existence quiet. Ten years later, the landowners James and Lois Kartchner, sold the caverns for $1.5 million to the Arizona State Parks, and their presence was made public. Ten years after the sale and following very careful development in order to keep them pristine (including a series of chambers visitors must pass through to preserve the humidity within the caves), the caves were opened to the public.

You'll begin your journey in the 23,000-square-foot Discovery Center, which houses exhibits, a replica of the cave, and (most interesting to me) a re-creation of a Shasta Ground Sloth, whose remains were found within the caverns. This 6- to 7-foot-long bear-like creature, whose head is mostly nose, lived about 80,000 years ago. All tours into the cave itself are guided, and at press time it was necessary to make reservations months in advance, although a handful of tickets are held back for walk-ins. Your best bet in acquiring these is to arrive before the morning opening.

The tour takes you via electric train to the cave entrance. You begin walking through a series of chambers, then into the first room, the Rotunda, which is about the size of a football field with a classic dome shape. Here you'll see long, thin soda straws and shields with crab leg-like stalactites hanging off. Next comes a long passageway, which you'll duck slightly to get through. Here you'll see lovely flowstone, with pinks, tans, and purples melding together, as well as drapery and what's called "bacon" hanging on the walls. The passage winds along with some close-up views of the lovely formations. The next room is the Throne Room, named for the very dramatic 58-foot tall Kubla Kahn column. The name for the column came from the famous Samuel Taylor Coleridge poem "Kubla Khan," which speaks of the Mongolian warrior and his home in "Xanadu." Apparently, the cavers who discovered the caverns used the name Xanadu whenever they spoke to each other about it in order to keep their find secret. Here visitors sit and watch a spectacular light show play across the large formation and others surrounding it. Be aware that at this writing the largest chamber, the "Big Room," was still unopened, so the order of the tour may change.

CLIMBING

One of the most beautiful of the sky islands in southeastern Arizona is the Dragoon Mountains, home of **Cochise Stronghold,** where, in the late 1800s the famed Apache leader hid out with his band. Within this area is an incredible maze of granite domes and cliffs perfect for vertical exploration. Some call the nearly 500 traditional routes the best climbing in the state. For detailed route descriptions consult *Backcountry Rock Climbing in Southern Arizona* by Bob Kerry (Backcountry Books of Arizona, 1997) and *Rock Climbing Arizona* by Stewart M. Green (Falcon, 1999).

Cochise Stronghold is divided into two main areas: East and West. The East has numerous domes, including Entrance Dome, Out-of-Towners Dome, and Stronghold Dome, with face routes up to 700 feet long. Also worth checking out there is the Rockfellow Dome, most noted for its crack and face routes. The West Stronghold is noted for its multi-pitch slab routes up Westworld and Whale domes. To get to East Stronghold, drive south of I-10 on U.S. 191 for 17 miles to Ironwood Road in Sunsites. Turn west onto Ironwood where the sign says "Cochise Stronghold." Follow this road 7 miles to the national forest boundary and a cattle guard. Some of the climbs are in the canyon to the right, reached by taking the first right at the cattle guard. Others are reached near the Cochise Stronghold Campground, 2 miles past the cattle guard. To reach the West Stronghold, follow the directions to Isle of You below, except continue past the Isle of You to the Cochise Trail trailhead. Follow the trail for 100 yards, then turn left and follow a dry creek for a mile to the domes.

South of the Stronghold is the sport climbing area **Isle of You,** and the **Sheepshead** area, also called the Southwest Stronghold. The Isle of You is made up of numerous ribs, fins, buttresses, and faces along an escarpment. The main area has three granite cliffs—Trad Rock, Rad Rock, and Glad Rock, with some 27 single-pitch bolted routes ranging in difficulty from 5.6 to 5.11. Climbers like to camp in the area and spend days climbing there, particularly October to May, though be aware that with an elevation of 5,000 feet, winters can be cold. Access the area off AZ 80 near Tombstone via Middlemarch Road. Follow this gravel road to FS 687 to the West Stronghold. Some of these routes in the Dragoons are closed during spring for falcon nesting.

FISHING

Anglers know all too well that a warm water fish tastes nothing like a cold water species. Perch, catfish, bass, bluegill, and crappies for example have a firm, flaky white meat while the salmon family of cold water fish like trout have a more refined and delicate meat. Warm water fish are great in a fish fry; cold water fish are delicious poached or sautéed. If it's a fish fry you're craving, head to **Patagonia Lake** to catch some warm water species. Anglers catch crappie, bass, bluegill, and catfish. Trout is stocked every three weeks from November until late February. It's located south of Patagonia on AZ 82. Ideal for fly fishers, Patagonia's 264-acre surface waters are easily accessed by wading, kick-boating, or float-tubing. Part of the lake is also has a no-wake speed limit. The lake has a store with gas, as well as a campground. Be aware that in summer this lake gets very crowded, and can also become weedy.

Rose Canyon Lake in the Santa Catalina Mountains is heavily used, but does offer decent fishing close to Tucson. Since boats are not allowed here, all fishing is done from shore. The 7-acre lake, at 7,200 feet and surrounded by ponderosa forest and granite outcroppings, is stocked with rainbow trout. There is a 1-mile trail leading around the lake that provides access for anglers and others. When the campground closes in October, gates are locked, drinking water is turned off, and garbage service is curtailed. However, fishing and picnicking are still allowed for those willing to walk in. If you visit during this off-season, you must pack out everything you pack in. From Tucson, take Tanque Verde Road east to the Catalina Highway. Turn left (north) onto Catalina Highway, and drive 4.2 miles to the forest boundary. Then continue up the Highway 17.5 miles. Turn left the Rose Canyon Lake Campground.

Parker Canyon Lake, located south of Sonoita via AZ 83, is set within a little valley surrounded by hills. The lake's biggest draw are the rainbow trout stocked October through March, giant-sized largemouth bass, and channel catfish. There are 64 campsites. The Parker Canyon Lake Store can set you up with fishing needs, including a boat and a cup of coffee.

HIKES & BACKPACK TRIPS

Romero Canyon in the Santa Catalina Mountains

2–14.5 miles. Moderate. 1,000–3,200-ft. elevation gain. Allow 1–8 hrs. Access: In Tucson, from the Ina intersection, go north on Oracle for 6 miles to the Catalina State Park entrance on your right. Continue to the Day Use Area. $4 entrance fee.

This hike takes you quickly up into the cactus-covered rocky crags of these pristine mountains, just minutes from busy Tucson. The trail begins up a quite steep ramp, steeper than anything you'll encounter farther along. For the first mile after that it remains wide, with sandy parts that will give your calves a workout. Soon you come to the junction for the loop trail. If you'd like to stay in the lowlands, this is the easier option. However, you'll miss some awesome views. Soon the Romero Canyon Trail begins its ascent, often rambling over rocky sections. It climbs steadily (on a very hot day don't even attempt this climb) until it reaches a semi-saddle from which you can look down into an adjoining canyon. From there the trail skirts along a ridge, with views down both canyons as well as up at the rocky crags to the east. The trail drops down and then climbs again continuing in this fashion, reaching some refreshing pools. Then it continues farther into the Pusch Ridge Wilderness, an area set aside in 1978 primarily for the protection of lambing grounds for bighorn sheep, though unfortunately, due to pressure from Tucson, most of the sheep have migrated into nearby forestland. You can make this hike as long or short as you like. If you continue for 7.2 miles you'll come to the Mount Lemmon Trail.

Supertrail to Mount Wrightson

6.5–14 miles round-trip. Moderate to strenuous. 2,800–4,000-ft. elevation gain. Allow 3½–8 hrs to 2 days. Access: Drive south of Tucson on I-19 for 25 miles to the Continental exit. Head east on Madera Canyon Rd. for 12 miles to the Roundup Picnic Area parking lot where you'll find the Supertrail Trailhead. Map: USGS Mount Wrightson or USFS Coronado National Forest (Santa Rita Mountain).

This is a truly spectacular hike through mountainous terrain, with glimpses of bold granite peaks and long views of southwestern Arizona. I'm really listing two hikes here. The first is a nice day hike to Josephine Saddle; the second is a long and strenuous day hike or a nice overnight hike to the top of Mount Wrightson.

The Supertrail lives up to its name. Meandering around mountains, it's smooth and broad with no steep sections. It begins through oak forest, then moves into ponderosa pine. The trail winds around edges of mountains with views off toward the north and the west, and incredible glimpses of Mount Wrightson. At mile 4 the trail arrives at Josephine Saddle, where there's a sad memorial to three Boy Scouts who died of hypothermia in November 1958. Not far from where the Supertrail comes upon the saddle you'll find the Old Baldy Trail, a decent route down, though not nearly as scenic as the Supertrail. It descends a rocky hillside and doesn't offer many views along the way. However, at 2.5 miles, it's a much quicker way down.

The climb to the top of Mount Wrightson will be a long day hike; you may want to do an overnight and camp at Josephine Saddle. In either event, if you'd like the scenic route, follow the directions above to Josephine Saddle. If you're in a hurry, you can save a couple of miles by hiking up the Old Baldy Trail. Just before Josephine Saddle on the Supertrail you'll encounter Sprung Spring, usually a source of water, but don't count on it completely. At Josephine Saddle turn left onto Trail 78; hike about 0.25 miles and turn left again onto Trail 94. (Trail 78 is a longer, less steep route to the summit.) The trail will come to (oft dry) Bellows Spring, then proceed up to Baldy Saddle. From there it heads south, climbing into Mexican white pine and Douglas fir. Finally, it switchbacks to the top of the rocky summit. From there you'll have views of the Santa Ritas and the surrounding desert, as well as the Mount Hopkins telescope, visible to the west. To make the return interesting, you may want to take Trail 78 back down, which crosses (oft dry) Baldy Spring. Along the way keep your eyes to the trees; more than 170 species of birds have been recorded in this area. You may see red-shafted flickers, sulphur-bellied flycatchers, and the rare elegant trogon.

Sendero Esperanza Trail in Saguaro National Park West

3.5–6.4 miles round-trip. Moderate. 600-ft elevation gain. Allow 1½–3½ hrs. Access: In Tucson, follow the directions to Saguaro National Park West as listed in "Parks & Other Hot Spots" earlier in this chapter. The trailhead is approximately 6 miles from the Red Hills Visitor Center: On Kinney Rd. drive past the visitor center to Hohokm Rd. Turn right and follow this one-way road until it intersects with two-way Golden Gate Rd. Turn right and continue for 1.5 miles until you come to the trailhead on your right. $6 entrance fee.

This is an excellent introduction to Saguaro National Monument West, what some people believe to be the better of the two Saguaro parks. Here you'll get a taste of the intense beauty of the Sonoran Desert, with views from on high. The trail begins through a wash along an old mining road. Then it heads up a series of switchbacks. Note the variations in the cactus populations from the north and south-facing slopes. Soon (mile 1.7) the trail comes to the top of a saddle west of Amole Peak. From here you have a few choices. Heartier ones like to turn left here and hike approximately 2 more miles to the top of Wasson Peak, at 4,687 feet, the highest in the Tucson Mountains. Another option is to continue on the Sendero Esperanza Trail over the top of this saddle and down the other side. You'll note that on the other side the south-facing cactus stands are much thicker. This option will take you 1.4 miles to Mam-a-Gah picnic area (named after a Tohono O'odham Indian Chief) and the King Canyon Trail. You can either turn around here and head back, or if you've arranged a shuttle, follow the King Canyon Trail for 0.9 miles to Kinney Road. You'll come out just across from the Arizona–Sonora Desert Museum.

Aravaipa Canyon
4–22 miles round-trip. Easy. 200-ft. elevation gain. Allow 3 hrs. to 2–3 days. (There are both east and west entrances; I will describe the most accessible hike, from the west.) Drive south from Winkleman on AZ 77 for 11 miles to Aravaipa Rd. Turn left and drive 12 miles on this dirt road to the trailhead. *Note:* A permit is required to enter the canyon. Obtain one by calling the Safford BLM at ☎ 520/348-4400. A fee of $5 per day is payable at the trailhead. Maps: USGS Brandenburg Mountain, Booger Canyon. Dogs aren't allowed in the canyon.

This hike takes you into a lush and colorful box canyon that is, at points, 1,000 feet deep, and is surrounded by Sonoran Desert. The area is rich with wildlife such as bighorn sheep and coatimundis, and bird life such as black- and zone-tailed hawks, yellow-billed cuckoo, and northern beardless tyrannulet. From the parking lot you'll head down a rocky trail that takes you by a sign that says there's no maintained trail and that much of the route will be through the river, which isn't necessarily the case. Although there's not a *maintained* trail, there is a route that's been beaten through the woods. In order to find that and take advantage of it, you'll need to do the following: The rocky trail will lead to a wash, and the wash will lead about 100 yards paralleling the river, and then it will lead to the river. Right at that point, cross the river. That will put you onto the trail that pretty much runs along the right side of the river. The trail leaves the side of the river in various places. The only time it's on the left side is when it's on the very edge—you're almost wading in the river. *Note:* At times the only way to get anywhere is to wade in the river. Those times are pretty apparent; when it's not those times, you really want to watch that right bank for the trail—if you try to make your way along the left side you'll be bushwhacking like crazy and will be totally frustrated. When the river starts taking some more sharp turns, there's no choice but to be in the river, which is generally only about ankle deep. As the canyon walls narrow you'll be in the river more and more. It took me about 45 minutes to get to the place where the canyon narrows and gets really beautiful, after about 2 miles. From there it continues to be narrow with lovely painted walls of sandstone. At times it broadens, with sandy banks on the side—good for camping if you're doing an overnight. The water is cold so you'll want to wear good footgear. River sandals won't provide enough insulation in winter, and rubber boots will likely fill with water, as will hiking boots, so your best bet might be to wear insulated socks with old running shoes. These will provide some insulation and agility, but won't collect as much water as rubber or hiking boots will. Though be aware that if you're backpacking, you'll want the support of good boots to negotiate the occasionally precarious footing.

Echo Canyon Loop in Chiricahua National Monument
3.3-mile loop. Moderate. 700-ft. elevation gain. Allow 2 hrs. Access: From the Chiricahua National Monument Visitor

Center drive the Bonita Canyon Drive almost to the end at Massai Point (8 miles). Watch for the Echo Canyon parking lot on your right. $6 entrance fee. Map: Chiricahua National Monument Hiker's Map.

Many consider this the best hike in the monument to really get a feel for the Chiricahua. The reason? It has great variety. It begins in the elaborate rock gardens high on a canyon rim, then makes its way down into lush riverside forest, then back up into the rocks. You'll definitely want to do this loop counter-clockwise in order to take advantage of the views and to leave you in the shade for the hike back up. Therefore, at the first juncture, where signs point both directions for Echo Canyon, turn right. The trail makes its way along a ridge, winding around rock formations, then descends into the canyon. At 1.6 miles it meets up with the Hailstone Trail, which you'll follow to your left. At 2.4 miles it meets up with the Ed Riggs Trail, which you'll follow to the left. These later sections trace the canyon bottom and then ascend back to the trailhead.

Heart of Rocks Loop

7.5 miles round-trip. Difficult. 800-ft. elevation gain. Allow 4 hrs. Access: From the Chiricahua National Monument Visitor Center, drive the Bonita Canyon Drive for 8 miles to Massai Point. Map: Chiricahua National Monument Hiker's Map.

If you long to spend a full day meandering through the formations at Chiricahua, this hike offers such a chance. It begins at Massai Point where you can view the canyons from above. Along the trail you'll see the most massive balanced rock in the monument and rock caricatures of people and animals. Be sure to pick up a hiking map at the visitor center before setting out. The route descends, meeting up with the Ed Riggs Trail and heading into a shady canyon bottom. After 1 mile it meets up with the Mushroom Rock Trail, onto which you'll turn left. Follow this for 1.2 miles to the juncture with the Inspiration Point Trail. This 1-mile side trip provides spectacular views of Rhyolite Canyon, but if it's a hot day you may want to conserve your energy. At the Inspiration Point Trail juncture the main trail becomes the Big Balanced Rock Trail and, after almost a mile, comes to the towering formation with that name. Shortly the trail comes to the junction for the 1.1-mile Heart of Rocks Loop, where you'll see such likenesses as Duck on a Rock and Punch and Judy, as well as Pinnacle Balanced Rock. Returning to the main juncture, continue west on the Sarah Deming Trail for 1.6 miles to the juncture with the Upper Rhyolite Trail. Turn right and follow that trail for 1.1 miles to the Hailstone Trail, which you'll follow for 0.8 miles back to the Ed Riggs Trail. Turn right onto Ed Riggs and travel 1.1 miles to the next trail juncture where you'll turn right and ascend back to Massai Point.

Cochise Stronghold

4–6 miles round-trip. Moderate. 1,000-ft. elevation gain. Allow 2–3 hrs. Access: From Wilcox, drive west on I-10 about 10 miles, and turn south on U.S. 191; travel about 17 miles to Sunsites. Just north of the village, turn west (right) on the signed road to Cochise Stronghold. Follow this mostly dirt road 9 miles to the trailhead.

This hike provides a glimpse into the rugged area that served as a natural fortress and hide-out for Apache Indians of the Chiricahua clan led by Cochise. He was born in these Dragoon Mountains around 1815. From 1860 to 1872 he and his band battled the U.S. Cavalry. It is believed that Cochise was buried somewhere in the stronghold.

The hike begins with awesome views of some of the amazing rock formations that are most prevalent right at the beginning of the canyon. As you head deeper into the canyon the rock continues to be striking and beautiful. The canyon's narrowness and ruggedness make it easy to imagine why this was a stronghold. I could even imagine Apaches stationed up along the rim ready to skewer enemies. The trail continues to follow the drainage, climbing gradually, at times making its way down into the mostly dry creek, at other times meandering through large rock formations. At mile 2 it arrives at a spring, a good destination if you don't feel like hiking the whole way in. Here you'll find a little shade and a little water and, probably, a lot of flies. Later the trail swings left onto the south slopes of the canyon and contours to the pass at the head of this stronghold canyon. At the divide there are good views down the canyon.

Miller Peak Trail

10.6 miles round-trip. Moderate. 2,916-ft. elevation gain. Allow 6 hrs.–2 days. Access: From Sierra Vista, drive south on AZ 92 for 15 miles and turn south on Coronado Rd. (watch for signs to Coronado National Memorial). This road becomes Montezuma Rd., which you follow to the top of Montezuma Pass, about a 20-minute drive. Just before you enter the parking area for Montezuma pass, look for a sign for the Crest Trail, the trail you'll take to Miller Peak. Map: USGS Miller Peak, Montezuma Peak or USFS Coronado National Forest Huachuca Mountains.

This unique hike traverses along the borderland, with spectacular views of the San Pedro Valley and the San Pedro and Montezuma Peaks, as well as the Sierra Madre in Mexico. Once at the top you'll stand on the highest point in the Huachuca Mountains.

The trail begins traversing along a mountainside in fairly open, hot country, coming to a saddle, then switchbacking up a south-facing slope. The grade these first 2 miles is steady but not too difficult. At mile 2 the trail comes into more forested terrain, and the going gets easier and shadier. It follows the main ridge (the crest for which the trail is named) north toward Miller Peak, winding through rough granite terrain. After passing the junction with the Huachuca Crest Trail, it makes a final dash up a few final switchbacks to the summit. Return the way you came.

Carr Peak

6 miles round-trip. Moderate. 2,000-ft. elevation gain. Allow 3 hrs. Access: From Sierra Vista drive south 7 miles on AZ 92; turn right on the signed Carr Canyon Rd. Follow this fairly steep and rough road for 5 miles to the Old Sawmill Spring trailhead across from the entrance to Reef Townsite Campground, or a mile farther to the Ramsey Vista Campground, where there's also a trailhead. (Though this road is only 5–6 miles long, it took me a good ½ hour to get to the trailhead.) Maps: USGS Carr Peak; USFS Coronado National Forest Huachuca Mountains.

The big bonus to this hike is that the trailhead is so high you can get to the second highest peak in the Huachuca Mountains without too much effort. Besides that, it's a lovely hike through a recovering burn area then through pines to the summit. I did the hike from the Reef Campground, mostly because I was tired of dirt-road driving; if you're not, you can start from the Ramsey Campground. Either option makes for a good hike. From the Reef Townsite Campground, the trail climbs quickly, then enters a beautiful canyon with a variety of trees. It then traverses a hill, still making its way across the burn, so you don't have shade but you do have tremendous views off to the north and east. At mile 1, the trail comes to the junction for the trail that starts from the Ramsey View Campground; turn left and continue following up toward the peak. On the north side of the peak, the trail passes through aspen stands, then swings to the south slopes, where the forest survived the fire. Look for a signed junction, where the Carr Peak Trail branches right and the main trail continues on toward

Miller Peak. Continuing to Miller Peak is a good option if you're looking to do a longer hike; you'll want to arrange a shuttle at Montezuma Pass. It's 0.2 steep miles to the Carr Peak summit. One of the stops on the southeastern Arizona birding trail, Carr Peak is a great birdwatching destination.

South Fork Trail 243

6.8 miles one-way. Easy to difficult. 3,440-ft. elevation gain. Allow 1–4 hrs. one-way. Access: From Portal head west on FS 42 for 2 miles to the South Fork turnoff. Turn right (south) and continue 1 mile to the trailhead. Map: USGS Portal Peak.

This sweet trail is a birder's paradise. In fact, many people who travel it barely make it more than a few miles, so much is there to see and hear en route. It traverses the South Fork of Cave Creek, with clear pools, big boulders, and lots of trees and birds. The forest is rich and varied—walnut, sycamore, and cypress predominate. Brightly colored birds flit about almost any time of year, but particularly in the spring and fall. Look for bluethroated hummingbirds, painted redstarts, and red-faced warblers. Along the way you'll catch glimpses of stunning orange cliffs high above the forest canopy. At 1.6 miles the trail comes to Maple Camp, continuing in the shadow of steep cliffs. Soon it heads up a side canyon toward the high country. It makes its way into aspen and Douglas fir forest, past Burnt Stump Trail, to a junction with the Crest Trail. From there, it's a little over a half-mile to the summit of Sentinel Peak, the site of an old lookout and a great place to catch some views of the Chiricahuas.

While I hiked the trail, two women stopped to say they had seen an elegant trogon up the trail (see the "Elegant Trogon" feature earlier in this chapter). I became determined to find it, so I continued up the canyon. Little did I know how quickly word would spread throughout the area. With no luck in my own endeavor, I headed back down to the trailhead. When I arrived at my car, many birders had arrived and were gearing up to locate that trogon. I hope they had better luck than I did.

Rucker Canyon Trail 222

2–4.6 miles one-way. Easy. 1,460-ft. elevation gain. Allow 1–3 hrs. one-way. Access: From Douglas head north on U.S. 191 for 34 miles to Rucker Canyon Rd. (FS 74). Turn right and drive this graded dirt road for 16 miles to the junction with Leslie Canyon Rd. Turn left (still Rucker Canyon Rd.) and drive 9 miles to FS 74E. Turn left and drive 4.7 miles to the Rucker Forest Camp. The trailhead is at the end of the camp. Map: USGS Chiricahua Peak.

This is a lovely meander up Rucker Creek, through a deep forest of Arizona sycamore and cypress and ponderosa, Apache, and Chihuahua pine. This area is at the very heart of the Chiricahua, a place so remote I wondered how so many people had made it into the campground. Rucker Creek is a perennial stream, with some lovely pools that serve as home to a small, introduced population of trout. The one disadvantage of this trail is that it's far from pristine. Heavy foot traffic from the campground deposits bits of trash, which lessens the farther you get up the trail. A few miles into the hike the trail switchbacks steeply up the canyon's east slope to join the Red Rock Canyon Trail, providing some excellent views. This trail accesses the Crest Trail via the Price Canyon Trail. The canyon was named for Lieutenant Rucker from Fort Bowie at the north end of the Chiricahuas, who in the late 1800s led an Army detachment in search of Apaches. He didn't find the Apaches, but he did come across traces of copper near what is now Bisbee. Later this turned out to be one of the richest ore bodies in the world, though Rucker didn't share in the wealth.

Raspberry Ridge Trail 228 (and Crest Trail 270)

4.6 miles one-way. Moderate to difficult. 3,257-ft. elevation gain. Allow 3 hrs.–many days one-way. Access: Follow directions to the Rucker Canyon Trail above. The trail begins near the Rucker Canyon Trailhead. Map: USGS Chiricahua Peak, Rustler Park; USFS Coronado National Forest.

This trail provides a pristine climb through a richly forested canyon onto a spectacular ridge, which leads to 9,537-foot Monte Vista Peak, one of the best viewpoints in the Chiricahuas. The trail follows Bear Canyon for the first half of its route. Going is moderate and lovely with plenty of birds to entertain and inspire you. At the top of the canyon, the trail switchbacks steeply to razorback Raspberry Ridge, which it follows northwesterly. From the ridge you'll have occasional views of Rucker Lake, which was dry when I visited, but may be full when you're there. The trail follows the ridge to a junction with the Crest Trail 270, near Monte Vista Peak. Turn left and take a spur trail for 0.2 miles to the summit. The panorama includes much of southeastern Arizona including several of its sky island mountain ranges.

This is a good trail to use to connect to the Crest Trail 270. The Crest Trail is actually a system of trails, spurs, and side loops that sits like an inverted "Y" on the central ridge of the Chiricahuas. The trails offer access to diverse forests, meadows, and summits. Since much of the trail wanders along a wide and easy-to-follow trail, with only a moderate gradient, it can make for a good overnight (or multi-day) route. If you do explore the 6.3-mile route from Monte Vista Peak to the northern boundary of the Chiricahuas (or start north and head south), you'll access Chiricahua Peak, Anita Park, and Flys Peak. The northern access point for the Crest Trail is in the vicinity of Chiricahua National Monument. Take FS 42 12 miles up Pinery Canyon to FS 42D. Drive about 2.5 miles to the Rustler Park Campground where you'll find the trailhead.

Silver Peak Trail 280

2–9 miles round-trip. Difficult. 3,075-ft. elevation gain. Allow 1–6 hrs. Access: From Portal, drive west on FS 42 for about 1 mile. You'll pass the Cave Creek Visitor Center on your right. Shortly after, look for a small pull-out on your right, where you'll find the trailhead. You can also park at the visitor center and access the trail from there. Maps: USGS Portal.

This is an excellent way to get a bird's-eye-view of the Cave Creek Canyon area. The trail takes you quickly up into the rocky crags and on to the 7,975-foot summit of Silver Peak. Because the route is steep and shadeless, I recommend that you attempt this hike only during cooler hours. The trail starts on a sweet desert path through sotol and agave. On this early leg of the trail I encountered a couple that had spent the morning birding here. The woman had an arm-long list of birds they'd seen, which she took great care in relating to me in its entirety. After that lengthy encounter, while the heat rapidly came to the morning, I made tracks on a rigorous and nonstop ascent. The trail crosses a lovely meadow full of prickly pear and yucca. After awhile it comes into the Douglas fir forests of the Canadian zone. From there you can see the eastern slopes of the Chiricahuas, including the canyons that Cave Creek, the South Fork of Cave Creek, and East Turkey Creek have cut into the mountain range. To the east the grasslands of the San Simon Valley stretch to the Peloncillo Mountains. On the summit are remains of the Silver Peak Lookout, which burned in October 1992. Return the way you came.

HORSEBACK RIDING

With its Wild West background, southeastern Arizona is one of the nation's top guest ranch regions. It's so Western, in fact, that many films have been set in the area. In 1939, an Old West town was built to film the movie *Arizona*. So elaborate was the set that this mock Western town remains. Known as Old Tucson Studios, it's still used for film and video productions. Movies filmed there include *Tombstone;* John Wayne's *Rio Lobo, Rio Bravo,* and *El Dorado;* and Clint Eastwood's *The Outlaw Josey Wales,* and many others. South of Tucson, the Patagonia area has also hosted Westerns, including *Oklahoma* and *Red River,* and the television shows *Little House on the Prairie* and *The Young Riders.*

One of Arizona's best guest ranches, the **Circle Z** (☎ 888/854-2525 or 520/394-2525; www.circlez.com or e-mail: info@circlez.com) offers rides through diverse terrain in the Patagonia area on the ranch's 5,000 acres. We started in the lush riparian banks of the Sonoita Creek and worked our way into mesquite and ocotillo forests, back down to the creek again for a romp through the water, then a barbeque under the shade. One of the best features of this place is the children's riding program, which allows them to ride as they please and allows parents a more quiet riding experience. Other activities include hiking and birding on the lovely grounds and at nearby Patagonia-Sonoita Creek Preserve (guided tours arranged by the ranch). There are also tennis courts and a swimming pool. The ranch rooms are charmingly Old West; all have a sunny Southwestern ranch feel. The dining is very upscale, served in a hacienda-style room that looks out onto a patio. If it weren't for the testy wrangler, I'd call this place heaven. Prices range from $910 to $1,070 per week, with day rates available but with a minimum 3-night stay.

Two guest ranches take visitors into the sky-island regions of southeastern Arizona. **Sunglow Guest Ranch** (☎ 520/824-3334; www.soarizona.com/sunglow or e-mail: sunglow@vtc.net) has in recent years come under new ownership. With it the ranch has moved away from the straight dude ranch experience to a more rounded guest-ranch experience. The ranch is surrounded on three sides by 330,000 acres of Coronado National Forest and wilderness area. As well as riding for both guests and non-guests, the ranch offers hiking, bird watching, fishing, hay rides, painting, photography, and wildlife viewing. In the 1880s, this was a logging boomtown. One building from that era remains, an adobe building that now houses the dining hall. A replica of a mission-style church houses the recreation hall, where the phone and VCR are located. The accommodations are rustic: Guest rooms are large, and most have kitchenettes with woodstoves. A small lake lies downhill from the ranch buildings. The accommodations aren't as upscale as the Circle Z, but neither are the prices. Sunglow can also arrange multi-day ranch-to-ranch riding. The ranch is located near the junction of AZ 181 and 186.

Though the **White Stallion Ranch** doesn't rank with the Circle Z in Patagonia or the K El Bar in Wickenburg, it is a good choice for those looking for a mainstream dude ranch experience. Owned by the same family since 1965 and situated on 3,000 acres, this ranch has much to offer. Best of all is the riding terrain—since the ranch borders Saguaro National Park West, some of the rides traverse this spectacular desert setting. This ranch also offers weekly rodeos and interesting evening programs such as bird presentations. The ranch has tennis courts, a heated pool, hot tub, ping-pong and pool tables, basketball, volleyball, horseshoes, shuffleboard, and a petting zoo. The accommodations are in white adobe-style cottages, some newly built and quite comfortable and efficient, others built in the 1940s with a more traditional ranch feel. All sit amidst gardens of oversized prickly pear and saguaro cacti, and have porches looking out upon the desert. The ranch's proximity to Tucson, just 35 minutes away, makes it possible to sightsee in the city. The only real drawback here is there's a mass-production quality to the riding, since the ranch handles up to 75 guests at a time. Meals—three a day—are decent but not gourmet. Prices range from $125 to $148 per person per night to $1,036 to $1,176 per person per week, depending on the season and type of room. Call ☎ **888/977-2624** or 520/297-0252 for current prices.

Though **Grapevine Canyon Ranch** (☎ **800/245-9202** or 520/826-3185; www.gcranch.com) doesn't have the quality of accommodation or food that the Circle Z and the K El Bar ranches have, the riding is interesting and worthwhile. Tailored especially for those who can handle a horse, some of the rides head up into Chiricahua National Monument and into Cochise Stronghold, so if you like all-day rides where you get to canter a fair amount, this is a good place to go. The ranch has nice secluded cabins that are sorely in need of remodeling, and single units that are more up-to-date. A sweet little pool and hot tub offer welcome respite after a day in the saddle. Prices range from $135 to $270 per person per night.

Don Donnelly Stables, (☎ **800/346-4403** or 480/982-8895; www.dondonnelly.com), based in the Superstition Mountains outside Phoenix, offers a number of riding vacations throughout Arizona. One of note in this region is a 5-day ride exploring Bisbee and Tombstone. Another takes riders into the Chiricahua Mountains, and another explores the area around Patagonia. Prices range from $690 per person for a 3-day trip to $1,920 per person for the most expensive 7-day trip.

If you're in the Amado area and want to ride in the foothills of the lovely Santa Rita Mountains, call **Rex Ranch Stables**. The Rex Ranch wranglers have a strong reputation, and the horses are summered in Idaho, so they're not likely to be overworked. Prices range from $20 for 1 hour to $50 for a half-day. Contact the ranch at ☎ **520/398-2914,** www.rexranch.com, or e-mail: info@rexranch.com.

If you like to get way out into the wilderness but don't relish carrying your life on your back, you might want to try hiking with goats. **Purple Mountain Pack Goats** (☎ **520/886-7721;** www.azpackgoat.com or e-mail: azpackgoat@aol.com) provides custom day hikes, overnight camping, and educational field trips, letting the animals do the work. Overnight trips travel into the scenic Dragoon Mountains east of Tucson. The walking speed of a goat is about the same as a person, so they're good travel companions. This is an excellent way to hike with young kids.

MOUNTAIN BIKING

If you're looking for a guided mountain biking experience or you just want to rent a bike, you're in luck in the Tucson area. **Arizona Off-Road Adventures** (☎ **520/822-9830;** www.azora.com) offers both front and full-suspension rentals, which include bikes, water bottles, snack, helmet, gloves, and map; it also offers half-day, full-day, and multi-day tours. Tours head through ghost towns, along dirt roads, and single track. The company caters to beginner through expert riders. Overnight tours feature fully supported camping or lodging at hotels, usually a combination of the two. Off-Road Adventures can also do combination tours in which participants hike, bike, and bird-watch. The guide, Paul Pineo, is a former bike racer, a cook, and bike mechanic. Call for prices and tour dates.

Starr Pass in the Tucson Mountains
7.5-mile loop. Moderate. 1,700-ft. elevation gain. Allow 2 hrs. Access: From I-10 head west on Speedway for just over 2 miles. Turn left on Greasewood and travel a half-mile to Anklam. Turn right and travel 0.8 miles to Player's Club. Turn left and travel 1 mile to Starr Pass. Turn left and travel 0.1 miles to Deer Meadow. Turn right and drive 0.3 miles to the trailhead.

Despite possibly the longest wash in the world, this is a primo ride through saguaro forest, up and over a saddle and around a butte. Except for the wash it's all fun, fast single track with a few rocky, technical sections just to keep you on your toes. The ride starts along a double-track road and makes its way through the first of the gravelly wash sections. Soon it turns to single track and climbs up through a gate, entering the Tucson Mountains Park. It levels out at a small pass and begins descending into pristine Sonoran Desert on fast and fun winding single track. This turns into a treacherously rocky section that you'll want to be wary on, particularly one ledge well worth walking your bike over, unless you want to do the over-the-handle-bars trick my friend Lex did here, with scars on his hands to attest to the feat.

The trail makes its way between two peaks and leaves the park through a gate, skirting the edge of a residential district. Soon it passes through another gate and begins its ascent around the side of the butte. It goes over a section where there are some funky washes that force you down into ruts, then you'll come to some pavement. Watch for a gate to your right here. After passing through the gate, the trail heads up around the butte and through another pass, the most scenic part of the trip. A nice technical, rocky section here will test your skills and your wind. Then you descend down into the world's longest wash. Fortunately it's comprised of gravel rather than sand so you'll likely make it through without having to push your bike. Once you're through it, though, you'll feel as though you've completed a major feat. The trail winds along and soon comes to a fork. Follow the sign for the Yetman Trail (bear left), which will take you backtracking on the main stretch of trail to the first pass, the gate, and to your car.

Cactus Forest Trail Loop in Saguaro National Park East

5.5 miles. Easy. Allow 1½ hrs. Access: In Tucson, head east on Speedway Blvd. Turn right on Old Spanish Trail, which will lead to the visitor center.

This is an excellent way to enjoy the park. The ride begins on paved roads, then cuts onto the only allowed bicycle single track within either of the Saguaro Parks. The terrain is lovely hills adorned with towering saguaros. From the visitor center, head southeast on the Cactus Forest Loop. On weekends and holidays, beware—this paved road may be busy. As you go, be sure to obey traffic signs, especially those regarding direction of travel on this one-way 8-mile road. At about mile 0.75 you'll note the Cactus Forest Trail on your left. This trail is also open to hikers and horseback riders, to whom cyclers need to yield. The well-marked trail travels 2.5 miles across the desert; be sure to stay on the it and avoid veering off into washes. The trail meets back up with the Cactus Forest Loop; turn left and follow the loop back to the visitor center.

Elephant Head

2–24 miles round-trip. Strenuous. 2,500-ft. elevation gain. Allow 1–6 hrs. Access: Drive south of Tucson on I-19 for 25 miles to the Continental exit. Head east on Madera Canyon Rd. for 11 miles to Proctor Rd., a dirt road that varies in temperament and leads 1.5 miles to the trailhead.

This very scenic grind of a ride takes you through the Santa Rita foothills, along the base of the stunning formation called Elephant Head, then up to some radio towers, where the panorama of southwestern Arizona spreads out for miles. It's an out-and-back, so you can go for as long or short a ride as you'd like. The route starts on single track, and then breaks onto double track and some Forest Service road. You'll definitely want to do this ride during the cooler months.

The trail starts through a gate at the end of Proctor Road. It travels along the foothills below the distinctive Elephant Head formation for 3.4 miles, then passes through a gate and goes left onto a jeep road. It really begins climbing here, continuing on the jeep road for 2.8 miles before passing through another gate. The trail turns to single track again, climbing steeply; watch for trail signs in this 0.9-miles-long section. The trail meets up with FS 183; turn left and follow this rough road up to the radio towers. From here you'll have spectacular views of the Santa Cruz Valley and across to the Tumacacori Mountains. Head back the way you came.

Perimeter Trail Loop 138
8 miles. Difficult. 1,500-ft. elevation gain. Allow 2 hrs. Access: Drive south of Sierra Vista on AZ 92 for 9 miles to Miller Canyon Rd. Follow it for 1 mile to the Perimeter Trailhead. This trail can be difficult to follow without a map. Call the Forest Service (☎ 602/378-0311) to acquire one.

This is Sierra Vista's best mountain bike ride. It traverses varied terrain, mostly single track except for a grunt of a climb up Carr Canyon Road for a stretch. All along you'll find views east from the Huachucas. When I rode it the loop was marked with yellow signs so it was easy to find the way, but this may not always be the case. Begin heading up the Perimeter Trail, contouring the foothills en route to Carr Canyon Road, which it meets at 3.75 miles. Turn left and grunt your way up past the Carr House, over a bridge, and to the Clark-Springs Trail at 5.45 miles. Turn left and contour back around the mountains. At the edge of the Miller Peak Wilderness Area, veer left onto the John Cooper Trail. This trail was built in the name of a boy who was killed in a car accident just after high school graduation. It goes around the wilderness where bikes are prohibited, allowing bikers to complete this loop. The trail varies between rocky and smooth, finally rejoining the Miller Trail. When you come to Miller Canyon Road, cross it and head across the parking area. On the other side you'll find a trail that parallels that road back to the car.

Brown Canyon Trail
5 miles round-trip. Moderate. 600-ft. elevation gain. Allow 2 hrs. Access: From Sierra Vista drive south on AZ 92 for 6 miles and turn west (right) on Ramsey Canyon Rd. Drive 2 miles; the trailhead is on the right.

The Brown Canyon Trail offers a fun single-track jaunt into a partially shaded area, rich with birdlife. The canyon has a false trailhead at the parking area about a mile from where the actual trail takes off. The road in between requires a high-clearance vehicle, so many choose to ride it. If you have a four-wheel-drive, you can continue on from the little parking area off the Ramsey Canyon Road to where the trail begins. Starting from the parking area, the ride follows mostly double track across some meadows then up a steep hill. From there, single track heads down into Brown Canyon, first traversing the side of the canyon and then along the canyon bottom. There you'll find some welcome shade. It cruises along the canyon bottom for many miles. Return the way you came.

San Pedro Riparian Conservation Area
1–16 miles. Easy. No elevation gain. Allow 1–3 hrs. Access: Drive AZ 90 east from Sierra Vista for 7 miles. Watch for the San Pedro on your right.

This makes for a good family ride or a relaxing break from intense single track. The trails parallel the San Pedro River, up above on the flat plains. Because of the lack of shade, during warm months you'll want to ride here only in the morning or in the evening. The San Pedro's lush stands of cottonwoods attract many birds and animals to the area, and you can pedal slowly while you watch and listen.

The trails take off from the San Pedro House, heading south. One loops east toward the river and makes its way back. Another continues south toward the village of Hereford and can be ridden for as long or short a ride as you'd like. I stayed on the loops close to the San Pedro House, but the volunteer at the house said you can ride 8 miles to Hereford, turn around and come back, though the trails will likely not be as maintained as they are near the San Pedro House.

ROAD BIKING

Cactus Forest Drive in Saguaro National Park East

8 miles. Easy. Allow 1 hr. Access: In Tucson, head east on Speedway Blvd. Turn right on Old Spanish Trail, which will lead to the visitor center.

The paved 8-mile Cactus Forest Drive in Saguaro East winds over hills of rich Sonoran Desert and through large stands of saguaro. If you hit it on off-peak times such as weekdays and non-holidays it can be a good family ride. Be sure to pick up a guidebook before embarking. This drive has picnic areas along the way, each with picnic tables, fire grills, and pit toilets. There is no drinking water.

AZ 82 from Sonoita East

40 miles one-way. Easy to moderate. Allow 3 hrs. one-way. Access: Begin in the village of Sonoita on AZ 82.

This ride is especially beautiful because it tracks through southeastern Arizona's cienegas, broad range land with tall, flowing grass, dotted with rounded and oddly shaped hills, with blue sky islands in the distance. The pavement is good, and much of the way there are decent shoulders. Except during weekends and holidays the traffic flow will be minimal, though around Sierra Vista it will pick up. The ride begins in the village of Sonoita and passes along the edge of the Empire Cienega Wildlife Preserve, where you may spot antelope. AZ 82 continues east skirting the north end of the Mustang Mountains, through Rain Valley to the intersection with AZ 90, which heads south to Sierra Vista. Continue east noting the views of the San Pedro River and its rich bosque as you go, across the river to the intersection with AZ 80. It's a 6-mile jaunt down to the village of Tombstone, if you care to see the O.K. Corral and staged gunfights. Either way, return the way you came.

SEA KAYAKING & RAFTING

Though you won't really find white water in this region, you will find awesome scenery. The **Gila River** runs lazily through the region, providing a calm and scenic float. It passes through desert landscape, areas full of wildlife. The trip runs mid-February through mid-October, from Dripping Springs to Winkelman. Oar or paddle rafts are available. This is a good family adventure; children who weigh over 30 pounds are invited. Contact **Chandelle River Tours** (☎ 800/242-6335 or 520/577-1824; www.arizonaguide.com).

SWIMMING

Patagonia Lake State Park has a nice beach along with changing and bathroom facilities. The day I visited this lake to swim, rangers stood at the entrance turning people away because it was full. That's how popular this 640-acre spread of water can be on a hot spring day, and I'm sure that summer is even worse. Your best bet is to hit it on weekdays and non-holidays. From Tucson, take Interstate 19 south to AZ 82 and head northeast for 12 miles to Patagonia Lake Road. The park is open 4am to 10pm; the entrance fee is $5.

WALKS & RAMBLES

Signal Hill Petroglyphs Trail in Saguaro National Park West

0.5 miles round-trip. Easy. Allow 30 min. Access: Follow the directions to the park as given in the "Parks & Other Hot Spots" section earlier in this chapter. On

Kinney Rd. drive past the Red Hills Visitor Center to Hohokm Rd. Turn right and follow this one-way road until it intersects with two-way Golden Gate Rd. Turn left and drive just over a mile to the trailhead on your right.

This short trail takes you down through a wash and then up through saguaro and paloverde forest to the top of a small hill, where you can view ancient petroglyphs. From the hilltop you'll have spectacular views across the monument to the southeast. There are many notable glyphs. One is shaped like a wheel, which some believe may be a representation of life or season cycles. There's also a goat with long horns and a great snakelike circular pattern, which some say symbolizes the migration. Another wheel has a human-like figure attached to it. Also on the hilltop are placards telling about the prehistoric Hohokum, the people who historians believe were the artists of these works. These hunter-gatherers lived in the area from A.D. 200 until 1450. Yet another placard tells about the Spanish Conquest.

Tohono Chul Park
1 mile. Easy. Allow 45 min. Access: In Tucson, heading west on Ina Rd., go past Oracle to the first stoplight; turn right; 7366 N. Paseo del Norte. Grounds open 7am–sunset; Tea Room open daily 8am–5pm. Call ☎ **520/742-6455** for more information.

So you're in Tucson and you're hungry for both some food and some nature—where do you go? To this privately owned park, complete with cafe. Put your name in with the hostess, and you'll probably have about 45 minutes to cruise around either the 0.75-mile south trail, which meanders through gardens, exhibits and washes, or the 0.25-mile north trail, which makes its way through a tract of relatively undisturbed desert. Either option will expose you to many varieties of cacti, including not only the fairly common prickly pear and cholla, but also the less common South American cereoid and the hedgehog. If you're looking for birds you may see pyrrhuloxia, curve-billed thrashers, or cactus wren. A geology wall demonstrates the unique formation of the Santa Catalina Mountains, and a nursery will sell you any number of types of cacti. When your name comes up in the restaurant you'll enjoy an eclectic selection of salads and sandwiches, and some of the biggest desserts in these parts.

Massai Point in Chiricahua National Monument
0.25 miles. Easy. Allow 20 min. Access: From the Chiricahua National Monument Visitor Center, drive the Bonita Canyon Drive to the end at Massai Point (8 miles).

There's no better place to view the vast and odd rock formations of the Chiricahua than Massai Point. From this high point you can see off across the rocks as well as west toward Sugarloaf Mountain, which at 7,310 feet is the tallest point in the monument, and north toward Cochise Head, a mountain that eerily resembles the Chiricahua leader. Geologists believe that about 27 million years ago volcanic eruptions from Turkey Creek caldera spewed ash that cooled and formed a dark layer of rhyolite. Erosion took over and sculpted the rock into the fascinating formations. The trail is short and simple, with sweeping views all along the way, including one of a huge balanced rock. Interpretive signs highlight the geology of the monument.

Cochise Stronghold Nature Walk
0.4-mile loop. Easy. Allow 20 min. Access: From Willcox, drive west on I-10 about 10 miles, and turn south on US 191; travel about 17 miles to Sunsites. Just north of the village, turn west (right) on the signed road to Cochise Stronghold. Follow this mostly dirt road 9 miles to the trailhead.

This nature walk provides a glimpse into the rugged area that served as a natural fortress and hideout for Apache Indians of the Chiricuahua clan led by Cochise. The walk offers good views of some of the amazing rock formations that are most prevalent right at the beginning of Stronghold Canyon. Along the way are interpretive signs identifying plants and animals.

Coronado Peak Trail

0.8 miles round-trip. Easy. Allow 40 min. Access: From Sierra Vista, drive south on AZ 92 for 15 miles and turn south on Coronado Rd. (watch for signs to Coronado National Memorial). This road becomes Montezuma Rd., which you follow to the top of Montezuma Pass, about a 20-min. drive.

This is a quick route to a high point with spectacular views in almost every direction. The route starts from the placard at the top of Montezuma Pass and heads up a short, easy-to-follow trail. From the top you can see the San Pedro Valley, San Pedro Peak, Montezuma Peak, and the Sierra Madre in Mexico. It's an awesome feeling to stand so near the border of the United States and Mexico and look far into each country's reaches.

Vista Point in Cave Creek Canyon

0.5 miles. Easy. Allow 30 min. Access: From Portal drive west on FS 42 for 1.5 miles and watch for the trailhead on your right.

When I headed up this little trail, I couldn't imagine how, in the base of the canyon, it could lead to a good vista point. You'll probably be just as skeptical as you make your way through the woods, with little ascent at all. But suddenly, the brush diminishes, and you're on top of a pinnacle looking west into the canyon. Cathedral Rock stands before you surrounded by the massive walls that Cave Creek has left as it has carved its way through the Chiricahuas.

WILDLIFE VIEWING

This region has abundant wildlife, from desert to mountain dwellers. **Saguaro National Park** is home to such nocturnal creatures as the cactus mouse and the Western diamondback rattlesnake. Others that feed at night are the desert tortoise and the Gila monster. If you do travel into the desert at night to see these creatures (Saguaro National Park West is open 24 hours), be sure to carry a flashlight and walk gingerly, always watching for cacti and creatures that might do you harm. In this dry land that receives less than 12 inches of rainfall in a typical year, you'll also find animals that are out at midday and have special adaptations for dissipating heat and retaining moisture. For example, the jackrabbit radiates heat from its oversized ears; the kangaroo rat never needs to drink water since it gets all it needs from seeds it eats.

Outside Tucson, the **Santa Catalina Mountains** were once an important breeding ground for desert bighorn sheep. Unfortunately, the herd of 75 to 80 head has dwindled to nothing. With pressure from Tucson and an inability to range, inbreeding may have set in. That factor along with predation has either killed the herd or driven the sheep into bordering national forest lands. However, you may see other desert dwellers in the Santa Catalinas such as coyotes and javelinas.

The **Chiricahua Mountains** are home to a broad range of species from mule deer to black bear. Also watch for species that are more commonly found in Mexico such as the Chiricahua fox squirrel, the coatimundi, and the peccary (a largely gregarious nocturnal animal related to a pig).

Empire Cienega near Sonoita offers a very unique wildlife viewing and hiking experience. This is a great way to get a sense of the savanna-like rangeland in this part of Arizona. A small herd of pronghorn was introduced here in the 1980s. If you find a wash and bushwack to a hill, you might just spot them. This land is not grazed much, so it's covered by knee-high golden grass stretching for miles and miles to the mountains.

Campgrounds & Other Accommodations

CAMPING

Patagonia Lake State Park
From Tucson, take I-19 south to AZ 82 and head northeast for 12 miles to Patagonia Lake Rd. ☎ 520/287-6965. 72 developed sites, 34 with hookups. Rest rooms, showers, picnic area, boat ramps, marina and camp supply store, dump station, creek trail. Pets on leash accepted. $10–$15 per night.

Amidst the rolling hills of southeastern Arizona lays this hidden treasure. The 72 campsites overlook a man-made lake where anglers catch crappie, bass, bluegill, and catfish. Trout are stocked every three weeks from November until late February. Creek Trail offers bird-watchers a close peek at canyon towhee, Inca dove, black vulture, and several species of hummingbirds.

Chiricahua National Monument Bonita Canyon Campground
On AZ 86, 30 miles southwest of Wilcox. ☎ 520/824-3560. www.nps.gov/chir. 25 sites, rest room, picnic tables, grills, water. $6 entrance fee, $8 camping fee. Pets on leash accepted.

This campground sits within lovely oak forest at the base of the Chiricahua Mountains within walking distance of some of the odd rock formations that make this monument famous. The campground is open year-round; particularly spring through fall it fills up quickly and operates on a first-come, first-served basis. It's worth the effort to get a site here. Though the sites aren't exactly private, a few at the top of the campground provide a very isolated feel, with access to some rock formations you can climb upon in the evening to watch the sunset. RVs share the space, but quiet hours from 8pm to 8am are enforced so you won't have to listen to generators. Wood gathering is prohibited.

Cochise Stronghold Campground
From Wilcox, drive west on I-10 about 10 miles, and turn south on U.S. 191; travel about 17 miles to Sunsites. Just north of the village, turn west (right) on the signed road to Cochise Stronghold. Follow this mostly dirt road 9 miles to the campground. 18 sites, picnic tables, fireplaces, composting toilets, but no water. $10 fee.

This lovely campground sits under a canopy of oaks, with mourning doves perched above. At times this can be a bit of a rowdy campground since climbers hang out a lot at Cochise, though when I was there in the spring only two other sites were occupied. The campground has excellent access to hikes in the Cochise Stronghold.

Rucker Forest Camp
From Douglas head north on U.S. 191 for 34 miles to Rucker Canyon Rd. (FS 74). Turn right and drive this graded dirt road for 16 miles to the junction with Leslie Canyon Rd. Turn left (still Rucker Canyon Rd.) and drive 9 miles to FS 74E. Turn left and drive 4.7 miles to the campground. 13 sites. Picnic tables, fireplaces, vault toilets. $10 fee.

This is a pretty place near Rucker Lake (which is at times dry) and along Rucker Creek. Unfortunately, due to the heavy use from the city of Douglas, the area can at times be trashed.

Stargazing

A combination of low humidity and little light pollution make southern Arizona one of the prime stargazing sites in the world. Fortunately, there's a special spot in this region that accommodates all levels of gazers, from novices to full-on astronomers. The **Vega-Bray Observatory**, part of the **Skywatcher Inn** (see "Inns & Lodges" below), offers guided tours of the night sky. Be sure to reserve in advance (starting at about $85 for up to 5 people). You'll start at sunset, getting a basic knowledge of the sky and where the major planets and constellations are located. As the night progresses you can move on to more specific stargazing, viewing nebulae and clusters through a variety of world-class telescopes. The observatory is equipped with a sliding-roof observing room with a 14.5-inch Newtonian telescope, a 6-inch refractor, two computerized 12-inch Schmidt-Cassegrains, and two Dobsonian telescopes, 8- and 12-inches. A separate observing room with a 14-inch electronically controlled dome houses a 20-inch Maksutov telescope. Contact ☎ **520/615-3886** or log on to www.communiverse.com/skywatcher for reservations and more information.

INNS & LODGES

Amado Territory Inn Bed & Breakfast
3001 E. Frontage Rd. (P.O. Box 81), Amado, AZ 85645. ☎ **520/398-8684** or 888/398-8684. www.amado-territory-inn.com. 9 units. A/C. Summer $90–$105 double; winter $105–$135 double. MC, V.

This inn just off I-19 provides a comfortable, quiet stay, with views of the Santa Rita and the Tumacacori Mountains. Rooms in this two-story pitched-roof building are large and bright with pine floors and territorial-style furniture. They open off a hallway, and most have shared porches. The only drawback is that each room doesn't have its own thermostat. A big delicious breakfast is served in a sunny atrium from which over 53 species of birds have been spotted. The inn shares grounds with a nursery and restaurant.

Casa Tierra
11155 West Calle Pima, Tucson, AZ 85743. ☎ **520/578-3058**. E-mail: casatier@azstarnet.com. 4 units. A/C TV TEL. $95–$300 double. Prices include breakfast. MC, V.

It's difficult to pinpoint what's best about this bed & breakfast—its location, 30 minutes from downtown Tucson at the edge of Saguaro National Monument West, or its ambiance, created by hand-sculpted adobe walls, viga ceilings, and red-brick floors. The rooms are situated around a very Mexican-style courtyard complete with fountain, and each has its own private patio with desert views as well. A Jacuzzi under the stars rounds out the luxurious experience. The only drawback here is that noise travels from room to room; however, the place does quiet down at night. A full gourmet breakfast is served in the courtyard during warm months and in a sunny dining room during cooler ones.

Hacienda del Sol Guest Ranch Resort
5601 N. Hacienda del Sol Rd., Tucson, AZ 85718. ☎ **800/728-6514** or 520/299-1501; www.haciendadelsol.com. 33 units. A/C TV TEL. $75–$195 double, depending on the season and type of room; includes an elaborate continental breakfast. AE, MC, V.

If you really want to get a feel of traditional Tucson, this is the place to stay. Built in the 1929 as a girls school, this small resort is so full of Spanish tile, adobe, cactus, and wildflowers, visitors are constantly strolling the grounds snapping photos. Rooms vary in size from the small historical rooms to the larger hacienda rooms to casitas, all decorated with bright Mexican colors, all with mini-refrigerators and large TVs. The property is comprised of a series of quaint courtyards; off the main one is a sunny pool with a view of the Santa Catalina Mountain. In addition there are tennis and croquet courts and a whirlpool. The on-site restaurant has a good reputation and serves three delicious meals. On the grounds is a riding stable where guests can take short rides through the desert.

Aravaipa Farms
HCR Box 4252, Winkleman, AZ 85292. ☎ 520/357-6901. 2 casitas. A/C. $225 double. Price includes 3 meals. No credit cards.

This inn near one of the few perennial streams in southern Arizona is a menagerie of creativity. The charming casitas are adorned by hand-carved birdhouses, hand-painted tile, and bent willow furniture, blended with the richness of kilim rugs and antique American quilts. Bright banks of windows look out upon a peach orchard. Innkeeper Carol Steele, who formerly operated restaurants in the Scottsdale area, serves purely gourmet meals. Breakfast is a simple, serve-yourself affair in your own room, which is equipped with mini-refrigerator and coffeemaker. Most people head to Aravaipa Canyon for a hike and take along one of Carol's lunches; mine included a perfect tuna sandwich and sides. In the evening guests sit around an outdoor fireplace, drinking wine, and swapping canyon stories. Dinner is spectacular—during our stay, we had salmon grilled to perfection, Caesar salad, asparagus, and memorable sourdough bread.

Skywatcher's Inn
South of Benson. (Mailing address: 5655 North Via Umbrosa, Tucson, AZ 85750.) ☎ 520/615-3886. www.communiverse.com/skywatcher. 4 units. A/C TV TEL. $75–$110 double. Rates include full breakfast and afternoon treats. MC, V.

This isn't so much a night's stay as an adventure. The order of business here is stargazing, and whether you're a novice or an expert you will be completely entertained. The accommodations themselves have an exotic elegance; such rooms as "The Egyptian," "Garden," and "Galaxy" hold tightly to their themes. All are impeccably clean, with full amenities including televisions with satellite reception. Since most visitors stay up well into the night, mornings can be slow-moving affairs, with gazers trading sightings over a gourmet breakfast. For the best use of the attached Vega-Bray Observatory, be sure to reserve a guide for an additional cost (starting at about $85 for up to 5 people). You'll start at sunset, getting a basic knowledge of the sky, where the major planets and constellations are. As the night progresses you can move on to more specific stargazing, viewing nebulae and clusters through a variety of world-class telescopes. Below the inn is a small lake with a paddleboat, excellent for wiling away hot afternoons.

Vineyard Bed & Breakfast
92 S. Los Encinos Rd. (P.O. Box 1227) Sonoita, AZ 85637. ☎ 520/455-4749. www.virtualcities.com. 4 units. $95–$110 double. Rates include a full breakfast. No credit cards.

Set within a 1916 adobe, the oldest house in Sonoita, this inn offers simple and comfortable rooms surrounded by grasslands that once held vineyards. Most rooms have early American decor, while the casita is more Southwestern in style. Mornings and evenings bring hundreds of birds to the gardens, which guests can overlook from broad windows in the living room or from near the coy pond. Breakfasts are big enough to keep you going through much of the day and tasty enough so you'll remember them long after you've left.

San Pedro River Inn
8326 S. Hereford Rd., Hereford, AZ 85615. ☎ 520/366-5532. www.sanpedroriverinn.com. E-mail: sanpedroriverinn@juno.com. A/C, TV, TEL. 4 houses. $95 double. Price includes continental breakfast. No credit cards.

Though these houses aren't as refined as some of the B&Bs listed above, they do provide plenty of comfort in a remarkable setting. Within walking distance of the San Pedro Riparian area, these four houses sit upon large lawns with trees full of birds. The decor is simple and practical, the rooms and bathrooms generally on the small side. Each has a full kitchen. With all the outdoor space and the variety of types of houses, this is an exceptional choice for families. If you like to brush elbows with fame, this is where author Barbara Kingsolver stayed while she wrote a *National Geographic Magazine* article on the San Pedro.

Ramsey Canyon Inn Bed & Breakfast
26 Ramsey Canyon Rd. Hereford, AZ 85615. ☎ 520/378-3010. www.tnc.org/ramseycanyon/ramseycanyoninn. E-mail: lodging@theriver.com. 6 units, 2 apartments. $110–$132 double. Full breakfast and afternoon pie included in the price of the rooms, but not the apartments. MC, V.

The rooms at this inn owned and operated by the Nature Conversancy are generally booked 6 months in advance; that's how special the place is. The inn itself is quaint and comfortable, a modern building with Victorian decor. Rooms and bathrooms are medium-sized and decorated with antiques and designer linens. The adjacent duplex houses apartments that have smaller rooms and bathrooms, but do come with a kitchen. This is a good option for families, whereas only children 16 and older are welcome at the inn. The real draw to the place is the 24-hour access to Ramsey Canyon Preserve. There's also a lovely porch to lounge on during warm months, and a great room with a welcome fireplace for cold ones.

Casa de San Pedro
8933 S. Yell Lane, Hereford, AZ 85615-9250. ☎ 800/588-6468 or 520/366-1300. www.naturesinn.com. E-mail: casadesanpedro@naturesinn.com. 10 units. A/C. $100–$139 double. Rates include full breakfast and afternoon pie or cobbler. DISC, MC, V.

Planned and built by a group of avid birders, this inn, just steps from the San Pedro Conservation Area, is comfortable and well planned and executed. Set around a lush courtyard, the rooms are large with handcrafted furniture and medium-sized bathrooms with showers. The great room carries on the hacienda theme, with comfortable couches, a good birding library, and a computer with a *Thayer Birds of North America* program. Breakfast is served family-style early to accommodate serious birders in a large dining room with windows looking out to feeders where birds congregate. This inn has good access for travelers with disabilities.

Portal Peak Lodge
P.O. Box 364, Portal, AZ 85632. ☎ 520/558-2223. www.portalproductions.com/portalpeaklodge. 16 units. A/C TV TEL. $75 double. AE, DISC, MC, V.

The only game in town, this clean, efficient, Motel 6-feeling place will give you a comfortable night's sleep and a decent meal in the store next door, but not much else. Most guests are birders, who head out early in the morning and stay out into the evening, so they don't mind. Rooms are medium-sized with a small bathroom. They open out onto a center deck. Though the hotel is made up of portable buildings, masqueraded as red wood, the rooms are surprisingly quiet.

8

New Mexico Indian Country

I'm always amazed when my adventures in my home state rival the ones I've enjoyed in the "exotic" places I've traveled, such as Borneo and Bolivia. But in New Mexico's "Indian Country," they do, because the region is so mysterious, unpredictable, and culturally rich. At Acoma, I peeked through a hole in the wall of an ancient cemetery on a mesa hundreds of feet above the ground. The hole had been left there so the spirits of some children who were taken from the pueblo could return. In Grants, a former uranium-mining boomtown, I traveled deep into a mine. In Gallup, self-proclaimed "Indian capital of the world" and a mecca for silver jewelry shoppers, I jogged along Route 66 and on top of a pink mesa overlooking the city. In Farmington, center of the fertile San Juan Valley and gateway to the Four Corners region, I slept in a cave.

Each was an adventure in its own right, but what really made them special for me were the reminders that northwestern New Mexico's greatest asset is the prevalence of Native American culture. My Zuni friend Jim met me at El Malpais National Monument, where we hiked deep into lava caves. During our journey, he spoke of his efforts to conserve the traditions of the tribe into which he was born. In Farmington, I stumbled upon a couple of old childhood friends, who took me biking on the Road Apple Trails, some of the smoothest single track in the Southwest, while telling me stories of what it's like to live and work in a land where Native American culture is so predominant.

Every time I travel to northwestern New Mexico I'm pleasantly surprised by the number of Pueblo, Navajo, and Apache who inhabit it. In some pockets, they are the majority, and they set the pace and tone of the place. The Zuni, Acoma, and Laguna Pueblos are each located within a short distance of I-40. Acoma's "Sky City" has been continually occupied for more than nine centuries. A huge chunk of the northwest is taken up by a part of the Navajo Reservation, the largest in America, and the Jicarilla Apache Reservation stretches 65 miles south from the Colorado border. All share their arts and crafts as well as their distinctive cultures with visitors, but they ask that their personal privacy and religious traditions be respected.

The past lives here, too. The Pueblo people believe their ancestors' spirits still inhabit the ruins. Chaco Culture National Historical Park, with 12 major ruins and hundreds of smaller ones, represents the development of Puebloan civilization, which reached its peak in the 11th century. Aztec Ruins National Monument and the nearby Salmon Ruins are similarly spectacular Pueblo preservations. The most interesting thing I learned while traveling here is that the contemporary Puebloan tribes no longer want to use the word *Anasazi* to refer to the people who once inhabited the ruins of Chaco, Salmon, Aztec, Mesa Verde, and others. Anasazi is a Navajo word meaning "ancient ones," or possibly "ancient enemies." The Pueblo tribes, believed to be the ancestors of the Anasazi, prefer the term *ancestral Puebloan people*.

This new consciousness about language is just one example of the many ways in which Native Americans are reclaiming their heritage. With the passing of the Native American Graves and Repatriation Act in 1990, tribes all over the country began claiming rights to ancient religious and burial artifacts. You may note these changes in museums throughout the region, where pottery has been claimed by tribes or simply removed from exhibits. During my visit to the Aztec Ruins National Monument, one large space stood empty. A warrior's remains had been exhibited there, and now a sign informs visitors that to the native people such a display of the dead was offensive. Though I would have liked to see the warrior, in some ways his absence spoke even more eloquently to me, and I hope it will to others, about the nature of these people and their struggle to maintain their beliefs amid the overpowering culture surrounding them.

Two other national monuments in northwestern New Mexico also speak of the region's history. El Morro is a sandstone monolith known as "Inscription Rock," where travelers and explorers documented their journeys for centuries. El Malpais is a volcanic badland with spectacular cinder cones, ice caves, and lava tubes.

Northwestern New Mexico can be best appreciated by hikers who love stepping along trails that have been used for a millennium by native people, and those who appreciate viewing living cultures very different from their own. It's also a good place for mountain biking, particularly in the area around Farmington. Fly fishers come from all over the world to test the waters of the San Juan below Navajo Lake. Additionally, along the northern border of the region is the flat area known as Four Corners, the only place where four states adjoin. Kids and adults love to stand on the concrete slab and occupy all four states at once.

Your trip through New Mexico Indian Country will undoubtedly weave you into the lives of the Navajo, Zuni, and Jicarilla Apache tribes, whether you're strolling the streets of Gallup, climbing onto the mesa at Acoma, or fishing in the lakes at Dulce. All three groups are deeply linked to the land, and it's important for visitors to realize while traversing the deserts, buttes, and canyons of the region that for these Native Americans every bit of the land and sky, and all the forces acting upon them, are sacred.

The Lay of the Land

This region sits atop the Colorado Plateau, a relatively stable landmass that stretches from northwestern New Mexico across northern Arizona, southern Utah, and western Colorado. It's characterized by its high elevation (usually between

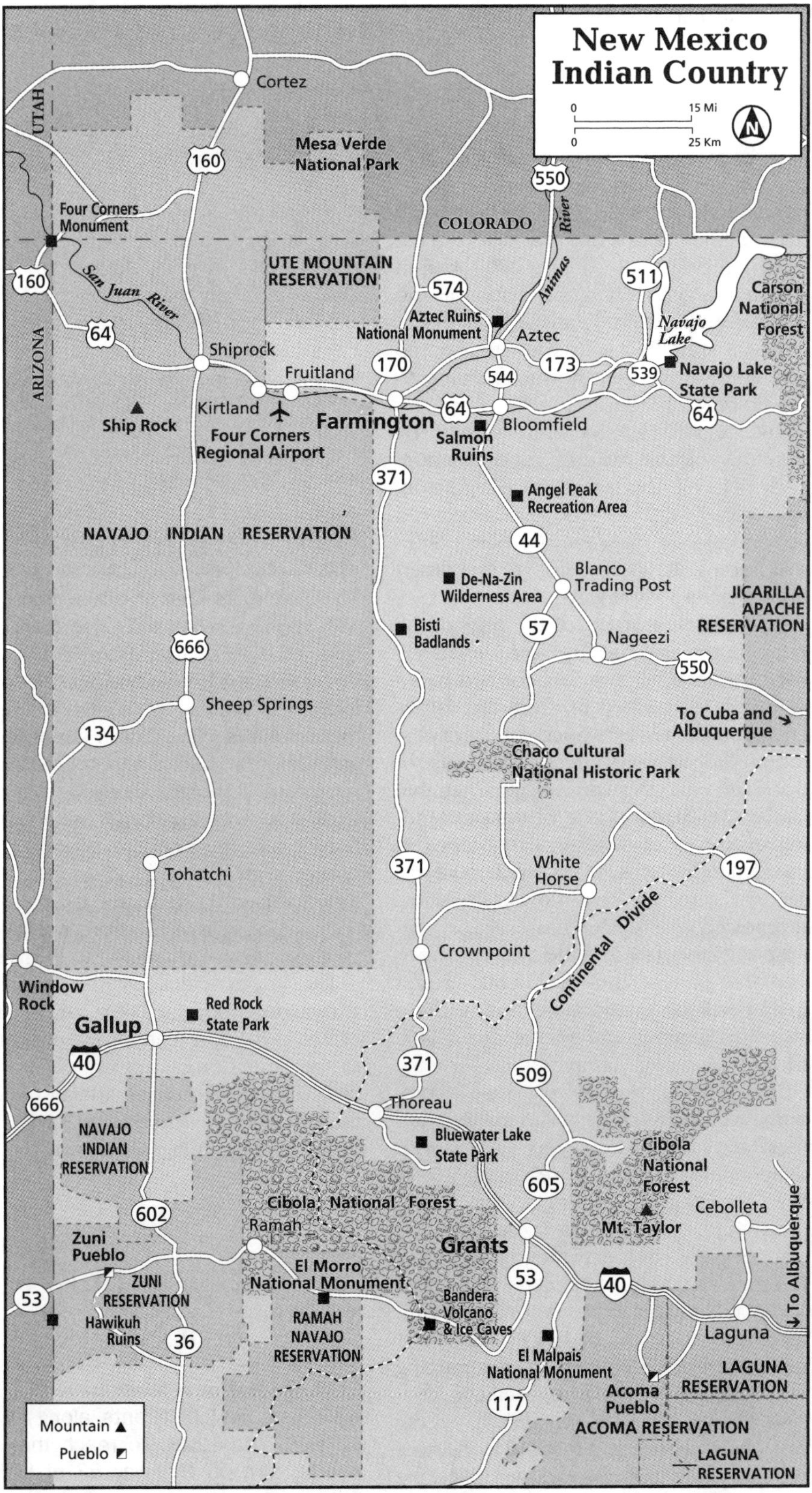

New Mexico Indian Country
0
15 Mi
0
25 Km
N
UTAH
ARIZONA
COLORADO
Cortez
160
Mesa Verde National Park
550
Four Corners Monument
San Juan River
Animas River
UTE MOUNTAIN RESERVATION
574
511
Carson National Forest
Navajo Lake
Aztec Ruins National Monument
Aztec
64
Shiprock
Fruitland
170
173
539
Navajo Lake State Park
544
Kirtland
Ship Rock
Farmington
Bloomfield
Four Corners Regional Airport
Salmon Ruins
371
Angel Peak Recreation Area
NAVAJO INDIAN RESERVATION
44
De-Na-Zin Wilderness Area
Blanco Trading Post
JICARILLA APACHE RESERVATION
Bisti Badlands
57
Nageezi
666
Sheep Springs
134
To Cuba and Albuquerque
Chaco Cultural National Historic Park
White Horse
197
Tohatchi
Continental Divide
Crownpoint
Window Rock
Red Rock State Park
Gallup
40
509
Thoreau
NAVAJO INDIAN RESERVATION
Bluewater Lake State Park
Cibola National Forest
605
Cibola National Forest
Mt. Taylor
Cebolleta
602
Ramah
Grants
To Albuquerque
Zuni Pueblo
El Morro National Monument
53
ZUNI RESERVATION
Bandera Volcano & Ice Caves
Laguna
Hawikuh Ruins
36
RAMAH NAVAJO RESERVATION
El Malpais National Monument
LAGUNA RESERVATION
Acoma Pueblo
117
ACOMA RESERVATION
Mountain
Pueblo
LAGUNA RESERVATION

5,000 to 10,000 feet) and its vast tracts of open range, which are interrupted by angular mesas. Within this mass of high country lies the San Juan Basin, a circular basin 110 miles wide, that contrasts with the uplifted blocks that characterize the rest of the plateau country. This barren region was generally ignored until oil and gas were discovered below its surface. Now it's sprinkled with wells that pump and grind away from north of Gallup to the Colorado border.

The region is also distinguished by stunning volcanic features, especially hogback ridges in the vicinity of Farmington, and volcanic necks—eroded hearts of old volcanoes—the most famous being Shiprock, rising 1,100 feet above the desert floor west of Farmington.

In the southern part of the region, the Zuni Mountains rise up from relatively flat surroundings. They are formed by an anticline that pushed up from the earth's crust and then was striped away, exposing its Precambrian granite core. East of the Zunis lie the almost impenetrable lands of El Malpais, one of the outstanding examples of volcanic landscapes in the United States. The area contains 115,000 acres of lava flows, the most recent only 1,000 years old.

Spring and fall are the best times to visit this part of the world; hiking and biking will be comfortable during these seasons. Summer and winter are a little trickier. Summer temperatures average 87°F; however, the lack of shade combined with high-intensity sun means summer days can get very hot, with temperatures at times reaching 100°F. With elevations averaging in the 6,500-foot range, New Mexico Indian Country can get quite cold in winter, often below freezing. Anytime between November and May you can expect snow, and winter temperatures can be below freezing at night, with daytime temperatures ranging from the 30s to the 60s. Unlike central New Mexico where mountains play a big role, here there's a bit more consistent elevation. The coldest area will likely be along the Arizona border where the Chuska Mountains reach an elevation of nearly 10,000 feet.

Note: Your greatest concern in the region is the summer monsoon. During July, August, and September, thunderheads build over the higher landmasses and dump rain that can race down the canyons and make roads impassable. Flooding can also occur during the spring snowmelt. Generally April, May, and June receive the least precipitation.

Orientation

The eastern border of this region is U.S. 550, running along the edge of Santa Fe National Forest from Bernalillo north to Cuba; then the border becomes NM 537 up to the Dulce area. The southern border of the region lies at the Catron County boundary, about 30 miles south of Interstate 40, which cuts through the region from east to west. The western border is the Arizona border, and the northern boundary is the border with Colorado. The other major thoroughfare through the region is U.S. 550, cutting diagonally from northwest to southeast from Farmington to Bernalillo.

The major cities in the region are Farmington (pop. 36,000), a rich farming center in the San Juan Valley and gateway to the Four Corners region; Gallup (pop. 20,000), self-proclaimed "Indian Capital of the World"; and Grants (pop. 8,900), a former uranium-mining boomtown.

Parks & Other Hot Spots

El Morro National Monument
43 miles west of Grants along NM 53. ☎ 505/783-4226. To reach the visitor center, turn off Highway 53 at El Morro

sign, and travel approximately 0.5 miles. The visitor center is open daily 9am–7pm in summer; 9am–5pm in winter. Trails are open daily 9am–6pm in summer, 9am–4pm in winter. The park is closed on Christmas and New Year's Day. Admission $4 per car or $2 per person. Allow 2–4 hrs. to visit the museum and hike a couple of trails. Self-guided trail booklets are available at the visitor center.

Travelers who like to look history straight in the eye are fascinated by "Inscription Rock." Looming up out of the sand and sagebrush is a bluff 200 feet high, holding some of the most captivating messages in North America. Its sandstone face displays a written record of the many who inhabited and traveled through this land, beginning with the ancestral Puebloan who lived atop the formation around 1200. Carved with steel points are the signatures and comments of almost every explorer, conquistador, missionary, army officer, surveyor, and pioneer emigrant who passed this way between 1605, when Gov. Don Juan de Oñate carved the first inscription, and 1906, when it was preserved by the National Park Service. Oñate's inscription, dated April 16, 1605, was perhaps the first graffiti left by any European in America.

A paved walkway makes it easy to walk to the writings, and there is a stone stairway leading up to other treasures. One reads: "Year of 1716 on the 26th of August passed by here Don Feliz Martinez, Governor and Captain General of this realm to the reduction and conquest of the Moqui." Confident of success as he was, Martinez actually got nowhere with any "conquest of the Moqui," or Hopi, peoples. After a 2-month battle, they chased him back to Santa Fe.

Another special group to pass by this way was the U.S. Camel Corps, trekking past on its way from Texas to California in 1857. The camels worked out fine in mountains and deserts, outlasting horses and mules 10 to 1, but the Civil War ended the experiment. When Peachy Breckinridge, fresh out of the Virginia Military Academy, came by with 25 camels, he noted his passage on the stone here.

El Morro was at one time as famous as the Blarney Stone of Ireland—everybody had to stop by and make a mark. But when the Santa Fe Railroad was laid 25 miles to the north, El Morro was no longer on the main route to California, and from the 1870s the tradition began to die out.

Atop Inscription Rock via a short, steep trail are ruins of a Puebloan pueblo occupying an area of 200 feet by 300 feet. Its name, Atsinna, suggests that carving one's name here is a very old custom indeed: The word, in Zuni, means "writing on rock."

A museum at the visitor center features exhibits on the 700 years of human activity at El Morro. A 15-minute video gives visitors a good introduction to the park. Also within the visitor center is a bookstore where you can pick up souvenirs or educational and informational books.

CAMPING Though it isn't necessary to camp here in order to see most of the park, a nine-site campground at El Morro is open from Memorial Day to Labor Day, and costs $5 per night. There are no supplies available within the park, so if you're planning on spending a night or two, be sure to arrive well equipped.

One nearby private enterprise, **El Morro RV Park** (HC 61, Box 44, Ramah, NM 87321, ☎ 505/783-4612), has cabins, RV and tent camping, and a cafe.

Cíbola National Forest
Contact Mount Taylor Ranger District, ☎ **505/287-8833** or Cíbola National Forest, ☎ **505/346-2650**. Bird watching, hiking, mountain biking, wildlife viewing.

This is actually a combination of parcels of land throughout the state that total more than 1.6 million acres. Elevation varies from 5,000 to 11,301 feet, and the forest includes the Datil, Gallinas, Bear, Manzano, Sandia, San Mateo, and Zuni Mountains.

Two major pieces of the forest flank I-40 on either side of Grants, near the pueblos and monuments described in this section. To the northeast of Grants, NM 547 leads some 20 miles into the San Mateo Mountains. The range's high point, and the highest point in the forest, 11,301-foot Mount Taylor, is home of the annual Mount Taylor Winter Quadrathlon in February. The route passes two campgrounds, Lobo Canyon and Coal Mine Canyon. Hiking, enjoying the magnificent scenery, and elk hunting are popular in summer, cross-country skiing in winter.

To the west of Grants run the Zuni Mountains, a heavily forested range topped by 9,253-foot Mount Sedgewick. Ask at the Grants/Cíbola County Chamber of Commerce, 100 N Iron Ave. (☎ **800/ 748-2142** or 505/287-4802), or the Mount Taylor Ranger District (see phone number above) in Grants for the *Zuni Mountain Historic Auto Tour* brochure. This describes a 61-mile loop (about a half-day trip) that winds through Zuni Canyon into Agua Fria Valley, to the historic town of Sawyer, and loops back to Grants by way of Bluewater Lake. The route includes more than 45 miles of unpaved road with no gas or water en route. It gives unusual insight into the region's early 20th-century logging and mining activities. It's also a good mountain biking route.

On the northern slope of the Zuni Mountains, but outside of the national forest, is **Bluewater Lake State Park.** At 7,400 feet, this forested recreational site offers fishing for rainbow trout and catfish, boating, hiking, picnicking, and camping, and ice fishing is popular in winter. To reach the park, 18 miles west of Grants, leave I-40 at Exit 63 and continue south for 7 miles. For more information, see the "Fishing" section later in this chapter.

Aztec Ruins National Monument
Approximately 0.5 miles north of U.S. 550 on Ruins Rd. (County Rd. 2900) on the north edge of the city of Aztec. Ruins Rd. is the first street immediately west of the Animas River Bridge on Hwy. 516 in Aztec. ☎ **505/334-6174**, ext. 30. The monument is open daily in summer (Memorial Day to Labor Day) 8am–6pm and in winter 8am–5pm; closed Thanksgiving, Christmas, and New Year's Day. Admission $4 adult, free for children ages 17 and under.

What's most striking about these ruins is the central kiva, which visitors can enter and sit within, sensing the site's ancient history. The ruins of this 450-room Native American pueblo, left by the Puebloan ancestors 7 centuries ago, are located 14 miles northeast of Farmington in the town of Aztec on the Animas River. Early Anglo settlers, convinced that the ruins were of Aztec origin, misnamed the site. Despite the fact that this pueblo was built long before the Aztecs of central Mexico lived, the name persisted.

The influence of the Chaco culture is strong at Aztec, as evidenced in the pre-planned architecture, the open plaza, and the fine stone masonry in the old walls. But a later occupation shows signs of Mesa Verde (who flourished from 1200 to 1275) influence. This second group of settlers remodeled the old pueblo and built others nearby, using techniques less elaborate and decorative than the Chacoans.

Aztec is best known for its Great Kiva, the only completely reconstructed ancestral Puebloan great kiva in existence. About 50 feet in diameter, with a main floor sunken 8 feet below the surface of the surrounding ground, this circular ceremonial room rivets the imagination. It's hard not to feel spiritually overwhelmed, and perhaps to feel the presence of people who walked here nearly 1,000 years ago. (Though, be aware that doubt has been cast on the reconstruction job performed by archaeologist Earl H. Morris in 1934; some believe the structure is much taller than the original.)

Visiting Aztec Ruins National Monument will take you approximately 1 hour, even if you take the 0.25-mile self-guided trail and spend some time in the visitor center, which displays some outstanding examples of ancestral Puebloan ceramics and basketry, as well as such finds as an intact Pueblo ladder, turkey feather woven cloth bound with yucca cordage, and most importantly, an empty case where a warrior's remains had been, but were removed because the Pueblo people felt the display was offensive. Add another half-hour if you plan to watch the video imaginatively documenting the history of native cultures in the area.

CAMPING Camping is not permitted at the monument. Nearby, KOA Bloomfield (☎ 505/632-8339), on Blanco Boulevard, offers 83 sites, 73 full hookups, tenting, cabins, laundry and grocery facilities, picnic tables, grills, and firewood. The recreation area has coin games, a heated swimming pool, basketball hoop, playground, horseshoes, volleyball, and hot tub.

Salmon Ruin and San Juan County Archaeological Research Center
6131 U.S. Hwy. 64, Farmington. ☎ 505/632-2013. www.more2it.com/salmon. E-mail: salmonruin@outerbounds.net. Open daily 9am–5pm in summer, Mon–Sat 9am–5pm and Sun noon–5pm in winter. Admission $3 adults, $2 seniors, $1 children ages 6–16, free for children 6 and under.

What really distinguishes the 150 rooms of these ruins 11 miles west of Farmington near Bloomfield is their setting on a hillside surrounded by lush San Juan River bosque. But before you get to the site, you'll pass through the museum, where a number of informative displays range from one showing the variety of types of ancestral Puebloan vessels from pitchers to canteens, to an exhibit about the wild plants the Puebloan people harvested. Like the ruins at Aztec, here there are two strong architectural influences visible. First the Chacoan: They built the village around the 11th century, with walls characterized by an intricate rubble-filled core with sandstone veneer. The more simple Mesa Verde masonry was added in the 13th century. A trail guide will lead you to each site. There's a marvelous elevated ceremonial chamber or "tower kiva" and a Great Kiva, now a low-lying ruin but with some engaging remains such as the central fire pit and an antechamber possibly used by leaders for storage of ceremonial goods.

One of the most recently excavated ruins in the West, the site today is only 30% excavated by design. It's being saved for future generations of archaeologists, who, it's assumed, will be able to apply advanced research techniques. For now, the archaeological research center studies regional sites earmarked for natural-resource exploitation. There is also a photograph exhibit of Navajo pueblitos and rock art.

Built in 1990, **Heritage Park** on an adjoining plot of land comprises a series of reconstructed ancient and historic dwellings representing the area's cultures, from a paleoarchaic sand-dune site to an ancestral Puebloan pit house, from Apache wickiups and teepees to Navajo hogans, and an original pioneer homestead. Visitors are encouraged to enter the re-creations. In the visitor center you'll find a gift shop and a scholarly research library.

Acoma Pueblo
To reach Acoma from Grants, drive east 15 miles on I-40 to McCartys, then south 13 miles on paved tribal roads to the visitor center. From Albuquerque, drive west 52 miles to the Acoma-Sky City exit, then 12 miles southwest. ☎ 800/747-0181 or 505/470-4966. Open daily 8am–7pm in the summer and daily 8am–4:30pm during the rest of the year. Admission $9 adults, $8 seniors ages 60 and over, $6 children ages 6–17, free for children under 6. Group discounts apply to parties of 15 or more, and there's also a discount for Native American visitors. $10 fee for taking still photographs; no videotaping, sketching, or painting is allowed except by special permission.

The spectacular Acoma Sky City, a walled adobe village perched high atop a sheer rock mesa 367 feet above the 6,600-foot valley floor, is said to have been inhabited at least since the 11th century—it's the longest continuously occupied community in the United States. Native history says it has been inhabited since before the time of Christ. Both the pueblo and its mission church of San Esteban del Rey are National Historic Landmarks. When Francisco Vásquez de Coronado visited in 1540, he suggested that Acoma was "the greatest stronghold in the world"; those who attempt to follow the cliff-side footpath down after their guided tour, rather than take the bus down, might agree.

About 50 to 75 Keresan-speaking Acoma (pronounced *Ack*-oo-mah) reside year-round on the 70-acre mesa top. Many others maintain ancestral homes and occupy them during ceremonial periods. The terraced three-story buildings face south for maximum exposure to the winter sun. Most of Sky City's permanent residents make their living off the throngs of tourists who flock here to see the magnificent church, built in 1639 and containing numerous masterpieces of Spanish colonial art, and to purchase the thin-walled white pottery, with brown-and-black designs, for which the pueblo is famous.

Many Acomas work in Grants, 15 miles west of the pueblo, in Albuquerque, or for one of Acoma's business enterprises such as Sky City Casino; others are cattle ranchers and farm individual family gardens.

SEEING THE HIGHLIGHTS You absolutely cannot wander freely around Acoma Pueblo, but you can start your tour of Acoma at the visitor center at the base of the mesa. One-hour tours begin every 30 minutes, depending on the demand; the last tour is scheduled one hour before closing. The pueblo is closed to visitors on Easter weekend (some years), June 24 and 29, July 9 through 12 or 10 through 13, and the first or second weekend in October.

While waiting, peruse the excellent little museum displaying Acoma history and crafts, or buy snacks at the nearby concession stand. Then board the tour bus, which climbs through a rock garden of 50-foot sandstone monoliths and past precipitously dangling outhouses to the mesa's summit, where you'll disembark for the walking tour. There's no running water or electricity in this medieval-looking village; a small reservoir collects rainwater for most uses, and drinking water is transported up from below. Wood-hole ladders and mica windows are prevalent among the 300-odd adobe structures. As you tour the village on foot there will be many opportunities to buy pottery and other pueblo treasures. Pottery is expensive here, but you're not going to find it any cheaper anywhere else, and you'll be guaranteed that it's authentic if you buy it directly from the craftsperson. Along the way, be sure to sample some Indian fry bread topped with honey.

DANCES & CEREMONIES The annual San Esteban del Rey feast day is September 2, when the pueblo's patron saint is honored with a midmorning mass, a procession, an afternoon corn dance, and an arts-and-crafts fair. A Governor's Feast is held annually in February; and 4 days of Christmas festivals run from December 25 to 28. Still cameras are allowed for a $10 fee, and guided tours do not operate on the mesa during feast days.

Other celebrations are held in low-lying pueblo villages at Easter (in Acomita), the first weekend in May (Santa Maria feast at McCartys), and August 10 (San Lorenzo Day in Acomita).

Laguna Pueblo
From Grants, take I-40 east for 32 miles. The pueblo is 50 miles west of Albuquerque along I-40. ☎ **505/ 552-6654.** Visitors are welcome during daylight hours year-round. No admission or photo fee, but some restrictions apply from village to village.

This major Keresan-speaking pueblo consists of a central settlement and five smaller villages not far from Acoma Pueblo and just over a half-hour from Grants. In fact, Lagunas are closely related to the Acomas who live just 14 miles away. Founded after the 1680 revolt by refugees from the Rio Grande Valley, Laguna is the youngest of New Mexico's pueblos and has about 7,000 residents. Today many Lagunas are engaged in agriculture or private business, including a tribal-operated commercial center. Federal funds brought modern housing facilities and scholarship programs, one of which helped start the career of famous Laguna author Leslie Marmon Silko. The employment rate here is high, and this is widely considered one of New Mexico's wealthiest pueblos.

SEEING THE HIGHLIGHTS New to the pueblo and surrounding area are organized tours; call ☎ **505/552-9771** for the latest information. You can also wander around (respecting the fact that this is home to thousands of people) on your own at your leisure. The outlying villages of Mesita, Paguate, Paraje, Encinal, and Seama are interesting in their own rights, but the best place to visit is the old pueblo where you can see the massive stone church, San Jose de Laguna, built in 1699 and famous for its interior. It was restored in the 1930s.

DANCES & CEREMONIES Pueblo and Navajo people from throughout the region attend St. Joseph's Feast Day (September 19) at Old Laguna Village. The fair begins in the morning with a mass and procession, followed by a harvest dance, sports events, and a carnival. New Year's Day (January 1) and Three Kings Day (January 6) are also celebrated at the pueblo with processions and dances. Each smaller village has its own feast day between July 26 and October 17; call the pueblo office for details.

AN ATTRACTION NEAR LAGUNA **Seboyeta,** the oldest Hispanic community in western New Mexico, is 3.5 miles north of Paguate, outside Laguna Pueblo. It still shows ruins of adobe fortress walls built in the 1830s to protect the village from Navajo attack. The Mission of Our Lady of Sorrows was built in the 1830s, as was the nearby Shrine of Los Portales, built in a cave north of town.

Zuni Pueblo

38 miles south of Gallup via NM 602 and 53. ☎ **505/782-4481,** ext. 401. Visitors are welcome daily from dawn to dusk. Although there is no time when the pueblo is completely closed to visitors, certain areas may be off limits during ceremonies, and all photography may be prohibited at times. Free admission. No sketching or painting is allowed, but still photography is permitted for a $5 fee, and videotaping for $10. As at all Indian reservations, visitors are asked to respect tribal customs and individuals' privacy.

Because of its remoteness and its fierce clinging to its roots, Zuni is one of the most interesting pueblos in New Mexico. When the Spanish first arrived, there were approximately 3,000 Zunis living in six different villages, and they had occupied the region for more than 300 years.

One of the main villages amid the high pink and gold sandstone formations of the area was **Hawikuh.** It was the first Southwestern village to encounter Europeans. In 1539 Fray Marcos de Niza, guided by the Moor Esteban (who had accompanied Cabeza de Baca in his earlier roaming of the area), came to New Mexico in search of the Seven Cities of Cíbola, cities Baca said were made of gold, silver, and precious stones. Esteban antagonized the inhabitants and was killed. De Niza was forced to retreat without really seeing the pueblo, although he described it in exaggerated terms upon his return to Mexico, and the legend of the golden city was fueled.

The following year Coronado arrived at the village. Though the Zunis took up arms against him, he conquered the village easily and the Zuni fled to Towayalane ("Corn Mountain"), a noble mile-long sandstone mesa near the present-day pueblo, as they would later do during the 1680 Pueblo Revolt.

At the time the Zunis had a sophisticated civilization, with a relationship to the land and to each other that had sustained them for thousands of years. Today, the tribe continues efforts to preserve its cultural heritage. They've recovered valuable seed strains once used for dryland farming, they're teaching the Zuni language in schools, and they're taking measures to preserve the wildlife in the area that's critical to their faith.

The Zunis didn't fully accept the Christianity thrust upon them. Occasionally they burned mission churches and killed priests. Though the Catholic mission, dedicated to Our Lady of Guadalupe, sits in the center of their village, clearly their primary religion is their own ancient one, and it's practiced most notably during the days of Shalako, an elaborate ceremony that takes place in late November or early December and is a reenactment of the creation and migration of the Zuni people to Heptina, or the "Middle Place," which was destined to be their home.

SEEING THE HIGHLIGHTS Most of the pueblo consists of modern housing, so there isn't really that much to see; nevertheless, you'll get a feeling for time gone by if you take a walk through the old pueblo. Make a stop at the Catholic mission, dedicated to Our Lady of Guadalupe. Within you'll find a series of murals that depict events in the Zuni ceremonial calendar. In addition, there are some Native American archaeological ruins on Zuni land that date from the early 1200s, but you must obtain permission from the Tribal Office well in advance of your visit in order to see them.

Today, Zuni tribal members are widely acclaimed for their jewelry, made from turquoise, shell, and jet, set in silver in intricate patterns called "needlepoint." The tribe also does fine beadwork, carving in shell and stone, and some pottery. Jewelry and other crafts are sold at the tribally owned **Pueblo of Zuni Arts and Crafts** (☎ 505/782-5531). Look especially for the hand-carved fetishes as well as the acclaimed "needlepoint" jewelry.

If you're planning your visit for late August, call ahead and see if you're going to be around during the pueblo's annual fair and rodeo.

Navajo Indian Reservation
From Gallup, U.S. Route 666 goes directly through the Navajo Indian Reservation up to Shiprock. From there you can head over to Farmington on U.S. 64. *Warning:* U.S. 666 between Gallup and Shiprock has been labeled America's "most dangerous highway" by *USA Today*. Drive carefully! Contact the Navajo Tourism Department ☎ 520/871-6436.

Navajos comprise the largest Native American tribe in the United States, with more than 200,000 members. Their reservation, known to them as Navajoland, spreads across 24,000 square miles of Arizona, Utah, and New Mexico. The New Mexico portion, extending in a band 45 miles wide from just north of Gallup to the Colorado border, comprises only about 15% of the total area.

Until the 1920s, the Navajo Nation governed itself with a complex clan system. When oil was discovered on reservation land, the Navajos established a tribal government to handle the complexities of the 20th century. Today, the Navajo Tribal Council has 88 council delegates representing 110 regional chapters, some two dozen of which are in New Mexico. They meet at least four times a year as a full body in **Window Rock, Arizona,** capital of the Navajo Nation, near the New Mexico border 24 miles northwest of Gallup.

Natural resources and tourism are the mainstays of the Navajo economy. Coal, oil, gas, and uranium earn much of the Navajo's money, as does tourism, especially on the Arizona side of the border, which contains or abuts Grand Canyon and Petrified Forest National Parks, Canyon de Chelly, Wupatki, and Navajo National Monuments, and Monument Valley Navajo Tribal Park; and in Utah, Glen Canyon National Recreation Area, Rainbow Bridge and Hovenweep National Monuments, and Four Corners Monument.

The Navajos, like their linguistic cousins the Apaches, belong to the large family of Athapaskan Indians found across Alaska and northwestern Canada and in parts of the northern California coast. They are believed to have migrated to the Southwest around the 14th century. In 1864, after nearly two decades of conflict with the U.S. Army, the entire tribe was rounded up and forced into internment at an agricultural colony near Fort Sumner, New Mexico—an event still recalled as "The Long March." Four years of near-starvation later, the experiment was declared a failure, and the now-contrite Navajos returned to their homeland.

During the World War II, 320 Navajo young men served in the U.S. Marine Corps as communications specialists in the Pacific. The code they created—437 terms based on the extremely complex Navajo language—was never broken by the Japanese. Among those heroes was artist Carl Gorman, coordinator of the Navajo Medicine Man Organization and father of internationally renowned painter R. C. Gorman.

While Navajos express themselves artistically in all media, they are best known for their work in silversmithing, sandpainting, basketry, and weaving. Distinctive styles of handwoven rugs from Two Grey Hills, Ganado, and Crystal are known worldwide.

WHAT TO SEE & DO For more information on the Navajo Nation, see chapter 3. From September 6 to 10, the annual 5-day **Navajo Nation Fair** (☎ 520/871-6478) attracts more than 100,000 people to Window Rock for a huge rodeo, parade, carnival, Miss Navajo Nation contest, arts-and-crafts shows, intertribal powwow, concerts, country dancing, and agricultural exhibits. It's the country's largest Native American fair. A smaller, but older and more traditional, annual tribal fair is the early October **Northern Navajo Nation Fair** (☎ 520/871-6436), held 90 miles north of Gallup in the town of Shiprock.

The **Crownpoint Rug Weavers Association** has 12 public auctions a year, normally on Friday evening, about 5 weeks apart. This is a rich cultural event well worth the time. For more information, call ☎ 505/786-5302.

Shiprock Peak and Four Corners Monument

Located on the Navajo Indian Reservation southwest of Shiprock, 29 miles west of Farmington via U.S. 64.

This distinctive peak is known to the Navajo as *Tse bidá hi,* "rock with wings." Composed of igneous rock flanked by long upright walls of solidified lava, it rises 1,700 feet off the desert floor to an elevation of 7,178 feet. There are viewpoints off U.S. 666, 6 to 7 miles south of the town of Shiprock. You can get closer by taking the tribal road to the community of Red Rock, but you must have permission to get any closer to this sacred Navajo rock. Climbing is not permitted. The town named after the rock is a gateway to the Navajo reservation and the Four Corners region. There's a tribal visitor center here.

From Shiprock, you might want to make the 32-mile drive west on U.S. 64 to Teec Nos Pos, Arizona, then north on U.S. 160 to the **Four Corners Monument.** A concrete slab here sits astride the only meeting point in the United States of four states—New Mexico, Colorado, Utah, and Arizona. Kids especially like the idea of standing at the center and occupying four states at once. There's a visitor center and crafts and food booths.

Bluewater Lake State Park
28 miles west of Grants via I-40 and NM 412. ☎ 505/876-2391. Camping, group campground, visitor center, drinking water, showers, rest rooms, RV dump station, boat ramp. Camping fees $8–$14. Boating, camping, fishing, hiking, water sports.

This 2,350-acre reservoir located between Gallup and Grants and surrounded by piñon/juniper-covered hills is one of the best places to fish in the area. In fact, some people believe it has the highest catch rate of all New Mexico lakes. Look to catch trout here. There's great summer sailing and water-skiing. Real die-hard anglers set up their tippets in winter and ice fish the frigid waters.

Navajo Lake State Park
Located 25 miles east of Bloomfield via U.S. 64 and NM 511. ☎ 505/632-2278. Visitor center, group campground, drinking water, showers, rest rooms, electric hookups, dump station, boat ramp and marina. Boating, camping, fishing, hiking.

With an area of 15,000 acres, Navajo Lake extends from the confluence of the San Juan and Los Pinos Rivers 25 miles north into Colorado. Navajo Dam, an earthen embankment, is 0.75 miles long and 400 feet high. It provides Farmington-area cities, industries, and farms with their principal water supply. It's also the main storage reservoir for the Navajo Indian Irrigation Project, designed to irrigate 110,000 acres.

This large lake, 450 feet at its deepest point, is a great place to take a cool dip or fish for trout, salmon, bass, and crappie. Navajo Lake State Park is comprised of three separate recreation sites—Pine River, Sims Mesa, and San Juan River (renowned for its world-class trout fishing). Water temperatures usually hover around a cool 70°F and are pretty murky. Like many New Mexico lakes, Navajo Lake's bottom is uneven and rocky, with steep drop-offs close to shore. The lake has boat ramps and several marinas (from which visitors can rent boats), picnic areas, and groceries for those who plan to make a day of it.

Red Rock State Park
Located 5 miles from downtown of Gallup on frontage road Route 66. ☎ 505/722-3839. Camping, hiking, wildlife viewing.

Red Rock State Park, with its natural amphitheater, is set against elegantly shaped red sandstone buttes. It includes an auditorium/convention center, historical museum, post office, trading post, stables, and modern campgrounds.

The 8,000-seat arena is the site of numerous annual events, including the Intertribal Indian Ceremonial in mid-August. Red Rock Convention Center accommodates 600 for trade shows or concert performances.

A nature trail leads up into these stone monuments, and makes for a nice break after hours on the road. See the "Campgrounds & Other Accommodations" section later in this chapter for camping information. There's also a playground, horseback riding trails, and a sports field. Park rangers take people on guided hikes every Saturday and Sunday during the summer months.

The **Red Rock Museum** has displays about prehistoric Puebloan and modern Zuni, Hopi, and Navajo cultures, including an interesting collection of very intricate kachinas. There's a gallery that features changing exhibits. In my most recent visit, there was a display of prayer and dancing fans, bold art made with blue and gold macaw feathers. The museum is open year-round. Monday through Friday from 7am to 6pm, Saturday and Sunday from 9am to 6pm. Suggested donation is $2 for adults, $1 seniors, and 50¢ for children.

Also at this site, in early December is the **Red Rock Balloon Rally,** a high point on the sporting balloonist's calendar. For information, call the Gallup–McKinley County Chamber of Commerce (☎ 505/722-2228).

The New Mexico Museum of Mining
100 N. Iron St. at Santa Fe Ave., Grants. ☎ 800/748-2142 or 505/287-4802. E-mail: discover@grants.org. Open Mon–Sat, 9am–4pm. Admission $3 adults, $2 seniors over age 60 and children ages 7–18, free for children ages 6 and under.

Though this museum isn't an "outdoor" attraction as most in this book are, it does take you on an adventure down into the stomach of the earth into a re-creation of a mine shaft, a thrilling and history-filled journey.

Your trip begins in an enormously interesting little museum with geological displays such as a fossilized dinosaur leg bone and a piece of Malpais lava. The world's only underground uranium-mining museum also gives you a sense of the context within which uranium was mined, through photos of the uranium-mining pioneers. "Word went out that uranium was in demand before people even knew why," reads one quote, which further explains that only scientists and physicists knew about its use as an explosive and fuel. Thus sets the stage for your walk into a mine-shaft-like doorway adorned with rusty metal hats.

An elevator takes you down into a spooky, low-lit place with stone walls. You begin in the station where uranium was loaded and unloaded and travel back into the earth through places defined on wall plaques with such interesting names as *track drift* (where ore comes up in cars from the mine) and *stope* (a room stripped of all ore and off-limits in an actual mine), and you learn the functions of equipment such as a *mucker* (a machine that digs the tunnel for tracks) and a *loaded round* (which blasts holes in rock). Most of all you get to sense the dark and dirty work that mining can be, and when the elevator pauses a moment before taking you to the surface, you may hold your breath in fear that you won't get to return from this strange underworld. If you call in advance, the museum will arrange for a tour guide from the local college. Those with claustrophobia will have to content themselves with the aboveground exhibits.

Chaco Culture National Historic Park

Far beyond the trading posts and towns of northwestern New Mexico, far beyond where the pavement ends sits this amazing ruin site, once the center of one of the world's great civilizations. The ruins are set within stark desert country that seems perhaps ill-suited as a center of culture. However, the ancient Puebloan people successfully farmed the lowlands and built great masonry towns, which connected with other towns over a wide-ranging network of roads crossing this desolate place.

What's most interesting here is how changes in architecture chart the area's cultural progress. These changes began in the mid-800s, when the ancestral Puebloans started building on a larger scale than they had previously. They used the same masonry techniques that tribes had used in smaller villages in the region, walls one stone thick with generous use of mud mortar, but they built stone villages of multiple stories with rooms several times larger than in the previous stage of their culture. Within a century, six large pueblos were underway. This pattern of a single large pueblo with oversized rooms, surrounded by conventional villages, caught on throughout the region. New

Chaco Culture National Historic Park

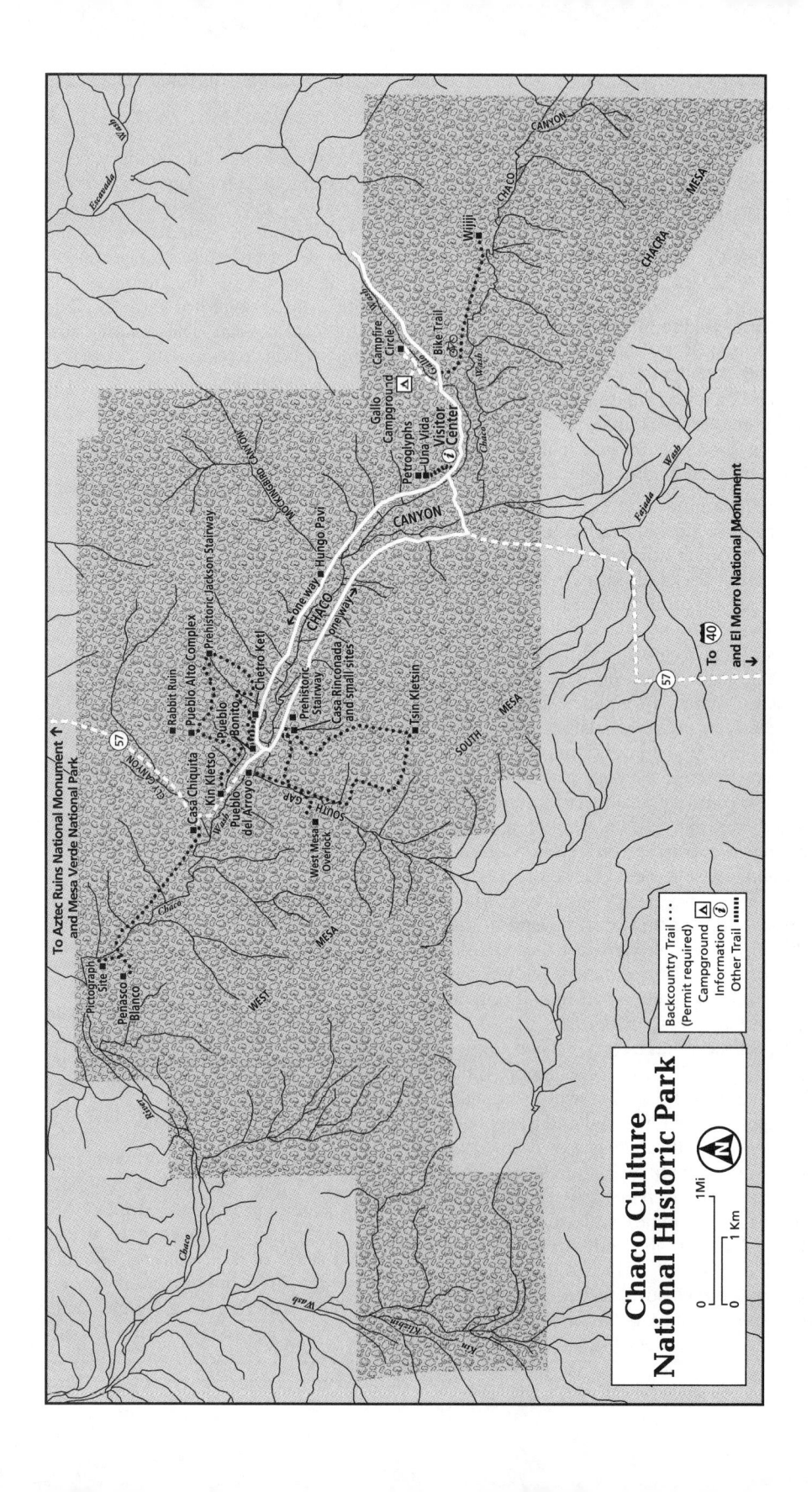

communities built along these lines sprang up. Old villages built similarly large pueblos. Eventually there were more than 75 such towns, most of them closely tied to Chaco by an extensive system of roads.

This progress led to Chaco becoming the economic center of the San Juan Basin by 1000. As many as 5,000 people may have lived in some 400 settlements in and around Chaco. As masonry techniques advanced through the years, walls rose more than four stories in height. Some of these are still visible today.

Chaco's decline after 1½ centuries of success coincided with a drought in the San Juan Basin between 1130 and 1180. Scientists still argue vehemently over why the site was abandoned and where the Chacoans went. Many believe that an influx of outsiders may have brought new rituals to the region, causing a schism among tribal members. Most agree, however, that the people drifted away to more hospitable places in the region and that their descendants live among the Pueblo people today.

This is an isolated area, and there are no services available within or close to the park—no food, gas, auto repairs, firewood, lodging (besides the campground) or drinking water (other than at the visitor center) is available. Overnight camping is permitted year-round.

GETTING THERE

There are two entrances, one on San Juan County Road 7900 and the other on NM 57. From Bloomfield, head southeast on U.S. 550 for 35 miles to the Nageezi Trading Post (last stop for food, gas, or lodging). Three miles east of Nageezi turn right on County Road 7900 and drive 5 miles. Turn right on CR 7950 and drive for approximately 20 miles (dirt road) to the park's visitor center. South entrance: From Crownpoint follow NM 9 east for 40 miles to Seven Lakes. Turn north on NM 57 and follow it about 20 miles (dirt road) into the park. Be aware that on rainy and snowy days these roads become slick and impassable. To inquire about road conditions or other information call ☎ 505/786-7014. There's also a 24-hour emergency assistance line at ☎ 505/786-7060, which connects directly to the homes of law-enforcement rangers in the park.

VISITOR INFORMATION

Admission is $8 per car, campsite extra. The visitor center, with a bookstore and a museum showing films on Puebloan culture, is open Memorial Day through Labor Day, daily from 8am to 6pm; the rest of the year it's open daily from 8am to 5pm. Trails are open from sunrise to sunset. Ranger-guided walks and campfire talks are available in the summer at the visitor center, where you can also get self-guiding trail brochures and permits for the overnight campground (which has non-potable water, tables, and fire grates; bring your own wood or charcoal).

SEEING THE HIGHLIGHTS

Exploring the ruins and hiking are the most popular activities here. A series of pueblo ruins stand within 5 or 6 miles of each other on the broad, flat, treeless canyon floor. Plan to spend at least 3 to 4 hours here driving to and exploring the different pueblos. A one-way road from the visitor center loops up one side of the canyon and down the other. Parking lots are scattered along the road near the various pueblos; from most it's only a short walk to the ruins.

You may want to focus your energy on seeing **Pueblo Bonito,** the largest prehistoric southwest Native American dwelling ever excavated. It contains giant kivas and in its final form had 600 rooms covering more than 3 acres. It's located on the loop road, about 3 miles up the canyon from the visitor center. Also, the **Pueblo Alto Trail** is a nice hike that takes you up on the canyon rim so you can see the ruins from above—in the afternoon, with thunderheads building, the views are spectacular. If you're a cyclist, there's a special map with ridable trails outlined—an excellent way to traverse the vast expanse while experiencing the quiet of these ancient dwellings.

Other ruins accessible directly from the auto road or via short walks are Chetro Ketl, Pueblo del Arroyo, Kin Kletso, Casa Chiquita, Casa Rinconada, Hungo Pavi, and Una Vida. Backcountry hikes (from 2 to 5 hours) are required to reach some ruins; they include Peñasco Blanco, Tsin Kletsin, and Wijiji.

Most ruins are on the north side of the canyon. **Chetro Ketl** had some 500 rooms, 16 kivas, and an impressive enclosed plaza. In its final form, **Pueblo del Arroyo** was a four-story, D-shaped structure. It had about 280 rooms and 20 kivas, many of which are still visible today. At it's peak, the village of **Kin Kletso** had three stories, 100 rooms, and 5 kivas, many of which are still visible. All three are located on the loop read near Pueblo Bonito. **Una Vida,** a short walk from the visitor center, was one of the first pueblos built and has been left only partially excavated; it had 150 rooms and 5 kivas. **Casa Rinconada,** on the south side of the canyon, is the largest "great kiva" in the park, and is astronomically aligned to the cardinal directions and the summer solstice. It may have been a center for the community at large, used for major spiritual observances.

Aerial photos show hundreds of miles of roads connecting these towns with the Chaco pueblos, one of the longest running 42 miles straight north to Salmon Ruin and the Aztec Ruins. Settlements were spaced along the road at travel intervals of 1 day. They were not simple trails worn into the stone by foot travel, but engineered roadways 30 feet wide with a berm of rock to contain the fill. Where the road went over flat rock, walls were built along the sides of it. It is this road network that leads some scholars to believe Chaco was the center of a unified ancestral Puebloan society.

The Chacoans' trade network, as suggested by artifacts found here, stretched from California to Texas and south into Mexico. Seashell necklaces, copper bells, and the remains of macaws or parrots were found among Chaco artifacts. Some of these items are displayed in the museum at the visitor center.

CAMPING

Gallo Campground, located within the park, is quite popular with hikers. See the "Campgrounds & Other Accommodations" section later in this chapter for information.

El Malpais National Monument

Designated a national monument in 1987, El Malpais (Spanish for "badlands") is considered one of the outstanding examples of volcanic landscapes in the United States. El Malpais contains 115,000 acres of cinder cones, vast lava flows, hundreds of lava tubes, ice caves, sandstone cliffs, natural bridges and arches, ancestral Puebloan ruins, ancient Native American trails, and Spanish and Anglo homesteads.

INFORMATION

There are two approaches to El Malpais, via NM 117 and NM 53. NM 117 exits I-40, 7 miles east of Grants; NM 53 exits I-40 just west of Grants. Admission to El Malpais is free (unless you're visiting the privately owned Ice Caves), and it's open to visitors year-round. The visitor center, located off NM 53 between mile markers 63 and 64, is open daily from 8am to 4:30pm. Here you can pick up maps of the park, leaflets on specific trails, and other details about exploring the monument. For more information, call ☎ **505/285-4641.**

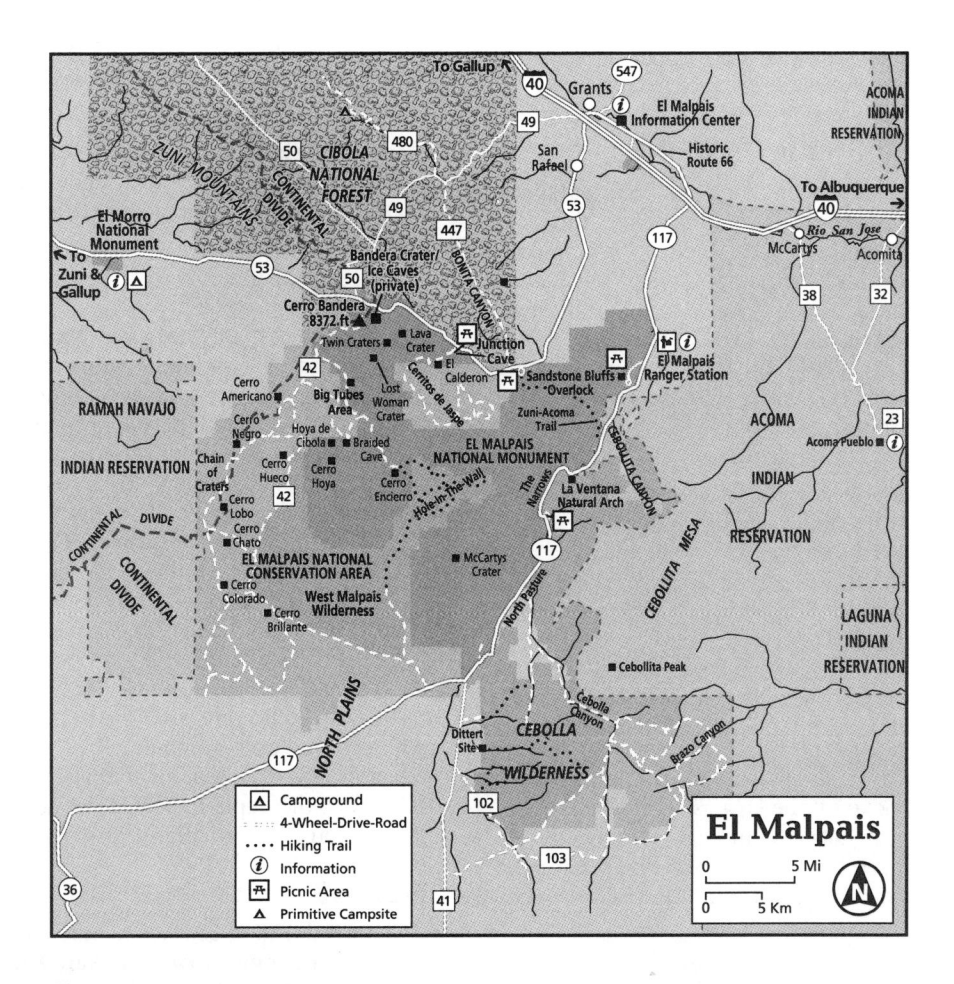

SEEING THE HIGHLIGHTS

From **Sandstone Bluffs Overlook** (10 miles south of I-40 off NM 117) many craters are visible in the lava flow, which extends for miles along the eastern flank of the Continental Divide. The most recent flows are only 1,000 years old; Native American legends tell of rivers of "fire rock." Seventeen miles south of I-40 is **La Ventana Natural Arch,** the largest accessible natural arch in New Mexico.

From NM 53, visitors have access to the **Zuni-Acoma Trail,** an ancient Pueblo trade route that crosses four major lava flows in a 7.5-mile (one-way) hike. A printed trail guide is available. **El Calderon,** a forested area 20 miles south of I-40, is a trailhead for exploring a cinder cone, lava tubes, and a bat cave. (*Warning:* Hikers should not enter the bat cave or otherwise disturb the bats.)

The largest of all Malpais cinder cones, **Bandera Crater** is on private property 25 miles south of I-40. The National Parks Service has laid plans to absorb this commercial operation, known as **Ice Caves Resort** (☎ **888/ICE-CAVE** or 505/783-4303; www.icecaves.com). For a fee of $7 for adults and $3.50 for children ages 5 through 12, visitors hike up the crater or walk to the edge of an ice cave. It's open daily from 8am until 1 hour before sunset; that means hikers can start out no later than 7pm in summertime or 4:30pm in midwinter.

Perhaps the most fascinating phenomenon of El Malpais is the lava tubes, formed when the outer surface of a lava flow cooled and solidified. When the lava river drained, tunnel-like caves were left. Ice caves within some of the tubes have delicate ice-crystal ceilings, ice stalactites, and floors like ice rinks.

HIKING & CAMPING

Several hiking trails can be found throughout El Malpais, including the above-mentioned Zuni-Acoma Trail. Most are marked with rock cairns; some are dirt trails. The best times to hike this area are spring and fall, when it's not too hot. You are pretty much on your own when exploring this area, so prepare accordingly. Be sure to carry plenty of water with you; do not drink surface water. Carrying first-aid gear is always a good idea; the lava rocks can be extremely sharp and inflict nasty cuts. Hikers should wear sturdy boots, long pants, and leather gloves when exploring the lava and caves. In addition, never go into a cave alone. The park service advises wearing hard hats, boots, protective clothing, and gloves, and carrying three sources of light when entering lava tubes. The weather can change suddenly, so be prepared; if lightning is around, move off the lava as soon as possible.

Primitive camping is allowed in the park, but you must first obtain a free backcountry permit from the visitor center.

What to Do & Where to Do It

BALLOONING

At Red Rock State Park in early December is the **Red Rock Balloon Rally,** a high point on the sporting balloonist's calendar. For information, call the Gallup–McKinley County Chamber of Commerce (☎ **505/722-2228**).

BIRD WATCHING

Located 5 miles north of Farmington via NM 170, **Jackson Lake Wildlife Area** is a 60-acre fishing lake, which attracts a broad variety of songbirds as well as, in winter, Canada geese and a wide range of ducks. **Bluewater Lake** in the Grants area is one of the best places in the region to see shorebirds such as cinnamon teal and Canada geese, and, if you're lucky, snow geese. The lake can be accessed off I-40 from either NM 412 or NM 612.

CAVING

Big Tubes at El Malpais National Monument is a great way to get acquainted with a relatively young lava flow. For a detailed description of the hike and the journey into the caves, see the "Hikes & Backpack Trips" section later in this chapter. You'll likely want to travel into the **Four Windows Cave,** a relatively simple trek where the chances of getting lost are low. Still, come prepared. Have on hand three sources of light, hard hats, sturdy hiking boots and long pants and shirtsleeves. Early on in the cave you'll come to roped-off areas where a unique community of green moss grows. The length of this cave is 1,207 feet, the depth 81 feet. Take note of the bulbous ice formations throughout.

FISHING

If you need fishing gear while in the area, contact **Duranglers on the San Juan,** 1003 Hwy. 511, Navajo Dam (☎ **505/632-5952**), or the nearby **Abe's Motel and Fly Shop,** 1791 U.S. 173, Navajo Dam (☎ **505/632-2194**).

The **San Juan River** is a world-renowned trophy river where, in the Quality Waters section, the average trout caught is 17 inches long. The fishing in these tailwaters is good for a variety of fishing abilities. Beginners will have plenty of room to practice casting, while veterans will be able to use their best tricks to lure in the trophies. The river has a variety of designations, each with special regulations so you'll want to find out the rules before you go. A good place to schmooze with the local fishers is at Abe's Motel and Fly Shop, not far from the river. Access the river from U.S. 550, U.S. 64 and NM 511. With water temperature controlled at between 42 and 44°F, fishing is good year-round. But you must wear waders!

Surrounded by piñon/juniper forest, the 2,350-acre **Bluewater Lake** is one of the best places to fish in the Grants area. Use caution if fishing from a small craft since big seas can blow up quickly on this lake. As the weather gets warmer, the bigger fish are generally found deeper and farther from shore. Your best bet is to fish for trout here. The lake can be accessed off I-40 from either NM 412 or NM 612.

North of Ramah via NM 53 sits the 1,300-acre **Ramah Reservoir** where one will find trout, bass, bluegill, and catfish. Trolling or drifting usually works best here. The reservoir was created in the late 1800s by Mormons for the purpose of irrigation, and it was privately owned until 1987 when it became available for public use. Known hatches on the lake are dragon and damsel fly. A record 30-pound channel catfish was pulled out of Ramah in 1995.

Located 5 miles north of Farmington via NM 170, **Jackson Lake Wildlife Area** is a 60-acre fishing lake, which attracts many anglers. Songbirds will likely serenade you while you're casting at this lake during its open season from April to November.

HIKES & BACKPACK TRIPS
Bisti De-Na-Zin Wilderness
1–5 miles. Easy. 150-ft. elevation gain. Allow 1–3 hrs. Access: From Farmington take NM 371 for about 30 miles to Bisti. Or, head east from Farmington for 13 miles on U.S. 64. At Bloomfield turn south on U.S. 550 and drive for about 20 miles to Huerfano Trading Post. Turn southwest (right) on County Rd. 7500, which will become Indian Reservation Rd. 7023 and lead you 12 miles to De-Na-Zin Wilderness. Map: USGS Alamo Mesa.

You'd almost expect to see elves and trolls in this magical land of hoodoos and toadstools, or at least some kind of hungry rock muncher with all the stone mushrooms and chocolate drops. Often referred to as Bisti Badlands (pronounced Bist-*eye*), this barren region may merit that name today, but it was once very different. Around 70 million years ago, large dinosaurs lived near what was then a coastal swamp, bordering a retreating inland sea. Today, their bones, and those of fish, turtles, lizards, and small mammals, are eroding slowly from the low shale hills.

Kirtland Shale, containing several bands of color, dominates the eastern part of the wilderness and caps the mushroom-shaped formations found there. Along with the spires and fanciful shapes of rock, hikers may find petrified wood sprinkled in small chips throughout the area, or even an occasional log. Removing petrified wood, fossils, or anything else from the wilderness is prohibited.

There are no designated trails here, and bikes and motorized vehicles are prohibited. There is also no water or significant shade; the hour just after sunset or, especially, just before sunrise is a pleasant and quite magical time to see this starkly beautiful landscape. Primitive camping is allowed, but bring plenty of water and other supplies.

The very nature of both places calls for all-out, unguided exploration. Grab a water bottle, compass, and map and keep tabs on where you're going as you head out along the washes and over hills. Beware, though—this area is very fragile, and you should definitely follow a "Leave No Trace" policy.

If you'd like more direction for your exploration than that, here goes: At the Bisti, begin at the Bureau of Land Management parking area on an old road that heads east along a wash. Explore both sides of the wash, especially the south side. Continue following the wash, careful not to get off on any of the ravines that branch off from it. Hike as far as you like, then return. From the De-Na-Zin parking area, strike out on a dirt road heading north, which will climb a low hill then drop into an arroyo at about 0.4 miles. Turn left in the arroyo and follow it into a shallow canyon. It will open up into a broader gorge at 0.9 miles, and then will intersect with a larger wash. Turn left and hike down that wash until you come to private land, a good place to turn around and backtrack to your car.

Pueblo Alto Trail at Chaco Culture National Historical Park
5.4-mile loop. Easy. 350-ft. elevation gain. Allow 2½ hrs. Access: You have a choice of two entrances, one on San Juan County Rd. 7900 and the other on NM 57. From Bloomfield, head southeast on U.S. 550 for 35 miles to the Nageezi Trading Post (last stop for food, gas, or lodging). 3 miles east of Nageezi turn right on County Rd. 7900 and drive 5 miles. Turn right on CR 7950 and drive for approximately 20 miles (dirt road) to the park's visitor center. South entrance: From Crownpoint follow NM 9 east for 40 miles to Seven Lakes. Turn north on NM 57 and follow it about 20 miles (dirt road) into the park. *Beware:* On rainy and snowy days these roads become slick and impassable. ☎ **505/786-7014** for road conditions or other information; ☎ **505/786-7060** for the 24-hour emergency assistance line, which connects directly to the homes of law-enforcement rangers in the park. Whichever way you come in, drive first to the Chaco visitor center, then drive to the Pueblo del Arroyo parking area, about 5 miles west of the visitor center. All trails close at sunset, so plan accordingly. Admission $8 per car, campsite extra. Map: Chaco Culture National Historic Park Brochure. All trips into the backcountry including this one require a free permit available at the visitor center. Collecting anything on these sites is prohibited, as is climbing on the ruins, and straying from designated trails.

On a warm summer day at Chaco, while thunderheads build in the distance, you may find yourself looking off of a pink cliff and time-traveling to another century. This trail climbs up on cliffs above Chaco Canyon and contours the rim, then heads farther onto the mesa, where it comes to Pueblo Alto, a ruin important as the junction of several prehistoric roads. The name Pueblo Alto means "high town" in Spanish, an apt name for the ruin that sits atop a mesa.

Beginning at the Pueblo del Arroyo parking area follow the path to the Kin Kletso ruin, where a sign marks the trailhead. The trail begins by climbing through a crack up on a bench. From there it runs east along Chaco Canyon rim, passing the return leg of the loop. From the rim there's a stunning view of Pueblo Bonito, the park's largest ruin. The trail ascends to the mesa top and soon comes to views of Chetro Ketl. From there the trail veers toward the north skirting along some of the prehistoric roads that converge at Pueblo Alto, though evidence of them is very subtle. Next it climbs along the prehistoric Jackson Stairway, carved in the sandstone. The trail turns west and soon comes to Pueblo Alto. As well as the ruins, you'll be able to see the La Plata Mountains to the north and Mount Taylor to the south. From the ruins, the trail heads south to complete the loop.

Peñasco Blanco at Chaco Culture National Historic Park
6.4 miles round-trip. Easy. 150-ft. elevation gain. Allow 3½ hrs. Access: See Pueblo Alto Trail access above. Map: Chaco Culture National Historic Park Brochure.

This trail will spark your imagination. It follows along cliffs where great concentrations of petroglyphs can be seen, culminating in a view of the "Supernova Pictograph," then ends at Peñasco Blanco, one of the earliest pueblos in the canyon, dating to around the middle of the 9th century.

The hike begins at the Pueblo del Arroyo parking area about 5 miles west of the visitor center. From the parking lot, walk past Kin Kletso to Casa Chiquito ruin. From there the trail runs north along

Chaco Wash. It travels along the base of cliffs where many petroglyphs adorn the sandstone. At mile 2 look for images of bighorn sheep and a human figure high on the canyon wall. Next the trail rejoins the road, which heads away from the cliff toward the center of the canyon. At mile 3, the trail leaves the road, drops into the wash, and comes to a trail junction. Bear right toward the pictograph site. Beware of crossing the wash after thunderstorms when water can tear through, sweeping everything in its path. This spur will take you to the "Supernova Pictograph" site. Here you'll see a red-painted crescent moon, a star, and handprint. Experts have correlated this to a supernova explosion that occurred in 1064. A written record of the supernova was also left by Chinese astronomers.

From the supernova, backtrack to the last trail junction and follow the signs for "ruins." The trail heads along the cliff face then up on ledges to reach the main trail. Turn right and follow the cairns high up on the mesa to Peñasco Blanco ("white rocky outcrop"). This "great house" village, inhabited from around A.D 913 until the great abandonment of Chaco Canyon in the mid-1100s, was three stories high and had about 160 rooms. To return, follow the signs, bypassing the spur trail to the pictograph.

The South Mesa Loop and Tsin Kletzin at Chaco Culture National Historic Park

5 miles round-trip. Moderate. 450-ft. elevation gain. Allow 2½ hrs. Access: See the Pueblo Alto Trail directions for access to the Park. Drive to the parking area for Casa Rinconada, about 5 miles from the visitor center. Map: Chaco Culture National Historic Park Brochure.

This trail takes you up to South Gap, which allows for views of the line-of-sight village placement, which operated in Chaco Canyon and was integral to the ancestral Puebloan communication system. The trail makes its way to Tsin Kletsin, ("charcoal house") a modest ruin site that sits 100 feet higher than any other ruin, with stunning views over Chaco Canyon. The trail begins south of the great kiva of Casa Rinconada. At the post marked "South Mesa Loop," turn right, paralleling the base of a cliff. The trail will pass an intersection with a trail from Pueblo del Arroyo. At 0.75 miles the trail comes to a spur trail that climbs to the South Gap signal station sitting above a wide break in the south wall of Chaco Canyon. If you'd like, take the 150-foot climb to the viewpoint from which you'll be able to see Pueblo Bonito and Pueblo Alto. Head back on the spur trail to the main trail and turn right. The trail follows a fence for a while, and soon switchbacks to the top of a ridge. As you climb, take note of the sandstone. Here you'll see evidence of the Menefee Formation, which consists of shale and coal deposits interspersed with sandstone. It's capped by the more erosion-resistant Cliff House sandstone. Once on top of the mesa, you'll come to Tsin Kletzin. Note how you can see across to other Chacoan villages: Kin Klizhin, Bas'sa'ani, Peñasco Blanco, Kin Kletso, Casa Chiquita, and Pueblo Alto. If Tsin Kletzin had been built even some 30 feet in any other direction the connection would have been lost. This ruin dates from the early 1100s. To complete the south Mesa Loop trail go to the northeast corner of Tsin Kletzin where you'll find the return trail. It passes through soft sand then descends steeply down layers of sandstone back to Casa Rinconada.

Mt. Taylor's Gooseberry Springs Trail

6 miles round-trip. Moderate. 2,000-ft. elevation gain. Allow 3 hrs. Access: From Santa Fe Ave. in Grants, head north on NM 547 (First St.) for 13 miles (you'll pass the Mt. Taylor Ranger Station en route, if you'd like to stop for information). At the end of the pavement, turn right onto FS 193 and drive 5 miles to the trailhead for Trail 77. Map: USGS Mt. Taylor or USFS Cíbola National Forest.

At a height of 11,300 feet, Mount Taylor stands like a lone sentinel on the western New Mexico landscape. Its mythic proportions have earned it a place in the cosmology of the Hopi, Zuni, and other Pueblo tribes, as well as the Navajo. This trail takes you to the summit of this extinct volcano, allowing for views out across the lava fields near Grants and much of the rest of the state as well. There is a forest service road that travels almost to the top, so you may find others on the summit who didn't work to get there, but rest assured they didn't experience the beauty along the way. Be sure to take plenty of water, as there's none available en route.

The trail begins paralleling a small drainage. At 0.25 miles it crosses the drainage and soon climbs through aspens, passing a steel tank at Gooseberry Springs at 0.75 miles. For the next 2 miles the trail passes through wide-open meadows surrounding the summit. Here you'll have long views to the south and east. Soon the trail begins a series of switchbacks, then passes through a gate and makes its final trek to the top. Note that the rim forms a horseshoe shape. The volcano has a long and violent history, including major eruptions occurring 2 to 4 million years ago. These and subsequent ones shaped the mountain, creating a high-rimmed crater draining to the east. The Navajos call this mountain Dzil Dotlizi, which translates as "turquoise mountain," while the Spanish settlers named it Cebollita, which means "tender onion." Following the Mexican War in 1846, it was renamed after a key general in that war, General Zachary Taylor, who later became president of the United States. Once you've enjoyed a break at the summit and have taken in the views, head back the way you came. Beware of thunderstorms in July through September. This trail is best traveled from late May through early November.

Zuni-Acoma Trail

7.5 miles one-way. Moderate to difficult. 15-ft. elevation gain. Allow 5 hrs. one-way. Access: From I-40 near Grants, take NM 117 south from for 15 miles. Look for the trailhead on the right. I recommend running a shuttle for this hike. To leave your vehicle, head south from I-40 on NM 53 for 18 miles. The trailhead is on the left. Map: El Malpais Recreation Guide Map.

This route was used since pre-Columbian times by Puebloan Indians going from Acoma to Zuni Pueblo. It traverses El Malpais, one of the most exceptional examples of volcanic landscapes in the United States. The area contains 115,000 acres of lava flows, ice caves, sandstone cliffs and natural bridges. Native American legends tell of rivers of "fire rock." The route starts into some of the youngest and most interesting lava flows. Throughout the hike footing can be precarious, and the landscape can be deceptive, so be careful. Carry a compass and don't leave one cairn without having spotted the next. The trail meanders past cinder cones, lava tubes and natural arches, finally reaching its terminus not far from the Zuni lands.

El Calderon in El Malpais National Monument

2–4 miles round-trip. Easy to moderate. 200-ft. elevation gain. Allow 1–2 hrs. Access: Take NM 53 west from Grants for 20 miles. The trailhead is on the left. Map: Obtain an El Calderon Area map and trail description from the El Malpais visitor center.

This easily accessed trail is a great introduction to El Malpais. It provides glimpses of many of the major features you'll find in this fascinating lavaland, including caves, sink holes, and a crater. Begin at the trailhead following the well-marked and maintained trail to the sign for the Junction Cave. Take this spur trail to the left to the first cave. If you're prepared with at least three sources of light, a hard hat, and very sturdy shoes, you can head down into the cave. If not, you simply might want to peruse the opening where you can get a sense of its depth and darkness. Head back to the main trail. At 0.25 miles you'll cross over a bridge between Double Sinkholes, the larger of which drops some 50 feet down. The trail continues to the Bat Cave. At one time home to over 40,000 Mexican free-tail bats, this cave is not quite the nesting spot it once was, as the use of pesticides and human disturbance have greatly decreased the numbers. Still, during the spring, summer, and fall, at dusk, the dark creatures of the night will fly. In order to protect the dwindling populations, the monument recommends hikers not enter this cave. The maintained trail ends here, but if you continue hiking straight ahead, you'll find an unmaintained trail that leads up to the Calderon Crater, well worth the 0.75-mile hike. Follow the path to a fence, turn right and keep the fence to your left. The path meets a road, upon which you'll turn right (watch for cairns, which will help you find your way back). Follow this road a short distance. It comes to a sunken lava tube then parallels its right bank. Watch to your left for two small cairns that mark an even less-discernible path still following the sunken tube. You'll come to a burned area. Directly across it is a red cinder hill. Ascend the hill to its summit and you'll find the crater, not the largest in the area, but the oldest, part of its flows dating to 115,000 years ago. Today the caldera is a lovely hole decorated with pines. Turn around to appreciate amazing views of chalk-colored cliffs in the distance. Retrace your path back. Or head back to the road and continue north until you meet a road heading easterly, which will take you back to the parking area.

Big Tubes at El Malpais National Monument

2 miles round-trip. Moderate. 20-ft. elevation loss. Allow 2 hrs. Access: Head west from Grants on NM 53 for 26 miles to CR 42 south. Turn left on CR 42 and travel 4.5 miles. Turn left and travel a short distance to the trailhead. *Beware:* CR 42 can easily become impassable when muddy. Map: Obtain a Big Tubes Area map and trail guide at the visitor center.

This amazing trail takes you across the most serious of lava flows, a place of undulating black rock, hard and relentless; one could easily get lost in this forsaken land, a fact that brings a sense of urgency to the hike. It's also a cave exploration hike, so come prepared. If you have yet to explore a cave on your own, this might be a good chance, since the Four Windows Cave is relatively simple, so your chances of getting lost are low. Still, come prepared. We had three sources of light, hard hats, sturdy hiking boots and long pants and shirtsleeves. The trip to the caves is as interesting as the caving.

My friend Jim from Zuni went with me into the Four Windows Cave. I was well into it before I realized that I'd never been caving before. (Guess walking along the paved and lighted paths at Carlsbad doesn't really count.) I also realized that I was scared. Just about that time, I tripped, and my lamp fell off my head and went black. Luckily we had plenty of back-up lighting. We continued on deep into the darkness; fortunately this cave has a fairly smooth floor upon which to walk. Others like Big Skylight are more dangerous because they require boulder-hopping within the darkness. In the Four Windows Cave we spent some time with our lamps off in the sheer darkness talking about how womb-like it is and what it would be like when we came back out into the world. On our way out (lights back on) we saw a rectangle of light hanging in the sky. We turned off our lights again. We realized the light was the way out, a perfect doorway sitting above us. How bizarre it looked, like a passage into some other world, a sort of silver light emanating from it. When we finally came back out, everything seemed new and oddly different.

You'll want to tour the whole Big Tubes area as well as enter the Four Windows Cave. From the trailhead, look for the first cairn and walk to it. Then locate the next one before heading toward it. You'll continue in this fashion for the whole hike, as it is very easy to get lost in the area. Soon you'll come to a trail junction. Head to the left and follow the cairns to the Caterpillar Collapse, a giant collapsed lava tube. Then, head back to the junction. What's before you is the Big Skylight Cave. Though you can go into this cave, the hiking is over boulders and therefore very rough. I recommend heading across the bridge over Big Skylight and following the cairns to Four Windows Cave.

Early on in the cave you'll come to roped-off areas where a unique community of green moss grows. From there bear right into a leg with cauliflower-like walls. The length of this cave is 1,207 feet, the depth 81 feet. You'll know when you reach the end. Take note of the bulbous ice formations throughout. Back out in the shiny new world, you'll want to travel back to the first trail juncture and follow the signs south to the Seven Bridges Collapse. This collapsed tube maintains a number of bridges, some with large ponderosa pines growing precariously on top. The trail continues back to the parking area.

Narrows Rim
6 miles round-trip. Moderate. 350-ft. elevation gain. Allow 3 hrs. Access: From I-40 near Grants turn onto NM 117 and drive 19 miles south. Look for the trailhead sign on the left (east) side of the road. Map: USGS North Pasture and Arrosa Ranch.

One of New Mexico's best secrets, the 376,000-acre Cebolla Wilderness is marked by bold golden cliffs called the Narrows, which sit above El Malpais National Monument. This trail takes you along the rim of these stunning cliffs to an overlook of New Mexico's second-largest natural arch. The easy-to-follow route climbs up onto the Zuni sandstone bluffs on a rocky trail. It follows the bluffs through piñon-juniper forest, allowing for some views across the vast lava flow to the west. Finally, the trail reaches the overlook of La Ventana. Reminiscent of formations at Arches National Monument in Utah, La Ventana (Spanish for "the window") is carved of salmon-colored and white sandstone and spans 165 feet. Return the way you came.

HORSEBACK RIDING

The Mt. Taylor Ranch and Guest Lodge (☎ 800/432-2237 or 505/552-6530), located near Mt. Taylor on Laguna Pueblo, caters especially to hunters and fishers, but equestrians can enjoy daylong trail rides into impressive southwest country. For $50, guides will take you around the nearby trout lakes and through pine and aspen forest. Or if you want to stay out longer photographing the surrounding area, these laid-back guides will encourage you to do so. The ranch house itself is 15,000 square feet and has 16 rooms, all double occupancy with a shared Jacuzzi. Double occupancy is $125, which doesn't include riding. The ranch is located north of Cubero, on County Road 6 off exit 104 from I-40.

MOUNTAIN BIKING

Your home base for cycling in the Four Corners area is **Cottonwood Cycles,** in Farmington at 3030 E. Main St., Unit T2 (☎ 505/326-0429). This shop offers bike maintenance and good maps and directions to area trails.

Canyon Floor Loop at Chaco Culture National Historic Park
8 miles. Easy. No significant elevation gain. Allow 3 hrs. Access: You have two options. From Bloomfield, head southeast on U.S. 550 for 35 miles to the

Nageezi Trading Post (last stop for food, gas, or lodging). 3 miles east of Nageezi turn right on County Rd. 7900 and drive 5 miles. Turn right on CR 7950 and drive for approximately 20 miles (dirt road) to the park's visitor center. South entrance: From Crownpoint follow NM 9 east for 40 miles to Seven Lakes. Turn north on NM 57 and follow it about 20 miles (dirt road) into the park. *Beware:* On rainy and snowy days these roads become slick and impassable. ☎ **505/786-7014** for road conditions or other information; ☎ 505/786-7060 for the 24-hour emergency assistance line, which connects directly to the homes of law-enforcement rangers in the park. Admission $8 per car, campsite extra.

Cycling is the perfect way to experience the quiet and beauty of this history-filled canyon. This easy pedal along paved road, great for families, will take you by the major ruins, with views of the canyon along the way. The ride begins at the visitor center, where you can get a good idea of the historic scope of Chaco Canyon. A short walk from there is the first ruin, Una Vida, where there are about 150 rooms and 5 kivas. From there pedal along the one-way road to Chetro Ketl. This ruin contains more than 500 rooms and 16 kivas. The enclosed plaza is typical of great houses from the period around 1054. The next stop is Pueblo Bonito, the largest of the great houses. Built in stages, in its final form this pueblos reached heights of four stories and had some 600 rooms and 40 kivas, any of which are still visible today. A spur trail near there leads out to the Pueblo del Arroyo, Kin Kletso, and Casa Chiquita Ruins. You'll ride a little ways on a road, then hike the rest of the way. Pueblo del Arroyo was a D-shaped great house that rose three and four stories toward the rear, stepping down to one story in front. Kin Kletso had about 100 rooms and 5 enclosed kivas, and Casa Chiquita, as the name implies, is one of the smaller houses. Back on the road, the next stop is Casa Rinconada and a prehistoric stairway. Casa Rinconada is the largest "Great Kiva" in the park, and one of the largest in the Southwest. From there the road heads back to the visitor center to complete the ride.

Wijiji Trail at Chaco Culture National Historic Park
6 miles round-trip. Easy. No significant elevation gain. Allow 2 hrs. Access: To get to the park, see directions for Canyon Floor Loop above. From the visitor center drive east for 1.5 miles to the Wijiji Trailhead. Before taking this ride, acquire a free permit from the visitor center.

This maintained trail, the only off-road trail in the park, is a fun double-track ride to an interesting ruin. It begins at the confluence of Chaco and Gallo Wash (both dry; beware of flooding during rainy or monsoon season). The trail is well marked and follows Chaco Wash as it extends east through Chaco Canyon. It leads to the Wijiji Ruin; leave your bike at the edge of the ruin and make your way around on foot. This ruin was built around the year 1100. It differs from others in the canyon in that it appears to have been built during one construction stage rather than many. This is noticeable in the symmetry of the masonry and the uniformity of the rooms. Northeast of the ruin along the canyon wall is a rock art panel. Once you've made your way through the ruin, turn around and head back on the same trail.

Mount Taylor
18.8-mile loop. Difficult. 1,033-ft. elevation gain. Allow 5 hrs. Access: From Santa Fe Ave. in Grants, head north on NM 547 (First St.) for 13 miles (you'll pass the Mt. Taylor Ranger Station en route, if you'd like to stop for information). The paved road turns to a dirt road, and NM 547 becomes FS 239. This is where you'll park. You'll also note that FS 193 comes in from the south; this is the route upon which you'll complete the loop.

This trail takes you first on forest service roads, then on single track to the summit of this extinct volcano, at 11,300 feet, one of New Mexico's most prominent peaks, allowing for views out across the lava fields near Grants and much of the rest of the state. The route down follows some romping single track, finishing on forest service road.

Begin riding up FS 239 along the northwestern side of the mountain. At 3.5 miles the roads splits. Be sure to veer to the right onto FS 453. Here the road climbs up through La Mosca Canyon, finally emerging onto La Mosca Saddle at about mile 8. If you continue on FS 453 at this point, you'll go to La Mosca Peak, one of the forest service's highest fire lookout points. Back on the main route, you'll come to another fork. Bear right on FS 570, still contouring the mountain. Follow FS 570 for 2 miles until you come to a saddle just below the summit. Look to the right side of the road for Trail 77, the Gooseberry Springs Trail, and take this up to the top. Note that the rim forms a horseshoe shape. Once you've enjoyed a break at the summit and have taken in the views, continue on Trail 77 as it makes its way steeply down and then carves across broad meadows with views to the south and east. At mile 3, the trail intersects with FS 193. Turn right and head downhill for about 5 miles back to your car. This trail is best traveled from late May through early November. Beware of thunderstorms during the late summer monsoon season. Also be aware that a lot of climbing is involved in this ride.

Alien Run Trail

9 miles. Moderate to difficult. 300-ft. elevation gain. Allow 2½ hrs. From Aztec, drive north on U.S. 550 to mile marker 164 and turn right on County Rd. 2770. Follow that gravel road for 3 miles and watch for a sign that reads "Bike Trail." Turn left and go 0.5 miles up a hill and over a cattle guard. Just past the cattle guard, turn right and follow a two-track road about 0.25 miles to the trailhead.

This new trail built by the Bureau of Land Management and area enthusiasts is a nice technical single-track route with a fun bit of payoff. At its halfway point is an alleged UFO crash site, complete with a plaque explaining the details of the crash. A year after the 1947 Roswell crash that has put that dusty little town on the map, a spacecraft allegedly crashed down outside Aztec, killing its passengers on impact. The U.S. military supposedly descended upon the scene, whisked up the bodies and debris and took them to Los Alamos, where they've remained hidden ever since. Though there's little to see at the site, the story does stir the imagination. This area is full of gas wells, and some of them lie along the route, breathing an eerie sound into the air that, if you use your imagination, can add to the undercurrent of the ride. However, if you like a more wilderness experience, they'll ruin your fun here.

The first part of the trail makes its way along a slickrock rim and through piñon/juniper forest. At this writing the whole trail was marked with little flags tied to the trees, which I hope will remain. On the slickrock areas it is, at times, difficult to find your way, but watch for cairns here and there. Before you get to the site you'll pass along the base of some cliffs and encounter some spots that are technical enough for even experienced riders to have to walk. When you get to the UFO plaque, continue straight ahead up the hill, rather than backtracking and continuing on the trail you were on. Above all, don't do as I and many others have done and go through a barbed wire gate near the crash site or you'll lose the trail completely. If you come to that gate, turn around and look behind you for the trail. The route back has some steep sections through piñon/juniper forest that require some careful riding. They bring you into sage forest where the going gets much faster, finally delivering you back to the car. I heard some locals complain that this trail isn't fun because it isn't fast. If you like fast, try the Road Apple Trail mentioned below.

Road Apple Trail of the Glade Trail System

30-mile loop with a total of 50 miles to explore. Easy to difficult. Allow 2–6 hrs. Access: Lions Wilderness trailhead: From Main St. in Farmington, take 30th St. west 0.5 miles to College Blvd. Turn right and drive 2 miles to the Lions Wilderness area. Just past the entrance to the paved parking area for Lions Wilderness you'll see an overlook pullout on your right, park there. Ride up the same road for 0.8 miles and watch for a single-track route to branch off to the right. Foothills trailhead: Follow Main St. east to Piñon Hills Blvd. and turn left. Immediately turn right onto Foothills Drive. Follow Foothills 3 miles to its end, where the trails begin.

This is some of the most primo desert riding in the region. The area offers miles of rolling single track with some good technical ascents and descents for those who like to push themselves. In the description below I try to give a sense of where the trails go, but your best bet may be to pick up a map at Cottonwood Cycles and explore. If you don't have a map and aren't an expert, you may want to start at the Foothills trailhead where there are some easier routes to explore.

From the Lions Wilderness trailhead you'll begin on an intermediate trail called Mainly Whoops. It leads to Trey's Air Time, an advanced trail. After this section, watch for the Windmill Cutoff to your right. This will take you down to the lower trails and makes for a nice 15-mile loop back around on what's known as Kinsey Ridge. If you'd like a challenge, continue northeast from Trey's Air Time to the Clay Hills and Imperial Walkers sections. At the end of Imperial Walkers, you'll pass through a cattle guard and follow a road, which will take you to the Road Apple Trail (watch on your right), the section for which the annual Farmington race is named. You'll head southwest on this trail, which has some advanced technical sections as well as some smooth intermediate ones. This will take you to the Kinsey Trail, most of which is smooth, fast single track. The Kinsey Trail takes you to the Foothills trailhead, from which you can ride County Road 3807 back to your car. If you intend to do this whole loop, you'll definitely want to pick up a map at Cottonwood Cycles to help guide you.

If you'd like a little less challenge, I recommend riding the Kinsey Trail. Once you find the Foothills trailhead (see above), you'll find smooth rolling single track for miles along this ridge. The trail makers have tried to make this into a loop so that you ride a more difficult trail called Rigor Mortis on the way out and the Kinsey Trail on the way back, though I'm not certain people abide by the regulations. Most of all you'll want to keep your ears peeled for the sound of motorbikes, which also use these trails. From the Kinsey Ridge there are a couple of loop rides off to the east that offer more technical challenge. These include the Kenny's Revenge and the Seven Sisters Loop. With over 50 miles of maintained trails to ride here, you really can't go wrong; your best bet is to explore.

ROAD BIKING

Ruins Road Ride

40 miles round-trip. Moderate. Allow 3 hrs. Access: Begin on NM 516 in Farmington.

This is a 40-mile out-and-back on nice pavement that takes you from Farmington to Aztec, up toward the ruins and then back. Ride out of town heading east on NM 516 and turn right immediately after the cemetery onto the old Aztec Highway (CR 3520). When this comes to a T intersection at CR 3500, turn left. Just before the light, turn right onto CR 3050. This runs into NM 516 outside of Aztec. Follow NM 516 to the second light and turn left on Ruins Road. Turn right just before Aztec Ruins and follow U.S. 550 north to

Cedar Hill. Turn around and return on the same route. *Note:* At the time of this writing, the highway numbers had recently changed names. U.S. 550 between Farmington, and Aztec had just become NM 516. Be aware that there still may be some confusion.

SWIMMING

Navajo Lake State Park, located 25 miles east of Bloomfield via U.S. 64 and NM 511, is one of the few places to take a dip in this highly desertic region. Though you won't find many sandy beaches, you will find plenty of clean, cool water at many spots within a short distance of the road that runs along the edge of the lake. The often-murky water usually hovers around a cool 70°F in summer. Like many New Mexico lakes, Navajo Lake's bottom is uneven and rocky, with steep drop-offs close to shore. The lake has boat ramps and several marinas (from which visitors can rent boats), picnic areas, and groceries for those who plan to make a day of it.

WALKS & RAMBLES

Sandstone Bluffs Overlook

1–2 miles. Easy. 300-ft. elevation gain. Allow 1 hr. Access: Off I-40 7 miles east of Grants, take NM 117 south for 10 miles.

The Sandstone Bluffs Overlook allows for panoramic views across El Malpais National Monument. The area contains 115,000 acres of cinder cones, lava flows, hundreds of lava tubes, ice caves, sandstone cliffs, natural bridges and arches. The most recent flows are only 1,000 years old. There's no designated trail at this overlook, but you can simply hike north, contouring close to the rim. You can explore the eroded formations along here until you reach a break, allowing a descent to the valley below. There you'll find a dirt track along the lava's edge heading back to the base of the bluffs. Scramble a little and you'll be back on top.

La Ventana Natural Arch

0.5 miles. Easy. No elevation gain. Allow 30 min. Access: Off I-40 7 miles east of Grants, follow NM 117 17 miles south.

Just north of the stunning bluffs called the Narrows, which contour the edge of the equally stunning El Malpais, this hidden treasure is reminiscent of formations at Arches National Monument in Utah. The second largest such formation in New Mexico, La Ventana is carved of salmon-colored and white sandstone and spans 165 feet. (Snake Bridge in western New Mexico is the largest at 204 feet long, but it is on the Navajo Indian Reservation and generally inaccessible to the public.) A short trail leads up to the base of the arch, where cholla cacti attempt to block passage, thereby protecting it. Return the way you came.

Aztec Ruins National Monument

0.25 miles. Easy. Allow 1 hr. Access: On the north edge of Aztec (14 miles northeast of Farmington), drive 0.5 miles north of U.S. 550 on Ruins Rd. (County Rd. 2900). Open daily in summer (Memorial Day to Labor Day) 8am–6pm, in winter 8am–5pm; closed Thanksgiving, Christmas, and New Year's Day. Admission $4 per adult, free for children ages 17 and under.

This is a fun way to be out in the northern New Mexico sun, while traveling 7 centuries back in time. The walk, along with a stop at the visitor center, will take you on a self-guided trail meandering through ruins of this 450-room pueblo spread out across a meadow on the Animas River, culminating at the central kiva, the most striking feature of these ruins. Visitors can enter and sit within the kiva to collect a sense the site's ancient history. Early Anglo settlers, convinced that the ruins were of Aztec origin, misnamed the site. Despite the fact that this pueblo was built long before the Aztecs of central Mexico lived, the name stuck. To find out more about Aztec Ruins National Monument, see the "Parks & Other Hot Spots" section earlier in this chapter.

INDIAN COUNTRY PAWN

In this region, the simple word "pawn" is used to describe older, high-quality Native American jewelry. In fact, when my mother first came to New Mexico in the early 1950s she used to travel through Indian Country, camping out and stopping at pawnshops and trading posts in search of pawn, jewelry that then cost a pittance and is now extremely valuable.

What most people don't realize is that pawnshops in New Mexico provide a surprising range of services for their largely Native American clientele and have little in common with the pawnshops of large American cities. Indian Country pawnbrokers in essence are bankers, at least from the Navajo and Zuni viewpoint. In fact, they're an integral part of the economic structure of the Indian Country area.

Security systems in Navajo hogans and Zuni pueblos are nonexistent, and banks won't take jewelry or guns as loan collateral, so pawnshops provide such services as the safekeeping of valuable personal goods and making small-collateral loans. Native Americans hock their turquoise and silver jewelry, ceremonial baskets, hand-tanned hides, saddles, and guns for safekeeping. The trader will hold onto the items for months or even years before deeming them "dead" and putting them up for sale. Less than 5% of items ever go unredeemed. For their part, the Native Americans may accept a payment far less than the value of the goods, because the smaller the amount of the loan, the easier it is to redeem the items when they are needed.

If you're shopping for jewelry, you may want to explore some of the pawnshops in the area as well as the trading posts. Look for silver concho belts, worn with jeans and Southwestern skirts; cuff bracelets; and necklaces, from traditional squash blossoms to silver beads and *heishi*, very fine beads worn in several strands. Earrings may be made only of silver, or they may be decorated with varying stones. Also be on the lookout for bolo ties and belt buckles of silver and/or turquoise. Silver concho hatbands go great on Stetson hats. Handwoven Native American rugs may be draped on couches, hung on walls, or used on floors. Also look for pottery, kachinas, and sculpture. Most shops in Indian Country are open Monday through Saturday from 9am to 5pm.

Salmon Ruin and San Juan County Archaeological Research Center

0.5 miles round-trip. Easy. Allow 1 hr. Access: Off U.S. 64 15 miles east of Farmington at Bloomfield. Open daily during regular business hours except on winter Sundays, when they're open only in the afternoons. Adults $3, seniors $2, children ages 6–16 $1.

This is a lovely meander through 150 rooms of these ruins, which sit on a hillside surrounded by lush San Juan River bosque (Spanish for forest). You'll begin in the museum, where you'll want to pick up a trail guide. Like the ruins at Aztec, here there are two strong architectural influences visible. First the Chacoan: They built the village around the 11th century, creating walls with an intricate rubble-filled core with sandstone veneer. The more simple Mesa Verde masonry was added in the 13th century. There's a marvelous elevated ceremonial chamber or "tower kiva" and a Great Kiva, now a low-lying ruin, but with some engaging remains such as the central fire pit and an antechamber possibly used by leaders to store ceremonial goods. For more information about the site, see the "Parks & Other Hot Spots" section earlier in this chapter.

You may want to take the trail through the Heritage Park. Built in 1990 on an adjoining plot of land, it comprises a series of reconstructed ancient and historic dwellings representing the area's cultures, from a paleoarchaic sand-dune site to an ancestral Puebloan pit house, from Apache wickiups and teepees to Navajo hogans, and an original pioneer homestead. Visitors are encouraged to enter the re-creations.

WHITE-WATER KAYAKING

The **Farmington Whitewater Course** is a recent addition to northwestern New Mexico boating. Designed by a notable Denver white-water expert, it is very short (about 100 yards), but has some interesting features. When I was there the water was low, but there were two glassy waves, one at the top and one at the bottom. At higher water, play holes are created in the middle, and a long pour-over occurs along one side toward the top. At low water this is a definite class II section of river, but it pushes into class III at higher water.

WILDLIFE VIEWING

Navajo State Park and the San Juan River, located 17 miles east of Aztec via NM 173, has plenty of varied terrain, from high, open plains to riparian habitat. Watch for mule deer, coyotes, and elk in the area. Watch for those same creatures 5 miles north of Farmington via NM 170 at **Jackson Lake Wildlife Area**, a 60-acre fishing lake, which attracts a broad variety of visitors.

The area's almost impenetrable nature makes **El Malpais** a great preserve for many species. Once while crossing along the fringes of the region on I-40, I saw a bobcat crossing the highway. This is also home to mule deer and coyotes, as well as scorpions, rattlesnakes, and bullsnakes.

Campgrounds & Other Accommodations

CAMPING

Gallo Campground
Located within Chaco Culture National Historic Park about 1 mile east of the visitor center (see "Parks & Other Hot Spots" earlier in this chapter). 64 sites (group sites are also available), with fire grates (bring your own wood or charcoal), central toilets, and non-potable water. Drinking water is available only at the visitor center. $10 per night. *Note:* The campground cannot accommodate trailers over 30 feet.

This campground at the base of Chaco Canyon is an ideal spot to sleep within centuries of history. Many find waking in the canyon with views out across the sandstone and the ancient ruins to be a spiritual experience; others find it merely lovely.

There's no place to stock up on supplies once you start the arduous drive to the canyon, so if you're camping, make sure to be well supplied, especially with water.

Navajo State Park, San Juan River
Located 17 miles east of Aztec via NM 173. ☎ 505/632-2278. 23 campsites, rest rooms, RV sites, electric hookups, and dump station.

Within Navajo State Park is Cottonwood campground located on the San Juan River. The 23 campsites along the river are located in a forest of cottonwoods. Anglers come to this world-class fishing river to fish the Quality Water Section of the San Juan.

Angel Peak Campground
Located 15 miles south of Bloomfield on U.S. 550; the last 7 miles of access are over a graded dirt road. ☎ 505/599-8900. 6 primitive sites, a pit toilet, picnic tables, and grills. Open year-round. No fees.

This small, primitive campground is set atop a mesa in a juniper/piñon forest with overlooks of the impressive Kutz Canyon Badlands—white and gray sedimentary rock comprised of shale and silt stones that make up magical land formations. This canyon resembles the badlands of the Dakotas—beautiful yet forlorn in its starkness. At almost 7,000 feet, the views of the San Juans in Colorado and Angel Peak to the west from the campground are stunning. Legend has it that Angel Peak was originally given this moniker because it resembled an angel, at least until a plane crashed into the top and altered its face forever. No reservations accepted—it's first-come, first-served.

Red Rock State Park Campground
Located 5 miles east of downtown Gallup, on frontage road Route 66. ☎ 505/722-3839. 106 campsites, 36-person group campground, primitive camping, electrical hookups, flush toilets, hot showers, drinking water, trading post, phones, nature trails, natural amphitheater, and stables. $8–$14 camping fee.

Red Rock State Park campground looks like a miniature Sedona, Arizona, with its unique red rock spires, smoothed and worn by weather. This gorgeous campground was once the site of an 1885 trading post, which traded sheep, cattle, pelts, and other necessities of the era. The original trading post sign, engraved into a boulder, was recently discovered by rangers while performing trail maintenance. From the campground, visitors can hike past the sign and to Native American petroglyphs. Park rangers take campers on guided hikes every Saturday and Sunday during the summer months.

INNS & LODGES

Inn at Halona
23B Pia Mesa Rd., Zuni, NM 87327-0446. ☎ 800/752-3278 or 505/782-4118. www.halona.com. E-mail: halona@nm.net. 8 units. A/C TEL. $79 double. Rates include full breakfast. MC, V.

When checking into this inn I felt as though I were on an adventure in a foreign land. Situated in the center of Zuni, its front desk is at an old trading post/store. The inn itself fills two homes, one built in 1920, the other in 1940. I recommend the main house (built in 1920) since it is the brighter of the two and was remodeled in 1998. Both are filled with local art and decorated with handcrafted furniture. Most rooms are fairly small, and some rooms share bathrooms, so you'll want to reserve accordingly. All rooms have good linens and comfortably firm beds. My favorite, the penthouse room, is small but very sunny and quaint. Over a full and delicious breakfast served family-style in the dining room or out on the lovely patio, the innkeepers Roger Thomas and Elaine Dodson Thomas will delight you with stories of living at Zuni, where Elaine's Dutch family started the first trading post in 1903.

El Rancho Hotel & Motel
1000 E. 66 Ave., Gallup, NM 87301. ☎ 800/543-6351 or 505/863-9311. www.elranchohotel.com. E-mail: elrancho@cnet.com. 100 units. A/C TV TEL. $47–$65 double; $76 suite. AE, DISC, MC, V. Pets are welcome.

This historic hotel owes as much to Hollywood as to Gallup. Built in 1937 by R. E. "Griff" Griffith, brother of movie mogul D. W. Griffith, it became the place for film companies to set up headquarters while filming here. Between the 1940s and 1960s, a who's who of Hollywood stayed here. Their autographed photos line the walls of the hotel's cafe. Spencer Tracy and Katharine Hepburn stayed here during production of *The Sea of Grass;* Burt Lancaster and Lee Remick were guests when they made *The Hallelujah Trail.* The list goes on and on: Gene Autry, Lucille Ball, Jack Benny, Humphrey Bogart, James Cagney, Errol Flynn, Henry Fonda, the Marx Brothers, Ronald Reagan, Rosalind Russell, James Stewart, John Wayne, and Mae West all stayed here.

In 1986, Gallup businessman Armand Ortega, a longtime jewelry merchant, bought the then run-down El Rancho and restored it to its earlier elegance. The lobby staircase rises to the mezzanine on either side of an enormous stone fireplace, while heavy ceiling beams and railings made of tree limbs give the room a hunting-lodge ambience. The hotel is on the National Register of Historic Places.

Rooms in El Rancho differ one to the next, and are named for the stars who stayed in them. Most are long and medium-sized, with wagon wheel headboards and good heavy pine furniture stained dark. Bathrooms are small, some with showers, others with shower/bathtub combos. All have lovely small white hexagonal tiles. Many rooms have balconies. There are also 10 full-service apartments with kitchenettes available.

El Rancho has a lounge, a full-service restaurant, and gift shop. Services and facilities include a 24-hour desk, courtesy car (by request), a seasonal outdoor pool, and guest Laundromat.

Sands Motel
112 McArthur St., Grants, NM 87020. ☎ **800/424-7679** or 505/287-2996. 24 units. A/C TV TEL. $43 double. Continental breakfast included. AE, CB, DC, DISC, MC, V. Pets are welcome for a $5 fee.

On first glance you may wonder why anyone would want to stay at this older motel rather than the newer chain motels near the interstate, and yet the Sands draws crowds. Mostly, the price is good, and the rooms are clean and spacious, though the furnishings and carpet aren't as new as at those more recent competitors. Located a block from Route 66 in the center of town, it gives travelers a break from the noise of the interstate. Rooms are spacious with a table, chairs, and refrigerator; the beds are comfortable; and the bathrooms are clean. The parking area is enclosed by a wall, and you can park right in front of your room to keep an eye on your belongings.

Step Back Inn
103 W. Aztec Blvd., Aztec, NM 87410. ☎ **800/334-1255** or 505/334-1200. www.aztecnm.com. E-mail: stepback@ cyberport.com. 39 units. A/C TV TEL. May 15–Nov 1 $68–$72 double; Nov 2–May 14 $58–$62 double. Rates include cinnamon Danish pastry, juice, and coffee. AE, MC, V.

This inn offers Victorian charm in a brand new building with modern conveniences. Though it's a fair-sized hotel, it has a cozy inn feel and plenty of amenities. The building was designed by the same architect who built the Inn of the Puebloan in Santa Fe, and the tastefulness and functionality are apparent in the layout of the large rooms and good-sized bathrooms, as well as in the quietness, which is due to good insulation. The rooms have pretty touches such as wallpaper and early American antique replica armoires, which hold the television. Each is named after an early pioneer family of the area, with a small booklet in the room recounting their story; some are the ancestors of the hotel's owner. The beds are firm, and the linens are good. Each room has a hair dryer and shampoo. Breakfast time brings a warm, delicious cinnamon roll as large as a plate served in a quiet tearoom.

Casa Blanca
505 E. La Plata St., Farmington, NM 87401. ☎ **505/327-6503**. 6 units. A/C TV TEL. $68–$150 double. AE, DISC, MC, V.

Located within a residential neighborhood just a few blocks from the shops and restaurants of Main Street, this inn provides a touch of elegance that you wouldn't expect to find in Farmington. Run by professional innkeepers, the inn combines old-world elegance with contemporary amenities. It was built in the 1940s by a wealthy family that traded with the Navajos.

Now, each of the spacious rooms has its own bent, from one with a four-poster pencil-post bed (the Aztec) to another with an elaborate hand-carved headboard and French doors leading out to a lushly landscaped yard (the Caballero). All have very comfortable beds and nice bathrooms, each with a tub, except for the

Aztec, which has a shower. A two-room casita is a new addition to the property. Breakfasts include such delicacies as peach-melba waffles and eggs Benedict. Mine started with a fruit plate that included mango, blueberries, strawberries, and yogurt.

Kokopelli's Cave
206 W. 38th St., Farmington, NM 87401. ☎ 505/325-7855. www.bbonline.com/nm/kokopelli. E-mail: koko@cyberport.com. 1 unit. TV TEL. $180 double; $210 for 3–4 people. Closed Dec–Feb. AE, MC, V.

After a long day of sightseeing, I lay on a queen bed under 200 feet of sandstone, listening to Beethoven, with a sliding glass door open to a view hundreds of feet down to a river snaking across a valley. It began to rain, slow big drops that made the air smell like wet sage. It suddenly struck me: I was staying in a cave. I can't overstate how cool an experience it was.

Here's the story: Retired geologist Bruce Black wanted to build an office in a cave, so he gave some laid-off Grants miners $20,000 to bore as deeply as they could into the side of a cliff face. This luxury apartment was the result. Through time it worked better as a living space than a workspace, and that is how it functions today. Built in a semicircle, both the entry hall and the bedroom have wide sliding glass doors leading to little balconies, beyond which the cliff face drops hundreds of feet below. This really is a cliff dwelling, one that you must hike a bit down to, though there are good guardrails to guide you.

The apartment is laid out around a broad central pillar, and the ceilings and walls are thick, undulating stone. There's a stove, refrigerator, coffeemaker, microwave, and washer/dryer. The dining area has a table and six chairs set on flagstone next to a mock kiva, used for storage. The living room has a TV, VCR, and futon couch. This and the bedroom are on a carpet-covered platform that provides an elegant feel. Best of all is the bathroom. Water pours off rocks above, creating a waterfall, and if that's not enough, there are Jacuzzi jets in the flagstone tub. Golden eagles nest in the area, and ring-tailed cats tend to wander onto the balcony. There's a grill outside, as well as chairs where you can relax in the mornings and evenings. Fruit, juice, coffee, and pastries comprise a self-serve breakfast.

9

New Mexico's Rocky Mountains

Physically, north central New Mexico is defined by the Rocky Mountains, which jut up through the center, forming a rich and varied land full of surprises. But there's much to experience in the region beyond the grandness of those mountains. This area is imbued with a mystical quality, certainly created by the ecological beauty, but also by the presence of the Native Americans, who have inhabited this land for over a millennium, and the Hispanic populations, who have lived here for over 400 years.

Your outdoor adventures here will take you into the very heart of the history of the region. In the Jemez Mountains, you might backpack to unexcavated ruins containing symbolic petroglyphs holding cryptic messages, or climb pueblo–style ladders high up to a cave to find a ceremonial kiva. Even in the most remote regions of the Pecos Wilderness in the Sangre de Cristo Mountains you might stumble upon a sacred lay of rocks used by Native Americans to tell direction. While paddling a kayak down the Rio Grande, you may pass through Hispanic farming villages where people still speak an ancient form of Spanish and still live on what they grow in their fields.

You may understand these experiences more if you know that the Pueblo tribes of the upper Rio Grande Valley are believed to be descendants of the Anasazi, who from the mid-9th to the 13th centuries lived in the Four Corners Region. The Anasazi built spectacular structures such as those at **Chaco Canyon** (see chapter 8) and **Mesa Verde** in Colorado. Archaeologists speculate about why the Anasazi abandoned those homes. Some believe it was due to drought; others claim social unrest. Whatever the reason, they moved from these sites to areas such as **Bandelier** and **Puye** in this region, where they built villages resembling the ones they had left behind. Then several hundred years later, for reasons not yet understood, they moved down from the canyons onto the fertile plains next to the Rio Grande. By the time the Spaniards arrived in the 1500s, the Pueblo culture was well established throughout what would become northern and western New Mexico.

In 1540 Francisco Vásquez de Coronado led an expedition in search of the fabled Seven Cities of Cíbola, coincidentally introducing horses and sheep to the region. Neither Coronado nor a succession of fortune-seeking conquistadors could locate the legendary cities of gold, so they determined that the wealth was actually in the land itself. Thus the Spanish concentrated their efforts on establishing rule over the region. Their strategy involved the use of immense cruelty, forcing the Native Americans to till fields and build missionary churches under slave-like conditions. Convinced that they were divinely commissioned to convert conditions. Convinced that they were divinely commissioned to convert the Native American to Christianity, the Spaniards also set about that task, filling them with fear of damnation and denying them their traditional practices.

The first Anglos to spend time in the upper Rio Grande Valley were mountain men—hunters, trappers, and traders. Trailblazers of the U.S. westward expansion, they began settling in New Mexico in the first decade of the 19th century. Other settlers followed along the ruts of the **Santa Fe Trail,** which started 800 miles east in Independence, Missouri, and ended at the Santa Fe Plaza. With the completion of the **Atchison, Topeka & Santa Fe Railway** in 1879, the gateways to the region swung open completely, and people and goods poured in. Albuquerque in particular blossomed in the wake of a series of major gold strikes in the Madrid Valley, close to ancient Native American turquoise mines. By the time the gold lodes began to shrink in the 1890s, cattle and sheep ranching had become well entrenched. The territory's growth culminated in statehood in 1912.

During World War II, the federal government purchased an isolated boys' camp west of Santa Fe and turned it into the **Los Alamos National Laboratory,** where the Manhattan Project and other top-secret atomic experiments were developed and perfected. (For more information on the Los Alamos lab, see the "Los Alamos: The A-Bomb's Birthplace" feature later in this chapter.) The science and military legacy continues today: Albuquerque is among the nation's leaders in attracting defense contracts and high technology.

With all this history about, it's important to remember that much of the adventure in northern New Mexico happens en route to your destination. While heading up to Taos to mountain bike, you'll pass by many pueblos where Native Americans still cling to their traditional beliefs; before a grueling trek up to the Truchas Peaks, you may stop at the Santuario de Chimayo, where you can dip your fingers in dust that's believed to have healing powers. Everywhere you'll see little altars decorated with plastic flowers called *descansos,* which mark the place where someone has died, and ancient *camposantos* (cemeteries) sitting on mesa tops as reminders that our presence here is but a precious few moments, and we'd best use them well.

The extremes of this land give it an edginess that's not immediately apparent. Those coming from Colorado or Wyoming might scoff at any notion that the outdoors here could be threatening—but it sometimes is. Despite the fact that there are lush forests in the highlands, this is mountain desert. It can be hot and dry in summer, with flash floods rushing down arroyos and washing cars and people away. In winter, with peaks topping 13,000 feet and much of the area's elevation in the 7,000-foot range, temperatures and snow conditions can be extreme, often catching visitors off-guard and necessitating rescue operations.

But there's a hospitable nature to the region as well. Unlike the more jagged peaks of the northern Rockies, the mountains here have a gentler line. The weather that at one moment can be so tortuous may suddenly surprise you. You'll be backpacking through a hailstorm and moments later pull off your shirt to sunbathe during lunch. Many kayakers paddle the Rio Grande at Pilar south of Taos year-round. Once, while paddling that section in March, I found myself so hot that I took snow from the bank to rub on my face.

The Lay of the Land

When you visualize this region, you might want to picture a "V" shape. The San Pedro and Jemez Mountains form the western arm, and the Sangre de Cristos form the eastern arm, with the Sandia Mountains forming the southern part of the eastern arm. Down the middle runs the Rio Grande River, at some points (west of Taos) flowing through a gorge 700 feet deep. Taos is the northernmost city in the area. Sixty miles south of Taos and nearly at the region's center is Santa Fe, with a population of about 70,000. Another 50 miles south lies New Mexico's largest city, Albuquerque, where some 700,000 people live.

Seventy million years ago the Rocky Mountains began lifting skyward, over time forming the high-alpine summits and glacier-carved valleys that now stretch from Canada down into New Mexico. In this state, the range's southern terminus, they're called the Sangre de Cristo Mountains, though they developed in a completely different way. Formed 270 million years after the Rockies, these mountains to the west came about through cataclysmic volcanic eruptions. Today they reach to about 10,000 feet. Within them lie the remains of one of the largest volcanic calderas in the United States, the Valles Caldera, a piece of land recently purchased by the U.S. government, with plans to allow public access there. Between these ranges lies the Rio Grande Rift, a sedimentary flood plain through which the Rio Grande River carves.

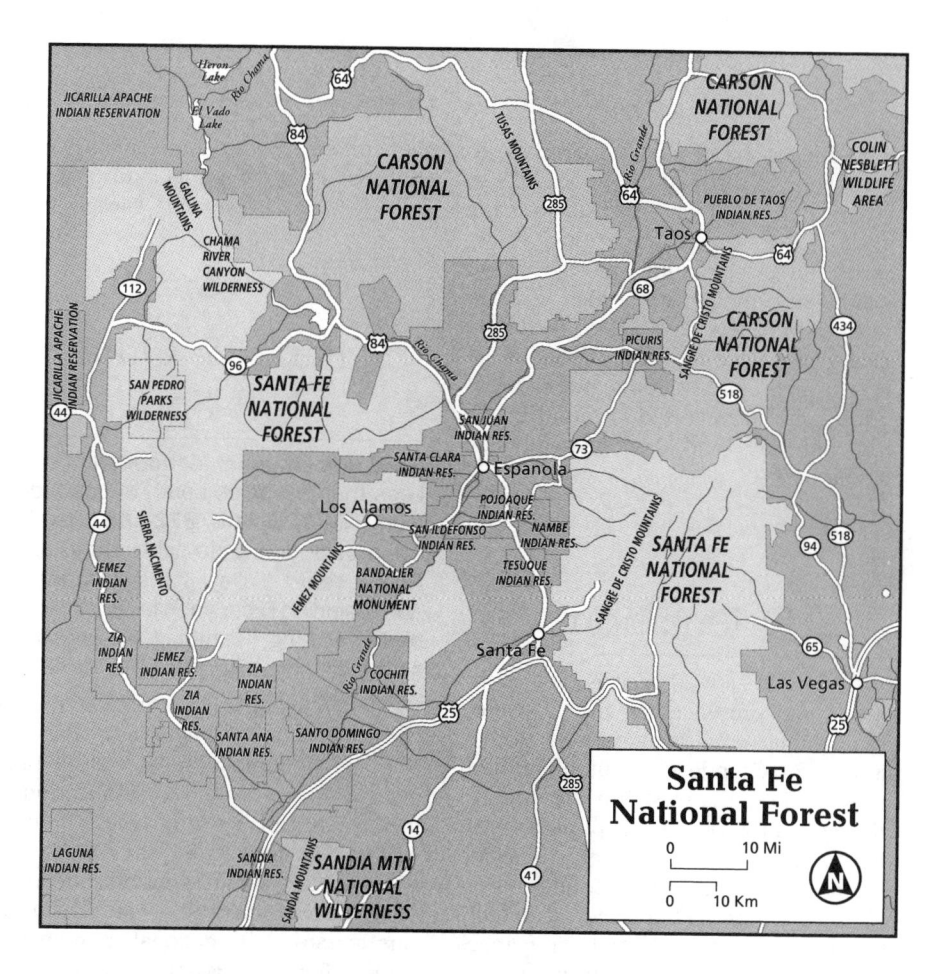

The climate in north central New Mexico varies greatly, but the biggest disparity lies in the elevation difference between Albuquerque and surrounding areas at 5,200 feet, and Santa Fe and Taos at 7,000 feet. In Albuquerque, the average summer temperatures are 90°F, which makes activity during mid-day too hot. Spring and fall are ideal times to be outdoors, with temps running in the 70s. The area's mild winters, with temperatures in the 50s make it a great place to hike and bike during winter, though the Sandia Mountains can be much colder and accumulate enough snow to ski and snowshoe. From the Santa Fe area north, expect temperatures about 10 degrees cooler than those in Albuquerque. That makes for decent hiking, biking, and fishing through the summer, and much of the spring and fall as well. Winter brings plenty of snow, great for all kinds of sports. Be aware that all depends heavily on elevation, and you have great gains in this region, from the base of about 7,000 feet to the peaks at 13,000. When hiking in the mountains you'll always want to bring weather gear—for rain in summer, and for snow and hail in the other three seasons. As you head farther north and climb in elevation, winters become harsher, until you reach the Valle Vidal area along the border with Colorado, where winter temperatures remain below 40°F much of the time.

The biggest bit of advice I can give to any traveler to this part of the world is to avoid canceling plans because of the weather. I've woken to spring snowstorms and gone boating anyway only to find the sun shining by the time I got to the river. Very few days are so cold here that skiing is uncomfortable. Biking is the one exception, unless you're one of those people who likes to slide around in the mud and clay (and there certainly are those around).

Orientation

North Central New Mexico is defined by the strong presence of the V-shaped mountainous area I mentioned above, with the Rio Grande River cutting through its center. Both the west and east sides of this region drop off quickly to high desert and eastern plains, respectively. Interstate 40 runs east-west along the southern portion of the region. Interstate 25 initially cuts the region in half, until it reaches Santa Fe, where it abruptly turns east and then north again, helping to define the eastern boundary of the region. From Santa Fe, U.S. 84/285 heads straight north and is the route you'll follow to many of the activities listed in this book. At Espanola, U.S. 84 splits to the west heading into the Abiquiu and Chama areas. From Espanola NM 68 heads north to Taos, becoming NM 522 in its dash to the Colorado border.

One of the best information sources in the area is the **Public Lands Information Center,** located on the south side of Santa Fe at 1474 Rodeo Rd., Santa Fe, NM 87505 (☎ **505/438-7542**). Under one roof, adventurers can find out what's available on lands administered by the National Forest Service, Bureau of Land Management, National Park Service, and a number of other state and federal bureaus. The Information Center also collaborates with the New Mexico Department of Tourism. Its main Web site address is www.publiclands.org, with links to over 261 separate sites.

Parks & Other Hot Spots

Bandelier National Monument
Less than 15 miles south of Los Alamos along NM 4. ☎ **505/672-3861,** ext 517. Open daily during daylight hours, except New Year's Day and Christmas. Admission $10 per vehicle. Backpacking, bird watching, camping, cross-country skiing, fishing, hiking, wildlife viewing.

Hidden in lush pockets within 46 miles of canyon-and-mesa wilderness, Bandelier National Monument represents one of the most extensive and picturesque ruins of the ancient cliff-dwelling ancestral Pueblo culture (Anasazi) in the Southwest. During busy summer months head out early, as there can be a waiting line for cars to park. The national monument is named after the Swiss-American archaeologist Adolph Bandelier, who explored here in the 1880s.

After an orientation stop at the visitor center and museum to learn about the culture that flourished here between 1100 and 1550, most visitors follow a trail along Frijoles Creek to the principal ruins (see the "Walks & Rambles" section later in this chapter). The pueblo site, including an underground kiva, has been stabilized. The biggest thrill for most folks, though, is climbing hardy ponderosa pine ladders to visit an alcove—140 feet above the canyon floor—that was once home to prehistoric people. Tours are self-guided or led by a National Park Service ranger. Be aware that dogs are not allowed on trails.

On summer nights, rangers offer campfire talks about the history, culture, and geology of the area. Some summer evenings, the guided night walks reveal a different, spooky aspect of the ruins and cave houses, outlined in the two-dimensional chiaroscuro of the thin cold light from the starry sky. During the day, nature programs are sometimes offered for adults and children. The small museum at the visitor center displays artifacts found in the area.

Elsewhere in the monument area, 70 miles of maintained trails lead to more tribal ruins, waterfalls, and wildlife habitats. However, a recent fire has decimated parts of this area, so periodic closings will take place in order to allow the land to reforest.

The separate **Tsankawi** section, reached by an ancient 2-mile trail close to the town of **White Rock,** has a large unexcavated ruin on a high mesa overlooking the Rio Grande Valley. The town of White Rock, about 10 miles southeast of Los Alamos on NM 4, offers spectacular panoramas of the river valley in the direction of Santa Fe; the White Rock Overlook is a great picnic and climbing spot.

Within Bandelier, areas have been set aside for picnicking and camping. Past Bandelier National Monument on NM 4, beginning about 15 miles from Los Alamos, is the **Valles Caldera,** a vast meadow 16 miles in area—all that remains of a volcanic caldera created by a collapse after eruptions nearly a million years ago. When the mountain spewed ashes and dust as far away as Kansas and Nebraska, its underground magma chambers collapsed, forming this great valley—one of the largest volcanic calderas in the world. However, lava domes that pushed up after the collapse obstruct a full view across the expanse. Valles Caldera, also known as the Baca Ranch, has recently been purchased by the U.S. government, with plans to allow for public use.

Valle Vidal

Take NM 522 north from Taos 40 miles to Costilla. Turn east on NM 196. It will become FR 1950, which will lead to the campgrounds and trailheads. Bird watching, camping, cross-country skiing, fishing, hiking, mountain biking, wildlife viewing.

This 100,000-acre parcel of Carson National Forest is an unspoiled land of pines and broad meadows inhabited by some 60 mammal species including black bear, mountain lion, and many elk, as well as 200 species of birds. Over the years it has remained pristine through private ownership. Only in 1982 did these become public lands. Before that they were part of the 492,560-acre Vermejo Park Ranch, and before that they were part of the 1,714,765-acre Maxwell Land Grant, at the time the largest single landholding in the Western Hemisphere.

Today much of the land grant has been scattered among various owners. The Vermejo Park ranch is owned by media mogul Ted Turner, as are two other large landholdings in southern New Mexico. There are few designated hiking trails traversing these lands, but that shouldn't stop you from exploring. Once while driving through I saw a massive elk herd just off the forest road. I parked and made my own hike, quietly following them toward the high country. If you do such a thing, be sure to take a map. The USGS Abreu Canyon, Ash Mountain, Van Bremmer Park, Red River Pass, Comanche Point, and Baldy Mountain quadrangles will be helpful. Be aware that you may encounter hunters during deer and elk seasons. For other activities in the area see the fishing, hiking, cross-country skiing, mountain biking, and wildlife viewing sections of this chapter.

Jemez State Monument

From Albuquerque, take NM 44 to NM 4, and then continue on NM 4 for about 18 miles. ☎ **505/829-3530.** Open daily 8:30am–5pm. Closed New Year's Day, Easter, Thanksgiving, Christmas. Admission $3 adults, free for children 16 and under. Bird watching, hiking.

A stop at this small monument takes you on a journey through the history of the Jemez people. The journey begins in the museum, which tells the tale of Giusewa, "place of boiling waters," the original Tewa name of the area. Then it moves out into the mission ruins whose story is told on small plaques, which juxtapose the first impressions of the missionaries against the reality of the Jemez life. The missionaries saw the Jemez people as barbaric and set out to settle them. Part of the process involved hauling up river stones and erecting 6-foot-thick walls of the Mission of San José de los Jemez in the early 17th century (founded in 1621). Excavations in 1921 to 1922 and 1935 to 1937 unearthed this massive complex through which you may wander. You'll enter through a broad doorway to a room, which once held elaborate fresco paintings; the room tapers back to the nave, with a giant bell tower above. The setting is startling next to a creek, with steep mountains rising behind.

Wild Rivers Recreation Area

North of Taos (about 3 miles north of Questa), turn west off NM 522 onto NM 378; travel 8 miles on a gravel road. ☎ **505/770-1600**. Backpacking, biking, bird watching, camping, fishing, hiking, horseback riding, mountain biking, swimming, wildlife viewing.

Here, where the Red River enters the Rio Grande gorge, you'll find 22 miles of trails, some suited for biking and some for hiking, a few traveling 800 feet down into the gorge to the banks of the Rio Grande River. Forty-eight miles of the Rio Grande, which extend south from the Colorado border, are protected under the National Wild and Scenic River Act of 1968. Information on geology and wildlife, as well as hikers' trail maps, may be obtained at the visitor center here. Ask for directions to the impressive petroglyphs in the gorge.

El Vado Lake State Park

14 miles southwest of Tierra Amarilla on NM 112. ☎ **505/588-7247**. Backpacking, camping, fishing, hiking, horseback riding, powerboating, sailing.

A favorite place for many northern New Mexicans to boat and water-ski as well as fish and camp during the summer months, this lake stretches across 3,200 acres and is surrounded by mountain forest. It has 50 developed campsites and room for 150 tents. It's also a good place for cross-country skiing and ice fishing in winter.

Heron Lake State Park

11 miles west of Tierra Amarilla via U.S. 64 and NM 95. ☎ **505/588-7470**. Bird watching, boardsailing, camping, canoeing, coastal and wetlands birding, cross-country skiing, fishing, hiking, powerboating, sailing, swimming, wildlife viewing.

With a no-wake speed limit for motor vessels, this 5,900-acre mountain lake is especially appealing to those interesting in fishing, sailing, windsurfing, canoeing, and swimming. The park has an interpretive center, plus camping, picnic sites, hiking trails, and cross-country skiing in the winter. Many like to camp along the shore. The scenic 5.5-mile Rio Chama trail connects Heron with El Vado Lake.

What to Do
& Where to Do It

BALLOONING

The **Kodak Albuquerque International Balloon Fiesta,** the world's largest balloon rally, brings together more than 1,000 colorful balloons and includes races and contests. There are mass ascensions at sunrise, and "balloon glows" in the evening. Various special events are staged all week.

Balloons lift off at Balloon Fiesta Park (at I-25 and Alameda NE) on Albuquerque's northern city limits during the second week in October. For information, contact ☎ 800/733-9918 or www.balloonfiesta.com.

Also in October, the **Taos Mountain Balloon Rally,** the Albuquerque fiesta's "little brother," offers mass dawn ascensions, tethered balloon rides for the public, and a Saturday parade of balloon baskets (in pickup trucks) from Kit Carson Park around the plaza. Call ☎ 800/732-8267 for more information.

Visitors not content to just watch the colorful craft rise into the clear-blue skies have a choice of several Albuquerque hot-air balloon operators. Rates start at about $130 per person per hour. Contact **Rainbow Ryders,** 11520 San Bernardino NE (☎ 505/823-1111); and **World Balloon Corporation,** 4800 Eubank Blvd. NE (☎ 505/293-6800).

BIRD WATCHING

Just a short drive from the Santa Fe Plaza, the **Randall Davey Audubon Center** (☎ 505/983-4609) offers a great chance for bird lovers to wander. Named for the late Santa Fe artist who willed his home to the National Audubon Society, this wildlife refuge occupies 135 acres at the mouth of the Santa Fe Canyon. More than 100 species of birds live here at various times of year, including broad-billed, black-chinned, and rufous-tailed hummingbirds, Steller's and Western scrub jays, Cooper's and sharp-shinned hawks, northern flickers, and mountain chickadees. There are also 120 types of plants, and many mammals, including black bears, mule deer, mountain lions, bobcats, raccoons, and coyotes. Trails winding through a sanctuary are open to day hikers, but not to dogs. There's also a natural history bookstore on-site. It's located at 1800 Upper Canyon Road. Drive up Upper Canyon Road until it turns to dirt; then go straight at the Dead End sign. Trail admission is $1 for adults, 50¢ for children; it's open daily 9am to 5pm. House tours are conducted sporadically during the summer for $3 per person; call for hours.

The **Rio Grande Nature Center State Park** (☎ 505/344-7240), located just a few miles north of Old Town in Albuquerque, spans 270 acres of riverside forest and meadows, which include stands of 100-year-old cottonwoods and a 3-acre pond. Located on the Rio Grande Flyway, an important migratory route for many birds, it's an excellent place to see sandhill cranes, Canada geese, and quail—over 260 species have made this their temporary or permanent home. In a protected area where dogs aren't allowed (you can bring dogs on most of the 2 miles of trails) you'll find exhibits of native grasses, wildflowers, and herbs. Inside a building built half above and half below ground, you can sit next to a pond in a glassed-in viewing area and comfortably watch ducks and other birds in their avian antics. There are 21 self-guided interpretive exhibits as well as photo exhibits, a library, a small nature store and a children's resource room. On Saturday mornings you can join in a guided bird and nature walk. Other weekend programs are available for adults and children including nature photography and bird and wildflower identification classes. Call for a schedule. It's located at 2901 Candelaria Rd. NW. Admission is $1 for adults, 50¢ for children 6 and older, and free for children under 6. The park is open daily from 8am to 8pm. The center is open daily 10am to 5pm in winter, 10am to 8pm in summer. Both are closed New Year's Day, Thanksgiving, and Christmas.

The **Hawk Watch Trail** takes birders to a platform in the Sandia Mountains where members of a raptor conservations group called Hawk Watch International observe as many as 20 species of raptors including hawks, falcons, eagles, and rare birds such as zone-tailed hawks and black-shouldered kites. It's a 4-mile round-trip hike to see the site. See the "Hikes & Backpack Trips" section later in this chapter for details.

BOARDSAILING

Since this is the high desert, you won't find an abundance of waters upon which to ply your board, but there are a few spots. Many beginners like to go to 1,200-acre **Cochiti Lake** between Santa Fe and Albuquerque. Here often-gentle winds will push you out and only occasionally not allow you to come back in. *Beware:* Strong winds can come on, and come on quickly. Access is off NM 22.

The setting of **Abiquiu Lake** is unparalleled. Full of pink and yellow buttes and azure mountains, this is the land that Georgia O'Keeffe made famous in her haunting paintings of northern New Mexico. Seven miles north of the village of Abiquiu on U.S. 84, the 12,000-acre lake is used mostly by fishers and jet skiers, though I've done some swimming and picnicking here as well.

Because of no-wake boat restrictions **Heron Lake State Park,** 11 miles west of Tierra Amarilla via U.S. 64 and NM 95, is one of the region's premier spots for all types of sailors. Winds on the lake can be brisk, as can water temperatures except during mid-summer. This 5,900-acre mountain also has nice campsites and hiking trails.

CLIMBING

With its many and varied mountains (the Sangre de Cristos, Jemez, and Sandias, to name a few), northern New Mexico has lots of rock to climb, and lots of variety of rock. From pockety basalt to grippy tuft, there's plenty here for most levels of climbing expertise. Best of all, many of the areas are climbable year-round, with the sweetest conditions from April through November. A good all-around source for the area is *Rock Climbing New Mexico and Texas,* by Dennis R. Jackson (Falcon Press, 1996), though for even more specific directions note the guides I mention within the text below. For guided climbing or lessons call **Southwest Climbing Resource** in Santa Fe (☎ 505/983-8288) or **Mountain Skills** in Taos (☎ 505/776-2037).

When the **Sandia Mountains** crashed up from the earth, their steep, rugged western face exposed some 4,000 feet of Precambrian granite. And to this feat of nature today's climbers salute, for it left them with some of New Mexico's best and most challenging traditional climbing. Climbers who tackle this area should be adept at route finding, gear placements, and self-rescue. The Shield, Needle, and other climbs are best accessed from the top of Sandia Crest. Access the Crest from I-25, 10 miles north of Albuquerque. Turn on NM 165 and drive 20 miles, part of which is dirt road (this road is closed in winter). Or, from the backside of the Sandias, take NM 14 to NM 536, which meets up with NM 165 to the Crest.

The largest and most popular of the formations is the **Shield,** rising more than 1,000 feet at the north end of the Sandias. Climbers will find 20 designated routes ranging from 5.4 to 5.11a in difficulty and 5 to 13 pitches in length. Note that the area is closed between March and August to protect peregrine falcon nest sites. Access the Shield via the North Crest Trail for a mile then bushwhack toward the west.

South of the Shield, the next major formation is the **Needle.** This spire has 10 routes ranging from 5.4 to 5.8 in difficulty and from 3 to 15 pitches in length. The approach takes at least 2 hours. It begins at the Crest parking area. Follow the North Crest Trail, then head down to a saddle to the east of the Needle. From there bushwhack to the base of the Southwest Ridge. Other climbs in the range include Muralla Grande, Torreon, and Mexican Breakfast. For more detailed information about these climbs, the *Hikers & Climbers Guide to the Sandias,* by Mike Hill (University of New Mexico Press, 1993), is a good source, available at REI and other area climbing stores.

Also in the Sandias at their northern end is **Palomas Peak,** with over 70 bolted sport routes on a 50-foot madera limestone cliff band. With only a handful of 5.8 and 5.9 climbs and many 5.10 through 5.13 ones, the area is especially desirable to experienced climbers. From I-25 about 15 miles north of Albuquerque, take Exit 242 and head east on NM 165 for 14 miles (through Placitas) to a parking area on your left (look for 3 large concrete railings). From the parking lot hike down into a little valley, then north toward the crags. Allow for 20 to 30 minutes on this well-defined trail

Cochiti Mesa at the southeast edge of the Jemez Mountains is New Mexico's best-known and one of the state's most easily accessible sport climbing areas. These routes range in difficulty from moderately steep (5.8) to slightly overhanging (13c), and vary in length from 30 feet to 80 feet. Be aware that most of the routes range in the more difficult end of the scale, so the area is most fun for experienced climbers. At Cochiti you're climbing on welded tuff, a soft rock formed from volcanic ash flow with a thin, hard surface. Climbing is possible year-round on these faces but April to mid-June and September to mid-November are ideal (unfortunately, the road to access them isn't always open; check road conditions by calling the **Jemez Ranger District** at ☎ **505/ 829-3535**). Access is south of Santa Fe off I-25. Head west on NM 22 for about 16 miles until you come to FS 289. Depending upon where you stop on this road, a number of faces in the area are available for climbing. These include Eagle Canyon, Jimmy Cliff, Vista Point Overlook, Cacti Cliff, Disease Wall, and Cochiti Mesa itself.

Also in the Jemez Mountains, in the area of **White Rock,** are a number of choice climbing areas. In most of these you'll be climbing on basaltic rock, and the area is warm enough to climb year-round. This is a wide face overlooking the spectacular Rio Grande River hundreds of feet below. Climbs range in difficulty from 5.8 to 5.13b, and are 30 to 50 feet long. Though for years this was a traditional climbing area, sports climbers have made headway here, particularly on the faces between cracks. Trad crack enthusiasts will find plenty to play on here as well. The site is located 30 miles northwest of Santa Fe and 10 miles southeast of Los Alamos in the town of White Rock. Reach it by taking NM 285 north from Santa Fe to NM 502. Take the White Rock exit onto NM 4 and drive 4.1 miles and turn left on Rover Boulevard. Take the first left onto Meadow Lane and follow it to Overlook Regional Park. From the parking area walk out the ridge of the escarpment and scramble down to the trail below. This leads to the faces called the Overlook and the Underlook. Other faces can be reached by remaining on Meadow Lane (rather than turning into the Overlook Park entrance) for 0.25 miles to a paved access trail, which leads down to the west. There you'll find climbs named the Old New Place, the Sununu Place, Below the Old New Place, the Doughnut Shop, and the Playground.

If you like to climb in plush meadow surroundings—maybe even with a stream nearby for a cooling dip—head to **Las Conchas,** a rhyolite formation also in the Jemez Mountains. Unfortunately, on weekends this spot gets pretty crowded. Here you can climb from late spring to early fall on mostly bolted routes ranging from 5.8 to 5.13c. Crags here include Roadside Attraction, Cattle Call Wall, Gateway Rock, Chilly Willy Wall, Love Shack Area, Gallery Wall, Dream Tower, the Sponge, and the Leaning Tower. Access is directly off NM 4. From Los Alamos take NM 501 to NM 4 and head west toward Jemez Springs. Drive about 12 miles to the Las Conchas parking area. From White Rock, you can simply continue on NM 4 westward through the Valle Grande Caldera to the Las Conchas parking area. Roadside Attraction and Cattle Call Wall are north of the road and just east of the parking area, while all the other rocks can be accessed by walking northwest (downstream). For a more detailed account of these climbs read *Sport Climbing in New Mexico* by Randal Jett and Matt Samet, published by the authors in 1991 and available in most New Mexico climbing stores and at the Public Lands Information Office in Santa Fe.

The **Taos area** is known for its variety of climbing, from sport routes hanging above the meandering Rio Grande to a multi-pitch peak ascent at Questa Dome. **John's Wall,** also called Hondo Cliffs, is an easily accessible 70-foot basalt cliff just east of the John Dunn Bridge at the base of the 650-foot-deep Rio Grande Gorge. It's known for its fine crack and face routes and offers both sport and trad climbing. Unfortunately, vandals have splattered an oil-based substance along the bottom, detracting from some of the routes. One nice thing about this site is that you can climb here year-round, though spring and fall are the best seasons. There are 13 designated routes ranging in difficulty from 5.7 to 5.12. Access the climb by driving north of Taos on NM 522 for 7 miles to the village of Arroyo Hondo. Turn west on NM 577. Drive 2 miles and look for John's Wall on the north side of the road where the road crosses over the Rio Hondo.

Dead Cholla Wall, also known as Pilar, is another Rio Grande Gorge climb, but this one is nestled along the rim. It's a great place to go if you like views with your climbing, for the Rio Grande meanders below and the Sangre de Cristos stand like a blue wave to the east. Composed of vertical and overhanging basalt, the site has more than 20 sport routes, most in the 5.10 through 5.11 range, all equipped with new ⅜-inch bolts. Some crack climbing is also available here. Even top-roping is available, though many of the anchors are well below the top of the cliff. Access the area from the village of Pilar, which is on NM 68, midway between Taos and Española. At the Rio Grande Yacht Club turn on NM 570 and follow the Rio Grande 6 miles to the Taos Junction Bridge. Cross the bridge and continue about 1.6 miles up what has turned into NM 567 until the road becomes pavement again. Travel 0.2 miles on the pavement and turn at the first dirt track to the right. The parking area is 0.3 mile down this road above the Gorge's western rim. Look for the trail leading off the cliff's top. It drops down to the crag's southern end.

East of the Rio Grande Gorge, **Tres Piedras Rocks** ("tres piedras" is Spanish for "three rocks") jut up dramatically from the mesa. Here you'll find single-pitch climbing on vertical and overhanging walls, as well as some fine crack routes. Locals like the area because it's granite, and it's surrounded by forest, so it stays relatively cool in summer. Over time this area has had mostly traditional climbs, but some sport routes have appeared. Some of the existing bolts are old, so come prepared with your own rack. Climbs here range from 5.7 through 5.12, with lengths ranging from 70 feet to 150 feet in height. Part of this climbing area is on private land, the rest on U.S. Forest Service land. The private owner isn't too receptive to climbing activity, so conduct yourself responsibly while in the area. Access the area from Taos by heading north on U.S. 64 for 30 miles to the junction of U.S. 285. From Santa Fe, follow U.S. 285 north through Española, and continue on it to the village of Tres Piedras. From the junction of U.S. 64 and U.S. 285, travel 0.7 miles west on U.S. 64 past the ranger station (where you can get a map to the site) and look for an unmarked dirt road on the right. Turn and go right past a water tower and continue 0.4 miles to a T intersection. Turn left and travel a short ways to the parking area. About 100 yards to the north you'll see South Rock, on private land. Walk around its west end and you'll come to the most popular area,

Mosaic Rock. Crags here also include Middle Rock, West Rock, Sundeck Wall, and North Rock.

In the midst of the Latir Wilderness north of Taos sits the **Questa Dome.** Within a remote alpine setting, this 500-foot granite crag has 6 routes that vary from 2 to 5 pitches, all traditional climbing on cracks and faces. These climbs are in the 5.10 through 5.12 range. The area is for those who know what they're doing. Routes often have long runouts, and serious fall potential is high. The closest medical facilities are in Taos. Access this area by driving north from Taos on NM 522 to the village of Questa. Continue 7 more miles north of the village until you come to a road heading east toward El Rito. The trailhead is 2.1 miles from the highway on a 4-wheel-drive road. At 0.9 miles a road joins from the left. Continue straight. At a T junction go right for 0.2 miles to the parking area. The trail climbs steadily, close to the creek. Allow about 40 minutes for the approach.

CROSS-COUNTRY SKIING

Cross-country skiing conditions in north central New Mexico are definitely bittersweet. On the one hand you have light, airy powder, but then you also have a very strong and warm sun. The sun makes for glorious adventures even at the height of winter, but it also warms the snow and creates very uneven conditions. Rarely do I long for the steady, relentless cold of more northern climes, but once in awhile when I'm clawing my way up a slope of ice, I actually do. But if you can accept the yin/yang of it, you'll have an awesome time at either the groomed areas listed below or the more independent trails.

Groomed Trails

Enchanted Forest Cross Country Ski Area
22 miles. Easy to difficult. 500-ft. elevation gain. Allow 2–8 hrs. Access: East of Red River on State Highway 38. ☎ **505/754-2374**. Open 9am–4:30pm. Map: Trail map available.

This is the closest you'll find in New Mexico to the over-the-river-and-through-the-woods kind of skiing people enjoy in New England. The 22 miles of groomed trails wind through 600 acres of forest, crossing meadows, through woods, and for the daring, down narrow drops. Though the area is geared for beginning and intermediate skiers, there are a few advanced runs left ungroomed. A small hut at the base provides shelter and hot drinks. You won't have to worry about crowds here; they haven't yet found the sport or the place. Equipment rentals and lessons can be arranged at **Millers Crossing** ski shop on Main Street in Red River (☎ **505/754-2374**). The shop offers instruction in ski skating, mountaineering, and telemarking. In addition to cross-country ski and snowshoe rentals, the ski area also rents "pulk sleds," high-tech devices in which children are pulled by their skiing parents. The ski area offers a full snack bar, with hot lunches available.

Ungroomed Trails

Sandia Mountains
10K Trail
5–10 miles. Moderate to difficult. 900-ft. elevation gain. Allow 2–5 hrs. Access: On the east side of the Sandia Mountains. From Albuquerque head east on I-40 to the Cedar Crest/Tijeras exit and follow the signs for NM 14 north. In 6 miles, turn left on NM 536. Continue 12 miles to the trailhead along the side of the road. Maps: USGS Placitas, Sandia Crest, and Tijeras quads.

This trail runs either north or south from NM 536. I recommend heading north. Here you'll find some of the best snow in the Sandias. Follow the blue markers up and down across Las Huertas Canyon to Canon Media, where a spur trail leads east to Media Spring. From there you can ascend a steep hill to another roadcut, which leads north all the way to the ridgeline of the Sandias. If you'd like you can connect with the Survey Trail or the

North Crest Trail, both of which will take you back to NM 536. However, these loops are long and suited for more experienced skiers.

North Crest Trail

11 miles. Moderate to difficult. 400-ft. elevation gain. Allow 2–6 hrs. Access: On the east side of the Sandia Mountains. From NM 14 turn northwest on NM 536 and drive for 14 miles until you come to the Sandia Crest parking lot. Map: USGS Placitas, Sandia Crest, and Tijeras quads.

Conditions on this trail can vary greatly due to the wind blowing across it. However, if you catch it after a fresh snow on a relatively calm day, it's one of the most spectacular skis you'll ever do, because it traverses the Crest of the Sandias, with views hundreds of miles in all directions. The trail is only moderately steep. You'll head north from NM 536 on trail no. 130 below television and radio antennas and power lines. Then you'll come to some exhilarating descents through trees. You'll reach the Cañon del Agua Overlook at mile 2. Here you'll have views across the Rio Grande Valley to Mount Taylor, Cabezon, and the Jemez Mountains. At this point you have the option of doing a loop heading back on the 10K trail or the Survey Trail. The North Crest Trail continues to a second overlook, then heads back into the trees as it leaves the rim of the mountains. You can continue from here to the north Del Agua Overlook at about mile 3. Then the trail leaves the rim and begins switchbacks down the east side of the mountains into Gambel oak forests and later into piñon-juniper; however these lower elevations don't generally maintain good snow pack. On a good snow year you can follow this trail all the way to Tunnel Springs near the village of Placitas, accessed from FR 231. If you decide to make a loop with the 10K trail you'll have to follow the paved road for 2 miles back to the Crest.

Carson National Forest

Numerous popular Nordic trails exist in the Carson National Forest in the area surrounding Taos. If you call ahead (☎ 505/753-6200), the forest service will send you a booklet titled *Where to Go in the Snow*, which gives cross-country skiers details about the maintained trails.

Amole Canyon

3 miles groomed. 300-ft. elevation gain. Allow 2 hrs. Access: From Taos, follow State Hwy. 518 south about 14 miles (2 miles past U.S. Hill). Parking is on the east side of the highway at FS 4 entrance.

This high, very scenic trail offers plenty of fun groomed miles for beginning skiers with gentle slopes and open ponderosa pine stands and meadows. There are a few steeper grades for those who like more challenge, and each has a detour around it. If you're looking for still more adventure, there are over 13 miles of ungroomed sections, called the Lower and Upper Loops. These follow old logging roads and the historic Comales Sheep Driveway. The Driveway was used for many years by local sheepmen to drive their flocks from winter range near Taos to summer range in the high country. The Lower Loop (6 miles) is rated as "most difficult" due to the 0.25 miles of 20% grade. This portion is narrow and not recommended unless one has mastered steep, narrow courses. The Upper Loop (7.2 miles) has a more gentle nature. Near the head of Amole Canyon there are approximately 200 yards of 20% grade. Recommended direction of travel for both the Upper and Lower Loops is up Amole Canyon. There are signs at intersections, and blue diamonds designate the courses. Be aware that there is no patrol in this area.

Santa Barbara Canyon

2.4 miles round-trip, with options for longer distances. Easy to difficult. 600-ft. elevation gain, with option for more.

Allow 1–4 hrs. Access: Drive to Peñasco via NM 75. At Peñasco turn on NM 73 heading southeast. Drive 1.5 miles to the junction with FS 116. Turn left and follow the signs 4 miles to Santa Barbara Campground. Maps: USGS Jicarita Peak and Pecos Falls; USFS Pecos Wilderness.

The Rio Santa Barbara watershed is the most pristine in New Mexico. The river's clear waters are dazzling any time of year. This trail starts along forest service roads and moves up onto mountain trails. Beginning skiers might want to start their tour along FS 116 anywhere that strikes their fancy. It's a lovely winter road following the Rio Santa Barbara through meadows and stands of aspens. For those who would like a more challenging route drive in to the Santa Barbara Campground and begin there. You'll ski 1.2 miles before the entrance to the Pecos Wilderness. This is easy skiing, a fun jaunt for novices. Once you enter the wilderness, however, the trail gets more difficult. You'll cross a bridge over the river and begin a gentle climb along the east slope of the canyon. From here you can ski your heart out. Some like to go snow camping and do 20 or so miles to and from No Fish Lake. Keep in mind that these are not groomed trails, and that the weather in the Pecos Wilderness can be precarious. Since this trail is rarely traveled in winter, those venturing into the Pecos Wilderness should have gear, maps, compass and strong mountaineering skills.

Jemez Mountains

You'll find plenty of trails in the Jemez Mountains, particularly in the area of La Cueva where NM 4 and NM 126 intersect.

East Fork Ridge Cross-Country Ski Trail

4.5 miles. Easy. 400-ft. elevation gain. Allow 2–4 hrs. Access: From the La Cueva intersection of NM 4 and NM 126, head east on NM 4 for 6.5 miles until you see the sign for the East Fork Recreation Area on the left side of the road.

This isn't so much a single trail as it is a vast web of abandoned logging roads winding through the forest with minimal elevation gain and a few nice overlook spots. Anyone with prior cross-country experience will be comfortable here. After 0.5 mile the trail intersects with the Mistletoe Canyon Trail, a nice alternate route, but with fewer views. At 2.5 miles the East Fork Ridge Trail reaches a large clearing with a spectacular view of Redondo Peak. Then, after a short climb the trail gradually descends and again meets the Mistletoe Canyon Trail, which can provide a return loop to the trailhead. Farther east the East Fork Trail intersects with the Burn Trail and the East Fork National Recreation Hiking Trail. All the trails are well marked with blue markers. Be aware that snow conditions in the Jemez can vary greatly.

Santa Fe National Forest
Norski Tracks de Santa Fe

3 miles. Easy to moderate. 200-ft. elevation gain. Allow 2 hrs. Access: Drive northeast of Santa Fe on Hyde Park Rd. for 14.5 miles. About 0.5 miles before the Santa Fe Ski Area parking lot you'll see the trailhead and parking lot on the left.

This loop trail winds blissfully through towering Aspen stands and fir forests. Laid out in 1985 by a Santa Fe ski touring club, it is well marked with blue diamond blazes, and has a trailhead map, distance markers, and a beginner and intermediate loop. Be aware that you cannot bring dogs on the trail.

Begin the loop on the right leg. You'll head into thick conifer forest and descend into aspens. Here you'll encounter some crossover signs where the trail returns. Bear right until you come to a sign directing beginners back to the trailhead. A "more difficult" sign directs those who have good downhill skills to head onward. This area is fun if you want to try a few tele turns, though at times the trail can be icy, leaving you screaming downhill. Fortunately the hill ascends shortly, giving you a chance to reduce your speed. The rest of the way back you'll ascend toward the east, finally meeting up with the beginner trail and making your way back to the parking lot.

Aspen Vista, Forest Road 150
6–10 miles. Moderate to difficult. Elevation gain up to 2,000 ft. Allow 3–5 hrs. Access: Take Hyde Park Rd. toward the Santa Fe Ski Area 15.5 miles to the Aspen Vista Recreation Site where Forest Rd. 150 begins.

This run is a local favorite. Though it begins with a forever climb and then has a fast descent, it offers spectacular views and can be a short to a quite long run. Basically you begin at the parking lot, from which you'll have some flat ground on which to warm up. Then you'll begin a series of ascents interspersed with more flat skating areas. There's no way to get lost here, so just continue higher and higher. You'll move out of aspen forest into spruce-fir at about the 3.5-mile mark. If you go all the way to the top, you'll come to some radio towers. The route down is swift, and you'll have to negotiate those upwardly mobile skiers. At times there's just enough room for a few tele turns, but often the track is rutted single track making it hard to slow down. From the top skiers can access Santa Fe Ski Area trails.

Windsor Trail
10 miles. Difficult. 1,000-ft. elevation gain. Allow 5 hrs. Access: Take Hyde Park Rd. northeast 15 miles to the Santa Fe Ski Area parking lot. The trailhead is at the north end of the lower lot. Be aware that during ski season these lots will be quite full. If all else fails you should be able to park at the Norski Trailhead and ski to the Windsor Trailhead. Maps: Santa Fe National Forest–Pecos Wilderness Map.

This is where the big boys and girls go to play in the snow. The Windsor Trail meanders into the Pecos Wilderness, where backcountry skiing abounds. However, be aware that these areas can be very remote. Be prepared with proper gear, maps, water, and some duct tape to repair broken bindings.

The trail begins in a steep series of switchbacks for a half-mile until it reaches the Pecos Wilderness boundary. This first half-mile is the most difficult part of the trail. When you enter the wilderness you'll descend in a gentle glide east through trees. Here the area opens out, and you'll revel at views of the Jemez Mountains to the west. The trail continues with this awesome kick and glide terrain for about 2.5 miles, crossing the Rio Nambe along the way. Next the trail turns northward and ascends another series of switchbacks (be careful to follow the trail; at times snow can blow away previous tracks) until it reaches a spectacular high meadow called Puerto Nambe. From here you can turn around and see Santa Fe Baldy to the north and Penitente and Lake Peaks to the south, and much of northern New Mexico as well. This is a good point to turn around, or for those who'd like to do an overnight a good place to stop before continuing across the wilderness to the village of Cowles. Be careful on the switchbacks when descending from Puerto Nambe. Then enjoy the not-so-tough uphill for awhile, finally descending more switchbacks to the Ski Area parking lot.

Valle Vidal

Powderhouse–Little Costilla Peak Trail
Variable mileage—20 miles maximum. Moderate to difficult. 3,000-ft. possible elevation gain. Allow 2–10 hrs. Access: Take NM 522 north from Taos to Costilla. Turn east on NM 196 until you come to the junction of FR 1950 and FR 1900. Stay on FR 1950 and drive (or if the road is impassable ski) 3 miles to the trailhead, which is marked. Map: USGS Quad Ash Mountain.

This is a trail for those off-the-beaten-path types. You're not likely to see other skiers in the Valle Vidal area, though some do snowmobile there (not on this trail). Its lack of popularity has to do with its remoteness. On the edge of the Colorado–New Mexico border, the area is miles from any city. Access is further hindered by the fact that the forest roads are not plowed. Additionally, the forest service closes areas of Valle Vidal during the elk migration. Be sure to check with the district office for snow conditions and migration schedules (☎ **505/586-0520** or 505/758-6230). However, if you do decide to make the trek, it will be worth it. This area is especially known for the huge herds of elk that live in the area. I've seen hundreds grazing meadows and moving up into the woods.

The forest service calls this a "thru" trail because it runs like a horseshoe from one forest road to another. Only those carrying camping gear will probably make it "thru," though, because the trail is so long. One trailhead is located about 3 miles south of Comanche point on Forest Road 1950. The other is located north of Comanche Point on Forest Road 1900 near the Valle Vidal boundary. Both trailheads are signed. From either end you'll follow old logging roads (ungroomed trail) about 10 miles and reach Little Costilla Peak. From there and other places along the trail views of Big Costilla Peak and the Latir Peaks are spectacular. The logging roads do tend to fork so you'll want to take along a map.

Chama

With more meadows and gentle slopes than you'll find in the Sangre de Cristo Mountains, the Chama area offers a very complete backcountry experience. For rentals, service, and information, contact **Chama Ski Service** (☎ **505/756-2492**), a small company in its 22nd season located 1 mile up NORA Coop Road in the center of Chama. As well as renting cross-country equipment, it also rents sleds and snowshoes.

Southwest Nordic Center (☎ **505/758-4761**) offers rental of a large *yurt* (Mongolian-style hut) 2 miles above Taos Ski Valley, at 10,800 feet, in Bull of the Woods Meadow. This yurt is spacious for a group of 4 and can handle up to 10 people. Access is up a steep trail, and skiing in the area takes you through what Southwest Nordic Center terms "steep and deep" terrain, a good place for adrenaline and endorphin junkies. Less extreme skiers will enjoy the Nordic Center's four other yurts in the Rio Grande National Forest near Chama. All yurts are insulated and fully equipped, each with a stove, pots, pans, dishes, silverware, mattresses, pillows, a table and benches, and wood-stove heating. Skiers trek into the huts, carrying their clothing and food in backpacks. Or some choose to go from hut to hut, spending a night in each. The area around the Chama huts is excellent for both touring and telemark skiing, with many fun trails and some nice bowls. Guide service is provided, or people can on in on their own, following directions on a map. Prices range from $85 to $125 per night per group. Call for reservations. Book all of the yurts as much in advance as possible as they do fill up. The season runs from mid-November through April, depending on snow conditions.

The Norski Meadows

12 miles. Easy to moderate. 400-ft. elevation gain. Allow 2–6 hrs. Access: Head north from Chama on NM 17 for 8.5 miles. Just before you reach Cumbres Pass, you'll see a plowed parking area on the west side of the highway.

This series of trails winds across some lovely high meadows and through stands of Douglas fir. The loop heads northwest from the highway along railroad tracks until it reaches a 1-kilometer marker. Here the trail turns south, then southeast. The route winds through varied terrain, and at the 2-kilometer mark allows you, if you'd like, to return via a spur trail. The main trail comes back around toward the highway and the trailhead. There is no fee, and the trail is not groomed except in February when there's a local race here.

Though snowmobiles are allowed in the area, you'll rarely see them on this trail. Your best bet here is to explore. You're not likely to get lost since the course is set between the highway and some steep cliffs. For further exploration, continue up to the top of 10,200-foot Cumbres Pass, which is all National Forest land, ripe for adventuring on skis.

DOWNHILL SKIING & SNOWBOARDING

When newcomers to New Mexico first sample the skiing here, they're often surprised at how good it is. In fact, Taos is often named by industry magazines as one of the top resorts in the world. Other areas provide a less radical experience. The main reasons the skiing is so good here is that New Mexico's snow is usually dry, and the days are often warm, making for a comfortable and fun experience. For snow conditions call the **New Mexico Snow Phone** (☎ **505/984-0606**), which gives statewide reports. For profiles of the individual resorts, try www.skinewmexico.com; and to request a brochure contact info@skinewmexico.com. All the alpine ski areas listed below are open daily 9am to 4pm from around Thanksgiving (sometimes a little later) to Easter (sometimes a little earlier).

Taos Ski Valley

On NM 150 north of Taos. ☎ **505/776-2291**. www.skitaos.org. 72 trails (24% beginner, 25% intermediate, 51% expert); 11 lifts including 5 double chairs, 1 triple, 4 quads, and 1 surface tow; 2,612-ft. vertical drop. Full-day tickets cost from $31–$45 for adults.

This is the preeminent ski resort in the southern Rocky Mountains. It was founded in 1955 by a Swiss-German immigrant, Ernie Blake. According to local legend, Blake searched for 2 years in a small plane for the perfect location for a ski resort comparable to what he was accustomed to in the Alps. He found it at the abandoned mining site of Twining, high above Taos. Today, under the management of two younger generations of Blakes, the resort has become internationally renowned for its light, dry powder (as much as 320 inches annually), its superb ski school, and its personal, friendly service.

Taos Ski Valley, however, can best be appreciated by the more experienced skier. It offers steep, high-alpine, high-adventure skiing. The mountain is more intricate than it might seem at first glance, and it holds many surprises and challenges—even for the expert. The *London Times* named the valley "without any argument the best ski resort in the world." And, if you're sick of dealing with yahoos on snowboards, you will be pleased to know that they're not permitted on the slopes of Taos Ski Valley (the only ski area in New Mexico that forbids them). The quality of the snow here (light and dry) is believed to be due to the dry Southwestern air and abundant sunshine.

With its children's ski school, Taos Ski Valley has always been an excellent location for skiing families, but the 1994 addition of an 18,000-square-foot Kinderkafig Center made it even better. Kinderkafig offers many services, from equipment rental for children to baby-sitting services. Call ahead for more information.

Taos Ski Valley has many lodges and condominiums with nearly 1,500 beds. All offer ski-week packages; four of them have restaurants. There are three more restaurants on the mountain in addition to the many facilities of Village Center at the base. For reservations, call the **Taos Valley Resort Association** (☎ **800/776-1111** or 505/776-2233).

I have heard skiers accustomed to more glitzy resorts such as Vail and Aspen complain of the lack of high-speed quads at Taos. Be aware that you won't be whisked up the mountain here—as of this writing, Angel Fire has the only high-speed quads in the state. Most days you won't encounter large crowds except during holidays such as Christmas and New Year's,

SHREDDERS UNITE!

As you drive around the area you may see graffiti proclaiming "Free Taos" on the sides of buildings or on bumper stickers. With recent developments in Montana and Texas, you might think that these are the marks of a local separatist militia. On the contrary, they are part of a campaign by mostly young people (with many of the area's lodge owners behind them) to open the ski area up to snowboarders. Traditional downhill skiers don't look kindly on sharing the mountain with the shredders, who they claim make the sport more dangerous. Currently, Taos is one of only a handful of ski resorts in the West that bans boarders completely from its slopes. However, many of the area's lodge owners feel they are losing out on significant business from families and young adults who enjoy snowboarding. In the spring of 1997, the "Free Taos" message appeared in 100-foot-high letters emblazoned in the snow across an open slope above the ski area. In more recent years, an organization called **Free the Snow** (www.freethesnow.com) has formed to promote the cause. They argue that since Taos is on national forest land, the area should be open to skiers and boarders. The resort argues that since they lease the land, they are responsible for how it is used. The campaign continues to heat up: During the 1999–2000 ski season, advocates relayed their "Free Taos" message via a billboard between Santa Fe and Taos. Most recently it has gained momentum, with sponsors such as Burton Snowboards and Nike ACG joining in to "liberate" not only Taos, but also Ajax in Colorado and Alta in Utah. The "Free Taos" bumper stickers have become so popular that comic offshoots have arisen, the most notable one using the same black-and-white lettering proclaiming "Free Tacos."

and during spring break. Weekdays are usually very calm. Most of the time, however, you can find peace in the heights.

Between the 11,819-foot summit and the 9,207-foot base, there is little flat terrain for novices to gain experience and mileage. However, many beginning skiers find that after spending time in lessons they can enjoy the **Kachina Bowl,** which offers spectacular views as well as wide-open slopes. (It should be noted that Taos Ski Valley has one of the best ski schools in the country. This school specializes in teaching people how to negotiate steep and challenging runs.) Intermediates skiers will also enjoy the Kachina Bowl. More extreme skiers enjoy hiking to up to the **Ridge,** a half-hour hike (longer to Kachina Ridge) where steep, often powdery runs drop quickly into Kachina Bowl and the West Basin. Much of this is chute skiing, where fast, narrow turns are the only way down, reserved for expert skiers. The front side of the mountain offers excellent bump skiing on such runs as the renowned Al's and its neighbor Snakedance.

Sandia Peak Ski Area
20 miles northeast of Albuquerque, via Interstate 40, NM 14 and NM 536. ☎ **505/242-9133;** 505/857-8977 for snow report. 30 trails (35% beginner, 55% intermediate, 10% expert); 6 lifts including 4 doubles and 2 surface; 1,700-ft. vertical drop. Full-day adult tickets $34.

The best thing about this ski area is that it's convenient. Albuquerquians are known to sneak away from the office afternoons and take a few runs, just because it's so close. It's also a good place for families; with its 1,700-foot vertical drop, family members won't get into too much trouble in steeps. If you're looking for more challenge, though, you'll want to head north to Santa Fe or Taos. There is a day lodge and ski-rental shop. On weekends and holidays this mountain can be quite crowded. The season runs from mid-December to mid-March. You can combine a skiing day with a ride up the tramway (☎ **505/856-7325;** www.sandiapeak.com). And you may want to reserve dinner at the High Finance Restaurant at the top of the tram.

Ski Santa Fe

16 miles northeast of Santa Fe via Hyde Park Road. ☎ **505/982-4429;** 505/983-9155 for snow report. 39 trails (20% beginner, 40% intermediate, 40% advanced); 7 lifts including 1 quad, 1 triple, 2 doubles, 3 surface; 1,650-ft. vertical drop. Full-day adult ticket $42.

This mountain can surprise you. Just when you think you have its 39 runs laid out in your mind, you'll find yourself cruising through a grove of trees or launching down a chute that you've never even seen before. If Taos weren't up the road, I'd probably be content with my many days of skiing Santa Fe just because of the variety. The mountain averages 225 inches of snowfall, often the light, fluffy kind, and it has a reputable ski school as well as a strong reputation for contributing to the local community in the form of special fundraising events.

Weekends and holidays can be miserably busy here, mostly because the mountain is so close to Santa Fe, a major tourist destination. Weekdays you won't wait in a lift line. Beginners will find plenty to do on the quad chair at the bottom, while intermediate and advanced skiers will want to head to the "triple chair" that goes up to the 12,000-foot summit. If you like to ski the trees, you'll find some fun runs off to the north (left) such as Tequila Sunrise and Columbine. Cruisers can get their fill by turning right and heading to Gayway or Parachute. Your best bet might be to ask a local to lead you for a run or two so you can discover some of the hidden tree and chute runs. Snowboarders will find plenty to do on this mountain, which has a snowboard park. Base facilities center around La Casa mall, with a cafeteria, lounge, ski shop, and boutique. Another restaurant, Totemoff's, has a mid-mountain patio. The season generally runs from Thanksgiving through Easter.

Ski packages are available through **Santa Fe Central Reservations** (☎ **800/776-7669** or 505/983-8200).

Red River Ski Area

On NM 38, 36 miles northeast of Taos. ☎ **800/331-7669** for reservations, 505/754-2223 for information. 57 trails. (32% beginner, 38% intermediate, 30% expert); 7 lifts include 2 triples, 4 doubles, 1 surface; 1,600-ft. vertical drop. Full-day adult tickets $42.

It was in Red River that I first heard a joke that went something like this: "What are an inexperienced skier's last words? 'Watch this!'" Actually, the joke was told using a Texan and the punch line delivered with full accent, but I'd like to go easy on our friends to the east, a number of whom are my relatives. Though my relatives don't ski at Red River, the rest of Texas probably does, mostly because it's a fairly easy drive from the Panhandle, and because the town really caters to the southern crowd. Most are attracted to the fact that almost anywhere you stay in Red River you can step out of your door and be at the slopes in minutes. Like Aspen, it is a real village at the base of the mountain. Don't be fooled, however: It doesn't have the sophistication of anything close to Aspen. It's sort of the *Green Acres* version of Aspen.

One thing that draws people to this 37-year-old family-oriented area is that its trails are geared toward the beginner and intermediate skier, and there's snow early and late in the season thanks to snowmaking equipment that can dust 75% of the runs. Be aware, though, that this snow can be icy, and the mountain is full of inexperienced skiers, so you have to watch your back.

Families are especially drawn to Red River because there are plenty of amenities for them. There's an adventure run that takes kids by a mining cabin and through a teepee, and the lodgers offer family packages that are dirt cheap. Due to the inordinate number of beds in the community, this somewhat remote place can get very crowded on holidays. There's a good day-care program and a free trolley system that runs up and down the main street.

Angel Fire Resort

Off U.S. 64, 21 miles east of Taos. ☎ 800/633-7463 or 505/377-6401. 68 trails (31% beginner, 48% intermediate, 21% advanced); 4 lifts including 2 high-speed quads, 2 double chairs; 2,200-ft. vertical drop. Full-day adult tickets $42.

If you like the convenience of a resort ski town, you might find happiness at Angel Fire. Built in 1960, it's a Vail-style condo village set in the broad Moreno valley. The runs are well-groomed and geared toward intermediate and beginning skiers and snowboarders. The snow here can be light northern New Mexico powder, though this mountain doesn't get quite the footage Taos does.

Under new ownership, the mountain has received more than $7 million in improvements in recent years. Two new high-speed quads whisk skiers up the mountain quickly, but they still don't cure the crowd problems during holidays. You'll especially want to avoid getting caught at the base of lift #6, where long lines can develop. Still, for more advanced skiers and those who like adventure, that's were you'll want to ski or board. Off the top of lift #3 the ski area has opened up some new hike-access advanced runs; however, the hike is substantial. For boarders, the resort has a large and well-equipped snowboard park with a banked slalom course, rails, jumps, and other obstacles.

Facilities are good, and they include day care. The snowmaking capabilities here are excellent, and the ski school is notable, though I hear so crowded it's difficult to get in during spring break. This is a good spot for families with varying interests. While some ski and board, others can cross-country ski, fish, and even ride horses if weather permits.

Pajarito Mountain Ski Area

8 miles west of Los Alamos on NM 4. ☎ 505/662-5725. 37 trails (20% beginner, 50% intermediate, 30% expert); 6 lifts including 1 quad, 1 triple, 3 doubles, 1 surface; 1,200-ft. vertical drop. Lift hrs: 9am–4pm on Wed, Sat, Sun, and federal holidays. Open daily from Christmas–New Year's. Full-day adult lift tickets $34.

For years this was a private mountain run by a ski club that never advertised, and though anyone could ski the area, few non-egghead-Los-Alamos-scientist types did. Recently, the club has begun promoting the mountain more, but it still retains its secretive ambiance, highlighted by very few people and sparsely groomed runs. With a breakdown of 30% expert, 50% intermediate and 20% beginner runs you can see why this place doesn't appeal to the masses. On a good year you'll find plenty of snow here, but since the base elevation is only 9,031 feet, the ski area may not even open on a dry year.

The mountain has a very simple layout. Runs come down one north-facing slope. For those who like the workout a good bump run provides, you'll be elated with this mountain. Intermediate and beginner skiers might be disappointed in the lack of broad, groomed runs here, and thus may want to head to somewhere more resorty like Angel Fire. Or if you'd prefer to push yourself, the ski school is good, and the new lodge at the base will provide a little rest after the torture.

Sipapu Ski and Summer Resort

25 miles southeast of Taos on NM 518 in Tres Ritos Canyon. ☎ 505/587-2240. 20 trails (20% beginner, 60% intermediate, 20% advanced); 3 lifts including 1 triple and 2 surface; 865-ft. vertical drop. Full-day adult tickets $31.

The oldest ski area in the Taos region, founded in 1952, Sipapu prides itself on being a small local area, especially popular with schoolchildren. Unfortunately, beginners are limited to only a few runs here, as are advanced skiers. Still, it's a nice little area, tucked way back in the mountains, with excellent lodging rates. Be aware that since the elevation is fairly low, runs get very icy.

Ski Rio

50 miles north of Taos on NM 522 and NM 196 in the village of Costilla. ☎ 800/2-ASK-RIO or 505/758-7707. 83 trails (30% beginner, 50% intermediate, 20% expert); 6 lifts include 3 chairs and 3 surface lifts; 2,150-ft. vertical drop. Full-day adult lift tickets $30.

Just south of the Colorado border in Costilla is Ski Rio, a broad (and often cold and windy) ski area that can't quite get over its financial problems. In fact, you'll want to call before driving up there, as the resort has been open intermittently over the years. It's a pity because there's a lot on this mountain. It ranges over a broad mountain area with lots of catwalk trails winding about and leading to some nice wide runs. There are also snowboard and snow-skate parks, as well as 13 miles of cross-country trails. The resort has one of the best snowboard parks in the area, and occasionally holds national competitions. You won't likely find crowds, even on holidays. At the ski base you can rent skis, snowboards, snowshoes, and snow skates. Also at the base are lodgings, restaurants, and a sports shop. Sleigh rides, dogsled tours, and snowmobile tours are also available. The ski school offers private and group clinics (for adults and children) in cross-country and downhill skiing, snow skating, and snowboarding.

FISHING

Within this small region of the Rocky Mountains are over 4,000 miles of coldwater streams suitable for trout, along with many lakes and reservoirs. With that many miles of streams you can usually find a place to fish any time of year. Along with the fine fishing, many of the spots listed below are within spectacular scenery, with plenty of wildlife about.

Your contact for fly-fishing in this area is **High Desert Angler,** 435 S. Guadalupe St. (☎ **505/98-TROUT**), not far from the Plaza in Santa Fe. A very congenial and knowledgeable staff there can provide you with guide service and excellent instruction, equipment rental, all manner of tackle and accessories, and friendly, expert advice. An additional excellent source for fly-fishing in northern New Mexico is *Fly-Fishing in Northern New Mexico,* edited by Craig Martin (UNM Press, 1991).

East of Santa Fe the **Pecos River** flows down from 13,000-foot peaks of the Sangre de Cristo Mountains. Within these waters is some of New Mexico's best rainbow and brown trout fishing. Many of these streams are accessed by trails only. To reach these sections you'll want to take off from any of the campgrounds near Cowles, which is near Pecos, off I-25 east of Santa Fe. Others, however, have easy road access, also in the area of Cowles. The area from the village of Terrero to the village of Cowles provides excellent mountain stream fishing, but can get crowded with fishers. However, if you hike away from the road a little ways you'll find solitude.

Also in the Sangre de Cristo range, but toward the north end of the Pecos Wilderness is the **Rio Santa Barbara.** Named for the patroness of those who faced danger and sudden death, the river has a wild quality, but it's not hazardous. Instead you'll find it to be broad, clear, and rambling. The area has seen little logging and is full of wildlife, pines, and native trout—some of the best cutthroat fishing in New Mexico. You can park at the Santa Barbara Campground reached from NM 75 in Peñasco and NM 73, to FS 116, the latter of which is a well-maintained all-weather road. You'll probably want to fish the 3 miles of river below the campground. While the area adjacent to the campground is heavily fished, the river holds plenty of fish to accommodate. Another option is to fish the upper Santa Barbara, reached not by hiking along the river but by hiking on Trail 24. You'll have the option of fishing the Middle Fork, which is steep and makes catching fish difficult, or the more gentle West Fork, as well as the narrow canyon before you reach the forks. The hike into these waters is well worth it on a summer day when the cutthroats are biting and the wildflowers are blooming against the backdrop of mountain peaks. As well as cutthroats you'll find rainbows and browns. With most of the Santa Barbara watershed above 9,000 feet, the prime season for fishing here is after spring run-off from July through September.

The **Jemez River** area north of Albuquerque and west of Los Alamos offers a number of lovely trout streams. Though at the height of the season these easily accessed waterways can get crowded, on weekdays and evenings you're likely to find solitude, especially if you fish here in winter, which is a good time to be on these sunny banks. Don't expect crystal clear streams, though. Various factors, including the presence of volcanic ash, make these waters fairly turbid. To fish the Jemez River itself you can pull off of NM 4 at a number of places. Here you'll likely catch 8- to 12-inch rainbows and possibly some wild browns. You'll also find rainbows and wild browns nearby in the **East Fork of the Jemez River,** accessed on NM 4 between Los Alamos and Jemez Springs. What's outstanding about this stream is that it runs through the middle of a volcanic crater 14 miles in diameter that originated in a series of eruptions that scattered debris as far away as Oklahoma about a million years ago. Especially for novice fishers who like plenty of open space for casting, the upper section of the **Rio San Antonio** is a good spot. Here you'll find average length 9-inch rainbow and brown trout. The uppermost 2 miles of public water on the Rio San Antonio are designated Special Trout Water. Access is from NM 126 and FS 376, about 5 miles in on a well-maintained dirt road.

For those who like their fishing doused with a bit of culture, the mighty **Rio Grande** offers up trout and history in handsome doses. One of the best ways to catch a bit of both is by fishing in the area around Pilar. Though most fishers find it a very challenging river, it is quite fishable. One of the best features of the Rio Grande is you can fish year-round. Because of the geology of the area and the amount of water that is irrigation return, the Rio is rarely clear, but don't let the cloudiness deter you. You'll pass through a charming northern New Mexico village, full of adobe houses, centuries-old apple orchards, and tiny cornfields, and step onto shores much more accessible than those of the Rio Grande Gorge (which I discuss below). This section, the Orilla Verde Recreation Area, is located just off of NM 68 between Española and Taos. You'll turn on NM 570 at the village of Pilar. There's plenty of streamside parking and developed campsites available. Most of the fish in this area are stocked rainbows in the 8- to 20-inch range. You're also likely to catch browns here as well as cutthroat-rainbow hybrids. Some like to try their luck fishing for the voracious carnivores Northern Pike on the Rio, best fished with good heavy equipment from late December into the spring. This section is best fished in October, November, January, and February, times when the run-off has subsided and the waters are cool.

As one of this river's most notable sections, the **Rio Grande Gorge** was named the country's first National Wild and Scenic River in 1968. Even with such movement toward protection, the Rio faces a precarious future. With increased urban and farming pressure to use its waters, at times the river barely flows at all. And yet, in the waters described below, you'll find it's New Mexico's wildest trout stream, with many lunker brows, rainbows, and cutbows in a spectacular setting.

This rocky and steep terrain may require an 800- to 1,000-foot descent to the river and ascent back out. The entire section has been designated Special Trout Water. One of the most accessible ways into the Gorge is through the Wild and Scenic River Recreation Area, accessed by NM 522 north of Taos. Turn on NM 378 and follow the signs. Here you'll hike about 1 mile from rim to river along switchbacks that put the angler within range of 4 miles of stream. Except during spring run-off this section can be fished year-round. The **La Junta Run** is a legendary 10-mile long section that runs from the river's confluence with the Red River downstream to the John Dunn Bridge. This section is remote, with lots of boulders to climb over, but it has some excellent fishing for trout that average 16 inches or more. You can reach the La Junta section at the river's confluence with the Red River, or from the Cebolla Mesa Campground south of Questa. But the best fly-fishing is at **Cedar Springs,** located in the middle of the run. Get there by crossing the John Dunn Bridge and following the rim road north for 3.5 miles until you reach the Cedar Spring trailhead. If you'd like to float this section of the river, contact a commercial outfitter or the **BLM (☎ 505/438-7400)**. Below this section runs the Taos Box, 18 miles of river most known by rafters and kayakers. Access is difficult, but experienced guides do take fishers in through several difficult trails. One access point is at John Dunn Bridge at the north end of the Box as well as from NM 570 on the south end of the section at the BLM's Orilla Verde Recreation Area. If you're interested in floating the Taos Box, see the "White-Water Kayaking" and "White-Water Rafting" sections later in this chapter.

Flowing down from the 13,161-foot Wheeler Peak, and meandering through the resort town, which is its namesake, the **Red River** is a good place to go if you're looking for large trout. Basically there are two main sections of interest. The upper section is a classic freestone stream, descending fairly rapidly often through narrow canyons. Nearer to its confluence with the Rio Grande it takes on a character like its mother river, flowing through a canyon, steep and gorgy. Ten miles of the Red have been killed by the Molycorp Molybdenum Mine, beginning at the mine and going down to the Red River Hatchery near the town of Questa. The upper section of the Red can be reached through the town of Red River on NM 38, while the lower section can be reached either from the Red River Hatchery on NM 515, or from the Rio Grande Wild and Scenic Recreation Area north of Questa, via NM 522 and NM 378. From the La Junta or the El Aguaje campgrounds hike a mile from the rim to the river, descending about 800 feet. Best times for fishing are mid-June to July and September to March.

Farther north still, anglers can find sheer bliss in the little-traveled area of **Valle Vidal,** reached from NM 522 to NM 196. In this mountainous, elk-filled country you'll find two creeks of note as well as many smaller tributaries. Be aware, though, that the season for Valle Vidal is limited to July 1 through December 31 in order to protect the native cutthroats during their spawning season. The cutthroats are further protected by a catch-and-release designation for all waters within Valle Vidal. Only flies and artificial lures with single, barbless hooks, are permitted and all fish must be immediately released. Your first option is **Costilla Creek,** an especially nice flow of water during summer when other New Mexico streams are too low and warm for fishing. The Costilla runs through high mountains, across meadows and into canyons, and is best fished from July to late September.

Nearby is **Comanche Creek,** an excellent place to find cutthroats, but they are wily, so take care in your approach. Access is about 2 miles from the Carson National Forest boundary on FS 1950. You'll find fishing along the road as well as more secluded areas upstream. Don't expect to find big fish here; most of the cutthroats are in the 7- to 11-inch range. If you're interested in landing some monsters, though, head to **Shuree Ponds,** also in the Valle Vidal. Oversized rainbows and hybrid Rio Grande cutthroats can run 20 inches or more. These are also maintained as Special Trout Waters, and the same season applies. The daily bag and possession is 2 fish over 15 inches. There's a pond here designated especially for children under 12.

The **Rio Chama** and **Rio Brazos** offer some of the most lush and scenic surroundings of any rivers in New Mexico. The Chama has many identities, from a small tumbling stream where it crosses the border from Colorado to a heavier-flowing river that carves through deep canyons. Along its way it passes through the El Vado Lake and Abiquiu Lake. Likewise, it runs through both public and private land. The Upper Rio Chama runs from beneath Chama Peak to the Rio Chama Wildlife Area, a 50-mile stretch, reached from various points around the town of Chama. Fishing is best here from late spring through early fall, and the catch will be mostly rainbows and wild browns. Downstream are various tailwater fisheries of the Rio Chama, the most notable being the one below El Vado Dam reached through the El Vado Ranch, from U.S. 84 and NM 112, an area that can be heavily fished but is also heavily stocked. The **Rio Brazos** is most known for its wild brown trout. Unfortunately, the river runs mostly through private land; there's only about 1 mile of river open to the public. This stretch is located off U.S. 64 and NM 512. But many private lodges in the area offer fishing packages worth checking out. A couple of note are **The Timbers at Chama** (see the "Campgrounds & Other Accommodations" later in this chapter) and **The Lodge at Chama.**

Some of the best fly-fishing in the state can be found on the **Jicarilla Apache Indian Reservation** north of Chama. In order to fish on waters such as the **Navajo River** or the **Jicarilla Lakes,** you must purchase a tribal fishing permit at the Best Western Jicarilla Inn, the General Store, or the Tribal Game and Fish Office, all in Dulce accessed via U.S. 64. The fees vary. While on the reservation, be sure to respect the customs and traditions of the tribe.

For those who enjoy lake fishing there are a number of options as well. North of Taos at **Cabresto Lake** wild cutthroat and brook trout swim, and can be caught after a 20-minute drive on a rough dirt road. This 15-acre lake is easily fishable from shore. It can get crowded, so the very best times are in May and September, when summer crowds have left. Access the lake from the village of Questa via NM 38, FS 134, and FS 134A. Some sources name the **Eagle Nest Lake** situated in the broad Moreno Valley not far from Taos one of New Mexico's best trout lakes. Under its 1,500 surface acres of water are plenty of cutthroat trout, rainbows, and kokanee salmon that can be fished from miles of public shoreline or from a boat. Access the lake off U.S. 64 northeast of Taos. The best fishing is May to early July and September to October, though some enjoy ice fishing in midwinter as well. If you're careful to miss the busy summer season, **Fenton Lake,** west of Los Alamos, is a pretty 30-acre mountain reservoir full of rainbow and brown trout. No motor boats are allowed, and there is plenty of shore fishing. The lake is well equipped for anglers with disabilities, with easily accessed fishing piers. Your best bet here is to fish in May and September to November. Access is from NM 4 and NM 126.

Even though it sits at 9,800 feet, **Hopewell Lake** in the Chama area is easily accessed by paved road. It's located directly off U.S. 64, 20 miles east of Tierra Amarilla. At this 15-acre reservoir you'll find lots of brook trout biting early in the season and rainbows throughout the warmer months. There's plenty of room to cast from shore, and boating is limited to electric trolling motors or oars. This is a good family lake, with a safe trail leading around it, where kids can explore. It's best fished from May to September.

Canjilon Lakes is comprised of 6 small ponds at 9,900-foot elevation. Located 12 miles northeast of Canjilon (south of Tierra Amarilla) via FS 559 and 129, these lakes have fair to good fishing, but not great. The lakes tend to get weedy as the summer grows hotter. These ponds are put and take, meaning the local hatchery regularly puts in rainbow, and the anglers take them out. A fishing derby is held in early June.

Lake Katherine, Spirit Lake, and **Stewart Lake** are hidden back in the reaches of the Pecos Wilderness. Lake Katherine is a glacial lake at the base of Santa Fe Baldy, while Spirit and Stewart are pine-surrounded lakes formed in mountain depressions. In all three, casting is easy from the banks, and you'll find stocked rainbows and cutthroats. Since these lakes are so high they're best fished in June to August. All three can be reached on the Windsor Trail either from the Windsor Creek Campground near Cowles or from the Santa Fe Ski Area.

If you like a challenge and long to fish for wild cutthroats, you may want to head to **Latir Lakes** north of Taos. Since these nine lakes that stair-step down the steep sides of Latir Peak are owned by the Rio Costilla Cooperative Livestock Association, you'll need to obtain a permit from its office in Costilla. While there, ask which lake has the current best fishing. Access is via NM 518 and NM 196, 6 miles past Ski Rio; from there it's a 6-mile very rough 4-wheel drive in to the lakes, best fished from June to September. **San Gregorio Reservoir** is an easily accessed meadow-framed lake in the San Pedro Parks Wilderness Area in the Jemez Mountains. A 20-minute hike in discourages the hoards, leaving the more fleet-footed plenty of hatchery-raised rainbows and some cutthroat hybrids. Access is easiest from Cuba. Follow NM 126 and FS 164. Best fishing is from April to May and September.

HIKES & BACKPACK TRIPS

Take one glance at a good map of north central New Mexico and you'll quickly see why this is such a great place to hike. Much of the area is national forest and wilderness. In fact, 3 of the state's 5 national forests lie within this region, including the Carson, with 1.5 million acres; the Santa Fe, with 1.5 million acres and over 1,000 miles of trails; and the Cíbola, with 1.6 million acres. Each holds many acres of designated wilderness as well. What this amounts to besides plenty of land to explore is a good dispersion of people, allowing hikers many options. If you like to hit the must-do hikes in an area, you can expect to find some crowds, but if you like to get away from it all, you can head to a more remote region. I've tried to include a little of both here.

Piedra Lisa Spring Trail

1–10 miles round-trip. 2,000-ft. elevation gain. Allow 1–4 hrs. Access: From I-25, 15 miles north of Albuquerque take the Placitas exit. Drive east for just over 3 miles (watch for 3-mile marker) to FS 445. Turn right on FS 445 and drive 2 miles to a sign pointing to the Piedra Lisa Spring trailhead parking lot. The trail leaves from the south end of the parking lot. Map: Cíbola National Forest–Sandia Mountain Wilderness.

This is one of those treks that gets more and more exciting as you go along. It traverses the Sandia Mountain foothills, providing hikable conditions almost year-round. The trail begins through a wash. Shortly it starts its ascent through a small canyon. The route throughout is fairly steep and, at times, rocky. As it makes its way into the mountains the bold Sandia Crest breaks into view, as do other peaks, shard-like slabs of granite that stop you in your tracks. The trail works its way south, paralleling the crest for some miles, until it reaches the Rincon Saddle and drops back down toward the Juan Tabo Picnic Area on the north end of Albuquerque. This is a good place to start the trek as well, though more hikers will be on this part of the trail. Either direction provides a good point-to-point hike (if you have a shuttle inclination) or an out-and-back, since the views heading down are as pretty as those on the way up.

Hawk Watch Trail

2 miles round-trip. Moderate to difficult. 1,185-ft. elevation gain. Allow 2 hrs. Access: Drive east from Albuquerque on I-40 to the Carnuel exit (about 10 minutes from town center). Take NM 333 east into Tijeras Canyon for 2 miles, looking for a development on the left named Montecello. Turn into the development and follow the signs about 1.5 miles (turning left onto FS 522 en route) to the Three Gun Spring Trail 194. Map: Cíbola National Forest–Sandia Mountain Wilderness.

This steep hike into the Sandia Mountains is a birder's dream; from early March through early May these arid lands are the playground for innumerable hawks, kites, falcons, eagles, and other raptors, who spend their days riding the currents that blow up this old volcanic face. Most are migrating northward, and members of the Hawk Watch team are there to monitor their course and their count. The trail leads up to a stone platform where volunteers sit for at least 7 hours a day counting birds. On another outcropping above the platform, other volunteers sit within a blind, with nets rigged to catch the raptors so they can band them and thus track their health and habits. These Hawk Watch team members are very friendly; in fact they may be just bored enough up there day after day to welcome company. They will show you a board listing their bird counts—when we were there around mid-season, they'd already had 139 golden eagle sightings. That day, which was slow, they had banded 4 birds; on a good day they will band 30 birds; but the typical count is about 12.

Begin at the Three Gun Springs Trail 194 and hike for 0.5 miles until you enter the wilderness. At that point turn right at the Hawk Watch sign and head first down into a wash, then fairly relentlessly up hill. The trail does some switchbacking, climbs through some large granite boulders, and finally reaches the pedestal on the left. Ask the team members permission to see if you can go up to the banding blind, though be aware that the hike up is very steep with poor footing. Return the way you came.

North Crest Trail

11 miles or less. Moderate. 400-ft. elevation gain. Allow 2–5 hrs. Access: On the east side of the Sandia Mountains. From NM 14 turn northwest on NM 536 and drive for 13.6 miles until you come to the Sandia Crest parking lot. Map: USGS Placitas, Sandia Crest, and Tijeras quads.

This trail takes you along the crest of this spectacular formation allowing views of both the steep west side and the gradually sloping east side. You'll pass bold granite crags and marvel at 360° views of New Mexico. *Beware:* The wind can howl up here, especially in spring, so wear appropriate gear.

The trail is only moderately steep. It heads north from NM 536 on Trail 130 below television and radio antennas and power lines. Then it descends through trees, reaching the Cañon del Agua Overlook at mile 2. Here you'll have views across the Rio Grande Valley to

Mount Taylor, Cabezon, and the Jemez Mountains. At this point you have the option of doing a loop, heading back on the 10K trail or the Survey Trail, but I prefer to do an out-and-back, and enjoy the views. The North Crest Trail continues to a second overlook, then heads back into the trees as it leaves the rim of the mountains. You can continue from here to the north Del Agua Overlook at about mile 3. Then the trail leaves the rim and begins switchbacks down the east side of the mountains into Gambel oak forests and later into piñon-juniper. If you're making this an overnight, you can follow this trail all the way to Tunnel Springs near the village of Placitas, accessed from FS 231. However, for that trip you'll need to arrange a shuttle. If you decide to make a loop with the 10K trail you'll have to follow the paved road for 2 miles back to the Crest. If you're doing an out-and-back, you can turn back anywhere. Just be aware of your time and canteen levels.

A much longer variation on this hike begins at the trailhead for the South Crest Trail off I-25 at Canyon Estates and eventually connects with the North Crest Trail. The trail travels 28 miles over the arced crest of the Sandias and ends at Tunnel Springs. This is a rigorous 2- to 3-day backpack trip, for which you'll want to carry plenty of water, as springs are few.

La Luz Trail

15 miles round-trip, or 9 miles with tramway ride. Strenuous. 3,900-ft. elevation gain. Allow 1 full day. Access: From I-40 take the Tramway Blvd. exit and follow that road north 9.8 miles to paved FS 333. Follow FS 333 for 2.5 miles to the trailhead at the upper end of the Juan Tabo Picnic Ground. Tramway Blvd. can also be accessed from I-25 north of Albuquerque. Map: Cíbola National Forest–Sandia Mountain Wilderness.

This is the most notable hike in the Sandias because the trail scales the jagged exposed side of these mountains created from massive faulting. You'll pass through several of the West's major life zones, from the semi-arid grasslands and piñon-juniper forests of the Upper Sonoran to the ponderosa pines of the Transition, to the Douglas fir, aspen, and blue spruce of the Canadian Life Zone. On the crest you'll come to the Engelmann spruce and sub-alpine firs, which characterize the Hudsonian Zone. And you'll be able to see across much of New Mexico and bordering states. Such an elevation gain comes with a cost. Here it is strenuous hiking that is relentless. Trail 137 is well marked and well-worn; be aware that you will likely encounter plenty of other hikers along the way.

You'll begin with a moderate grade and soon come to many switchbacks. At about mile 3 the trail crosses La Cueva Canyon where you may find some running water, but don't depend on it. The trail gets steeper, making its way up a canyon through towering cliffs of reddish granite. At about mile 7, you'll reach the junction with Trail 84, the Crest Spur Trail, which you'll want to follow to Sandia Crest, a steep 0.5 miles more. Here you'll find lots of people, a gift shop, and radio towers. If you're hiking the whole way, you'll descend the way you came.

There are a few other options. One is to eat dinner at the High Finance restaurant, which has spectacular views overlooking the Rio Grande Valley. If you do that, or even if just don't want to hike down, you'll want to either have arranged a car shuttle down the back side, or you can catch the tram down and hike 2 miles along the base of the Sandias back to your car. To reach the restaurant and the tram, you won't hike all the way to the Crest. Instead, when you reach the junction with Trail 84, don't turn, but instead continue on the La Luz Trail for an additional 1 mile to the tramway. The ride lasts 15 minutes and is quite spectacular. When you reach the base, you'll find the return trail (Tramway #82) at the northeast corner of the parking lot. Head through a forest of granite boulders and skirt along the foot of the Sandias passing near homes. After about 2 miles this trail intersects with the La Luz Trail, which will lead you back to your car.

Tent Rocks Canyon Trail
3 miles round-trip. Easy. 200-ft. elevation gain. Allow 2–4 hrs. Access: Take I-25 south from Santa Fe or North from Albuquerque to the Cochiti Exit, number 264. Head west on NM 16 for about 8 miles until you reach a T intersection. Turn right onto NM 22 and follow this road for 1.8 miles. Turn right on FS 266. Drive this bumpy but passable (for most cars) road for 4.8 miles, where you'll see the BLM sign and parking area for Tent Rocks. $5 self-pay fee. Map: USGS Cañada.

This is where the Martians who landed in Roswell set up camp, or so it seems when you first lay eyes on the eerily shaped land formations, a scape of stone teepees and wind- and rain-sculpted labyrinthine canyons. Though this hike is relatively short in terms of distance, I've spent many hours here simply gawking. The trail begins at the parking area and follows National Recreation Trail signposts about 100 yards to a junction. Bear right here. At about 0.5 miles you'll head into an arroyo, which leads into the narrowing canyon. Just before reaching the mouth of the canyon the trail splits; the left fork will take you along the tops of the cliffs, while the right will go into the canyon. Either route is spectacular, but I prefer the lower one, which takes you into the labyrinth. The trail widens and narrows, passing between high walls of banded volcanic deposits. At one point you'll have to crawl under a boulder. At 1.2 miles, a primitive trail continues up a razorback ridge to the upper mesa and a lookout point, and the end of the hike. Those with children or without incentive may want to stop the hike and head back without ascending. However the view from the top will give you a look at the formations from above as well as at the nearby Tetilla Peak and Cochiti Lake.

Atalaya Mountain
6 miles round-trip. Moderate. 1,800-ft. elevation gain. Allow 3–4 hrs. Access: From downtown Santa Fe, take Alameda heading east. You'll pass through a number of stop signs and up a long hill. Turn left at the entrance to St. John's College. Take your first right toward the college, then make a quick left into the parking lot. At the east end of the parking lot is the trailhead. Map: USGS Santa Fe.

If you're in Santa Fe and don't have time to head deeper into the mountains, this is an ideal hike. It gets you up and away from life's complexities very quickly and offers incredible views of Santa Fe and much of western New Mexico. Because the sun shines on the trail, it's hikable year-round, though summer months can be hot. The trail dives quickly down to an arroyo, which you'll follow, watching to the east (left) for the trail markers, which will begin your ascent. At 0.9 miles it crosses a dirt road, where cars move quickly, so watch your dogs. At mile 1.4 it intersects Trail 170, an alternate branch of the Atalaya Trail. Make a note of this intersection; on the way down you do not want to veer off that way or you'll end up at another trailhead. Continue upward as the trail contours around the southwest slope of the mountain. The trail is obvious the rest of the way until you get to the ridgeline at mile 2.5. There you'll turn left and continue 0.4 miles to the summit, where you can sit on one of the outcroppings and enjoy the view.

Borrego Trail
4-mile loop. Easy to moderate. 760-ft. elevation gain. Allow 2–3 hrs. Access: Take Hyde Park Rd./NM 475 northeast of Santa Fe (toward Santa Fe Ski Area). Drive 8.3 miles to the trailhead. Look for a small parking area on the left. Map: USGS Aspen Basin.

Though this trail offers few views, it does traverse through a variety of types of terrain from thick Douglas fir forest down through ponderosas, to sparse desert and mountain riparian. It's also a great trail run. The trail makes 150 twists down through the woods and becomes wide, descending slowly. After about a half-mile, it forks, with the Borrego Trail to the right; you'll return on the left fork. The trail is well marked. It climbs for awhile, then descends, switchbacking, down to Tesuque Creek. Cross the creek and you'll soon come to the Windsor Trail, where you turn left. Travel down this trail for a mile (you'll think you've gone too far) watching for the Bear Wallow sign to turn you back to your left. You'll cross the creek again and head up switchbacks for awhile until you enter the deep forest again. The ascent from here is gradual and the old conifers and aspens lovely. After a mile you'll come to the fork that took you to the right before. Continue straight back to your car.

Windsor Trail to Spirit Lake, Santa Fe Baldy, & Lake Katharine

6–14 miles round-trip. Strenuous. 2,760–3,200-ft. elevation gain. Allow 1 full day–2 days. Take Hyde Park Rd./NM 475 northeast of Santa Fe 15 miles to the parking area at the base of Santa Fe Ski Area where a sign indicates the trailhead for the Windsor Trail 254. Map: USGS Aspen Basin.

I'm lumping these three hikes together because they share the Windsor Trail to a high meadow called Puerto Nambe and then branch out from there. Any of the three will offer spectacular views and lush mountain meadows. All three will be relatively crowded. Since these trails are so accessible to Santa Fe, they are popular destinations especially on weekends and holidays. Spirit Lake is the easiest of the three, with some steep switchbacks in two points but lots of easy trail in between. Though it's a bit of a strain to the 12,622-foot peak of Santa Fe Baldy, this is an ideal day hike if you're really looking for a workout. As for Lake Katharine, I've hiked there and back in a day, but it was a strain. It's the one of the three I'd plan for an overnight.

The Windsor Trail 254 climbs steeply for the first half-mile, levels off into some high meadows and crosses the Rio Nambe and a few of its tributaries, then climbs switchbacks to a lovely high meadow known as Puerto Nambe. You will have traveled 4 miles. To get to Spirit Lake, stay on the Windsor Trail 254 heading east. The trail drops slowly, traversing a forested south-facing slope. A mile from the saddle, cross a short spur ridge, then drop down into the lake basin. As is the policy with most water sources in the Pecos Wilderness, you must camp at least 200 feet from shore.

To get to Lake Katharine and Santa Fe Baldy (from Puerto Nambe) turn left (north) at the junction with the Skyline Trail 251. The trail switchbacks to an 11,600-foot saddle. To get to Santa Fe Baldy, turn left at the saddle and follow a ridge to the summit (there's no real trail here). The last section is the most strenuous, climbing more than 1,000 feet in 1 mile. Once on top you'll enjoy 360° views across Northern New Mexico. To the north you'll see Wheeler Peak, New Mexico's highest at 13,161, and to the south, sitting alone in the center of the Rio Grande Rift, 11,301-foot Mount Taylor.

To get to Lake Katharine (from the saddle), continue north, and down into the impression on the other side. The descent is steep and leads to a clear mountain lake surrounded by pines. As is the case with Spirit Lake, you'll have to camp at least 200 feet from shore. Fly fishers enjoy the trout in the lake, and those who like cold water will be invigorated by a dip. These trails are accessible to hikers from mid-June to Mid-September, and are best hiked in June and early July before the monsoon season turns late afternoons electric with thunder action.

Pecos Baldy and the Truchas Peaks

17–27 miles round-trip. Difficult. 3,679–4,062-ft. elevation gain. Allow 2–4 days. Access: From Santa Fe take I-25 north toward Las Vegas for 15 miles. Exit at Glorieta Exit 299. Follow the signs toward Pecos. At Pecos village turn left on NM 63, which leads north into the Pecos River Valley. Drive to the village of Cowles. Continue past Cowles until you reach the Jack's Creek Campground. Map: Santa Fe National Forest Pecos Wilderness.

Pecos Baldy is renowned for the number of big horn sheep that feed in the area. The population is so dense the sheep can even be a nuisance, disturbing any gear left unattended. Considerably farther along, the Truchas Peaks dominate the skyline. These massive land formations are set around a tremendous bowl, the peaks held together by vast saddles. From atop them you can see well into Colorado, Utah, and Arizona, as well as down into the lush Rio Grande Valley.

From Jack's Creek Campground, take Trail 25 climbing northeast through pine forest to the wilderness boundary. At about mile 2 you'll reach the junction with Trail 257, where you'll turn left. Continue through meadows and aspen groves until you cross Jack's Creek. Shortly you'll come to another trail junction. Bear right staying on Trail 257, which will lead you right up to Pecos Baldy Lake. Before the lake, however, you'll come to the junction with Trail 251 to your left. This will lead you to Trail 275, which climbs steeply along a series of switchbacks to the top of 12,529-foot East Pecos Baldy. If you intend to continue north to the Truchas Peaks, you'll back track to Pecos Baldy Lake and head north from there on Trail 251. Some people choose to set up a base camp near the lake (regulations 200 feet away) and make their trip to the Truchas Peaks a day hike. In any event, you'll head north, pass through long, level meadows atop the ridge known as Trail Riders Wall. At 7.1 miles Trail 251 ends at Truchas Lakes. Though you can't camp at the lakes, you'll find plenty of spots nearby. To the west of the lakes you'll find a faint trail winding steeply up to a saddle on the ridge of the peaks. From here you can reach both Middle Truchas Peak, 13,064 feet and South Truchas Peak, 13,102 feet. You'll have to scramble some to ascend North Truchas, 13,024 feet. From the peaks you'll look down into a perfectly formed bowl below.

Hamilton Mesa, Beatty's Cabin, and Pecos Falls

6–16 miles round-trip. Easy to difficult. 1,000–1,640-ft. elevation gain. Allow 3 hrs.–2 days. Access: From Santa Fe take I-25 north toward Las Vegas for 15 miles. Exit at Glorieta Exit 299. Follow the signs toward Pecos. At Pecos village turn left on NM 63, which leads north into the Pecos River Valley. Drive 18.5 miles to the village of Terrero, pass it and watch for FS 223 on your right, which goes to the Iron Gate Campground. You'll travel this steep, rough road for 4 miles. If the road is wet or muddy you'll need four-wheel drive. Once you reach Iron Gate, continue to the far end of the campground where you'll see the trailhead for Trail 249. Maps: USFS Pecos Wilderness; USGS Elk Mountain.

If you're a sucker for high mountain meadows, this is your hike. In fact, one of the most beautiful scenes I've ever encountered remains etched in my memory. The phenomenon happens each June, and the window of opportunity only lasts about a week. It's the wild iris blooming. After hiking broad and well-used trails for 2.5 miles, the terrain opens out onto Hamilton Mesa, a vast meadow reminiscent of *The Sound of Music* that's full—and I mean full—of lovely purple irises, as well as lots of wild onions worth munching as you make your way across, with the oft-snow covered peaks (Pecos Baldy, Santa Fe Baldy, and Lake Peak) marking the western skyline. Whether you manage to catch the irises blooming or not, though, this is a lovely hike. The Hamilton Mesa day hike can end anywhere you choose to plop down for lunch or a snack on this broad meadow, or you can choose to venture onward.

From the start of Trail 249 the route gently zigzags through the woods in a broad trail with a slight rise. At 0.5 miles the trail turns left and parallels a ridge. At 1.5 miles you'll reach the intersection with Trail 250. Take the left fork. At 2 miles from the start, pass through a gate, and soon you'll leave the aspens and get your first glimpse of these magnificent high meadows. This meadow is long and broad, and you'll continue across it for another mile to a trail junction. At this point you can decide whether to go to Beatty's Cabin or Pecos Falls. To get to Beatty's Cabin, bear left on Trail 260 toward the northwest. You'll enter the woods and descend for about 2 miles to the Pecos River. Cross the river and find a spot on the grass to eat lunch. If you intend to camp, you'll want to continue on the trail climbing at least 200 feet above the river basin, per wilderness guidelines. Fishing in the Pecos is good, as is bathing if you like icy water. Don't look for a cabin, though—there no longer is one.

If you decide to take the longer trip from Hamilton Mesa to Pecos Falls, you'll take the right fork, continuing on Trail 249. The trail follows a 10,200-foot contour through meadows and aspen groves for about 5 miles to the falls. During spring run-off these falls can be spectacular. You'll enjoy this hike most in early June when the irises are blooming and in late September when the aspens burn yellow and orange. From late October through April snow will make it impassable.

Wheeler Peak

15 miles round-trip. Difficult. 3,700-ft. elevation gain. Allow 10–12 hrs. Access: From Taos, head north on U.S. 64 for 3 miles to the junction with NM 150. Turn right and follow the signs for the Taos Ski Area. Drive 15 miles and park in the upper lot at the ski area near an information board. Maps: USGS Wheeler Peak; USFS Latir and Wheeler Peak Wilderness.

This is a good hike for those of us who like to get to the highest point, no matter where we are, just so we can see the true lay of the land. Unfortunately, lots of people like to get to the top of Wheeler, so it can be a busy place. Many people climb this 13,161-foot peak, New Mexico's highest, in one day. Others prefer an overnight, camping at William's Lake. There are two routes to the top. The most preferable begins in the upper parking lot of Taos Ski Valley on Bull of the Woods Trail 90. For the first 2 miles you'll climb fast on a rocky trail, which is crossed by other trails, but easy to follow because it's so worn. At mile 1.9, you'll come to a fork at Bull of the Woods Pasture where a sign points you toward the right. The next 4 miles to the summit are easy to follow. The last stretch hugs an exposed ridge, not a desirable place to be amidst a lightning storm, so take care. If you're climbing in late summer, make your ascent early in the morning, so you can avoid afternoon electrical storms. Snowstorms can hit this peak even in May and October. Another less marked route ascends from William's Lake and heads steeply up scree slopes to the top. The peak was named for U.S. Army Major George M. Wheeler, who, between 1871 and 1878 mapped much of New Mexico.

Bandelier National Monument

Few places in the world allow the luxury of backcountry wilderness hiking with encounters with ancient culture. However this kind of time-traveling is available all over northern New Mexico, but nowhere more than Bandelier. The ruins dated between 1100 and 1550 are situated in a series of three large canyons, with smaller canyons crossing them. The main excavated ruins and the visitor center are located in Frijoles Canyon. The steep-walled canyons are home to deer and elk, as well as other wildlife. They are lush with cottonwoods, box elders, ponderosa pines, and chokecherries. Hikes range from easy day-trips to strenuous 2- to 3-day backpack trips. There are many unexcavated sites in Bandelier. Remember do not walk or sit on walls or remove anything from the sites. Collecting cultural resources is a criminal offense subject to imprisonment and/or fines up to $100,000.

Yapashi Ruins, Stone Lions, and Frijoles Canyon
18-mile loop. Strenuous. 2,500-ft. elevation gain. Allow 2–3 days. Access: From Santa Fe, travel north on U.S. 84/285 to Pojoaque, then west toward Los Alamos on NM 502. At the junction with NM 4, turn south toward White Rock. Continue on NM 4 until you come to the sign for Bandelier. If you do this hike as an overnight, you must obtain a free permit at the visitor center. Entrance fee $10 per vehicle. Maps: USGS Frijoles; Trails Illustrated Bandelier National Monument.

This hike will take you on a large loop into the heart of the Bandelier Wilderness. On it you'll visit one of the largest pueblos on the Pajarito Plateau, now a series of mounds of rubble mingling with cholla cactus. The trail also passes by the sacred Stone Lions shrine, a site the Native Americans called the "Pueblo ruin where the mountain lions lie." It passes through steep canyons and along a rich riparian streambed.

Begin the hike from the trailhead across the creek from the visitor center. It starts with a steep climb out of Frijoles Canyon. Here, in the first third of the hike you'll embark on the most difficult climbs, crossing several steep canyons and arid plateaus. In this stretch you'll cross Alamo Canyon; at 600 feet deep, it's one of the toughest obstacles on the trip.

The trail crosses one more small canyon before arriving at the Yapashi Ruins. At this point you will have traveled 5.5 miles from the trailhead. These ruins offer a good chance to see what archaeologists first encounter, a rubble puzzle that the imagination must piece together. This pueblo was multistoried, and there were several kivas, which are visible. It is believed that the pueblo was occupied from 1200 to 1475. The Cochiti Indians regard it as one of their ancient homes. Another half-mile and you'll come to the Shrine of the Stone Lions. An enclosure of boulders surrounds two mountain lions carved into the tuff. Many of the details in the carvings have eroded, but the forms are still recognizable. The shrine served Indians from a large area, including the Keres, Tewa, and Jemez, as well as the Zuni far to the west. Native Americans in the area still leave offerings here. No camping is allowed within 0.25 miles of the ruins.

At the ruins, the trail forks. Stay right, following the sign to the Upper Crossing. A few hundred yards farther, the trail forks again. Stay right. The next half-mile climbs steeply up onto a high mesa, through a ponderosa forest. You'll continue hiking to the Upper Alamo Canyon crossing, about 9 miles into the hike (check at the visitor center before embarking to see if it is flowing). This is a good place to camp, but you'll want to move away from the stream. Continue following signs toward Upper Crossing for about 3 miles farther until the trail drops back down into Frijoles Canyon. From there the trail follows a stream while descending easily for 6 miles back to the visitor center. Along the way you'll pass the Ceremonial Cave, a spectacular kiva perched 140 feet above the canyon floor, accessed by pueblo-style ladders. No dogs or campfires are allowed in the canyons. This trail is hikable year-round, but is very hot in summer and cold in winter.

Cebolla Mesa

2–8 miles round-trip. Moderate. 1,300-ft. elevation gain. Allow 1½–4 hrs. Access: On U.S. 522 north of Taos, drive 16 miles to FS 9. Turn left onto this dirt road, passable to all vehicles when dry, and drive to its end and the trailhead, about 3.5 miles. Map: USGS Guadalupe Mountain.

The Rio Grande Gorge, one of New Mexico's most prominent features, 60 miles long and in places 1,000 feet deep, can be best experienced by hiking down into it. Carved by the Rio Grande River over thousands of years, it lays bare great sheets of lava that emanated from the volcanoes of the Taos Plateau. A good place to start a trip into the gorge is from Cebolla Mesa. The trail takes you fast into canyon's fold. It switchbacks down, passing a variety of vegetation, from Yucca to Douglas firs, for 1 mile, when it reaches the river. If you're looking for a short hike that's a good workout, you can turn around here. If you'd like to go longer, continue on and you'll come to a footbridge crossing the Red River into La Junta Campground. The trail climbs through the shelters and over a low ridge. It continues north past the Little Arsenic shelters. At 3.5 miles the trail ascends over a rock fall, then descends into Big Arsenic Campground, where there are shade trees and more shelters. To return, backtrack the way you came.

Valle Vidal

McCrystal Ranch Site

7 miles round-trip. Easy. 600-ft. elevation gain. Allow 2½–3 hrs. Access: Take NM 522 north from Taos 40 miles to Costilla. Turn east on NM 196. It will become FR 1950, which you'll follow to the McCrystal Creek Campground. You can also access FR 1950 from U.S. 64 northeast of Cimarron. Maps: USGS Van Bremmer Park and Ash Mountain.

This hike will take you into the heart of this mountainous region, following a creek lush with plant and animal life. From the campground, walk west along FR 1950 for 0.25 miles to a dirt road heading northwest. Bear right and you'll pass through a gate. Hike about 1 mile and you'll come to McCrystal Creek. The trail follows this creek, at one point passing by ruins of an old sawmill. While walking the creek keep an eye open for some of the 33 species of reptiles and amphibians and 15 kinds of fish that inhabit the Valle Vidal area. Follow the creek until it comes to another creek called Can Creek, at mile 2.6. Follow this for 0.25 miles as it descends down to the ruins of the John McCrystal Homestead, settled in the late 1800s. Return the way you came.

Ghost Ranch

One of artist Georgia O'Keeffe's haunts, this ranch is now owned by the Presbyterian Church. Its name is derived from local Spanish folklore and is called *El Rancho de los Brujos*, "Ranch of the Witches." There are three hikes well worth taking here. You'll park at the headquarters where you'll want to stop in at the Florence Hawley Ellis Museum of Anthropology and the Ruth Hall Museum of Paleontology. At the Ruth Hall Museum you'll meet Coelophysis, the earliest known dinosaur. In the museum you can watch a paleontologist dust away stone to find the small bones of this dinosaur known for its speed.

Kitchen Mesa

5 miles round-trip. Easy. 600-ft. elevation gain. Allow 3 hrs. Access: Take U.S. 84 north from Espanola about 25 miles to Abiquiu Dam. Continue for 6.3 miles to a sign on the right that reads Ghost Ranch on the north side of the highway. Follow the road to the office and let the staff know you're hiking. Continue on the road past the office and bear left toward the Teepee village. A sign will direct you to Kitchen Mesa, Box Canyon, and the parking lot for both trails. Map: USGS Ghost Ranch.

This is the classic Ghost Ranch hike. It follows along pale buttes, then climbs onto a high mesa, which offers views out across the Chama River Valley. From the parking area follow the dirt road a few yards down a short hill to the trailhead. The trail drops down a bank, across a bit of a stream, and through a small grove of trees. This trail is well marked with blue-painted coffee cans nailed onto wooden posts. It follows the riverbank, then joins a dirt road up a hill, then descends down to the valley floor. Next it climbs over a steep ridge. You'll stay along the base of sculpted Entrada sandstone cliffs, crossing an arroyo and then heading up a steep slope. Avoid taking any of the dead-end branches in this steeper section—follow the cans. Toward the top you'll have to scramble up a narrow passage between boulders, which is a bit of a technical move, especially for a dog or child who you might have to boost. From there the trail veers right, crosses an arroyo and ascends sandstone ledges to the top of the mesa. You'll see blue arrows painted on the rocks. Follow those across the chalky white sand of the Todilto Formation. Made of gypsum, it was deposited by a lake that evaporated millions of years ago. It's crumbly stuff, so don't poke your toes over the edges of the cliffs here unless you want an extra fast trip down and to the hospital. Once on the mesa you'll have views of Ghost Ranch, well-protected down in the canyon; Cerro Pedernal, the flat-topped peak to the south, made famous by painter Georgia O'Keeffe; and Los Viejos, the blue mesa to the northwest. All around you you'll see millions of years of geologic history laid out like giant time sandwiches, from the reddish purple Chinle Formation at the base to the tree-topped Dakota sandstone at the rim.

Chimney Rock

3 miles round-trip. Moderate. 700-ft. elevation gain. Allow 1½ hrs. Access: See Kitchen Mesa hike above. Map: USGS Ghost Ranch.

This hike offers a spectacular introduction to Ghost Ranch country, with startling views in all directions. The hike starts behind the maintenance shed near the visitor center and makes its way through an arroyo. It crosses through a gate and climbs on top of a mesa. Here, with spectacular desert views to distract you, you'll follow the well-marked trail across surreal landscapes painted white, red, and green. The trail is easy to follow. Once you arrive at the foot of the next mesa step, avoid turning left immediately. Instead keep your eye on the trail. It will slowly climb up the backside of the mesa and deliver you to the top. From there you make your way across to the lookout point above Chimney Rock. The experience can only be described as spiritual. This is a good winter hike, or spring and fall.

Rim Vista Trail

4.5 miles round-trip. Easy to moderate. 1,200-ft. elevation gain. Allow 2½–3 hrs. Access: Take U.S. 84 west from Española 37 miles to the junction with FR 151. Turn west and travel 0.7 miles to a sign reading Trail 15. Turn right and follow a two-track road 0.2 miles north to a rough parking area and the trailhead. The trail is marked by blue diamonds on trees. Map: USGS Echo Amphitheater.

This trail explores one of the most enchanting canyon areas in the Southwest, with stunning colors laid out in defined layers. You'll hike through 100 million years of polychrome sedimentary history beginning in the bold red of the Chinle formation climbing into the darker red of the Dakota. Though the best introduction to this area is by boat (a class II paddle; see the Chama River in the "White-Water Kayaking" section later in this chapter), this trail offers its own rewards, including views of much of northern New Mexico. The trail begins by crossing an arroyo, then ascends through piñon-juniper forests. At mile 1.2 it swings south, then west again. A mile more and it climbs a

LOS ALAMOS: THE A-BOMB'S BIRTHPLACE

Sitting atop the 7,300-foot Pajarito Plateau about 35 miles north of Santa Fe, Los Alamos is an odd community known worldwide for its secret World War II bomb making. But its history stretches far back before the Manhattan Project. Pueblo tribes lived in this rugged area for well over 1,000 years, and an exclusive boys' school operated here from 1918 to 1943. Then, the **Los Alamos National Laboratory** was established in secrecy—Project Y of the Manhattan Engineer District, the hush-hush wartime program that developed the world's first nuclear weapons.

Project director J. Robert Oppenheimer, later succeeded by Norris E. Bradbury, worked with a team of 30 to 100 scientists in research, development, and production of the weapons. Today, more than 10,000 people work at the Los Alamos National Laboratory, making it the largest employer in northern New Mexico. Still operated by the University of California for the federal Department of Energy, its 32 technical areas occupy 43 square miles of mesa-top land.

The laboratory is known today as one of the world's foremost scientific institutions. It's still oriented primarily toward defense research—the Trident and Minuteman strategic warheads were designed here, for example—but it has many other research programs, including international nuclear safeguards and nonproliferation, space and atmospheric studies, supercomputing, theoretical physics, biomedical and materials science, and environmental restoration.

---

broad bench, then turns north to parallel the Dakota sandstone cliffs above. At a few points it makes its way through pine-tree shade, but overall it's a very sunny hike. At mile 2 it requires a bit of a scramble, finally reaching the mesa top, from which you'll see Abiquiu Lake and some of the formations Georgia O'Keeffe made famous such as the flat-topped Cerro Pedernal as well as the Sangre de Cristo and Jemez Mountains in the distance.

Ojitos Trail

12 miles round-trip. Moderate. 1,900-ft. elevation gain. Allow 1–2 days. Access: Take U.S. 84 west from Española 37 miles to the junction with FR 151. Turn left (west) and travel 8.5 miles to Skull Bridge on the Rio Chama and park. *Beware:* These clay roads become extremely slick in rainy weather, at times trapping travelers within the Chama Canyon. Map: USGS Laguna Peak.

Other than boating through this area, this trail is the only way to really penetrate the Chama River Canyon Wilderness. The trail is excellent for either a long day hike or an overnight backpack trek. It will take you through lush canyons and stark mesa country decorated with the stunning layers of Mesozoic rocks, which fill this 50,000-acre wilderness area. This is one of northern New Mexico's only completed sections of the Continental Divide Trail, so it is well marked and has plenty of backcountry campsites. The creek within Ojitos Canyon trickles throughout most of the year. Begin the hike by crossing Skull Bridge and following the dirt road heading south. Soon you'll find the trailhead and enter the wilderness. The trail passes along the mouth of Ojitos Canyon, enters a gap, edges around a mudstone mesa and over a low saddle before dropping into the main canyon. It passes through a hiker's gate at mile 2.1. Bear right and watch for the next trail marker. Now you'll follow the canyon bottom where you'll find the *ojitos,* "little springs" for which the canyon was named. At 4.5 miles the trail leaves the canyon and climbs a series of switchbacks up the wall of Mesa del Camino, where the trail ends at a road on a ledge below the mesa's top. To the left is a protected campsite. Return the way you came.

HORSEBACK RIDING

To give you an idea of the awesome riding available in this region, take it from those who really know scenery—the producers of films. In this area they've captured some of the most scenic and touching moments in the Western genre. *Butch Cassidy and the Sundance Kid* was filmed in Taos and Chama, *City Slickers* was filmed in Abiquiu, and *The Cowboys* was filmed in Chama and Galisteo, to name only a few. So if you're hankering for a taste of the Old West, you've come to the right place.

If you hook up with **Cerro Blanco Adventures,** P.O. Box 153, Gallina, NM 87017 (☎ **505/638-5462** or 505/638-5468), two gritty guides, Juan Chavez and Gene McCracken, will saddle up their surefooted Appaloosas and take you into some of the most scenic and remote country in New Mexico. You'll begin your journey in Gallina, a tiny, poetic town nestled in the Jemez Mountains between Cuba and Abiquiu. Heading into the highlands, you'll ride through dense forests and across wild-grass meadows to the tops of the San Pedro Wilderness. From there you can see almost 360° to the snowy peaks of Ute Mountain in Utah and the La Plata in Colorado to the sprawling deserts of Arizona. In the evenings your guides will treat you to campfire fajitas and other delicacies while regaling you with stories. One favorite is when they took the whole cast and crew of the Santa Fe Opera's *Barber of Seville* on a ride. "The lead singer barely sang real soft," says McCracken. "I guess it takes hours just for her to warm up, so she has to be careful with her voice." Prices range from $55 for a 2-hour day-trip to $600 for a 5-day camping trip.

There are a couple of places in the Albuquerque area that offer guided or unguided horseback rides. At **River Horse Rentals,** 85 Jarales Rd., Belen, NM (☎ **505/861-0766**), you'll ride on shady trails by the Rio Grande. Half-day trips cost $60, and full-day ones cost $100. The horses are healthy and gentle enough for the whole family. In addition, **Turkey Track Stables, Inc.,** 1306 U.S. 66 E. Tijeras (☎ **505/281-1772**), located about 15 miles east of Albuquerque, offers rides on trails in the Manzano foothills at costs ranging from $25 to $65.

Broken Saddle Riding Company in Cerrillos on the Turquoise Trail (☎ **505/470-0074**) offers riding through the spectacular Galisteo Basin southeast of Santa Fe at prices ranging from $45 for 1½ hours to $70 for 3 hours.

Taos Indian Horse Ranch, on Pueblo land off Ski Valley Road just before Arroyo Seco (☎ **505/758-3212**), offers a variety of guided rides. Open by appointment, the ranch provides horses for all types of riders (English, Western, Australian, and bareback) and ability levels. Call ahead to reserve. Rates start at $32 and go up to $65 to $95 for a 2-hour trail ride (depending on the number of people in your party). Horse-drawn hay wagon rides are also offered in summer. From late November to March, the ranch provides afternoon and evening sleigh rides to a bonfire and marshmallow roast. The ranch also has what's called the Paddle and Saddle Club. Designed for the adrenaline junkie, the event combines riding with a raft trip.

Horseback riding is also offered by the **Shadow Mountain Guest Ranch,** 6 miles east of Taos on U.S. 64 (☎ **800/405-7732** or 505/758-7732), and **Rio Grande Stables** (☎ **505/776-5913**), with prices ranging from $35 for a half-day up to $120 for a more elaborate outing. Call for further details.

A fascinating adventure you may want to try is a 1-hour, 1-day, or overnight horseback trip with **Roadrunner Tours** (☎ **505/377-6416;** www.rtours.com). Nancy and Bill Burch guide adventurers on horseback from Angel Fire through private ranch land into the high country. The cattle-drive trip is no bland trail ride: On the first day, you'll travel 15 miles through ponderosa forests, across meadows of asters and sunflowers, with bald peaks in the distance. Once at camp, riders bed down in an authentic mountain cowboy cabin. On the second day, you'll move as many as 300 cows through the Moreno Valley. One-hour rides cost $25, day rides $165, and cattle drives $200 (price includes overnight stay in a cow camp). Cattle drives take place in July and August; space is limited, so book early.

For a taste of the unusual, you may want to have a llama carry your gear and food, allowing you to walk and explore, free of any heavy burdens. They're friendly, gentle animals that have a keen sense of sight and smell. Often, other animals, such as elk, deer, and mountain sheep, are attracted to their scent and will venture closer to hikers if the llamas are present. **El Paseo Llama Expeditions** (☎ 800/455-2627 or 505/758-3111; www.elpaseollama.com) offers llama expeditions from May to mid-October, and day hikes are scheduled year-round. Gourmet meals are provided. Half-day hikes cost $54, day hikes $74, and 2- to 8-day hikes run up to $899. **Wild Earth Llama Adventures** (☎ 800/758-LAMA or 505/586-0174; www.llamaadventures.com; e-mail: llamatrek@aol.com) offers a "Take a Llama to Llunch" day hike—a full day of hiking into the Sangre de Cristo Mountains, complete with a gourmet lunch for $75. Wild Earth also offers a variety of custom multi-day wilderness adventures tailored to trekkers' needs and fitness levels for $215 per person per day. Children under 12 receive discounts, and children under 5 come along for free. Camping gear and food are provided. Their knowledgeable and experienced guides provide information about native plants and local wildlife, as well as natural and regional history of the area. The head guide doubles as a chef in the off-season, so the meals on these treks are exceptional.

MOUNTAIN BIKING

After recent travels to Moab and Sedona I came back raving to my Santa Fe friends about the *real* biking at those destinations, only to find some of them quite taken aback. Northern New Mexico is as good as those places, easily, they said, and I cocked my head and thought that maybe I'd taken my home for granted. I expanded my repertoire and came to agree with them, with one caveat: In order to really appreciate the biking in this region you need to be in excellent shape. A lot of the riding is, indeed, *mountain* bike riding, lots of steep climbs and steep descents. Still, I've managed to include some less extreme ones in the book for people such as me who like to sit back and enjoy the scenery.

In Albuquerque you can rent bikes and get good maintenance at **Rio Mountain Sport**, 1210 Rio Grande NW (☎ 505/766-9970), and they come with helmets, maps, and locks. A great place to bike is Sandia Peak in Cíbola National Forest. You can't take your bike on the tram, but chairlift #1 is available for up- or downhill transportation with a bike. If you'd rather not rent a bike from the above-mentioned sports store, bike rentals are available at the top and bottom of the chairlift. The lift ride one-way with a bike is $7; all day with a bike will cost you $12. Helmets are mandatory. Bike maps are available; the clearly marked trails range from easy to very difficult. Mountain Bike Challenge Events are held on Sandia Peak in May, July, August, and September.

Your contact in the Santa Fe area is **Bike n' Sport**, 1829 Cerrillos Rd. (☎ 505/820-0809), a shop that offers maintenance and can set you up with good maps and directions. If you'd like a guided biking experience, there are a few options. Located in the village of Cerrillos south of Santa Fe, **Mountain Bike Adventures** (☎ 505/474-0074; www.bikefun.com) offers a variety of day and multi-day trips through old mining towns, to an ancient turquoise mine, Indian ruins, and high into mountain terrain. Its trips range from $50 to $700. **Sun Mountain Bike Company,** 107 Washington Ave. (☎ 505/820-2902), rents bikes and also runs bike tours from April through October to some of the most spectacular spots in Northern New Mexico. Trips range from an easy Glorieta Mesa tour to my favorite, the West Rim Trail, which snakes along the Taos Gorge, to the technical Glorieta Baldy, with prices from $60 to $109. All tours include bikes, transportation, and a snack.

For biking in the Taos area, inquire at the **National Forest Service office,** 208 Cruz Alta Rd. (☎ 505/758-6200) for excellent materials that map out trails; tell you how to get to the trailhead; specify length, difficulty, and elevation; and inform you about safety tips. You can no longer purchase the Taos Trails map (created jointly by the Carson National Forest, Native Sons Adventures, and Trail Illustrated) from the forest service office, but you can still find it at area bookstores. (This is a great map that's worth looking for—it's even designed to withstand water damage.) Once you're out riding in Carson National Forest, you'll find trails marked in green (easy), blue (moderate), or gray (expert).

Bicycle rentals are available from the **Gearing Up Bicycle Shop,** 129 Paseo del Pueblo Sur (☎ 505/751-0365). **Native Sons Adventures,** 1033-A Paseo del Pueblo Sur (☎ 800/753-7559 or 505/758-9342), also rents bikes and car racks, and they can help arrange shuttles.

Albuquerque Foothills Trail

7 miles one-way. Easy to moderate. 300-ft. elevation gain. Allow 2 hrs. Access: From downtown head east on Montgomery Blvd. past the intersection with Tramway Blvd. Go left on Glenwood Hills Dr. and head north for about 0.5 miles before turning right onto a short road that leads to the Embudito Trailhead. You may also reach this trail from the Elena Gallegos Picnic Area in Albert G. Simms Park, farther north off Tramway Blvd.

On first glance, Albuquerque's foothills appear as barren as much of the land surrounding New Mexico's largest city. However, this series of trails stretching 7 miles along the base of the Sandia Mountains will surprise you. Sure these well-maintained single track trails start out on dusty open desert, but soon enough they climb (easily) into piñon-juniper forest, descend (gently) into arroyo basins lush with cottonwoods, and wind (slowly) through cholla cactus stands. A good strategy is to follow the trails closest to the mountains on the way out and then take it easy on the less hilly lower trails en route back. Watch out for hikers and horseback riders. Also take care: At times run-off from the steep face of the Sandia Mountains can erode the trail. This trail offers year-round biking.

Volcano and Petroglyph Tour

3–10 miles round-trip. Easy to moderate. Approximately 500-ft. elevation gain. Allow 2–3 hrs. Access: Head east on I-40 and take the Unser Blvd. exit. Follow Unser Blvd. 3 miles north to 6001 Unser; follow the signs to the visitor center.

This ride takes you around bases of ancient volcanoes and along a ridge where you can leave your bike and explore some Pueblo-ancestral petroglyphs. The trail traverses hard-packed dirt roads and offers spectacular views of the Jemez, Sandia, and Manzano Mountains and Mount Taylor. Riders can elect to ascend or descend some more technical trails around the most northern and most southern volcanoes. You'll begin the ride at the visitor center and ride out to the volcanoes via Atrisco Drive, which will take you up on the mesa. From there you'll see many dirt roads heading across the top of the Mesa. The left-most road will take you along the edge of the ridge, below which are the petroglyphs. The others will take you along the base of the five volcanoes, created as basalt lava pushed up hundreds of feet below the earth's crust along fissures created by the Rio Grande rift. On the north side of the Bond Volcano is a cave in which evidence of human existence from 10,000 years ago was found. The monument is adamant that bikers stay on the trails on the mesa, and not ride those that traverse the petroglyphs, so when you're ready to explore, you'll want to leave your bike and hike down along the ridge where thousands of vivid pictures have been drawn on stone. This trail can be ridden year-round, though during the late-summer monsoon watch for thunderstorms. The mesa is very exposed.

Rio Grande Nature Center
2–10 miles round trip. Easy. Allow 1–3 hrs. Access: From I-40, take the Rio Grande Blvd. Exit and travel north to Candelaria. Turn left and drive to the road's end, where you'll see the parking lot: 2901 Candelaria Rd. NW.

If you're looking for a gentle day riding through riparian terrain, this partly paved route should be your choice. The trails traverse the bosque along the Rio Grande for miles. You can't take your bike into the Nature Center per se, but you can take it out beyond the Nature Center to the paved trail that parallels a large irrigation ditch. This is a good place to bring kids, as the trail goes for miles. You'll encounter plenty of horseback riders and hikers along the away, to whom you ought to yield. Near the Rio Grande Nature Center the trail veers down to the river—a good spot to view the mighty Rio, and a good spot to see how little water is left after local farmers irrigate their crops.

La Tierra Torture Trail
3–12-mile loops. Moderate to strenuous. 400-ft. elevation gain. Allow 1–3 hrs. Access: From Santa Fe, drive north on U.S. 84/285 for 1 mile to the Santa Fe Relief Route exit. Follow the Relief Route 2 miles and turn right on County Rd. 85. Drive 0.7 miles; you'll see a green water tower to your right. Turn left and drive less than 0.5 miles on this dirt road, watching for dirt mounds to your left. Turn toward these bike jumps and park beyond the last mound. The trail starts in either direction from there. You'll see the single track heading east and west through the trees.

With such a delicious nomenclature, you'd think this trail west of Santa Fe would be tortuous. It only is for those participating in the annual September La Tierra Torture Race, because they ride at speeds that make crashing common. The biggest danger here is that the trail is a favorite spot for motorbikes. Their sounds sometimes echo through the route, often seeming ominously close, and sometimes a bike will surprise you around a corner. All that aside, the trail is most popular because it's one of the few in the Santa Fe area that traverses hilly terrain rather than mountainous terrain. It also has amazing views of the Sandia, Jemez, and Sangre de Cristo Mountains. Unfortunately, this terrain is quickly falling prey to Santa Fe's housing boon, which at this writing had recently eaten away a chunk of the course. The area is also party central on weekends, so beware of broken beer bottles.

In the months following the race the trail is well marked with orange ribbons, but as the year passes those marks fade away. Your best bet with this spaghetti bowl of trails is simply to explore. All of them criss-cross the power line road adjacent to the jumps. Use the Sangre de Cristo Mountains to the east as a bearing.

Windsor Trail System
4–17 miles. Moderate to strenuous. 760–1,400-ft. elevation gain. Allow 1½–5 hrs. Access: Take Hyde Park Rd./NM 475 northeast of Santa Fe. Drive 8.3 miles to the Borrego Trailhead. Look for a small parking area on the left.

This rugged river of trails runs on the western slope of the Sangre de Cristo Mountains from the Santa Fe Ski Area down to Tesuque Village north of Santa Fe with lots of tributaries, most of which lead to the Ski Area Road. The most popular and controversial route is the downhill ride from the ski area to Tesuque Village. I must admit it's a gripping piece of single track, known as one of the best downhill romps in the United States. This trip is not for novices. I've seen people seriously hurt on this run. Most conscientious locals frown on the practice of running it because of the erosion such fast downhill riding can cause. Much more respected are those who start in Tesuque and ride the grueling 17 miles up to the top and then descend. This is one way of riding it, but there are some 14 stream crossings, most of which require getting off your bike to climb over logs and sandbars. Therefore, I've included here the Borrego Trail as a good entry point to the Windsor. It is a fun and scenic ride and offers a variety of courses once you get onto the system.

Trail 150 starts at the end of the parking lot and twists down through the woods and becomes wide, descending slowly. About a half-mile in it forks. Go right on the well-marked trail. It climbs for awhile then descends in switchback down to Tesuque Creek. Cross the creek and you'll soon come to the Windsor Trail. From here, you have many options. You can ride up to the ski area or down to the Chamisa Trail, out to the Ski Area Road and back on pavement to your car. Or you can travel down Windsor Trail for a mile and turn back on the Bear Wallow trail in a 4-mile loop back to your car. If you choose the latter option, you'll cross the creek again and head up switchbacks on the Bear Wallow Trail for awhile until you enter the deep forest again. The ascent from here is fairly relentless and the old conifers and aspens lovely. After 1 mile you'll come to the fork, which took you to the right before. Continue straight back to your car.

Aspen Vista

2–12 miles round-trip. Moderate to strenuous. 500–2,000-ft. elevation gain. Allow 1–3 hrs. Access: Take Hyde Park Rd./NM 475 northeast of Santa Fe. Drive 13 miles to the trailhead. Look for a long parking area on the right.

This is an unparalleled fall ride, with thousands of aspen trees shedding their colors on the somewhat rocky Forest Road 150 that has amazing views; in the spring and summer it's also a beautiful trek. It is an out-and-back ride (with a paved loop option) that means a fairly relentless climb, then a complete coast back down. From the trailhead begin your ascent and continue for the first 2.5 miles through glades of aspens. Then you'll pass into fir and spruce forest, and later into tundra-like vegetation that characterizes alpine life zones. Once you reach the radio towers on Tesuque Peak, you'll turn around and return in a fast romp the way you came. You'll want to watch your speed since lots of hikers use the lower section of the trail. Or, you may want to make your way down one of the Santa Fe Ski Area Trails to the parking area and its intersection with Hyde Park Road. Follow the paved road back to your car.

El Devisadero Loop

5-mile loop. Difficult. 1,100-ft. elevation gain. Allow 2–3 hrs. Access: From Taos drive out of town on U.S. 64 to your first pullout on the right just as you enter the canyon at El Nogal Picnic Area.

This is techno-head land, a trail with loose dirt, steep grades, and amazing views. All of it is single track, with short, rocky sections that roam through piñon-juniper forest in foothills of the Sangre de Cristo Mountains. It begins directly across U.S. 64 on a short access trail that meets the loop. Bear left when you get to the loop and continue in a clockwise direction. You'll skirt along Devisadero Peak with an elevation of 8,304 feet and spectacular views in all directions including Maestas Ridge to the south.

South Boundary Trail
20 miles one-way. Strenuous. 2,000-ft. elevation gain. Allow 1 very full day. Access: From Taos, drive east on U.S. 64 and then south on NM 434. Go past Angel Fire Ski Area and continue to the village of Black Lake and turn right on County Road B1. When this road forks, bear right and continue for not quite 2 miles to where the road makes a sharp left. You'll see markers for FS Trail 164. Maps: Carson National Forest or USGS Osha Mountain, Shadybrook, and Rancho de Taos.

If you're one of those people who can't get enough single track, this tour from Angel Fire to Taos across the Rockies just might satiate your hunger. Be aware, though, that the journey should not be embarked upon lightly. This one-way trek hovers from 7,200 to 10,770 feet, with many long, steep grades. It's a full-day, one-way ride that traverses what once was the boundary between the Taos and Rio Grande del Rancho land grants. Be sure to bring plenty of water, food, weather gear, a first-aid and bike repair kit, and a compass. You'll want to watch for summer thunderstorms, and take precautions if you encounter one. It's also a good idea to notify the Carson National Forest Camino Real Ranger District at (☎ 505/587-2255) and give them your travel plans. Be aware that even riders who have traveled this route a few times have had difficulty finding their way. You may want to offer a local dinner in payment for guiding you. **Native Sons Adventures** (☎ 800/753-7559 or 505/758-9342) can help with directions and a shuttle.

You'll begin the ride in Angel Fire, on the eastern slope of the Sangre de Cristo Mountains, and ride to Taos. The first 5 miles of the ride are a climb, and the last 15 are rolling single track. En route you'll pass across ridges, through valleys, and over several peaks, through conifer forests and thick stands of aspen. If you can time it right, do this ride in the fall when the trees create a world of gold.

From the trailhead you'll find FS Trail 164 marked. But understand that it does cross and align itself with a few forest roads. Early on you'll cross over FS 76. Your next encounter will be FS 438 on which you'll turn right. Follow FS 438 until you reach FS 437. Turn right on 437. It will lead you to FS 445, where you turn left. This will take you to your final descent (a gnarly one) into the El Nogal Campground on U.S. 64 where your ride should meet you.

Taos Box Canyon West Rim
6 miles one-way. Easy. No discernable elevation gain. Allow 2 hrs. Access: From U.S. 84/285 turn west at the village of Pilar onto NM 570. Travel along the river for 6.2 miles. Cross the bridge and drive to the top of the ridge. From there, watch for the trail marker on your right.

This is a great family ride or a ride for those who feel like enjoying distant views rather than focusing on a technical trail. It follows an old jeep road along the very brink of the rim. It's an out-and-back trail so you can go as long as you like and turn around. Views in both directions are unique and spectacular.

Goose Lake near Red River
16-mile loop. Moderate to strenuous. 2,968-ft. elevation gain. Allow 4 hrs. Access: Ride or drive east out of Red River on NM 578. At about 0.7 miles turn right (south) on Forest Service Road 486, the beginning of the trail.

This is a fun ride south of the village of Red River through a section of Carson National Forest. You'll travel up a forest service road to a scenic mountain lake below the 12,711-foot Gold Hill. On the way down you'll romp along a 7-mile stretch of single track. The first section of the road is steep, but bear with it, as it will get easier. As you climb keep your sights on FS 486 rather than taking some of the intersecting side roads. At 8 miles you'll reach the lake. On the far side of the lake near an outhouse, you'll find FS Trail 65 that follows Goose Creek down.

Shortly after heading down you'll come to a fork in the trail. Head left down the drainage and continue on the single track until you reach NM 578. Turn left and ride back to town.

Costilla Pass in Valle Vidal
13 miles round-trip. Easy to moderate. 570-ft. elevation gain. Allow 3 hrs. Access: Take NM 522 north from Taos to Costilla. Turn east on NM 196. It will become the dirt FS 1950. Follow FS 1950 for 8 miles until you reach a fork at Comanche Point. Bear right continuing on FS 1950 for 4.5 miles to a dirt road that goes to the right. Turn onto this road and follow it for 0.5 miles to a dirt parking area. You can also access FR 1950 from U.S. 64 northeast of Cimarron.

The 100,000-acre Valle Vidal in Carson National Forest is an unspoiled land of pines and broad meadows inhabited by some 60 mammal species including black bear, mountain lion and many elk, as well as 200 species of birds. Over the years it has remained pristine through private ownership. Only in 1982 did these become public lands. Be aware that you may encounter hunters during deer and elk seasons. Also, the area contains various areas protected as elk calving grounds, so they remain closed through the spring and into July. Therefore this is a late summer/fall ride.

The ride will take you through the heart of this wild country up one creek bed and down another. Ride out of the parking area past a gate on a road that follows Comanche Creek. At 2 miles you'll reach a fork; go left, around a gate and continue past Clayton Camp. The road becomes a little obscure for awhile then comes to another fork. Bear right, following the road that parallels the Vidal Creek. At mile 8 you'll reach Costilla Pass, at 9,762 feet, where you may want to stop for a break. When you're ready to go again, head northwest off the pass. Ignore the gate on the left and several forks heading off to the left. Bear right, taking the road that descends through the Comanche Creek drainage, finally returning to Clayton Camp. Turn left and head back to your car.

Jemez Mountains
For those many riders who prefer smooth trails with less grade, the Jemez Mountains offer beauty and variety. Most of the best trails originate in the area of La Cueva, at the intersection of NM 4 and NM 126. I've had luck just clipping in at various trailheads in the area and seeing where fate leads me. However, if you'd like more structure, head to the East Fork Cross-Country area just off NM 4, 6.6 miles east of La Cueva.

East Fork Ridge Cross-Country Ski Trail
4.5 miles. Easy. 400-ft. elevation gain. Allow 1–3 hrs. Access: From the La Cueva intersection of NM 4 and NM 126 head east on NM 4 for 6.5 miles until you see the sign for the East Fork Recreation Area on the left-hand side of the road.

This isn't so much a single trail as it is a vast web of abandoned logging roads winding through the forest with minimal elevation gain and a few nice overlook spots. Anyone with prior single-track experience should be comfortable here. After a half-mile the trail intersects with the Mistletoe Canyon Trail, a nice alternate route, but with fewer views. At 2.5 miles the East Fork Ridge Trail reaches a large clearing with a spectacular view of Redondo Peak. Then, after a short climb the trail gradually descends and again meets the Mistletoe Canyon Trail, which can provide a return loop to the trailhead. Farther east the East Fork Trail intersects with the Burn Trail and the East Fork National Recreation Hiking Trail, the latter of which will take you down to NM 4, which you can ride back to the parking lot. I prefer to just follow the blue markers that guide you on all these trails and see where I end up. Trails are available for biking only in the summer and fall.

San Antonio Canyon

17 miles. Moderate. 1,000-ft. elevation gain. Allow 3 hrs. Access: From the village of La Cueva at the intersection of NM 4 and NM 126 go northwest about 4 miles to where FS 376 takes off across a cattle guard on the right-hand side of the road.

If you like to ride with a destination in mind, San Antonio Canyon offers one—though it's not exactly the best destination for the middle of a bike ride. It heads to one of the Jemez' best hot springs. Begin the ride on Forest Road 376, climbing gently for a mile, then descending into San Antonio Canyon for about 4 miles. At mile 5 the road forks. Go straight ahead up the canyon. (Or if you'd like to take a break and soak in the hot springs, turn right here. The springs are about a 250-foot hike above San Antonio Creek on the east wall of San Diego Canyon. Since they are on private property you'll need to ask permission to use them, though this doesn't seem to be a problem, as there are always people using the springs.) The next 2 miles take you on single track along some bizarre and beautiful volcanic rock formations, and across some stream crossings. Then you'll come to a 3-pronged fork; go left up a road that will climb steeply for less than 1 mile to where it meets FS 144. Go left onto FS 144 and ride this rolling road downhill for almost 7 miles to where it ends at the pavement of NM 126. Turn left again and head downhill to where you left your car at the beginning of FS 376.

ROAD BIKING

As far as scenery and variety go, northern New Mexico is an ideal spot to clip in and cruise. Unfortunately, the region is not very hospitable to cyclers. Drivers remain fairly naïve about who has the right-of-way, and many are known to honk, just to let you know they're there. (Thanks buddy!) That means that when you do ride here, be very aware. Never assume a driver sees you, and even if you're sure he does, don't assume he'll give you your hard-earned right-of-way. For your biking needs, check the mountain bike section for area shops. Annual touring events include Red River's **Enchanted Circle Century Bike Tour** (☎ 505/754-2366) on the weekend following Labor Day.

High Road to Taos

80 miles one-way, with variations. Difficult. Allow 7–10 hrs. or 2 days. Access: You can ride this straight out of Santa Fe or begin at the junction of U.S. 84 and NM 503, 16 miles north of Santa Fe.

A favorite route for riders and drivers alike is the High Road or King's Road from Santa Fe to Taos. This spectacular 80-mile route into the mountains between Santa Fe and Taos takes you through red painted desert, villages bordered by apple and peach orchards, and the foothills of 13,000-foot peaks. You can stop in Chimayo, known for its weavers, and Cordova, known for its woodcarvers. At the fabled Santuario de Chimayo, you can rub healing dust between your fingers. You'll also pass through Truchas, a village stronghold on a mountain mesa 1.5 miles above sea level. Often bikers like to park at the corner of U.S. 84 and NM 503, the turn-off to Nambe, about 16 miles north of Santa Fe. From there you'll pedal north on 503. *Take note:* These villages are not known for their hospitality toward outsiders. Be aware while riding. Here's a rundown of the villages you'll pass through.

Chimayo

Travel NM 503 to NM 520 and turn left heading down into the historic weaving center of Chimayo. It's approximately 16 miles past the beginning junction, at the junction of NM 520 and NM 76. In this small village, families still maintain the tradition of crafting handwoven textiles initiated by their ancestors 7 generations ago, in the early 1800s. One such family is the Ortegas, and both **Ortega's Weaving Shop** and **Galeria Ortega** (at the corner of NM 520 and NM 76) are fine places to take a close look at this ancient craft. Another is **Trujillo Weavings** on NM 76. If you're lucky enough to find John Trujillo in, you might get a weaving history lesson. John can show you a 75-year-old loom he learned to weave on and a 95-year-old shuttle that his father's uncle carved from apricot wood.

You may want to take a break at **El Santuario de Nuestro Señor de Esquipulas** (the Shrine of Our Lord of Esquipulas), better known simply as "El Santuario de Chimayo." Ascribed with miraculous powers of healing, this church has attracted thousands of pilgrims since its construction in 1814 to 1816. Up to 30,000 people participate in the annual Good Friday pilgrimage, many of them walking from as far away as Albuquerque. When most arrive they dip their fingers in the earth in the anteroom, which is presumed to have healing powers.

A good place to stop for a quick bite, **Leona's Restaurante de Chimayo** is right next door to the Santuario de Chimayo. Leona herself presides in this little taco and burrito stand with plastic tables inside and, during warm months, outside. Leona has gained national fame for her flavored tortillas—the raspberry and chocolate ones really are tasty.

From Chimayo head east about 7 miles on NM 76 to the village of Cordova, noted for its wood-carvers. (If you want to cruise, you may just want to look down upon this enchanting little village, but if you want to explore, you can ride down the hill into town.) Just a short way through this truly traditional northern New Mexico town is a gem of a gallery. **The Castillo Gallery,** 1 mile into the village, carries moody and colorful acrylic paintings by Paula Castillo, as well as her found-art welded sculptures. It also carries the work of Terry Enseñat Mulert, whose contemporary woodcarvings are treasures of the high country. En route to the Castillo, you may want to stop in at two other local carver's galleries. The first you'll come to is **Sabinita Lopez Ortiz;** and the second, her cousin, **Gloria Ortiz.** Both are descendents of the well-noted José Dolores Lopez. Carved from cedar wood and aspen, the works range from simple statues of saints (santos) to elaborate scenes of birds.

Truchas

You'll climb 4 hard miles onto an 8,000-foot high mesa where this enchanting village sits. Robert Redford's 1988 movie, *The Milagro Beanfield War,* featured the town of Truchas (Spanish for "trout"). A former Spanish colonial outpost, it was chosen as the site for the film in part because traditional Hispanic culture is still very much in evidence. Subsistence farming is prevalent here. The scenery is spectacular: 13,101-foot Truchas Peak dominates one side of the mesa, and the broad Rio Grande Valley dominates the other.

About 6 miles east of Truchas on NM 76 is the small town of **Las Trampas,** noted for its San José Church, which some call the most beautiful of all churches built during the Spanish Colonial period. Near the intersection of NM 75 and NM 76, is the **Picuris (San Lorenzo) Pueblo** (☎ **505/587-2519** or 505/587-2957). The 375 citizens of this 15,000-acre mountain pueblo, native Tiwa speakers, consider themselves a sovereign nation: Their forebears never made a treaty with any foreign country, including the United States. Thus, they observe a traditional form of tribal council government. A few of the original mud-and-stone houses still stand and are home to tribal elders. A striking aboveground ceremonial kiva called "the Roundhouse," built at least 700 years ago, and some historic excavated kivas and storerooms are open to visitors. The **annual feast day** at San Lorenzo Church is August 10.

Dixon & Embudo

Taos is about 24 miles north of Peñasco via NM 518. But bikers from Santa Fe can loop back to the capital by taking NM 75 west from Picuris Pueblo. Anyone who has ridden down from this high area into Dixon raves about the drop, a fast scream down into desert land punctuated by apple groves. Dixon, approximately 12 miles west of Picuris, and its twin village Embudo, 1 mile farther on NM 68 at the Rio Grande, are home to many artists and craftspeople who exhibit their works during the annual autumn show sponsored by the Dixon Arts Association. If you manage to get to Embudo at mealtime, stop in at **Embudo Station** (☎ 800/852-4707 or 505/852-4707), a restaurant right on the banks of the Rio Grande River. During mid-April through October—the only time it's open—you can sit on the patio under giant cottonwoods and sip the restaurant's own microbrewed beer (try the green-chile ale, its most celebrated) and signature wines while watching the peaceful Rio flow by.

Two more small villages lie in the Rio Grande Valley at 6-mile intervals south of Embudo on NM 68. **Velarde** is a fruit-growing center; in season, the road here is lined with stands selling fresh fruit or crimson chile ristras and wreaths of native plants. **Alcalde** is the site of Los Luceros, an early 17th-century home that is to be refurbished as an arts and history center. The unique **Dance of the Matachines**, a Moorish-style ritual brought from Spain by the conquistadors, is performed here on holidays and feast days.

Be aware, though, if you intend to do this loop back to Santa Fe or the Nambe turn-off where you left your car, the ride on U.S. 84/285 is not a safe one. Though there are good shoulders the whole way, this corridor is notorious for having lots of automobile accidents. It's a busy section of road. Another option is to continue on from Penasco to Taos via NM 518 though Ranchos de Taos and arrange a shuttle back to Santa Fe or return on the high road the following day. The trip back will offer a whole new set of views. Though I've described this route leaving from Santa Fe and going *to* Taos, some believe it's even prettier to start in Taos and ride to Santa Fe. I tend to agree, particularly regarding the section from Truchas to Chimayo.

Enchanted Circle

90-mile loop. Moderate to difficult. Substantial elevation gain at some points. Allow 1–2 days. Access: Begin at the north end of Taos and the junction of NM 150 and 522.

If you're in the mood to explore, take this 90-mile loop north of Taos through the old Hispanic villages of Arroyo Hondo and Questa, into a pass the Apaches, Kiowas, and Comanches once used to cross through the mountains to trade with the Taos Indians. You'll come to the Wild West mining town of Red River, pass through the expansive Moreno Valley, and along the base of some of New Mexico's tallest peaks. Then, you'll skim the shores of a high mountain lake at Eagle Nest, pass near the resort village of Angel Fire, and head back to Taos along the meandering Rio Fernando de Taos. Along the way you'll encounter good pavement, some grinding climbs, and hopefully, if you take the direction laid out here, favorable winds. Here's a rundown of the villages you'll pass through.

Arroyo Hondo

Travel north from Taos via NM 522 for 9 miles to this village, the remains of an 1815 land grant along the Rio Hondo. Along the dirt roads that lead off NM 522, you may see a windowless Morada or two, marked by plain crosses in front, places of worship for the still-active Penitentes, a religious order known for self flagellation. This is also the turn-off point for trips to the Rio Grande Box, an awesome 1-day, 18-mile white-water run for which you can book trips in Santa Fe,

Taos, Red River, and Angel Fire. Arroyo Hondo was also the site of the New Buffalo commune in the 1960s. Hippies flocked here looking to escape the mores of modern society. Over the years, the commune members have dispersed throughout northern New Mexico, bringing an interesting creative element to the food, architecture, and philosophy of the state.

Questa

Next, Highway 522 passes through Questa, most of whose residents are employed at a molybdenum mine about 5 miles east of town. Mining molybdenum (an ingredient in lightbulbs, television tubes, and missile systems) in the area has not been without controversy. The process has raked across hillsides along the Red River, and though Molycorp, the mine's owner, treats the water it uses before returning it to the river, studies show it has adversely affected the fish life. Still, the mine is a major employer in the area, and locals are grateful for the income it generates. To the west is the Rio Grande Gorge, some 48 miles of the Rio Grande, south from the Colorado border, which is protected under the national Wild and Scenic River Act of 1968.

Red River

To continue on the Enchanted Circle loop, turn east at Questa onto NM 38 for a 12-mile climb to Red River, a rough-and-ready 1890s gold-mining town that has parlayed its Wild West ambience into a pleasant resort village that's especially popular with families from Texas and Oklahoma. Though it can be a charming and fun town, Red River's food and accommodations are mediocre at best. Its patrons are down-home folks, happy with a bed and a diner-style meal.

Eagle Nest

The next stretch is the most grueling. You'll travel 16 miles over the 9,850-foot Bobcat Pass to this village, resting on the shore of Eagle Nest Lake in the Moreno Valley. Gold was mined in this area as early as 1866, starting in what is now the ghost town of **Elizabethtown** about 5 miles north; Eagle Nest itself (pop. 200) wasn't incorporated until 1976. The 4-square-mile lake is considered one of the top trout producers in the United States and attracts ice fishermen in winter as well as summer anglers. From Eagle Nest, continue southwest on U.S. 38 and U.S. 64 to Agua Fría and Angel Fire.

Shortly before the Agua Fría junction, you'll see the **DAV Vietnam Veterans Memorial.** It's a stunning structure with curved white walls soaring high against the backdrop of the Sangre de Cristo Range. Consisting of a chapel and underground visitor center, it was built by Dr. Victor Westphall in memory of his son, David, a marine lieutenant killed in Vietnam in 1968. The chapel has a changing gallery of photographs of Vietnam veterans who lost their lives in the Southeast Asian war, but no photo is as poignant as this inscription written by young David Westphall, a promising poet:

> *Greed plowed cities desolate.*
> *Lusts ran snorting through the streets.*
> *Pride reared up to desecrate*
> *Shrines, and there were no retreats.*
> *So man learned to shed the tears*
> *With which he measures out his years.*

Angel Fire

You'll probably cruise by this resort village without taking the time to venture into it, which is okay because unlike many of the others you've passed through there's not much to see here. From here it's 20 miles back to Taos on smooth pavement through a lovely narrow canyon on a winding road.

SNOWSHOEING

New Mexico will never be a snowshoeing mecca. There just isn't enough snow to require the use of the oft-clumsy attachments. In fact, I've found myself slogging along with them, only to realize going would be much easier without them. I've also found myself thigh-deep in snow wishing I'd strapped some on. Your best bet before embarking is to check with local outdoor shops to be sure the conditions warrant use of snowshoes. If they do, some favorite adventures are in the **Pecos Wilderness.** One long and strenuous route is up the Windsor Trail to **Santa Fe Baldy,** a trail along which, even if you don't make it to the top, you'll encounter pristine meadows and expansive views. If you'd rather enter the Pecos Wilderness from the Pecos side, and if the road is passable to Cowles, snowshoe to **Hamilton Mesa.** In the Taos area, some head up from the ski area toward **Bull of the Woods.** In the Jemez Mountains, you may want to snowshoe into the **San Antonio Hot Springs.** Each February, snowshoers compete in a mountain run outside Santa Fe.

SWIMMING & TUBING

Since this is the high desert, water in which to swim or float on an inner tube is rare. Most of the water is too shallow for the former and too rocky for the latter. However, there are a few spots where a dip in the cool will do. One is **Abiquiu Lake.** Surrounded by the land pink buttes and desiccated bones that Georgia O'Keeffe memorialized in her paintings, the lake is an oasis of sorts. Unfortunately, mostly powerboaters and jet skiers take advantage of it. But, if you cross the dam and drive along the east shore you'll find some nice spots to dunk in. There are also cliffs to dive off of. If you're like me and enjoy the shock of cool alpine water, head into the Pecos Wilderness to **Lake Katherine** (see the "Hikes & Backpack Trips" section earlier in this chapter). On hot summer days I've also made the plunge into **Navajo Lake** and **Heron Lake;** the latter, however will be quite cold.

The Abiquiu area is also your best bet for tubing. Some people have been known to float the stretch from the Christ in the Desert Monastery down to Big Eddy on the **Chama River** (see the "White-Water Kayaking" section later in this chapter). However, since some of the rapids in the lower section of this run are Class II+, I would only recommend tubing on the flat sections; a safer mode of transportation for the whole run would be a raft or an inflatable kayak. Similarly, the state park on the **Rio Grande** near Pilar is a flat-water float with a few class II riffles.

WALKS & RAMBLES

Mesa Point Trail at Petroglyph National Monument

1 mile. Moderate. Access: Take Interstate 40 west to the Unser Blvd. Travel 3 miles north to 6001 Unser Blvd. Visitor center and Boca Negra area (where this trail is) open daily 8am–5pm; other sites open during daylight hours. Closed New Year's Day and Christmas.

In the past few years this monument has made national news, and for good reason; a struggle has raged in U.S. Congress over whether or not to allow a road through these lava flows that were once a hunting and gathering area for prehistoric Native Americans, who left a chronicle of their beliefs etched on the dark basalt boulders. The issue is heated not only because such a road would disturb the 15,000 petroglyphs, but also because it would set a precedent that might allow roads through other national monuments around the country. One ranger said he sees Albuquerque expanding so fast that the monument is "like a speed bump in the development of the West mesa." This trail climbs quickly up the side of a hill offering many petroglyph sightings as well as an outstanding view of the Sandia Mountains. If you're traveling with your dog, you can't bring him or her along on this trail but you can on the nearby

Rinconada Trail (located a few miles south of the visitor center), where finding the petroglyphs is a bit more of a task.

Sandia Peak Tramway

10 Tramway Loop NE. Access: Take I-25 north to Tramway Rd., then proceed east about 5 miles on Tramway Rd. Or from I-40, take Tramway Blvd. approximately 8.5 miles. Turn east the last mile on Tramway Rd. ☎ 505/856-7325. Open summer 9am–10pm, with more limited operation hours the rest of the year. Admission $14 adults, $10 seniors and children ages 5–12; free for children under 5.

On this 15-minute trip up the world's longest "jig-back" tram, you'll leave the cholla cactus and piñon-juniper forest lands and pass over seven life zones as you rise more than 4,000 feet to the pine-covered summit, a full 10,678 feet above sea level. The ride provides good access to hiking trails; one along the rim is about a mile long and leads to Sandia Crest House, a small gift shop and snack bar. There is also access to Sandia Peak Ski Area. Plan your ride at dusk to get the full force of those legendary New Mexico sunsets.

Main Ruins Trail and Ceremonial Cave at Bandelier National Monument

1.5–2 miles. Easy. Access: From Santa Fe, travel north on U.S. 84/285 to Pojoaque, then west toward Los Alamos on NM 502. At the junction with NM 4, turn south toward White Rock. Continue on NM 4 until you come to the sign for Bandelier.

This is a good family trail, leading through well-preserved ancestral Puebloan ruins in a lovely riparian canyon. The hike also allows you to get a view of the excavated Bandelier ruins before heading into the backcountry. The visitor center offers guided tours in season, and the trail has plaques identifying canyon plants, birds and mammals. The route leaves from the visitor center, where you ought to stop to see the sights and to pick up a detailed guide to the trail and the history its ruins represent. The ancient dwellings that this trail traverses are representative of every type of ruin found in the monument. It leads though the Tyuonyi Pueblo ruins, including its plaza, and past sacred places such as the Snake Kiva. You'll pass cave rooms and petroglyphs. A leg off the trail takes you to the Ceremonial Cave, a must-see for those who are agile and don't fear heights. You climb on pueblo-style ladders 140 feet above the canyon floor to a kiva, which you can enter. From this cave you may look out across the canyon and possibly sense the hundreds of busy lives that once inhabited it.

High Road to Taos

80-mile drive. Access: From Santa Fe take U.S. 285 to NM 503, which heads east. Follow that highway to NM 76. Take a short leg on NM 75 to NM 518, which puts you on the outskirts of Taos. For a detailed description of this route see the "Road Biking" section earlier in this chapter.

This spectacular 80-mile route into the mountains between Santa Fe and Taos takes you through red painted desert, villages bordered by apple and peach orchards, and the foothills of 13,000-foot peaks. You can stop in Cordova, known for its wood-carvers, or Chimayo, famous for its weavers. At the fabled Santuario de Chimayo, you can rub healing dust between your fingers. You'll also pass through Truchas, a village stronghold on a mountain mesa 1.5 miles above sea level.

Rio Grande Gorge Bridge

Access: Take U.S. 64, 10 miles west of Taos.

This impressive bridge, west of the Taos airport, spans the Southwest's greatest river. At 650 feet above the canyon floor, it's one of America's highest bridges. If you can withstand the vertigo, it's interesting to come more than once, at different times of day, to observe how the changing light plays tricks with the colors of the cliff walls. A curious aside is that the wedding scene in the controversial film *Natural Born Killers* was filmed here. The Rio Grande has cut down through layered lava flows of the Taos Plateau. The lava layers are broken by columnar joints that formed as the lava cooled. Reddish baked soil zones show between some layers. Note that when the wind blows hard, you can feel the bridge move slightly under you.

Echo Canyon Amphitheater
1 mile round-trip. Easy. Allow 10 min. Access: 3 miles north of Ghost Ranch on U.S. 84.

The natural "theater," hollowed out of sandstone by thousands of years of erosion, is a natural artwork with layers of stone ranging from pearl-color to blood red. The walls send back eerie echoes and even clips of conversations. The Little Echo Trail winds into a smaller canyon where the erosion is industriously working to form a new amphitheater (at press time the Little Echo Trail was closed). This is also a U.S. Forest Service campground and picnic area.

WHITE-WATER KAYAKING

People are often surprised that this high desert has some notable white water. Well, it does. Though there aren't a lot of runs, what we do have is very scenic and entertaining, and some of it such as the **Taos Box** is quite challenging as well. Above all this is a great place to learn to kayak because the waters here can be fairly mild, and one of the best teachers around is here. Mike Hanselman with **Wolf Whitewater** takes beginners on a 4-day journey from pool to lake to river, teaching all the basics. He also offers one-day clinics. Prices range from $45–$275. Besides the great instruction, Hanselman will perform some of the sickest moves you've seen on water, and make you laugh until your guts hurt. Your central river store in Santa Fe is **Active Endeavors**, 328 S. Guadalupe St. (☎ 505/984-8221). They'll provide you with rental and demo gear, as well as directions and guidebooks.

Class I/II

"State Park" or Orilla Verde Recreation Area
The **Rio Grande River** is northern New Mexico's most substantial waterway, so somehow the river gods gave it broad appeal, with runs ranging from Class I to V. The State Park, a 6-mile run from the John Dunne Bridge to the village of Pilar, offers lovely scenery of the Lower Box and a few riffles for excitement. The run generally takes about 2 hours. The river meanders around wide turns through forests of Tamarisk. You'll likely scare up ducks and possibly geese. A few nice beaches and grassy spots make for good picnic sites. At the bottom of the run you'll have to cross a small spillway over which you'll want to be careful. Don't attempt to take out before it, as locals will complain and possibly even draw a shotgun bead on you. You'll take out at Quartzite parking lot.

The **Taos County Line to Embudo Station** run meanders lazily through the lovely northern New Mexico farm country. You'll see Penitente (a Catholic religious sect known for self-flagellation) crosses atop sandstone outcroppings, apple orchards, and small cornfields, all on the shores of lush *bosque* (Spanish for "forest"). You'll put in at the Country Line parking area and paddle to Embudo Station. The restaurant there won't complain about your taking out if you stop to have a beer and a bite to eat, and it's well worth the trip. Beware of bridges, which can collect debris and form strainers. This run is best in May and June, when the water is over 1,000 CFS (cubic feet per second), but it can be run at almost any level.

Class II/III

People are often surprised at the flamboyance of the **Rio Grande**. Nowhere is this river's dynamic personality more obvious than along the **Race Course at Pilar**. A favorite day run for locals, and an early season run for many who come down from Colorado and Utah, the 5-mile stretch has lots of fun play features especially during spring run-off in April, May, and early June. You'll put in at the Quartzite parking area just south of Pilar. The major features are Albert's Falls, a section with a few big holes worth missing at high water; the Narrows, a long section of white water where you won't want to swim unless you like swimming for awhile; Big Rock, one of northern New Mexico's few forays into rapids with big boulder features; and Souse Hole, an easy sneak to the left at almost any level, but a bit of a keeper through the center at big water. Many kayakers take out just after Souse, but the carry is steep up awkward stone steps. Another mile downstream is County Line, where there's a very accessible beach. If you run it straight through you'll finish quickly—in a few hours. However, I've been known to stay on this stretch for 7 hours playing on features. Your choice.

Truly one of the most spectacular places I've ever traveled to is the **Chama River Canyon** in this part of New Mexico. In the summer the green grass, sage and piñon trees juxtaposed against the reds and pinks of the sandstone canyon will entertain you for days.

In order to run the upper part of the Chama River, which has a Wild and Scenic Rivers designation, a permit is required. Apply by contacting the Bureau of Land Management Taos Field Office (☎ **505/758-8851**) to request an application. There's a $6 fee, and applications are due by the end of January. Notification takes place in early February. You can write for a permit from the BLM at 226 Cruz Alta Rd., Taos, NM 87571. If you do acquire a permit, you'll want to spend 1 or 2 nights out on the river. (Two nights make for a very leisurely trip.) With the Wild and Scenic Rivers designation, this area has pristine campsites; be sure to leave them that way. You'll put in at El Vado Ranch, off El Vado Reservoir Road 112, and take out off FS 151. The first day and a half you'll paddle mostly flat water, with a few riffles along the way. Watch for deer and even mountain lions in the area. When you see the Christ in the Desert Monastery on your left, you know you're nearing the Class II section described below.

If you'd like to do just a day run, you'll take FS 151 to the take-out. You may want to bring two cars or a bicycle to run the shuttle, as there's no main road on which to hitchhike. You'll continue up FS 151 to the put-in at a small well-marked launch below Christ in the Desert Monastery. Along the way to the put-in, look toward the river and you'll likely find a good campsite to stay the night. This is an excellent place to camp along a river and do day runs. You may even want to bring your bike in order to ride the dirt roads. *Beware:* During the rainy season (July into early September), the red clay roads become very slick, and those without four-wheel-drive are known to get stranded.

The run below the Monastery begins with some broad meandering curves and passes by sandbars. Be aware that mosquitoes in this area can be relentless; be sure to lather up with your favorite flavor of DEET or Avon. Also be aware that you'll want to do these runs on weekends in spring and summer, when the BLM is releasing water. The flows will range from 800 to 1200 CFS then, but will be an anemic 200 CFS or so at other times.

The only sizable rapids you'll encounter will be a stretch above Skull Bridge, with a good play hole about 10 feet before the bridge. A short distance later you'll encounter a long undercut wall with some good-sized waves at the gauging station, and finally, a "screaming" left-hand turn shortly before the take-out. When the flows are up, some people class these as III.

Class III/IV

The **Lower Taos Box** run takes you into the **Rio Grande's** mouth with a gradient averaging 28 feet per mile—but much steeper for long stretches—gargles you around between 700-foot-high canyon walls that jut straight up, and spits you out 18 miles later. It's one of New Mexico's most popular runs. Though some grumble about long stretches of flat water, most find the trip picturesque enough to endure those quiet times in order to savor Powerline Falls, a runable fall with a few imperative technical moves, and Rock Garden, a continuous 4-mile stretch. This is best run from April through July, and you'll want the water to be above 1,000 CFS. At very high water, this becomes a Class V run. The shuttle can be long since you have to go quite a ways away from the river, through Taos. I suggest enlisting a shuttle at the Rio Grande Yacht Club (☎ **505/758-9072**). In any event you put in at John Dunn Bridge west of Arroyo Hondo and take out at Taos Junction Bridge off Highway 96. Most do this run in a day; plan for 4 to 8 hours, depending on the water level.

Class IV/V

The **Upper Taos Box** on the **Rio Grande** is where New Mexico's hair boaters hang out. Kayakers like Ed Lucero, who is the star of some of the world's most risky kayak films, and many of his boating friends, test their skills on this stretch. It's a narrow, boulder-choked canyon, part of which is named the Razor Blade run (for the sharp rocks in the channel). It's best to do this run above 1,500 CFS. This 5-mile, approximately 2-hour run that drops 80 feet per mile is best run in May through July. You access it through Lee Trail near Sunshine Valley. Avoid the Class VI section, which is so treacherous it's basically unrunnable, between the Chiflo and Little Arsenic Springs campgrounds.

There are a few creek runs that feed into the Rio Grande, most notably the Embudo River and the Rio Pueblo de Taos. Both are extremely dangerous and should be run by experts only. The **Rio Pueblo de Taos** is a short run that begins in pastoral country, where you might meet up with fences, and then descends into a deep canyon with fast flows and lots of hazardous features. This section is rated Class IV to VI. The creek drops 60 feet per mile, and the last 0.75 miles greatly exceeds this. It's best run in April and May. Beware of diversion dams, low bridges, and fences. Upper NM 240 has a number of bridges that make for decent put-in points. For the take-out, the Taos Junction Bridge is easily accessible.

The **Embudo River** (some say Embudo Creek) is a favorite creek run for many hair boaters. It's a very fast run—approximately 15 miles and some sources say it can take as little as 1 hour. The upper section is class II and III for 4 or 5 miles, then turns to Class IV, V, and VI. Be prepared for portages. It's best run at 150 to 250 CFS. The lower section is continuous Class II and III, and is very fast. It's most runable in May and adjoining months on wet years. There are a number of accesses, most of them difficult, but the Rio Lucio Bridge on NM 75 toward Peñasco is one option. You can take out at the bridge in which the Embudo passes under NM 68, though parking is difficult. Watch for diversion dams, bridges, fences, logs, and strainers.

WHITE-WATER RAFTING

As with kayaking, people are often surprised that this high desert has white water. In fact, the notorious **Taos Box** is known across the nation as a highly scenic, challenging, and varied run. And there are other notable floats as well. Here's how to get there and what to look for.

Half- or full-day white-water rafting trips down the Rio Grande and Rio Chama originate in Taos and can be booked through a variety of outfitters in the area. The wild **Taos Box,** a steep-sided canyon south of the Wild Rivers Recreation Area, offers a series of class IV rapids that rarely lets up for some 17 miles. The water drops up to 90 feet per mile, providing one of the most exciting 1-day white-water tours in the West. May and June, when the water is rising, are good times to go. Experience is not required, but you will be required to wear a life jacket (provided), and you should be willing to get wet.

Most of the companies listed run the Taos Box ($69 to $89 per person) and **Pilar Racecourse** ($30 to $35 per person) on a daily basis. A full-day Pilar trip takes a more leisurely route before getting to the Racecourse and usually includes lunch ($69). Some companies (see Rio Grande Rapid Transit, listed below) also offer evening dinner floats—great for older people, little kids, or people with disabilities. These have no white water, but plenty of scenery (about $30). They take out at Embudo Station, where rafters can dine and drink microbrewed beer.

I highly recommend **Los Rios River Runners** in Taos, P.O. Box 2734 (☎ **800/ 544-1181** or 505/776-8854). Other safe bets are **Native Sons Adventures,** 1033-A Paseo del Pueblo Sur (☎ **800/ 753-7559** or 505/758-9342); **Far Flung Adventures,** P.O. Box 707, El Prado, 87529 (☎ **800/359-2627** or 505/ 758-2628), and **Rio Grande Rapid Transit,** Box A, Pilar, 87531 (☎ **800/ 222-RAFT** or 505/758-9700).

Safety warning: Taos is not the place to experiment if you are not an experienced rafter. Do yourself a favor and check with the **Bureau of Land Management** (☎ **505/758-8851**) to make sure that you're fully equipped to go white-water rafting without a guide. Have them check your gear to make sure that it's sturdy enough—this is serious rafting!

WILDLIFE VIEWING

Any of the hikes within the **Valle Vidal** area will expose you to wildlife. Sixty mammal species including black bear, mountain lion and many elk, as well as 200 species of birds inhabit this 100,000-acre parcel of Carson National Forest. The reason for so much wildlife is that all of it is carefully managed. There is even limited access to the area during the elk calving season in the spring. There are few designated hiking trails traversing these lands, but that shouldn't stop you from exploring. You're likely to even see large herds of elk from your car. Similarly in the **Pecos Wilderness** you're likely to see plenty of elk and Rocky Mountain bighorn sheep, but that has not always been the case. In the late 1800s elk had been exterminated in the Pecos country, and by 1900 they were gone from the rest of the state. Bighorn sheep had also disappeared from the area by 1900. It took the leadership of Elliott Barker, who had grown up on a ranch near the wilderness and went on to work in the Carson National Forest under the supervision of conservationist Aldo Leopold, to reintroduce bighorn sheep, elk, and beavers into the Pecos. He lobbied hard for better game protection and management laws, and helped organize the National Wildlife Federation. Today the bighorn sheep are so plentiful backpackers complain of them eating gear left unattended. Within the wilderness you're also likely to see mule deer.

Diamondback rattlesnakes inhabit many parts of northern New Mexico, generally lands below 8,000 feet. The **Sandia Mountains** is in rattlesnake habitat, as are many of the areas around Abiquiu. The reptiles generally want to avoid confrontation, so don't get carried away trying to view them, but you will find the intricate design on their skin is as lovely as any artwork you'll ever see. Scorpions and tarantulas are some of northern New Mexico's most exotic creatures, both of which exist in the state's warmer regions, and neither of which is lethal. The **Albuquerque** area is a likely site for scorpions. Generally nocturnal creatures, these pinkish/yellowish creatures with a slender tail ending in a sting can be found in dark places. Tarantulas seem to like the warmth of the Albuquerque area and the piñon/juniper forests in the lower lands surrounding Santa Fe and Taos.

Campgrounds & Other Accommodations

CAMPING

Carson National Forest
208 Cruz Alta Rd., Taos, NM 87571. ☎ 505/758-6200.

There are 9 national forest campsites within 20 miles of Taos, all open from April or May until September or October, depending on snow conditions. For information on other public sites, contact the **Bureau of Land Management,** 226 Cruz Alta Rd., Taos, NM 87571 (☎ 505/758-8851).

Cebolla Mesa Campground
On U.S. 522 north of Taos, drive 16 miles to FS 9. Turn left onto this dirt road, passable to all vehicles when dry, and drive to its end and the campground, about 3.5 miles. 6 primitive sites (RV trailers 32 ft. and under are welcome), picnic tables, fire rings, and rest rooms. Camping, fishing, hiking.

Cebolla Mesa Campground, located in Carson National Forest, sits within a piñon forest at a 7,300-foot elevation on the rim of the Rio Grande Gorge, with amazing views down into the canyon. This is a little-used campground so you should find plenty of solitude. A 1.25-mile trail starting at the campground drops you 600 feet down to the Rio Grande River. On the rare occasion that it rains, the clay road heading into the campground becomes quite slick. Four-wheel drive is your safest option during the monsoon season, July through September.

Enchanted Moon Campground
7 Valle Escondido Rd. (on U.S. 64 E.), Valle Escondido, NM 87571. ☎ 505/758-3338. 69 sites. Full RV hookups, picnic tables, water. Closed Nov–Apr. $18 per day with hook-up, $13 tent site.

At an elevation of 8,400 feet, this campground is surrounded by pine-covered mountains and sits up against Carson National Forest. Hiking trails are nearby, as well as forest roads on which to ride mountain bikes. Since it's located about 13 miles outside Taos, it has good access to activities in that town as well as in Angel Fire.

Twining Campground
Travel north from Taos on NM 522 to the Ski Valley Road NM 150; turn right and drive approximately 15 miles to Twining. 4 primitive campsites, picnic tables, rest rooms.

Twining Campground is not much to look at (it butts right up against the Taos Valley Ski Area parking lot), but with the cars aside, the campground is a jumping off point for Wheeler Peak hike or Hondo Canyon. Wheeler Peak, at 13,164 feet, is the highest peak in New Mexico. If camping near a parking lot doesn't thrill you, three less developed campgrounds are located nearby—the Lower Hondo, Cuchilla del Medio and the Upper Cuchilla. The Hondo Creek runs near these primitive-site campgrounds.

Cimarron Campground in Valle Vidal
Travel north of Questa about 20 miles to Costilla. Turn east and drive approximately 17 miles to Valle Vidal's west

boundary. It's another 10 miles to the campground. 36 primitive campsites, picnic tables, drinking water, and rest rooms. Camping, fishing, hiking, wildlife viewing.

With a grand ponderosa pine forest enveloping the campground, Cimarron feels private and remote. However, there are only a handful of primitive campsites operated under a first-come, first-served policy, so it's best to be there early in the morning to garner a site. Rangers ask that campers keep tents on gravel pads in order to prevent vegetation from being destroyed from too much use. Just a short hike from the campground, campers have access to the Shuree Ponds that are stocked with trout. One of the ponds is designated for children only, and fishing is not allowed for adults. But in the other ponds, there's a two-fish limit, with catches averaging 15 to 16 inches. If you get up early enough and head down to the water, you may see elk having breakfast. No overnight camping is permitted at the ponds. *A note of caution:* If you suffer from asthma or altitude sickness, this campground, at 9,400 feet, may be too high for you.

Canjilon Lakes Campground
Located 12 miles northeast of Canjilon via FS 559 and 129. ☎ 505/684-2486. 40 campsites, primitive campground, drinking water, rest rooms, and RV sites.

Canjilon Lakes is comprised of 6 ponds in which 40 campsites are located. Ponds are stocked with rainbow trout, and fishing is fair to good. Throughout the area are lovely aspen and pine stands. This is truly an enchanting place.

In & Around Santa Fe National Forest
Santa Fe National Forest
P.O. Box 1689, Santa Fe, NM 87504. ☎ 505/438-7840 or 505/753-7331 (but be patient; this is the number for the Española Ranger Station, and they're not as helpful as they could be). www.publiclands.org.

There are two National Forest campgrounds along NM 475 going toward the Santa Fe Ski Basin. All are open from May to October. Overnight rates start at about $10, depending on the particular site.

Black Canyon Campground, with 44 sites, is located just before you reach Hyde State Park (see listing below). It is one of the only campgrounds in the state for which you can make a reservation; to do so you must go through a national reservation system (☎ 877/444-6777 or www.reserveusa.com). The sites sit within thick forest, with hiking trails nearby. The campground has potable water and sites for trailers up to 32 feet long. **Big Tesuque,** a first-come, first-served campground, with 10 newly rehabilitated sites, is about 12 miles from town. The sites here are closer to the road and sit at the edge of aspen forests. Both Black Canyon and Big Tesuque campgrounds, located along the Santa Fe Scenic Byway, NM 475, are equipped with vault toilets.

Hyde Memorial State Park
8 miles up Hyde Park Rd., east of Santa Fe. 740 Hyde Park Rd., Santa Fe, NM 87501. ☎ 505/983-7175. 44 sites. RB hook-ups, shelters, picnic tables, water. Open year-round. $14 with hook-up, $10 tent site.

About 8 miles from the city, this pine-surrounded park offers a quiet retreat. Its campground includes shelters, water, tables, and vault toilets. Seven RV pads with electrical pedestals and an RV dump station are available. There are nature and hiking trails and a playground as well as a small winter skating pond.

INNS & LODGES
The Lodge at Red River
P.O. Box 189, Red River, NM 87558. ☎ 800/91-LODGE or 505/754-6280. www.redrivernm.com/lodgeatrr. 24 units. $42–$78 double. AE, DISC, MC, V.

This lodge offers decent hotel rooms in a town not known for its high standards. The lower priced ones don't tend to have windows opening to the outside so you may want to pitch for a little more. Knotty pine throughout, the accommodations are clean and comfortable. Downstairs, the restaurant serves standard breakfasts and family-style dinners: fried chicken, steaks, trout, and pork chops.

Taos Area
Little Tree Bed & Breakfast
P.O. Drawer II, Taos, NM 87571. ☎ 505/776-8467. www.littletreebandb.com. 4 units. $95–$145 double. Rates include breakfast and afternoon snack. AE, DISC, MC, V.

Little Tree is one of my favorite Taos bed-and-breakfasts, partly because it's located in a beautiful, secluded setting, and partly because it's constructed with real adobe that's been left in its raw state, lending the place an authentic hacienda feel. Located 2 miles down a country road about midway between Taos and the ski area, it's surrounded by sage and piñon. The rooms are charming and cozy, with radiant heat under the floors. All rooms feature queen-size beds, private bathrooms, and access to the portal and courtyard garden, at the center of which is the little tree for which the inn is named. In the main building, the living room has a traditional viga-and-latilla ceiling and tierra blanca adobe (adobe that's naturally white; if you look closely at it you can see little pieces of mica and straw). Visiting hummingbirds enchant guests as they enjoy a healthy breakfast on the portal during warmer months.

Abominable Snowmansion Skiers' Hostel
476 Taos Ski Valley Rd. (Hwy 150), Arroyo Seco (P.O. Box 3271), Taos, NM 87571. ☎ 505/776-8298. http://taoswebb.com/hotel/snowmansion. E-mail: snowman@newmex.com. 60 beds. $14–$20 for bed; $40–$54 private double, depending on size of accommodation and season; $16 cabins and tepees; $10 camping. Rates include continental breakfast in winter. DISC, MC, V.

Since I was a kid, I've traveled past this hostel and marveled at the name; it was a treat for me to finally experience the inside. Set in the quaint village of Arroyo Seco, about 8 miles north of Taos and 10 miles from the Taos Ski Valley, it offers clean beds for reasonable prices, and a nice community experience. The common room has a pool table, piano, and circular fireplace. The dorm rooms (2 men's and 2 women's) have 8 to 10 beds, and sheets, towels and blankets are provided free in winter or for a small fee in summer. Each dorm room has its own shower and bathroom. The private rooms are spacious, though the decor is only passable. Best of all are the tepees, which sit out around a grassy yard. They sleep 2 to 4 people and have an outdoor kitchen, showers, and toilets nearby.

Between Taos & Santa Fe
Casa Escondida
P.O. Box 142, Chimayo, NM 87522. ☎ 800/643-7201 or 505/351-4805. 8 units. $80–$140 double. Price includes full breakfast. AE, MC, V.

On the outskirts of Chimayo, between Santa Fe and Taos, this inn offers a lovely retreat and a good home base for exploring the Sangre de Cristo Mountains and their many soulful farming villages. This hacienda-feeling place has a cozy living room with a large kiva fireplace. Decor is simple and classic with mission-style furniture lending a colonial feel. The breakfast room is a sunny atrium with French doors that open out in summer to a grassy yard spotted with apricot trees. The rooms are varied; all of my favorites are within the main house. The Sun Room catches all that passionate northern New Mexico sun upon its red brick floors and on its private flagstone patio as well. It has an elegant feel but is versatile; it connects with a smaller room, so it's a good choice for families. The Vista, on the second story, has dormer windows, which create a uniquely shaped roof. The casita adjacent to the main house has a kiva fireplace, a stove, and mini-refrigerator, as well as nice meadow views.

Albuquerque
Hacienda Antigua
6708 Tierra Dr. NW, Albuquerque, NM 87107. ☎ 800/201-2986 or 505/345-5399. www.haciendantigua.com. E-mail: info@haciendantigua.com. 6 units. A/C TEL. $95–$159 double. Extra person $25. Rates include breakfast. AE, DISC, MC, V.

Located on the north side of Albuquerque, just off Osuna Road, is this 200-year-old adobe home that was once the first stagecoach stop out of Old Town in Albuquerque. Fortunately, the owners have been careful to preserve the building's historic charm while transforming it into an elegant bed-and-breakfast. The artistically landscaped courtyard, with its large cottonwood tree and abundance of greenery (including a large raspberry patch), offers a welcome respite for today's tired travelers. The rooms are gracefully and comfortably furnished with antiques. There's La Capilla, the home's former chapel, which is furnished with a queen-size bed, a fireplace, and a carving of St. Francis (the patron saint of the garden); and there's la Sala, with a king-size bed and a large hot tub with a view of the Sandia Mountains. All the rooms are equipped with fireplaces, signature soaps, hair dryers, coffeemakers, and unstocked mini-refrigerators. A gourmet breakfast is served in the garden during warm weather and by the fire in winter. Guests also have use of the pool (in summer) and hot tub. *Light sleepers beware:* The Santa Fe Railroad runs by this inn, with one to three trains passing in the night, the duration of noise lasting a few minutes.

Between Albuquerque & Santa Fe
Galisteo Inn
HC 75 Box 4, Galisteo, NM 87540. On NM 41, 15 miles from Cerrillos via the dirt County Road 42. ☎ 505/466-4000. E-mail: galisteoin@aol.com. 12 units, 4 with TV. $80–$200 double. DISC, MC, V.

Set on grassy grounds under towering cottonwood trees, this 250-year-old hacienda has thick adobe walls and plenty of quiet. Rooms are decorated with Latin art of the Americas, and though most are not sunny, they stay very cool in summer. The Inn serves a full breakfast daily for guests, as well as a *prix-fixe* dinner (at an extra cost) for guests and others on Wednesday through Sunday nights. There's a lovely pool large enough to swim laps, a hot tub, and guided horseback riding.

Santa Fe
Bishop's Lodge
Bishop's Lodge Rd. (P.O. Box 2367), Santa Fe, NM 87504. ☎ 505/983-6377. 144 units. A/C TV TEL. Midwinter $120–$270 double; fall and spring $175–$350 double; summer $240–$525 double; additional person $15. Children 3 and under stay free in parents' room. Ask about packages that include meals. AE, DC, DISC, MC, V.

This resort holds special significance for me, as my parents met in the lodge and were later married in the chapel. It's a place rich with history. More than a century ago, when Bishop Jean-Baptiste Lamy was the spiritual leader of northern New Mexico's Roman Catholic population, he often escaped clerical politics by hiking into this valley called Little Tesuque. He built a retreat and a humble chapel (now on the National Register of Historic Places) with high-vaulted ceilings and a hand-built altar. Today, Lamy's 1,000-acre getaway has become Bishop's Lodge. Purchased in 1918 from the Pulitzer family (of publishing fame) by Denver mining executive James R. Thorpe, it remained in his family's hands until 1998, when an Australian real estate company purchased it. The company is in the midst of an $17 million renovation including the addition of 56 guest rooms, a spa, and 10,000 square feet of meeting space as well as replacement of bedding and other furnishings, all planned to be completed by summer 2001. The lobby, lounge, and restaurant are also being renovated.

The guest rooms, spread through many buildings, feature handcrafted furniture and regional artwork, though some have more flair than others. Standard rooms are spacious and many have balconies, while deluxe rooms feature traditional kiva fireplaces, a combination bedroom/sitting room, and private decks or patios. All rooms have coffeemakers, robes, and in-room safes, and receive a morning newspaper. The newest rooms are luxurious, and some have spectacular views of the Jemez Mountains. The Lodge is an active resort three seasons of the year; in the winter, it takes on the character of a romantic country retreat. There's a restaurant and café, seasonal cookouts, and breakfast rides. There's also an outdoor pool with a seasonal lifeguard, tennis courts, and a spa with a hot tub, sauna, and steam room, as well as hiking and self-guided nature walks, daily guided horseback rides, supervised skeet and trap shooting, a stocked trout pond for children, Ping-Pong, and a summer daytime program with counselors for children.

El Rey Inn

1862 Cerrillos Rd. (P.O. Box 4759), Santa Fe, NM 87502. ☎ **800/521-1349** or 505/982-1931. www.elreyinnsantafe.com. 94 units. A/C TV TEL. $70–$155 double; $99–$199 suite. Rates include continental breakfast. AE, CB, DC, DISC, MC, V.

Staying at "The King" makes you feel like you're traveling the old Route 66 through the Southwest. The white stucco buildings of this court motel are decorated with bright trim around the doors and handpainted Mexican tiles on the walls. Opened in the 1930s, it received additions in the 1950s and remodeling is ongoing. The lobby has vigas and tile floors decorated with Oriental rugs and dark Spanish furniture. No two rooms are alike. The oldest section, nearest the lobby, feels a bit cramped, though the rooms have style, with art-deco tile in the bathrooms and vigas on the ceilings. Some have little patios. Be sure to request to be as far back as possible from Cerrillos Road. The two stories of suites around the Spanish colonial courtyard are the sweetest deal I've seen in all of Santa Fe. These feel like a Spanish inn, with carved furniture and cozy couches. Some rooms have kitchenettes. Complimentary continental breakfast is served in a sunny room or on a terrace in the warmer months. There's also a sitting room with a library and games tables, outdoor swimming pool, Jacuzzi, sauna, picnic area, children's play area, and Laundromat. For its cheaper rooms, El Rey is Santa Fe's best moderately (and even inexpensively) priced accommodation.

Riverdancer Retreat and Bed & Breakfast

16445 Scenic Highway 4, Jemez Spring, NM 87025. ☎ **800/809-3262** or 505/829-3262. www.riverdancer.com. E-mail: reservations@riverdancer.com. 7 units. A/C TV TEL. $350–$405 double; includes breakfast and light lunch or supper, and massage. DISC, MC, V.

"Eventually the watcher joined the river, and there was only one of us. I believe it was the river," wrote Norman Maclean in *A River Runs Through It.* This was my experience while sitting on cottonwood-shaded bench at this inn. The inn/retreat sits on a long bow of the Jemez River, a small, fast-flowing stream lined with cottonwoods. Built in 1994, the inn has clean lines and comfortable rooms, each named after Native American tribe. I stayed in the Hopi room, a queen that wasn't large but was well-planned, with built-in drawers and many amenities. All rooms have sliding glass doors that open out to a patio where there's a fountain. The beds are comfortably firm, with good reading lights, and each room has radiant heated Saltillo tile floors a tub/shower, hair dryer, and razors. Everything is done with an eye for conservation, including the bulbs, many of which are luminescent—not to my liking—but conscientious nonetheless. The Great Room has a cozy welcoming feel, as well as a large table where breakfast is served family style. We had both buckwheat pancakes and a artichoke heart quiche, with fruit and juice as well. The inn offers massage and body treatments, guided nature walks, art classes, yoga, dance, and drumming.

10

New Mexico High Plains

Much of my growing up took place on the oft-dusty, oft-lush plains of northeastern New Mexico, the region north of Interstate 40 and east of the Sangre de Cristo Mountains, where dinosaurs and buffalo once roamed. My family has a ranch here along the Cimarron cutoff of the Santa Fe Trail. I grew up with the ghost of Samuel Watrous, who once had a store on that historic trade route. Listed on the National Register of Historic places, the building is now my family's home. For a time, I slept in the room where Watrous was said to have committed suicide, though he was found with not one but two bullet holes in his head. For many years I searched one corner of our property for his grave, which was said to be where the Mora and Sapello Rivers meet. One day I did find a heavy chiseled stone among the *bosque* (Spanish for forest) there. Whether you believe in ghosts or not, historical characters are present throughout this part of the state, and that's part of the eerie fun of coming here.

Northeastern New Mexico is still the land of cowboys. My family raises cattle, and I long ago learned that ranchers tend to be stoic and use words only when necessary. They're comfortable with long silences in conversation, which for me defines the nature of this part of the state: There are many things to see here, but there are long, seemingly barren silences in between.

The long miles through the mountains from Las Vegas to Cimarron or across the plains from Raton to Clayton are worth the drive. The history is everywhere, from evidence of Coronado's passage during his 16th-century search of Cíbola, to the Santa Fe Trail ruts on the prairie made some 300 years later. In Cimarron you'll see evidence of the holdings of cattle baron Lucien Maxwell, who controlled most of these prairies as his private empire in the latter half of the 19th century. During his era, this was truly the Wild West. Cimarron attracted nearly every gunslinger of the era, from Butch Cassidy to Clay Allison, Black Jack Ketchum to Jesse James. Bullet holes still decorate the ceiling of the St. James Hotel.

Established long before its Nevada namesake, Las Vegas was the largest city in New Mexico at the turn of the 20th century, with a fast-growing cosmopolitan population. Doc Holliday, Bat Masterson, and Wyatt Earp walked its wild streets in the 1880s. A decade later, it was the headquarters of Teddy Roosevelt's Rough Riders, and early in the 20th century, it was a silent film capital (Tom Mix made movies here) and the site of a world heavyweight boxing match. Today, with a population of approximately 17,000, it is the region's largest city and the proud home of 900 historic properties.

Two national monuments and one national historical park are particular points of interest. Fort Union, 24 miles north of Las Vegas, was the largest military installation in the Southwest in the 1860s and 1870s. Visitors can stroll among the ruins and even into the jail. Capulin Volcano, 33 miles east of Raton, last erupted 60,000 years ago; visitors can now walk inside the crater. Pecos National Historical Park was once the home of the most feared Puebloan warriors, whose ghosts still may inhabit the now-serene mesa at the base of the Sangre de Cristo Mountains. One other place of note is the Kiowa National Grasslands, which preserves 136,000 acres of pure prairie.

Drained by the Pecos and Canadian Rivers, northeastern New Mexico is otherwise notable for the number of small lakes that afford opportunities for fishing, hunting, boating, camping—even scuba diving. There are 11 state parks and about a half-dozen designated wildlife areas within the region. Philmont Scout Ranch, south of Cimarron, is known by Boy Scouts throughout the world.

This region can be best appreciated by the history buff. It is not the place to go if you're longing for great hiking adventures; much of the hiking is within small state parks, except for Hermit's Peak, one of New Mexico's premier hikes, and the Skyline Trail into the Pecos Wilderness, a little-traveled route for those adept with a compass and topo map. Nor will you find many mountain biking trails here. However, bird-watchers and wildlife enthusiasts will have plenty to do.

The Lay of the Land

From the foothills of the Sangre de Cristo Mountains stretching eastward into Oklahoma and Texas are broad plains and rolling hills interrupted by bluffs and river valleys, all part of the stable interior of the continent. As compared to the Rio Grande Rift region to the west, these lands have a simple geologic makeup, with only a few faults and folds. Most of the complexity comes from erosion by the Pecos and Canadian Rivers and their tributaries that cut through the region.

There are, however, hundreds of small volcanoes here in a variety of shapes, from cinder cones to shield volcanoes to small lava domes, most notably Capulin Volcano to the north. This 8,182-foot peak was last active about 60,000 years ago, when it sent out the last of four lava flows. Today a trek around its rim offers panoramic views of these high plains as well as of other volcanic peaks in the region.

Also prominent within the region are sinkholes, such as the Blue Hole near Santa Rosa, formed from a partial collapse of an underground cavern. The hole is 60 feet wide and 81 feet deep. Three thousand gallons of 61°F water flow through it each day, making it a clear and clean haven for scuba divers.

Within broad depressions and folds along the plains, humans have created many lakes, most notably by damming the Canadian River to form Conchas Lake, a 25-mile long reservoir, and Ute Lake, which is 20 miles long. These are popular with fishers, water-skiers, and jet boaters.

The northeastern plains have a relatively mild climate. Summers are warm and dry, with cool nights. The highs are in the 70s and 80s with a few days in the low 90s. In winter the climate is generally sunny with highs in the 40s and 50s. However, lows can get into the 10s and 20s, often with nights below freezing. Hikers can enjoy the foothills of the Sangre de Cristos from spring to fall; however, winters will prove cold and snowy. West of the mountains the climate is warmer, making summers hot for hiking, but allowing some hiking in winter.

Orientation

This region's western border follows the base of the Sangre de Cristo Mountains, and its southern border follows Interstate 40 running east to west. The northern boundary is the Colorado border, and the eastern boundary is the border with Oklahoma and Texas.

With a population of approximately 17,000 Las Vegas is the region's largest city, while Raton (population 7,500), on I-25 in the Sangre de Cristo foothills, is the gateway to New Mexico from the north. Clayton (population 2,500), Tucumcari (pop. 6,831), and Santa Rosa (population 2,500) are all transportation hubs and ranching centers along the eastern border.

Parks & Other Hot Spots

Capulin Volcano National Monument
The monument is located 30 miles east of Raton via U.S. 64/87 and north 3 miles on NM 325. ☎ **505/278-2201.**

ROUTE 66 REVISITED: REDISCOVERING THE MOTHER ROAD

Everyone's heard of Route 66. The highway that once stretched from Chicago to California was hailed as the road to freedom. During the Great Depression, it was the way west for farmers escaping Dust Bowl poverty out on the plains. If you found yourself in a rut in the late 1940s and '50s, all you had to do was hop in the car and head west on Route 66.

Of course, the road existed long before it gained such widespread fascination. Built in the late 1920s and paved in 1937, it was the lifeblood of communities in eight states. Nowadays, however, U.S. 66 is as elusive as the fantasies that once carried hundreds of thousands west in search of a better life. Replaced by other roads, covered up by interstates (mostly I-40), and just plain out of use, Route 66 still exists in New Mexico and Arizona, but you'll have to do a little searching and take some extra time to find it.

Motorists driving west from Texas can take a spin (make that a slow spin) on a 20-mile gravel stretch of the original highway running from Glenrio (Texas) to San Jon. From San Jon to Tucumcari, you can get your kicks on nearly 24 continuous paved miles of vintage 66. In Tucumcari, the historic route sliced through the center of town along what is today Tucumcari Boulevard. Santa Rosa's Will Rogers Drive is that city's 4-mile claim to the Mother Road. In Albuquerque, U.S. 66 follows Central Avenue for 18 miles, from the 1936 State Fairgrounds, past original 1930s motels and the historic Nob Hill district, on west through downtown.

One of the best spots to pretend you are a 1950s road warrior crossing the desert, whizzing past rattlesnakes, teepees, and tumbleweeds, is along NM 124, which winds 25 miles from Mesita to Acoma in northwestern New Mexico. You can next pick up old Route 66 in Grants, along the 6-mile Santa Fe Avenue. In Gallup, a 9-mile segment of U.S. 66 is lined with restaurants and hotels reminiscent of the city's days as a Western film capital from 1929 through 1964. Just outside Gallup, the historic route continues west to the Arizona border as NM 118.

Route 66 continues through the Arizona town of Holbrook, where the landmark Wigwam Motel beckons guests to sleep in rooms shaped like teepees. In Flagstaff, Route 66 through town is lined with court motels, often with period neon signs still blinking. This town is so hyped about the route it has a Route 66 Festival the first weekend in June.

Sixty-five miles west of Flagstaff the longest remaining stretch of old Route 66 extends for 160 miles from Ash Fork to Topock, passing through remote country as well as through towns such as Seligman and Kingman. In the latter town, the Historic route 66 Association of Arizona holds forth, working to raise money for a Route 66 museum in the city.

Route 66 makes a pass through the rugged Sacramento Mountains cruising through Oatman, an old mining town, now the site where wild burros roam the streets and rhinestone cowboys stage mock gunfights. The route drops out of the mountains, where it once crossed a metal bridge. Today the bridge still stands, but travelers have to content themselves with the speed and efficiency of Interstate 40 as it dashes west to freedom.

For more information about Route 66, contact the Grants/Cíbola County Chamber of Commerce (☎ 800/748-2142) or the New Mexico Department of Tourism (☎ 800/545-2040).

---

www.nps.gov/cavo/. The visitor center, located at the base of the northern side of the volcano, is open daily Memorial Day through Labor Day 7:30am–6:30pm; the rest of the year, daily 8am–4pm. Admission $4 per car or $2 per person. All golden passports are honored.

Capulin Volcano National Monument offers visitors the rare opportunity to walk inside a volcanic crater. A 2-mile road spirals up from the visitor center more than 600 feet to the crater of the 8,182-foot peak, where two self-guiding trails leave from the parking area: an energetic and spectacular 1-mile hike around the crater rim and a 100-foot descent into the crater to the ancient volcanic vent. One of its most interesting features here is the symmetry of the main cinder cone. The volcano was last active about 60,000 years ago, when it sent out the last of four lava flows. Scientists consider it dormant, with a potential for future activity, rather than extinct. As far back as 1891 public settlement on Capulin Mountain was prohibited by Congress. In 1916 it was protected by presidential proclamation as Capulin Mountain National Monument for its scientific and geologic interest. The final name change came in 1987.

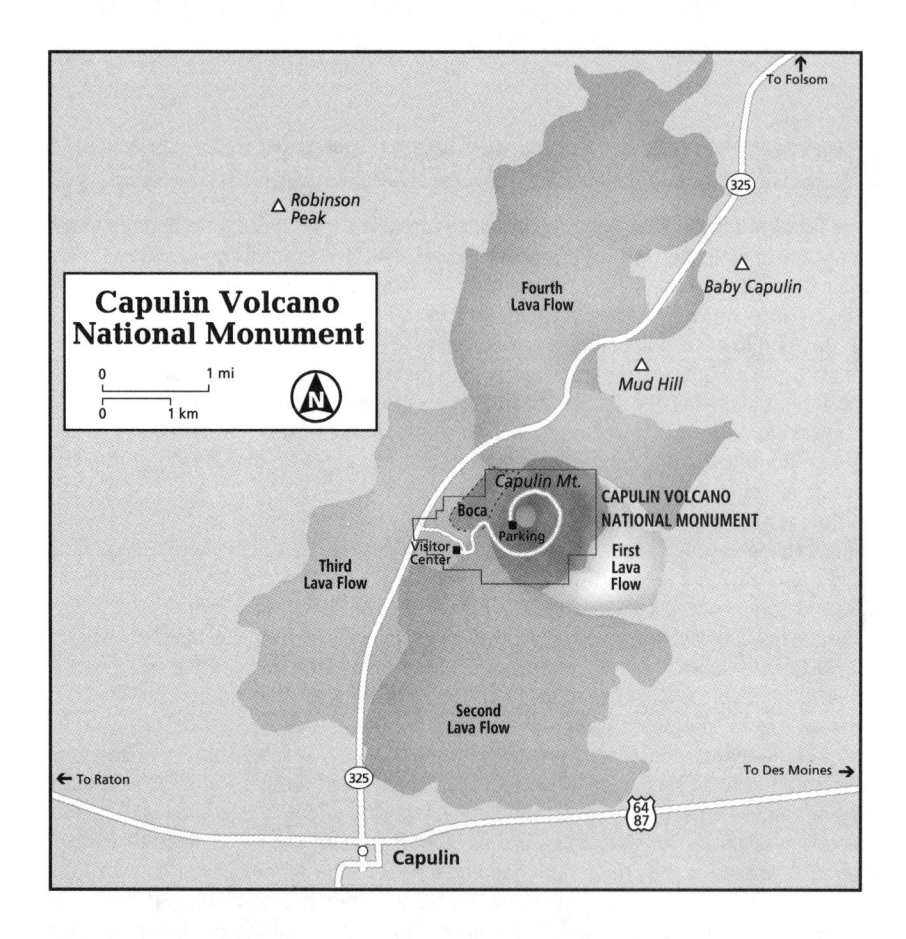

Because of the elevation, visitors should wear light jackets in the summer and layers during the rest of the year. Be aware that the road up to the crater rim is frequently closed due to weather conditions. Plan on spending 1 to 3 hours at the volcano; a more in-depth exploration could take several days, but camping is not permitted.

A short nature trail behind the center introduces plant and animal life of the area and is great for kids and accessible to people with disabilities. There's also a longer hike from park headquarters up to the parking lot at the crater rim. The crater rim offers magnificent panoramic views of the surrounding landscape, the Sangre de Cristo Mountains, and, on clear days, portions of four contiguous states: Kansas, Texas, Colorado, and Oklahoma. During the summer, the volcano attracts swarms of ladybird beetles (ladybugs). Camping is not permitted inside the monument; however, camping facilities are available 24 hours a day, only 3 miles away in the town of Capulin (try the **Capulin RV Park** at ☎ **505/278-2921**), as well as in the neighboring towns of Raton and Clayton.

Pecos National Historic Park

Head east from Santa Fe on I-25 for 20 miles to the Rowe exit; travel north on NM 63 for 4 miles. ☎ **505/757-6414.** Open daily Memorial Day to Labor Day, 8am–6pm; the rest of the year, daily 8am–5pm. Closed Jan 1 and Dec 25. Admission $2 per person, $4 per carload.

Pecos National Historical Park contains the ruins of a 15th-century pueblo and 17th- and 18th-century missions. The walk through these ruins offers spectacular views of green *vegas* (meadows) with the bald peaks of the Pecos Wilderness as a backdrop. Coronado mentioned Pecos Pueblo in 1540: "It is feared through the land," he wrote. With a population of about 2,000, the Native Americans farmed in irrigated fields and hunted wild game. Their pueblo had 660 rooms and many kivas. By 1620, Franciscan monks had established a church and convent. Military and natural disasters took their toll on the pueblo, and in 1838, the 20 surviving Pecos went to live with relatives at the Jemez Pueblo.

The E. E. Fogelson Visitor Center tells the history of the Pecos people in a well-done, chronologically organized exhibit, complete with dioramas. A 1.5-mile loop trail begins at the center and continues through Pecos Pueblo and the Misión de Nuestra Señora de Los Angeles de Porciuncula (as the church was formerly called). This excavated structure—170 feet long and 90 feet wide at the transept—was once the most magnificent church north of Mexico City.

En route to the park you'll pass through Glorieta Pass, site of an important Civil War skirmish. In March 1862, volunteers from Colorado and New Mexico, along with Fort Union regulars, defeated a Confederate force marching on Santa Fe, thereby turning the tide of Southern encroachment in the West. Pecos, a quaint town, well off the beaten track since the interstate was constructed, is the site of a noted Benedictine monastery. About 26 miles north of there on NM 63 is the village of Cowles, gateway to the natural wonderland of the Pecos Wilderness. There are many camping, picnicking, and fishing locales en route.

Fort Union National Monument

To reach the site from Las Vegas, drive 18 miles north on I-25 to the Watrous exit, then another 8 miles northwest on NM 161. ☎ **505/425-8025.** Open daily Memorial Day through Labor Day 8am–6pm; the rest of the year, daily 8am–5pm. Closed Christmas and New Year's Day. Admission $4 per car or $2 per person for persons ages 18–62.

Established in 1851 to defend the Santa Fe Trail against attacks from Plains Indians, Fort Union was expanded in 1861 in anticipation of a Confederate invasion, subsequently thwarted at Glorieta Pass, 20 miles southeast of Santa Fe. Its location on the Santa Fe Trail made it a welcome way station for travelers, but when the railroad replaced the trail in 1879, the fort was on its way out. It was abandoned in 1891. Today Fort Union, the largest military installation in the 19th-century Southwest, is in ruins. Though the site now contains only low adobe walls, chimneys, and a stone jail, the ruins do give an idea of the impressive scope of the fort. Santa Fe Trail wagon ruts can still be seen nearby. Follow the 1.6-mile self-guided interpretive trail that wanders through the ruins and imagine yourself a weary 19th-century wagon traveler stopping for rest and supplies.

The national monument has a small visitor center and museum with exhibits and booklets on the fort's history. Visitors should allow 2 hours to tour the ruins. There is a gift shop that carries a wide selection of books on New Mexico history, women's history, and frontier military books. Camping is not available at the monument, but there are facilities in nearby Las Vegas.

Cimarron Canyon State Park
Take U.S. 64 west from Cimarron for 13 miles. ☎ 505/377-6271. Campgrounds with toilets, water. Fishing, hiking, wildlife viewing.

The 32,000-acre designated state wildlife area sits at the foot of spectacular crenellated granite cliffs, 800 feet high in some areas, known as the Palisades. Also at the park are a river and the park lakes, which attract anglers; for the best fishing, move away from the heavily populated campgrounds. Rock climbing is allowed throughout the park except in the Palisades area.

Just east of Cimarron, County Road 204 offers access to the Carson National Forest's Valle Vidal recreation area (see chapter 9), an incredible place to hike and backpack and see hundreds of elk.

Villanueva State Park
Located 31 miles southwest of Las Vegas via I-25 and NM 3. ☎ 505/421-2957. 35 campsites, group campground, drinking water, showers, rest rooms, RV sites, dump station. Camping, fishing, hiking, horseback riding.

Villanueva State Park offers good hiking, camping, and picnicking between red sandstone bluffs in the Pecos River Valley. The state park is located at the base of a 400-foot-deep canyon on the banks of the Pecos River in a picturesque Hispanic farming valley. It has some decent fishing holes as well as shady spots to take a snooze. Nearby are the Spanish Colonial villages of Villanueva and San Miguel del Vado; the latter is a national historic district built around an impressive 1805 church. Be aware that this isn't the quietest park around. On weekends in particular, locals like to picnic while listening to ranchero music on their car stereos.

Coyote Creek State Park
Located 14 miles north of Mora via NM 434. ☎ 505/387-2328. Group campground, visitor center, picnic area, drinking water, showers, rest rooms, dump station. Camping, fishing, hiking.

Set in a secluded canyon with a trout stream and wildflowers, Coyote Creek State Park is a good place to stop for a picnic or for a longer sojourn. It has numerous shelters and an open meadow for tent camping near the stream dotted with beaver ponds. The fishing is good, and a few well-marked hiking trails head into the mountains.

Morphy Lake State Park
From Las Vegas, head northwest on NM 518 to Mora; turn left on NM 94 and drive south for 4 miles. ☎ 505/387-2328. Camping, fishing, hiking, picnicking, wildlife viewing.

Located on the edge of the Pecos Wilderness, this pretty lake is set in a basin of pine forest; it offers primitive camping, swimming (though mossy conditions) and trout fishing, and is a good starting point for hikes into the wilderness. Check on driving conditions before going; the road to the park is rough and best suited for four-wheel-drive vehicles, although usually passable by cars.

Storrie Lake State Park
Located 4 miles north of Las Vegas via NM 518. ☎ 505/425-7278. 20 sites with electricity, 23 sites without, primitive camping in an open area close to the lake, visitor center, picnic area with grills, playground, historic exhibits, drinking water, showers, rest rooms, dump station and boat ramp. Boardsailing, boating, camping, fishing, water sports.

This lake, set in the outskirts of Las Vegas on a meadow in the foothills of the Sangre de Cristo Mountains, is where the local kids used to go to make out at night when I was in high school, and I hear that's still the case, so you could list that as one of the park's activities. More noteworthy, though, are this lake's winds. With steady breezes blowing off the mountains and plains, the 1,100-acre lake is the top sailboarding spot in the state. When the winds calm a little, it becomes a playground for water-skiers. The fishing is good, with bass, catfish, rainbow and brown trout stocked regularly. The swimming, however, is marginal. Since the lake has no designated swimming area, and lots of steep natural drop-offs, park rangers suggest that swimmers wear life jackets. In winter, watch for Canada geese.

Sugarite Canyon State Park
Located 10 miles east of Raton via NM 72 and NM 526. ☎ **505/445-5607**. 2 campgrounds with a total of 40 campsites, visitor center, exhibits, cultural/historic sites, group campground, drinking water, rest rooms, RV sites, boat ramp. Camping fees $10–$18. Boating, camping, fishing, hiking, horseback riding, wildlife viewing.

Sugarite Canyon State Park, along the Colorado border, is one of the most picturesque parks in the state and a good spot for fly-fishing. It's comprised of a steep aspen-, oak-, and pine-covered canyon with wildflower-filled meadows. Black bear, elk, deer, turkey and other wildlife come to drink from one of the two trout-stocked lakes. Swimming is not allowed, but anglers can be sure to find a quiet spot on the lake where they'll most likely catch rainbow and golden trout. Lake Alice is the best place in the park for fly-fishing. Numerous hiking trails meander through the park, and a museum at the visitor center traces the canyon's mining history.

Clayton Lake State Park
12 miles north of Clayton off NM 370, near the distinctive Rabbit Ears Mountains. ☎ **505/374-8808**. 7 campsites with electric and water, table, shelter, and grill; 30 sites with table, shelter, and grill; rest rooms; hot showers Mar–Oct. Boating, camping, fishing, hiking, swimming. Fishing and boating allowed Mar–Oct; other activities allowed year-round.

Tracks from eight species of dinosaurs can be clearly seen next to this oasis sitting on the broad plains. The lake is crystalline blue, strange to come upon after driving across these pale prairies. A half-mile trail on the southeast side of the lake leads across the dam to an exhibit describing the types of dinosaurs that roamed this area. From there, you can wander along a boardwalk to the amazingly intact dinosaur tracks. Another trail starts on the north side of the lake and is 1.5 miles long; if hikers wish they can follow it farther to the dinosaur tracks, making for a 3.5-mile hike.

Santa Rosa Lake State Park
From the main street in Santa Rosa, Will Rogers Dr., turn north on North Second St. This will turn into NM 91; drive 7 miles on NM 91 to the lake. ☎ **505/ 472-3110**. 75 campsites (⅔ with electric hookups), visitor center, picnic area with grills, historic exhibits, drinking water, showers, rest rooms, dump station, and a boat ramp. $4 day-use fee; $10–$14 camping fee. Boating, camping, fishing, hiking, horseback riding, water sports.

Santa Rosa Lake State Park, on a dammed portion of the Pecos River, is a sweet spot surrounded by prairie and piñon/juniper forest. The park has camping year-round and excellent fishing. Swimming in the

---

Door of the Moon
Ten miles south of Santa Rosa via NM 91, the village of **Puerto de Luna** (Door of the Moon) is a 19th-century county seat with a mid-1800s courthouse and church, Nuestra Señora del Refugio. Francisco Vásquez de Coronado was believed to have camped here as he traveled en route to Kansas. For insight into village life here, read Rudolfo Anaya's *Bless Me, Ultima* (Warner, 1999), a tale of growing up on the *llanos* (plains) of the area.

lake is permitted but not encouraged because of its uneven bottom and lack of beaches; children would be safer swimming in Park Lake in Santa Rosa.

Conchas Lake State Park
Located 34 miles northwest of Tucumcari via NM 104. ☎ 505/868-2270. Visitor center, group campground, tent camping, shelters, drinking water, showers, rest rooms, RV sites, dump station, boat ramp and marina. Boating, camping, fishing, water sports.

I spent a lot of my youth sailing, waterskiing, and diving off cliffs at this 25-mile long reservoir situated on the Canadian River. It offers a lovely respite within the dry northeastern plains, with often-glassy water in the mornings and good winds in the afternoons. The lake sits within a desert environment, with lots of sand and little shade. A marina on the northern side provides facilities for boating, fishing, and water-skiing. Nearby is a store, cafe, RV park with hookups, and trailers available to rent. Anglers come to fish for crappie, bass, walleyed pike, and catfish. Scuba divers come to this fairly clear-water lake to get their certification. At the south side of the lake is Conchas Lodge and Resort, which is managed by a private concessionaire, and has a campground and boat-launch facilities.

Ute Lake State Park
Located 22 miles northeast of Santa Rosa on US 54, near the town of Logan. ☎ 505/487-2284. 200 campsites, RV sites with electric hookups, group shelter, visitor center, little league baseball parks, full-service marina, docking facilities, picnic tables, drinking water, rest rooms, showers, dump station, and rental boats. Boating, camping, fishing, horseback riding, water sports.

Much like its neighbor, Conchas Lake, 8,200-acre Ute Lake sits out on the open plains of northeastern New Mexico. The lake itself has about 12.5 miles of water fit for boating, plus another 5 miles on Ute Creek, creating plenty of space for fishers and water-sports enthusiasts. Parts of the lake have groves of cottonwoods and desert willow, including some campsites shaded by those trees. This reservoir on the Canadian River is filled with walleye, bass, catfish, and crappie. A 1.5-mile nature trail runs down through a canyon north of the park.

La Cueva National Historic Site and Salman Ranch
Off NM 518, 6 miles east of Mora. ☎ 505/387-2900. Open summer Mon–Sat 9am–5pm, Sun 10am–5pm; call first in winter, when hours are limited. Free admission.

Each fall I make a bit of a pilgrimage to this spot in a lush valley along the Mora River. Its history is rich, dating from the early 1800s when a man named Vicente Romero began farming and raising sheep here. He completed an elegant two-story northern New Mexico home that still stands, and a mill that ground flour and supplied electricity for the area (the real draw). Just north of these historic sites is the San Rafael Mission Church, with exquisite French Gothic windows. Recently restored by local people, it's now painted blue and white. The trip through these sites is worth the time during any season, but in the fall, the raspberries ripen and turn this into a must-do trip. The ranch's current owner David Salman planted 20 acres of the delectable fruit and now sells it by the basket or crate, as well as in jams and over soft vanilla ice cream. Delicious.

Victory Ranch
1 mile north of Mora on NM 434. ☎ 505/387-2254. www.victoryranch.com. E-mail: alpacas@victoryranch.com. Open daily 10am–4pm, with tours at 11am, 1 and 3pm. Admission $2 adults, $1 children under 12.

CIMARRON: THE WILD WILD WEST

Few towns in the American West have as much lore or legend attached to them as Cimarron, 41 miles southwest of Raton via U.S. 64. Nestled against the eastern slope of the Sangre de Cristo mountain range, the town (its name is Spanish for "wild" or "untamed") achieved its greatest fame as a "wild and woolly" outpost on the Santa Fe Trail between the 1850s and 1880s and a gathering place for area ranchers, traders, gamblers, gunslingers, and other characters.

Frontier personalities including Kit Carson and Wyatt Earp, Buffalo Bill Cody and Annie Oakley, Bat Masterson and Doc Holliday, Butch Cassidy and Jesse James, painter Frederic Remington and novelist Zane Grey, all passed through and stayed in Cimarron—most of them at the **St. James Hotel** (see "Campgrounds & Other Accommodations" later in this chapter). Even if you're not planning an overnight stay here, it's a fun place to visit for an hour or 2.

Land baron Lucien Maxwell founded the town in 1848 as base of operations for his 1.7 million-acre empire. In 1857, he built a mansion at his **Maxwell Ranch,** furnishing it opulently with heavy draperies, gold-framed paintings, and two grand pianos. In the gaming room the tables saw high stakes, as guests bet silver Mexican pesos or pokes of yellow gold dust. Gold was struck in 1867 on Maxwell's land, near Baldy Mountain, and the rush of prospectors that followed caused him to sell out 3 years later.

The ranch isn't open for inspection today, but Maxwell's 1864 stone grist mill, built to supply flour to Fort Union, is. The **Old Mill Museum,** a grand, three-story stone structure, well worth visiting, houses an interesting collection of early photos and lots of memorabilia, from a saddle that belonged to Kit Carson to dresses worn by Virginia Maxwell. It's open in May and September, Saturday from 9am to 5pm and Sunday from 1 to 5pm; from Memorial Day to Labor Day, Friday to Wednesday from 9am to 5pm. Admission is $2 adults, $1 seniors and children.

Cimarron has numerous other buildings of historic note, and a walking tour to see them only takes about a half-hour. A walking tour map is included in the Old Mill Museum brochure, which you can pick up at the museum.

Few things surprise me in this strange part of the state, where images of Jesus are known to appear upon stucco walls, and ghosts are said to inhabit old haciendas, but I must say that my head turned when I saw alpacas grazing in a meadow here. I stopped immediately and stepped out of my car just in time for a tour. With a small cup of feed I purchased for 25¢, I followed a young boy out to some lush pens where the odd South American Andean creatures greeted us with a harmonica-like hum. Very friendly, they ate from our hands while the babies roamed about, heads held high, marble-clear-blue eyes looking quizzical. Also on-site is a store that sells sweaters and shawls made from alpaca wool, as well as a loom where visitors can try weaving.

What to Do & Where to Do It

BIRD WATCHING

The **Las Vegas National Wildlife Refuge** (☎ **505/425-3581**), just a few miles outside of Las Vegas center, is a year-round home to such birds as prairie falcons and hawks, while during late fall and early winter migratory birds such as sandhill cranes, snow geese, Canada geese, and bald and golden eagles frequent the area. In all, more than 240 species can be seen. Take Las Vegas exit 345 and head west on

NM 4 for 1 mile until you come to NM 281. Turn south and drive 5 miles to the refuge.

The **Maxwell National Wildlife Refuge** (☎ 505/375-2331), near Raton, also has a rich population of migratory birds, including raptors and bald eagles. Also look for golden eagles, sandhill cranes, pelicans, ducks of all sorts, great blue heron, snowy egrets, gulls, and lots of small birds and shorebirds. It's located west of I-25 near the town of Maxwell.

BOARDSAILING & SAILING

Storrie Lake, 6 miles north of Las Vegas, via NM 518, benefits from strong winds blowing off the eastern plains. This 1,000-acre water body is large enough to travel around upon, and yet small enough so you won't get lost. A much larger water body, **Conchas Lake,** located 34 miles northwest of Tucumcari via NM 104, often has strong winds in the afternoons, particularly in the spring and early summer, though they aren't as consistent as they are at Storrie.

CLIMBING

Though not a developed site, **Cimarron Canyon State Park** has the notable and lovely 800-foot Palisades, which rangers discourage climbing upon since they're composed of flaky rock. However, climbing is available on several small granite cliff faces, a half-mile up Maverick Canyon, and behind a spring on the east end of the canyon. Access is off US 64 west of Cimarron.

FISHING

Fishing in northeastern New Mexico is a popular pastime, and there are many lakes and a few good streams where anglers catch a broad range of fish from bass to trout to bluegill. Some call the **Cimarron River** the best fly-fishing water in the state. Wild brown trout, German Brown trout, and stocked rainbows measuring 10 to 14 inches in length, make their homes in this river fed by Eagle Nest Lake. Because much of the river runs through private land you'll want to trek to the section below the mouth of Tolby Creek in the Colin Neblett Wildlife Area, managed by the New Mexico Department of Game and Fish. The river gets crowded, but you can always find your own private spot. Beginners may have trouble, however, because of the heavy brush. The best fishing is June through September. It's located 3 to 10 miles east of Eagle Nest via U.S. 64.

There's excellent summer fly-fishing and winter ice fishing for fish as big as 14 inches on **Eagle Nest Lake,** located along U.S. 64 northeast of Taos. This lake is also known for being one of the state's premiere kokanee and trout lakes.

Sugarite Canyon State Park, just north of Raton at the Colorado border, is a good spot for fly-fishing. Two lakes are stocked with rainbow and golden trout; the southern lake, Lake Alice, is the better of the two for catching with flies. The park is located 10 miles east of Raton via NM 526.

A small, lightly fished lake with a good population of bass and trout is **Maxwell Lake 13,** which sits on a 3,800-acre prairie site. This area attracts bird-watchers and anglers. Located 3 miles north of the Maxwell exit from I-25 via NM 445, Maxwell Lake is one of the best lakes for float tubes and for catching big trout (in the vicinity of 16 to 24 inches) and largemouth bass. Back in 1995, a 2-pound ring perch was snatched out of the lake. Maxwell Lake is closed November 1 until March 1 to accommodate migrating waterfowl.

An oasis of blue surrounded by miles of high grasslands, **Clayton Lake** is where fishers go for channel catfish and trout. Most people fish from the rocky shore. Fly-fishing is best during early spring or late fall, but as the waters heat up, worm fishing works to entice the fish that have gone deeper. The lake is located about 15 miles north of Clayton via NM 370.

Catfish in the 15- to 20-pound range known as lunkers dominate the **Canadian River** in the Mills Canyon Campground located southeast of Springer at Canadian River Canyon via US 56, NM 39, and County Road U1. There are also some bass and walleye. Fishers find nice 8- to 9-foot fishing holes along this stretch of river.

With 450 surface acres, anglers can catch lunkers in **Springer Lake** like the 36-pound pike caught in 1978. Today, pike are more in the range of 25 pounds. The lake is located about 5 miles due west of Springer. The best fishing is done from April to June and September to October.

Charette Lakes, 100- and 300-acres in size, are located on a mesa 23 miles southwest of Springer via I-25 and NM 569. These delightful lakes usually offer good fishing, with rainbows and perch nearing 14 inches. The lakes are closed November 1 until March 1 to accommodate migrating waterfowl.

With steady breezes and 1,100-acre surface area, **Storrie Lake,** beckons plenty of fisherman to gather along its shores. Four miles north of Las Vegas via NM 518, this lake has good fishing for bass, catfish, and rainbow and brown trout, which are stocked regularly.

McCalister Lake, part of the Las Vegas National Wildlife Refuge, is a bird-watchers' paradise in winter and a fine trout lake in summer. The lake is closed to fishing from October 31 through March 1, but when this 100-acre lake opens, float tubers catch plenty while enjoying the sight of eagles and hawks flying overhead. The lake is stocked with rainbow trout and has a very good early season for big fish. Boats traveling at trolling speed are permitted. Winds can make casting difficult. Access the lake from Las Vegas to NM 104 and NM 281.

Santa Rosa Lake, located 10 miles north of I-40 out of Santa Rosa on a dammed portion of the Pecos River is usually a fishing mecca on the high plains of eastern New Mexico, but during drought years it is less productive. When the fishing is good, there are walleye, bass, catfish and crappie. Santa Rosa Lake is surrounded by juniper and piñon trees and rolling hills. Fishing by boat is preferred.

With 8,200 surface acres, **Ute Lake** on the Canadian River has walleye, bass, catfish and crappie. The lake has about 12.5 miles of boatable water, plus another 5 miles on Ute Creek, creating plenty of space for fishers and other water-sports enthusiasts.

Built for flood control, irrigation, and water supply, **Conchas Lake** is a good spot for crappie, bass, walleyed pike, channel catfish, bluegill and largemouth bass. On this 9,600-acre U.S. Corps of Engineers impoundment are marinas on the northern and southern sides, which provide facilities for boating and fishing. The lake is located 32 miles northeast of Tucumcari via NM 104.

Ice-Skating

If you're in the mood to go ice-skating while you're in northeastern New Mexico, you're in luck. Set below a huge basaltic cliff on the Gallinas River, the **Montezuma Ice Pond** offers smooth ice throughout much of the winter. Though there are no skate rentals, those who have their own can skate for free. A Zamboni ice cleaner even keeps the ice glassy. Access the pond off NM 65 west of Las Vegas.

Lake Maloya at Sugarite Canyon State Park is the place to go in the Raton area to skate. A 60- by 100-foot space is cleared for skating, which takes place from mid-December though March. No rentals are available. The lake is 10 miles east of Raton via NM 72 NM 526.

Fourteen-inch rainbows have been snagged from the **Pecos River,** located along NM 63 north of Pecos Village. For more information on fishing this popular stretch of water, see chapter 9. East of there, the Pecos meanders through a picturesque Hispanic farming valley, where **Villanueva State Park** offers up some good fishing. Here you'll find quiet fishing holes as well as shady spots to take a snooze. The park is located 31 miles southwest of Las Vegas via I-25 and NM 3.

HIKES & BACKPACK TRIPS

In this region of New Mexico most hikes are within state parks, so their distance is limited to generally 6 miles or less. However, an adventurous person could access the Pecos Wilderness from the Mora area and put together some nice backpacking. I personally have yet to do so, but I have a goal to leave from the vicinity of Morphy Lake southwest of Mora and hike Trail 274 to the **Skyline Trail,** Trail 251 (both in the Pecos Wilderness) to the Truchas Peaks. Trail 251 traverses the entire length of the Santa Barbara Divide, past Barbara Peak and along the south face of Chimayosos Peak, altogether about 15 miles to the base of the Truchas Peaks. The trail is so little used that anyone attempting it should be proficient at map and compass reading and route finding.

With some imagination, the Hermit's Peak hike listed below could easily be turned into a multi-day trip into the Pecos Wilderness. **Clear Creek Canyon** in Cimarron Canyon State Park is another good area to explore.

Hermit's Peak

8 miles round-trip. Strenuous. 2,740-ft. elevation gain. Allow 4 hrs. Access: Take NM 65 about 15 miles northwest out of Las Vegas to the El Porvenir Campground. Maps: El Porvenir and Rociada.

This elephant-shaped peak stands as a unique backdrop for much of eastern New Mexico, and its history is tantalizing.

In 1863, Italian immigrant Giovanni Marie Augustini arrived in Las Vegas on the Santa Fe Trail. The recluse climbed to the top of the peak and set up residence and a small healing practice in a cave. His presence there became known, and people came to him for healings and to trade for wooden crosses he carved. He became so popular that in 1867 he resigned his solitary post and headed south across the desert to the rugged Organ Mountains. There he was murdered in 1869. Since then the peak has been named for him—*El Solitario,* or Hermit's Peak.

Trail 223 is well marked and well-worn. It climbs out of the canyon onto a bench that slopes up toward Hermit's Peak. You'll climb steadily on the rocky trail that grows steeper and steeper. It crosses a small stream a few times, then begins switchbacking up a canyon, the steepest and rockiest part of the trip. Just when you feel like gravity has defeated you, at about mile 3.5, you'll break out onto a ridge, and sigh not so much out of gratitude but at the view out across the plains. The last half-mile to the summit is fairly easy walking. You'll pass some campsites in a wooded area. On the summit, you'll find a short trail that leads to the Hermit's Cave. You'll also find spectacular views of eastern New Mexico. You may even be able to see tracks from the Santa Fe Trail, which carve through the vast plain from the north. If you'd like to turn this into a longer backpack trip, you'll find the markers for Trail 223 at the summit. This trail continues on to Lone Pine Mesa, Beaver Creek, El Porvenir Canyon, and back to the trailhead.

Canyon Trail at Villanueva State Park

2.25-mile loop. Moderate. 400-ft. elevation gain. Allow 1½ hrs. Access: 35 miles south of Las Vegas via I-25 and NM 3. Map: Villanueva State Park map.

Half the fun of this hike is getting to the trailhead. Once you turn off I-25, for 14 miles you meander along the Pecos River through lovely northern New Mexico faming villages with names such as El Pueblo and San Miguel. You'll pass the oddly named Sad Café, a good place to get some lunch, and by Madison Winery, where you might want to stop and have a sip. You'll meander along cornfields where, in summer, farmers sell ears from card tables along the road. You'll pass by enchanting Colonial churches and then you'll see the 400-foot high cliffs of Villanueva Canyon.

The trail starts at the group campground site right across from the visitor center. Cross the footbridge over the Pecos River, turn right (south), and head up the bank. The rocky trail climbs gradually above the river. Be aware that during the summer, this part of the hike might be noisy, as plenty of locals use the park to swim in the river and play music on their boom boxes. But as you head higher, the sounds will die away. After about 0.25 miles, the trail meets up with some turn-of-the-century ruins and interpretive signs explaining them. These 19th-century Spanish Colonial ruins include a threshing floor, used in processing grain, and some lovely stone corrals. The trail makes a switchback to the north and climbs a little more steeply to the top of the canyon. Right when you arrive at the top, you'll see a trail heading off to the left. This is your route along the rim and down. But first visit the picnic ramadas and viewpoint farther up the trail. The view to the west from there across the cornfields is amazing, as is the view to the east toward the plains. Backtrack to the trail you passed at the canyon rim. It travels along the rim, and then descends steeply to the river, which it follows south back to the bridge.

Kiowa National Grasslands
1–12 miles one-way. Moderate. Allow 1–6 hrs. Access: Located at the Mills Canyon Campground, southeast of Springer at Canadian River Canyon accessed via US 56, NM 39, and County Road U1. Map information is not available. Rangers recommend a high-clearance vehicle to enter the canyon.

The 263,954-acre Kiowa National Grasslands is a project to reclaim once-barren prairie land, the result of over-farming in the late 19th and early 20th centuries and the Great Plains Dustbowl of the 1930s. Today the plains are often green, and the area provides food, cover, and water for a wide variety of wildlife, such as antelope, bear, Barbary sheep, mountain lion, wild turkey, pheasant, and quail.

There are two portions, one near Clayton and the other near Springer. This route is in the Springer portion. Though there are no established trails, there are jeep roads and cow trails through lovely 800-foot-deep Mills Canyon. The Canadian River runs through and is a good place to fish. Your best bet is to head from the campground into the canyon and explore, returning the way you came.

Opportunity and Ponderosa Ridge Trails at Sugarite Canyon
6-mile loop. Moderate. 500-ft. elevation gain. Allow 3 hrs. Access: Located 10 miles east of Raton via NM 72 NM 526. Map: Sugarite Canyon State Park brochure.

This hike takes you through locust, ponderosa pine, and oak forests to a high point in the region at 8,400 feet, with lovely views of Sugarite Canyon. The trail leaves from the north end of the Soda Pocket Campground. Take the Opportunity Trail northwest. At 0.5 miles you'll come to Little Horse Mesa Trail, a 0.25-mile spur to the top of a mesa with 360° views. There's some as-yet undeveloped rock climbing there. Back on the Opportunity Trail you'll continue hiking, arriving at a series of switchbacks at about 1.5 miles. Another few miles and the Opportunity Trail intersects with the Ponderosa Ridge Trail from which views are available down toward Lake Maloya.

BOY SCOUTS OF AMERICA

Cimarron is the gateway to the **Philmont Scout Ranch** (☎ 505/376-2281), a 137,000-acre property donated to the Boy Scouts of America by Texas oilman Waite Phillips, beginning in 1938. Scouts from all over the world use the ranch for backcountry camping and leadership training from June through August and for conferences the remainder of the year. On my recent visit, after touring the incredible Villa (worth seeing even if you have no interest in scouting), I got a flat tire. If you're going to get a flat tire anywhere in the West, this is probably the place to do it. Two young Scouts, an Eagle Scout, and two girls who were working at the camp for the summer came to my rescue, and I was back on the road in a half-hour.

There are three museums on the ranch, all open to the public. For hours and tour information call the number listed above. **Villa Philmonte,** Phillips's lavish Mediterranean-style summer home, was built in 1927 and remains furnished with the family's European antiques. Located 4 miles south of Cimarron, it's open for guided tours for a small fee. The **Philmont Museum and Seton Memorial Library** commemorates the art and taxidermy of Ernest Thompson Seton, the naturalist and author who founded the Boy Scouts of America, and has exhibits on the varied history of the Cimarron area. Admission is free. The **Kit Carson Museum,** 7 miles south of Philmont headquarters in Rayado, is a period hacienda furnished in 1850s style. Staff members in historic costumes lead tours. Admission is free.

Complete the loop back to your car; en route watch for mule deer, elk, mountain lions, and black bears.

HORSEBACK RIDING

From May 15 to end of September **Rancho Cañon Ancho** (☎ 505/666-2004; www.straddleasaddle.com), a working cattle ranch, takes people trail riding and cattle driving across the plains and canyon country near Wagon Mound. Activities are tied to what's happening on the ranch during the days you're there. You might find yourself branding or doctoring cattle, or just riding up and down river checking on the bovines. Guests stay in little line-shack cabins that sleep up to four. These are relatively primitive digs, without electricity. What fuel is needed is propane. There's a bathhouse and a cowboy hot tub heated with a snorkel stove. For lunch and dinner guests have a sit-down family-style meal. Midday brings a "saddle-bag" lunch out on the range. Other activates to occupy visitors are fishing and tubing in the stream and hiking to old caves and overhangs in the canyon. Rates run $165 per day per person. The ranch also offers day rides. To get there from I-25 take exit 387 at Wagon Mound. Go straight past the Phillips 66 station, across the railroad tracks, and then take the first right. This will take you past the rodeo grounds for 18 miles to the ranch.

MOUNTAIN BIKING

Unfortunately, thus far, northeastern New Mexico lacks mountain biking trails. I'm sure that in coming years some will develop, but for now, your best bet after trying the couple I've mentioned here is to head to north central New Mexico, where trails abound (see chapter 9).

Glorieta Mesa

10 miles round-trip. Easy. 800-ft. elevation gain. Allow 2–3 hrs. Access: From Santa Fe drive east on I-25 for 7.5 miles to the Lamy exit. From the bottom of the exit, turn left and drive under I-25 to a stop sign. Turn right (east) and take the frontage road (Old Las Vegas Highway) for about 2 miles to County Road 51. Turn right on this paved-becoming-dirt road and drive under the freeway and

across some railroad tracks. Turn right and head up onto the mesa. Continue on this road for 3.5 miles to where it forks; bear left onto FS 326. Drive 1 mile on FS 326 to a fenceline and a sign marking National Forest Land, where you'll park.

This ride, a favorite of Santa Fe locals and a good place to bring kids, takes you across the top of a lovely mesa, with views of the Pecos Wilderness and the broad eastern New Mexico plains. From the parking area follow the dirt double track up a short hill. Through here you'll be traveling northeasterly across high mesa country speckled with piñon and juniper trees. Watch for mule deer, jackrabbits, and cattle. You'll traverse up and down not-too-steep hills for 4 miles, with views becoming more outstanding as you go. Many side roads lead off from this route; if you feel like exploring, you might want to follow some, but be careful not to become confused in this open country. After about 4 miles, make a left turn onto FS 612, which will keep you heading northeast. You'll encounter a rocky, technical section that levels off quickly. Ride less than 1 mile to the edge of the mesa, where you'll take in more views and turn around to head back the way you came.

Ponderosa Ridge and Opportunity Trails at Sugarite Canyon
6-mile loop. Moderate. 500-ft. elevation gain. Allow 2 hrs. Access: Located 10 miles east of Raton via NM 72 NM 526.

This ride takes you to the highest point in Sugarite Canyon State Park at 8,400 feet, with lovely views of Sugarite Canyon. The trail leaves from the north end of the Soda Pocket Campground. Your best bet is to ride in a clockwise direction. Take the Opportunity Trail northwest. At 0.5 miles you'll come to Little Horse Mesa Trail, a 0.25-mile spur to the top of a mesa with 360° views. There's some as-yet undeveloped rock climbing there. Back on the Opportunity Trail you'll continue riding through ponderosa pine and oak. At about 1.5 miles you'll begin switchbacks, climbing swiftly up to the height of the ride. The Opportunity Trail intersects with the Ponderosa Ridge Trail, from which views are available down toward Lake Maloya. Complete the loop back to your car.

ROAD BIKING
Raton to Capulin Volcano National Monument
90 miles round-trip. Moderate. Allow 6 hrs. Access: Begin at the public parking lot along Raton's First St.

This is a lovely ride across northeastern New Mexico plains to a 1,300-foot-high volcano. Begin riding north on First Street to its end and turn right under the railroad tracks. Turn east onto Sugarite Avenue (NM 72), which you'll follow out of town. At mile 10 the road gains some 800 feet in elevation as it makes its way atop basalt-capped Johnson Mesa. On top the road levels out. Watch for cinder cones along the route as well as antelope and elk and the Folsom Man historic marker. At 38 miles, you'll descend into Folsom. Turn right on NM 325 and ride 6 miles to Capulin Volcano National Monument, where water is available. If you're feeling energetic you can ride 2 miles to the top of the volcano. Return the way you came.

Sugarite Canyon to the Colorado Border
25 miles. Moderate. Access: Begin in Raton on First Street; see the Raton to Capulin Volcano ride above.

This ride takes you from downtown Raton up through the picturesque Sugarite Canyon State Park, passing two lakes en route to the Colorado border. On NM 72, 6 miles from Raton, turn north on NM 526. This will take you through Sugarite Canyon State Park, a lush canyon bordered by meadows. You'll pass by rocky cliffs and scree fields set within oak scrub forest. Black bear, elk, deer, turkeys, and skunk come to drink from

FOLSOM MAN

If you have any curiosity about human origins, one clue to the mystery is in the town of Folsom. Near there, cowboy George McJunkin discovered the 10,000-year-old remains of "Folsom Man." The find, excavated by the Denver Museum of Natural History in 1926, represented the first association of the artifacts of prehistoric people (spear points) with the fossil bones of extinct animals (a species of bison). Basically, what McJunkin found was a spear point lodged in the bone of an ancient bison. The site is on private property and is closed to the public, but some artifacts (prehistoric as well as from the 19th century) are displayed at the **Folsom Museum,** Main Street, Folsom (☎ **505/278-2122**) in summer, 505/278-3616 in winter), a funky little place presided over by locals full of tall tales about the area. The museum does not, however, contain any authentic Folsom points, only copies. The museum has limited exhibits on prehistoric and historic Native Americans of the area, as well as Folsom's settlement by whites. Hours are 10am to 5pm daily from Memorial Day through Labor Day, winter by appointment. Open weekends only in May and September. Admission is $1 for adults, 50¢ for children ages 6 to 12, and free for children under 6. To get to Folsom, take NM 325 off the Clayton Highway (U.S. 64/87, running 83 miles east-southeast from Raton to Clayton), 7 miles.

---

the lakes. When you reach the Colorado border, turn around and return the way you came.

NM 3 through Villanueva
10–58 miles one-way. Easy to moderate. Allow 1–4 hrs. one-way. Access: Begin at the intersection of NM 3 and I-25, 25 miles southwest of Las Vegas.

This road meanders for 14 miles along the Pecos River Valley through lovely northern New Mexico farming villages with names such as El Pueblo and San Miguel. You'll pass the oddly named Sad Café, a good refueling stop, and by Madison Winery. You'll pedal along cornfields and past Colonial churches and then you'll see the 400-foot high cliffs of Villanueva Canyon. If you intend to continue on NM 3, ride through the village of Villanueva south by Jacinto Mesa to the intersection with Interstate 40, where you can turn around and ride back. NM 3 doesn't have shoulders, but it has little traffic, so riding should be safe.

SCUBA DIVING

There couldn't possibly be scuba diving in this dry, arid, landlocked state, could there? Yes, there is, with the best at Santa Rosa, where you'll find the **Blue Hole,** an 81-foot-deep artesian well that's a favorite of divers from throughout New Mexico and neighboring states. Fed by a subterranean river that flows 3,000 gallons per minute at a constant 61°, it's deep enough to merit open-water certification. Actually most of the divers you see here will be in the process of obtaining certification, since shops from Colorado, Oklahoma, and Texas use this as their teaching hole. In fact, I got my certification here. It follows that divers must be certified, or dive with a certified instructor, and they must purchase a permit from the Santa Rosa Police Department. For those accustomed to diving in the ocean, it doesn't provide much room for exploration. The experience reminds me of swimming in a fish bowl, often with a number of other fish (divers) swimming about. No permit is required for swimming or snorkeling, however, and there's a bathhouse on-site. The best place to rent equipment is at the **Santa Rosa Dive Center** on Blue Hole Road (☎ **505/472-3370**).

SNOWSHOEING

In the Las Vegas area, **Hermit's Peak** can make for a steep but magnificent winter hike. For directions to the trailhead see the "Hikes & Backpack Trips" section earlier in this chapter. Intrepid snowshoers can access the **Pecos Wilderness** from Morphy Lake State Park southwest of Mora.

SWIMMING

Some of the best swimming in the area is at **Conchas Lake**, where swimmers like to jump off cliffs near the dam. The lake's many beaches provide good access as well. Other lakes in the region worth dipping into are **Clayton Lake, Morphy Lake** (though it will be chilly), **Storrie Lake**, and **Ute Lake**.

Park Lake (☎ 505/472-3763), in the middle of Santa Rosa, serves as the town's municipal pool. It's a lovely spot to take the kids. They can swim with the geese while you cool off under the elm trees. The lake offers free swimming, picnicking, and fishing, and contains a softball field and playground.

Though it's an indoor rather than outdoor experience, the new **Las Vegas Recreation Center's swimming pool**, located at 1751 North Grand Avenue, is an especially good place to take kids. It's Olympic-sized and has an incredible slide that will keep kids busy for hours. There's also a tot pool. Call ☎ **505/426-1739** for more information.

WALKS & RAMBLES

Clayton Lake State Park's Dinosaur Tracks

0.5 mile. Easy. Allow 1 hr. Access: 12 miles north of Clayton off NM 370, near the distinctive Rabbit Ears Mountains.

Tracks from eight species of dinosaurs lie on the shores of this small lake sitting on the plains. A half-mile trail on the southeast side of the lake leads across the dam to an exhibit describing the types of dinosaurs that roamed this area. From there, a boardwalk leads out across a sandstone bed to some 500 amazingly intact dinosaur tracks, dating back from more than 100 million years. Another trail starts on the north side of the lake and is 1.5 miles long; if hikers wish they can follow it farther to the dinosaur tracks, making for a 3.5-mile hike.

Crater Rim Trail at Capulin Volcano

1 mile. Easy. Allow 45 min. Access: The monument is located 30 miles east of Raton via U.S. 64/87 and north 3 miles on NM 325.

This amazing trail takes you along the rim of the Capulin Volcano, which at an elevation of 8,182 feet protrudes some 1,300 feet above the plains. The mountain is made up of loose cinders, ash, and other rock debris that were spewed out 60,000 years ago in eruptions that sent firework-like "rooster tails" of glowing cinders into the air. Despite this mountain's rugged birth, it is now calm and rich with wildlife. As you circumnavigate the rim you may see thousands of ladybugs that swarm on the park's plants in summer, chokecherry (*capulin* in Spanish) trees, or even mule deer hiding out on the slopes below. Once you complete the loop, or before, you'll definitely want to make your way 0.2 mile down to the bottom of the crater and the vent.

Sugarite Canyon Coal Camp Trail

1.5 miles. Easy. Allow 1 hr. Access: Located 10 miles east of Raton via NM 72 and NM 526.

This trail follows along a mountain stream to ruins of the old Sugarite Canyon Coal Camp. The camp operated between 1910 and 1941 and at its peak had a population of 1,000, many of whom were European and Asian immigrants. From the camp the trail leads up to an abandoned mine, where it connects with the River Walk Trail, which loops back to the visitor center.

A Walking Tour of Old Las Vegas

1 mile. Easy. Allow 2 hrs. Access: Begin from the front of the Plaza Hotel in Las Vegas.

Though this isn't a mountain-blazing experience, it, like the Old Mesilla walking tour in Las Cruces, provides a completely entertaining jaunt through centuries of history.

Before embarking on this tour of what's called West Las Vegas, you may want to stop in at the chamber of commerce on Grand Avenue to pick up a map of the self-guided historic-district walking tour (though you will find adequate directions below). If you do, take the time to head next door to the Rough Riders Memorial and City Museum (727 Grand Ave.; ☎ 505/454-1401, ext 283). The largest contingent of the First U.S. Volunteer Cavalry, also known as the Rough Riders, was recruited from New Mexico to fight in the 1898 Spanish-American War. This museum chronicles their contribution to U.S. history and also contains artifacts relating to the history of the city. A new permanent exhibit documents architectural and cultural changes in northern New Mexico. Admission is free; the museum is open Monday through Friday from 9am to 12pm and 1 to 4pm, and weekends 10am to 3pm (May through October only), except holidays.

What's most notable in this tour is the town's early Spanish history, with adobe buildings dating back to the first Spanish visits in the 16th century still standing alongside the ornate structures of the late 1800s. In addition, you'll rarely see such a well-preserved collection of Territorial-style buildings.

Most of the interesting structures can be found in the Plaza–Bridge Street historic district. Begin at the northwest corner of the plaza at the **Veeder Buildings.** The building to the right, built in 1880, is an example of Italianate architecture. The left building, built in 1895 by the Veeder brothers, was built with a Romanesque style, giving it a Moorish look.

Heading east, the **Plaza Hotel,** 230 Old Town Plaza, was the finest hotel in the New Mexico Territory back in 1881. Its three-story facade topped with a fancy broken pediment decoration was the town's pride and joy, and it has been happily restored. (See the "Campgrounds & Other Accommodations" section later in this chapter.) Next door, the **Charles Ilfeld Building,** at 224 Old Town Plaza, began as a one-story adobe store in 1867, grew to two stories in 1882, and finally reached three stories with an Italianate facade in 1890.

Nearby, the **Louis Ilfeld Building** shows the classic architecture coming into favor at the turn of the century in a storefront now serving as a bookstore. Though the low adobe building known as the **Dice Apartments,** 210 Old Town Plaza, is unimpressive, its history is. It is the sole building on the plaza that predates the Mexican-American War of 1846. In that year, General Stephen Kearney, commander of the Army of the West, stood on a one-story building on the north side of the plaza (probably this one) to address the town's population, claiming New Mexico for the United States.

Turning south on the plaza, you'll see **Our Lady of Sorrows,** one of the last remaining adobe buildings on the plaza. Its curving parapet on the facade dates from the 1930s. On the corner, the **Romero Building** is now Plaza Drugs, where you may want to stop for a lemonade and some ice cream. The building was erected in 1919 by Secundino Romero, a wealthy political leader.

Heading east on Bridge Street, you'll come to the **Rough Rider Trading Company** at 158 Bridge St., a good place to browse. You'll find Southwestern furniture, Western art, and old saddlebags here. Next, on the same side of the street, you'll come to the 1884 **Anicito Baca Building,** now Estella's Cafe, a good place for some authentic New Mexican food. The building's Italianate commercial style is exemplified in the fancy arched windows modeled after Italian palazzos.

PEACE COLLEGE

The Armand Hammer United World College, 5 miles west of Las Vegas via NM 65 (☎ 505/454-4200), is an international school with students from more than 70 countries. It is housed in the former **Montezuma Hotel,** a luxury resort built by the Santa Fe Railroad in the 1880s and now a historic landmark. Three U.S. presidents, Germany's Kaiser Wilhelm II, and Japan's Meiji Emperor Mutsuhito stayed in the multistoried, turreted, 270-room "Montezuma Castle," as it came to be known. It was abandoned during the Depression and purchased in 1981 by Armand Hammer, philanthropist and past chair of the Occidental Petroleum Corporation. Hammer, along with England's Prince Charles, created the school, one in a series of campuses across the globe whose mission is to foster peace by opening dialog between various nationalities.

Also on the campus are the **Montezuma Hot Springs.** The springs, which are free and open to the public, have attracted health-seekers for more than 1,000 years; there are legends that ancient Aztecs, including chief Montezuma II, journeyed here from Mexico in the early 16th century, long before the arrival of the Spanish.

Continue down the street to the 1879 **Stern and Nahm Building,** at 114 Bridge Street, where you'll note cast-iron columns and pressed and folded sheet-metal ornaments above. Next you'll come to the bridge crossing the Gallinas River with a plaque that notes that Francisco Vásquez de Coronado crossed the river here in 1541. A lush riverside park has some shade—a good place for a breather.

Crossing the street to the south side you'll note the **Kiva Theater,** an old stone structure where movies are still shown. Next door is a candy shop with good fudge. Soon you'll come upon the decorative brickwork adorning the 1895 **Winternitz Block,** a good example of local decorative brickwork. It now houses the El Rialto, with some of the best chile in New Mexico. Heading back to the plaza, you'll come to the **E. Romero Hose and Fire Company,** put up in brick in 1909. It has banded piers capped by pressed-metal capitals with dentils in a strange neoclassical architecture.

The 1882 Italianate-style **Hedgcock Building,** at 157 Bridge St., has arched window hoods like those of the Baca building, and has served both as police station and jail as well as shoe factory, saloon, and store. On the corner, is the **First National Bank.** Built around the 1880s, it features a contrasting combination of Italianate architecture and local sandstone block work. Finally, the **Courtroom Building** at 213 Old Town Plaza was erected in 1882 and served as a courtroom for 3 years. Continue on around the plaza and you'll come to **Plaza Antiques,** a fun place to browse for antique clothing and kitchen tables.

WILDLIFE VIEWING

In the **Las Vegas** and **Cimarron** vicinity, out on the eastern plains, watch carefully for pronghorn, more commonly known as antelope. Well-adapted to their environment, they blend in almost perfectly with the meadow grass, so you'll have to watch closely. To see them racing across the plains at speeds up to 45 miles per hour is truly a treat.

Not far off I-25, **Maxwell National Wildlife Refuge,** on the Canadian River 24 miles southwest of Raton, has a rich resident and migratory bird population and numerous native mammals. More than 200 species of birds have been recorded in the refuge. Also look for mule and white-tailed deer, fox, weasel, coyote, porcupine, and possums. You'll find primitive camping by Lake 13, where there is some of the best trout fishing in the state.

South of U.S. 56 via NM 39 is the western of the two parcels that comprise **Kiowa National Grasslands** (☎ 505/374-9652). The 263,954-acre area is a project to reclaim once-barren prairie land, the result of over-farming in the late 19th and early 20th centuries and the Great Plains Dustbowl of the 1930s. Today the plains are often green, and the area provides food, cover, and water for a wide variety of wildlife, such as antelope, bear, Barbary sheep, mountain lion, wild turkey, pheasant, and quail.

Another portion of the grasslands is located east of there, along U.S. 56/412, near the town of Clayton just west of the Oklahoma border. In the early 19th century, the Cimarron Cutoff of the Santa Fe Trail passed through here. This area was also the site of numerous bloody battles between Plains Indians and Anglo settlers and traders. Clayton is most known as the town where the notorious train robber Thomas "Black Jack" Ketchum was inadvertently decapitated while being hanged in 1901 (a doctor carefully reunited head and body before Ketchum was buried here).

Campgrounds & Other Accommodations

CAMPING

Sugarite Canyon State Park Campgrounds
Located 10 miles east of Raton via NM 72 and NM 526. ☎ **505/445-5607.** Two campgrounds (Soda Pocket and Alice Lake) with a total of 40 campsites, visitor center, exhibits, cultural/historic sites, group campground, drinking water, rest rooms, RV sites, and boat ramp. $10–$18 camping fee.

Sugarite Canyon State Park, just north of Raton at the Colorado border, has two of the most picturesque campgrounds in the state. The verdant canyon is laden with wildflower-strewn meadows. The views from Soda Pocket campground of the lush valley set within the stark, brown prairie is impressive. Both campgrounds are surrounded by valley walls with rocky cliffs and scree fields and are set within an oak scrub forest. Black bear, elk, deer, turkeys, and skunk come to drink from the two trout-stocked lakes. Swimming is not permitted, but anglers can be sure to find a quiet spot on the lakes where they'll most likely catch rainbow and golden trout. Numerous hiking trails meander through the park.

Coyote Creek State Park Campground
Located 14 miles north of Mora via NM 434. ☎ **505/387-2328.** 50 campsites, group campground, visitor center, picnic area, drinking water, showers, rest rooms, and dump station. $8–$14 camping fee.

Set a secluded canyon with a trout stream running through, this 83-acre park offers a lovely taste of greenery. The landscape is comprised of oak, aspen, and ponderosa pine. The park has numerous shelters plus an open meadow for tent camping near the stream. The fishing is good here. Summers get busy, but by early fall the only noise campers will hear is the gurgle of the creek or the drill of a woodpecker's beak.

Villanueva State Park Campground
Located 31 miles southwest of Las Vegas via I-25 and NM 3. ☎ **505/421-2957.** 35 campsites, group campground, drinking water, showers, rest rooms, RV sites, and dump station.

Villanueva State Park offers decent hiking, camping, and picnicking between red sandstone bluffs in the Pecos River Valley. The state park is located at the base of a 400-foot canyon on the banks of the Pecos River in a picturesque

Hispanic farming valley. There are great fishing holes as well as shady picnic spots. Nearby are the Spanish Colonial villages of Villanueva and San Miguel del Vado; the latter is a national historic district built around an impressive 1805 church.

INNS & LODGES
Casa de Gavilan
Located 6 miles south of Cimarron on Highway 21. P.O. Box 518, Cimarron, NM 87114. ☎ 800/GAVILAN or 505/376-2246. www.casadelgavilan.com. 4 units. $75–$130 double. AE, DISC, MC, V.

This sprawling adobe villa, built in 1910 on a broad hill overlooking Philmont Scout Ranch and the mountains beyond, provides a quiet Southwest ranch-style experience. The common areas have high ceilings with thick vigas and wooden floors, and the hallways are painted bright Southwestern blue and green. The rooms lie around a central courtyard, a nice place to sit and relax in the cool evenings. The rooms are spacious, with comfortably firm beds and plenty of antiques. The bathrooms are medium-sized and maintain an old-style charm, with touches such as tiny white tile on the floors but with new fixtures. The two-bedroom suite, which is housed in what's called the Guest House is good for families, though lower ceilings give it a slightly newer feel. There isn't a television on the premises, but there is a hiking trail just off the courtyard. Breakfast is served in a big, sunny dining room; you'll find such specialties as baked French toast with ham and fruit salad and a baked apple pancake served with sausage.

St. James Hotel
Rte. 1, Box 2, Cimarron, NM 87714. ☎ 800/748-2694 or 505/376-2664. 23 rooms. Hotel $90 double; $120 suite; motel $60 double. AE, DISC, MC, V.

This landmark hotel offers travelers a romantically historic stay in this Old West town. It looks much the same today as it did in 1873, when it was built by Henri Lambert, previously a chef for Napoleon, Abraham Lincoln, and General Ulysses S. Grant. In its early years, as a rare luxury hotel on the Santa Fe Trail, it had a dining room, a saloon, gambling rooms, and lavish guest rooms outfitted with Victorian furniture. Today, you will find lace and cherry wood in the bedrooms, though, like the Plaza in Las Vegas, the feel is frontier elegance rather than lavishness. Rooms don't have televisions or phones—the better to evoke the days when famous guests such as Zane Grey, who wrote *Fighting Caravans* at the hotel, were residents. Annie Oakley's bed is here, and a glass case holds a register with the signatures of Buffalo Bill Cody and the notorious Jesse James. The beds are comfortably soft, and the bathrooms are small and basic. One room just off the lobby is left open so those not staying the night can have a peek.

The St. James also was a place of some lawlessness: 26 men were said to have been killed within the 2-foot-thick adobe walls, and owner Perry Champion can point out bullet holes in the pressed-tin ceiling of the dining room. The ghosts of some are believed to inhabit the hotel still.

Next door are 12 more rooms in a motel, which I don't recommend. These rooms are narrow and cheaply made, though they do provide TV and telephone for those who prefer the 21st century.

Lambert's at the St. James serves good food in an atmosphere that doesn't quite bridge the century gap. The molded tin ceiling and textured wallpaper are lovely, but the tables and chairs are contemporary. The menu is short but good, with dishes such as pasta primavera and filet mignon priced from $14 to $25. A separate coffee shop serves three meals daily, purveying large portions of tasty New

Mexican food. The hotel also offers a tour desk, an outdoor patio with bar and grill, gift shop, and package store.

Budget Host Melody Lane Motel

136 Canyon Dr., Raton, NM 87740. ☎ 800/421-5210 or 505/ 445-3655. 27 rooms. A/C TV TEL. Mid-May to Labor Day $54 double; Labor Day to mid-May $45 double. Rates include continental breakfast. AE, CB, DC, DISC, MC, V. Small pets are permitted for $1 per pet per night.

Though not much on the outside, this cinder-block hotel provides large, very well cared for rooms close to downtown at a decent price. All rooms have been recently painted, and many have new air conditioners. The rooms are very clean, most with a hair dryer, and many with a steam shower (be sure to request one of these enclosed bathtubs that fills with steam; there's no extra charge). Rooms are especially quiet, with medium-firm beds and good reading lights. Bathrooms are small but have a changing room and sink/vanity. Courtesy transportation is available from Amtrak and the bus station.

Plaza Hotel

230 Plaza, Las Vegas, NM 87701. ☎ 800/328-1882 or 505/425-3591. www.worldplaces.com/plaza/. E-mail: plazahotel@worldplaces.com. 36 units. A/C TV TEL. $68–$98 double; $115–$130 suite. AE, DC, DISC, MC, V.

A stay in this hotel offers a romantic peek into the past with a view of the plaza. The windows look out on the spot where, in 1846, a ceremony led by General Stephen Kearny marked the takeover of New Mexico by the United States. The inn was built in Italianate bracketed style in 1882, in the days when Western towns, newly connected with the East by train, vied with one another in constructing fancy "railroad hotels," as they were known. Considered the finest hotel in the New Mexico Territory when it was built, it underwent a $2 million renovation exactly 100 years later. Stately walnut staircases frame the lobby and conservatory (with its piano); throughout the hotel, the architecture is true to its era.

As with most renovations in northern New Mexico, don't expect to see the elegance of the Ritz. Instead, expect a more frontier style, with antiques a bit worn, and old rugs a bit torn. Rooms are a variety of sizes, but most are average size, with elegantly high ceilings, and furnished with antiques, with comfortably firm beds, and armoires concealing the televisions. All have coffeemakers. The bathrooms also range in size; most are small, with lots of original tile, but with up-to-date fixtures. The rooms are built around a central air duct, leaving those on the outside with views and those on the inside with more quiet, so reserve accordingly. The rooms all open onto spacious hallways with casual seating areas.

The hotel offers limited room service from its Landmark Grill, which has good food, especially the New Mexican dishes, in a period setting. Notice the walls of the Landmark. The original 19th-century stenciling has been restored. The restaurant is open for lunch and dinner. A continental breakfast is included in the price of the room. There's often live music in the evenings at Byron T's 19th-century saloon on weekends.

Star Hill Inn

Located 10 miles north of Las Vegas on Interstate 25. P.O. Box 1-A, Sapello, NM 87745. ☎ 505/425-5605. www.starhillinn.com. E-mail: stay@starhillinn.com. 7 cottages and 1 house. $95–$145 double (cottage); $310 for four people (house). $10 each additional guest over 12 years old. Minimum 2-night stay. Credit cards are not accepted.

Located "in the Orion Spiral Arm of the Milky Way Galaxy," this inn is a haven for astronomers, stargazers, and anyone else in search of a peaceful mountain retreat. Owner Phil Mahon picked the site in the late 1980s for its nighttime darkness and frequently clear skies. On 195 pine-covered acres at the base of the Sangre de Cristo Mountains, this large property has seven cottages with plenty of space between them. Each unit is furnished with a fully equipped kitchen (including a range/oven, refrigerator, coffeemaker, and toaster), a covered porch, and small fireplace. Comfortable beds and clean, functional bathrooms round out the experience. The cottages are decorated with photos, taken on-site, of the Hale Bopp Comet. The recently added 3-bedroom house has two bathrooms and similar amenities and furnishings as the cottages. Meal service is not provided, but there are grocery stores and restaurants 20 minutes away in Las Vegas.

Star Hill rents a variety of astronomical observing equipment. Telescopes can be rented by the night or the week, and camera mounts and tripods are also available. One-hour "sky tours" are available for $20 to demonstrate the telescopes and introduce visitors to the intricacies of the night sky.

11

New Mexico Gila Country

Take one glance at a map of southwestern New Mexico and you'll get a good idea of its character. The entire center of it is green, denoting national forestland, much of which carries official wilderness area status. This region is home of the Gila Wilderness, the first designated wilderness in the United States and the place that noted naturalist Aldo Leopold saved, opening a new chapter in the methods of land management both in this country and in the world, since this was also the first place ever to be set aside solely to protect its natural environment.

The Gila is not an extremely rugged place like many western wilderness areas. Instead it is characterized by mountains with smoother lines, with tallgrass meadows and deep canyons. That's not to say it's a completely hospitable place. Its size alone—twice the size of the next-largest New Mexico wilderness area, the Pecos—makes it wild in a way few land parcels in the United States are. It spans a half-million acres and is bordered by even more forestland, part of the 3.3-million-acre Gila National Forest. It has peaks reaching above 10,000 feet, and animals ranging from the recently reintroduced Mexican gray wolf to mountain lion.

The beauty and richness of this land has attracted humans for centuries, at least. Most notable is the Mogollon (pronounced *MUG*-e-own) culture that emerged about 100 to 400 B.C. They farmed maize, beans, and squash in the lowlands and lived in pit houses bermed into the ground. Their descendants lived aboveground around A.D. 1000, some in masonry structures within caves high on cliff faces. They also created vivid pottery decorated with whimsical animals and geometric designs.

Around 1300 these people who had lived here for centuries left the area. Their departure is as mysterious as the dispersement of the Puebloan culture to the north in the Four Corners region, which happened around the same time. A visit to the Gila Cliff Dwellings National Monument near the center of the wilderness is a heartfelt adventure into the lives of the

New Mexico Gila Country

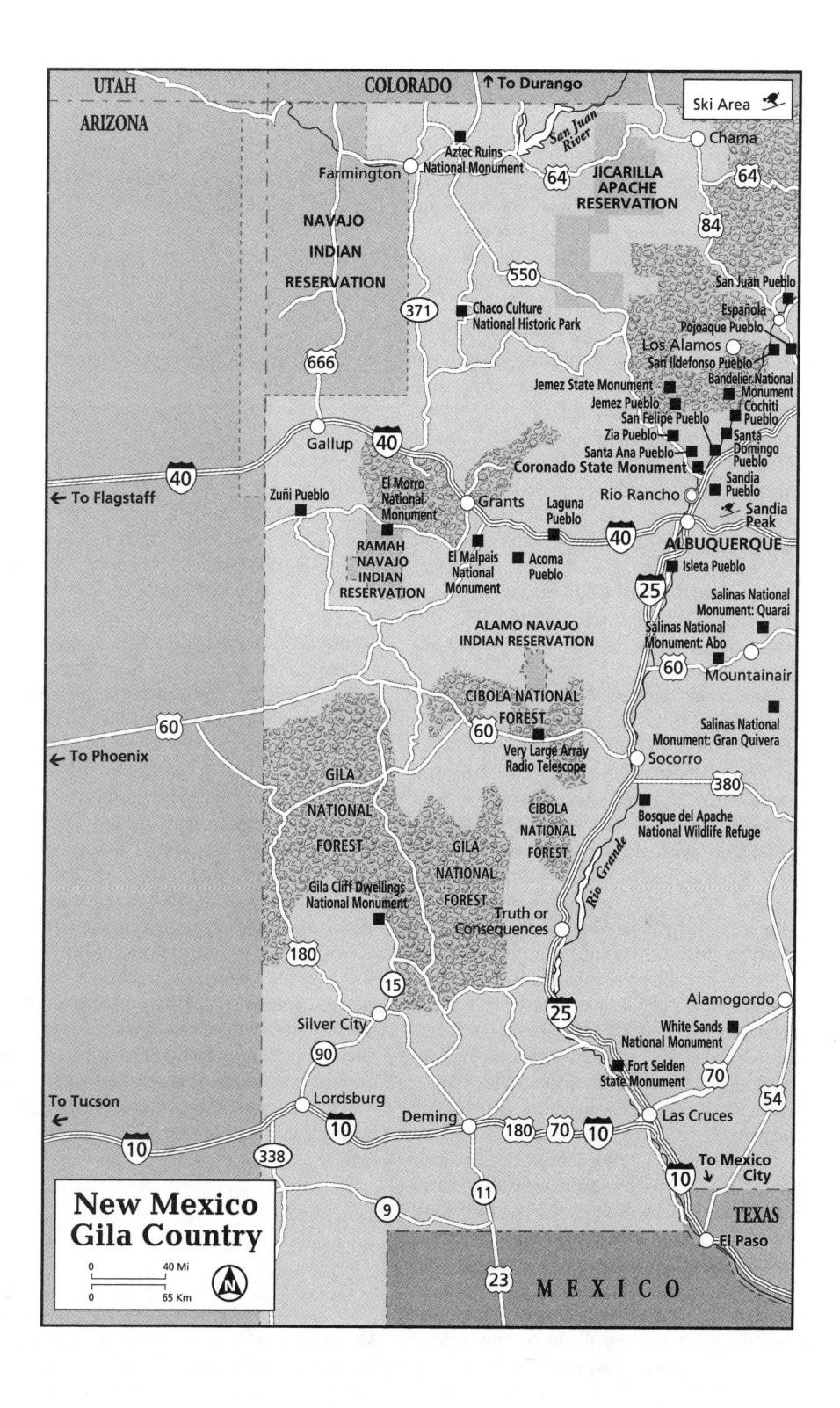

Mogollon. Their homes have remained well protected within the dry caves, allowing the imagination to wander across hundreds of years of history.

By the 16th century, Apaches roamed the area, and in the 19th century this region, along with southeastern Arizona, was a refuge for the Chiricahua Apaches, including Geronimo. His bands did their best to quell pioneer expansion. But despite the resistance, in the 1860s Mormon ranchers settled here. In 1870, a group of prospectors discovered silver, and the rush was on, with mining towns springing up inviting hordes of money-hungry prospectors. In 10 short months, the newly christened Silver City grew from a single cabin to more than 80 buildings. Early visitors included Billy the Kid, Judge Roy Bean, and William Randolph Hearst.

This comparatively isolated community kept pace with every modern convenience: telephones in 1883, electric lights in 1884 (only 2 years after New York City installed its lighting), and a water system in 1887. Typically, the town should have gone bust with the crash of silver prices in 1893. But unlike many Western towns, Silver City did not become a picturesque memory. It capitalized on its high, dry climate to become today's county seat and trade center. Copper mining and processing are still the major industry. But Silver City also can boast a famous son: the late Harrison (Jack) Schmitt, the first civilian geologist to visit the moon, and later a U.S. senator, was born and raised in nearby Santa Rita.

Southwestern New Mexico is also noted for its plains, especially the plains of San Agustin, which spread out north of the Gila region. Best viewed from such sky islands as the Magdalena Mountains, these plains are most noted for the presence of the Very Large Array (VLA), the world's most powerful radio telescope, a series of saucer-shaped receivers that gather radio signals from space, allowing scientists to hear sounds emitted millions and even billions of years ago that are just now reaching earth.

Though there are few large cities within the area, the most settled part is down the center of the state where the Rio Grande marks a distinct riparian line. Throughout history this river has nourished the Native American, Hispanic, and Anglo settlers who have built their homes beside its banks. The river land was especially fertile around modern Las Cruces; the settlement of La Mesilla was southern New Mexico's major center for three centuries. In that vicinity, the Organ Mountains with their spectacular jagged peaks—the Grand Tetons of the Southwest—are rich with plant and animal life.

Hikers and mountain bikers will most appreciate southwestern New Mexico. Of course the Gila Wilderness is the favorite destination of many backpackers, but the national forestland surrounding the wilderness also provides many biking opportunities. The Magdalena Mountains offer both hiking and biking, while the Organ Mountains have some of the loveliest hikes I've ever experienced. Bird-watchers will also appreciate this region: Located to the north, the Bosque del Apache Wildlife Refuge is one of the Southwest's prime birding spots, with literally thousands of snow and Canada geese wintering there. The area around Silver City is nationally known for its road biking, with many scenic miles of asphalt. It is there that the U.S. Cycling Federation holds the Tour of the Gila, a multi-day race that takes place in May.

The Lay of the Land

Much of this region lies upon the Datil-Mogollon Highlands. These are characterized by volcanic activity that happened in the Tertiary period, before the great Ice

Age, when volcanoes poured out vast quantities of silicic lava and volcanic ash. Some of the volcanoes that erupted then collapsed into their magma chambers, leaving calderas as much as 30 miles across.

Cutting across the Datil-Mogollon area are the Plains of San Agustin, a broad, flat, mountain-bordered valley that is geologically a sunken block that formed between parallel faults. It was once the site of a 50-mile-long Pleistocene lake. Now it is home to the Very Large Array (VLA) radio telescope. East of the VLA, the Magdalena Mountains rise up off the plain's floor, an excellent and quite remote place to hike and bike, and the home of an interesting enterprise.

Sitting atop 10,783-foot South Baldy Mountain, the **Langmuir Research Laboratory** studies thunderstorms and atmospheric electricity from June through August. There is a visitor center with exhibits. The research center can be reached by high-clearance vehicles only; visitors should call ☎ **505/835-5423** in advance to check on road conditions.

South of there, the vast mountainous region of the Gila Country came about some 65 million years ago from volcanic eruptions that produced a huge caldera, created when empty magma chambers collapsed. From very high above the Gila one can note the outline of this huge caldera, its rim stretching in the Mogollon, Diablo, and Jerky Mountains within the wilderness. Evidence of the area's volcanic past is visible throughout the region in the form of tuff, an often soft, ashy, gray stone visible along cliff faces.

The Continental Divide winds through the region to the south in the Silver City area. South of there, en route to Deming, lie the strange and beautiful formations of City of Rocks State Park, 680 acres of monolithic blocks of stone sitting in grassy foothills, formed by more than 30 million years of wind and rain eroding what was once a mammoth block of stone, an excellent place for bouldering. Farther south, in the area of Las Cruces are the Organ Mountains. These striking granite shards, which stick up some 9,119 feet at Organ Peak, their tallest point, are a product of upliftment followed by erosion along vertical joints.

And finally, running along the eastern side of the region is the Rio Grande Rift—a sedimentary flood plain through which the Rio Grande River carves, supporting a rich agricultural tradition that goes back some 400 years to the time of the Spanish Conquest of New Mexico.

The region's southern latitude coupled with its high peaks makes it suitable for outdoor fun year-round. The lower lands in the areas of Socorro, Las Cruces, and Deming often have summer temperatures in excess of 100°F. This makes hiking and biking during summer oppressive. However, in spring, fall, and winter, these areas provide comfortable temperatures for many outdoor activities. Within a half-hour, travelers can be up in the mountains in the region and find temperatures averaging 10 to 15°F cooler in summer and much more in winter. Enough snow sometimes falls on the Gila to allow for cross-country skiing and to prohibit hiking and biking in the area in winter. However, during spring, summer, and fall the highlands become green and cool, perfect oases for those escaping the heat of below. Travelers to the area should be aware of the monsoon season in July, August, and early September, when thunderclouds build up in the highlands by noon, and pour rain often into the night. Also be aware that these lowlands are desert, and nights can get cold.

Orientation

The north boundary of Catron Country, about 30 miles south of Interstate 40 defines the region to the north, connecting

ALDO LEOPOLD & THE GILA WILDERNESS

"We reached the old wolf in time to watch a fierce green fire dying in her eyes. I realized then and have known ever since, that there was something new to me in those eyes—something known only to her and to the mountain."

—Aldo Leopold

In the early 1900s, with the trigger of his own gun, naturalist Aldo Leopold killed a Mexican gray wolf and saved millions of acres of land. As he watched the life drain from the wolf's eyes, he was struck by the notion that he had helped alter nature's perfect balance of predator and prey with his own hands. He vowed that this wolf would be his last.

"I was young then and full of trigger itch; I thought that because fewer wolves meant more deer, that no wolves would mean hunters' paradise. But after seeing the green fire die, I sensed that neither the wolf nor the mountain agreed with such a view."

Leopold stopped hunting wolves, but his passion for deer hunting persisted. He wanted nothing more than to be able to head out into an area so grand that, "it could not be traversed without mechanical means in a single day," He wanted to be able ride for two weeks without seeing a road or a person.

Like hunter, preservationist, and former president Theodore Roosevelt, who made it his mission to set great swaths of the West aside for the avid hunter and gamer, Leopold made southwestern New Mexico's volcanic mountains, with their pine-covered canyons, old growth forests, and natural hot springs, his calling. Serving for the National Forest Service in charge of operations at Albuquerque, he became a wilderness advocate, pressing for the preservation of the Gila Country.

On June 3, 1924, the Gila Wilderness was officially designated a wilderness area, the first land in the United States to be set aside solely for preservation. Leopold saved the Gila in order to allow people to "step back in time." Today the wilderness spans 557,873 acres, and is part of the 3.3 million-acre Gila National Forest.

As well as his acts of preservation, Leopold is known for his books on the subject; most notable among them is his 1949 *Sand County Almanac* (Ballantine, 1991), in which he penned, "Man always kills the thing he loves, and so we the pioneers have killed our wilderness. Some say we had to. Be that as it may, I am glad I shall never be young without wild country to be young in. Of what avail are forty freedoms without a blank spot on the map?"

---

with Interstate 25 south of Albuquerque. I-25 runs south all the way to the U.S. border with Mexico (the region's southern border) at the Texas city of El Paso. En route it connects with I-10 at Las Cruces, the most major highway cutting through the region from east to west. The western border of the region is, of course, the border with Arizona. The only other thoroughfare of note is U.S. 60, running east-west across the northern part of the region from Socorro to Springerville, Arizona.

Mining and outdoor recreation, centered in historic Silver City (pop. 11,508), are now the economic stanchions of the region. But dozens of mining towns have boomed and busted in the past 140 years, as a smattering of ghost towns throughout the region attest. Las Cruces, at the foot of the Organ Mountains, is New Mexico's second largest city, with 73,600 people. It's a busy agricultural and education center. North up the valley are Truth or Consequences (pop. 7,500), a spa town named for the 1950s radio and TV game show, and Socorro (pop. 9,000), a historic city with Spanish roots. West, on the I-10 corridor to Arizona, are the ranching centers of Deming (pop. 14,500) and Lordsburg (pop. 3,010).

Parks & Other Hot Spots

Elephant Butte Lake State Park
Located 7 miles north of Truth or Consequences via I-25. ☎ 505/744-5421. 29 campsites, group campground, drinking water, showers, rest rooms, RV dump station, boat ramp, marina, exhibits, and visitor center. Open year-round. $8–$14 camping fee. Camping, fishing, hiking, powerboating, water sports.

Forty-three miles long, Elephant Butte Lake is the largest body of water in New Mexico. The lake is heaven for water sports enthusiasts. Anglers, boaters, water-skiers, and swimmers flock to these waters when oppressive heat in other parts of the state has driven them out. Look to catch white bass, black bass, catfish, walleye, crappie, and stripers here. Three ramps provide boating access to the lake, and there are also launching areas for smaller vessels. The park is extremely crowded on all weekends from Memorial Day to Labor Day. The best time to come is during the week. During that time and in spring and fall, the beaches here can be quiet and lovely. It's nothing like the 9-mile stretch of white that characterizes Grand Cayman, but you will find some soft sand and some calm water worth dunking into.

Caballo Lake State Park
Located 18 miles south of Truth or Consequences via I-25. ☎ 505/743-3942. Over 100 campsites in 2 separate camping areas, group campground, picnic area, drinking water, showers, rest rooms, RV dump station, boat ramp, visitor center, and exhibits. $8–$18 camping fee. Boating, camping, fishing, hiking, water sports, wildlife viewing.

This 11,500-acre lake offers anglers a choice of small and largemouth bass, stripers, bluegill, crappie, catfish, and walleye fishing. Caballo Lake State Park which, like Elephant Butte, has year-round water sports, fishing, swimming, and campsites, sits at the base of a lofty ridge of the Caballo Mountains just to the east of the lake, which makes a handsome backdrop. Park facilities include a full-service marina with a shop for boaters and full hookups for recreational vehicles.

City of Rocks State Park
Located 28 miles northeast of Deming via U.S. 180 and NM 61. ☎ 505/536-2800. 50 campsites, 10 with electric hookups (tenting is available), picnic tables, drinking water, showers, rest rooms, cultural/ historic sites and exhibits. The park is open year-round; the visitor center is typically open daily 10am–4pm, but hours vary depending on the size of its volunteer staff. Day use is allowed 7am–9pm for $4 per vehicle. $10–$14 camping fee. Camping, climbing, hiking, wildlife viewing.

City of Rocks State Park is an area of fantastically shaped volcanic rock formations, formed in ancient times from thick blankets of ash that hardened into tuff. This soft stone, eroded by wind and rain, was shaped into monolithic blocks reminiscent of Stonehenge. For some, the park resembles a medieval village; for others, it is a collection of misshapen, benign giants. Complete with a desert garden, the park offers excellent camping and picnic sites. Rock climbers and rock hounds alike frequent this park on weekends. It's particularly popular with those who like to boulder, with many problems in a range of levels of difficulty. There are good hiking trails within the park.

Rockhound State Park
Located 14 miles southeast of Deming via NM 11 and NM 141. ☎ 505/546-6182. Camping in 2 separate areas with tent and RV sites and hookups,

group campground, shelters, picnic area, drinking water, showers, rest rooms, RV dump station, and exhibits. Open year-round. Camping, hiking, picnicking, wildlife viewing.

Rockhound State Park is unique because visitors are actually encouraged to take away relics of early volcanic activity spread on the slopes of the Little Florida Mountains. This park is very picturesque, with desert plants such as Spanish dagger, mesquite, and prickly pear dotting the hillsides. A mineral collecting paradise, rock hounds may find agates, quartz, geodes, multihued chalcedony, gray and black perlite, and agate-colored spherulite. Unfortunately the areas near the campgrounds are picked clean, so you'll have to hike along some of the trails into remoter areas to find stones.

Pancho Villa State Park
In Columbus, 35 miles south of Deming via NM 11. ☎ 505/531-2711. 61 campsites with and without hookups, group campground, picnic area, drinking water, showers, rest rooms, RV dump station, playground, and cultural/historic sites. Open year-round; the park is staffed daily 8am–5pm. $8–$14 camping fee. Camping, picnicking.

The Pancho Villa State Park marks the last foreign invasion of American soil. In 1916 the notorious Pancho Villa, along with 600 Mexican revolutionaries, cut through the boundary fence at Columbus and attacked a temporary fort, where a tiny garrison was housed in tents. Eighteen Americans were killed, 12 wounded, and an estimated 200 Mexicans died. The Mexicans immediately retreated across their border. An American punitive expedition, headed by General John J. Pershing, chased them into Mexico, but failed to catch them. Villa restricted his banditry to Mexico after that, until his assassination in 1923. The state park includes ruins of the old fort and a visitor center with exhibits and a film. The park also has a strikingly beautiful desert botanical garden, which alone is worth the trip.

Very Large Array National Radio Astronomy Observatory (VLA)
54 miles west of Socorro via U.S. 60. ☎ 505/835-7000. Open year-round daily 8am–sunset. Free admission.

At this world-renowned site 27 dish-shaped antennae, each 82 feet in diameter, are spread across the plains of San Agustin, forming a single gigantic radio telescope. Many are familiar with the site because it was the research station in the 1997 movie *Contact* starring Jodie Foster. Photographs taken are similar to the largest optical telescopes, except that radio telescopes are sensitive to low-frequency radio waves. All types of celestial objects are photographed, including the sun and its planets, stars, quasars, galaxies, and even the faint remains of the "big bang" that scientists say occurred some 10 billion years ago. You'll begin in the visitor center, viewing a film describing the reason for the VLA, how it came about, why it's located where it is, and what it does. In the museum you'll also see how radio waves can be transformed into space pictures and why this is such an effective method of exploration. On the outdoor self-guided walking tour, you'll have a chance to get a closer look at the massive antennas, which resemble giant TV satellite dishes. Don't miss the whispering display, where you can sample firsthand how a dish collects and transmits sound.

Gila Cliff Dwellings National Monument

Though the drive to Gila Cliff Dwellings is long and intense following a winding mountain road, it's definitely worth the trip. First-time visitors are inevitably awed by the sight of the remains of an ancient civilization set in the mouths of caves, abandoned for seven centuries. You'll reach the dwellings on a 1-mile moderate hike, along which you'll catch first glimpses of the ruins. This walk is an elaborate journey into the past. It winds its way into a narrow canyon, from which you get first glimpses of the poetic ruins perched in 6 caves, 180 feet up on the canyon wall. Then the ascent begins up innumerable steps and rocks until you're standing face-to-face with these ancient relics. They offer a glimpse into the lives of Native Americans who lived in the cliffs from the late 1270s through the early 1300s. Tree-ring dating indicates their residence didn't last longer than 30 to 40 years.

However, the earliest ruin that has been found within the monument is a "pit house" dated to between A.D. 100 and 400. This pit house dwelling below ground level was an earlier type of home occupied by the Mogollon people who grew corn and beans, hunted, and gathered wild plant food.

What's remarkable about the journey through the cliff dwellings is the depth of some of the caves. At one point you'll climb a ladder and pass from one cave into the next, viewing the intricate little rooms (42 total) and walls that once made up a community dwelling. Probably not more than 10 to 15 families (about 40 to 50 people) lived in the cliff dwellings at any one time. The inhabitants were excellent weavers and skilled potters.

The cliff dwellings were discovered by Anglo settlers in the early 1870s, near where the three forks of the Gila River rise. Once you leave the last cave, you'll head down again traversing some steep steps to the canyon floor. Be sure to pick up a trail guide at the visitor center.

GETTING THERE

From Silver City take NM 15 44 miles to the Gila Cliff Dwellings. Travel time from Silver City is approximately 2 hours. Keep in mind that there are no gas stations between Silver City and Gila Cliff Dwellings, so plan accordingly. Once you

---

Gila National Forest Hot Springs

Due to its volcanic origins, the Gila National Forest has many hot springs. In the vicinity of the Gila Visitor Center there are three places where people like to soak:

The most accessible is **Lightfeather Hot Springs,** 0.5 miles up the Middle Fork of the Gila River on Trail 157. The round-trip journey requires four river crossings. Access the trail at the far end of the visitor center parking lot and turn right.

The **Jordan Hot Springs** can be accessed either via Little Bear Canyon (6 miles one-way) or via the Middle Fork (8 miles one-way). Both have many river crossings. These can be linked in a loop hike. For the Little Bear Canyon Trail, park at the TJ Corral trailhead, 1 mile from the visitor center on the road to the Cliff Dwellings and take Trail 729, following the signs to Middle Fork. Cross the Middle Fork and head upstream. The springs are on the northeast side of the canyon, just beyond and above a marshy area. *Beware:* Do not enter this canyon during flash flood weather—it is very narrow. To get to Jordan Springs via the Middle Fork, park at the Middle Fork trailhead (Trail 157) just north of the visitor center. The trail follows the river for 6 miles, until its junction with the trail descending from Little Bear Canyon. From this juncture, follow the directions above.

Melanie Hot Springs (about 3 miles one-way) is accessed on a difficult hike down Trail 788 from the Alum Camp Trailhead located off NM 15, approximately 2.5 miles south of Gila Hot Springs village. The descent and subsequent ascent is over 1,000 feet. Upon reaching the Gila River, follow Trail 724 upstream, crossing the river four times, to the springs on the east side of the river. Obtain more information from the Gila Cliff Dwellings National Monument visitor center.

get to the monument, you should know that vehicles are permitted on paved roads only.

INFORMATION

Contact the park at ☎ **505/536-9461.** Admission is $3 per person, with children ages 8 and under admitted free. The visitor center, where you can pick up detailed brochures, is open from daily 8am to 5pm Memorial Day to Labor Day, and daily from 8am to 4:30pm the rest of the year. The cliff dwellings are open daily from 8am to 6pm in the summer, and daily from 9am to 4pm the rest of the year. Pets are not allowed within the monument, but they can be taken on trails within the Gila Wilderness.

SEEING THE HIGHLIGHTS

Today, the dwellings allow a rare glimpse inside the homes and lives of prehistoric Native Americans. About 75% of what is seen is original, although the walls have been capped and the foundations strengthened to prevent further deterioration. It took a great deal of effort to build these homes: The stones were held in place by mortar, and all of the clay and water for the mortar had to be carried by hand up from the stream, as the Mogollon did not have any pack animals. The vigas for the roof were cut and shaped with stone axes or fire.

The people who lived here were farmers, as shown by the remains of beans, squash, and corn in their homes. The fields were along the valley of the west fork of the Gila River and on the mesa across the canyon. No signs of irrigation have been found.

A 1-mile loop trail, rising 175 feet from the canyon floor, provides access to the dwellings. See the "Walks & Rambles" section later in this chapter.

Near the visitor center, about a mile away, the remains of an earlier (A.D. 100 to 400) pit house, built below ground level, and later pit houses (up to A.D. 1000), aboveground structures of adobe or wattle, have been found.

OTHER ADVENTURES

Gila National Forest, which offers some of the most spectacular mountain scenery in the Southwest, comprises 3.3 million acres in four counties. Nearly one-fourth of that acreage (790,000 acres) comprises the **Gila, Aldo Leopold,** and **Blue Range Wildernesses.** Its highest peak is Whitewater Baldy, 10,892 feet. Within the forest six out of seven life zones can be found, so the range of plant and wildlife is broad. You may see mule deer, elk, antelope, black bear, mountain lion, and bighorn sheep. Nearly 400 miles of streams and a few small lakes sustain healthy populations of trout as well as bass, bluegill, and catfish. Anglers can head to Lake Roberts, Snow Lake, and Quemado Lake. For more information on the national forest, contact the **U.S. Forest Service,** ☎ **505/388-8201.**

Eighteen campgrounds can be found in the national forest, seven with drinking water and toilets. Car and backpack camping are also permitted throughout the forest.

HIKING & BIKING

Within the forest are 1,490 miles of trails for hiking and horseback riding, and in winter, cross-country skiing. Outside of the wilderness areas, trail bikes and off-road vehicles are also permitted. Hiking trails in the Gila Wilderness, especially the 41-mile Middle Fork Trail, with its east end near Gila Cliff Dwellings, are among the most popular in the state, and can sometimes be crowded. If you are more interested in communing with nature than with fellow hikers, however, you will find plenty of trails to suit you, both in and out of the officially designated wilderness areas.

Most of the trails are maintained and easy to follow. Trails along river bottoms, however, have many stream crossings (so be prepared for hiking with wet feet) and may be washed out by summer flash floods. It's best to inquire about trail conditions before you set out. More than 50 trailheads provide roadside parking.

Some of the best hikes in the area are the West Fork of the Gila, The Catwalk and Beyond, Gila Crest Trail, and the Black Range Crest Trail. The Gila National Forest contains several wilderness areas that are off-limits to mountain bikes, including the Gila, Aldo Leopold, and the Blue Range Primitive Area. However, cyclists can access quite a few trails. Some to look for are the Continental Divide, Fort Bayard Historical Trails, and Signal Peak.

CAMPING

Camping and picnicking are encouraged in the national monument, and there are four developed campgrounds (see the "Campgrounds & Other Accommodations" section later in this chapter). Overnight lodging can be found in Silver City and in the nearby town of Gila Hot Springs, which also has a grocery store.

What to Do & Where to Do It

BIRD WATCHING

Bosque del Apache National Wildlife Refuge (☎ 505/835-1828) is a haven for migratory waterfowl such as snow geese and cranes. It's located 90 miles south of Albuquerque on I-25, and is well worth the drive. You'll find 7,000 acres of carefully managed riparian habitat, which include marshlands, meadows, agricultural fields, and old-growth cottonwood forests lining the Rio Grande River. The experience is particularly thrilling if you're here from November through March, not only because of the variety of birds—of which there are over 300 species—but for the sheer numbers of them. Huge clouds of snow geese and sandhill cranes take flight at dawn and dusk, the air filling with the sounds of their calls and wing flaps. In early December, the refuge may harbor as many as 45,000 snow geese, 57,000 ducks of many different species, and 18,000 sandhill cranes. You may even be fortunate enough (as I was on my last visit) to see a whooping crane or two. There are also plenty of raptors, including numerous red-tailed hawks and northern harriers (sometimes called marsh hawks), Cooper's hawks and kestrels, and even bald and golden eagles. The refuge has a 15-mile auto-tour loop, which you should drive very slowly. The southern half of the loop travels past numerous water impoundments, where the majority of the ducks and geese are, and the northern half has the meadows and farmland, where you'll see roadrunners and other land birds, and where the cranes and geese feed from mid-morning through the afternoon.

People come from all over the world to attend the **Festival of the Cranes,** a bird-watching event that takes place at Bosque del Apache National Wildlife Refuge, always the weekend before Thanksgiving. Call ☎ **505/835-0424** for information.

The **Gila National Forest** in the Silver City area is a renowned bird-watching site. With diverse ecosystems ranging from riparian to piñon-juniper woodlands to ponderosa pines and mixed-conifer and aspen forests, the region is home to more than 100 species of birds including the great horned owl and the Harris hawk, among many others. Some of the hot spots are the riparian area of Cherry Creek and the riparian, piñon/juniper, and ponderosa pine areas of Fort Bayard Wildlife Refuge. Other riparian areas of note are the Gila River area, Bill Evans Lake, Hart Bar, Lake Roberts, and the Catwalk at Whitewater Canyon. If you're interested in a birding vacation, complete with guides, visit the **Bear Mountain Guest Ranch** (see the "Inns & Lodges" section later in this chapter), where

Nature Conservancy guides are on hand to teach about the bird life and other fauna, as well as the flora of the Gila.

The **Gila Bird and Nature Festival** takes place in late April to early May and features guided bird field trips, including information on archaeology, geology, native and medicinal plants, and reptiles and amphibians. Guides include specialists from the Gila National Forest and Western New Mexico University. For more information, contact the Silver City Chamber of Commerce at ☎ **505/ 538-3785.**

BOARDSAILING & SAILING

Though you'll want to avoid the lakes during weekends at the height of summer, Elephant Butte Lake State Park and Caballo Lake State Park both have plenty of surface water upon which to ply your sails. Particularly during spring when winds are up, these lakes provide good sailing, as well as good access from sandy beaches.

CLIMBING

Few people are aware of the bouldering paradise at **City of Rocks State Park,** which, of course, makes it even more of a paradise. The 680-acre area is littered with hundreds of 10- to 30-foot welded volcanic tuff formations, in the form of strangely shaped rocks, the result of volcanic activity some 30 million years ago. Often compared to the rock at Hueco Tanks, though without the diversity and quality of that southwest Texas site, the bouldering here is mostly undeveloped—meaning there are no named and rated problems, making this an ideal spot for real adventurers. Since many roads and trails traverse the park, it has excellent access. A good place to start is above the campsites on the east of the one-way road. Another good bet is above the campsites at the Suburb, on the far northwest end of the park. To reach the park drive 23 miles north of Deming on U.S. 180, then turn right on NM 61 and drive 3 miles to the park entrance.

New Mexico climbers often speak of "Datil" with a whispered reverence. It is considered by many to be *the* place to climb within the state. The reason? The **Enchanted Tower** and its satellite crags offer steep bolted cliffs composed of welded volcanic tuff, a fun material that can be strenuous and pumpy. Another reason for the area's fame is that it currently holds New Mexico's hardest route at 5.14a. The Enchanted Tower itself is a 110-foot semi-detached spire sitting within Thompson Canyon in the Datil Mountains north of the small village of Datil. The tower and the surrounding cliffs (Frog Prince Wall, Rapunzel's Wall, Humpty Dumpty Wall, Sleeping Beauty Wall, Captain Hook Area, Midnight Pumpkin Wall, and Pogue's Cave Area) offer more than 51 routes ranging in difficulty from 5.8 to 5.13. To reach the area, take U.S. 60 out of Socorro for 62 miles to Datil. From the blinking light in town continue west for 5.2 miles to a right turn (north) on a dirt road. Drive 0.8 miles to a left curve onto FS 59A. Soon you'll come to a sign that reads Thompson Canyon. Drive 1.8 miles to the crag. For route descriptions, pick up *The Enchanted Tower, Sport Climbing Socorro and Datil, New Mexico* by Solomon Maestas and Matthew Jones, 1993.

Though not exactly one of New Mexico's premier climbing areas, the **Socorro Box** does offer some fun and challenging climbing. In fact, this was the place where I did my first multi-pitch climb, an exciting venture for me even though it was just a two-pitch and I only cleaned. The area consists of 5 cliffs on the east and west side of Box Canyon, 7 miles west of Socorro on U.S. 60. One notable point about the area is that it has New Mexico's second hardest climb, Keeping Up With the Joneses (5.13d), a distinction shared with Snake Dance (also

5.13d) at Palomas Peak in the Sandia Mountains near Albuquerque. The routes in Box Canyon range from 5.7 to 5.13d, and there's also some excellent bouldering. The faces are composed of rhyolite, a fine-grained, hard volcanic rock, with sharp edges and small positive holds on steep to overhanging routes. Watch for Waterfall Wall, a top-rope area directly across from the parking area, as well as Fillet a Papillon Wall, with its many difficult and overhanging bolt-protected routes. Also of note is Red Wall, where the longest routes lie—up to 2 pitches long and from 5.6 to 5.11 in difficulty with some gear placement required. Other faces include the North Wall, the East Wall, and, 2 miles away, 3 other walls. Much of the traffic traveling in and out of this canyon (really, not much at all) consists of boulderers. At the far end of the Box, near the highway, the "Streambed" provides some excellent, pumpy problems, almost all overhanging. For specific route information, pick up the Maestas and Jones book mentioned in the Enchanted Tower section above.

An area reserved for experienced climbers who like their adventures served in big portions is the **Organ Mountains** near Las Cruces. This jagged, toothy range that marks the Las Cruces skyline is remote and dry, with few roads and trails traversing it. You can expect long approaches, long multi-pitch routes, and confounding descents in this range composed mostly of granite with some sedimentary and volcanic rock in the lowlands. Much of the climbing here requires traditional skills; be prepared for long days. Climbing areas include the Citadel, a 400-foot crag on the west side of the Organs, with a variety of moderate climbs, ranging from 5.9 to 5.10c/d; Southern Comfort Wall, a locals' favorite, with a relatively easy approach and fun routes ranging from 5.7 to 5.11; the Tooth, with a steep approach, offers long routes (up to 6 pitches) Grade III, 5.10 in difficulty; and Sugarloaf, on the east side of the Organs, an 800-foot granite spire that's well worth checking out. Finding these crags isn't easy and may require help from locals. Access the west side faces from the Baylor Canyon Road that parallels the Organ's west side, which can be accessed from U.S. 70 about 11 miles east of its junction with I-25. For specific route information refer to Dick Ingraham's compilation available at the New Mexico State University Library or from local shops in Las Cruces. The area was featured in *Rock and Ice* issue 48.

Not far away are the **Doña Ana Mountains,** a small range north of Las Cruces, which has pockets of excellent climbing. With easily accessible routes, and faces ranging from 1 to 3 pitches, as well as a 500-foot crag on Doña Ana Peak, there's plenty to do here. There's also some good bouldering in the area. There's only one sport route in the area, so it's a traditional climber's spot, one that's remote and dry, with rattlesnakes prevalent. Access the Doña Anas off U.S. 70/82 toward Alamogordo. Turn north onto Jornada Road. For specific route information, refer to the materials listed for the Organ Mountains.

FISHING

The **Gila River** flows through the 557,873-acre Gila Wilderness, offering anglers a chance to be alone with their thoughts and their tackle. The main Gila below the forks has mostly smallmouth bass. The water around the town of Gila Hot Springs gets summer and fall rainbows. Parts of the river are best accessed by horseback or on extended backpacking trips. The rare Gila trout is now only found in a few protected headwater streams, closed to fishing. The Gila Wilderness is located 25 miles north of Silver City, west of Continental Divide, within Gila National Forest.

Located northwest of Mimbres via NM 35, 72-acre **Lake Roberts** on the Sapillo Creek was drained in 1997 to allow for repairs to the dam. With work complete and the lake re-filled there is now fair year-round fishing for 10- to 14-inch rainbow trout, crappie, catfish and some bass at this meadow- and pine-surrounded lake.

The scenic 100-acre **Snow Lake** adjoining Gila National Forest has excellent fishing for stocked rainbow trout. Located southeast of Reserve via NM 435 and FS 141, 28, and 142, the place is very remote and surrounded by mountains. The lake has a boat ramp and primitive camping facilities.

North of there, and also surrounded by forest, 130-acre **Quemado Lake** is located 23 miles south of Quemado via U.S. 60, NM 32 and FS 13. This lake has very good fishing during early March and April, predominately for rainbow trout.

Twenty-one miles south of Truth or Consequences via I-25 and NM 187 is **Percha Dam State Park.** This 80-acre reservoir is located at the joining of Caballo Lake and the Rio Grande. Some anglers catch walleye, small- and largemouth bass, bluegill, crappie and a few trout. This is rumored to be one of the best mid-elevation lakes in the state to catch rainbow trout.

Some 30 miles northwest of Silver City and about 4 miles southwest of U.S. 180 is **Bill Evans Lake.** Anglers have pulled out record-sized smallmouth and largemouth bass in the 15-pound range from this water body. The lake is stocked with rainbow trout. It has a boat ramp and primitive camping facilities.

Eleven-thousand-acre **Caballo Lake** offers anglers a choice of small- and largemouth bass, stripers, bluegill, crappie, catfish, and walleye fishing. Florida-strain bass also are established here. The lofty ridge of the Caballo Mountains just to the east of the lake makes a handsome backdrop. Caballo Lake is located 16 miles south of Truth or Consequences via I-25.

Elephant Butte Lake, located 7 miles north of Truth or Consequences via I-25, is the place to go to catch trophy-sized fish of many types. Forty-three miles long, this lake is the largest body of water in New Mexico, nearing 40,000 surface acres in good water years. Anglers flock to this hourglass-shaped lake when oppressive heat in other parts of the state has driven them out. The lake has big upper and lower sections connected by a 4-mile stretch of Rio Grande. Look to catch white bass, black bass, channel catfish, blue catfish, flathead catfish, walleye, crappie, and stripers here. Three ramps provide boating access to the lake, and there are also launching areas for smaller vessels. The park is extremely crowded on weekends from Memorial Day to Labor Day.

The tiny 25-acre **Bear Canyon Reservoir,** with its clear water and wooded surroundings, is home to many catfish, crappie, bass, and sunfish as well as stocked rainbow trout. The lake is located 2 miles north of Mimbres via NM 35. It has a boat ramp, rest rooms, and primitive campsites.

HIKES & BACKPACK TRIPS
Magdalena Crest Trail
11 miles round-trip. Moderate to difficult. 1,100-ft. elevation gain. Allow 5–6 hrs. Access: Take U.S. 60 west from Socorro about 16 miles to FS 235. Turn left, following the signs for Water Canyon Campground. At 5 miles you'll drive though the campground onto a dirt road, which you'll follow for 8 miles to the trailhead just below the Langmuir Research Laboratory. Maps: USGS Magdalena and South Baldy.

This is the perfect way to experience one of New Mexico's great volcanic upliftments, from one end to the other, without much elevation gain. The road to the trailhead is long but scenic and generally in pretty good condition, though I recommend a high-clearance vehicle. The trail takes off to the west onto a little saddle then dives down into dense forest. It surfaces on the crest, allowing for the first real views north to Mount Taylor, east to the Sandia Mountains, and west toward Arizona. The trail doesn't immediately follow this ridge, though. Watch for cairns heading down this little saddle near where it surfaced. The trail parallels the crest for a while through aspen forest, then surfaces again at another saddle. Soon it passes through a rough scree field, then finds its way to yet another saddle. It continues this way, dipping into the forest just below the crest, then resurfacing at saddles, for the rest of the 5 miles to North Baldy. It's a 500-foot fast uphill grind to the summit where there are spectacular views into Copper Canyon, the eastern Magdalenas, and the Rio Grande Valley. Return the way you came. *Beware:* This crest is no place to be during a thunderstorm. You'll want to avoid it during the afternoon monsoons in July through September. In fact, Langmuir is a lightning observatory, strategically placed on a mountain range known for its thunderstorms.

West Fork of the Gila River

6 miles or more. Easy to moderate. 500-ft. elevation gain. Access: Head north from Silver City on NM 15 for 44 miles to the Gila Cliff Dwellings National Monument. This is a winding and very scenic road; expect the drive to take about 2 hours. The trailhead is just to the right of the Gila Cliff Dwellings trail.

This lovely trail follows the Gila River upstream through broad meadows and into a deep canyon with strikingly painted walls, arriving at a small cliff dwelling. It begins with a few easy river crossings (which may be difficult during spring runoff), then crosses a broad meadow past which you can see the red cliffs of the Gila Canyon in the distance. It enters the wilderness and comes to a larger stream crossing, where hikers need to cross by stepping on logs and rocks. (*Note:* During the spring this river may be considerably higher, so expect to wade.) At this point look for a short side trail south to some homesteader ruins where a grave is marked by this cryptic message, a relic of a feud that locals still talk about: "William Grudging waylaid and murdered by Tom Wood Oct. 8 1893 age 37 years 8 mos." Soon the trail climbs to a plateau above the river, offering amazing views of the cliffs on the opposite side of the river. At mile 3 you'll come to Three-Mile Ruin, a fragile cliff dwelling in a shallow cave on the river's west side. This is a good place to turn around. If you'd like to extend this trip, there are plenty of ways to do so. The trail itself travels 34 miles, eventually ending at the Willow Creek Campground.

Crest Trail to Mogollon Baldy Trail 182

6 miles one-way. Moderate to difficult. 1,763-ft. elevation gain. Allow 3 hrs. one-way–2 days round-trip. Access: Drive 3.5 miles north of Glenwood on U.S. 180, then 9 miles east on NM 159, a narrow mountain road that takes a good 25 min. to negotiate. Continue another 8 miles to the trailhead at Sandy Point. Maps: Grouse Mountain and Mogollon Baldy Peak.

The drive to this trail is almost as fun as the hike. It takes you through the village of Mogollon, an almost-ghost town that bears witness to silver and gold mining booms beginning in the late 19th century, and to the disastrous effects of floods and fire in later years. For the first few miles the broad and well-maintained trail makes its way through dense mixed conifer forest, with huge Douglas firs, and lots of birds such as hummingbirds and woodpeckers.

For the first 2.5 miles the trail ascends gradually, then it heads steeply to a ridge, which it follows through spruce-fir forest and aspen groves to the scenic Hummingbird Saddle. Next it passes over 10,895-foot Whitewater Baldy, which has an observation tower worth checking out. From there the trail makes its way up and down past 10,535-foot Center Baldy to its end at 10,770-foot Mogollon Baldy. Water will likely be available at Bead Spring,

Hummingbird Spring, Hobo Spring, Little Hobo Spring, and Blacktail Spring. Return the way you came.

Rain Creek Trail 189

1.5–8.5 miles one-way. Difficult. 2,000-ft. elevation gain. Allow 1–5 hrs. one-way. Travel north from NM 293 on FS 147 for approximately 13 miles. A short spur road leads to the east accessing the trailhead. You will pass through a gate, which is adjacent to FS 147. Rangers urge hikers not to park on private land and to close all gates. Maps: USGS Shelly Peak and Rice Ranch.

This is a trail for those who like isolation, physical challenge, and exceptional mountain vistas. It enters the Gila Wilderness's south side, the least-used and most rugged portion. Since it's so lovely I recommend hiking it even if you only make it 1.5 miles down to Rain Creek, a good turn-around spot. If you go the full 8.5 miles in, you will climb from Rain Creek over a divide down into Mogollon Creek, so the trip involves 2 descents into creeks and corresponding steep ascents. Also be aware that this trail is narrow, with steep descents, some approaching 20% to 30%. The trail is also rough and rocky; if you intend to carry weight, you should be very experienced with doing so under adverse conditions.

From the lovely and broad Sacaton Mesa and the trailhead, the trail traverses the side of a canyon through piñon/juniper forest, with beautiful views of craggy peaks in all directions particularly toward the end of the canyon. It continues a steady descent down to Rain Creek at mile 1.5, where there's usually water. Then it follows Rain Creek for a short distance before climbing steeply to the southeast to the divide between Rain Creek and the West Fork of Mogollon Creek. During that section the trail makes its way into some ponderosa pine, where the air will likely be cooler. From the divide, the trail descends rapidly to the West Fork of Mogollon Creek. There it intersects with Trail 224, which travels up the creek. Trail 189 crosses the West Fork of Mogollon Creek and continues over to Bud's Hole, located on Mogollon Creek. These trails can be linked with other trails for multi-day backpacking adventures. One interesting option is to take Trail 224 to Mogollon Baldy and connect up with the Crest Trail 182 to Sandy Point.

Black Range Crest Trail to Hillsboro Peak

10 miles round-trip. Moderate. 2,100-ft. elevation gain. Allow 5 hrs. Access: From Silver City head east on NM 152 for 40 miles (or from I-25, 31 miles) to the Emory Pass Vista. Maps: USGS Hillsboro Peak or USFS Aldo Leopold Wilderness.

This hike heads into the heart of the huge Aldo Leopold Wilderness, which spans the crest of the Black Range. It offers romantic views of the more remote reaches of these mountains, making it one of New Mexico's classic peak hikes. Begin hiking the Crest Trail 79, past a helispot and through a gate. From there the trail climbs moderately and steadily toward the peak with frequent views to the north and east. It enters the Aldo Leopold Wilderness at about 2 miles. At mile 3 it reaches a saddle, then climbs the west side of the ridge. From this point you can begin to see the peak. At just over 3.5 miles it comes to an intersection; continue straight. The trail makes its way to the south side of the peak. At mile 4.8, be sure to stay on the Crest Trail and avoid the trail to Granite Peak. Soon you'll find yourself on the broad, flat summit, a place with many decent campsites, and a fire lookout, which offers great views. If you'd like, you can arrange a shuttle, and that way continue on the Crest Trail and then down to the Railroad Canyon Campground (5 miles west of Emory Pass Vista on NM 152). Otherwise, return the way you came.

Catwalk National Recreation Area

1–5 miles round-trip. Easy. 700-ft. elevation gain. Allow ½–2½ hrs. Access: Drive 68 miles north of Silver City on U.S. 180;

then 5 miles east of Glenwood via NM 174. (*Beware:* During spring runoff stream crossings on this road may be impassable.)

Kids are especially thrilled with this hike; much of it traverses a hanging catwalk over a river. The catwalk follows the route of a pipeline built in 1897 to carry water to the now-defunct town of Graham and its electric generator. The trail begins on the north side of the creek at the Gila National Forest's Whitewater Picnic Area. About 0.25 miles above the parking area is the beginning of the striking metal causeway clinging to the sides of the boulder-chocked Whitewater Canyon, which in spots is 20 feet wide and 250 feet deep. Along the way you'll find water pouring through caves formed from boulders, and waterfalls spitting off the cliff side. Farther up the canyon, a suspension bridge spans the chasm. At mile 2.4 the trail intersects with Trail 212 where the South Fork meets White Water Creek. If you bear right onto 212 and cross the stream, you'll find the remains of a power-generating station. If you'd like to extend the hike, you can continue on Trail 212 or Trail 207; if not, backtrack to your car.

Baylor Pass

2–6 miles one-way. Easy to moderate. 1,480-ft. elevation gain. Allow 1–3 hrs. one-way. Access: From Las Cruces, head east on U.S. 70 14 miles to the turn off to Aguirre Springs Recreation Area. Turn right and drive this narrow, winding, paved road 6 miles to the Baylor Pass Trailhead. If you do this trek one-way, leave your shuttle vehicle at the southern trailhead by driving east on U.S. 70 for 11 miles; turn right onto Baylor Pass Rd. Drive 1.8 miles to the trailhead. Maps: USGS Organ and Organ Peak.

This is one of the prettiest hikes in southern New Mexico. The pass is named for Confederate Colonel John Baylor who in 1862 barely fought off Union troops at the pass. The trail leaves from just below the Aguirre Springs campground. It contours along the base of the Organ Mountains, allowing for more and more spectacular views of the peaks as you go, with the awesome Tularosa Basin spread out below. At just over 1 mile it skirts the upper edge of a drainage where there may be cool little pools of water. The trail continues, slowly gaining elevation until just after mile 2 when it heads over the pass and down toward Las Cruces. This upper meadow during monsoon season can be filled with wildflowers and is a great turn-around point if you don't care to do the whole trail. If you do want to do the rest (you may want to arrange a shuttle to pick you up on the other side), continue on the trail as it switchbacks down through white-thorn acacia and manzanita. At points the footing will be loose, so take care as the trail makes its way along more switchbacks onto the alluvial fan at the mouth of Baylor Canyon and into the open desert and the south trailhead. You can do what I saw one woman doing, just trucking her way along to the end and turning around and heading back. She wasn't even winded.

Pine Tree Trail

4.5-mile loop. Moderate to strenuous. 1,600-ft. elevation gain. Allow 2½ hrs. Access: From Las Cruces, head east on U.S. 70 14 miles to the turnoff to Aguirre Springs Recreation Area. Turn right and drive this narrow, winding, but paved road 6 miles; you'll pass by the campground before arriving at the Pine Tree Trailhead. Pay a small fee at a self-pay station. Maps: USGS Organ and Organ Peak.

This hike is a great introduction to the Organ Mountains. As a loop it takes you through this surprisingly lush desert with views in all directions. It begins a bit precariously, with a few signs that seem to contradict each other. I made my way in a counter-clockwise fashion and found arrows to help me stay oriented. As you go you can watch the rich desert vegetation dominated by huge alligator junipers.

HATCH CHILE: YOU SAY CHILI, WE SAY CHILE

North of Las Cruces, the town of **Hatch**, 39 miles via I-25 or 34 miles via NM 185, calls itself the "chile capital of the world." It is the center of a 22,000-acre agricultural belt that grows and processes more chile than anywhere else in the world. The annual **Hatch Chile Festival** over the Labor Day weekend celebrates the harvest. For information, call the Hatch Chamber of Commerce (☎ 505/267-5050).

Visiting Hatch is a great way to experience the very unique experience of chile. You'll never see "chili" on a menu in New Mexico. New Mexicans are adamant that chile, the Spanish spelling of the word, is the only way to spell it—no matter what your dictionary might say. I'm inclined to think chile with an "e" is listed as a secondary spelling only as a courtesy to New Mexicans. We have such a personal attachment to this small agricultural gem that in 1983 we directed our senior U.S. senator, Pete Domenici, to enter New Mexico's official position on the spelling of chile into the Congressional Record. That's taking your chiles seriously.

Chiles are grown throughout the state, in a perfect climate for cultivating and drying the small but powerful red and green New Mexican varieties. But it is the town of Hatch that has the most chile in production. Regardless of where you travel in the state, chiles appear on the menu. Virtually anything you order in a restaurant is topped with a chile sauce. If you're not accustomed to spicy foods, certain varieties of red or green chiles will make your eyes water, your sinuses drain, and your palate feel as if it's on fire—all after just one forkful. *Warning:* No amount of water or beer will alleviate the sting. Drink milk. A sopaipilla drizzled with honey is also helpful.

But don't let these words of caution scare you away from genuine New Mexico chiles. The pleasure of eating them far outweighs the pain. Start slow, with salsas and chile sauces first, perhaps *rellenos* (stuffed peppers) next, followed by *rajas* (roasted peeled chiles cut into strips). Before long, you'll be buying *chile ristras* (chiles strung on rope) and hanging them up for decoration. Perhaps you'll be so smitten that you'll purchase bags of chile powder or a chile plant to take home. If you happen to be in New Mexico in the fall, you'll find fresh roasted green chile sold. In the parking lots of most grocery stores and at some roadside stands, you'll smell the scent of roasting chile and see large metal baskets full of peppers rotating over flames. If you have a means of freezing the chile before transporting it home, you can sample the delicacy throughout the year. This will certainly make you an expert on the difference between chile and chili.

As the trail climbs, the vegetation turns to ponderosa forest. Approximately 80 species of mammals, 185 species of birds, and 60 species of reptiles and amphibians inhabit this area. Watch for Gambel's quail, mule deer, cottontail rabbits, tree lizards, and Western diamondback rattlesnakes. En route back you'll enjoy outstanding views of the Sacramento and White Mountains, White Sands, and the broad Tularosa Basin.

HORSEBACK RIDING

The **Double E Guest Ranch** (☎ 505/535-2048; www.doubleeranch.com) offers authentic ranch riding in the southwestern New Mexico desert and forestlands. Since the ranch is a working cattle ranch, it has an authentic feel, and its guest capacity of only 12 adds to the authenticity. Trail rides and cattle drives range across 30,000 acres, which adjoin the legendary Gila Wilderness. The ranch sits on a shady bend of Bear Creek, a place that draws plenty of wildlife. Rocky Mountain bighorn sheep, javalina, and black bear are a few of the denizens. Three tasty and plentiful meals daily are served family-style with chemical-free beef and buffalo as well as organic vegetables. The accommodations are in old ranch buildings, which range from cozy to expansive. My favorite has old saddles hanging from the rafters. These are not luxury rooms; instead they're real ranch lodgings. The ranch doesn't offer a children's program but it makes accommodations for kids. Double E also has special "Nature Expeditions" that include luxury accommodations some nights (at nearby Casitas de Gila—see the "Inns & Lodges" section later in this chapter) combined with overnight campout rides.

Circle S Stables (☎ 505/382-7708), has operated for the past 20 years in the Organ Mountains outside Las Cruces. Proprietor Kirk Storey takes riders out on his 14 head of horses. For the more inexperienced riders, Storey recommends heading into the desert, where the earth is smooth and easy. For the experienced rider, he recommends the rough, rocky, and rugged trail up to Baylor Pass where riders can look down on White Sands and the Tularosa Basin. One-hour rides run $20; two-hour rides are $30; half-day rides cost $45, and daylong rides are $75. Lunch and water are not included, but saddle bags are. Circle S is open November through May. The ranch is located 11 miles east of Las Cruces on Hwy. 70. Take Baylor Canyon Road, which runs along the bottom of the Organ Mountains, and turn on the second road on the right.

Though **Happy Trails** (☎ 505/527-8471) is a B&B, it does have stables, and the proprietors will set visitors up with horses and take them through the irrigated alfalfa fields surrounding the village of Mesilla to the Rio Grande River. The inn is a 60-year-old adobe cluttered—I mean, decorated—with all manner of Southwestern knickknacks, from day-of-the-dead heads to Mexican blankets. If you reserve a room, ask for the Aspen, which opens out onto a sunny porch. The porch, in turn, opens out onto a courtyard where the pool and Jacuzzi are located. Out back are the stables, where an occasionally available wrangler can saddle up horses and take you for a ride. If he's not around, the inn will make other riding arrangements for you. The inn serves a full breakfast and is located minutes away from Old Mesilla Plaza. Children and pets are welcome.

MOUNTAIN BIKING

Your home base in the Silver City area is **Gila Hike and Bike,** 103 E. College (☎ **505/388-3222**). There you can get equipment as well as directions to trailheads. While in the area you might be tempted to purchase *Trails of the Gila* (1994), a book written and published by Bryan Thomas. Unfortunately, I can't recommend this book until a new edition comes out. Directions to some trails are so outdated you may end up four-wheeling while trying to find the trailhead rather than two-wheeling on the trails. In Las Cruces, you'll get very personal service and good directions from **The Bike House,** 1900 S. Espina, Suite A (☎ **505/527-9918** or 505/621-4321). In Socorro, stop in at **Desert Cycles,** 105 Plaza (☎ **505/835-4085**) for repairs and directions, and possibly to hook up with some locals who want to ride. Next door to the shop at the Socorro Chamber of Commerce you can purchase the *Fat Tire Trail Book,* a locally written and published booklet that lists 30 trails in the area.

Fort Bayard Wagon Road and Big Juniper Loop

6 miles round-trip. Moderate. 500-ft. elevation gain. Allow 1½ hrs. Access: From Silver City head east on U.S. 180 8 miles to the town of Central. Turn north following the signs toward Fort Bayard. Stay right bypassing around the manicured grounds. The road will become FS 536. Drive this dirt road for 3 miles to the Fort Bayard Historical Trails parking area. Once on your bike, backtrack to FS 536, and head north (left) passing through 3 gates onto a rough jeep track—this is your trail.

Though this trail is jeep road, it's not exactly a road on which your granny is going to drive her Ford sedan. The route has lots of fun technical climbs and descents. It crosses some smooth slickrock-like stuff but it's tuff, not sandstone, so it's not real grippy. A rule of thumb: Bear left at every juncture. The trail passes through three gates next to a Ranger Outpost and then begins a slow ascent. At mile 2.1 you'll note a cairn to the right. This rough and rocky trail can make for fun exploration. It heads to the "wagon wheel ruts" less than 0.25 mile uphill, then continues all the way to Signal Peak. If you intend to ride this route be sure to pick up a map from Hike and Bike. Continue to bear left at all junctures. Keep riding until you come to a sign that reads Sawmill. If you'd like to go see the "Big Tree," which I highly recommend, turn right here. You'll find plenty of fun single track all over this area, so you may want to stretch your ride and explore. The trail heads up a short climb to a three-prong fork; take the right prong down a hill, across a meadow, through a creek, through another meadow with a little corral, then back through the trees. Along the way you'll ask yourself, is that the Big Tree? Is that it? Then, suddenly, you'll practically run into the trunk of a giant juniper tree, the second largest in the United States, according to the American Forestry Association. You can almost miss it because it's so big that the foliage is very high up. It's surrounded by a rickety pine fence. Heading home, backtrack to the main trail, then follow that downhill and watch for two cairns on the right and a sign that directs you back to the trailhead. This last bit of single track has some fun rocky technical descents and one ascent that has a lot of erosion protection (you may have to walk your bike up). The last section is fun single track.

Continental Divide Trail

2–20 miles. Moderate. 1,100-ft. elevation gain. Allow 1–4 hrs. Access: If you'd like to ride this as a 20-mile loop, you'll begin in town near the junction of Alabama St. and U.S. 180. However, I recommend riding the Continental Divide Trail as an out-and-back, mostly because I'm not much of a dirt-road rider. Either way, you'll follow Alabama St.; it will become Cottage San Rd., also known as Bear Mountain Rd. Continue for 3 miles until the pavement ends. At a 3-prong fork, bear left, continuing on Bear Mountain Rd., which becomes FS 853. Follow this for 3 more miles until you come to the Continental Divide Trailhead on your right.

This is a primo southern New Mexico trail, traversing the Pinos Altos Range. It combines single track and double track that is technical and at times rocky, with, if you do the loop, some paved and graded dirt road. If you start at the trailhead, rather than doing the loop ride mentioned above, the trail climbs steeply for 0.75 miles to the top of Bear Mountain, then drops down to the east along a rolling ridgeline. The single-track trail continues to climb and fall for another 5 miles, heading up Stewart Peak and down again, until it intersects with FS 506. If you parked at the trailhead, this is a good place to turn around and head back; if you're riding the loop, however, go right onto FS 506 and head downhill. You'll come to a T intersection where you'll go right, continuing to follow FS 506, past Little Walnut Campground. FS 506 will become Little Walnut Creek Road, which will take you back to U.S. 180 and to your car.

Magdalena Mountain

12 miles. Difficult. 2,000-ft. elevation gain. Allow 4 hrs. Access: Take NM 60 west from Socorro for 15 miles to FS 235. Turn left toward the Magdalena Mountains and drive about 4 miles to the Water Canyon Campground.

From the Water Canyon campground begin riding up and don't stop until you die. That's how I would describe this ride, though those riders who really appreciate going uphill would differ with me. I'm assuming there are other riders like my friend Dave who, upon completing a long grueling stretch that I've cussed my way up, stops and says, "Man, that felt good." This ride is for all of you Daves out there. Basically, you follow FS 235 for 9 miles to just below the summit of South Baldy. You definitely won't miss the trailhead sign for Trail 11—you'll be going so slow because much of this grind is steep. The trail takes off to the right and jams for 3 miles downhill. The single track is generally nice, though there are some rocky places to be aware of. The trail joins up with FS 235 and continues its fast jaunt back to the campground. Along the way both up and down there are amazing views out to the north and east of the Magdalenas. I find it hard to believe, but this is a very popular ride for Socorro locals.

Sierra Vista Trails
2–15 miles one-way. Moderate. 300-ft. elevation gain. Allow 1–3 hrs. one-way. Access: From I-25 in Las Cruces, take University Blvd. east 5 miles; turn right on Soledad Canyon Rd. and follow it (it will take a sharp left bend) for 3.7 miles to the trailhead on your right; park on the grass.

This trail heads south, skirting the foothills of the Organ Mountains. It's all single track, a nice narrow trail winding through prickly pear and barrel cacti—south, south, south. That's the mantra of the trail builders who hope one day to connect it up with the notorious Franklin Mountain Trail system in El Paso. At this writing it progresses in that direction for 15 miles. You'll pass along the base of Rattlesnake Ridge, then pass Pyramid Peak and Bishop Cap, at times dipping in and out of drainages or around knolls with a gradual loss of elevation on the way out. When you get tired, you can return the way you came.

A Mountain Trail
4-mile loop. Difficult. 300-ft. elevation gain. Access: In Las Cruces, just east of the intersection of University Ave. and I-25, turn onto Las Alturas Dr. Go south about 0.5 miles and turn left onto Geothermal Rd. Drive this paved-to-gravel road for 1.8 miles until you see a "No Trespassing" sign on your right. Continue 25 ft. or so and park behind the sign (see below for explanation and disclaimer).

You'll be singing, "She'll be comin' 'round the mountain when she comes . . . ." as you ride this sweet trail which circumnavigates A Mountain just east of New Mexico State University. It's a big bald mountain with "No Trespassing" signs to ward off the less serious of riders. I was assured by local bike shops that riders can enter the area without being prosecuted, but if you're very law-abiding you might want to avoid this. And if you do get caught, don't blame me. Blame the bike shops that told me about the ride. Actually, what tips me off that trespassing is okay is the fact that New Mexico State University holds an intramural biking event here each year.

Anyway, the usual route is counterclockwise, starting just after the asphalt a little way up the side of the mountain. Start riding from the parking area up the road climbing the mountain. Look for an odd bit of black asphalt to form. Then watch for the trail to your right. It descends a bit, then begins its trek around, rising and descending. Once you round the backside you'll have nice views of the Organ Mountains, and there you'll pass a few ocotillo bushes, but otherwise this is pure, desolate desert. All along the way you'll encounter some challenging obstacles, including loose rock and just plain rock to climb over. At the ¾ point the trail skirts along just above University Avenue. It climbs the side of the mountain, allowing for a scream back to your car.

ROAD BIKING
Silver City to Glenwood
65 miles one-way. Moderate to difficult. Allow 4–5 hrs. one-way. Access: Begin on U.S. 180 in Silver City and travel west toward Glenwood.

This ride takes you over long rolling hills of the Gila National Forest on excellent highway with good shoulders. Though U.S. 180 is a United States Highway, this portion's remote locale doesn't have a lot of traffic. What makes this most appealing is that it is one of the races in the Tour of the Gila, a U.S. Cycling Federation race that has been designated a "National Prestige Classic." The ride cruises through open country with vast views in all directions. The forest closes in around the area of Glenwood. If you'd like to really do the race the U.S. Cycling Federation maniacs do, continue north of Glenwood 3.5 miles to NM 159 and ride 6 miles to the top of the pass above Mogollon. The finish line for this race was at the highest point before the road heads down into Mogollon.

Gila Cliff Dwellings National Monument

44 miles one-way. Moderate to difficult. Allow 4 hrs. Access: Head north from Silver City on NM 15.

This is a windy and very scenic road that leads through the heart of the Gila Wilderness to amazing Mogollon Cliff Dwellings. It is another road raced by members of the U.S. Cycling Federation during the Tour of the Gila each May. Unfortunately, everyday bikers won't be sheltered from traffic on this shoulderless road the way the racers were, so this is a risky ride. I'd avoid it during peak tourist seasons such as summer. The rest of the year there will likely be little traffic, but you'll still want to watch and listen for cars that may come screaming around the many tight turns. If you're up for the adventure, this trip will take you through some of the most spectacular mountain and canyon country in New Mexico.

Emory Pass

40 miles one-way. Difficult. Allow 3–4 hrs. one-way. Access: Begin in Silver City on NM 152.

This trip follows NM 152 through the lush and dense forests of the Black Range, over Emory Pass to the quaint artist town of Hillsboro. It is a serpentine route, with some tough climbs and fun descents. Much of the way the road has decent shoulders and little traffic, though you'll still want to beware around the many blind curves.

Silver City to Lordsburg

50 miles one-way. Moderate. Allow 3½ hrs. one-way. Access: Begin on NM 90 in Silver City.

This lovely ride follows NM 90 south, skirting along the edge of the lower portion of the Gila National Forest, with views of 8,035-foot Burro Peak. It crosses the Continental Divide, then settles onto the flatter desert plains of southern New Mexico. The road has little traffic, rolling hills, with some decent climbs and good shoulders.

Bosque del Apache Wildlife Refuge

16 miles round-trip. Easy. Allow 1½ hrs. Access: Begin in San Antonio heading south on NM 1.

A good ride in the Socorro area, though only 16 miles, takes you on NM 1 from the Owl Bar in San Antonio (which is noted for its green chile cheeseburgers) south through the Bosque del Apache Wildlife Refuge (see the "Bird Watching" section earlier in this chapter), where you'll likely see all manner of fowl, from hawks to snow geese. Follow this road 8 miles to the end of the pavement, and turn around and return. This is a beautiful ride on little-used road. Though there aren't shoulders, the road isn't heavily traveled except during the peak of winter when the bird-watchers are out. You can add mileage by starting on NM 1 in Socorro.

SWIMMING

Your best bet for swimming in the region is **Elephant Butte Lake State Park** and **Caballo Lake State Park**. Some of the best beaches at both reservoirs are boat-in ones in remote parts of the lake. However, if you're bound to an automobile try Cow Camp at Elephant Butte, not far below the Quality Elephant Butte Inn. There's a small pier there good for jumping off, and some decent sand, though not of the Hawaii variety. Be aware that in summer the drive-on beaches will be full of people, but in spring, fall, and winter, they'll be quiet.

WALKS & RAMBLES

Gila Cliff Dwellings National Monument

1 mile. Moderate. 180-ft. elevation gain. Allow 1 hr. Access: Head north from Silver City on NM 15 for 44 miles to the Monument. This is a windy and very scenic road; expect the drive to take about 2 hrs. You'll pay a nominal fee at the trailhead.

This 1-mile walk is an elaborate journey into the past. It winds its way into a narrow canyon, from which you get glimpses of the poetic ruins perched 180 feet up on the canyon wall. Then the ascent begins up innumerable steps and rocks until you're standing face-to-face with these ancient relics. They offer a peek into the lives of the Mogollon people, who lived at the site from the late 1270s through the early 1300s. However, the earliest ruin that has been found within the monument is a pit house dated to between A.D. 100 and 400. This dwelling below ground level was an earlier type of home occupied by the Mogollon people who grew corn and beans, hunted, and gathered wild plant food in the area. What's remarkable about this journey through the cliff dwellings is the depth of some of the seven caves. At one point you'll climb a ladder and pass from one cave into the next, viewing the intricate little rooms (40 total) and walls that once made up a community dwelling. Once you leave the last cave, you'll head down again traversing some steep steps to the canyon floor. Pets are not allowed within the monument, but they can be taken on trails within the Gila Wilderness. Be sure to pick up a trail guide for this walk at the visitor center.

A Walking Tour of La Mesilla in Las Cruces

1 mile. Easy. Allow 1 hr. Access: From I-10 in Las Cruces, take NM 28 south to Calle de Santiago; turn right and drive two blocks to the Plaza.

Though not in the great outdoors, this walk through the village of La Mesilla is such a wonderful trip back in time, I'm including it as a walk. You'll especially enjoy this walk if you appreciate the feel of a 16th-century plaza or you're a Wild West fanatic. Begin at the **San Albino Church** on the plaza of Mesilla. From here you can get a view of the plaza and even peek down the side streets leading away, where some of the old adobe houses have been restored and painted bold pinks and greens. Head east on Calle de Santiago until you come to **Silver Assets.** Located in the old Valles Gallegos building (1880s), it was once a carpentry shop.

Turn south on Avenida de Mesilla and go to Boutz Street, east on which you'll come to the **Gadsden Museum,** a grand old house full of memorabilia. In the back of the museum parking lot is a replica of the old Mesilla jail, a dismal storage shed with original jail doors that once helped to incarcerate Billy the Kid.

Travel back west along Boutz Street and you'll see a sign for **Country Living Antiques** at the corner of Avenida de Mesilla and Calle de Parian. This 1860s building housed the customs house for the area. Country Living Antiques and the other three antiques shops in the complex are great for browsing.

Continuing west on Calle de Parian, and you'll come to the **William Bonney Gallery.** Here you'll find some nice local paintings as well as some less desirable curios. Across the street is **La Posta de**

GOLD, SILVER & COPPER IN THEM THAR HILLS

If there ever was a boom-to-bust region of the southwestern United States, this part of New Mexico is it. Starting in the late 1800s many towns sprung up due to mining of mostly silver and gold, thrived, and then died. If you seek the ghostly sense of battered buildings and broken windows you're in luck here.

The scenic ghost town of Mogollon is 3.5 miles north of Glenwood on U.S. 180, then 9 miles east on NM 159, a narrow mountain road that takes a good 25 minutes to negotiate. The village bears witness to silver and gold mining booms beginning in the late 19th century, and to the disastrous effects of floods and fire in later years. Remains of its last operating mine, the Little Fanny (which ceased operation in the 1950s), are still visible, along with dozens of other old buildings, miner's shacks, and mining paraphernalia. An art gallery and museum are found along Mogollon's main street. The movie *My Name Is Nobody,* starring Henry Fonda, was shot here.

The virtual ghost town of Pinos Altos, straddling the Continental Divide, is 6 miles north of Silver City on NM 15. Dubbed "Tall Pines" when it was founded in the gold- and silver-rush era, Apache attacks and mine failures have taken their toll. The adobe Methodist-Episcopal Church was built with William Randolph Hearst's money in 1898 and now houses the Grant County Art Guild. The Pinos Altos Museum displays a ¾-scale reproduction of the Santa Rita del Cobre Fort and Trading Post, built at Santa Rita copper mine in 1804 to protect the area from Apaches. (It was renamed Fort Webster in 1851.) The town also has the Log Cabin Curio Shop and Museum located in an 1866 cabin and the Buckhorn Saloon and Opera House.

South of Silver City 12 miles on NM 90 is the Phelps Dodge Open Pit Copper Mine, a modern mining facility that tells a old story. Some 80 million tons of rock are taken out every year. Phelps Dodge consolidated its Tyrone holdings in 1909 and hired famous architect Bertram Goodhue to design a "Mediterranean-style" company town. Tyrone, later referred to as the Million Dollar Ghost Town, was constructed between 1914 and 1918. A large bank and shop building, administration office, mercantile store, and passenger depot were grouped around a central plaza. Eighty-three single and multiple-unit dwellings, accommodating 235 families, were built on the nearby hillsides; and a school, chapel, garage, restaurant, justice court, hospital, morgue, and recreation building were added. A drop in copper prices caused it to be abandoned virtually overnight.

After a pre-World War II incarnation as a luxurious dude ranch, Tyrone lay dormant for years until the late 1960s, when the town made way for the present-day open pit mine and mill. A new town site was created 7 miles north. Most of the original homes and major buildings were removed between 1967 and 1969; today, the only remaining structures are Union Chapel, the justice court, and the pump house. The copper mine supplies copper concentrates to the modern Hidalgo Smelter near Playas, southeast of Lordsburg.

East of Silver City, the oldest active mine in the Southwest, and among the largest in America, is the Chino Mines Co. Open Pit Copper Mine at Santa Rita, 15 miles east of Silver City via U.S. 180 and NM 152, a sad sight for land lovers. The multicolored open pit is 1 mile wide and 1,000 feet deep, and can be viewed from an observation point. Guided tours, lasting 3½ hours, are offered weekday mornings at 9am.

Apaches once scratched the surface for metallic copper at this site. By 1800, the Spanish, under Colonel Jose Manuel Carrasco, were working "Santa Rita del Cobre." Convict labor from New Spain mined the shafts, while mule trains full of ore went down the Janos Trail to Chihuahua, Mexico. An impressive adobe fort was built near the mine, along with smelters and numerous buildings, but Apache raids finally forced the mine's abandonment. In the late 19th century, the mine was reopened, and the town of Santa Rita was reborn. The huge open pit, started around 1910, soon consumed Santa Rita. Today, giant-sized machines scoop the ore from the earth and huge 175-ton ore trucks transport it to the reduction mill to the southwest of the pit.

About 40 miles from Truth or Consequences are the precarious remains of Winston and Chloride, two so-called ghost towns—abandoned mining centers that nevertheless do have a few residents. Exploring these towns makes for a nice side-trip off I-25. You may want to include a visit to the Very Large Array (VLA) and the old mining town of Magdalena in the trip. However, be aware that if you do, much of the journey from Winston to the VLA is on graded dirt road. Winston, 37 miles northwest of Truth or Consequences on NM 52, was abandoned in the early 1900s when silver prices dropped and local mining became unprofitable. Some of the original structures are still standing from that era. A similar fate befell Chloride, 5 miles west of Winston on a side road off NM 52, where famed silver mines had such names as Nana, Wall Street, and Unknown. Chloride also figured in many battles in the turn-of-the-century war between cattle-ranching and sheep-ranching interests. In the very center of town is the "hanging tree," where the town used to tie drunks to "dry" in the sun.

Shakespeare Ghost Town (☎ 505/542-9034) is a for-profit enterprise south of Lordsburg. A national historic site, Shakespeare was once the home of 3,000 miners, promoters, and dealers of various kinds. Under the name of Ralston, it enjoyed a silver boom in 1870. This was followed by a notorious diamond fraud in 1872 in which a mine was salted with diamonds in order to raise prices on mining stock; many notables were sucked in, particularly William Ralston, founder of the Bank of California. It enjoyed a mining revival in 1879 under its new name, Shakespeare. It was a town with no church, no newspaper, and no local law. Some serious fights resulted in hangings from the roof timbers in the Stage Station.

Since 1935, it's been privately owned by the Hill family, which has kept it uncommercialized with no souvenir hype or gift shops. Six original buildings and two reconstructed buildings survive in various stages of repair. Two-hour guided tours are offered on a limited basis, and reenactments and living history are staged on the fourth weekends of April, June, August, and October if performers are available. Phone to confirm the performances.

To reach Shakespeare, drive 1.3 miles south from I-10 on Main Street. Just before the town cemetery, turn right, proceed 0.6 miles and turn right again. Follow the dirt road 0.4 miles into Shakespeare. Admission is $3 for adults, $2 for children ages 6 to 12; free for children 5 and under; for shoot-outs and special events $4 for adults, $3 for children ages 6 to 12, free for children 5 and under. Open 10am and 2pm on the second Sunday and preceding Saturday of each month. Special tours by appointment.

Another privately owned town, **Stein's Railroad Ghost Town** (☎ 505/542-9791), 19 miles west of Lordsburg, started as a Butterfield Stage stop, and then was a railroad town of about 1,000 residents from 1880 to 1955. It was so isolated that water, hauled from Doubtful Canyon, brought $1 a barrel!

Today there remain 12 buildings, with 16 rooms filled with artifacts and furnishings from the 19th and early 20th century. There is also a petting zoo for kids and the Steins Mercantile shop. Recently the owners began offering horseback and stagecoach rides from Wednesday through Sunday; they hope to continue offering them. Admission is $2.50 for those over 12 years of age; children under 12 are admitted free of charge. Open daily from 9am until dusk.

Mesilla Restaurant, a decent place to stop for a meal, though not the best in the area. The building dates from the mid-18th century, and is the only surviving stagecoach station of the Butterfield, Overland Mail route from Missouri to San Francisco. Kit Carson, Pancho Villa, and Billy the Kid all were here.

Then continue west around the plaza to the **Nambé Showroom,** a shop displaying handcrafted tableware by Nambé Mills in Santa Fe. It's a great place to shop for gifts. On the southwest corner of the plaza is the oldest documented brick building in New Mexico built by Augustin Maurin in 1860. It has a sad history of its proprietors being murdered by robbers.

Continue north along the plaza and be sure to stop at the **Bowlin's Mesilla Book Center.** Housed in a historic mercantile building (ca. 1856), the building has tall ceilings with elaborate vigas and latillas. The bookstore has a strong selection of Southwestern books and children's titles. A few doors down is **El Platero,** a store selling mostly tourists trinkets, but also large snow cones, perfect to cool you off after a walking tour.

If you prefer a guided historic walking tour, contact **Preciliana Sandoval** (☎ 505/647-2639). This bold artist/historian, a fifth-generation Mesilla Valley native, will regale you with stories of ghosts and historic battles in the area.

WILDLIFE VIEWING

My best wildlife encounter during the course of researching this book took place in southwestern New Mexico in the Magdalena Mountains west of Socorro. At the end of a long day, I was sitting in the doorway of my tent at Water Canyon Campground typing away on my laptop. Suddenly my dog, Alma, barked and ran toward my left. I thought, "Not now, girl,"—and I turned to see a big brown bear chasing her straight toward me. I grabbed Alma and her dish of food, putting both in the car. Then I ran to the back of my 4-Runner to close the tailgate so the bear couldn't get at the food, but the damn thing wouldn't close. I was shaking as the bear drew nearer. Finally the tailgate closed, and I jumped in the front seat. The bear returned to the tent, sniffed at the computer, at Alma's water dish, and then stood by the camp for quite awhile. Alma had a low growl going in the car. Finally he turned and walked up the hill. I got out of the car and, with hands shaking, returned to my writing, when suddenly Alma barked again. We looked over a little knoll to see the bear eating apples at a tree there. We jumped back in the car and waited and watched while the bear ate and ate the apples—really a beautiful sight. After he had his fill, though, he headed back over to my camp, where he sniffed at my tent, and then opened his mouth to take a bite of it. I yelled at him, but he only moved around to the front and opened his mouth again. At that point I honked the horn. I honked and honked, until he moved about 20 yards away and stayed there. At this point it was apparent that I was camped near his apple tree, and he wasn't going to leave. So I jumped out of the car, collapsed the tent, threw it in the back of my car and hit the road. Later I learned that because of drought conditions many bears had come down from the high country in mountains all over New Mexico. So the point of the story is, the **Magdalena Mountains** are a good place to see brown bears.

Gila National Forest, which offers some of the most spectacular mountain scenery in the Southwest, comprises 3.3 million acres in 4 counties. Nearly one-fourth of that acreage (790,000 acres) comprises the **Gila, Aldo Leopold,** and **Blue Range Wildernesses.** Its highest peak is Whitewater Baldy, at 10,892 feet. Within the forest six out of seven life zones can be found, so the range of plant and wildlife is broad. You may see mule deer, elk, antelope, black bear, mountain lion, and bighorn sheep. Nearly 400 miles of streams and a few small lakes sustain healthy populations of trout as well as bass, bluegill, and catfish.

Also in the Silver City area is the **Fort Bayard Wildlife Refuge,** east of town, where you'll likely see mule deer, bobcat, and black bears on lovely trails that wind through piñon/juniper woodlands, ponderosa pine forest, and riparian areas.

Though the major sight at **Bosque del Apache National Wildlife Refuge** is waterfowl such as snow geese and cranes, it's also a great place to see other wildlife such as coyotes and mule deer and many reptiles. It's located 90 miles south of Albuquerque on I-25, and is well worth the drive.

Campgrounds & Other Accommodations

CAMPING

Mesa Campground

Located 30 miles northeast of Silver City via NM 15 or 35. ☎ **505/536-2250.** Cultural/historic sites, developed campground, drinking water, rest rooms, RV sites, and boat ramp. Open May–Sept.

Surrounded by tall ponderosa pines, juniper, and piñon, these campsites are located near Lake Roberts, though they don't have a view of the lake. Lake Roberts is clear blue since it was drained in 1998 and then restocked with trout. Only boats with electric motors are allowed on the lake.

Scorpion Campground

Located 45 miles north of Silver City via NM 15. ☎ **505/536-2250.** Visitor center, cultural/historic sites, developed campground, drinking water, rest rooms, and RV sites.

Scorpion Campground sits on the Gila River and is the closest campground to the Gila Cliff Dwellings built by the Mogollon people who inhabited the area from around A.D. 300 to 1300. Because of its close proximity to the cliff dwellings, the campground can get very busy. If you're looking for something quieter, try the Fork or Grapevine Campgrounds about 4.5 miles south of the Gila Cliff Dwellings. Great hikes are just minutes away.

Willow Creek Campground

Located 31 miles northeast of Glenwood via U.S. 180 and FR 159. ☎ **505/533-6232.** 6 primitive campsites. Picnic tables and rest rooms.

Nestled between steep canyon walls are these six campsites on Willow Creek at the edge of the Gila Wilderness. There's good trout fishing in the creek and hiking and horseback riding nearby.

Juniper Campground

Located 23 miles south of Quemado via U.S. 60, NM32, and FS 13. ☎ **505/533-6232.** Developed campground, drinking water, rest rooms, RV sites, electric hookups, and boat ramp.

Open May 1 to September 31, Juniper Campground is situated on Quemado Lake, among piñon/juniper forest. You can always find a fairly shady spot here with a lake view. The campground is nicely kept, bathrooms are clean, and the grounds are tidy. A host is there to greet guests, to keep the campground looking good, and to answer any questions you might have. The fishing is fair. Only boats with electric motors are allowed on the lake. There's an easy 3-mile hike around the lake.

Water Canyon Campground

Take U.S. 60 west from Socorro about 16 miles to FS 235. Turn left and drive 5 miles to the campground. 6 tent sites, 3 RV sites, picnicking sites with BBQ grills, vault toilets. Open year-round. Free.

This is the campground where I had my bear adventure (see "Wildlife Viewing" earlier in this chapter), so aside from being chased away by a bear, I found it to be one of the prettiest sites in the region. It sits on the banks of an oft-dry creek, bordered by cottonwoods and ponderosa pines. Some of the sites are on soft meadowgrass below the trees. Generally, it is a very quiet place. When I camped there in the middle of summer, I had the place to myself.

Aguirre Springs Campground
From Las Cruces, head east on U.S. 70 for 14 miles to the turn off to Aguirre Springs Recreation Area. Turn right and drive this narrow, winding, paved road 6 miles to the campground. ☎ **505/520-4300**. 55 sites, picnic tables, fireplaces, rest rooms. Water and firewood are available from the campsite host en route to the campground. $3 camping fee.

This is one of the loveliest places I've ever camped. Set at the very foot of the Organ Mountains, high above the Tularosa Basin, it's a series of sites that are overused by picnickers and underused by campers, so you can often count on solitude during the night. One problem, though, is that the heavy day-use leaves the place a bit trashed and flies dominate. Every time you gaze in any direction you'll forget the trash and pests and be mesmerized. Best of all: Two of the best trails in the Organs leave from the campsite, so those early morning and late evening desert hikes are yours for the taking.

INNS & LODGES

Quality Inn at Elephant Butte
NM 195 (P.O. Box 996), Elephant Butte, NM 87935. ☎ **505/744-5431**. www.hotelchoice.com/res/hotel/nm086/. 48 units. A/C TV TEL. Mid-Sept–April $70–$75 double; May–early Sept $75–$90 double. AE, CB, DC, DISC, MC, V.

This inn, owned by the people who own Goulding's Lodge in Monument Valley, offers a comfortable and unique experience. It sits above Elephant Butte Lake and has panoramic views as well as a relaxing resort-like feel. Recent years have brought a complete facelift to the whole place. It caters to boaters, fishers, and other relaxation lovers. Rooms are standard-sized, furnished with medium-firm king- or queen-size beds. Bathrooms are small but functional. All rooms come with coffeemakers, irons and ironing boards, hair dryers, and data ports. I recommend the lakeside view, which costs a little more but is worth it, as there's a big grassy lawn stretching down to tennis courts. The inn has a restaurant, swimming pool, room service, and offers golf packages with the Oasis Golf Course, a 5-minute drive away.

River Bend Hot Springs Hostel
100 Austin St., Truth or Consequences, NM 87901. ☎ **505/894-6183**. 16 dormitory beds, 2 apartments. A/C. Dorm beds $13–$15; apartments $32–$45 double. AE, DISC, MC, V.

This pleasant hostel is clean and comfortable with an inviting Southwest hippie atmosphere. Outdoor communal hot mineral baths on the premises overlook a swampy section of the Rio Grande. There are kitchenette units, family units, and couples can be accommodated. There is also a campground on the property ($12 per person). Campers may use the hostel facilities. A guest laundry is available, and day tours of area attractions can be arranged. RV parking is available.

The River House
P.O. Box 131, Gila, NM 88038. ☎ **505/535-2383**. www.gilanet.com/estamler. E-mail: estamler@gilanet.com. 1 house. TV TEL. $90–$125 double. No credit cards. 2-night minimum stay required.

A friend at the Nature Conservancy introduced me to this sweet house nestled near the bosque along the Gila River. The house is for those who don't really want the interaction of a B&B, but want the comfortable feel of a home. Sparsely and tastefully decorated, it has two complete bedrooms with large bathrooms, a large kitchen and sitting area, as well as a desk. The bedding could be better throughout the place as could the mattress in what the owners refer to as the "children's room," but otherwise, with its full kitchen, it's a dream of a stay.

Casitas de Gila
310 Hooker Loop (P.O. Box 325), Gila, NM 88038. ☎ 505/535-4455. www.casitasdegila.com. E-mail: info@casitasdegila.com. 5 casitas. TEL. $110–$150 double. Price includes continental breakfast. AE, DISC, MC, V.

If you're really looking for a remote and peaceful stay in the quintessence of southern New Mexico terrain, this inn is for you. Set on a little bluff above Bear Creek, these five casitas epitomize Southwestern style. The adobe dwellings are inventively decorated with Spanish-style furniture and Mexican rugs, each with a full kitchen, with stove, microwave, refrigerator and coffeemaker, and medium-sized bedrooms and bathrooms. Each also has a small porch with a chiminea fireplace and a grill. On hand is a hot tub with a view of the creek, canyon, and sky. The area is great for bird watching and hiking, and there's a horse ranch nearby where riding can be arranged.

Bear Mountain Lodge
Cottage San Rd., Silver City, NM 88061. To reach the ranch, turn north off U.S. 180 on Alabama St. (0.5 miles west of NM 90 intersection). Proceed 2.8 miles (Alabama becomes Cottage San Rd.) to a dirt road turnoff to left; the lodge is another 0.6 miles. ☎ 877/620-BEAR. www.bearmountainlodge.com. 10 units. A/C TEL. $108–$135 double. Rates include a full breakfast. Box lunches available for an extra charge. MC, V.

Set on 160 acres just 3.5 miles northwest of downtown Silver City, this lodge recently acquired and renovated by the Nature Conservancy is ideal for outdoors enthusiasts, from birders to bikers. Scheduled to reopen in March 2001, the lodge was previously the passion of Myra McCormick, a salty outdoorswoman who continued to run the place into her 90s. Her recent death saddened many of us, but her bequeathing the ranch to the conservancy assures its future. The 1920s guesthouse offers large rooms with maple floors, high ceilings, and French windows. Each is equipped with modern amenities, including country-inn Southwestern décor and comfortable beds. Four rooms have private balconies. This is a nature lover's delight. On-site Nature Conservancy staff members are on hand to inform visitors about the flora and fauna of the area, and also conduct guided trips. What's best here is that you can count on complete quiet.

Casa Blanca
P.O. Box 31, San Antonio, NM 87832. ☎ 505/835-3027. 3 units. $60–$90 double. Closed Memorial Day–Labor Day. MC, V. Rates include continental breakfast. Children and pets are welcome. No smoking.

The ideal situation in this part of the world is to be just a few minutes away from the Bosque del Apache National Wildlife Refuge. That way, you only have to get out of bed a half-hour or so before sunup in order to get to the refuge to see the morning flight. This is the place to stay for this reason. It's a cozy Victorian farmhouse and home to proprietor Phoebe Wood, a schoolteacher. The place has a real home quality—comfortable and well maintained. The best room is the Crane, light and airy, with a queen-size bed and private bathroom. Breakfast is simple and can be eaten early on the way out to the Bosque or upon return later. Fruit, cereals, and home-baked muffins are served in a home-style kitchen. There are mountain bikes for rent. Smoking is not permitted.

Lundeen's Inn of the Arts
618 S. Alameda Blvd., Las Cruces, NM 88005. ☎ 888/526-3326 or 505/526-3326. www.lundeen@innofthearts.com. 24 rooms. A/C TV TEL. $72 double;

$78–$130 suite. Rates include breakfast. AE, CB, DC, DISC, MC, V. Pets welcome.

This inn within the city of Las Cruces offers a Barcelonan type of stay in a late 1890s adobe home, with whitewashed walls, narrow alleys and arched doorways. It's a complex composite of rooms stretching across 14,000 square feet of floor space, that at some moments seems completely orderly and at others a bit unkempt. There's a wide range of rooms, each named for an artist. My favorites are in the main part of the house, set around a two-story garden room, with elegant antiques and arched windows. Most rooms are medium-sized with comfortably firm beds dressed in fine linens. Bathrooms are generally small and simple but clean. My favorite rooms are the Maria Martinez (the only room without a TV), which has wood floors and a working fireplace, and gets lots of sun. The Frederic Remington has a more masculine feel and includes a kitchenette with a microwave, mini-refrigerator, stove, and coffeemaker. Other rooms have similarly equipped kitchenettes. The inn is also an art gallery, displaying the works of about 30 Southwestern painters, sculptors, and potters.

Breakfast includes fresh fruit and such specialties as pumpkin waffles and huevos rancheros. Guests get reduced rates at a local health club, and Gerry Lundeen will take them on architectural walking tours of nearby Old Mesilla. The inn is surrounded by a 10-foot stone privacy wall with iron gates. Services include laundry service, baby-sitting, and secretarial services.

Martha's Bed & Breakfast

Main and Lima Sts., Columbus, NM 88029. ☎ **505/531-2467.** 5 units. A/C TV TEL. $55 double. Breakfast included. MC, V. Children and pets are welcome.

If you'd like to add a little Mexico adventure to your southern New Mexico stay, head south of Deming 30 miles and stay with Martha. She has a two-story stucco pueblo-style adobe painted cream and green, with Victorian touches inside. Built in 1991, it's just 3 miles from the Mexican border town of Las Palomas. The place is furnished with some nice antiques as well as furniture made in her family's *maquiladora* (manufacturing plant) across the border. The medium-sized rooms have comfortably firm beds and good bedding. Each has French doors and a balcony. Bathrooms are medium-sized and basic, with showers, and are very clean. This is not a luxury B&B, nor is great care taken in making your stay perfect, but Martha is a complete character and enjoys being a host, which is worth a lot. She'll fill you with stories of border-town life, and tell you exactly when and how to see what. Breakfasts are simple and full—I had fruit, egg-toast, and Canadian bacon. If you're lucky you'll arrive on one of the two weeks of the year when the Tumbleweed Theater has a melodrama performance, held in back of the inn, with Martha presiding.

12

New Mexico Cave Country

Southeastern New Mexico is a place of high drama. During my travels in the region, I have been both startled and deeply moved by the landscapes. Possibly more than any part of the southwestern United States, the region has undergone great shifts over time, from the recent lava flows of the Valley of the Fires, which have left elaborate black lands full of tubes and rich with foliage growth, to farther back in time. As part of the Basin and Range Province, innumerable volcanic upliftments have created truly breathtaking mountain ranges such as the Whites and the Capitans. Meanwhile, erosion has worked upon the surfaces of the mountains, moving particles that were later transformed into the lovely rhythmic beauty of White Sands National Monument. Below the surface, water has trickled over vast periods of time through layers of limestone. It has dripped and pooled, and thereby created the immense chambers and intricate hallways of Carlsbad Caverns. And located farther to the south is a place that I will borrow from our neighbor Texas: Guadalupe Mountains National Park, the world's largest ocean reef, which juts up from the great Chihuahuan Desert, creating an oasis.

For outdoor adventurers this area is best explored on foot, through odd kinds of hikes into deep caverns and across sands where your feet tend to sink, slowing progress. Hiking in the Valley of Fires is also a slow but interesting process, across lava flows where you have to watch every step. Similarly, at Three Rivers Petroglyph site, you'll find the going slow because you'll want to enjoy the beauty of the many vivid pictures drawn on the rocks. However, many of the highlands hikes provide excellent passageway to incredible views. This is also a key place for horse enthusiasts, who enjoy the trails of the high country, especially in the White Mountain Wilderness. Those who love winter sports can find some fun here, but they'd be better off heading to north central New Mexico to ski Taos and the surrounding ski areas.

ATOMIC BOMBS & RADIOACTIVE WASTE

TRINITY SITE

The world's first atomic bomb was exploded in the desert never-never land of White Sands Missile Range on July 16, 1945. The site is strictly off-limits to civilians—except twice a year, on the first Saturday of April and October. A small lava monument commemorates the explosion, which left a crater a 0.25 miles across, 8 feet deep, and transformed the desert sand into a jade green glaze called "Trinitite" that remains today. The McDonald House, where the bomb's plutonium core was assembled 2 miles from Ground Zero, has been restored to its 1945 condition. The site is on the west slope of Sierra Oscura, 90 air miles northwest of Alamogordo. For more information, call the public affairs office of **White Sands Missile Range** (☎ **505/678-1134**).

TRANSURANIC TRASH

If you're interested in world history in the making, you'll want to look into the **Waste Isolation Pilot Plant,** located 26 miles from Carlsbad. Our nation's first deep-geologic repository for permanent disposal of radioactive waste is embedded in a 225 million-year-old salt formation. In 1999, the facility received its first shipments of waste, stored 2,150 feet (almost a half-mile) underground. At this site, the U.S. Department of Energy disposes of transuranic waste (trash from the production of nuclear materials) from more than 20 temporary storage sites nationwide. For more information stop by the **WIPP Information Center** at 4021 National Parks Highway (☎ **800/336-9477**; www.wipp.carlsbad.nm.us) in Carlsbad, where you'll find a reading room. WIPP is now offering free tours of the site Monday through Thursday and every other Friday from 8am to 12pm. Call at best 2 weeks to 1 month in advance to book a tour, and when on the tour, wear long pants and sturdy walking shoes.

For centuries humans have played out dramatic histories in this region. This is the place where Billy the Kid, the notorious 19th-century outlaw, was incarcerated and finally killed and buried, just one chapter in the history of the bloody Lincoln County War. It was fought between various ranching and merchant factions over the issue of beef contracts for Fort Stanton near Ruidoso. A sharp-shooting teenager named William Bonney—soon to be known as Billy the Kid—took sides in this issue and became an odd sort of hero revered throughout the world.

This is also the place where Robert Oppenheimer, creator of the first atomic bomb, watched while his creation was detonated. The event took place in the predawn hours of July 16, 1945, the result of more than 2 years of intensive nuclear research at Los Alamos Scientific Laboratories. Because it was top secret, it was known as the "Manhattan Project," and the bomb itself was called "Fat Man." The incident produced a blinding flash of light followed several seconds later by the sound and shock wave, a wave felt over a radius of at least 160 miles. The atomic weapon was then used to bomb Hiroshima and Nagasaki, Japan. The site is generally closed to the public except for two annual tours on the first Saturdays of April and October. Southeastern New Mexico is also the home of the Waste Isolation Pilot Project, our nation's first deep-geologic repository for permanent disposal of radioactive waste, a controversial project over 20 years in the making that received its first shipments in

New Mexico Cave Country

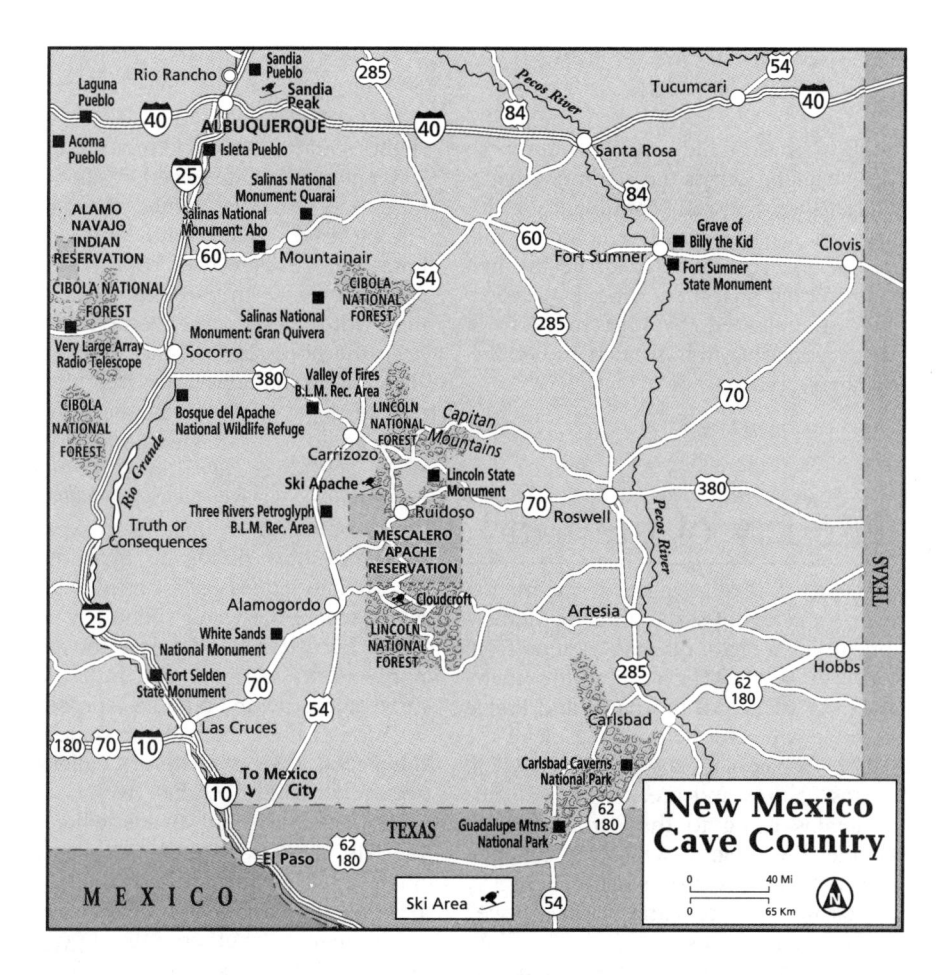

1999. For more information on visiting the sites of the Manhattan Project and the Waste Isolation Pilot Project, see the "Atomic Bombs & Radioactive Waste" feature in this chapter.

Throughout the region, as with much of the southwestern United States, Native Americans have been an enduring presence, from the stunning petroglyphs carved at Three Rivers near Alamogordo, to the thriving culture of the present-day Jicarilla Apache tribe that inhabits the mountains south of Ruidoso. These people of Athapascan lineage, relatives of the Navajos, arrived in the southwestern United States sometime in the 15th century. They wandered the northern and eastern plains until around the 17th century when they settled in northeastern New Mexico, growing beans, corn, and squash. By the mid-19th century they'd moved closer to the Rio Grande River, where they were known to raid American wagon trains on the route from Santa Fe to Taos. Because of the raiding, the U.S. government forced them to move from place to place. They gathered what they could from the land, but nearly starved in the process. In 1887 the government deeded them the land they now occupy in the Ruidoso area. What was thought to be fairly useless acreage has turned out to be rich with fossil fuels as well as hungry tourists. As you pass through the area, you may see Apaches astride horses, which they still use for hunting and, at times, transportation. Herds of wild horses roam the Apache lands as well.

While traversing these lands you'll likely touch upon these important pieces of history. Wherever you go you'll see signs of The Kid, including places he drank or shot or hid out. You may note while walking across the starkness that is White Sands National Monument that it's that very starkness and remoteness that led the government to detonate the first atomic bomb near there. Above all, you'll likely be startled by the mastery of nature, so visible in this harsh and enduring landscape.

The Lay of the Land

A glance at a relief map of the region reveals a series of sky islands that almost appear like a chain running easterly from north to south. These, like the many other sky islands of the Basin and Range Province, were formed as a result of the extending nature of the province, which creates fissures and breaks, the volcanic mountains rising to the surface. These include the Capitan, White, Sacramento, and San Andreas Mountains. These sky islands are full of bird and wildlife as well as abundant streams.

The southern end of the chain, the Guadalupe Mountains, has a little different history. They are part of the largest fossil reef in the world that 10 to 12 million years ago uplifted and tilted, revealing the spectacular structures that they are today. The reef was formed during the Permian age, from about 280 to 230 million years ago, when a shallow sea covered the area. The reef builders were lime-secreting algae, sponges, bryozoans, and brachiopods. The work they performed has, millions of years later, proven to be a wonder for geologists to explore.

Beneath the Guadalupes, and formed through the same process but with the forces of erosion putting in their time, is one of the largest and most spectacular cave systems in the world, Carlsbad Caverns. Upliftment in the great reef formation caused small fractures through which ground water, having acquired a slight acidity from trickling through the soil, entered and dissolved cavities in the limestone. The labyrinth of some 80 known caves filled with intricate and immense formations allows either the casual hiker or the serious caver a lifetime worth of sites to experience.

To the north of Carlsbad, White Sands National Monument preserves the best part of the world's largest gypsum dune field, an area of 275 square miles of pure white sand reaching out over the floor of the Tularosa Basin in wavelike hills. They were formed over millions of years by rain and snow dissolving gypsum from nearby mountains and depositing it in lakes, where the water eventually evaporated. Persistent winds blow the crystals northeasterly, forming the dunes, which move and grow in an endless procession.

Through the center of the region runs the Pecos River, with fertile valleys and scenic lakes. East of the river, the land opens out to the high plains, where people talk like Texans and ranching is the mainstay. This area, part of the Permian Basin, is also rich with oil fields.

The region's southern latitude coupled with its high peaks makes it suitable for outdoor fun year-round. The lower lands in the areas of Carlsbad and Roswell often have summer temperatures in excess of 100°F. The heat makes hiking and biking during summer oppressive. However, in spring, fall, and winter, these areas provide comfortable temperatures for many outdoor activities. Within a half-hour, travelers can be up in the mountains in the region and find temperatures averaging 10 to 15°F cooler in summer and much more in winter. Enough snow generally falls on Sierra Blanca to allow for skiing and to prohibit hiking and biking in the area in winter. However, during spring, summer, and fall the highlands become green and cool, perfect oases for those escaping the heat below.

At no time is this phenomenon so pronounced as during the monsoon season in July, August, and early September, when thunderclouds build up in the highlands by noon, and pour rain often into the night. One July day when I was traveling in the region, I finally fled the Cloudcroft area where I intended to camp just because the rain would not stop falling. Immediately when I dropped down toward Alamogordo the sun shone and dried my wet gear. Then the clouds hanging on the peaks presented a spectacular rainbow over the sheer cliffs of the Sacramento Mountains.

Also be aware that these lowlands are desert, and nights can get cold. One winter when I headed to White Sands to camp, many inches of snow fell, the temperature dropped into the teens, and I ended up in a motel. Go tell.

Orientation

The main population center in this region is Roswell (pop. 50,000), famous as the purported landing place of an unidentified flying object (see "The Incident at Roswell" feature later in this chapter for details). Carlsbad (pop. 27,800), 76 miles south of Roswell, and Alamogordo (pop. 31,000), 117 miles west of Roswell, are of more immediate interest to travelers. Ruidoso (pop. 8,500), in the mountains between Alamogordo and Roswell, is a booming resort town. Other sizable towns are Clovis and Hobbs, both on the Texas border, and Artesia, between Roswell and Carlsbad.

This region is defined to the north by Interstate 40, which runs east-west, and to the west by Interstate 25, which runs north-south. Nearly paralleling I-25 is U.S. 54 running along the western flank of the White and Sacramento Mountains. Parallel to U.S. 54 is U.S. 285, which connects the towns of Roswell, Artesia, and Carlsbad. Cutting across the center of the region running east-west are two major thoroughfares: U.S. 380 and, south of that, U.S. 82.

Parks & Other Hot Spots

Carlsbad Caverns National Park
Take U.S. 62/180 south from Carlsbad. The scenic entrance road to the park is 7 miles long and originates at the park gate at Whites City. Van service to Carlsbad Caverns National Park from Whites City, south of Carlsbad, is provided by **Sun Country Tours/Whites City Services** (☎ 505/785-2291). 3225 National Parks Hwy., Carlsbad, NM 88220. ☎ **800/967-CAVE** for tour reservations, 505/785-2232, ext. 429, for information about guided tours, or 505/785-2107 for recorded information. Open daily from Memorial Day to mid-Aug from 8am–7pm; the rest of the year from 8am–5:30pm. Admission $6 for adults, $3 for children 6–15, and free for children under 6. Admission is good for 3 days and includes entry to the 2 self-guided walking tours. Guided tours range in price from $6–$20 depending on the type of tour, and reservations are required. Backpacking, biking, bird watching, camping, caving, hiking, mountain biking, wildlife viewing.

One of the largest and most spectacular cave systems in the world, Carlsbad Caverns National Park is comprised of some 80 known caves that snake through the porous limestone reef of the Guadalupe Mountains. Fantastic and grotesque formations fascinate visitors, who find every shape imaginable (and unimaginable) naturally sculpted in the underground world—from frozen waterfalls to strands of pearls, from soda straws to miniature castles, from draperies to ice-cream cones.

Although Native Americans had known of the caverns for centuries, they were not discovered by whites until about a century ago, when settlers were attracted by sunset flights of bats from the cave.

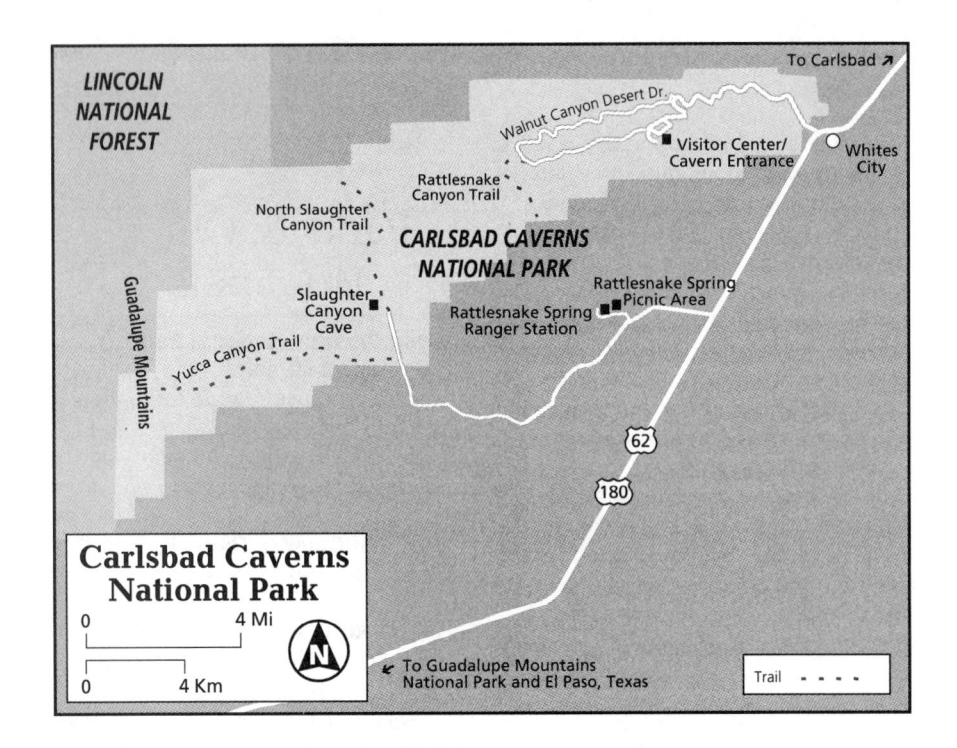

Jim White, a guano miner, began to explore the main cave in the early 1900s and to share its wonders with tourists. By 1923, the caverns had become a national monument, upgraded to a national park in 1930.

Aside from the caves, the national park offers a 10-mile one-way scenic loop drive through the Chihuahuan Desert to view Rattlesnake and Upper Walnut Canyons. Picnickers can head for Rattlesnake Springs Picnic Area, on County Road 418 near Slaughter Canyon Cave, a water source for hundreds of years for the Native Americans of the area. Backcountry hikers must register at the visitor center before going out on any of the trails in the 46,766 acres of the park. For information on seeing the caves, see the "Caving" section later in this chapter.

White Sands National Monument

15 miles southwest of Alamogordo on U.S. 70/82. (*Note:* Due to missile testing on the adjacent White Sands Missile Range, this road is sometimes closed for up to 2 hours at a time.) P.O. Box 1086, Holloman, AFB, NM 88330-1086. ☎ **505/479-6124.** When driving near or in the monument, tune your radio to 1610 AM for information. From Memorial Day to Labor Day the visitor center is open daily 8am–7pm, and Dunes Dr. is open daily 7am–9pm. During the rest of the year, the visitor center is open daily 8am–4:30pm, and Dunes Dr. is open daily 7am–sunset. Ranger talks and sunset strolls are given nightly at 7 and 8:30pm during summer. $3 for adults 17 and over. Backpacking, camping, hiking, wildlife viewing.

Arguably the most memorable natural area in this part of the Southwest, White Sands National Monument occupies part of the world's largest gypsum dune field, an area of 275 square miles of white sand. Plants and animals have evolved in special ways to adapt to the bright white environment here. Some creatures have a bleached coloration to match the whiteness all around them, whereas some plants have evolved means for surviving against the smothering pressures of the blowing sands.

The surrounding mountains—the Sacramentos to the east, with their forested slopes, and the serene San

Andres to the west—are composed of sandstone, limestone, sedimentary rocks, and pockets of gypsum. Over millions of years, rains and melting snows dissolved the gypsum and carried it down into Lake Lucero. Here the hot sun and dry winds evaporate the water, leaving the gypsum to crystallize. Then the persistent winds blow these crystals, in the form of minuscule bits of sand, in a northeastern direction, adding them to growing dunes. As each dune grows and moves farther from the lake, new ones form, rank after rank, in what seems an endless procession.

The dunes are especially enchanting at sunrise and under the light of a full moon, but you'll have to camp here to experience these extraordinary sights (see the "Campgrounds & Other Accommodations" section later in this chapter). If you're not camping, you'll probably want to spend only a couple of hours here. Refreshments and snacks can be purchased at the visitor center, along with books, maps, posters, and other souvenirs; however, there are no dining or grocery facilities available here.

Seeing the Highlights

A 16-mile **Dunes Drive** loops through the "heart of sands" from the visitor center. Information available at the center will tell you what to look for on your drive. Sometimes the winds blow the dunes over the road, which must then be rerouted. The dunes are in fact all moving slowly to the northeast, pushed by prevailing southwest winds, some at the rate of as much as 20 feet a year.

In the center of the monument, the road itself is made of hard-packed gypsum. (*Note:* It can be especially slick after an afternoon thunderstorm, so drive cautiously!) Visitors are invited to get out of their cars at established parking areas and explore a bit; some like to climb a dune for a better view of the endless sea of sand. If you'd rather taste the park by hiking rather than on the long drive, a good trail right near the entrance is the Big Dune Trail (see "Walks & Rambles" later in this chapter). It will take you on a 45-minute loop along the edges of the dunes and then into their whiteness, ending atop a 60-foot-tall one.

Safety tips: The National Park Service emphasizes that (1) tunneling in this sand can be dangerous, for it collapses easily and could suffocate a person; (2) sand-surfing down the dune slopes, although permitted, can also be hazardous, so it should be undertaken with care, and never near an auto road; and (3) hikers can get lost in a sudden sandstorm should they stray from marked trails or areas.

Valley of Fires Recreation Area

On U.S. 380 4 miles west of Carrizozo. ☎ **505/648-2241.** 19 campsites with picnic shelters, tables, grills, and water. RV electrical hookups at 14 sites. RV dump station and wheelchair-accessible campsites and rest rooms. Open year-round. $3 per person or $5 per car for day use; $5–$11 camping fee. Bird watching, camping, hiking, wildlife viewing.

At this amazing park you'll find what is considered one of the youngest and best-preserved lava fields in the United States. Among the black lava formations, there's a 0.75-mile self-guided nature trail, which is well worth the walk. Part of it is wheelchair accessible. You'll discover a strange new landscape that at first glance appears inhospitable, but really is rich with plant and wildlife. Be sure to walk far enough to see the 400-year-old juniper wringing itself from the black stone. A small visitor center with a bookstore is near the park campground.

Oliver Lee Memorial State Park

15 miles southeast of Alamogordo via U.S. 54 and Dog Canyon Rd. 409 Dog Canyon Rd., Alamogordo, NM 88310. ☎ **505/437-8284.** Picnic and camping

grounds, with showers, electricity, and dump station. Backpacking, bird watching, camping, hiking, wildlife viewing.

Nestled at the mouth of Dog Canyon, a stunning break in the steep escarpment of the Sacramento Mountains, this site has drawn human visitors for thousands of years. Springs and seeps support a variety of rare and endangered plant species, as well as a rich wildlife. Hiking trails into the foothills are well marked; the park also offers a visitor center with excellent exhibits on local history. **Dog Canyon** was one of the last strongholds of the Mescalero Apache, and was the site of battles between Native Americans and the U.S. Cavalry in the 19th century. Around the turn of the 20th century, rancher Oliver Lee built a home near here and raised cattle; guided tours from the visitor center to his restored house give a taste of early ranch life in southern New Mexico.

Three Rivers Petroglyph National Recreation Area

From U.S. 54 30 miles north of Alamogordo, take FS 579 and follow the signs 4.5 miles to the site. ☎ 505/525-4300. Picnicking and camping. The National Forest Service also has a campground in the area, about 5 miles east via a gravel road. Day use or camping fee $3 per vehicle. Backpacking, bird watching, camping, hiking, wildlife viewing.

There are some 20,000 individual images here, carved by Mogollon peoples who lived in the area centuries ago. A trail about 0.8 miles long links many of the more interesting petroglyphs, while the view surrounding the area, with mountains to the east and White Sands to the southwest, is outstanding. Be sure to go far enough to see site 7, a vividly depicted bighorn sheep pierced with three arrows. The park also includes the partially excavated ruins of an ancient Native American village, including a multi-room adobe building, pit house, and masonry house that have been partially reconstructed.

Bottomless Lakes State Park

Located 16 miles southeast of Roswell via NM 409 off U.S. 380. ☎ 505/624-6058. Campsites for trailers or tents, shelters, showers, rest rooms, drinking water, a RV dump station, a sandy beach, a concession area with vending machines and paddleboat rentals (open Memorial Day–Labor Day 9am–6pm). Open year-round daily 6am–9pm. $10–$18 camping fee. Boating, camping, fishing, hiking, horseback riding, water sports.

Bottomless Lakes State Park is a chain of seven small, deep lakes surrounded by red stone bluffs. It got its name from early cowboys, who tried to fathom the lakes' depths by plumbing them with lariats. No matter how many ropes they tied together and lowered into the limpid water, they never touched bottom. In truth, though, none of the lakes is deeper than 100 feet. The largest, Lea Lake, is so clear that scuba divers frequent it. Another, aptly called Devil's Inkwell, is so shaded by surrounding bluffs that the sun rarely reaches it. Mirror, Cottonwood, Pasture, and Figure 8 Lakes got their monikers with similar logic; No Name Lake, which apparently didn't have anything to distinguish it, has been renamed Lazy Lagoon. This park is a popular recreation site for Roswell residents. There's good rainbow trout fishing and a 2-mile horse trail. Horses are allowed overnight in primitive camping areas only.

Brantley Lake State Park

Located 12 miles north of Carlsbad via U.S. 285. For reservations call ☎ 877/664-7787 or 505/457-2384 (half of the sites can be reserved). 51 RV sites with or without hook-ups, primitive campsites, picnic area with grills, drinking water, showers, rest rooms, RV dump station, boat ramp, recreational facilities and visitor center. $8–$14 camping fee. Boating, camping, fishing, horseback riding, swimming.

This 2,800-acre lake in the desert is sought out by windsurfers who favor its consistent desert winds. Boating and lake fishing are also popular here. The water gets to a tepid 80°F in July and August, making swimming quite comfortable. However, the reservoir's rocky bottom can be tough on the soles of the feet. Primitive camping sites are located among the salt cedars along the reservoir's coastline. But because it is a reservoir, the water level fluctuates dramatically, affecting where you may set up your tent that evening.

Sumner Lake State Park

Located 16 miles northwest of Fort Sumner (10 miles north on U.S. 84 and 6 miles west on NM 203). ☎ 505/ 355-2541. Campsites with or without electric and water hookups, drinking water, showers, rest rooms, RV dump station, and boat ramps. Boating, camping, fishing, horseback riding, wildlife viewing.

This 4,500-acre lake resting on the flat plains of southeastern New Mexico is popular with anglers, boaters, swimmers, and water-skiers. It has four launching ramps, making access to the water convenient and accessible. Also on this large acre property are tennis courts, a playground, nature trail, and a lakeside restaurant. In winter, hunters come to hunt waterfowl.

A SIDE TRIP TO TEXAS

Guadalupe Mountains National Park

Take U.S. 62/180, 55 miles southwest of Carlsbad. ☎ 915/ 828-3251. Visitor center open June–Aug daily 8am–6pm, Sept–May daily 8am–4:30pm. Free admission. Backpacking, bird watching, camping, hiking, wildlife viewing.

Some 250 million years ago, the Guadalupe Mountains were an immense reef poking up through a tropical ocean. Marine organisms fossilized this 400-mile-long Capitan Reef as limestone; later, as the sea evaporated, a blanket of sediments and mineral salts buried the reef. Then, just 10 to 12 million years ago, a mountain-building uplift exposed a part of the fossil reef. This has given modern scientists a unique opportunity to explore earth's geologic history and outdoor lovers a playground for wilderness experience.

The steep southern end of the range makes up the park, and includes Guadalupe Peak (the highest in Texas at 8,749 feet), while the northern part lies within Lincoln National Forest and Carlsbad Caverns National Park. Deer, elk, mountain lion, and bear are found in the forests, which contrast strikingly with the desert around them. In these isolated basins and protected valleys is a proliferation of vegetation rare elsewhere in the southwestern United States.

Most of the national park's 86,416 acres are reached only by 80 miles of foot or horse trail through desert, canyon, and high forest. There's no lodging, restaurants, stores, or gas within 35 miles of the park. Backcountry hikers require water and permits; camping must be in designated areas. For information on camping see the "Campgrounds & Other Accommodations" section later in this chapter. Pets are permitted on a leash only in campground parking area.

The visitor center offers a variety of exhibits and slide programs telling the story of the Guadalupe Mountains, as well as ranger-guided walks and lectures. Information, maps, and backcountry permits can also be obtained at McKittrick Canyon Visitor Center (10 miles northeast via U.S. 62/180 and a side road) and Dog Canyon Ranger Station (reached through Carlsbad via NM 137 and County Road 414, about 70 miles).

McKittrick Canyon, protected by its high sheer walls, with a green swatch of trees growing along the banks of its spring-fed stream, is a beautiful location. It is a great spot for bird watching and viewing other wildlife, and an especially lovely sight during fall foliage time, late October to mid-November.

What to Do & Where to Do It

BIRD WATCHING

Fifteen miles northeast of Roswell, on the Pecos River, is the **Bitter Lake National Wildlife Refuge,** where a great variety of waterfowl—including cormorants, herons, pelicans, sandhill cranes, and snow geese—find a winter home. The refuge, reached via U.S. 380 and NM 265 from Roswell, comprises 24,000 acres of river bottomland, marsh, stands of salt cedar, and open range. Seven gypsum sinkhole lakes, covering an area of 700 acres, are of a peculiar beauty. If you're here between December and February, don't miss seeing the sky actually darken with birds. Once threatened with extinction, the sandhill crane now appears, along with puddle and diving ducks every winter. Snow geese were unknown here 20 years back, but now turn up to the tune of some 40,000 every winter. All told, over 300 species of birds have been sighted. You can get information at the headquarters building at the entrance, or call ☎ **505/622-6755.**

Also of note is **Bluff Springs** (☎ **505/682-2551**), south of Cloudcroft, a good place to see wild turkeys and hummingbirds. If you find turkey vultures particularly fascinating, **Rattlesnake Springs** (☎ **505/785-2232**), located south of Carlsbad, is the place to go.

BOARDSAILING

Located 12 miles north of Carlsbad via U.S. 285, **Brantley Lake State Park** is a 2,800-acre lake in the desert sought out by windsurfers because the winds tend to blow consistently and, at times, strongly. Boating and lake fishing are also popular here. The water gets to a tepid 80°F in July and August, making boarding quite comfortable. However, the reservoir's rocky bottom can be tough on the feet. Primitive camping sites are located among the salt cedars along the reservoir's coastline.

CAVING

For those *real* cavers—the kind who go down with their own lights to explore little-known underground worlds—there are options besides Carlsbad (listed below). The Roswell Bureau of Land Management manages three caves in the area north of Ruidoso. The **Fort Stanton Cave** is the second or third largest in New Mexico. It and the **Crockett Cave** forge through limestone similar to what you see at Carlsbad, and both have large rooms and lengthy tunnels. The **Torgac Cave** is considered the premier gypsum cave in the world. Unfortunately, only one permit per month is issued for that cave, so it's tough to get a permit. Access to the other two caves is limited as well, so a permit is required. Cavers must be experienced and have all the necessary gear. For information and permits, contact the **Bureau of Land Management** (☎ **505/627-0272** or 505/627-0278). Cavers should have in mind two or three dates in case their first choice is filled.

Carlsbad Caverns National Park

Take U.S. 62/180 south from Carlsbad. The scenic entrance road to the park is 7 miles long and originates at the park gate at Whites City. Call ☎ **800/967-CAVE** for tour reservations, 505/785-2232, ext. 429, for information about guided tours, or 505/785-2107 for recorded information. The visitor center and park are open Memorial Day–mid-Aug daily 8am–7pm; the rest of the year daily 8am–5:30pm. General admission to the park is $6 for adults, $3 for children ages 6–15, and free for children under 6. Admission is good for 3 days and includes entry to the two self-guided walking tours. Guided tours cost $6–$20 depending on the type of tour, and reservations are required.

THE INCIDENT AT ROSWELL

Best known as a destination for UFO enthusiasts and conspiracy theorists, Roswell has become a household name in the last few years thanks to Mulder, Scully, and their friends. And even if you're not glued to your set for *The X-Files* every week, you might remember Roswell as the setting for major scenes from the 1996 blockbuster *Independence Day*. Government cover-ups, alien autopsies, and cigarette-smoking feds—this is the place to find them in the UFO capital of the world.

What I find most interesting about the incident at Roswell and about a visit to the local museums there is how plausible it all seems; and yet, with each fact presented there remains plenty of room for doubt. It's a fun journey though your own psyche, noting how much you *do* believe. The "incident" took place in 1947. On July 8, a local rancher named MacBrazel found unusual debris scattered across his property. Initially, the U.S. military released a statement saying the debris was from a spaceship crash, but they quickly retracted the statement saying the debris was from a weather balloon. The military story was plausible. After all, Robert Goddard had been working on rockets in this area since the 1930s, and the Roswell Air Base was in the area as well. However, those who saw the debris were convinced that it was from some form of alien craft.

Actually, two crafts were said to have ended up in the area: one that broke apart and was the source of the debris on MacBrazel's ranch, and another that crash landed, leaving the bodies of four aliens. Believers say the bodies were whisked away by the military never to be seen again. With growing popularity on the issue, and the 50th anniversary of the crash at hand, the U.S. Air Force made a statement in 1997. It said the most likely explanation for the unverified alien reports might be that people were simply remembering and misplacing in time a number of life-sized dummies dropped from the sky during a series of experiments in the 1950s.

The main place to go in Roswell to learn more about the incident is the **International UFO Museum and Research Center** (☎ **505/625-9495**), located in the old Plains Theater on Main Street. Staffers will be more than happy to discuss the crash and the alleged military cover-up. There's an hour-by-hour timeline, as well as a videotape in which an alleged witness tells his account. The museum is open daily in winter from 10am to 5pm, in summer from 9am to 5pm; admission is free.

If you want to see the two "crash sites," call **Bruce Roads** at ☎ **505/622-0628**. He gives one short tour that covers 53 miles, takes 3 hours, and costs $75 for 1 to 3 people. He also gives a long tour to the debris site. It's approximately 123 miles, takes about 5 hours, and costs $125 for 1 to 3 people.

Roswell hosts a **UFO Festival** every year during the first week in July. Some of the special events include guest speakers, the Crash and Burn Expo Race, concerts, out-of-this-world food, a laser light show, and an alien invasion at the Bottomless Lakes recreation area. For details on the event, contact the visitor center at ☎ **888-ROSWELL**.

Two caves, Carlsbad Cavern and Slaughter Canyon Cave, are open to the public. The National Park Service has provided facilities, including elevators, to make it easy for everyone to visit the cavern, and a kennel for pets is available. Visitors in wheelchairs are common.

In addition to the tours described below, inquire at the visitor center information desk about other ranger-guided tours, including climbing and crawling "wild" cave tours. Be sure to call days in advance because some tours are only offered one day per week. Spelunkers who seek access to the park's undeveloped caves require special permission from the park superintendent. For more information about Carlsbad Caverns, see the "Parks & Other Hot Spots" section earlier in this chapter.

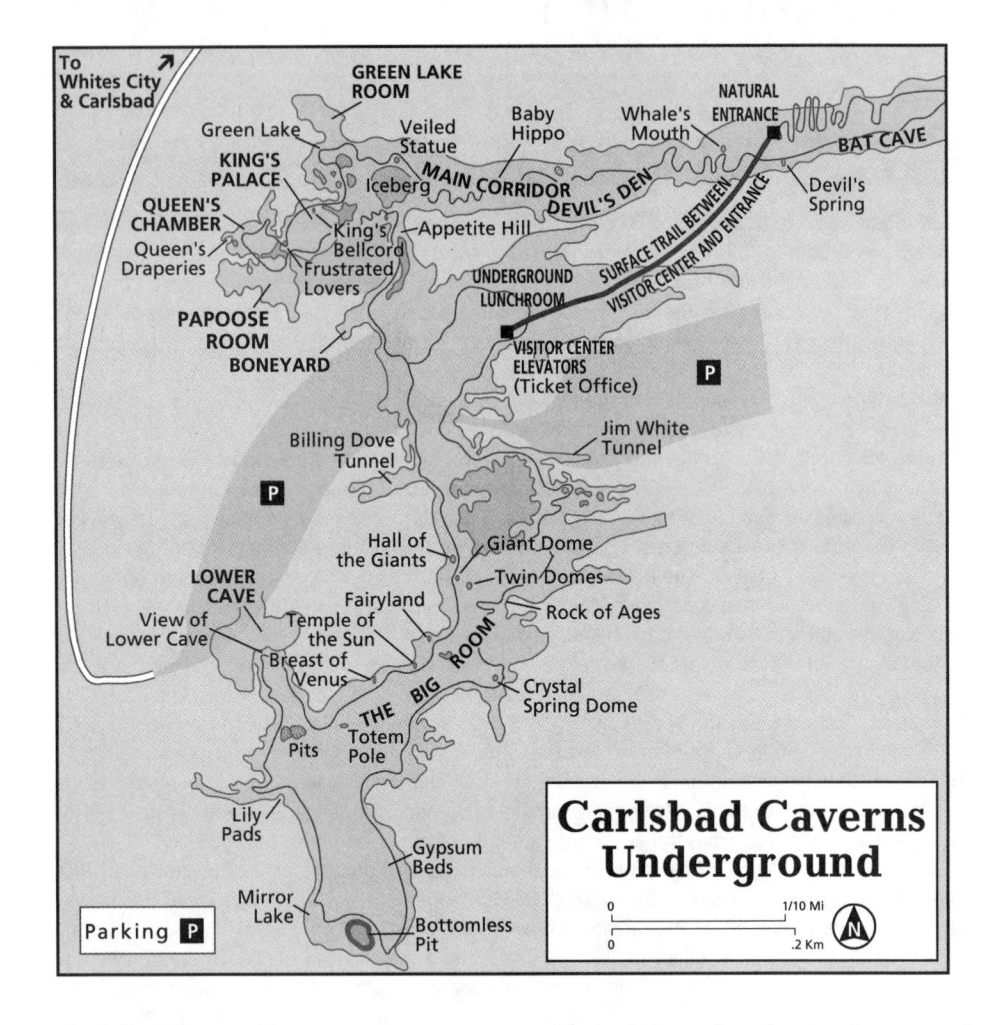

Carlsbad Cavern Tours

You can tour the caverns in one of three ways, depending on your time, interest, and level of ability. The first, and least difficult, option is to take the elevator from the visitor center down 750 feet to the start of the self-guided tour of the Big Room. More difficult and time-consuming, but vastly more rewarding, is the 1-mile self-guided tour along the Natural Entrance route, which follows the traditional explorer's route, entering the cavern through the large historic natural entrance. The paved walkway through the natural entrance winds into the depths of the cavern and leads through a series of underground rooms; this tour takes about an hour. Parts of it are steep. At its lowest point, the trail reaches 750 feet below the surface, ending finally at an underground rest area.

Both visitors who take the elevator and those who take the Natural Entrance route begin the self-guided tour of the spectacular Big Room near the rest area. The floor of this room covers 14 acres; the tour, over a relatively level path, is 1¼ miles in length and takes about an hour.

The third option is the 1½-hour ranger-guided Kings Palace tour, which also departs from the underground rest area. This tour descends 830 feet beneath the surface of the desert to the deepest portion of the cavern open to the public. Reservations are required, and an additional fee is charged.

Tour Tips: Wear flat shoes with rubber soles and heels because of the slippery paths. A light sweater or jacket feels good in the constant temperature of 56°F, especially when it's 100°F outside in the sun. The cavern is well lit, but you might want to bring along a flashlight as well. Rangers are stationed in the cave to answer questions.

Slaughter Canyon Cave Tour

Slaughter Canyon Cave was discovered in 1937 and was mined for bat guano commercially until the 1950s. It consists of a 1,140-foot-long corridor with many side passageways. The lowest point is 250 feet below the surface, and the passage traversed by the ranger-guided tours is 1.75 miles long, but more strenuous than hiking through the main cavern. There is also a strenuous 500-foot-rise hike from the parking lot to the cave mouth. The tour lasts about 2½ hours. No more than 25 people may take part in a tour, and then by reservation only. Everyone needs a flashlight, hiking boots or shoes, and a container of drinking water. Slaughter Canyon Cave is reached via U.S. 180, south 5 miles from Whites City, to a marked turnoff that leads 11 miles into a parking lot.

Other Guided Tours

Be sure to ask about the Left Hand Tunnel, Lower Cave, Hall of the White Giant, and Spider Cave tours. These vary in degree of difficulty and adventure, from Left Hand, an easy half-mile lantern tour; to Spider Cave, where you can expect tight crawlways and canyon-like passages; to Hall of the White Giant, a strenuous tour in which you're required to crawl long distances, squeeze through tight crevices, and climb up slippery flow-stone–lined passages. Call in advance for times of each tour. All of these tours depart from the visitor center.

CLIMBING

This region of the state has little in the way of developed climbing areas. Most serious climbers bypass it en route to **Hueco Tanks** in Texas, one of the most renowned climbing spots in the southwestern United States. A trip there is well worth the long drive. The park can be reached by traveling 32 miles northeast of El Paso just off U.S. Highway 62/180, then turning north on Ranch Road 2775 (☎ **915/857-1135**). Be aware that a Public Use Plan effective in 1998 limits the number of climbers allowed in the area as well as the range of climbs available. Outside the Ruidoso area climbers are covertly developing a place called **The Tunnel.** Located between Cloudcroft and Alamogordo, the spot sits above U.S. 82 near a tunnel. Area climbers fear they may eventually be barred from the spot because of the danger of rocks falling on the highway. On the eastern edge of the **Capitan Mountains** climbers are also developing routes.

New Mexico's newest and one of its best sport climbing areas is **Sitting Bull Falls** near Carlsbad. Not an area for novices, routes here range from 5.10 to 5.13b in difficulty. Much of the area is composed of tufa, or travertine, a limestone that is riddled with pockets and holes. Together the Rosebud Wall and the Big Horn Wall have 14 routes, and climbers are not allowed on any other walls in the area. From Carlsbad, drive on U.S. 285 12 miles north to NM 137. Take 137 for 20 miles to a signed right turn toward Sitting Bull Falls. Follow this road 8 miles to the picnic area. The climbing area is behind the rest rooms. There is currently no published guide to this area, though you might check the Internet for any local write-ups that will likely appear in upcoming years.

DOWNHILL SKIING & SNOWBOARDING

"Skiing in *southern* New Mexico?" you might ask in disbelief. Oh ye of little faith. Yes, there's skiing here, and it's good enough to draw crowds from Texas to the Ruidoso area. Though there are two areas of note in the area, **Ski Apache** and **Ski Cloudcroft,** the latter hasn't opened for long in past years, so it deserves only a mention.

Ski Cloudcroft is a small ski area that is open only some winters. The mountain has 21 runs and a 700-foot vertical, served by one double chair and two surface lifts. It appeals primarily to beginning skiers. When there's snow (usually December through March), it's open daily from 9am to 4pm. Snowboarding is permitted. For information, contact the **Cloudcroft Chamber of Commerce** (☎ 505/682-2733).

Ski Apache

20 miles northwest of Ruidoso in the Mescalero Apache Reservation. ☎ **505/257-9001** for snow report, or 505/336-4356 for information; skibum@skiapache.com. 55 trails (20% beginner, 35% intermediate, and 45% advanced); 11 lifts including 1 four-passenger gondola, 2 quads, 5 triples, 1 double, 2 surface. 1,900-ft. vertical drop. Full-day tickets $42–$45.

Situated on an 11,500-foot ridge of the 12,003-foot Sierra Blanca, this ski resort has some broad bowls up high, many difficult runs down one face, interwoven with some nice intermediate runs. There's a day lodge, sport shop, rental shop, ski school, first-aid center, four snack bars, and a lounge. Though its location seems remote, a lot of skiers fill this mountain during weekends and holidays. Your best bet is to ski during the week. What's especially unique about the mountain is that, since it is owned and run by the Apaches, you can experience another culture while skiing. The mountain is open Thanksgiving to Easter daily from 8:45am to 4pm. Lift-and-lodging packages can be booked through the **Inn of the Mountain Gods** (☎ 800/545-9011).

FISHING

The town of Ruidoso was named "noisy" because of the tumbling stream that runs through it. The **Rio Ruidoso** is a popular spot for stream fishers, with plenty of rainbow and brook trout swimming within the "noise." Locals and visitors fish the stream from a number of spots within town, as well as on the outskirts. North of Ruidoso, surrounded by scenic Lincoln National Forest, **Bonito Lake** has excellent trout fishing from April through November in a lovely mountain setting. Be aware that during mid-summer the lake gets extremely crowded, with fishers scattered all along the banks. Access the lake from NM 37 north of Ruidoso; turn left on FS 107. There is forest service camping nearby at South Fork Campground.

Feeding the lake is the **Rio Bonito,** a small stream good for trout fishing. To reach fishing spots continue up FS 107 toward the Argentina Canyon trailhead. **Silver Lake,** on NM 244 near Cloudcroft, is a lovely mountain lake on the Jicarilla Apache Reservation that gets too many visitors during much of its season. I mention it mostly because I thought it might be a good place to camp and fish, but when I was there it was fairly trashed from the heavy weekend crowds that come to party and fish. It's stocked with rainbows though the summer. **Bottomless Lakes State Park,** located 16 miles southeast of Roswell via NM 409 off U.S. 380, has good trout fishing in the spring, summer, and fall. It is a chain of seven small, deep lakes surrounded by red stone bluffs. Despite their name, none of the lakes is deeper than 100 feet. The largest, Lea Lake, is so clear that scuba divers frequent it. Another, aptly called Devil's Inkwell, is so shaded by surrounding bluffs that the sun rarely reaches it. Mirror, Cottonwood, Pasture, and Figure 8 lakes got their monikers with similar logic. This park is a popular recreation site for Roswell residents. The park is open year-round from 6am to 9pm daily. **Brantley Lake State Park,** located 12 miles north of Carlsbad via U.S. 285, has decent trout fishing, though the water gets very warm in summer (80°F). **Sumner Lake State Park,** located 16 miles northwest of Fort Sumner (10 miles north on Hwy. 84 and 6 miles west on paved State road 203) is a 4,500-acre lake that's popular with anglers, boaters, swimmers and waterskiers. The lake has four launching ramps.

The tiny 14-acre fishing oasis **Green Meadow Lake** is located 2 miles northwest of Hobbs via NM 18. Overall the fishing here is fair to good, and great after it has been stocked with large 1- to 2-pound catfish in summer and rainbow trout in winter. The lake is only about 8 to 10 feet deep.

HIKES & BACKPACK TRIPS

Alkali Flat Trail at White Sands National Monument

5 miles round-trip. Easy. 100-ft. elevation gain. Allow 3 hrs. Access: 15 miles southwest of Alamogordo on U.S. 70/82. (*Note:* Due to missile testing on the adjacent White Sands Missile Range, this road is sometimes closed for up to 2 hours at a time.) From the park entrance drive 7 miles on the Dunes Rd. to the Heart of the Sands and the well-marked trailhead. ☎ **505/479-6124**. When driving near or in the monument, tune a radio to 1610 AM for information on what's happening. From Memorial Day–Labor Day the visitor center is open daily 8am–7pm, and Dunes Dr. is open 7am–9pm. During the rest of the year, the visitor center is open daily 8am–4:30pm and Dunes Dr. is open 7am–sunset. Admission is $3 for adults 17 and over.

Hiking in White Sands is a completely unique experience. Every footstep can be an adventure if you have your senses working full throttle. Not only is the stark and undulating landscape awesome, but what lies below your feet and around you is thrilling as well. You'll likely see fox or centipede prints on the sand, or those of many other creatures who inhabit this inhospitable land. (For more information about the monument see the "Parks & Other Hot Spots" section at the beginning of this chapter.)

Above all be aware of the dangers of hiking here. Always wear sunscreen and dark glasses, carry water, and have sturdy shoes—some people find running shoes work best. Be sure to register at the trailhead and return by sunset. It's also a good idea to orient yourself on the San Andreas Mountains to the west and the Sacramentos to the east. If the wind doesn't blow over your tracks, you'll likely be able to follow them back to the trailhead.

The trail starts to the west and is marked with orange and white posts. Beware of moving forward until you spot the next post. The trail traverses the dunes and interdunal basins heading toward the San Andreas Mountains. At just over 2 miles it reaches Alkali Flat, where some of the sand is formed for the dunes. Then it continues out onto the lakebed. Return by the same route.

Three Rivers Petroglyph Site

3 miles round-trip. Easy. 200-ft. elevation gain. Allow 2 hrs. Access: From U.S. 54 30 miles north of Alamogordo, take FS 579 and follow the signs 4.5 miles to the site. Map: USGS Golondrina Draw. A small self-service fee is charged.

This trail meanders through some 20,000 individual images, carved by Mogollon peoples who lived in the area centuries ago. As you go you'll want to wander to many of the side trails where you'll find more petroglyphs. At the trailhead there is a brochure pointing out some of the more interesting images. Be sure to go far enough to see site seven, a vividly depicted bighorn sheep pierced with three arrows. As you hike you'll have incredible views of the surrounding area, with Sierra Blanca to the east and White Sands to the southwest. The park also includes the partially excavated ruins of an ancient Native American village, including a multi-room adobe building, pit house, and masonry house that have been partially reconstructed.

Capitan Peak

4–14 miles round-trip. Moderate to difficult. 700-ft. elevation gain. Allow 8 hrs. for whole route. Access: From Capitan, take NM 246 for 32 miles (or 53 miles from Roswell) to a dirt road on the right (south) with signs saying Boy Scout Mountain. Follow this rough dirt road 4 miles to the Capitan Peak Trail 64. Maps: USGS Arabela and Capitan Peak.

This is one of the more remote hikes in the region, climbing to the peak of the Capitans, standing 5,000 feet above the surrounding plains. Views from the top and along the way are spectacular, and even the drive presents great granite faces that will keep you rubbernecking your way to the trailhead. Unfortunately, the first half-mile of the trail parallels along some vacation homes, which detract from the remote quality you'll find on the rest of the hike. The trail enters the Capitan Wilderness and switchbacks 2 miles up a canyon to lovely view of Chimney Rock, a gracefully balanced formation. This is a good turnaround point for day hikers. If you plan to continue on or to make this an overnight, be sure to take along plenty of water, as springs are scarce and traveling here can be hot and strenuous. The trail comes to a narrow ridge, then traverses Douglas-fir forest, coming to a viewpoint of Sunset Peak to the east at a little over 4 miles. At a little over 5 miles the trail intersects with the Summit Trail 58. Bear right and follow the signs for Capitan Peak. A series of broad switchbacks leads to the summit ridge. Continue climbing, crossing a wildflower-strewn sloping meadow (a good place to camp) to the peak, where you'll find 360° views. Return the way you came. *Beware:* During the summer, the monsoon hits this area as early as noon. You'll want to hike early in the day to avoid dangerous thunderstorms.

Argentina Canyon–Bonito Canyon Loop

5.6 miles. Moderate. 1,140-ft. elevation gain. Allow 3 hrs. Access: From NM 37 north of Ruidoso, turn left on FS 107 toward Bonito Lake and travel 8 miles to the trailhead. Maps: USGS Nogal Peak and/or USFS White Mountain Wilderness.

This is a favorite of Ruidoso locals, and for good reason. It climbs fairly easily up either of two often wet and lush canyons and takes you onto the White Mountain crest (one of the most lovely crests I've ever experienced, with views out across White Sands in the distance and numerous sky islands to the west), as well as Sierra Blanca and its lush rolling mountainsides to the east. It's debatable whether it's better to start up Argentina Canyon or up Bonito. The book I read said it was easier going to start with Argentina; I did so and met some local hikers on the trail who said they much preferred the other way around. Take your pick. My directions will follow the way I went.

The trail makes its way along a creek up Argentina Canyon, a moderately steep grade much of the way. Toward the top of the canyon it comes to a juncture with a shortcut trail over to Bonito Canyon. Don't take it—you'll miss the crest, the major reason for taking this hike. Continue up to the crest; just before it you'll come to some lovely old pine corrals, then onto a high meadow where signs will point you to the left onto the Crest Trail. Soon you'll come to the actual crest, with the views spread out before you. What sets this crest apart from many others I've hiked is its gentleness. It's a series of *The Sound of Music*-style meadows interrupted by aspen and pine stands. Once you get there you'll swear your next hike will be a multi-day covering the whole crest (see the White Mountain Crest Trail hike, below).

Travel along the crest for 1.25 miles, much of it with views. Those diminish as you make your way around Argentina Peak. The trail opens onto a small saddle with signs pointing various directions. Here you'll want to turn left (east) on Little Bonito Trail 38. This will take you down the canyon eventually to a junction with Bonito Trail 36. It's about 2.6 miles back to the parking lot. If you're doing this as a brief overnight, which would be well worth carrying the gear, there is a lovely campsite 0.25 miles west of the junction of the Crest Trail and the Little Bonito Trail.

Beware: During the summer the monsoon comes as early as noon to these mountains. In order to avoid dangerous thundershowers, start early in the day.

White Mountain Crest Trail

21 miles one-way. Moderate. 2,300-ft. elevation gain. Allow at least 3 days for whole route. Access: Drive north from

Ruidoso on NM 48 to the ski area turn-off (NM 532). Turn left and proceed for 1 mile to FS 117. Turn right and drive for 5.5 miles looking for a hiker marker on the left. Turn into the trailhead parking lot. Leave your shuttle vehicle at the northern trailhead: From NM 37, take FS 400 west into Nogal Canyon. Near its end take FS 108 south to the trailhead for the Crest Trail 25. Be aware that you can cut mileage from this trip by climbing down a canyon such as Argentina. For directions to that canyon see the Argentina Canyon–Bonito Canyon Loop above. Map: USFS Lincoln National Forest–White Mountain Wilderness.

Many call this the most spectacular crest hike in the southwestern United States, and I would venture to give it even higher accolades. It is simply lovely and very different from many crest hikes because the beauty is a gentle kind with views you won't find anywhere else, especially those out across the undulating land sea of White Sands and more blocky, black, shifty lava flows of Valley of the Fires. Because this hike is so close to Ruidoso it does get fairly heavy hiker and horseback rider traffic, but most enter and leave the crest from side trails and don't traverse the whole way. The White Mountain Wilderness gets a surprising amount of moisture, so there are water sources along the way. You'll still want to carry plenty of water with you, however.

The trail enters meadows almost immediately, giving you a taste of what's to come. It makes its way through aspens and spruce-fir forest through more meadows, gradually ascending to 10,400 feet as it passes along the west side of Buck Mountain, where there are radio towers. At this point you're about 5 miles into the hike. Shortly the trail turns northward passing by Elk Point, White Horse Hill, and Bonito Spring, a possible water source. There is a lovely campsite 0.25 miles west of the junction of the Crest Trail and the Little Bonito Trail. The trail traverses around the east side of Argentina Peak and then passes onto a spectacular high meadow. Then it swings east heading toward Nogal Peak and to its terminus.

Dog Canyon

9 miles round-trip. 3,100-ft. elevation gain. Difficult. Allow 2 hrs. for part of the hike; full day to complete it. Access: At Oliver Lee Memorial State Park; 15 miles southeast of Alamogordo via U.S. 54 and Dog Canyon Rd. Map: USGS Alamogordo South and Sacramento Peak.

This canyon presents a stark and vivid picture of life in the Chihuahuan Desert, from the sheer cliffs plunging into a wet canyon to the vast views out across the Tularosa Basin. Over the centuries it has served as a pass to the highlands for Mescalero Apaches, Mexican and American soldiers, and Texas ranchers. The notorious and narrow "eyebrow" section was strategic for the Apaches, who would lie in wait there ready to ambush. In fact, in 1880 they rolled boulders through the section, killing several men of the Ninth Cavalry.

The hike starts behind the visitor center, climbing steeply up onto the right wall of the canyon. Be aware that this sets the tone for the hike; it is steep and arduous, with no shade or water for the first 2.5 miles. The views along this section reveal White Sands and the jagged peaks of the Organ Mountains. At 0.6 miles the trail levels out along the canyon rim. Then the climb intensifies again, rising 400 feet over the next half-mile to a flat section, with boulders tumbled from the cliffs above. Shortly the trail reaches the stream and your first piece of shade, below cottonwoods. Be aware that camping is not permitted along the stream. The next section of the trail is the eyebrow, where it crosses a narrow ledge high above the canyon floor. From there the trail continues steeply up Joplin Ridge at mile 4, reaching FS 90B. Return on the same route.

Last Chance Canyon in the Guadalupe Mountains

10 miles round-trip. Moderate. 700-ft. elevation gain. Allow 5 hrs. Access: Travel on U.S. 285 12 miles north of Carlsbad to NM 137. Drive this paved road 24 miles to FS 276, the road to Sitting Bull Falls. Turn right and travel about 7 miles to the well-marked trailhead for Trail 226 on your right. You can also get to the trailhead by traveling south of Carlsbad on U.S. 62/180 to Dark Canyon Rd. and taking it to NM 137. Map: USGS Red Bluff Draw and Queen.

This canyon got its name in around 1881 when a group of ranchers pursuing some Apaches lost their way and ran out of water. They searched many canyons in the area to no avail. With little hope left, they found the stream that cuts through this canyon—their last chance, and so it was named. This canyon is especially popular because of the lovely limestone walls and the spring that, in places, invites swimmers. Beware when hiking this trail in summer, however; when I was there the biting flies were so bad that I had to cut my trip short. Carry plenty of DEET.

Unfortunately, the park has labeled the trails in this whole area in a very confusing way, with arrows pointing in two directions. Without a map, many travelers would be lost. When you leave the kiosk at the trailhead, you'll come to the signs. Turn right and head into the immediately apparent canyon opening out in that direction. Going left will take you along the road to Sitting Bull Falls. The trail enters the broad mouth of the canyon, with torrey yuccas, sotol, and prickly pear decorating the ground. Soon the trail drops down and at mile 1 crosses the stream and passes through a hiker's gate. The trail makes its way along limestone ledges, while the canyon walls squeeze in tighter. You'll pass a travertine wall at the mouth of White Oak Canyon. Then the canyon will widen. The trail continues to follow the canyon, at times up on very steep ledges (those who fear heights beware!), at times snaking along the bottom. Watch for pools in which to swim, one over 6 feet deep. Also watch for flat benches along the stream that serve as nice campsites. Toward the end of the route the trail switchbacks up the canyon wall, offering spectacular views in all directions. Return the way you came.

Before or after your hike, be sure to take the trip over to **Sitting Bull Falls,** where water pours 150 feet off a travertine wall, forming near-tropical pools below, filled with minnows. Another worthwhile hike is the **Sitting Bull Falls Trail,** which begins on NM 137 and makes its way to the falls.

McKittrick Canyon at Guadalupe National Monument

10.9 miles one-way. Easy to moderate. 2,380-ft. elevation gain. Allow 2–10 hrs. Access: Off U.S. 62/80, 11 miles south of the New Mexico border. Open daily 8am–6 pm in summer and 8am–4:30pm in winter. However, if you're planning an overnight, you can get a permit to leave your car after hours. Map: USGS Guadalupe Peak.

I'd heard about this canyon long before I came upon it. Its lushness and abundance of wildlife are legendary. To me, however, the more striking feature in the area is the great cliffs on the south end of the Guadalupe Mountains. If you make your way to the Guadalupe from the north, be sure to take the time to drive around the south side of the monument. Some 250 million years ago, the Guadalupe Mountains were an immense reef poking up through a tropical ocean. Marine organisms fossilized this 400-mile-long Capitan Reef as limestone; later, as the sea evaporated, a blanket of sediments and mineral salts buried the reef. Then just 10 to 12 million years ago, a mountain-building uplift exposed a part of the fossil reef. Erosion has helped lay bare the walls of this canyon, a multi-colored artwork. The biggest detraction from this hike is that a power line runs through the length of the canyon, a frustrating detail for those who like their wilderness to be wild.

This hike doesn't really begin until 1 mile in. Then suddenly you'll find yourself in a lush, steep-walled canyon. As the trail continues westward it grows more and more scenic as it follows a creek where you may see trout swimming; be aware that fishing is not allowed. At mile 2.3 the trail comes to Pratt Cabin, named for Wallace Pratt, who built a house there in the late 1920s. At mile 3.4 the trail comes to the Grotto Picnic area, a lovely shaded area set within limestone formations. The route continues climbing up the ridge away from the canyon floor. Even if you're just day hiking, plan to climb at least part way up so you can get a glimpse both up and down McKittrick Canyon. The climb to the ridge is arduous, ascending 2,380 feet in about 2 miles. If you're doing an overnight, you may want to camp at McKittrick Ridge Campsite at 7.4 miles. The trail continues along the ridge above South McKittrick Canyon, ascending to a high point of 7,916 feet and gradually descending to a junction with the Tejas Trail at 10.9 miles. Along the way you'll have spectacular views of the Bowl, Hunter Peak, and the Blue Ridge. For a point-to-point journey, you may want to combine this hike with the Tejas Trail, which leaves from Pine Spring Campground. Otherwise, return the way you came.

Guadalupe Peak
8.4 miles round-trip. Moderate. 3,000-ft. elevation gain. Allow 6 hrs. Access: Take U.S. 62/180, 55 miles southwest of Carlsbad. Map: USGS Guadalupe Peak.

If you manage to see Guadalupe National Park from the south, you'll know that you have to climb this mountain. The remains of an immense reef once a part of a tropical ocean, the giant faces jut up from the vast Chihuahuan Desert, with Guadalupe Peak at 8,749 feet, the highest point in Texas, dominating the view. Be aware that summer thunderstorms and high winds make this hike at times dangerous. Check with the ranger station about weather conditions before heading up.

The trail heads west from Pine Springs Campground, climbing steadily up the cliffs at the south side of the mouth of Pine Canyon. Along the way you'll have good views across to Hunter Peak, and later of Shumard Peak. About 1 mile from the summit you'll come to the Guadalupe Peak campsite within a small stand of juniper and pine. If you do camp, be aware that winds can be very strong here. When you make the summit you'll find a small monument erected by American Airlines in 1958, on the 100th anniversary of the completion of the first transcontinental mail route, a route that traversed Guadalupe Pass. From the top you'll have views of Bush Mountain and Shumard Peak, the second and third highest peaks in Texas.

HORSEBACK RIDING & PACK TRIPS

For those traveling with their own horses, there are many options in this area. In fact, especially in the area around Ruidoso, horses are very common. The area around **Bonito Lake** is especially popular, with trails heading up onto the White Mountain Crest Trail (see the Argentina Canyon–Bonito Canyon Loop hike above for details). **Fort Stanton** has a horse area on NM 214, a half-mile from the intersection of U.S. 380. The trails traverse the rolling hills in the vicinity of Rio Bonito.

If you're looking to rent horses and a guide, contact **Elite Outfitters** (☎ 505/354-7307 or 505/257-5379; eliteoutfitter.com). Elite specializes in small groups, and takes riders into the high country of the White Mountain Wilderness. Many rides go up Argentina Canyon to the Crest Trail, where you'll find magnificent views. Rides range from 2 hours to a full day, with prices ranging from $30 to $79.

Elite also does hunting and pack trips into the wilderness for about $100 per person per day. **Buddie's Stables (☎ 505/258-4027)**, very close to the town of Ruidoso, won't exactly introduce you to your inner Marlboro Man self, but they will provide families with an introduction to being a cowpoke. Set in Gavilon Canyon, the stables have sound horses that they saddle up and ride through a narrow stretch where houses haven't yet been built. When I was there, a mom dropped off three kids and went on her way, so I could tell this was a very kid-friendly place. You can expect no running of horses, just basically your single-file trail ride at reasonable rates.

Another option close to town is **Desert-High Country Stables (☎ 505/378-4559)**. In business for 32 years, this outfit takes riders into the Lincoln National Forest Hale Canyon area, where rides start in cedars and piñon, and move into the pines. Located near Ruidoso Downs on U.S. 70, High Country offers hourly rides in the same price range as Buddie's and is also kid-friendly. Prices start at $15 for a 1-hour ride and go to $60 for a 6-hour ride.

MOUNTAIN BIKING

Although I wouldn't call the trails in this region abundant, I would call what's here quality, especially those in the area around Cloudcroft, where single track is fast, and views are broad. **High Altitude (☎ 505/682-1229)** is your stop in both Ruidoso and Cloudcroft for trail directions, bike tune-ups, and cool clothes and candles. Run by a bunch of brothers—I quit counting how many—the store is fully equipped and generous with directions. The Cloudcroft shop rents bikes and will transport them to the Ruidoso store if you'd like. Another great contact is **Outdoor Adventures (☎ 505/434-1920)** in Alamogordo. In Carlsbad the **Bike Doc (☎ 800/391-3331** or 505/887-7280) will service your bike and give you directions.

Spaghetti Bowl

10 miles. Moderate. 300-ft. elevation gain. Allow 1–2 hrs. Access: Head north in Ruidoso on Mecham Dr. Just past the Smokey Bear Ranger Station (901 Mecham), turn left, and drive 0.5 miles to Cedar Creek Picnic area on the right. Midway through the grounds look for the cov-ered picnic tables on your right. The unmarked trailhead heads off into the forest.

This trail got its name because it is really many trails weaving around and through each other in a tangled, spaghetti-like fashion. All of them run through forest and meadows, mostly smooth, fun single track that you can really romp on, with a few whoop-tee-doos and jumps to keep things exciting. The trail starts from the covered picnic site and heads north making its way up a small canyon. You'll see trails leading off from it here and there. It climbs steadily, and there are more trails up at the top of the canyon. Basically, you'll want to explore the area and find the routes that suit you best.

Perk Canyon

6 miles. Easy to moderate. 300-ft. elevation gain. Allow 1½ hrs. Access: Head west on Sudderth in Ruidoso until it comes to a Y. Take the right fork, heading to Upper Canyon. Just after Story Book Cabins turn right on Ebarb and proceed to Perk Canyon Dr. Follow this road until it dead-ends at a small parking area. (Note that a rough dirt road continues to the right, but you don't.) Ride up the unmarked trail straight in front of your car.

This is a fun family-type ride up a lovely canyon. It's all single track, a nice rolling surface with a few bumps and small climbs to keep things interesting. When I was on this ride I passed a couple with their wide-eyed little boy in a jump seat on the back of the bike. That's the kind of gentle ride this is; it would be a great place for a novice to get the feel of real single track. Basically the trail starts right from the parking area and heads slowly up Perk Canyon. At a few points it dips into the streambed, which will be wet during spring runoff and monsoon season. It continues up through the forest, at a few points climbing the side of the canyon, at others opening out into small meadows. At the top of the canyon you'll turn around and have a blast coasting your way down.

Rim Trail
8 to as many as 56 miles round-trip. Moderate. 400-ft. elevation gain. Allow 2 hrs. or more. (The distance I describe takes 2 hours.) Access: Take NM 530 two miles south of Cloudcroft; turn right on the Sunspot Hwy. (NM 6562) and travel less than 0.25 miles to the trailhead for Trail T105 on the right.

This trail has a renowned reputation as one of the best in southern New Mexico, and it deserves the hype. It follows along a huge escarpment overlooking the Tularosa Basin. Winding through the forest, along the way it offers glimpses hundreds of miles to the west. Most incredible, White Sands National Monument glistens in the sun 5,000 feet below. I rode this trail during the monsoon season and had to jump on it between rainstorms (it rains a lot up in Cloudcroft during July and August—beautiful, cool, but *wet*). The trail was slick and fast, and I almost ate mud too many times. I don't recommend it unless you're one of those really sick bikers. Anyway, the best way to ride this is from south to north, so most locals recommend riding the Sunspot Highway up and jumping on the trail to head back to Cloudcroft. You can jump on at a number of points. I recommend riding to just above mile marker 4 where there's a gate to your right. You'll immediately be on the trail, which loosely follows the highway back toward Cloudcroft. The trail is well marked with little signs that say T105. It twists and turns, goes up and down through canyons that run off the rim, all awesome single track with enough rocks to keep you on your toes but not so many that you'll need dental work when finished. You'll come out at the gate where you left your car at the Slide Group Campground. If that's not enough single track for you, jump on the trail at the trailhead and ride up as long as you like (28 miles!) and then return either on pavement or on dirt. Be aware that the above-described section, which is closest to Cloudcroft, is the cleanest and most maintained. As you make your way into the hinterlands you'll have to be more cautious and work harder.

White Sands Loop
16 miles round-trip. Easy. Allow 3 hrs. Access: 15 miles southwest of Alamogordo on U.S. 70/82. (*Note:* Due to missile testing on the adjacent White Sands Missile Range, this road is sometimes closed for up to 2 hours at a time.)

Usually closed to bicycles, this loop is opened one time a year, at night, so that riders can marvel at the beauty of the full moon reflecting off the white sand. The event happens in the fall, generally on October. Call ☎ **505/679-2599** for reservations and information. A bicycle light and warm clothing are required, and a small fee is charged.

Grand View Trail
3 miles round-trip. Easy. 100-ft. elevation gain. Allow 1 hr. Access: From Cloudcroft, drive west on U.S. 82; turn left (north) on Cherry Way. Drive this paved road 0.2 miles to Cottage Row. Turn left and follow this paved road for 0.5 miles to the signed junction for Fresnal Canyon Rd., FS 162C. Turn right and drive less than 1 mile to a left-hand curve, watching for the trailhead on your left.

A former railway line restored by a local chapter of the New Mexico Rails-to-Trails Association, this route is part of the Cloud-Climbing Rail Trail, which runs through Lincoln National Forest at an elevation of about 6,000 feet. The Grand View Trail involves little elevation gain, so it's a good route for beginners. It follows a portion of the Alamogordo and Sacramento Mountain Railway that ended operation in 1947. Along the way the trail offers views of the Tularosa Basin and the San Andres Mountains. At about mile 1 the trail passes over a wooden drainage structure. A spur trail, T130A will add 0.3 miles to the trip, but this route is more difficult. Also part of the Cloud-Climbing Rail Trail is the **Mexican Canyon Trestle Trail,** a 2.5-mile trail that involves some steep ascents, but rewards riders with a spectacular view of a turn-of-the-century railroad bridge. For directions to this trail call the **Cloudcroft Ranger Station** (☎ **505/682-2551**).

La Cueva Trails
15 miles round-trip. Moderate to difficult. 400-ft. elevation gain. Allow 1–3 hrs. Access: From Carlsbad, drive south on U.S. 62/180 to the edge of town to Hidalgo Rd.; turn right and drive 2 miles to Standpipe Rd.; turn right and drive 0.3 miles to a dirt road on your left. Turn left; ignore roads leading off to the right, and drive 0.4 miles to a cleared parking area on your left. The trail leaves uphill from there. Look for brown BLM markers.

Recently built by the BLM and a local bike shop, this trail travels the vast area of the La Cueva Escarpment, a rocky hill jutting up south of Carlsbad. Though it's not the most scenic route around, it does provide some fun, smooth single track, with some rocky sections to keep you on your toes. The trails meander along the escarpment, some making the rough climb up to the top. Your best bet here is to take along a compass and pay attention and explore. It's not too easy to get lost since there are no trees, and your car will be visible from most of the trails. They travel though scrub desert of yucca and ocotillo, intermingling with gas wells along the way. This is a good spring, fall, and winter ride. It's possible to do a loop; just keep to the left at all intersections while riding in a clockwise fashion.

ROAD BIKING
Bottomless Lakes State Park Ride
35 miles round-trip. Easy to moderate. Allow 2½ hrs. Flat plains leading to a series of lakes. Access: Start at Roswell's Spring River Park and Zoo.

From the park, pedal 1 mile south on Atkinson Ave. (NM 256), and turn left (east) on U.S. 380. This is the main highway that connects Roswell with Lincoln to the west and not much but plains to the east. Travel on this route for 9 miles, passing through the lush farming areas along Pecos River, to NM 409. Turn right (south) and pedal 7 miles to the visitor center at Lea Lake, which is just one of the Bottomless Lakes. You may want to break up your trip with a dip in the lakes. You can take the park road up to a mesa top in a loop back to NM 409. Head back the way you came.

SWIMMING

Your best bet for taking a dip is at **Lake Carlsbad** on the east side of ·Carlsbad. Here the Pecos River has been dammed, creating a calm playland surrounded by grass. There's a small beach with a dock and changing rooms. From Canal Street in town turn right on Church Street, and travel five blocks to the park. You can rent paddleboats from the marina. Another great option is **Bottomless Lakes State Park,** a scenic series of very deep lakes southeast of Roswell (see the "Parks & Other Hot Spots" section earlier in this chapter). Travel U.S. 309 east from town to NM 409; turn south and drive 7 miles to the visitor center.

WALKS & RAMBLES

This region has plenty of interesting places to explore, whether you're into involved hikes or just want to meander. A few I'll mention briefly take you through the history of the area. The **Sacramento Mountains Historical Museum and Pioneer Village,** U.S. 82 east of downtown Cloudcroft (☎ **505/682-2932**), recalls the community's early days with several pioneer buildings, historic photos, and exhibits of turn-of-the-century railroad memorabilia, clothing, and other artifacts. Call for hours. Nearby, the **Lincoln National Forest** (☎ **505/ 682-2551**) maintains the unique **La Pasada Encantada Nature Trail,** a short foot path from Sleepygrass Campground, off NM 130 south of Cloudcroft, with signs in Braille inviting walkers to touch the various plants, leaves, and trees. A new trail is a several-mile moderate hike to the historic **Mexican Canyon Railroad Trestle.** The trailhead is in a U.S. Forest Service picnic area west of the junction of U.S. 82 and NM 130, where you'll also find a short walk to an observation point offering spectacular views across White Sands Missile Range and the Tularosa Basin. This picnic area also has tables, grills, drinking water, and rest rooms.

Valley of Fires Loop
0.75-mile loop. Easy. Allow 1 hr. Access: On U.S. 380 4 miles west of Carrizozo. The park is open year-round. Admission is $3 per person or $5 per car for day use.

Along this amazing loop you'll traverse part of one of the youngest and best-preserved lava fields in the United States. Though it is a short hike, you may find yourself spending hours here, squatting down to look at all that can grow within the nooks and crannies of a lava flow. Particularly during and after the summer rains the quantity and variety of plant and animal life are astounding. Be sure to walk far enough to see the 400-year-old juniper wringing itself from the black stone. A small visitor center and bookstore has more information about the landscape. Part of the trail is wheelchair accessible.

Big Dunes Trail at White Sands National Monument
1.5-mile loop. Easy. 60-ft. elevation gain. Allow 45 min. Access: 15 miles southwest of Alamogordo on U.S. 70/82.

(Note: Due to missile testing on the adjacent White Sands Missile Range, this road is sometimes closed for up to 2 hours at a time.) From the park entrance drive 5 miles on the Dunes Rd. to the well-marked trailhead. ☎ **505/479-6124.** When driving near or in the monument, tune a radio to 1610 AM for information. From Memorial Day–Labor Day the visitor center is open daily 8am–7pm, and Dunes Dr. is open daily 7am–9pm. Ranger talks and sunset strolls are given nightly at 7 and 8:30pm during summer. During the rest of the year, the visitor center is open daily 8am–4:30pm, and Dunes Dr. is open daily 7am–sunset. Admission is $3 for adults 17 and over.

One of the best ways to get a feel for White Sands is to be out in the dunes, and this trail takes you there fast. You'll climb along the sides of and over the tops of these great monuments of sand. Be aware that even on this short hike you'll want to wear sunscreen and sunglasses, carry water, and wear sturdy shoes; many find that running shoes work best. Before you head out, orient yourself on the San Andreas Mountains to the west and the Sacramentos to the east. Fortunately, there are orange maker posts along the way; be sure to locate the next marker before you proceed. From the trailhead the route goes south traversing the base of the dunes. In this area you'll get a sense of the vegetation that grows between the dunes such as the soaptree yucca. Also watch the sand for tracks of rodents, rabbits, foxes, coyotes, and porcupines that inhabit the sands. Friends of mine have been blessed to see white foxes with small spots of black on their tail and faces. Soon you'll climb up onto the dunes and nearly feel lost within their whiteness. Only a few landmarks are available along this section of the hike so heed the orange trail markers. Toward the end the trail climbs onto a 60-foot tall dune, from which you may slide your way back to your car.

Lincoln State Monument: A Walk in the Footsteps of Billy the Kid

1 mile. Easy. Allow 2 hrs. Access: 37 miles northeast of Ruidoso on U.S. 380. Open daily year-round 8:30am–5pm. Admission is $6.

I'm including this historic walk through the village of Lincoln because to me it is an amazing place. It's one of the last historic yet uncommercialized 19th-century towns remaining in the American West. What that means is it is all lovely adobe historic buildings—no McDonald's, no convenience stores. The last time I visited I did this walk in the dark under a waxing moon, and a skunk followed my dog and me the whole way! That should give you an idea of how little this town is developed. It lies in the valley of the Rio Bonito and has 70 residents, but it was once the seat of the largest county in the United States, and the focal point of the notorious Lincoln County War of 1878 to 1879. The entire town is now a New Mexico State Monument and a National Historic Landmark. Best of all, it was an important spot in Billy the Kid's journey.

Many of the original structures from that era have been preserved and restored by the Museum of New Mexico, the Lincoln County Historical Society, and an organization called **Historic Lincoln.** You'll begin your walk at the **Lincoln Historical Center,** where exhibits explain the role in Lincoln's history of Apaches, Hispanics, Anglo cowboys, and the black Buffalo Soldiers, and detail the Lincoln County War. A brief slide show on Lincoln history is presented in an old-fashioned theater. You can pick up a brochure describing the self-guided walking tour of the town. From there, head west passing more than a dozen buildings that witnessed much of the Lincoln County War. Make your way past the **torreon,** a circular stone tower the first settlers erected as a defense against raiding Apaches, and the **Tunstall Store.** Behind it, the Kid and his pals ambushed and killed the Lincoln County sheriff and his deputy in April 1878. West of there is the 12-room McSween Home, the Wortley Hotel, and, most importantly, the **Lincoln County Court House,** built in 1873 to 1874. There, Billy the Kid killed two guards and escaped, with bullet holes in the wall as a reminder. A few more historic buildings are farther west.

An annual **folk pageant,** *The Last Escape of Billy the Kid,* has been presented outdoors since 1949 as a highly romanticized version of the Lincoln County War. It's staged Friday and Saturday night and Sunday afternoon during the first full weekend in August as part of the **Old Lincoln Days** celebration. For details, call ☎ **800/263-5929.** The festival also includes living-history demonstrations of traditional crafts, musical programs, and food booths throughout the village.

Sitting Bull Falls

0.1 miles. Easy. Allow 30 min. to enjoy the falls, more for swimming in the pools. Access: Travel on U.S. 285 12 miles north of Carlsbad to NM 137. Drive this paved road 24 miles to FS 276, the road marked Sitting Bull Falls. Turn right and travel about 8 miles to the falls picnic area. You can also get to the trailhead by traveling south of Carlsbad on U.S. 62/180 to Dark Canyon Rd. and taking it to NM 137.

This short jaunt takes you to a platform overlooking these 150-foot high falls, where water pours off a travertine wall, forming near-tropical pools below, filled with minnows. It's a strange oasis in the midst of an oft-dry desert mountain range. You can hike down to the pools and even take a dip, though they're very shallow. You can also hike to the top of the falls and look down.

BILLY THE KID

In the late 1800s a young punk shot up some sheriffs and deputies in the Lincoln Country War, escaped from the town of Lincoln, and became a legend that even today has a strong following. He claimed he killed 21 men, 1 for every year he lived, but some sources say he only killed 4.

William Bonney, also known as Billy the Kid, was probably born in New York City sometime in 1859. In the 1870s, when he was still a child, his family moved to the southwestern United States. He had an unstable youth primarily because his mother died of tuberculosis, leaving him to a series of foster homes. One day he began petty thievery. In 1875, he was arrested and jailed, but he shimmied up a chimney and escaped to southeast Arizona. Along the road back to New Mexico he became a ranch hand, horse rustler, killed a blacksmith, and earned himself the moniker of "The Kid." What few people realize is that he was bright and literate—he loved books and music, drank little, and didn't smoke. He fought in the Lincoln Country wars and made a name for himself as a good marksman, but once the wars were over, he and his gang continued terrorizing the area. Legendary lawman Pat Garrett tracked him down, and arrested him. The Kid was sentenced to die by hanging in Lincoln. Less than a month before his hanging, he escaped, killing two guards, and helping five other prisoners out of the Lincoln Country Court House jail. Garrett tracked him down again, this time in Fort Sumner, where he killed The Kid, who was only 21 years old.

If you're interested in tracking The Kid yourself, start in Lincoln (see the "Walks & Rambles" section earlier in this chapter). Call ☎ 505/653-4372 for information. In the northern part of this region in Fort Sumner, visit the **Billy the Kid Museum** (☎ **505/355-2380**), 1 mile east of downtown Fort Sumner on U.S. 60/84. In its 48th year, it contains more than 60,000 relics of the Old West, including some recalling the life of young Bonney himself, such as his rifle. Admission is $4 for adults, $2 for children. You can also visit the **Old Fort Sumner Museum** (☎ **505/355-2942**) to see artifacts, pictures, and documents. It's a private enterprise that may not quite be worth the $3 admission. Behind the museum (you don't have to go through the museum) is the **Grave of Billy the Kid,** its 6-foot tombstone engraved to "William H. Bonney, alias 'Billy the Kid,' died July 16, 1881," and to two previously slain comrades with whom he was buried.

WILDLIFE VIEWING

One of the best places to get acquainted with the regional wildlife is at the **Living Desert Zoo and Gardens State Park,** 1504 Miehls Dr. (P.O. Box 100), Carlsbad, NM 88221-0100 (☎ **505/887-5516**). Situated within 1,200 acres of authentic Chihuahuan Desert, this park contains more than 50 species of desert mammals, birds, and reptiles, and almost 500 varieties of plants. Even for someone like me, who cringes at the thought of zoos, this was a pleasant 1.3-mile walk. You pass through displays with plaques pointing out vegetation such as mountain mahogany, and geologic formations such as gypsum sinkholes. You're likely to see lizards and other wild creatures, as well as the captive ones, and there's also a new nocturnal exhibit.

Rehabilitation programs provide the park's animals, which have been sick or injured and could no longer survive in the wild. You'll see golden eagles and great horned owls among the birds of prey in the aviary, and large animals such as deer and elk in outdoor pastures. An arroyo exhibit houses javelina, and you'll also see bears, bobcats, and cougars. A prairie dog town is a children's favorite, and a visitor center houses additional exhibits and a gift shop. Best of all is the "Succulents of the World" exhibit near the visitor center, a greenhouse that shelters such exotics as Kranz's Ball from Bolivia and velvet leaf from Madagascar.

The view from the park, high atop the Ocotillo Hills on the northwest side of Carlsbad, is superb. To get there, take Miehls Dr. off U.S. 285 west of town and proceed just over a mile. Admission is $4 for adults, $2 for children ages 7 to 12, and children 6 and under free. Group rates are available. The park is open Memorial Day weekend to Labor Day from 8am to 8pm, with last park entry by 6:30pm. The rest of year the park is open daily 9am to 5pm, with last park entry by 3:30pm. The park is closed December 25.

Southeastern New Mexico is a great place to see bats. In fact, if you look up at street lamps at night in towns such as Roswell and Alamogordo, you might just see some diving for insects. If just a few sightings only whet your appetite, head for **Carlsbad Caverns National Park.** Every sunset from early spring through October, a crowd gathers at the natural entrance of the cave to watch a quarter of a million bats take flight for a night of insect feasting. (The bats winter in Mexico.) All day long the Mexican free-tailed bats, approximately 1 million of them, sleep in the cavern; at night they hunt insects. A ranger program is offered about 7:30pm (verify the time at the Carlsbad Caverns visitor center) at the outdoor Bat Flight Amphitheater. On the second Thursday in August (usually), the park sponsors a Bat Flight Breakfast from 5 to 7am, during which visitors watch the bats return to the cavern. For contact information, see the Carlsbad Caverns National Park listing in the "Parks & Other Hot Spots" section earlier in this chapter.

Finally, one of the loveliest coyote choruses I've ever heard was in the White Mountain Wilderness north of Ruidoso. Also look here for mountain lions, mule deer, and elk.

Campgrounds & Other Accommodations

CAMPING

White Sands National Monument

15 miles southwest of Alamogordo on U.S. 70/82. (*Note:* Due to missile testing on the adjacent White Sands Missile Range, this road is sometimes closed for up to 2 hours at a time.) ☎ **505/479-6124.** 6 campsites. No facilities. When driving near or in the monument, tune a radio to 1610 AM for information on what's happening. From Memorial Day to Labor Day the visitor center is open daily 8am–7pm, and Dunes Dr. is open daily 7am–9pm. Ranger talks and sunset strolls are given nightly at 7 and 8:30pm during summer. During the rest of the year, the visitor center is open daily 8am–4:30pm, and Dunes Dr. is open daily 7am–sunset. Admission $3 for adults 17 and over.

I strongly recommend camping here, especially to see the dunes at sunrise or under a full moon. The park closes at dusk, and you'll have to leave if you're not camping. It doesn't reopen until after dawn, so there's no way you'll see the sunrise unless you camp. There are no actual campgrounds and no facilities, however, so this is strictly a backcountry adventure. Only tent camping is allowed, and you'll hike 0.75-miles to the campsite where you can pitch your tent. Be aware that on a full moon, the campsites go quickly; you may want to arrive early in the morning. At other times, availability shouldn't be a problem. In any event, you must register at the visitor center, get clearance, and pay a small fee.

Valley of Fires Recreation Area

On U.S. 380 4 miles west of Carizozo. ☎ **505/648-2241.** 19 campsites with picnic shelters, tables, grills, and water. RV electrical hookups at 14 sites. RV dump station, wheelchair-accessible campsites, and rest rooms. The park is open year-round. $3 per person or $5 per car for day use; $5–$11 camping fee.

Though there's not much shade here, it's an amazing place to spend the night, amidst one of the youngest and best-preserved lava fields in the United States. When you're not sleeping you'll enjoy exploring this landscape rich with plant and animal life.

Bonito Canyon

From NM 37 north of Ruidoso, turn left on FS 107 toward Bonito Lake and travel 7 miles to the riverside primitive campsites. Toilets at some sites. No camping fee.

Especially if you're headed up Bonito Canyon to hike the Argentina Canyon–Bonito Canyon Loop Trail, you'll probably want to camp in this canyon. Toward the end of it, you'll find all kinds of pretty sites along the Rio Bonito. Beware, though, this is big horse country. Some of the sites have been fairly trashed by horses that are corralled for days at them. When selecting a campsite, you'll want to find one away from the horse people, because the horses can be noisy at night, as can the big diesel trucks used to haul the horses. I had to move my site because the horse people were so intrusive. Some of the areas have toilet facilities, though no water.

Silver and Saddle Campgrounds

2 miles from the junction of NM 244 and U.S. 82 near Cloudcroft. 17 and 32 units respectively. Rest rooms and water.

Located just a few miles outside Cloudcroft, these are good campgrounds to cool your jets for a few days in the mountains. Of the two the Silver seemed to hold lots of RVs and have lots of kids around. Saddle was quieter, and Apache, below these two, is quieter yet. If you want an even quieter experience head to Pine Campground (see below).

Pine Campground

0.5 miles from the junction of NM 244 and road to U.S. 82 near Cloudcroft. 15 sites. Water. Primitive rest rooms.

This is my choice of Cloudcroft area campgrounds. It's set on a lovely meadow that's surrounded by pines. If you do stay here, camp as far back in the compound as possible to avoid listening to the campground host's generator. The Osha Trail can be accessed from a spur trail at the end of the campground.

Pine Springs Campground at Guadalupe National Park

Located just off U.S. 62/180 near the Headquarters Visitor Center. ☎ **915/828-3251.** 20 tent sites, 19 RV sites (without hookups). Pay phones, drinking water, picnic area, rest rooms, service sink. Pets on a leash accepted, but not allowed on the trails. $8 per night ($4 for Golden Age and Golden Access Passport holders).

Pine Springs Campground sits at the mouth of Pine Canyon, the jumping-off point to climb Guadalupe Peak, the highest point in Texas (8,749 ft.) The surrounding Guadalupe Mountains are a spectacular backdrop to this quiet little campground. Campsites are simple, clean, and have a few trees to break the desert heat, though they don't have enough leaves to really make shade. Winds can crank through this area so stake your tent well. The Guadalupe Mountains National Park has a vast array of plant life, from desert-blooming cactus to Douglas fir and aspen trees higher up. If you're looking for some solitude but still want the amenities of a campground, this one will suit you well. Quiet hours are enforced, and RVs may not run generators from 8pm to 8am. Charcoal and wood fires are not permitted.

Dog Canyon Campground at Guadalupe National Park

Located 65 miles south of Carlsbad right off Hwy. 137. ☎ **505/981-2418.** 9 tent sites, 4 RV sites (without hookups). Picnic area, ranger station, visitor horse corrals, drinking water, rest rooms. Pets on a leash accepted, but are not allowed on any of the hiking trails. $8 per night ($4 for Golden Age and Golden Access Passport holders).

Nestled in a forested canyon on the north side of Guadalupe Mountains National Park at an elevation of 6,300 feet is this secluded campground. Its small size and remote location (the nearest town, Carlsbad, is 2 hours away) make it an ideal getaway. Three hikes conveniently start from the campground: Indian Meadows Nature Loop, an easy half-mile round-trip loop that takes you through the flora and fauna of a meadow community; Tejas Trail, a moderate-to-strenuous 5.5-mile one-way hike that skirts along Lost Peak; and the Bus Mountain Trail, a 7.5-mile moderate-to-difficult one-way trail that leads to Blue Ridge Campsite. The Tejas Trail and the Bush Mountain Trail can be combined (along with the Blue Ridge Trail) to form a 15-mile loop hike. Lost Peak Trail, a moderate-to-strenuous hike that climbs out of Dog Canyon into a coniferous forest; and Marcus Overlook, which follows the Bush Mountain Trail.

Harry McAdams Park & Campgrounds

Located 4 miles north of Hobbs on NM 18. ☎ **505/392-5845.** 47 campsites; 35 with full hookups, visitor center, jogging trail, group shelter, rest room, showers, dump station, playground, and horseshoes. Pets on a leash accepted. $7 per night without hookup, $11 with hookup.

This charming little campground is centered around two ponds where tall desert grasses grow along its edge. The grounds look almost as well cared for as the 18-hole golf course across the street. Fishing is permitted for those aged 12 and under and 65 and older. Best of all for tenters are the grassy sites. Go and watch hang-gliders take off from a nearby field.

Oasis State Park

5 miles north of Portales via NM 467. ☎ **505/356-5331.** 26 campsites, 13 with hookups. Rest rooms, showers, drinking water, picnic area, dump station. Pets on a leash accepted. $4 day-use fee, $10 per night without hookup, $14 with hookup.

Fairly obvious from the name, Oasis State Park is a lush respite from the surrounding barren desert. The willowy cottonwood trees planted in 1902 shade campers from the scorching sun. Unfortunately you're not allowed to cool off in the tiny lake, but just being near water will make everything feel cooler. The park is busiest from November through March, when the New Mexico Department of Game and Fish stocks the pond with rainbow trout every two weeks. In the summer, the pond is stocked with channel catfish. There's a nice hike on the High Plains Trail that runs along the base of the dunes, through prairie grass. And if that's not enough to keep you busy, head over to nearby Blackwater Draw Museum and Site to see 11,000-year-old stone tools used by man to hunt saber-tooth tigers and wooly mammoths. Archaeologists believe that at the time, there was a large pond near the present-day campground that served as a water source for animals and a good hunting ground for humans.

INNS & LODGES

If you plan to stay in the Ruidoso area during the high seasons of summer and winter, heed the name of the town, which is the Spanish word for "noisy." I'd recommend instead staying in nearby Lincoln where there are two excellent accommodations.

Casa de Patrón Bed and Breakfast

On U.S. 380 (P.O. Box 27), Lincoln, NM 88338. ☎ **800/524-5202** or 505/653-4676. www.casapatron.com. E-mail: patron@pvtnetworks.net. 5 units, 2 casitas. $87–$117 double; casitas are $97 and $107. Rates include breakfast. MC, V.

The main building of Casa de Patrón, an adobe, was built around 1860 and housed Juan Patrón's old store (the home is on the National Register of Historic Places). In addition, Billy the Kid used part of the house as a hideout at some point during his time in the Lincoln area. Jeremy and Cleis Jordan have capitalized on the presence of that notorious punk by collecting portraits and photographs and hanging them throughout the cozy sitting and dining areas of the inn.

Rooms in the old part of the house are friendly, with a homey feel created by quilts and a major collection of washboards adorning the walls. More sophisticated are the Old Trail House rooms, one with a Jacuzzi tub, and the other for people with disabilities, both with fireplaces, wet bars, and mini-refrigerators. A short walk from there are the casitas, ideal and reasonably priced places for families to stay. The Casita Bonita has a vaulted ceiling, loft bedroom, and a kitchen with stove, oven, microwave and refrigerator, while the Casita de Paz is funkier—it's a 1960s New Mexico house added onto over the years and with a mini-refrigerator. If you choose to stay in a casita, a continental-plus breakfast is delivered to your door. If you stay in the main house or the recently added Old Trail House, Cleis and Jeremy will prepare you a full breakfast. Specialties include Dutch babies (a soufflé) served with apple compote and sausage, or stuffed French toast with piñon nuts.

Ellis Store and Co. Country Inn

U.S. 380 (P.O. Box 15), Lincoln, NM 88338. ☎ **800/653-6460** or 505/653-4609. 10 units (6 with bathroom). Pets are not permitted inside, but kennels are available. $79–$139 double. Rates include gourmet breakfast. AE, DC, DISC, MC, V.

With part of this house dating from 1850, this is believed to be the oldest existing residence in Lincoln County, and as a B&B it gives visitors a real taste of 19th-century living but with most of today's luxuries. The house has plenty of history. Billy the Kid spent several weeks here, although somewhat unwillingly, according to court records that show payment of $64 for 2 weeks' food and lodging for The Kid and a companion held under house arrest. Today, guests of innkeepers Virginia and David Vigil can come and go as they please, wandering over the inn's 6 quiet acres, or using the inn as a base while exploring Lincoln and nearby attractions.

Three rooms in the main house are a step back into the 1800s, with wood-burning fireplaces or stoves providing heat, antique furnishings, and handmade quilts. The separate Mill House, built of adobe and hand-hewn lumber in the 1880s, isn't quite as cozy as the main house, but definitely holds an Old West feel. A recent addition of two new suites provides an excellent place for families and others seeking solitude. Best of all are the breakfasts. I had an amazing stuffed French toast with baked apples, and smoked bacon. People are talking about the gourmet dinners served at Ellis, by reservation only.

Best Western Cavern Inn

17 Carlsbad Cavern Hwy. at NM 7 (P.O. Box 128), Whites City, NM 88268. ☎ **800/CAVERNS** or 505/785-2291. 63 units. A/C TV TEL. Pets are welcome. $65–$85 double. AE, CB, DC, DISC, MC, V.

Even though this is a motel and not an inn or lodge, I'm including it because it's really the only place to stay near Carlsbad Caverns. Be aware, though, that you'll want to reserve carefully. The lobby is within an Old West storefront, and the accommodations are across the street. The staff here seems to be overworked, so you may not get the service you would in Carlsbad. The motel has three sections. The best is the Guadalupe Inn. This section is built around a courtyard, and rooms have a rich feel, with vigas on the ceilings and nice Southwestern pine furniture. Bathrooms are roomy enough, and the beds are comfortably firm. In back is a big pool surrounded by greenery. Next door, the two-story Cavern Inn provides 1970s rooms that are adequate, with springy beds, and small bathrooms with jetted tubs. I cannot recommend the Walnut Canyon Inn, which is used for overflow. During my visit, these rooms were in dire need of a remodel, with soft and saggy beds, but the bathrooms were clean.

Most folks dine and drink across the highway at the Velvet Garter Saloon and Restaurant, although, as one local said, "teenagers are doing the cooking there." Between the Cavern Inn and its neighbor properties, there are two swimming pools, two hot tubs, a water park with two water slides and a court for tennis, volleyball, and basketball.

Hurd Ranch Guest Homes

P.O. Box 100 (mile marker 281) San Patricio, NM 88348. ☎ **800/658-6912** or 505/653-4331. www.wyethartists.com. 5 casitas. TV TEL. $125–$300 per casita (2-night minimum). AE, DISC, MC, V.

Located about 20 miles east of Ruidoso on 2,500-acre Sentinel Ranch, these attractive casitas are part of the Hurd–La Rinconada Gallery, which displays the work of well-known artists Peter and Michael Hurd, Henriette Wyeth Hurd, N. C. Wyeth, and Andrew Wyeth. The grounds also include the San Patricio Polo Fields, where matches take place from Memorial Day to Labor Day.

There are two older one-bedroom casitas, built in the early part of the century, and three new and much larger units. Of the smaller, the Orchard house is my favorite, sitting on the edge of an apple orchard, furnished in weathered Southwestern antiques (though some noise from the highway travels through its walls). Both of the larger units are elegant, especially the newer La Helenita, a pitched roofed adobe house large enough for two families. All have completely equipped kitchens, with stove, oven, refrigerator, microwave, dishwasher and satellite TV. They also have fireplaces and comfortable living areas, and are decorated with antiques, primitives, and art by the Hurd-Wyeth family. A stay here wins you access to fine fly-fishing along the Rio Ruidoso.

Inn of the Mountain Gods

Carrizo Canyon Rd. (P.O. Box 269), Mescalero, NM 88340. ☎ **800/545-9011** or 505/257-5141. www.innofthemountaingods.com. 253 units. A/C TV TEL. May–Labor Day $135 double, $145 suite; Labor Day–Oct $110 double, $120 suite; Nov–Apr $95 double, $105 suite. Golf, tennis, and ski packages available. AE, CB, DC, DISC, MC, V.

What's most impressive about this resort is its location, set on a grassy slope above a mountain lake on the Mescalero Apache Reservation, 3.5 miles southwest of Ruidoso. It is the successful dream of the former tribal president, Wendell Chino, who wanted to help his people get into the recreation and tourism business.

Nine interconnected brown-shake buildings comprise the hotel and an associated convention center, all built in 1975 with renovations ongoing. Guests cross a covered wooden bridge over a cascading stream to reach the three-story lobby, dominated by a huge, cone-shaped, copper fireplace. Modern tribal art and trophies of wild animals bagged on the reservation are on display. The property includes an 18-hole golf course designed by Ted Robinson, whose work includes the famed course at the Princess in

Acapulco. In winter, buses shuttle skiers to the Ski Apache resort, also owned by the tribe.

The guest rooms are spacious and comfortable, though I wouldn't use the term *luxurious,* which the inn bandies about. They do have high ceilings, tasteful furnishings, coffeemakers, and patios or balconies. Beds are comfortable and bathrooms are very clean and functional.

Lithographs on the walls depict typical 19th-century tribal scenes. On-site is a piano bar and Casino Apache, a smoky building filled with slot machines and card rooms. There's also a pool, hot tub, sauna, sundeck, outdoor tennis courts, volleyball, basketball, badminton, fishing lake stocked with rainbow trout, and boating (rowboats, pedal boats, and aqua cycles can be rented).

Index

A

A Mountain Trail, 333
Abe's Motel and Fly Shop, 216
Abiquiu, 267
Abiquiu Lake, 240, 278
Abominable Snowmansion Skiers' Hostel, 286
Abyss, the, 39
Accommodations, 23, 285. *See also specific accommodations*
    Arizona
        Grand Canyon Area, 59
        Indian Country, 85
        Red Rock Country, 137
        Sky Islands, 196
        West Coast, 108
        White Mountains, 163
    New Mexico
        Cave Country, 370
        Gila Country, 340
        High Plains, 311
        Indian Country, 229
        Rocky Mountains, 285
Ackre Lake Trail, 154
Acoma Pueblo, 205
Active Endeavors, 280
Adventures Out West, 115
Agassiz Peak, 47
Agate Bridge, 68, 80
Agate House, 68, 79
Aguirre Lake, 98
Aguirre Springs Campground, 340
Airlines, 4
Airports, 4, 30
Ajo, 91–92, 98, 108
Ajo Mountain Drive, 96, 102
Alamo Lake State Park, 93
Alamogordo, 347, 368
Alamogordo and Sacramento Mountain Railway, 364
Albuquerque, 284
    accommodations, 287
    ballooning, 238
    bird watching, 239
    horseback riding, 267
    mountain biking, 268
Albuquerque Foothills Trail, 269

Albuquerque International Sunport, 4
Alcalde, 276
Aldo Leopold Wilderness, 318, 322, 328, 338
Alice, Lake, 297, 300
Alien Run Trail, 224
Alkali Flat Trail, 357
Alpine Divide Campground, 162
Alpine, accommodations, 164
Amado Territory Inn Bed & Breakfast, 196
Amole Canyon, 244
Amtrak, 4
Anasazi, 54, 63, 65, 69, 71, 74, 77, 200, 204–205, 211, 214, 232, 269
Anderson Mesa, 29
Angel Fire Resort, 11, 251, 277
Angel Peak Campground, 228
Antelope Canyon, 64, 82
Antelope House Overlook, 80
Antelope Island, 20, 81
Apache Indians, 114, 140, 165, 172, 174, 180, 184, 194, 276, 316, 336, 345, 350, 359–360, 372
Apache Maid Trail, 121
Apache Stables, 49
Apache Trail, 131
Apache-Sitgreaves National Forest, 140
Aravaipa Canyon, 178, 183
Aravaipa Farms, 23, 197
Arboretum at Flagstaff, 29
Argentina Canyon, 358
Arivaca, 102–103, 105
Arivaca Creek, 98
Arivaca Lake, 99
Arivaca Road, 103
Arizona, 86
Arizona Off-Road Adventures, 189
Arizona Reel Time, 73
Arizona River Runners, 56
Arizona Snowbowl, 11, 37
Arizona Trail, 123, 168
Arizona's Salt River Tubing, 132

Arizona-Sonora Desert Museum, 168
Armand Hammer United World College, 309
Arroyo Hondo, 276
Aspen Sports, 35, 38
Aspen Vista, 246, 271
Atalaya Mountain, 259
Atchison, Topeka & Santa Fe Railway, 233
Aztec Ruins National Monument, 200, 204, 226

B

Back Bay Canoes and Kayaks, 103
Backcountry Information Center, 37, 39
Backpacking, 13. *See also* Hiking
    Arizona
        Grand Canyon area, 26, 38
        Indian Country, 73
        Red Rock Country, 118
        Sky Islands, 181
        West Coast, 99
        White Mountains, 148
    New Mexico
        Cave Country, 357
        Gila Country, 326
        High Plains, 302
        Indian Country, 217
        Rocky Mountains, 256
Bajada Loop Drive (Saguaro), 172
Bald eagles, 72, 96, 99, 113, 143, 178, 300
Ballooning, 7
    Arizona
        Red Rock Country, 114
        Sky Islands, 175
    New Mexico
        Indian Country, 216
        Kodak Albuquerque International Balloon Fiesta, 8, 238
        Red Rock Balloon Rally, 211, 216

INDEX **375**

Rocky Mountains, 238
Taos Mountain Balloon
Rally, 239
BalloonRidesUSA, 115, 175
**Bandelier National
Monument, 232, 236,
262, 279**
Bandera Crater, 215
**Basin and Range Province.
See Great Basin and Range
Province**
Baylor Pass, 329
Beaches. *See* **Swimming**
Bear Canyon Reservoir, 326
**Bear Mountain Lodge, 24,
324, 341**
**Bear Wallow Wilderness,
149–150**
Beatty's Cabin, 261
**Beatty's Miller Canyon Apiary
& Orchard Company, 178**
Bell Crossing, 121
Bell Rock Pathway, 126
**Best Western Cavern
Inn, 371**
Betatakin, 69–70, 75
**Betty's Kitchen Nature
Trail, 97**
Bicycle Showcase, 126
**Big Dunes Trail
(White Sands), 365**
Big Juniper Loop, 331
Big Lake, 145
**Big Springs Environmental
Study Area, 156, 161**
Big Tesuque, 285
**Big Tubes (El Malpais), 9, 216,
221**
**Bighorn sheep, 57, 95, 97,
105, 171, 181, 194, 261, 283,
322**
Bike & Bean, 126
Bike n' Sport, 268
Biking. *See* **Mountain biking;
Road biking**
Bill Evans Lake, 323, 326
**Bill Williams National
Wildlife Refuge, 97**
Bill Williams River, 97
**Bill Williams River
Canyon, 99**
**Billy the Kid, 316, 335, 344,
367, 371**
grave of, 367
museum, 367
walk in the footsteps
of, 366
Biosphere 2, 170

Bird watching, 8
Arizona
Grand Canyon area, 33
Indian Country, 72
Red Rock Country, 115
Sky Islands, 176, 178, 186
West Coast, 93, 96
White Mountains, 143,
161
New Mexico
Cave Country, 352
Festival of the Cranes,
8, 323
Gila Country, 316, 323
High Plains, 299
Indian Country, 216
Rocky Mountains, 239
Bisbee, 166
Bishop's Lodge, 287
**Bisti De-Na-Zin Wilderness,
217**
**Bitter Lake National Wildlife
Refuge, 352**
**Black Canyon Campground,
285**
Black Range Crest Trail, 328
Black River, 147, 160
Blue Hole, 20, 292, 306
**Blue Range Primitive Area,
145, 162**
**Blue Range Wilderness,
322, 338**
Blue River, 160
Blue Vista, 159
**Bluewater Lake State Park,
204, 210, 216, 217**
Bluff Springs, 352
Boardsailing, 9
Arizona
Sky Islands, 178
West Coast, 98
White Mountains, 143
New Mexico
Cave Country, 352
Gila Country, 324
High Plains, 300
Rocky Mountains, 240
Boating. *See* **Boardsailing;
Canoeing; Houseboating,
in Arizona; Kayaking;
Rafting; Sailing; White-water
kayaking**
Bonita Canyon, 174, 195
**Bonita Canyon Drive
(Chiricahua), 174**
Bonito Canyon, 358, 369
Bonito Lake, 356, 361
Bonito Lava Flow, 79
Bonito River, 356, 369

Bonney, William. *See* **Billy the
Kid**
Boot Hill Graveyard, 166
Borderland, 92
Borrego Trail, 259
**Bosque del Apache National
Wildlife Refuge, 8, 316, 323,
334, 339**
**Bottomless Lakes State Park,
350, 356, 364**
Bouldering. *See* **Climbing**
**Boy Scouts of America,
291, 304**
**Boyce Thompson Arboretum
State Park, 113**
Boynton Canyon, 118
Boynton Canyon Vortex, 128
Brahma Temples, 36
**Brantley Lake State Park, 350,
352, 356**
Brazos River, 255
Briar Patch Inn, 137
Bright Angel Canyon, 40–41
**Bright Angel Creek, 38,
40, 73**
**Bright Angel Lodge & Cabins,
59**
Bright Angel Point Trail, 54
Bright Angel Trail, 36, 39
Bright Angel Walls, 35–36
Broken Arrow, 127
**Broken Saddle Riding
Company, 267**
Brown Canyon, 98
Brown Canyon Trail, 191
Bruce Roads, 353
Buck Ridge Point, 52
Buckskin Gulch, 26, 44
**Buckskin Mountain State
Park, 107, 123**
Buddie's Stables, 362
**Budget Host Melody Lane
Motel, 312**
**Buenos Aires National
Wildlife Refuge, 97,
102–103, 106**
Buffalo Park, 36, 53
Bull of the Woods, 278
Bull Pasture Trail, 100
Buses, 5, 32

C

**Caballo Lake State Park, 319,
324, 326, 334**
**Cabeza Prieta National
Wildlife Refuge, 23, 98,
105–106**
Cabresto Lake, 255

INDEX

Cactus Forest Drive (Saguaro), 172, 192
Cactus Forest Trail Loop (Saguaro), 190
Calderon Crater, 215, 220
California condors, 8, 33–34, 72
Camelback Mountain, 124
Camino del Diablo, 98, 106
Camp Verde, 117
Camping, 23
  Arizona
    Grand Canyon Area, 57, 59
    Indian Country, 84
    Red Rock Country, 136
    Sky Islands, 174, 195
    West Coast, 95, 107
    White Mountains, 162
  New Mexico
    Cave Country, 368
    Gila Country, 322–323, 339
    High Plains, 310
    Indian Country, 203, 205, 214, 216, 228
    Rocky Mountains, 284
Canadian River, 291, 298, 301
Canjilon Lakes, 256, 285
Canoeing, 9. *See also* Kayaking
Canyon Creek, 148
Canyon de Chelly National Monument, 65, 69–70
  accommodations, 85
  biking, 80
  hiking, 74
  horseback riding, 78
Canyon del Muerto, 70, 78, 80
Canyon Explorations (Flagstaff), 56
Canyon Floor Loop (Chaco Culture), 222
Canyon Lake (Phoenix), 132
Canyon National Geographic Theater, 33
Canyon Trail (Villanueva), 302
Canyon View Center (Grand Canyon), 30
Canyoneering, 14. *See also* Climbing
  Arizona, 26
Cañada del Oro, 170
Capitan Mountains, 355
Capitan Peak, 357
Capulin Volcano National Monument, 291–292, 305, 307

Car rentals, 5
Car travel. *See also specific scenic drives*
  Arizona
    Chiricahua National Monument, 174
    Grand Canyon area, 28
    Grand Canyon National Park, 31
    Indian Country, 66
    Organ Pipe Cactus National Monument, 95
    Red Rock Country, 112
    Saguaro National Park, 172
    Sky Islands, 167
    West Coast, 91
    White Mountains, 140–141
  New Mexico
    Cave Country, 347
    Gila Country, 318
    High Plains, 292
    Indian Country, 202
    Rocky Mountains, 236
Carlsbad, 347, 362
Carlsbad Caverns National Park, 9, 343, 346–347, 352
  bats, 23, 368
  caving, 352
Carlsbad Lake, 364
Carr Peak, 185
Carson National Forest, 256, 272, 283. *See also* Valle Vidal
  camping, 284
  cross-country skiing, 244
  hiking, 272
  wildlife viewing, 283
Carson, Kit, 299, 304
Casa Blanca, 230, 341
Casa Chiquita, 223
Casa de Gavilan, 311
Casa de Patro[as]n Bed and Breakfast, 24, 371
Casa de San Pedro, 198
Casa Escondida, 286
Casa Rinconada, 214
Casa Tierra, 23, 196
Casitas de Gila, 341
Castillo Gallery, 275
Castle Rock Bay, 103
Catalina State Park, 170
Cataract Lake, 59
Cathedral Rock, 127, 134
Cattail Cove State Park, 98, 104
Catwalk National Recreation Area, 328

Cave Country, 343, 346, 348, 350, 353–354, 356, 358, 361, 363, 366, 370, 372
Cave Creek Canyon, 178, 194
Caving, 9
  Arizona
    Grand Canyon area, 35
    Sky Islands, 179
  New Mexico
    Cave Country, 352
    Indian Country, 216, 221
Cayuse Equestrian Area, 125
Cebolla Mesa, 264, 284
Cebolla Wilderness, 222
Cedar Springs, 254
Ceremonial Cave, 279
Cerro Blanco Adventures, 267
Chaco Canyon, 232
Chaco Culture National Historic Park, 200, 211, 214
  camping, 228
  hiking, 213, 218
  mountain biking, 222
Chama, 11, 247
Chama River, 22, 255, 278, 283
Chama River Canyon, 281
Chama River Canyon Wilderness, 266
Chama Ski Service, 247
Chandelle River Tours, 160, 192
Charette Lakes, 301
Chetro Ketl, 214, 223
Chevelon Canyon Lake, 147
Chevelon Creek, 147
Chicken Point Trail, 127
Chihuahuan Desert, 166, 343, 348, 359, 367
Chiles, about, 330
Chimayo, 274, 279
Chimney Rock, 265
Chinle, 85
Chinle Creek, 74
Chinle Formation, 67, 265
Chiricahua Mountains, 8, 165, 173, 194
Chiricahua National Monument, 172, 175, 189
  camping, 174, 195
  hiking, 174, 183
  walks and rambles, 193
Chloride, 337
Christmas Tree Lake, 146
Christopher Creek, 148, 150, 158, 159, 163
Cibola National Forest, 203
Cibola National Wildlife Refuge, 97, 99

Cimarron, 290, 299, 309, 311
Cimarron Campground, 284
Cimarron Canyon State Park, 296, 300, 302
Cimarron River, 300
Circle S Stables, 331
Circle Z Ranch, 17, 188
City of Rocks State Park, 317, 319, 324
Civil War, 114, 203, 295
Clayton, 292, 310
Clayton Camp, 273
Clayton Lake State Park, 297, 300, 307
Clear Creek, 38, 73
Clear Creek Canyon, 302
Cliff Canyon (Rainbow Bridge), 74
Climate, 5, 28, 65, 91, 111, 167, 171, 202, 235, 292, 317, 346
Climbing, 10
   Arizona
      Grand Canyon area, 35, 36
      Indian Country, 72
      Red Rock Country, 116
      Sky Islands, 180
   favorite climbs, 11
   New Mexico
      Cave Country, 355
      Gila Country, 324
      High Plains, 300
      Rocky Mountains, 240, 243
   resources, 10
Cloud-Climbing Rail Trail, 363
Cloudcroft, 362–363, 369
Cochise Stronghold, 165, 180, 184, 189, 193, 195
Cochise Stronghold Nature Walk, 193
Cochiti Lake, 240
Cochiti Mesa, 241
Cockscomb Loop, 128
Coconino National Forest, 49, 110, 136
Cody, Buffalo Bill, 299, 311
Colorado Plateau, 26, 64, 109–110, 200
Colorado River, 26, 40, 64, 68, 82, 90–92
   bird watching, 96
   fishing, Lees Ferry, 12, 38, 73
   geological history of, 26, 64
   rafting, 84
      Grand Canyon, 22, 55, 57
   swimming, 54
   through Grand Canyon, 55
      rafting, 22, 55, 57

Colorado River Valley, 97, 104
Comanche Creek, 255
Conchas Lake State Park, 292, 298, 300–301, 307
Condors. *See* California condors
Continental Divide, 317, 334
Continental Divide Trail, 266, 332
Cordova, 275, 279
Coronado National Forest, 170, 188
Coronado National Memorial, 123
Coronado Peak Trail, 194
Coronado Trail, 157, 159
Costilla Creek, 254
Costilla Pass, 273
Cottonwood, 117
Cottonwood Campground, 85
Cottonwood Cycles, 222
Cougar Springs, 48
Coyote Creek State Park, 296, 310
Coyote Pass Hospitality, 85
Coyotes, 83–84, 96–97, 105, 113, 170, 173, 194, 228–239, 309, 368
Crater Rim Trail (Capulin Volcano), 307
Crazy Jug Point, 51
Crescent Lake, 146
Crest Trail, 187, 327
Crockett Cave, 9, 352
Cross-country skiing, 11
   Arizona
      Grand Canyon area, 36–37
      White Mountains, 144
   New Mexico's Rocky Mountains, 243–248
Crownpoint Rug Weavers Association, 209
Crystal Forest, 68, 80
Crystal Forest Trail, 68, 80

D

Dairy Springs National Forest Campground, 59
Datil-Mogollon Highlands, 316
DAV Vietnam Veterans Memorial, 277
Davis Dam, 103
Day in the West, 125
Dead Cholla Wall, 242

Dead Horse Ranch State Park, 113, 117
Deadman's Pass Loop, 128
Deer. *See* Mule deer
Deer Creek, 38, 73
Deming, 317–318
Demotte Campground, 58
Desert Classic Trail (Phoenix), 129
Desert Cycles, 331
Desert Museum, Arizona-Sonora, 168
Desert View Drive (Grand Canyon), 31, 52
Desert View Loop (Organ Pipe Cactus), 104
Desert-High Country Stables (Ruidoso), 362
Devil's Bridge Trail, 134
Devil's Inkwell, 350, 356
Diablito Mountain, 102
Diamond Peak, 36
Dinosaur Tracks (Clayton Lake), 307
Diving. *See* Scuba diving
Dixon, 276
Doe Mountain Trail, 134
Dog Canyon, 350, 359, 370
Dogtown Lake, 38, 59
Don Donnelly Stables, 17, 78, 189
Doney Mountain, 72
Doña Ana Mountains, 325
Double D Ranch, 125
Double E Guest Ranch, 15, 16, 330
Double Springs National Forest Campground, 59
Downhill skiing. *See* Skiing
Dragoon Mountains, 180
Dry Lake Hills Loop, 53
Duck on a Rock, 173–174
Dude ranches. *See* Guest ranches
Dunes Drive (White Sands), 349
Duranglers on the San Juan, 216

E

Eagle Nest, 277
Eagle Nest Lake, 255, 277, 300
Eagletail Mountains, 116
East Fork of the Jemez River, 253
East Fork of the Little Colorado River, fishing, 145

INDEX

East Fork Ridge Cross-Country Ski Trail, 245, 273
Echo Canyon Amphitheater, 280
Echo Canyon Loop (Chiricahua), 183
Echo Canyon Trail (Camelback Mountain), 124
Ed Riggs Trail, 184
El Calderon, 215, 220
El Camino del Diablo, 98, 106
El Devisadero Loop, 271
El Malpais National Monument, 200, 202, 214, 216
    caving, 216
    hiking, 220
    walks and rambles, 226
    wildlife viewing, 228
El Morro National Monument, 200, 202
El Paseo Llama Expeditions, 18, 268
El Paso International Airport, 4
El Rancho Hotel & Motel, 229
El Rey Inn, 288
El Santuario de Nuestro Señor de Esquipulas (Chimayo), 234, 274–275
El Tovar Hotel, 59
El Vado Dam, 255
El Vado Lake State Park, 238, 255
El Vado Ranch, 255, 281
Elbow Canyon, 48
Elegant trogon, 171, 174, 176, 179, 186
Elephant Butte Lake State Park, 9, 319, 324, 326, 334, 340
Elephant Butte, accommodations, 340
Elephant Head, 190
Elevation, 6
Elite Outfitters, 361
Elizabethtown, 277
Ellis Store & Co. Country Inn, 24, 371
Embudo River, 282
Embudo Station, 276, 280
Emory Pass, 334
Empire Cienega Wildlife Preserve, 178, 192, 194
Enchanted Circle, 276
Enchanted Circle Century Bike Tour, 274
Enchanted Forest Cross Country Ski Area, 243

Enchanted Moon Campground, 284
Enchanted Tower, 324
Escudilla Mountain, 149
Espanola, 236
Estes Canyon Trail, 100

F

Far Flung Adventures, 160, 283
Faraway Ranch, 174, 175
Farmington, 199–200, 202, 230
Farmington Whitewater Course, 228
Fenton Lake, 255
Festival of the Cranes, 8, 323
Film sites. *See* Movie sites
First Mesa, 64
Fishing, 12
    Arizona
        Grand Canyon area, 38
        Indian Country, 73
        Red Rock Country, 116
        Sky Islands, 180
        West Coast, 98
        White Mountains, 145–146, 148
    licenses, 12
    New Mexico
        Cave Country, 356
        Gila Country, 325
        High Plains, 300
        Indian Country, 216
        Rocky Mountains, 252, 255–256
Flagstaff, 28
    accommodations, 60
    climbing, 36
    fishing, 117
    hiking, 38, 46, 47
    horseback riding, 50
    mountain biking, 50, 52
    road biking, 53
    skiing, 37
Flagstaff Arboretum, 29
Flagstaff Mountain Guides, 10, 35–36
Flagstaff Nordic Center, 37
Flash floods, 6, 15, 65
Flying Heart at Flagstaff, 50
Folsom Man, 306
Folsom Museum, 306
Forest Road 150 (Aspen Vista), 246
Fort Apache Indian Reservation, 139
Fort Bayard Wagon Road, 331

Fort Bayard Wildlife Refuge, 339
Fort Huachuca, 171
Fort Stanton, 361
Fort Stanton Cave, 9, 352
Fort Sumner, 367
Fort Union National Monument, 295
Fountain Hills Loop, 131
Four Corners, 65, 200
Four Corners Monument, 209
Four Corners Monument Navajo Tribal Park, 83
Four Windows Cave, 216, 221
Free the Snow, 249
Fremont Saddle, 124
Frijoles Canyon, 263

G

Gadsden Museum, 335
Galisteo Basin, 267
Galisteo Inn, 287
Gallina, 267
Gallinas River, 301
Gallo Campground, 228
Gallup, 199, 202, 229
Ganado, 66
Garden Canyon, 171
Gardens State Park (Carlsbad), 367
Garlands General Store, 133
Gearing Up Bicycle Shop, 269
Geronimo, 165, 174, 316
Ghost Ranch, 264
Giant Log (Petrified Forest), 68, 79
Gila Bird and Nature Festival, 324
Gila Cliff Dwellings National Monument, 316, 320, 322–323, 334, 335
Gila Country, 314, 317, 319–320, 324, 327, 329, 332, 334, 338–339, 341
Gila Hike and Bike, 331
Gila National Forest, 314, 318, 322–323
Gila National Forest Hot Springs, 321
Gila River, 321, 327, 339. *See also* West Fork of the Gila River
    fishing, 325
    rafting, 22, 192
Gila Wilderness, 23, 314, 318, 322, 325, 328, 338
Glade Trail System, 225

Glen Canyon Dam, 27, 63, 65–66
Glen Canyon National Recreation Area, 66
Glenwood, 333
Globe, 157, 163
Glorieta Mesa, 304
Glorieta Pass, 295
Gon' Fishen, 117
Goodding Research Center, 100
Goose Lake, 272
Gooseberry Springs Trail, 219, 224
Gouldings Lodge, 69, 86
Gouldings Trading Post, 69
Grand Canyon Airport, 30
Grand Canyon Caverns, 9, 35
Grand Canyon Country, 25–26, 29, 32, 35, 37, 40, 42, 46, 48, 53, 55, 57, 58, 60
Grand Canyon Expeditions Company, 56
Grand Canyon Lodge, 60
Grand Canyon Mule Rides, 49
Grand Canyon National Park 25, 27–28, 30–31. *See also* North Rim of the Grand Canyon; South Rim of the Grand Canyon
  accommodations, 31, 59
  bird watching, 35
  bus tours, 32
  climbing, 35
  cross-country skiing, 37
  fees, 30
  fishing, 12, 38, 73
  geological history of, 26
  hiking, 38–42, 123
    permits, 39
  history of, 25
  horseback riding, 49
  information, 30
  kayaking, 81
  maps, 39
  mountain biking, 50–52
  mule rides, 49
  rafting, 22, 55, 57
  transportation options, 31
  traveling to, 30
  weather, 28
  wildlife viewing, 57
Grand Canyon Railway, 54
Grand Canyon Village, 30
Grand Canyon West, hiking, 42
Grand Falls, 83

Grand View Trail, 363
Granite Dells, 124, 131
Granite Mountain, 116, 123, 136
Grants, 199, 204, 230
Grapevine Canyon Ranch, 189
Grasshopper Point, 116, 132
Gray wolf, Mexican, 23, 161, 314, 318
Great Basin and Range Province, 91, 109–110, 166, 343, 346
Great Basin Desert, 29
Green Meadow Lake, 356
Greenway (Grand Canyon), 31
Greer, 145, 163
Greer Lakes, 145, 162
Grey, Zane, 140, 299, 311
Guadalupe Mountains National Park, 343, 346, 351
  camping, 369
  hiking, 360
Guadalupe National Monument, 360
Guadalupe Peak, 361
Guest House Inn (Ajo), 108
Guest ranches, 15, 188. *See also* Horseback riding; *specific ranches*

H

Hacienda Alta, 138
Hacienda Antigua, 24, 287
Hacienda del Sol Guest Ranch Resort, 196
Hamilton Mesa, 261, 278
Hannagan Meadow Loop, 144, 154
Hannagan Meadows Lodge, 164
Hantavirus Pulmonary Syndrome, 5
Happy Trails, 331
Harry McAdams Park & Campgrounds, 370
Hassayampa River Preserve, 115
Hatch, 330
Hatch Chile Festival, 330
Haunted Canyon, 41
Havasu Canyon, 42
Havasu Falls, 43, 54
Havasu National Wildlife Refuge, 96
Havasu, Lake, 92
  camping, 107
  fishing, 98

  kayaking, 20, 103
  sailing, 9, 98
  swimming, 104
Hawikuh, 207
Hawk Watch Trail, 239, 257
Health concerns and precautions, 6
Heart of Rocks Loop, 184
Hellsgate Wilderness, 151, 155
Hermit Road, 31, 52
Hermit's Peak, 302, 306
Heron Lake State Park, 9, 238, 240, 278
High Altitude, 362
High Desert Angler, 252
High Gear Bike Shop, 126
High Plains, 290, 293–294, 296, 298, 300, 301, 303, 305, 307, 308, 311
High Road to Taos, 274, 279
Highline Trail, 150, 155
Hiking, 13–14
  Arizona
    Grand Canyon area, 26, 38–42, 45–49
    Indian Country, 73–74, 76
    Red Rock Country, 118–119, 121, 123, 125
    Sky Islands, 172, 174, 181, 182, 184–187
    West Coast, 96, 99, 101
    White Mountains, 148–149, 152
  favorite hikes, 14
  New Mexico
    Cave Country, 357, 359–361
    Gila Country, 316, 322, 326, 328–330
    High Plains, 292, 302, 304
    Indian Country, 213, 216–220, 222
    Rocky Mountains, 256–257, 259, 260, 262–264, 267
  permits, 39
  preservation, 24
  resources, 13
  safety tips, 6–7, 15, 38
Hillsboro, 334
Hillsboro Peak, 328
Hitchin' Post Stables, 50
Hohokum Indians, 124, 193
Holbrook, 66
Holiday Inn Express Grand Canyon, 59

Homolovi Ruins State Park, 65, 70
Hondo Cliffs, 242
Hoover Dam, 27, 30
Hopewell Lake, 256
Hopi Cultural Center Restaurant and Inn, 87
Hopi Indians, 47, 62, 64, 70, 77, 81, 203, 220
Hopilands, 63–64, 69, 71
  accommodations, 87
  walks and rambles, 81
Horseback riding, 14
  Arizona
    Grand Canyon area, 49
    Indian Country, 77
    Red Rock Country, 125
    Sky Islands, 172, 187
    West Coast, 101
    White Mountains, 152
  New Mexico
    Cave Country, 361
    Gila Country, 330
    High Plains, 304
    Indian Country, 222
    Rocky Mountains, 267
Horseshoe Bend Viewpoint, 82
Horseshoe Cienega Lake, 146
Horton Creek, 150, 154
Horton Creek Trail, 150, 154
Hot-air ballooning. *See* Ballooning
Hotels. *See* Accommodations; *specific hotels*
Houseboating, in Arizona
  Lake Havasu, 93
  Lake Powell, 67
H2O Houseboats, 93
Huachuca Mountains, 171, 185
Hualapai Indian Reservation, 56
Hualapai Mountain Park, 93, 107
Hualapai River Runners, 36, 56
Hubbell Trading Post, 69
Hueco Tanks, 355
Hummingbird Haven, 177
Hummingbirds, 98, 135, 176–178, 195, 327, 352
Humphreys Peak, 26–27, 47, 65
Hurd Ranch Guest Homes, 372
Hurricane Cliffs, 34
Hyde Memorial State Park, 285

I

Ice Caves Resort, 215
Ice skating, in New Mexico, 301
Immigrants, illegal, 92
Imperial National Wildlife Refuge, 97, 99, 104
Indian Country
  Arizona, 62, 65, 67, 70, 73, 75, 77, 80, 82, 84, 85
  New Mexico, 199, 202, 204, 206, 208, 213, 216, 218, 222, 224, 226, 228–229
Inn at 410 (Flagstaff), 23, 61
Inn at Halona, 229
Inn of the Mountain Gods, 356, 372
Inscription House, 69
International UFO Museum and Research Center, 353
Isle of You, 180

J

Jacks Canyon, 72
Jackson Lake Wildlife Area, 216–217, 228
Jacob Lake, 58, 123
Jacob Lake Inn, 60
Jacques Marsh Wildlife Area, 161
James, Jesse, 299, 311
Jasper Forest Overlook, 68, 80
Jemez Mountains, 232, 234
  climbing, 241
  cross-country skiing, 11, 245
  horseback riding, 267
  mountain biking, 273
  snowshoeing, 278
Jemez River, 253
Jemez Spring, accommodations, 288
Jemez State Monument, 237
Jerome State Historic Park, 114
Jicarilla Apache Indian Reservation, 199, 255
Jicarilla Lakes, 255
Jim Thompson–Midgley Bridge Trail, 127
John's Wall, 242
Jordan Hot Springs, 321
Junction Overlook, 80
Juniper Campground, 339

K

K El Bar Ranch, 15–17, 126
Kachina Bowl, 249
Kaibab Camper Village, 58
Kaibab Lake, 59
Kaibab Lodge, 60
Kaibab National Forest, 49–50, 58, 123
  camping, 59
Kaibab Plateau, 23, 27–28, 35, 57
Kaibab squirrels, 23, 51, 57–58, 161, 163
Kaibab Suspension Bridge, 40
Kartchner Caverns, 9, 179
Katherine, Lake, 256, 260, 278
Kay El Bar Ranch, 15–17, 126
Kayaking, 20. *See also* Whitewater kayaking
  Arizona
    Indian Country, 81
    Sky Islands, 192
    West Coast, 103
  New Mexico
    Indian Country, 228
Keet Seel, 69, 74
Kendrick Mountain, 47
K5 High Country Adventures, 16, 152
Kin Kletso, 214
Kingman, 91
Kinnikinick Reservoir, 117
Kinsey Trail, 225
Kiowa National Grasslands, 291, 303, 310
Kirtland Shale, 217
Kit Carson Museum, 304
Kitchen Mesa, 264
Kitt Peak National Observatory, 94
Kodak Albuquerque International Balloon Fiesta, 8, 238
Kofa Mountains, 88, 100
Kofa National Wildlife Refuge, 88, 91, 100, 108
Kohl's Ranch, 164
Kokopelli's Cave, 24, 231

L

La Cueva Canyon, 258
La Cueva Escarpment, 364
La Cueva National Historic Site, 298
La Cueva Trails, 364
La Junta Run, 254
La Luz Trail, 258
La Mesilla, 316, 335

INDEX 381

La Mosca Canyon, 224
La Mosca Peak, 224
La Pasada Encantada Nature Trail, 365
La Posada Hotel, 86
La Tierra Torture Trail, 270
La Ventana Natural Arch, 215, 226
Ladybug Trail, 152
Laguna Pueblo, 206
Lake Havasu City, 92, 104
Lake Havasu State Park, 92, 98, 107
Lake Mary Road, 53
Lake Mead National Recreation Area, 29, 38, 98
Lakeside, 142, 157, 159
Langmuir Research Laboratory, 317
Las Conchas, 241
Las Cruces, 316, 318, 335
Las Guijas Mountains, 103
Las Trampas, 275
Las Vegas, 291–292, 307, 309
  walking tour, 307
Las Vegas National Wildlife Refuge, 299, 301
Last Chance Canyon, 360
Last Escape of Billy the Kid (folk pageant), 366
Latir Lakes, 256
Latir Wilderness, 243, 262
Laughlin, Nevada, 90
Lava Flow Nature Trail (Sunset Crater), 72
Lava River Cave, 9, 35
Lazy Lagoon, 350
Le Petit Verdon, 36
Lea Lake, 350, 356, 364
Lee Valley Outfitters, 153
Lee Valley Reservoir, 146
Lees Ferry, 63
  fishing, 12, 38, 73
  swimming, 54
Lees Ferry Lodge, 86
Lenox Crater, 72
Leona's Restaurante de Chimayo, 275
Leopold, Aldo, 149, 283, 314, 318
Leupp Road (Navajo Indian Reservation), 79
Lightfeather Hot Springs, 321
Lincoln, 366
Lincoln Historical Center, 366
Lincoln National Forest, 356, 363, 365
Lincoln State Monument, 366
Lions Wilderness, 225

Little Colorado River, 71, 84, 140, 143, 146, 153
  East Fork of, fishing, 145
  West Fork of, 148
  snowshoeing, 21, 144
Little Costilla Peak Trail, 246
Little Florida Mountains, 320
Little Green Valley, 155
Little Tree Bed & Breakfast (Taos), 24, 286
Living Desert Zoo (Carlsbad), 367
Llama trekking, 17, 268
Lodge at Chama, 255
Lodge at Red River, 285
London Bridge, 90
London Bridge Beach, 104
Long Logs (Petrified Forest), 68, 79
Lordsburg, 334
Los Alamos National Laboratory, 234, 266, 344
Los Burros Campground, 162
Los Burros Loop, 156
Los Luceros, 276
Los Rios River Runners, 283
Lost Cabin Mine Trail, 101
Lost Dutchman State Park, 114, 132, 136
Lousley Hill Trail, 135
Lowell Observatory, 29
Lower Granite Gorge, 36
Lower Lake Mary, 117
Lower Oldham Trail, 53
Lower Salt River, 117
Lower Taos Box Canyon, 282
Luna Lake, 143, 153
  camping, 162
Lundeen's Inn of the Arts, 341
Lyman Lake State Park, 142–143, 146, 158

M

Magdalena Crest Trail, 326
Magdalena Mountains, 316–317, 332, 338
Main Ruins Trail (Bandelier), 279
Maloya, Lake, 301
Manhattan Project, 234, 266, 344
Marble Canyon, 34, 42
Marble Canyon Bridge, 73
Marble Canyon Lodge, 73, 86
Martha's Bed & Breakfast, 342
Martinez Lake Marina, 97
Mary, Lake, 117

Massacre Cave Overlook, 80
Massai Point, 184, 193
Mather Campground, 57
Maverick Canyon, 300
Maxwell Lake, 300
Maxwell National Wildlife Refuge, 300, 309
Maxwell Ranch, 299
McCalister Lake, 301
McCrystal Ranch Site, 264
McDonalds Ranch, 50
McDowell Competitive Track, 129
McDowell Mountains, 128, 131, 135
McKittrick Canyon, 351, 360
Mead, Lake, 28–29, 55
  fishing, 38, 98
Melanie Hot Springs, 321
Mesa Campground, 339
Mesa Point Trail, 278
Mesa Verde, 232
Mescalero, accommodations, 372
Meteor Crater, 81
Mexican Canyon Trestle Trail, 364–365
Mexican gray wolf, 23, 161, 314, 318
Midgely Bridge, 133
Midgley Bridge Trail, 127
Miller Peak, 186
Miller Peak Trail, 185
Miller Peak Wilderness Area, 191
Millers Crossing, 243
Mistletoe Canyon Trail, 245, 273
Mitten View Campground, 85
Mogollon Baldy, 327–328
Mogollon Baldy Trail, 327
Mogollon Creek, 328
Mogollon culture, 140, 143, 158, 314, 321, 335, 339, 350, 357
Mogollon Rim, 28, 110, 112, 123, 139, 140, 143, 150
  fishing, 147
  hiking, 150
  mountain biking, 154
  walks and rambles, 158
Mohave, Lake, 29
  fishing, 38, 98–99
  kayaking, 20, 103
  sailing, 9, 98
Moki Mac River Expeditions, 56
Monte Vista Peak, 187
Montezuma Castle National Monument, 133

382 INDEX

Montezuma Hot Springs, 309
Montezuma Hotel, 309
Montezuma Ice Pond, 301
Montezuma's Well, 132
Monument Canyon, 70, 80
Monument Valley, 64, 69
 accommodations, 86
 hiking, 76
 horseback riding, 77
 mountain biking, 78
Mora River, 298
Mormon Canyon, 127
Mormon Lake, 53, 59
Mormon Lake Ski Center, 37
Mormon Loop, 130
Morphy Lake State Park, 296, 307
Mount Baldy, 140–141, 144, 148
Mount Bangs, 48
Mount Elden, 36, 46, 53
Mount Humphreys, 26, 46
Mount Sedgewick, 204
Mount Taylor, 204, 219, 223
Mount Taylor Ranch and Guest Lodge, 222
Mount Wrightson, 182
Mountain Bike Adventures, 269
Mountain Bike Heaven, 126
Mountain biking, 17–19
 Arizona
  Grand Canyon area, 50–53
  Indian Country, 78
  Red Rock Country, 110, 126–129, 131
  Sky Islands, 189, 192
  West Coast, 102
  White Mountains, 153–157
 favorite rides, 19
 New Mexico
  Cave Country, 362–364
  Gila Country, 316, 322, 331, 333
  High Plains, 304
  Indian Country, 222, 225
  Rocky Mountains, 268–274
Mountain goat trekking, in Arizona, 17, 189
Mountain Ranch Stables, 50
Mountain sickness, 6
Mountain Skills (Taos), 10, 240
Mountain Sports (Flagstaff), 35, 38, 50
Mountaineering, 35. *See also* Climbing

Movie sites, 69, 188, 229, 267, 275, 280, 320, 336
Mule deer, 23, 29, 35, 47, 51, 57, 84, 105, 113, 115, 135, 149, 161, 194, 228, 239, 283, 305, 307, 322, 330, 338, 368
Mule rides
 Grand Canyon, 49
Mummy Cave Overlook, 80

N

Nageezi Trading Post, 213
Nankoweap Trail #57, 42
Narrows Rim (Cebolla Wilderness), 222
National Trail (Phoenix), 130
Native American Graves and Repatriation Act (1990), 200
Native Americans, 62, 106, 199–200, 232, 345, 350. *See also specific Indian tribes*
 dances and ceremonies, 206, 276
Native Sons Adventures, 269, 272, 283
Nava-Hopi Tours, 5
Navajo Indian Reservation, 79, 82, 199, 208–209
Navajo Indians, 47, 62, 64, 68–70, 77, 80, 83, 205, 208, 220, 227, 345
Navajo Lake State Park, 210, 226, 278
Navajo Mountain, 73
Navajo Nation Fair, 209
Navajo National Monument, 65, 74
 camping, 85
Navajo River, 255
Navajo State Park, 228
Navajo taco, 85, 87
Navajoland, 66, 208
Needle, the (Sandia Mountains), 240
New Mexico Museum of Mining, 211
New Mexico State University, 333
Newspaper Rock, 68, 80
No Fences on Moonlight Mesa, 126
Noftsiger Hill Inn, 163
Nordic ski trails. *See* Cross-country skiing
Norski Meadows, 247
Norski Tracks de Santa Fe, 245

North Crest Trail, 240, 244, 257
North Kaibab Trail, 40
North Rim Campground (Grand Canyon), 58
North Rim Drive (Canyon de Chelly), 80
North Rim Drive (Grand Canyon), 54
North Rim of the Grand Canyon, 28, 31
 accommodations, 60
 bird watching, 35
 camping, 58
 cross-country skiing, 37
 hiking, 38, 40–41
 information, 30
 mountain biking, 50
 snowshoeing, 21
 wildlife viewing, 57
Northern Light Balloon Expeditions, 115
Northern Navajo Nation Fair, 209

O

O.K. Corral, 166
Oak Creek, 113
 fishing, 117
 West Fork of, 118
Oak Creek Canyon, 112, 118
 camping, 136
 climbing, 116
Oak Creek Canyon Overlook, 116, 133
Oakley, Annie, 299, 311
Oasis State Park, 370
Observatories
 Kitt Peak National Observatory, 94
 Lowell Observatory, 29
 Vega-Bray Observatory, 196–197
 Very Large Array National Radio Astronomy Observatory (VLA), 320
Ojitos Trail, 266
O'Keeffe, Georgia, 240, 264–266
Old Baldy Trail, 182
Old Fort Sumner Museum, 367
Old Las Vegas, walking tour of, 307
Old Mill Museum, 299
Old Tucson Studios, 188
Oliver Lee Memorial State Park, 349, 359
Opportunity Trail, 303, 305

INDEX **383**

Organ Mountains, 316–317, 325, 331
 camping, 340
 hiking, 329
 mountain biking, 333
Organ pipe cactus, 91, 94–95, 101–102, 104
Organ Pipe Cactus National Monument, 91, 94, 96
 camping, 108
 hiking, 96, 100
 walks and rambles, 96, 104
Orilla Verde Recreation Area, 253–254, 280
Ortega's Weaving Shop, 274
Outdoor Adventures (Alamogordo), 362
Outdoors Unlimited, 56
Outfitters, 16. *See also specific outfitters*
 questions to ask, 16

P

Page, 27–28
Painted Desert, 63, 67
Painted Desert Trail (Imperial), 97, 104
Paiute Wilderness, 48
Pajarito Mountain Ski Area, 251
Pajarito Plateau, 263, 266
Palatki Ruin, 133
Palm Canyon, 99
Palm Lake, 115
Palomas Peak, 241
Pancho Villa State Park, 320
Papago Well, 98
Paradise Fork, 36
Paria Canyon, 26, 45
Paria River, 46
Park Lake (Santa Rosa), 298, 307
Parker Canyon Lake, 168, 181
Parsons Trail, 121
Patagonia Lake State Park, 168, 178, 181, 192, 195
Patagonia Sonoita Creek Preserve, 177
Pawnshops, 227
Payson, fishing, 147
Peace College, 309
Peavine Trail, 124, 131
Pecos Baldy, 261
Pecos Falls, 261
Pecos National Historic Park, 291, 295
Pecos River, 21, 252, 291, 297, 303, 346, 364
 fishing, 302

Pecos Wilderness, 232, 245, 246, 252, 256, 260–261, 278, 283, 302, 307
Pemberton Loop, 128
Peñasco Blanco, 218
Peralta Trail, 124
Percha Dam State Park, 326
Perimeter Trail Loop (Sierra Vista), 191
Perk Canyon, 362
Petrified Forest National Monument, 63, 67, 79
Petroglyph National Monument, 278
Phantom Ranch, 36, 49, 59
Phelps Dodge Open Pit Copper Mine, 336
Philmont Museum and Seton Memorial Library, 304
Philmont Scout Ranch, 291, 304
Phoenix, 113, 140
 accommodations, 138
 ballooning, 115
 camping, 136
 hiking, 124
 mountain biking, 126, 128
 road biking, 131
Picacho Peak State Park, 114, 137
Picuris (San Lorenzo) Pueblo, 275
Piedra Lisa Spring Trail, 256
Pilar, 253, 281
Pilar Racecourse, 283
Pima Point, 39
Pinaleño Mountains, 151, 158, 161
Pine Campground, 369
Pine Canyon, 151, 361, 369
Pine Canyon Trail, 150
Pine River, 210
Pine Springs Campground, 369
Pine Tree Trail, 329
Pinetop, 142, 157, 159
Pinos Altos, 336
Pintail Lake Wild Game Observation Area, 143, 162
Plateau Point, 49
Plaza Hotel (Las Vegas), 308, 312
Point Sublime, 36, 51
Poll Knoll Recreation Area Cross-Country Ski Trails, 144
Ponderosa Ridge Trail (Sugarite Canyon), 303, 305
Portal Peak Lodge, 198

Powderhouse–Little Costilla Peak Trail, 246
Powell, John Wesley, 26, 33, 55
Powell, Lake, 27, 63, 65–66
 accommodations near, 86
 bird watching, 72
 camping, 84
 kayaking, 20, 81
 sailing, 9
 scuba diving, 20, 80
 swimming, 54
Prescott
 accommodations, 137
 camping, 136
 hiking, 123
 horseback riding, 125
 mountain biking, 126, 130
Preservation, 24
Priest Draw, 36
Pronghorns. *See* Sonoran pronghorns
Public Lands Information Center, 236
Pueblo Alto, 218
Pueblo Alto Trail, 213, 218
Pueblo Bonito, 213, 223
Pueblo del Arroyo, 214, 218
Pueblo of Zuni Arts and Crafts, 208
Puerco Indian Ruins, 68, 80
Puerto Blanco Drive, 96, 102
Puerto de Luna, 297
Pupfish, 105
Purple Mountain Pack Goats, 18, 189
Pusch Ridge Wilderness, 181
Puye, 232

Q

Quality Inn at Elephant Butte, 340
Quartzite, 88
Quemado Lake, 322, 326, 339
Questa, 276, 277
Questa Dome, 243
Quitobaquito Warm Springs, 96, 105

R

Rafting, 22
 Arizona
  Grand Canyon, 22, 55, 57
  Grand Canyon Area, 55, 57
  Indian Country, 84
  Sky Islands, 192
  White Mountains, 160

Rafting *(cont.)*
  New Mexico's Rocky
    Mountains, 282
Rain Creek Trail, 328
Rainbow Bridge, 67, 73
Rainbow Rim Trail, 50
Rainbow Ryders, 8, 239
Ramah Reservoir, 217
Rambles. *See* **Walks and rambles**
Ramsey Canyon, 8, 176
Ramsey Canyon Inn Bed & Breakfast, 198
Rancho Cañon Ancho, 16, 304
Rancho de la Osa, 17, 101
Randall Davey Audubon Center, 239
Raspberry Ridge Trail, 187
Raton, 292
  accommodations, 312
  road biking, 305
Rattlesnake Springs, 352
Rattlesnakes, 84, 96, 110, 194, 228, 283, 325, 330
Raven Site Ruin, 158
Rawhide & Roses, 163
Rawhide Mountains Wilderness, 99
Red River, 238, 272, 274, 276–277
  fishing, 254
Red River Ski Area, 11, 250
Red Rock Balloon Adventures, 115
Red Rock Balloon Rally, 211, 216
Red Rock Country, 109, 112, 116, 119, 123–124, 126, 130, 132, 134, 136–137
Red Rock Museum, 210
Red Rock State Park, 113, 115, 210
  camping, 229
Red Rock–Secret Mountain Wilderness, 122, 133, 135
Red Setter Inn, 23, 163
Redstone Picnic Area, 30
Reservation Lake, 147
Rex Ranch Stables, 189
Rhyolite Canyon, 184
Rim Lakes Vista Point Trail, 158
Rim Trail (Mogollon Rim), 159
Rim Trail (Tularosa Basin), 363
Rim View Trail (Mogollon Rim), 155

Rim Vista Trail (near Española), 265
Rincon Mountains, 171–172
Rio Bonito, 356, 369
Rio Grande Flyway, 239
Rio Grande Gorge, 238, 277
  climbing, 242
  fishing, 253
  hiking, 264
Rio Grande Gorge Bridge, 279
Rio Grande National Forest, 247
Rio Grande Nature Center, 270
Rio Grande Nature Center State Park, 239
Rio Grande Rapid Transit, 283
Rio Grande Rift, 235, 260, 292, 317
Rio Grande River, 232, 234, 236, 264, 279
  fishing, 253
  horseback riding, 267
  kayaking, 280, 282
    Taos Box Canyon, 280
  rafting, 22
    Taos Box Canyon, 22, 254, 282
  tubing, 278
Rio Grande Stables, 267
Rio Grande Valley, 232–233, 276
Rio Mountain Sport, 268
Rio Pueblo de Taos, 282
Rio San Antonio, 253
Rio Santa Barbara, 245, 252
River Bend Hot Springs Hostel, 340
River Horse Rentals, 267
River House (Gila), 340
River Island (Buckskin Mountains), 107
River rafting. *See* **Rafting**
Riverdancer Retreat and Bed & Breakfast, 288
Road Apple Trail, 225
Road biking, 20
  Arizona
    Grand Canyon area, 53
    Indian Country, 79–80
    Red Rock Country, 131
    Sky Islands, 192
    West Coast, 103
    White Mountains, 157
  favorite rides, 20
  New Mexico
    Cave Country, 364
    Gila Country, 333
    High Plains, 305

  Indian Country, 225
  Rocky Mountains, 274–277
Roadrunner Tours, 15, 267
Roberts, Lake, 322, 326, 339
Rocamadour Bed & Breakfast, 23, 137
Rock climbing. *See* **Climbing**
Rockhound State Park, 319
Rocky Mountains, 232, 235, 237, 239, 243–244, 246, 249, 251, 254, 257, 260, 263, 266, 269, 271, 273, 275, 277, 279, 281, 284, 286, 287
Rocky Ridge Trail, 49, 53
Rolfe C. Hoyer Campgrounds, 162
Romero Canyon, 181
Romero Canyon Trail, 170, 181
Roosevelt Lake, 144
Roper Lake State Park, 143
Rose Canyon Lake, 181
Rose Spring Trail, 149
Roswell, 347, 353, 368
  UFO crash site (1947), 224, 353
Round the Mountain Trail, 151
Route 66, 199, 293
Ruby Road, 100, 105
Rucker Canyon Trail, 186
Rucker Creek, 186, 195
Rucker Forest Camp, 195
Rucker Lake, 195
Ruidoso, 345, 347, 356, 361
  accommodations, 370
Ruidoso River, 356
Ruins Road Ride, 225
Ruth Hall Museum of Paleontology, 264

S

Sacramento Mountains Historical Museum and Pioneer Village, 365
Sacred Monument Tours, 69, 76–77
Saddle Mountain Wilderness, 42
Saguaro cactus, 171, 173
Saguaro National Park, 123, 167, 171–172, 173
  hiking, 172, 182
  horseback riding, 172
  mountain biking, 190
  road biking, 192
  walks and rambles, 192
  wildlife viewing, 194

INDEX 385

Sailboarding. *See* Boardsailing
Sailing, 9
  Arizona
    Sky Islands, 178
    West Coast, 98
    White Mountains, 143
  New Mexico
    Gila Country, 324
    High Plains, 300
Salman Ranch, 298
Salmon Ruins, 205, 227
Salt River, 160
  tubing, 21, 132
Salt River Canyon, 22, 139, 160
San Agustin Plains, 317
San Andreas Mountains, 357
San Antonio Canyon, 274
San Antonio Hot Springs, 278
San Antonio River, 253
San Esteban del Rey, 206
San Francisco Mountains, 65
San Francisco Peaks, 26, 50
  cross-country skiing, 11
San Gregorio Reservoir, 256
San Juan Basin, 202, 213
San Juan County Archaeological Research Center, 205, 227
San Juan River, 12, 210, 227–228
  fishing, 216
San Lorenzo (Picuris) Pueblo, 275
San Miguel del Vado, 296, 311
San Pedro Mountains, 234
San Pedro Riparian Area, 8, 176, 191
San Pedro River, 167, 191
San Pedro River Inn, 198
San Pedro Wilderness, 267
Sandia Mountains, 283
  bird watching, 239
  climbing, 240
  cross-country skiing, 243
  hiking, 257
Sandia Peak Ski Area, 249, 279
Sandia Peak Tramway, 279
Sandpoint Marina, 98
Sands Motel, 230
Sandstone Bluffs Overlook, 215, 226
Sangre de Cristo Mountains, 232, 234, 252, 292
  cross-country skiing, 11, 247
  mountain biking, 270

Santa Barbara Canyon, 244
Santa Barbara River, 245, 252
Santa Catalina Mountains, 123, 167
  hiking, 181
  wildlife viewing, 194
Santa Fe, 234, 236
  accommodations, 287
  bird watching, 239
  climbing, 240
  fishing, 252
  hiking, 259
  mountain biking, 268
  skiing, 250
Santa Fe Baldy, 260, 278
Santa Fe Central Reservations, 250
Santa Fe National Forest, 202, 245, 256
  camping, 285
Santa Fe Trail, 233, 290, 295, 302
Santa Rita del Cobre, 336
Santa Rita Mountains, 123, 168
Santa Rosa, 292
Santa Rosa Lake State Park, 297, 301, 306, 307
Santuario de Chimayo, 234, 274–275
Sasabe, 103, 106
Scenic drives. *See* **Car travel;** *specific drives*
Schnebly Hill, 116
Schultz Creek Trail, 52
Scorpion Campground, 339
Scuba diving, 20
  Arizona, 80
  New Mexico, 306
Sea kayaking. *See* **Kayaking; White-water kayaking**
Seasons, 5, 65, 111, 167, 202, 235, 292, 317, 346
Seboyeta, 207
Secret Canyon, 36
Secret Mountain Wilderness, 122, 133, 135
Sedona, 111
  accommodations, 137
  ballooning, 115
  camping, 136
  hiking, 118–122
  horseback riding, 125
  mountain biking, 126
  walks and rambles, 132
Sendero Esperanza Trail, 182
Sentinel Ranch, 372
Shadow Mountain Guest Ranch, 267

Shakespeare Ghost Town, 337
Sheepshead, the (Southwest Stronghold), 180
Shield, the (Sandia Mountains), 240
Shilo Inn, 108
Shiprock, 209
Shiprock Peak, 202, 209
Shiva Temple, 36
Show Low, 156–157
Shredders, 249
Shuree Ponds, 255
Sierra Vista, 168
Sierra Vista Trails, 333
Signal Hill Petroglyphs Trail, 192
Silver City, 316, 318, 323
  accommodations, 341
  road biking, 333–334
Silver Lake, 356
Silver Peak Trail, 187
Sims Mesa, 210
Sinagua Indians, 71, 83, 109, 113, 122, 133
Sipapu Ski and Summer Resort, 251
Sitting Bull Falls, 355, 360, 366
Six Shooter Trail, 157
Ski Apache, 11, 355–356
Ski Cloudcroft, 355
Ski Rio, 252
Ski Santa Fe, 250
Skiing, 11. *See also* **Cross-country skiing**
  Arizona
    Grand Canyon Area, 37
    White Mountains, 145
  New Mexico
    Cave Country, 355
    Rocky Mountains, 248–249, 252
    Snow Phone, 248
    Taos, 11
Sky Harbor International Airport, 4
Sky Islands, 165, 167, 170, 173–174, 176, 181, 184, 187, 190–192, 194–197, 346
Sky Ranch Lodge, 137
Skyline Trail, 302
Skywatcher's Inn, 23, 196–197
Slaughter Canyon Cave, 355
Sled Dog Inn, 60
Slide Rock State Park, 21, 132
Sliding House Overlook, 80
Snow Lake, 322, 326

386 INDEX

Snowboarding, 11. *See also*
  Skiing
  Arizona's Grand Canyon
    Area, 37
  New Mexico
    Cave Country, 355
    Rocky Mountains, 248
Snowshoeing, 21
  Arizona
    Grand Canyon area, 36
    White Mountains, 144
  New Mexico
    High Plains, 306
    Rocky Mountains, 277
Soap Creek Canyon, 38, 41
Socorro, 318
Socorro Box, 324
Sonoita, 192
  accommodations, 197
Sonoita Creek, 177
Sonora Desert Museum, 168
Sonoran Desert, 29, 91, 95, 97, 110, 113, 125, 171, 174, 182
  ballooning, 115, 175
Sonoran pronghorns, 23, 105, 178, 195
South Boundary Trail, 272
South Fork Trail, 186
South Kaibab Trail, 36, 40
South Mesa Loop (Chaco Culture), 219
South Rim Drive (Canyon de Chelly), 80
South Rim of the Grand Canyon, 28, 31
  accommodations, 59
  climbing, 35
  hiking, 39–40
  horseback riding, 49
  information, 30
  mountain biking, 50, 52
  weather, 28
Southeastern Arizona Bird Observatory (SABO), 176
Southwest Climbing Resource, 10, 240
Southwest Nordic Center, 247
Southwest Stronghold, 180
Spaghetti Bowl, 362
Speckled Trout, 145
Spelunking. *See* Caving
Spider Rock, 78
Spider Rock Overlook, 70, 80
Spirit Lake, 256, 260
Springer Lake, 301
Springerville, 142, 145
  horseback riding, 152
  road biking, 157
  walks and rambles, 158

Springerville Volcanic Field, 140
Spruce Mountain, 130
Squirrels. *See* Kaibab squirrels
St. James Hotel, 299, 311
Star Hill Inn, 312
Stargazing. *See* Observatories
Starr Pass, 189
Stein's Railroad Ghost Town, 337
Step Back Inn, 230
Sterling Canyon, 122
Stewart Lake, 256
Stone Lions, 263
Stoneman Lake, 117
Storrie Lake State Park, 9, 296, 300–301, 307
Strawberry Crater, 83
Strawberry Crater Wilderness, 79, 83
Submarine Rock, 127
Sugarite Canyon Coal Camp Trail, 307
Sugarite Canyon State Park, 297, 300–301
  camping, 310
  hiking, 303
  mountain biking, 305
  walks and rambles, 307
Sumner Lake State Park, 351, 356
Sun Mountain Bike Company, 269
Sunburn, 6
Sunglow Guest Ranch, 17, 188
Sunrise Lake, 147
Sunrise Park Resort, 11, 145
Sunrise Resort, 21, 144
Sunset Crater Volcano National Monument, 71, 79
Sunset Trail, 47, 49
Sunset-Wupatki Loop Road, 79
Superstition Mountains, 114
  climbing, 116
  hiking, 123–124
  horseback riding, 189
Superstition Wilderness, 114
Supertrail (Mount Wrightson), 182
Swift Trail, 158
Swimming, 21
  Arizona
    Grand Canyon area, 54
    Red Rock Country, 132
    Sky Islands, 192

West Coast, 104
White Mountains, 158
New Mexico
  Cave Country, 364
  Gila Country, 334
  High Plains, 307
  Indian Country, 226
  Rocky Mountains, 278
Sycamore Canyon, 36, 47, 115, 119, 135
Sycamore Canyon Trail, 100
Sycamore Creek, 122
Sycamore Pass, 119
Sycamore Point, 36
Sycamore Rim Trail, 47

T

Taos, 234, 236
  accommodations, 286
  ballooning, 239
  climbing, 240, 242
  cross-country skiing, 11, 244
  horseback riding, 267
  mountain biking, 269
  road biking, 274
  skiing, 248
Taos Box Canyon, 272
  kayaking, 280, 282
  rafting, 22, 254, 282
Taos Indian Horse Ranch, 267
Taos Mountain Balloon Rally, 239
Taos Ski Valley, 11, 248, 286
Taos Valley Resort Association, 248
Tapeats Creek, 38, 41, 73
Taylor Cabin, 119
Teepees, the (Petrified Forest), 68, 80
10K Trail (Sandia Mountains), 243
Ten-X Campground, 58
Tent Rocks Canyon Trail, 259
Tesuque Creek, 260, 271
Third Mesa, 64
Three Rivers Petroglyph National Recreation Area, 343, 350, 357
Thumb Butte, 123, 130
Thumb Butte Loop Trails, 130
Thunder River Trail, 41
Thunderbird Lodge, 70, 85
Thunderstorms, 6
Timbers at Chama, 255
Tiyo Point, 36, 51
Tohono Chul Park, 193
Tohono O'odham Reservation, 90, 94
Tombstone, 166

INDEX

Tonto Creek, 148, 151
Tonto National Forest, 116, 123
Tonto Natural Bridge State Park, 114, 123
Torgac Cave, 9, 352
Tortilla Flats, 132
Totem Pole Rock, 173–174
Totem Pole Tours, 76, 77
Totsonii Ranch, 78
Tour West, 56
Trading posts, 69, 210, 213, 227
Trail Horse Adventures, 125
Trailer Village RV Park (Grand Canyon), 57
Train travel, 4
Traveling to Arizona and New Mexico, 4
Tres Piedras Rocks, 242
Trinity Site, 345
Truchas, 275, 279
Truchas Lakes, 261
Truchas Peaks, 234, 261
Trujillo Weavings, 275
Truth or Consequences, 318
  accommodations, 340
Tsankawi, 237
Tsegi Canyon, 65, 70, 75
Tsegi Overlook, 80
Tsin Kletzin, 219
Tuba City Truck Stop and Cafe, 87
Tubing, 21
  Arizona, 38
    Red Rock Country, 132
  New Mexico's Rocky Mountains, 278
Tucson, 142, 168
  mountain biking, 189
Tucson Botanical Gardens, 170
Tucson International Airport, 4
Tucson Mountains Park, 189
Tucumcari, 292
Tularosa Basin, 346
Tule Well, 98
Tumacacori Mountains, 102–103
Tunnel, the (Ruidoso area), 355
Turkey Track Stables, Inc., 267
Turkey Trot Trail, 156
Turkeys. *See* Wild turkeys
Turquoise Trail, 267
Tusayan, 30, 33
Tusayan Ruin Walk, 54

Tuzigoot National Monument, 117
Twin Finn Diving Center, 81
Twining Campground, 284
Tyrone, 336

U

UFO crash site, 224, 353
UFO Festival, 353
UFO Museum and Research Center, 353
Una Vida, 214
Upper Lake Mary, 117
Upper Taos Box Canyon, 282
Ute Lake State Park, 292, 298, 301, 307

V

Valle Vidal, 237, 296
  camping, 284
  cross-country skiing, 246
  fishing, 254
  hiking, 264
  mountain biking, 273
  wildlife viewing, 283
Valles Caldera, 237
Valley Drive (Monument Valley), 78
Valley of Fires Loop, 365
Valley of Fires Recreation Area, 343, 349, 365
  camping, 368
Vega-Bray Observatory, 196–197
Velarde, 276
Verde River, 117
Vermilion Cliffs, 27, 44
  bird watching, 8, 33–34
Very Large Array National Radio Astronomy Observatory (VLA), 320
Victoria Mine Trail, 101
Victory Ranch, 298
Villa Philmonte, 304
Villanueva, 306, 311
Villanueva State Park, 296, 302
  camping, 310
Vineyard Bed & Breakfast (Sonoita), 197
Virgin Mountains, 26, 48
Vishnu Schist, 26, 30, 40
Vista Point (Cave Creek Canyon), 194
Volcano and Petroglyph Tour, 269
Volunteer Canyon, 36
Vultee Arch, 122

W

Wahweap Campground, 84
Waldroup Canyon, 121
Walks and rambles, 21
  Arizona
    Grand Canyon Area, 54
    Indian Country, 81, 83–84
    Red Rock Country, 132–135
    Sky Islands, 192
    West Coast, 96, 104–105
    White Mountains, 158
  New Mexico
    Cave Country, 364–366
    Gila Country, 335
    High Plains, 307
    Indian Country, 226
    Rocky Mountains, 278
Walnut Canyon National Monument, 50, 83, 123
Waste Isolation Pilot Plant, 345
Waste Isolation Pilot Project, 344
Water Canyon Campground, 339
Water Holes Canyon, 76
Water, drinking, 7
Weather, 5, 28, 65, 91, 111, 167, 171, 202, 235, 292, 317, 346
Weaver's Needle, 116, 125
West Clear Creek, 117, 120
West Clear Creek Canyon, 21, 120, 121, 132, 135
West Elden, 36
West Fork of the Gila River, 322–323, 327
West Fork of the Little Colorado River, 21, 144, 148
West Fork of the Oak Creek, 118
Wet Beaver Creek, 21, 117, 121, 132, 135
Wet Beaver Wilderness, 121
Wheeler Peak, 262, 284
White House Overlook, 80
White House Ruin, 70, 74
White Mountain Apache Tribe, 145
White Mountain Crest Trail, 358, 361
White Mountain Trail System, 156

INDEX

White Mountains, 139, 142, 144, 146, 148, 151, 153, 155, 157, 159, 161–163
  cross-country skiing, 11, 144
  fishing, 145
  hiking, 148
  mountain biking, 153
  wildlife viewing, 23, 161
White River, 147
White Rock, 237, 241
White Rock Loop Trails, 130
White Sands Loop, 363
White Sands Missile Range, 345
White Sands National Monument, 343, 346, 348–349
  camping, 368
  hiking, 357
  walks and rambles, 365
White Stallion Ranch, 188
Whitehorse Lake, 59
Whites City, accommodations, 371
Whitewater Baldy, 322, 327
Whitewater Canyon, 323, 329
White-water kayaking, 22
  Arizona
    Grand Canyon Area, 55
    White Mountains, 160
  New Mexico
    Indian Country, 228
    Rocky Mountains, 280–282
White-water rafting. *See* Rafting

Wickenburg, horseback riding, 126
Widforss Trail, 40
Wijiji Trail, 223
Wild Earth Llama Adventures, 18, 268
Wild Rivers Recreation Area, 238
Wild turkeys, 23, 35, 54, 57, 143, 149, 154, 310, 352
Wilderness River Adventures, 84
Wildlife. *See also specific wildlife*
  safety tips, 7
  viewing, 23
William's Lake, 262
Williams, 47
  camping, 59
Williams Ski Area, 37
Williams Valley Winter Sports Area, 144, 153
Willow Creek Campground, 339
Willow Springs Lake, 148
Wilson Canyon Trail, 135
Wilson Mountain Trail, 122
Wind and Water Sports, 144
Window Rock, 66, 208
Window Rock Tribal Park, 84
Windsor Beach Unit, 104, 107
Windsor Trail, 21, 246, 256, 260, 270
Winslow, 66, 86

Winston, 337
Wire Pass Trail, 44
Wolf, Mexican gray, 23, 161, 314, 318
Woodland Lakes, 156
Woods Canyon Lake, 148
World Balloon Corporation, 8, 239
Wrather Canyon, 46
Wupatki Loop Road, 79
Wupatki National Monument, 65, 71, 79

X

X-Diamond & MLY Ranch, 153

Y

Yank Spring, 100
Yapashi Ruins, 263
Yavapai Campground, 136
Yavapai Indians, 113
Yuma, 92, 99
  accommodations, 108
Yuma Crossing State Historic Park, 93

Z

Zoroaster Temple, 36
Zuni
  accommodations, 229
Zuni Indians, 149, 207, 220, 227
Zuni Mountains, 202, 204
Zuni Pueblo, 207, 220
Zuni-Acoma Trail, 215, 220

FROMMER'S® COMPLETE TRAVEL GUIDES

Alaska
Amsterdam
Arizona
Atlanta
Australia
Austria
Bahamas
Barcelona, Madrid & Seville
Beijing
Belgium, Holland & Luxembourg
Bermuda
Boston
British Columbia & the Canadian Rockies
Budapest & the Best of Hungary
California
Canada
Cancún, Cozumel & the Yucatán
Cape Cod, Nantucket & Martha's Vineyard
Caribbean
Caribbean Cruises & Ports of Call
Caribbean Ports of Call
Carolinas & Georgia
Chicago
China
Colorado
Costa Rica
Denmark
Denver, Boulder & Colorado Springs
England
Europe
European Cruises & Ports of Call
Florida
France
Germany
Greece
Greek Islands
Hawaii
Hong Kong
Honolulu, Waikiki & Oahu
Ireland
Israel
Italy
Jamaica
Japan
Las Vegas
London
Los Angeles
Maryland & Delaware
Maui
Mexico
Montana & Wyoming
Montréal & Québec City
Munich & the Bavarian Alps
Nashville & Memphis
Nepal
New England
New Mexico
New Orleans
New York City
New Zealand
Nova Scotia, New Brunswick & Prince Edward Island
Oregon
Paris
Philadelphia & the Amish Country
Portugal
Prague & the Best of the Czech Republic
Provence & the Riviera
Puerto Rico
Rome
San Antonio & Austin
San Diego
San Francisco
Santa Fe, Taos & Albuquerque
Scandinavia
Scotland
Seattle & Portland
Shanghai
Singapore & Malaysia
South Africa
Southeast Asia
South Florida
South Pacific
Spain
Sweden
Switzerland
Thailand
Tokyo
Toronto
Tuscany & Umbria
USA
Utah
Vancouver & Victoria
Vermont, New Hampshire & Maine
Vienna & the Danube Valley
Virgin Islands
Virginia
Walt Disney World & Orlando
Washington, D.C.
Washington State

FROMMER'S® DOLLAR-A-DAY GUIDES

Australia from $50 a Day
California from $60 a Day
Caribbean from $70 a Day
England from $70 a Day
Europe from $70 a Day
Florida from $70 a Day
Hawaii from $70 a Day
Ireland from $60 a Day
Italy from $70 a Day
London from $85 a Day
New York from $80 a Day
Paris from $80 a Day
San Francisco from $60 a Day
Washington, D.C., from $70 a Day

FROMMER'S® PORTABLE GUIDES

Acapulco, Ixtapa & Zihuatanejo
Alaska Cruises & Ports of Call
Bahamas
Baja & Los Cabos
Berlin
California Wine Country
Charleston & Savannah
Chicago
Dublin
Hawaii: The Big Island
Las Vegas
London
Los Angeles
Maine Coast
Maui
Miami
New Orleans
New York City
Paris
Puerto Vallarta, Manzanillo & Guadalajara
San Diego
San Francisco
Sydney
Tampa & St. Petersburg
Venice
Washington, D.C.

FROMMER'S® NATIONAL PARK GUIDES

Family Vacations in the
  National Parks
Grand Canyon

National Parks of the
  American West
Rocky Mountain Park

Yellowstone & Grand Teton
Yosemite & Sequoia/
  Kings Canyon
Zion & Bryce Canyon

FROMMER'S® MEMORABLE WALKS

Chicago
London

New York
Paris

San Francisco
Washington, D.C.

FROMMER'S® GREAT OUTDOOR GUIDES

New England
Northern California

Southern California & Baja
Southern New England

Washington & Oregon

FROMMER'S® BORN TO SHOP GUIDES

Born to Shop: France
Born to Shop: Italy

Born to Shop: London
Born to Shop: New York

Born to Shop: Paris

FROMMER'S® IRREVERENT GUIDES

Amsterdam
Boston
Chicago
Las Vegas

London
Los Angeles
Manhattan
New Orleans

Paris
San Francisco
Seattle & Portland

Vancouver
Walt Disney World
Washington, D.C.

FROMMER'S® BEST-LOVED DRIVING TOURS

America
Britain
California

Florida
France
Germany

Ireland
Italy
New England

Scotland
Spain
Western Europe

THE UNOFFICIAL GUIDES®

Bed & Breakfasts in
  California
Bed & Breakfasts in
  New England
Bed & Breakfasts in
  the Northwest
Bed & Breakfasts in
  Southeast
Beyond Disney
Branson, Missouri

California with Kids
Chicago
Cruises
Disneyland
Florida with Kids
Golf Vacations in the
  Eastern U.S.
The Great Smoky &
  Blue Ridge
  Mountains

Inside Disney
Hawaii
Las Vegas
London
Miami & the Keys
Mini Las Vegas
Mini-Mickey
New Orleans
New York City
Paris

San Francisco
Skiing in the West
Southeast with Kids
Walt Disney World
Walt Disney World
  for Grown-ups
Walt Disney World
  for Kids
Washington, D.C.

SPECIAL-INTEREST TITLES

Frommer's Britain's Best Bed & Breakfasts
  and Country Inns
Frommer's Britain's Best Bike Rides
The Civil War Trust's Official Guide
  to the Civil War Discovery Trail
Frommer's Caribbean Hideaways
Frommer's Adventure Guide to Central
  America
Frommer's Adventure Guide to South
  America
Frommer's Adventure Guide to Southeast
  Asia
Frommer's Food Lover's Companion to
  France
Frommer's Gay & Lesbian Europe

Frommer's Exploring America by RV
Hanging Out in Europe
Israel Past & Present
Mad Monks' Guide to California
Mad Monks' Guide to New York City
Frommer's The Moon
Frommer's New York City with Kids
The New York Times' Unforgettable
  Weekends
Places Rated Almanac
Retirement Places Rated
Frommer's Road Atlas Britain
Frommer's Road Atlas Europe
Frommer's Washington, D.C., with Kids
Frommer's What the Airlines Never Tell You